THE KINGS AND THE PAWNS

Studies on War and Genocide

General Editors: Omer Bartov, Brown University; A. Dirk Moses, European University Institute, Florence / University of Sydney

THE KINGS AND THE PAWNS

Collaboration in Byelorussia during World War II

Leonid Rein

berghahn
NEW YORK · OXFORD
www.berghahnbooks.com

Published in 2011 by
Berghahn Books
www.berghahnbooks.com

Library of Congress Cataloging-in-Publication Data

Rein, Leonid.
The kings and the pawns : collaboration in Byelorussia during World
War II / Leonid Rein.
    p. cm. -- (War and genocide ; v. 15)
Includes bibliographical references and indexes.
ISBN 978-1-84545-776-1 (hardback) -- ISBN 978-0-85745-043-2
(institutional ebook) -- ISBN 978-1-78238-047-4 (paperback)--
ISBN 978-1-78238-048-1 (retail ebook)
1. World War, 1939-1945--Collaborationists--Belarus. 2. Belarus--
History--German occupation, 1941-1944. 3. Nazis--Belarus--History--
20th century. 4. Collaborationists--Belarus--History--20th century. 5.
World War, 1939-1945--Atrocities--Belarus. 6. Belarus--Politics and
government--1917-1945. 7. Belarus--Social conditions--20th century.
8. World War, 1939-1945--Belarus. I. Title.
D802.B38R45 2011
940.53'478--dc22
                                                        2011003050

British Library Cataloguing in Publication Data

A catalogue record for this book is available from the British Library
Printed in the United States on acid-free paper.

ISBN: 978-1-78238-047-4 paperback
ISBN: 978-1-78238-048-1 retail ebook

"The local self-administration has the sole task, to execute the orders of the responsible German offices"

from the Report of Major Oskar W. Müller, the liaison officer of the Reich's Ministry for the Occupied Eastern Territories by the Commanding General of the Security Troops and Commander of the Army Area "Center" to the political department of the Ministry for the Occupied Eastern Territories, 8 October 1942

"[T]he leaders of our homeland, Byelorussia, should themselves be Byelorussians. We've had enough of asking for German permission or bribing them with fat, vodka, and whores until we Byelorussians cannot find our own truth. The memorandum must bring to the forefront the question of transferring authority to Byelorussians everywhere and in all sectors, to the police, and to all Byelorussian institutions…"

Radaslaŭ Astroŭski at the meeting of the Baranoviči city administration, end of 1943

CONTENTS

ABBREVIATIONS

Here I have cited only those abbreviations that are not frequently encountered in historical literature. Such well known abbreviations as POWs, USSR or SS have been omitted.

A-A line   Archangels-Astrakhan line
Abt.   *Abteilung* (department)
AK   *Armija Krajowa* (Polish Home Army)
AOK   *Armeeoberkommando* (Supreme Command of an Army)
BA   *Bundesarchiv* (Federal Archives, Germany)
BA-MA   *Bundesarchiv-Militärarchiv* (Federal Archives-Military Archives, Freiburg im Breisgau, Germany)
Batl.   *Bataillon* (Battalion)
BCR   *Belaruskaja Central'nja Rada* (Byelorussian Central Council)
BDM   *Bund deutscher Mädels* (Union of German Girls)
BdS   *Befehlshaber der Sicherheitspolizei* (Commander of the Security Police)
Beauftragter d. Reichsm. f.d. bes. Ostgeb. b. Kommand. General d. Sich.-Tr. u. Befh. i. H. G. Mitte   *Beaftragter des Reichsministeriums für die besetzte Ostgebiete bei kommandierenden General der Sicherheitstruppen und Befehlshaber in Heeresgruppe Mitte* (Liason Officer of the Reich's Ministry of the Occupied Eastern Territories at the headquarters of the commanding general of security troops and commander of the Area of Army Group "Center")

BGMIVOV   *Belorusskij Gosudarstvennyj Muzej Istorii Velikoj Otechestvennoj Vojny* (Byelorussian State Museum for the History of Great Patriotic War)

BH   *Belaruskaja Hazeta* ("Byelorussian Newspaper")

BKA/BKO   *Belaruskaja Krajova Abarona* (Byelorussian Home Guard) (in Russian sources: *Beloruskaja Krajovaja Oborona*)

BKS   *Belorusskij Komitet Samopomoshchi* (Byelorussian Self-Aid Committee)

Bl.   *Blatt* (sheet)

BNP   *Belaruskaja Narodnaja Partyzanka* (Byelorussian People's Partisan Movement)

BNP   *Belaruskaja Nezaleİnickaja Partyja* (Byelorussian Independent Party)

BNR   *Belaruskaja Narodnaja Respublika* (Byelorussian People's Republic)

BNS/BS   *Belaruskaja Narodnaja Samapomač* (Byelorussian Popular Self-Aid Organization)

BP   *Belorusskoje Predstavitel'stvo* (The Byelorussian Representation)

BSA   *Belaruskaja Samaakhova* (Byelorussian Self-Defense, the full name Free Corps of Byelorussian Self-Defense)

BSSR   *Belorusskaja Sovetskaja Socialisticheskaja Respublika* (Byelorussian Soviet Socialist Republic)

Cheka   *Chrezvychajnaja Komissiya* (Extraordinary Commission, the forerunner of OGPU, NKVD, MGB and KGB)

CHGK   *Chrezvychajnaja Gosudarstvennaja Kommissija* (Extraordinary State Commission for Investigation of Nazi crimes)

CIS   Community of Independent States

DAF   *Deutsche Arbeiterfront* (German Workers' Front)

DNVP   *Deutsche Nationale Volkspartei* (German National People's Party)

DZO   *Deutsche Zeitung in Ostland* (German Newspaper in Ostland)

Feldgend.   *Feldgendarmerie* (military police)

FHO   *Fremde Heere Ost* (Department of "Foreign Armies East")

FK	*Feldkommandantur* (field command)
FZU	*Fabrichno-Zavodskoje Uchilishche* (Factory Workshop School)
GAMO	*Gosudarstvennyj Arkhiv Minskoj Oblasti* (State Archives of the Minsk Oblast)
GARB	*Gosudarstvennyj Arkhiv Respubliki Belarus* (State Archives of Republic of Belarus)
GARF	*Gosudarstvennyj Arkhiv Rossijskoj Federatsii* (State Archives of the Russian Federation)
GFP	*Geheime Feldpolizei* (Secret Field Police)
GG	*Generalgouvernement* (General-Government, the German-occupied part of Poland)
GK	*Generalkommissariat* (General Commissariat)
GKW	*Generalkommissariat Weißruthenien* (General Commissariat "White Ruthenia")
GPO	*Generalplan Ost* (General Plan "East")
Heu	*Heimatlos* (without a homeland), *Elternlos* (without parents), *Unterkunftslos* (homeless)
Hiwis	*Hilfswillige* ("auxiliary volunteers", local dwellers performing mainly logistic and sentry duties for German army)
HJ	*Hitlerjugend* (Hitler's Youth)
Hrsg.	*Herausgeber* (editor)
HSSPF	*Höherer SS- und Polizeiführer* (Supreme SS and Police Leader)
HstAS	*Hauptstaatsarchiv Stuttgart* (Main State's Archives, Stuttgart, Germany)
Ic	intelligence officer in German army
IMT	International Military Tribunal of the Main War Criminals (Nuremberg, 1946)
KdO	*Kommandeur der Ordnungspolizei* (commander of the order police)
KdS	*Kommandeur der Sicherheitspolizei* (commander of security police)
Kdt. r. A. Geb.	*Kommandantur der rückwährtigen Armeegebietes* (Commandant of Army's Rear Area)
KGB	*Komitet Gosudarstvennoj Bezopasnosti* (The Committee for State Security)
Komp.	*Kompanie* (Company)
Komsomol	*Kommunisticheskij Soyuz Molodjozhi* (Communist Youth Union)
KONR	*Komitet Osvobozhdenija Narodov Rossii* (Committee for Liberation of the Peoples of Russia)

KPB/KP(b)B	*Kommunisticheskaja Partija (bolshevikov) Belorussii* (Communist Party (Bolsheviks) of Byelorussia)
KPZB	*Kamunistychnaja Partyja Zakhodnjaj Belarusi* (Communist Party of Western Byelorussia)
LAF	Front of Lithuanian Activists
La-Führer	*Landwirtschaftsführer* ("agricultural leader")
LVF	*Légion des volontaires Française contre le Bolshévisme* (The counter-Bolshevist Legion of French volunteers)
MZ	*Minsker Zeitung* (the German-language version of *Menskaja Hazeta*, a forerunner of *Belaruskaja Hazeta*)
NARB	*Nacional'nyj Arkhiv Respubliki Belarus* (National Archives of Republic of Belarus)
NEP	*Novaja Ekonomicheskaja Politika* (New Economic Policy)
NKVD	*Narodnyj Komissariat Vnutrennikh Del* (People's Commissariat of the Interior)
NS	*Nasjonal Samling* (National Assembly, Nazi party, Norway)
NS	National Socialist
NSB	*Nationaal Socialistische Beweging* (National Socialist Movement, Holland)
NSV	*Nationalsozialistische Volkswohlfahrt* (National Socialist Popular Welfare Organization)
NU	*Nederlandsche Unie* (Netherlands Union)
Obkdo.	*Oberkommando* (Supreme Command)
OD	*Ordnungsdienst* (Order Service, local auxiliary police)
OGPU/GPU	*Objedinjonnoje Gosudarstvennoje Politicheskoje Upravlenije* (Joint State Political Department)
OKH	*Oberkommando des Heeres* (Supreme Command of the Army)
OKL	*Oberkommando der Luftwaffe* (Supreme Command of Luftwaffe)
OKW	*Oberkommando der Wehrmacht* (Supreme Command of Armed Forces)
Omi	*Ostministerium* ("Eastern Ministry", official name Reich's Ministry for Occupied Eastern Territories)
OSR	Operational Situation Report
OT	*Organization Todt* (Todt Organization)

OUN	*Organizatsija Ukrainskikh Natsionalistov* (Organization of Ukrainian Nationalists)
OUN-B	Organization of Ukrainian Nationalists headed by Stephan Bandera
OUN-M	Organization of Ukrainian Nationalists headed by Andrij Mel'nyk
PA	*Partijnyj Arkhiv Instituta Istorii Partii pri Central'nom Komitete KPB (*Party Archives of the Institute of Party History of the Central Committee of CPB)
PAW	*Propaganda-Abteilung Wehrmacht* (Wehrmacht's Propaganda Office)
PBNS	*Partyja Belaruskikh Nacyjanal-Sacyjalista?* (Party of Byelorussian National Socialists)
POB	*Parti Ouvrier Belge* (Belgian Labor Party)
Pol.	*Politik* (politics)
PPF	*Parti Populaire Français* (French People's Party)
PSR/Esery	*Partija Socialistov-Revolucionerov* (Social Revolutionary Party)
Pz. AOK	*Panzerarmeeoberkommando* (Supreme Command of the Tank Army)
Pz. Gren. Brig.	*Panzergrenadierbrigade* (Armored Infantry Brigade)
RAD	*Reichsarbeiterdienst* (Reich's Labor Service)
Reg.	*Regierung* (Government)
Res. Pol. Batl.	*Reservepolizeibattaillon* (Reserve Police Battalion)
Rev.	*Reserve* (Reserve)
Rgt./Regt./ Rgm.	*Regiment* (Regiment)
RJF	*Reichsjugendführer* (Reich's Youth Leader)
RK	*Rajonnyj Komitet* (Communist Party Rayon Committee)
RK	*Reichskommissariat* (Reich's Commissariat)
RKO	*Reichskommissariat für Ostland* (Reich's Commissariat [for] Ostland)
RKU	*Reichskommissariat für die Ukraine* (Reich's Commissariat [for] Ukraine)
RM	*Reichsmark*
RmfdbO	*Reichsministerium für die besetzte Ostgebiete* (Reich's Ministry for the Occupied Eastern Territories)

RONA	*Russkaja Osvoboditel'naja Narodnaja Armija* (Russian Liberation People's Army)
ROVS	*Russkij Obshchevoinskij Soyuz* (Russian Common-to-All-Arms Union)
RSHA	*Reichssicherheitshauptamt* (Reich's Main Security Office)
Rükw.	*Rükwärtiger* (rear)
russ.	*russische* (Russian)
San.-Stelle	*Sanitätsstelle* (medical unit)
SBM	*Sayuz Belaruskaj Moladzi* (Union of Byelorussian Youth)
Schuma	*Schutzmannschaft* (auxiliary police formation, literally 'guard unit')
SD	*Sicherheitsdienst* (Security Service)
Sich. Div.	*Sicherungsdivision* (security division)
SSPF	*SS- und Polizeiführer* (SS and Police Leader)
SWCA	Archives of Simon Wiesenthal Center (Jerusalem, Israel)
TLB	*Tätigkeits- und Lagebericht*
TVAZ	*Tapferkeits- und Verdienstauzeichnung* (Order for Bravery and Merit)
V-Leute	*Vertrauensleute* (literally "people of confidence", agents of German security organizations)
VS KONR	*Vooruzhonnyje Sily Komiteta Osvobozhdenija Narodov Rossii* (Armed Forces of Committee for the Liberation of Peoples of Russia)
Waff. Gren. Div. d. SS	*Waffen-Grenadier Division der SS*
WJW	*Weißruthenische Jugendwerk* (German name for Union of Byelorussian Youth)
WSW/BSW	*Weißruthenische Selbsthilfewerk* (German name for Byelorussian Self-Aid Organization)
YVA	*Yad Vashem Archives* (Jerusalem, Israel)
ZHO	*Zentralhandelsgesellschaft Ost* (Central Trade Society "East", full name is Central Trade Society "East" for Agricultural Marketing and Demand Ltd)

PREFACE

This book deals with a relatively obscure phenomenon of World War II, namely, the indigenous collaboration with German occupation authorities in one of the least prominent countries: Byelorussia.

The theme of collaboration during World War II as such is certainly one of the most difficult and controversial issues in historical research, primarily because it raises sensitive questions. It is especially problematic in the case of a country such as Byelorussia.

I grew up in Byelorussia and recall that even as a schoolchild I had a very clear—although as it later turned out, an inaccurate, or in fact, a much distorted—picture of World War II (or the *Great Patriotic War,* as it was called in the Soviet Union and as it is still referred to in the post-Soviet era). According to the official Soviet version, from the very first day of the German invasion, the Soviet people rose as one to fight against the Hitleristic hordes. Yet at the same time, everyone also knew about the so-called *polizai* (the word was a Russian distortion of the German word *Polizei,* i.e., police). The *polizai* were—again according to the official version—individuals who either sold out their motherland for personal gain or simply had personal reasons to hate Soviet rule. Their existence was virtually unmentionable, treated as a kind of "They-Who-Must-Not-Be-Named," to borrow a turn of phrase from the Harry Potter series. If referred to at all, in books, films, or plays, the *polizaj* (the singular form) was usually depicted as a rather dark figure, mostly drunken, wearing ragged clothes; an unprincipled, sadistic, lust-ful, and avaricious character. In Byelorussia, this perception of World War II remains largely intact to this day, a fact that is only partially related to the current political situation there.

In the current study, I wish to shed additional light on this period in history, and to analyze the controversial topic of Byelorussia's local collaboration with the Nazi regime. Few other countries under Nazi occupation were as hard hit by this occupation as Byelorussia. According to various data, between one and two million Byelorussian inhabitants were killed (of these, between a quarter million and a million were Jews), and some three million people were left homeless.[1] Most Byeloruss-ian cities lay in ruins at the time of liberation in 1944. Thou-sands of villages had been burned down during the so-called "anti-partisan operations." Byelorussia's industrial capacity in 1945 was only twenty per cent of its prewar levels, and the count of heads of cattle came to thirty-one per cent of the prewar num-bers.[2] During the German occupation, there existed as many as five different administrative units in what is now Byelorussia. German policies in Byelorussia resulted in a growing resistance movement, which towards the end of the occupation was the second largest in Europe, following Tito's resistance in Yugoslavia. This fact led the British historian Gerald Reitlinger to state that Byelorussia's "real history under German occupa-tion must be sought in the annals of Partisan warfare."[3] The official Soviet propaganda even dubbed Byelorussia "a partisan republic."

It would be false and ahistorical, however, as this book will demonstrate, to suggest that the entire period of Nazi occupa-tion in Byelorussia may be subsumed under the title of *resis-tance,* or even to say that the resistance movement was a forceful influence from the day Germany invaded the Soviet Union. The situation must be imagined as it was seen through the eyes of those living in this period. What the simple Soviet cit-izen witnessed in the hectic summer days of 1941 was the crum-bling of the Soviet doctrine that had been inculcated by propaganda during the years preceding the invasion, a message that prophesied a quick and practically bloodless Soviet victory over the invaders. Many people, not only Nazi leaders, both in the Soviet Union and beyond its borders, were certain that this was the end of the USSR. In reality, even from its very begin-ning, the German advance into the Soviet Union was no plea-sure trip; yet, to the "lay" observer, the Wehrmacht's advance towards Moscow looked quite impressive. Half a year would pass before this advance was brought to a standstill at the very gates of the Soviet capital.

The resistance was a reaction to the repressive policies of the occupying regime. It is undeniable that, practically from the outset, the Nazis did not hesitate to display the ugliest aspects of their rule in the Soviet territories. However, in the first weeks and months after 22 June 1941, Nazi terror was rather selective: in the first place, it was directed against Jews, who were in any case perceived by many Gentiles as outsiders; and in the second place, against communists, who also did not enjoy favorable public opinion. The latter's popularity and trustworthiness in particular sank even lower following the debacles of the first weeks and months of the German-Soviet war. Given the "selective" terror of the Germans, and their seeming invincibility, it would require a very good reason for any Byelorussian inhabitant to try to resist the Germans.

At the same time, quite a number of people who foresaw the imminent victory of Germany thought it wise to cooperate with the victors as a means of adapting to the new situation. Here it should be mentioned (a detailed explanation follows) that in Byelorussia, as in other Nazi-occupied Soviet territories, only a small minority of these people collaborated out of identification with the National Socialist ideology or owing to some nationalist aspirations. For the most part, working in the various institutions created by the occupying authorities presented—initially, at least—an opportunity to make the best, for themselves and for their families, of an unfortunate situation. It meant, inter alia, having a job at a time when there were almost no jobs to be had.

With the unfolding of the Nazi terror, collaboration, as well as resistance, became for many a matter of pure physical survival. For some, for example for the Poles in Byelorussia, who were members of the Home Army (Armija Krajowa), work in institutions such as the local self-administration and the auxiliary police was used both as a cover for subversive activities as well as a way of acquiring military training.[4]

The Germans needed some degree of local cooperation, because they came into the Soviet territories with very little personnel and with only a very vague knowledge of the conquered territories. At a later stage, as the radicalization and brutalization of the occupation policies increased, the Germans intended the local collaboration bodies to serve not only as propagandistic tools but also as a kind of lightning rod that would absorb the rage of the population. Finally, the Germans expected the collaborationist institutions to manage to rob the resistance movement of its manpower.

Thus, in Byelorussia, an entire web of indigenous institutions and organizations was created that cooperated—some willingly and others with reservations—with the German occupying authorities. To refute the existence of the phenomenon of Byelorussian collaboration means to deny the obvious facts. Byelorussian society was a normal one that found itself in an abnormal situation between 1941 and 1944; in this respect, its reactions were no different from those of other European societies in countries that had to live for a certain period under the Swastika. In all of these societies, there were individuals and groups of people who, impelled by various motives, thought it "convenient" or even "essential" to cooperate with the new authorities.

The history of indigenous collaboration in Byelorussia as well as in other occupied countries does not conjure up a halo of glory like the history of the resistance movement although, as we shall see, during World War II the line separating the two could be extremely thin; nevertheless, the phenomenon did occur and must be reconstructed and analyzed, because without it the picture of World War II would be incomplete.

For the sake of authenticity, the names of people in this work are presented in their Byelorussian form (for example, Astroŭski, Kušal). The decisive consideration for the presentation of place names was the site of the particular locality. Thus, localities situated during the occupation period in the Rear Area of Army Group "Center" where the predominant language was Russian are presented in their Russian form (for example, Mogiljov, Gomel, Bobrujsk), whereas the names of cities and villages that belonged to the *Generalkommissariat Weißruthenien*, where Byelorussification policies were pursued and where many documents were composed in Byelorussian, the Byelorussian form is presented (for example, Baranaviči, Hlybokaje, Navahrudak). In quotations from German documents, the German place names remain unchanged (for example, *Gebietskommissariat Baranowitsche, Gebietskommissariat Hansewitsche*). All translations from the German, Russian, Byelorussian, Hebrew, and Yiddish documents are my own, if not stated otherwise. Needless to say, any errors, factual or otherwise, that may be encountered in this work are solely my own.

The work on this book would not have been possible without the kind support of many people and organizations. First of all, I would like to thank Professor Ben-Cion Pinchuk and especially Dr. Gilad Margalit, who for three long years stood by my side and whose friendly advice, constructive comments, and extremely competent critiques contributed greatly to the shaping of my study.

My highest appreciation goes to the Bucerius Center for German History at Haifa University and to its head, Dr. Yfaat Weiss, for providing me with a half- year grant, enabling me to do part of my research in the German archives. In addition, I wish to thank the director of the Zentrum für Antisemitismusforschung at the Technical University (Berlin), Professor Dr. Wolfgang Benz, for the hospitality offered me by ZfA during my archive research in Germany.

As with every historical work, the assistance of the personnel of various archives is of crucial importance. At this point I wish to cordially thank all of those people at the Bundesarchiv (Berlin-Lichterfelde), Militärarchiv (Freiburg im Breisgau), Bundesarchiv (Dallwitz-Hoppegarten), and Yad Vashem archives (Jerusalem), whose names unfortunately I do not know, but who assisted me greatly in finding my way through the rich resources of their respective archives. Also, my warm thanks are due to the head of Jerusalem Office of the Simon Wiesenthal Center, Dr. Efraim Zuroff, who was kind enough to allow me to look through the records assembled by the Office.

I would like to thank also the Authority for Advanced Studies at Haifa University, for providing me with a grant that enabled me to focus on my research without being troubled by financial concerns.

I also wish to express my gratitude to Professor Dan Michman (Bar-Ilan University and the International Institute for Holocaust Research, Yad Vashem) for his extremely constructive review of my research work. In addition, my thanks are due to the anonymous reviewers of the *Holocaust and Genocide Study* journal, whose critiques were of immense value in the process of developing parts of this book.

I was granted the opportunity to work on this book during my stay in Germany, in the framework of my post-doctorate Minerva Fellowship at the Bibliothek für Zeitgeschichte (Stuttgart). My *Dankeschön* goes to the personnel of the Bibliothek, especially to its director, Professor Dr. Gerhard Hirschfeld, and to his secretary, Frau Edith Gruber, for their hospitality and assistance. Professor Dr. Hirschfeld, who is himself a specialist on the phenomenon of collaboration during World War II, was ready and able to provide me with hints and advice that contributed greatly to the work on this book as well as to its subsequent publication.

I wish to express my gratitude to Dr. Leonid Smilovitsky (Diaspora Institute, Tel Aviv University), for pointing me towards the works of Byelorussian historians that are not widely known outside Byelorussia.

My sincere appreciation also goes to Mrs Lee Cornfield and Mrs. Fern Seckbach, who spent many days making sure that the language of this volume looks and sounds like English.

Dr. Fania Oz-Salzberger (Haifa University), who employed me as a research and teaching assistant for many years, was not only an employer with whom it was a pleasure to work but also a friend who took a genuine interest in my research. My kind thanks are due to her.

Last but not least, I wish to thank my parents for providing me with unfaltering moral support throughout these years.

Notes

1. It is very difficult to establish with precision the human losses in Byelorussia during the period of Nazi occupation. In the Soviet period, it was routinely suggested that every fourth Byelorussian resident perished. For more than fifty years after World War II, the number of 2,200,000 people killed in Byelorussia was taken for granted (see for example, Ivan Kravchenko, "Nemecko-Fashistskij okkupacionnyj Rezhim v Bjelorussii," in *Nemetsko-Fashistskij Okkupatsionnyj Rezhim (1941–1944)*, ed. Yevgeny Boltin et al. (Moscow, 1965), 63). This number included 1,409,225 "peaceful inhabitants" and 810,091 Soviet prisoners-of war (POWs), not all of whom lived in Byelorussia before the war. Mainly owing to propagandistic reasons, the number 2.2 million was taken for granted. Only in the last decade were these numbers, which originally appeared in the 1944 report of the "Extraordinary Commission for the Investigation of the Crimes of German-Fascist occupants," revised somewhat by historians both within and outside Byelorussia. In the collection *Narysy historyi Belarusi* that appeared in Minsk in 1995, the Byelorussian historian Alexej Litvin assumed the number of the losses among Byelorussian population to be between 1.95 and 2 million people. According to Litvin, this number includes Byelorussians who perished in Byelorussian territory as well as at the front and during forced labor in Germany. In this case, the author takes into consideration the fact that the census carried out in Byelorussia in 1939, after the annexation of western areas, was falsified, and that the figure of 2.9 million people was simply added out of whole cloth. See Alexej Litvin, "K Voprosu o Kolichestve lyudskikh Poter' Belarusi v Gody Velikoj Otechestvennoj Vojny

(1941–1945 gg.)", in *Belarus v XX Veke*, ed. Yakov Basin (Minsk, 2000), 136–37. In the 2002 edition of the study *Zhertvy Dvukh Diktatur* dealing with the tragic fate of Soviet forced workers in the Third Reich, Russian historian Pavel Poljan quoted the summary report of the Extraordinary Commission, dated 1 March 1946. The report detailed the losses in Byelorussia for each of the twelve oblasts that existed at the time (after the war, the Soviet Union transferred to Poland a large part of prewar Bialystok oblast as well as three rayons of the Brest oblast. The remnants of the Bialystok oblast were renamed Grodno oblast). In this report 1,360,034 people were listed under the rubric "killed, tormented peaceful citizens." This number accounted for 22.4 % of the total Byelorussian population. See P. Poljan, *Zhertvy Dvukh Diktatur* (Moscow, 2002), 11, 737. Christian Gerlach, *Kalkulierte Morde* (Hamburg, 1999), 11, Litvin, "K Voprosu," 142.

2. Yury Turonak, *Belarus' pad njameckaj akupacyjaj* (Minsk, 1993), 198. Turonak quotes *Narodnoje Khozjaystvo Belorusskoj SSR* (Moscow, 1957), 14. Both Turonak and Nicholas Vakar, the author of the classic study about Byelorussia, accuse the Soviet authorities at least as much as the Germans for the deliberate destruction of the Byelorussian economy in the first weeks of Operation *Barbarossa*. Turonak even states explicitly that "the greatest destruction in Byelorussian industry occurred as a result of the evacuation to the east of machines and equipment as well as of the elimination through the partisans of the small businesses at the periphery" (198). It is difficult to prove or disprove such statements.

3. Gerald Reitlinger, *House Built on Sand* (London, 1960), 155.

4. See Martin Dean, "Polen in der einheimischen Hilfspolizei. Ein Aspekt der Besatzungsrealität in den deutsch besetzten ostpolnischen Gebieten," in *Die polnische Heimatarmee*, ed. B. Chiari (Munich, 2003), 355–68, esp. 359f.

INTRODUCTION

As early as 1972, the British historian David Littlejohn remarked that "[t]he literature of resistance is prolific; that of collaboration sparse indeed."[1] This statement is still accurate today. The very sensitivity of the topic has prevented researchers from approaching it for many years. Yet, as regards collaboration in the former Soviet territories, ideological considerations have also played a paramount role in preserving the topic's "untouchable" status. Immediately after World War II, when the Cold War threatened to turn into a hot one, a trend in Western historiography sought to draw lessons from the war, especially from the German experiences in the *Ostpolitik*. One such "lesson," which was practically taken for granted, was that Hitler's failure in the war against the Soviet Union was due chiefly to his inability to create and use the wide-scale anti-Soviet opposition inside the Soviet Union. Such views, voiced for the first time in 1949 in *Life* magazine in an article by Wallace Carroll, the former director of the London Office of the US Office of War Information, were not confined to the mass media, but were accepted readily by Western historians.[2]

Thus, for example, Alexander Dallin, in the first edition of his fundamental work *German Rule in Russia,* quoted Carroll's article no less than nine times. It is no wonder, therefore, that in this state of affairs and minds, the main focus of Western research was on the military aspect of collaboration on the part of Soviet citizens, as embodied in the various *Hilfswilligen* or *Hiwis* (literally: "voluntary auxiliaries") and the so-called "eastern troops" (*Osttruppen*) that served as both sentries and antipartisan fighters.[4]

Subsequent research interests were drawn to the so-called Vlasov movement. Until the beginning of the 1990s, a series of studies and memoirs by former German military and civilian officials had been produced in the West which focused on military collaboration on the eastern front during World War II and emphasized the "missed chances," but did not analyze the events.[4] Even then, critical voices opposed the perspective of "missed chances" and strove instead to analyze the phenomenon of collaboration in the former Soviet Union as it was, not as it might have been. One of these voices belonged to the British historian Gerald Reitlinger, who in his study, *The House Built on Sand,* harshly rebuked the existing tendency to instrumentalize the history of military collaboration in the Soviet Union in an attempt to gauge current political or strategic needs.[5]

From the beginning, other historians, like Dallin, perceived the occupied Soviet territories as a single monolithic body, without allowing for any differentiation among the various regions. As a result, prior to the fall of the Soviet Union, any consideration of the history of Byelorussia under German occupation was mentioned only sporadically in non-Soviet research.[6]

During the period when access to the Soviet archives was impossible for Western scholars owing to the general political situation, virtually all of the studies published were based solely on records available in Western archives. Many of these records were captured German documents, which provided a picture of Nazi occupation from the point of view of the occupiers and presented the local inhabitants as mere objects of the occupation policies.

On the other side of the "iron curtain," the theme of collaboration was taboo. Officially, it was deemed unthinkable that "decent Soviet people" would have cooperated with the enemy of the USSR. If mentioned at all, collaborators were usually described either as "traitors from among the nationalist bourgeoisie, a small group of renegades and secret agents of the fascist intelligence," or as people who were forced—by means of threats or deception—to collaborate with the Nazis. As the leading Byelorussian military historian, Alexej Litvin, noted, for a long time "priority" in the coverage of the theme of collaboration was afforded to "investigators rather than to researchers."[7]

Thus, it is not surprising that one of the first persons to refer to the problem of collaboration in Byelorussia during the Nazi occupation was Lavrentij Tsanava, the head of the NKVD (KGB) apparatus in Byelorussia in the postwar years.[8] The works that appeared during the 1960s, 1970s, and 1980s in Soviet Byelorussia were intended primarily to serve Soviet propaganda, demonstrating the "anti-national character" of collaborators, and their postwar role as "agents of international imperialism." In Minsk, in 1964, Vasilij Romanovskij published a book with the revealing title *Saŭdzel'niki ŭ zlachynstvakh* (Accomplices in the Crimes), which reported on the participation of Byelorussian collaborators in Nazi crimes. Its main function, however, was not to analyze the Byelorussian collaboration per se, even though it is based on rich documentary material and provides valuable facts. Rather, the intent of this work was to accuse "American imperialism" of using former "Nazi accomplices" for its own subversive activities against the Soviet Union.

The disintegration of the USSR and of the Eastern Bloc in the late 1980s and early 1990s marked a certain turn in the historiography dealing with the National Socialist occupation in the East. For the first time, Western historians gained access to Soviet archives (although that access was not—and still is not— complete), and they were able to cite the testimonies of the people who lived in the occupied territories during the period. This, in turn, allowed an insight into the society under occupation not only, as previously, from the perspective of the occupiers, but also from the point of view of the occupied, an opportunity to study their reactions to the conditions imposed by the occupation. Little wonder then that from the 1990s collaboration as a response to occupation also began to attract the attention of researchers dealing with the theme of the Third Reich's rule in the former Soviet territories. In fact, the sixteen-volume collection of articles *Europa unter Hakenkreuz* that appeared in Germany between 1994 and 1996 devotes much space to the debates on the subject.[9] At the same time, the previous "monolithic" approach to the occupation, as expressed by Dallin, gave way to a separate analysis of each region and its events.

In the 1990s, three studies appeared dealing specifically with Nazi occupation policies in Byelorussia (one in Polish and two in German).[10] Of these three, only the study by Christian Gerlach dealt with the entire Byelorussian territory, whereas Yuri Turonak's and Bernhard Chiari's works focused solely on the territory of *Generalkommissariat Weißruthenien* (the civil administration area), thus excluding from the scope of their research the large part of occupied Byelorussia, i.e., the military administration area and the territories attached to *Reichskommissariat Ukraine, Gen-*

eralbezirk Litauen, and *Bezirk Bialystok.* At the same time, Chiari
and Turonak concentrated on the social and political aspects of the
Nazi occupation of Byelorussia and therefore gave careful consideration to the phenomenon of collaboration, whereas Christian
Gerlach built his study around the German economic policy in
Byelorussia and therefore considered the phenomenon of collaboration only very briefly. Still, notwithstanding all the shortcomings
of these three studies, they can be seen as pioneering works in the
research of Nazi occupation policies in Byelorussia.

The three studies mentioned above were based to a great
degree upon sources from the Byelorussian archives and thus
the picture they presented of Byelorussia under the occupation
was as close to reality as was possible (this is especially true of
Turonak's and Chiari's studies) and free of any ideological considerations. Their main significance, as noted, was in their pioneering character. At the same time when treating the theme of
collaboration none of these studies devoted enough attention to
the variety of the motives for collaboration with the occupiers.
Similarly, they did not analyze the various forms and aspects of
collaboration in Byelorussia. Moreover, by concentrating primarily on the occupation period itself, these authors did not go
beyond it or gave only cursory treatment to the activities of the
various Byelorussian collaborationist bodies after the German
retreat from Byelorussia in 1944. For example, a topic such as
collaboration in the framework of Waffen-SS remained largely
outside the scope of all the aforementioned studies. In the current study, I am striving specifically to put the phenomenon of
Byelorussian collaboration, with its multiple forms and facets,
under a magnifying glass, to place it within the general context
of German occupation policies, and to provide an analysis of
Byelorussian collaboration beyond the occupation period as well.

Further impetus toward conducting a close analysis of the phenomenon of collaboration, especially of the collaboration in the
implementation of the "Final Solution of the Jewish Question,"
was provided in the 1990s by the studies of the American scholars
Christopher Browning, Daniel Jonah Goldhagen,[11] and Jan
Tomasz Gross.[12] The study by Martin Dean, *Collaboration in the
Holocaust* (2000), constituted a major contribution to the
research on the topic of collaboration in the execution of the
"Final Solution" in Byelorussia and the Ukraine. Based on an
abundance of factual material, it attempts to track the motives of
those local inhabitants who actively participated in the persecution of their Jewish neighbors, impelled apparently by more than

mere anti-Semitism or greed. Dean's study, however, important as it is, concentrates once again upon only one aspect of the indigenous collaboration, namely the police collaboration, which was probably the most "visible" form of collaboration as the local police were inter alia directly involved in the physical extermination of the Jews. Yet, as I will show in this study, even in relation to the Holocaust this was not the only form of local collaboration.

Although in Byelorussia itself the theme of the local population's collaboration with the Germans is still a rather marginal topic, a number of studies have appeared there dealing with this topic. Especially fruitful in this respect was the period of relative liberalization—covering approximately the first half of the 1990s—that followed the disintegration of the Soviet Union. Of note are such works as those of Alexej Solov'ev, dealing with the Byelorussian Central Council, and of Sergej Zhumar, dealing with the Byelorussian-language "legal press" (i.e., the press that published with the permission of the German occupying authorities), as well as the more recent studies by I. Servachinskij and byAlexej Litvin, which deal with the topic of Byelorussian collaboration at large.[13] Nevertheless, recent years have witnessed an emerging tendency inside Byelorussia to return to the old pattern of historiography.

Once again, the themes of resistance and partisan warfare are taking center stage in the local research on the occupation period in Byelorussia. Typical is the work of Vladimir Kuz'menko *Intelligenciia Belarusi v Period Nemecko-Fashistskoj Okkupacii (1941–1944)* (Byelorussian Intelligentsia in the Period of German-Fascist Occupation), which deals mainly with the participation and subsequent role of the Byelorussian intelligentsia in the resistance movement during the occupation period. Moreover, Byelorussian historiogrpahy, returns to the style of describing collaborators' characteristics, labeling them as "traitors, self-seekers, cowards, perjurers who, for miserable hand-outs and current interests, betrayed the most sacred of all: the homeland."[14] This approach has little to do with balanced historical analysis. A number of studies produced by Byelorussian authors living abroad, recently published in Byelorussia, are also of interest. Most often the theme of collaboration in such works is either mentioned very briefly, as in the study by Jan Zaprudnik, *Belarus' na Histarychnykh Skryzhavannjakh* (Minsk, 1996), or presented apologetically, as in the study by Lyavon Yurevič, whose work is based on the memoirs of former members of the Union of Byelorussian Youth.[15]

Reviewing the state of research in the field reveals the absence of a study analyzing the various aspects of the phenomenon of collaboration that covers the entire territory of Byelorussia, one that considers the motivations of the local collaborators as well as the perceptions of the German occupying authorities, military and civilian. This book aims to fill this lacuna in the historical research of World War II.

As in other occupied countries, collaboration in Byelorussia was not something monolithic; rather, it took various forms and included many spheres of life. At the same time, like every historical phenomenon, it was by no means static. In this case, its development (and variations) stretched over the entire occupation period. Moreover, the phenomenon of collaboration cannot be understood outside the context of the reality of the occupation. And finally, collaboration constitutes a perfect case study of the destructive social influences of the Nazi occupation, which resulted in the disintegration of all existing social ties. The present work takes all of these points into consideration.

To be sure, the phenomenon of collaboration was not unique to Byelorussia but existed in all countries that found themselves under Nazi occupation between 1939 and 1945. The first chapter of this work therefore provides a general overview of the phenomenon of collaboration in various occupied countries.

Obviously, readiness to collaborate with the invader did not appear out of a void, neither in Byelorussia nor in other Nazi-occupied territories. Collaboration with the Germans during World War II had its roots in the period preceding the German occupation, so the second chapter of this book is dedicated to an analysis of the historical background and the genesis of Byelorussian collaboration.

Since one of the chief factors that influenced the decision to collaborate with the German authorities was Nazi occupation politics themselves, the third chapter presents a general overview of these politics, so as to examine to what degree they did or did not encourage the collaboration.

Chapter 4 deals with political forms of collaboration in Byelorussia. The main focus here is on bodies such as the "local self-administration," the Byelorussian Self-Aid Organization (BNS), the Byelorussian Central Council (BCR), and the Union of Byelorussian Youth (SBM). Primarily the occupying authorities saw all these organizations as important tools for maintaining control of the population in Byelorussia as well as for exploiting local resources to supply the Germans' war needs.

But did these organizations have their own aims? If the answer is affirmative, how much did the occupation authorities know about these aims and how far were they prepared to tolerate them? This chapter aims at addressing these questions.

The fifth chapter considers the Church's view of the collaboration phenomenon in Byelorussia and its role in it. The Orthodox Church occupies the center of these discussions. Among other issues, this chapter considers the limits of collaboration as drawn by the Church's top officials.

Chapter 6 deals with so-called "ideological" collaboration. As this chapter demonstrates, a group of people in Byelorussia identified themselves almost completely with the goals of the occupying power. These people played an important part in the "legal" mass media, such as in the largest Byelorussian newspaper of the time, *Belaruskaja Hazeta*, and were supposed to provide propagandistic cover for various measures of the Nazi occupation authorities.

One of the main raisons d'être of the very existence of the collaboration movement in Byelorussia, as well as in other occupied countries, was the Nazis' need to maintain "peace and order" (*Ruhe und Ordnung*). In the main, this meant the elimination of "undesirable" elements. Chapter 7 analyzes the role of local collaborators in this process. Since Jews were at the top of the list of undesirables, this chapter is devoted mainly to Byelorussian collaboration in the Holocaust. Here it is important to examine to what extent the participation of local residents in Byelorussia accelerated the implementation of the "Final Solution." The chapter discusses the various forms this participation took, ranging from the denunciation of Jews to the seizing of their property, with some being murdered while others were still alive but left to perish. In addition, this chapter also analyzes the role of local collaboration bodies in the repression of other groups also defined by the Nazis as undesirables, including the Roma (gypsies), Soviet prisoners of war, and strangers (*Ortsfremde*).

The last chapter examines the role of Byelorussians in the Third Reich's military efforts during the different stages of World War II. The various military and paramilitary frameworks in which Byelorussian collaborators were integrated are delineated. The chapter's main thrust is on the policies of the German authorities towards the people serving in various auxiliary police and military bodies, and it describes the perpetual, unresolved Nazi conflict between reality and racially ideological dogmatism.

Notes

1. David Littlejohn, *The Patriotic Traitors* (London, 1972), xiii.
2. Wallace Carroll, "It takes a Russian to beat a Russian," *Life Magazine* (19 December 1949), 80–88, quoted in Gerald Reitlinger, *House Built on Sand* (London, 1960), 22–23.
3. The Hiwis were paramilitary formations created spontaneously by various Wehrmacht units at the very beginning of the offensive against the Soviet Union. Consisting chiefly of Soviet POWs, and civilians from among the local population, they performed mainly logistic duties.
4. See Peter Kleist, *Zwischen Hitler und Stalin* (Bonn, 1950); George Fisher, *Soviet Opposition to Stalin* (Cambridge, MA, 1952); Sven Steenberg, *Vlasov* (New York, 1970); Wilfried Strik-Strikfeldt, *Gegen Stalin und Hitler* (Mainz, 1970); the chapter "Soviet Union" in D. Littlejohn, *Patriotic Traitors* (London, 1972); Reinhard Gehlen, *The Service*, trans. D. Irving (New York, 1972; Russian translation quoted below); Jürgen Thorwald, *Die Illusion* (Zurich, 1974); Alex Alexiev, *Soviet Nationalities in German Wartime Strategy, 1941–1945* (Santa Monica, 1982) (Alexiev states in the preface to his work: "This study should be of interest to military and strategic planners who are beginning to address the Soviet nationality issue in a strategic perspective," iii); J. Lee Ready, *The Forgotten Axis* (Jefferson and London, 1987); Catherine Andreyev, *Vlasov and the Russian Liberation Movement* (Cambridge, 1987).
5. Reitlinger, *House Built on Sand*.
6. Among the studies that do touch upon this topic are Nikolas Vakar's *Belorussia: The Making of a Nation* (Cambridge, MA, 1956) as well as Ivan Lubachko's *Belorussia under Soviet Rule 1917–1957* (Lexington, 1972). Both works dedicate only two chapters to German occupation, significantly marginalizing the theme of local collaboration. The only work appearing in the West before 1991 that dealt exclusively with Byelorussian collaboration during the war was that of John Loftus, *The Belarus Secret* (New York, 1982), but the fact that it was written not by a historian but by the former federal prosecutor in the Office of Special Investigations of the Criminal Division of the US Justice Department made it more of an indictment than a piece of objective research.
7. Pjotr Pospelov et al. (eds.), *Istoria Velikoj Otechestvennoj Vojny Sovetskogo Sojuza 1941–1945* (Moscow, 1961). A. Litvin, "Kalabaracijnizm na Terytorii Belarusi ŭ Gady Vjalikaj Ajchynnaj Vajny: Da Prablemy Vyvuchennja," in *Akupacyja Belarusi (1941–1944)*, (Minsk 2000), 195–203.
8. Lavrentij Tsanava, *Vsenarodnaja Partisanskaja Vojna v Belorussii protiv Fashistskikh Zakhvatchikov*, Part II, (Minsk, 1951), 642–852.
9. See, for example, Hans-Heinrich Wilhelm, "Die Rolle der Kollaboration für die deutsche Besatzungspolitik in Litauen und 'Weißruthenien'," in *Europa unter Hakenkreuz*, ed. W. Röhr, Band: *Okkupation und Kollaboration* (Heidelberg, 1994), 191–216; Valentin Bojzow, "Aspekte der militärischen Kollaboration in der UdSSR von 1941–1944," in ibid., 293–317; Werner Röhr, "Okkupation und Kollaboration," in ibid., 59–84.
10. Yury Turonak, *Belarus' pad nyameckaj Akupacyjaj* (Minsk, 1993); Bernhard Chiari, *Alltag hinter der Front* (Dusseldorf, 1998); Ch. Gerlach, *Kalkulierte Morde* (Hamburg, 1999).

11. Christopher Browning, *Ordinary Men: Reserve Police Battalion 101 and the Final Solution in Poland* (New York, 1992). Daniel Jonah Goldhagen, *Hitler's Willing Executioners: Ordinary Germans and the Holocaust* (New York, 1996).

12. Jan Tomasz Gross, *Neighbors* (Princeton and Oxford, 2001). See Loftus' highly controversial book quoted above, note 6; Shalom Cholawski's *Be-Sufat ha-Killayon* (In the Eye of the Hurricane), (Tel Aviv, 1988). In German: Jürgen Matthäus, "'Reibungslos und Planmäßig'. Die zweite Welle der Judenvernichtung im Generalkommissariat Weißruthenien (1942–1944)," *Jahrbuch für Antisemitismusforschung*, 4 (1995), 254–74; M. Dean, "Polen in der einheimischen Hilfspolizei. Ein Aspekt der Besatzungsrealität in den deutsch besetzten ostpolnischen Gebieten," in *Die polnische Heimatarmee*, ed. B. Chiari (Munich, 2003). In English: M. Dean, *Collaboration in the Holocaust* (New York, 2000); Yehoshua R. Büchler, "Local Police Force Participation in the Extermination of Jews in occupied Soviet Territory 1941–1942," *Shvut* 4, no. 20 (1996), 79–99; Daniel Romanovsky, "Soviet Jews under Nazi Occupation in Northeastern Belarus and Eastern Russia," in Z. Gitelman, *Bitter Legacy* (Bloomington and Indianapolis, 1997). In Russian: D. Romanovsky, "Kholokost v Vostochnoj Belorussii i Severo-Zapadnoj Rossii Glazami Neevreev," *Vestnik Evrejskogo Universiteta* 2, no. 9 (1995), 56–92; Leonid Rein, "Otnosheniie belorusskogo naseleniia k evreyam vo vremya Katastrofy. 1941–1944 gody," *Evrei Belarusi. Istoriia i Kul'tura*, 6 (2001), 181–205; Ilya Altman, "Zhertvy Nenavisti" (Moscow, 2002); Emanuil Yoffe, *Belorusskije Evrei* (Minsk, 2003), 179–93.

13. Alexej Solov'ev, *Belorusskaja Tsentral'naja Rada* (Minsk, 1995); Sergej Zhumar, *Okkupatsionnaja Periodicheskaja Pechat' na Territorii Belarusi v Gody Velikoj Otechestvennoj Vojny* (Minsk, 1996); I. Servachinskij, *Kollaboracionizm na okkupirovannoj Territorii Belarusi* (Minsk, 1999); A. Litvin, *Akupatsyja Belarusi (1941–1944). Pytanni Supracivu i Kalabaracyi* (Minsk, 2000).

14. "V usluzhenii u gitlerovcev," *Belorusskaja Niva*, 18 September 1996, quoted in Lyavon Yurevič, *Vyrvanaja Bachyny*, (Minsk, 2001), 5.

15. Yurevič, *Vyrvanaja Bachyny*.

CHAPTER 1

COLLABORATION IN OCCUPIED EUROPE: THEORETICAL OVERVIEW

A study that aims to analyze the various forms of collaboration in Byelorussia under Nazi occupation requires two preliminary steps by way of introduction: the first is to define the term collaboration, and the second, to compare the phenomenon of collaboration in various countries under German occupation during World War II. Both of these goals are pursued in the brief description provided in this chapter, since a detailed comparative analysis is beyond the scope of this volume.

Defining the Collaboration

"Was Kollaboration ist, weiß jedermann," wrote German historian Hans Lemberg ironically in an article published in 1972.[1] Yet, to this day, historians focusing on this topic have not reached an agreement on the exact definition of the term *collaboration* nor on the activities that this term encompasses. The term as used in this work was first coined in a radio address to the French nation by the aged Marshal Pétain, the head of the Vichy regime, after his meeting with Hitler in Montoire-sur-le-Loir in October 1941. Pétain stated then that "collaboration had been envisaged between our two countries [that is, France and Germany—L.R.]" and that he "accepted it in principle."[2] What Pétain meant by "collaboration" was an arrangement between victorious Germany and defeated France, by which the latter wished to preserve as much independence as possible.[3]

As the occupation continued, the activities that could be defined as collaboration between victors and vanquished proceeded from the macro, i.e., the interstate level, to the micro, affecting spheres of life such as culture, the economy, and the individual. Such activities were not peculiar to France but were part of the occupation reality in every country that found itself under Nazi rule. Nevertheless, as the Polish historian Czesław Madajczyk demonstrated, during World War II the term collaboration as such was not widely used. The German wartime official correspondence speaks of "voluntary cooperation" (*freiwillige Mitarbeit*), calling those engaged in these activities "agents" (*Agenten*), "people in our confidence" (*Vertrauensleute*), "willing foreign nationals" (*willige Fremdvölkische*), "national administrations" (*nationale Verwaltungen*), and "anticommunist forces" (*antikommunistische Kräfte*).[4] The term collaboration was used only in the case of the final report of the German military administration in Belgium, referring to the cooperation between France and the "forces of the *New Order*."[5] Actually, France remained the only country where the term collaboration was already used during the war by both sides, that is, by the Germans as well as by the collaborators themselves.

The Allies, although aware of the phenomenon of collaboration in the German-occupied countries, refrained from using the term collaboration during the war to characterize it. Rather, the terms "Quislingism" and "Quislings," after the name of the most renowned collaborator, Norwegian Vidkund Quisling, were used, although the phenomenon of collaboration as such was considered an act of high treason warranting moral (and eventually judicial) condemnation.[6]

This approach dominated the attitude in various European countries even decades after the end of World War II. In both West and East, the term collaboration came to encompass a very broad set of activities, ranging from work in the "local administrations" to conducting love affairs with German soldiers. For example, in postwar Norway, the term *landsswick*, as introduced in judicial practices, included a "general conception of the crime against independence and security of the State (high treason), crime against the constitution and the Head of the State (state treason), and crime against the military articles of the Military

Criminal Code (military treason)." Even conducting business with the enemy could be punishable under the definition of landsswick.[7]

At the same time, a razor-sharp distinction was drawn between collaboration and resistance; specifically, it was assumed that those who did not collaborate with the occupying authorities almost automatically belonged to the resistance, and vice versa. Applying this approach, anyone who lived through the occupation period was immediately defined as a "good" or a "bad" Frenchman, Dutchman, Norwegian, and so on.[8] Thus, in Western European countries the term collaborator was frequently utilized in political struggles to discredit opponents.[9]

In light of the foregoing, it is not surprising that quite a long period the subject of collaboration remained beyond the scope of research dealing with Nazi occupation in various countries. It is likely that the moral implications of collaboration and the shame it aroused also served as a major deterrent to scholars, who refrained from addressing the issue for many years following the war. Only after several decades did historians dealing with the period of the Third Reich and World War II begin to address the issue of collaboration. Understandably, initial studies on the topic focused on Western European countries, where the democratic and pluralistic societies made it somewhat easier to discuss a theme as delicate as collaboration, and where access to primary sources was practically unrestricted. By the 1970s and 1980s, the research on France, where, as noted, the term collaboration was born, was especially prolific.[10] The history of collaboration in other countries, such as the Netherlands, Denmark, Norway, and Belgium, too, became the subject of historical analysis at quite an early stage.[11] The fall of the Socialist bloc in the late 1980s and early 1990s led to a growing interest in the topic in the former Socialist countries, although access to the archives there was—and still is—not without complications.

The rise of interest in the theme of collaboration naturally led to the necessity to define the term. Numerous attempts were undertaken to do so as well as to differentiate between its various forms. In my opinion, none of the definitions encountered in historical literature is totally convincing. Even the most basic definition provided by *The Oxford Companion to World War II*, namely, "working with the enemy" or "assisting the occupying power," is problematic.[12] On the one hand, it includes a judgment, which has nothing to do with objective historical analysis, while on the other, it disregards the wide variety of motives and

modes of conduct encompassed by the term collaboration and
portrays the collaborators as mere assistants or, more accurately, as accomplices to the occupying power, devoid of any goals
or interests of their own.

Using the French case, historian Stanley Hoffmann attempted
to differentiate between "*collaboration with Germany* for reasons
of state (*collaboration d'état*) that is to safeguard French interests
in interstate relations between the beaten power and the victor"
and "*collaborationism with the Nazis*, in the sense of an openly
desired co-operation with and imitation of the German regime."[13]
According to Bertram M. Gordon, a similar distinction already
existed during World War II. Thus, *collaborationists* were those
who cooperated with Germans out of ideological considerations,
while *collaborators* were those "who trafficked with the Germans
solely for material gain or personal advancement."[14] This distinction, however, is hardly convincing: for example, the French October 1940 anti-Jewish legislation, which was more radical than the
infamous Nuremberg Laws of 1935 (see below), was issued by
people in the Vichy government, who—were we to adopt the terminology of Hoffmann and Gordon—would be considered collaborators rather than collaborationists.

In his study dealing with collaboration in the Netherlands,
German historian Gerhard Hirschfeld differentiates between
two modes of conduct by the population in the occupied European countries: the so-called *attentisme*, which he defines as "a
cautious, waiting approach, a form of playing for time," characteristic of the period immediately following the German conquest; and *collaboration* per se, which expressed itself in various
spheres, such as politics, the economy, and the social fabric, and
which resulted from the desire "to reach an agreement on a
modus vivendi with the victors in the interests of maintaining
peace and order...."[15] This distinction too is not unproblematic.
It appears to be applicable only to Western European countries,
where the German occupation authorities did not confront the
population at once with brutal force, so that, at least initially,
the "wait-and-see" approach was possible. In Byelorussia, however, as well as in other occupied Soviet territories (with the possible exception of North Caucasus) and in Poland, almost from
the beginning of Nazi rule the population was faced with a
choice: either cooperate with German occupying authorities or
be treated as "partisan supporters."

Isaiah Trunk, in his classical study on Jewish Councils
(*Judenräte*), differentiates between forced *cooperation* with the

German authorities, which was undertaken in order to avoid the worst fate; and *collaboration* which was undertaken voluntarily out of either "sharing the National-Socialist ideology," "opportunity for personal gain (career, authority, etc.)," a desire "to let off pentup hatred toward the Jews," or "a lust to rob and kill."[16] According to Trunk, the collaborators included in their ranks non-Jews as well as "Jewish Gestapo agents," "the demoralized members of the [Jewish] Councils and the ghetto police who served the German authorities in order to gain privileges and material goods for themselves and their families."[17] Israeli historian Dan Michman, too, defines active collaboration as "active assistance to the government due to ideological identification or careerism."[18] For me, neither the distinction between cooperation and collaboration nor the reductive definition of collaboration as ideological identification or opportunism is convincing. First, depicting cooperation as a result of the desire to prevent the worsening of things to come presupposes that those who adopted this course of behavior knew the German plans and the type of future the Germans had in store for them. This assumption, however, is wrong, since the Germans never fully disclosed their ultimate plans regarding occupied Europe. Secondly, as will be seen from the example of orthodox clergy in Byelorussia, it is often difficult to draw a clear line between cooperation and collaboration. To illustrate this, although the Archbishop of Bialystok-Hrodna Venedikt (Benedict) issued the so-called "epistles" thanking Hitler and Nazi Germany for the "liberation of Byelorussia from the Bolshevist yoke," he also, in put forth calls to send labor forces to work in Germany, maintained that dispatching a specific number of workers from each region would save the majority of the population from German repression.[19] It is also true, as will be demonstrated in what follows, that not all collaborators were fascists or opportunists. Both in Byelorussia and in other occupied countries there were people who used collaboration with the Germans to attain their own goals, which did not necessarily coincide with those of the occupiers. One such example is the wing of the Organization of Ukrainian Nationalists (OUN) led by Stephan Bandera, which strove to build a Ukrainian state that would be a partner rather than a vassal of the Third Reich.[20]

Over recent decades, research in the field gradually came to the conclusion that it would be wrong to consider the conduct of the populations under occupation as either collaboration or resistance. Numerous attempts were made to differentiate

between various modes of behavior located in the "gray zone"
between active collaboration and active resistance. Czesław
Madajczyk, in the Polish-language study *Faszyzm i okupacje*
(Fascism and Occupation), distinguished between numerous
kinds of reactions to occupation:

1. Voluntary and conscious political *treason*
2. *Treason* forced through the use of violence or terror
3. Voluntary or forced *collaboration*
4. *Fraternization*
5. *Loyalty*, harmful for the interests of the occupied country
6. *Passivity*, connected to or resulting from the realities of
   war
7. *Passive resistance*, designated also as civil struggle or civil
   disobedience
8. *Self-defense* in case of threat to the national existence
9. *Participation in conspiracy or in armed resistance*
10. *Flight abroad*

Madajczyk defines treason and collaboration as "either an
offer made voluntarily to the occupying power or cooperation
with the occupier either in exchange for material or other
advantages or forced through torture or blackmail."[21]

Werner Rings, in his study *Life with the Enemy*, went even
further and differentiated between various kinds of collaboration in Nazi-occupied Europe according to the collaborators'
stance vis-à-vis the occupation regime.[22] He speaks of four different types of collaboration:

1. *Neutral collaboration*, i.e., collaboration out of self-inter-
   est, the desire to continue life as it was before the occupation without sharing a single tenet of National-Socialism
2. *Unconditional collaboration*, i.e., collaboration out of
   total identification with the principles and goals of
   National-Socialism
3. *Conditional collaboration*, i.e., collaboration integrating
   partial identification with Nazi doctrines and plans, but
   pursuing the goals of the collaborators. As an example of
   such conduct, the author refers to the activities of the
   Nederlandsche Unie (Netherlands Union), which on the
   one hand was ready to accept the role of Germany as a
   leader of "New Europe" (the prewar Dutch Prime Minister and leader of NU, Hendrik Colijn, likened Germany to

the conductor of a symphony orchestra), while on the other hand, it strove to preserve the autonomy of Holland.[23]

4. *Tactical collaboration*, i.e., collaboration intended either to damage the occupation rule from within or "to prevent the mass murder of innocent people whenever possible."[24]

Although this classification may appear somewhat artificial, it still depicts, more or less, the broad spectrum of collaboration in Nazi-occupied Europe. Often there are cases in a single country that correspond to either all four or at least to more than one of these collaboration types; frequently, different types of collaboration characterize different periods of the occupation.

Understandably, collaboration—like resistance—was to a very significant degree a reaction to the occupation, and it cannot be understood without the context of occupation politics. German historian Werner Röhr stated that in analyzing the phenomenon of collaboration one must ask foremost about the concepts applied by the occupiers themselves to local occupation politics; also, one has to probe the influence of collaboration upon these politics.[25] Thus, collaboration does not necessarily mean identification with the goals and interests of the conqueror. On the contrary, as stressed by Röhr, the existence of an individual's or a group's own interests and goals, whether economic profit or the establishment of a nation-state, make it necessary to speak about collaboration.[26]

As noted, it would be wrong to draw a sharp dividing line between collaboration and resistance. It was not unusual, especially in the later stages of the war when the ultimate victory of Germany appeared much less evident, for people to change sides or even to engage in activities that could be called collaboration and resistance simultaneously. One of the most prominent examples of changing sides (even more than once) is the *Druzhina* (see Chapter VIII), which consisted of Soviet soldiers who had become prisoners of war in the early stages of the German-Soviet war. The unit participated in numerous anti-partisan operations in the territory of Byelorussia, and yet in August 1943 defected en masse to the partisans. On the Soviet side it was renamed The 1st Anti-Fascist Partisan Brigade. At the same time, resistance did not necessarily mean an armed struggle against occupiers. Activities such as sheltering Jews, which of course contradicted Nazi ideology and practices, also fell into this category. One case to cite here is that of Andrij Szepticky,

Metropolitan of L'viv (today Ukraine), who both blessed the
members of the Ukrainian Waffen-SS Division "Halychyna," yet
simultaneously provided assistance to the persecuted Jews.[27]

It is indeed difficult, if not senseless, to provide what purports
to be an exact and all-encompassing definition of the term collaboration. Collaboration took on many faces and forms. It occurred
in virtually all spheres of life and was not relegated to any particular country. It affected all the countries that found themselves
under Nazi rule during World War II. Not unlike any other historical phenomenon, collaboration too had its roots, which should
be sought in the period preceding the Nazi occupation.

Comparative Overview

The Background

Readiness to collaborate with the occupiers did not occur on its
own. As the next chapter will show using the example of
Byelorussia, we must look for the sources of this willingness in
the period preceding German occupation. In the period between
the two world wars, Europe found itself in a political, intellectual, and economic crisis that reached its peak in the 1930s and
made the populations of various European countries susceptible
to radical ideas, such as those offered by Mussolini in Italy and
Hitler in Germany. World War I only hastened the social changes
introduced by the Industrial Revolution, which to a considerable
degree were sanctified—so to speak—by the ideas of the European Enlightenment. The new age witnessed the rise of new
elites and the destruction of traditional values. Occurrences
such as secularization or atomization of society, to name only
two, left a great number of Europeans confused. Many of those
who had belonged to traditional elites even spoke about the
decline of civilization. For such people, the ideologies of Nazism
or Fascism, which combined ultramodern and traditional elements, seemed to serve as defenders of this "civilization"; therefore, during the occupation they were quite ready to support the
occupation authorities, if not to actually collaborate with them.
Stanley Hoffmann describes the Vichy government in France as
representing "revenge, but one perpetrated by men who felt
that they were the natural governing elite of the French
state."[28]

Among the prominent collaborators were people who had
belonged to the radical left for quite some time, such as Jacques

Doriot, the head of the collaborationist Parti Populaire Français (PPF). He was the one-time communist mayor of the Paris suburb of Saint-Denis and former member of Comintern's Executive Committee. This fact needs some explanation. As vividly demonstrated by the Israeli scholar Zeev Sternhell, at the end of the nineteenth century some people in the Marxist movement began to be skeptical about the revolutionary potential of the proletariat. While a number of these skeptics abandoned the idea of revolution altogether and resorted to parliamentary struggle as a means of changing society (the most prominent example is, of course, German Social Democrats), others began to look for a vehicle other than the proletariat to realize their revolutionary visions and believed they would find it in the nation. The first among those who tried to integrate socialism and nationalism as early as the end of nineteenth and beginning of the twentieth century was the French publicist, George Sorel.[29] Both Sorel and his followers remained the sworn enemies of the existing "bourgeois" capitalist order, especially of occurrences linked to the modernization process, such as the "dehumanization" of people and the atomization of the society.

It is little wonder that the demand for a "corporatist state" became not only the official aim of the fascist regime in Italy, but also the cornerstone of the ideology of radical movements throughout Europe, from Charles Maurras' Action Française, the most influential radical right-wing movement in France before World War II, to the Walloon Rex movement in Belgium, all of which figured prominently in the support of collaborationism during the German occupation of their countries.[30] The majority of collaborationists in France described themselves as "socialists." However, as noted by Bertram M. Gordon, the researcher of French collaborationism, in this case "'socialism' became a term utilized by many who felt threatened by large scale capitalism... As in German National Socialism, the socialism of the collaborationists was that of the battlefield, a feeling of egalitarianism in that all had been exposed equally to the bullets at the front. This egalitarianism was combined with the hierarchy of military merit, symbolized by the uniform and the colored shirt."[31] The collaborationists saw themselves in the first place as young revolutionaries who came to overthrow the "rotten" and stalled liberal order of their parents, and in this respect they considered the Nazi movement in Germany and the Fascist movement in Italy their true models.

The fact that the totalitarian regimes in Italy and Germany of the 1930s succeeded in significantly obliterating the conse-

quences of an economic crisis made these regimes quite popular
not only inside their respective countries; they also definitely
enhanced the longing for a "strong hand" among various circles
beyond them. At the time though, very few people noted the
human cost or that this attainment derived from investing heavily in the armament industries. Moreover, onlookers' positive
sentiments and admiration for totalitarian governments also
gained strength from scandals that public opinion associated
with democratic governments, especially that of France. The
loudest of these scandals involved Serge Alexandre Stavisky, a
schemer of Jewish origin, whose machinations involving high-
ranking state officials continued for almost half a century. Ultimately, the disclosure of the Stavisky affair led to public riots at
the beginning of February 1934, which almost ended in an
assault on the Chamber of Deputies in Paris.[32] Moreover, the
Stavisky affair had a very strong anti-Semitic flavor. Stavisky
was a Jew and, more than that, he was a "foreign Jew." As will
be shown below, foreign Jews in France in the 1930s became the
prime target for widespread xenophobia. For many of those who
saw their world crumbling as a result of all the changes before
and after World War I, Jews—the traditional scapegoat of Christian societies—who after 1917 also came to be associated with
the Bolsheviks, were seen as the prime destroyers of this world.
Anti-Semitism thus became one of the central features in the
outlook of all Europeans who were susceptible to the solutions
proposed by Rome and later by Berlin.

In addition, for people outside Germany and Italy, these two
regimes radiated stability, a significant, attractive attribute for
inhabitants of France, where a widespread joke of the time
stated that even "dinner lasted longer than the government."[33]
Adding to this formula the almost obsessive fear of Bolshevism
that reigned in Europe between the two world wars, it appears
practically inevitable that pro-German attitudes would become
widespread even beyond rightist circles, with Nazi Germany
coming to be regarded as Europe's bulwark against Bolshevism.

Among the main issues plaguing Europe in the interwar
period was an ethnic one. The Wilsonian "right of nations for
self-determination" became a time bomb for Europe. Even in a
country like Belgium, conflict between Dutch-speaking Flemings
and francophone Walloons was rampant. In 1939, the ultrana-
tionalist Vlaamsch Nationaal Verbond (Flemish National Union),
which advocated Flemish separation from Belgium and the creation of a Greater Netherlands, succeeded in gaining almost

eight per cent of the votes in the national elections and some twenty-two seats in both chambers of the Belgian parliament.[34] The issue of nationalism, however, was much more salient in Central and Eastern Europe. At a time when the term *multicultural* had not yet been invented, it was common practice to subject the ethnic minorities to the title nation or even to assimilate them outright. The most extreme example of this was interwar Poland, which had the largest share of minorities. As will be shown in the next chapter using the example of the Byelorussians, almost from the very beginning and despite public declarations promising respect for the rights of minorities, the Polish authorities carried out discriminatory policies toward all non-Poles, especially those living in the Kresy Wschodnie (the eastern districts), that is, the territories that belonged to Poland according to the Treaty of Riga of 1921. These inequitable Polish policies created a real powder-keg effect that boomeranged and exploded immediately after the Soviet invasion of Eastern Poland in September 1939, and again during the Nazi occupation. Anti-Polish rhetoric became a significant element of various collaborationist bodies that emerged both in Western Ukraine and Western Byelorussia between 1941 and 1944.

Stalinist terror should also be mentioned as one of the factors that drove people in Soviet territories to side with the Germans. While it would be wrong to portray all collaborators in these territories as enemies of Soviet rule, undeniably the forced collectivization, the mass executions, and the deportations carried out in the Soviet Union in the 1930s and early 1940s embittered more than a few people against the Soviet regime, such that they greeted the Germans as liberators from the yoke of the Soviets. In fact, before the German invasion, many of these collaborators had been loyal Soviet citizens, and some had even occupied prominent positions in the Communist Party and state apparatus (see Chapter II).

Although democracy in many Western European countries was badly shaken during the interwar period, it still succeeded in holding on until the German invasion. In the eastern part of Europe, in the majority of cases, democracy did not withstand the challenge. Many of the eastern countries had only become independent states after World War I, previously having been part of the Russian, German, or Austro-Hungarian Empires. In countries such as Poland or the Baltic republics, the democracy initially established was merely a concession to the fashions of the time and therefore had a less than promising start. Not surprisingly, then, it was dispensed with in favor of authoritarianism at the earliest opportunity. In 1926, the Lithuanian leftist Populist government attempted to extend the limits of liberal democracy—apparently too far—with steps such as granting amnesty to political prisoners, dropping the clergy's salaries from the state budget, and attempting to normalize relations with the Soviet Union. This initiative was met by a military coup d'état that overthrew the democratic liberal government; ultimately, the President Smetona's authoritarian regime was established.[35]

In the interwar years, Goebbels' propagandist machine, as well as the number of agreements concluded between Germany and its neighbors after 1933, such as with Poland in 1934, persuaded politicians and broad sections of the population in various European countries that they were dealing with a "normal," that is, a peace-seeking regime. The Nazis did not hurry to disclose their plans, but rather camouflaged them with rhetoric on revision of the Versailles treaties, stating their desire to unite all Germans in one state and to create the "New Europe." As it turned out, this approach succeeded in giving many a false sense of security. Appeals and warnings, like those from the German-Jewish left-wing journalist and political scientist Franz Borkenau, for example, remained by and large unheeded.[36] As early as April 1939, shortly after the fall of Prague, Borkenau predicted that Germany would not stop there but would "continue her course of indeterminate aggression."[37] His voice and others' echoed in the wilderness of the World War I aftermath: the war had been so great a shock that many Europeans refused to give any credence to such dire predictions. Especially in France, pacifism was rampant in the late 1930s and was among the leading causes for the rapid collapse of the French Republic in the summer of 1940.[38]

The Nazi Attitude toward Collaboration

Hitler was well aware of all the dissatisfaction throughout interwar Europe and was quite eager to use it to his advantage. As early as 1932, that is, even prior to the Nazi ascendancy to power in Germany, during one of his conversations with the Nazi president of the Danzig senate, Hermann Rauschning, and Danzig's *Gauleiter* Albert Forster, he described his prospective methods of warfare:

> When I wage war, Forster, in the midst of peace, troops will sud-
> denly appear, let us say, in Paris. They will wear French uniforms.
> They will march through the streets in broad daylight. No one
> will stop them. Everything has been thought out, prepared to the
> last detail. They will march to the headquarters of the General
> Staff. They will occupy the ministries, the Chamber of Deputies.
> Within a few minutes, France, Poland, Austria, Czechoslovakia
> will be robbed of their leading men. An army without a general
> staff! All political leaders out of the way! The confusion will be
> beyond belief. But I shall long have had relations with the men
> who will form a new government—a government to suit me.... We
> shall find such men, we shall find them in every country. We shall
> not need to bribe them. They will come of their own accord.
> Ambition and delusion, party squabbles and self-seeking arro-
> gance will drive them.[39]

Even if this scenario existed merely in the Fuehrer's imagina-
tion, it nevertheless includes a list of the motives that did actually compel many of those who decided to collaborate with the
Germans in various European countries after 1939.

One of the main peculiarities of the National Socialist regime
was the vagueness of its plans and slogans, regarding both
domestic and international politics. Some of their declarations
were very appealing to social groups outside Germany. This was
especially true with regard to the term "New Europe," which
was proclaimed by the Nazis as they embarked upon their
aggressive policies. Characteristically enough, on 5 April 1940,
shortly before the German invasion of Scandinavia, Goebbels
stated before a group of German journalists, "If someone asks
today, 'what do you think of the New Europe?' we have to
answer that we don't know. Certainly we have an idea. But if we
put it into words, that immediately brings us enemies and
increases resistance. Let us first have the power, then people
will see, and we will see too, what we can make of it.... Today we
say: *Lebensraum*. People can make of that what they want."[40]
Indeed, this lack of a well-defined plan and the elusive meanings
of their public statements was one of the main factors that
brought about collaboration with the Nazi regime in various
European countries.

Essentially, on different levels, the Nazi authorities' attitude
toward local collaborators was duplicitous. Werner Röhr
remarks that in principle Hitler and his government did not
want any form of cooperation, but rather wished to deal only
with those who received the Germans' orders.[41] He also says

that the Nazis were not ready to provide collaborators, even those in subordinate positions, with the freedom to take actions or decisions of their own.[42] Even as late as 1942–43, Goebbels noted in his diary that "[t]alks about collaboration are intended only for a moment," while Göring informed the Reichskommissare and military commanders in the occupied territories in August 1942 that "I do not recognize any collaboration.[43] I see the collaboration of the French only as follows: when they supply us (*abliefern*, that is, provide us with products and war-relevant materials–L.R.) to the utmost of their ability (*bis sie selber nicht mehr können*), and they do so voluntarily, then I will say: collaborate!"[44]

Such views were widespread not only among the top echelons of the Nazi regime but also among the personnel in the occupied countries. Even at the beginning of 1944, half a year before the liberation of France, the High SS and Police Leader (HSSPF) in Belgium and Northern France, Carl Oberg, stated that "although outwardly the politics of cooperation must be carried out, I hereby declare that we shall never lose sight of the ultimate goal: the final destruction of France."[45] Italian Foreign Minister Count Galeazzo Ciano compared the attitude of German authorities in France toward the local collaborators to that of "a coachman toward his mule once he has tied it to a pole, and as he hits it with a stick, crying 'collaborate! Collaborate!'"[46] All of this does not mean that the Nazis were deaf to "collaboration proposals" (W. Röhr) in various occupied countries, but rather that they were ready to use this collaboration "exclusively as a means to achieve their own goals."[47] The aim of the German authorities was primarily to compromise the collaborators in such a way that they would be absolutely dependent upon the occupiers.[48]

A distinction, however, should be made between the official statements of Nazi functionaries and the real conditions that existed throughout occupied Europe. Quite soon after the beginning of the occupation, it became clear that without at least some degree of local collaboration it would be impossible to exploit the resources of the occupied countries for German war needs or to establish effective control over the populations of these countries. One should remember that "the main task of civil as well as of military administration" in all occupied countries "was to put at the disposal of German warfare as many resources of the occupied country as possible and to do so using only a minimal number of German forces to quell the resistance."[49]

In the specific countries, the German attitude toward collaboration varied according to the particular aims of the occupation in that country. Moreover, this attitude depended to a significant degree upon the officials who manned the German occupation administration. While it is difficult to speak of any coherent Nazi plans regarding occupied countries, when one looks at the map of occupied Europe, it is possible to discern several groups or even blocs of countries.[50] First noted are countries such as Holland and Belgium, which were allegedly included in the "Great Germanic Reich" (*Großgermanische Reich*), or Norway, which was supposed to be "tightly bound to the 'Great Germanic Reich.'"[51] In these countries, the highest possible level of collaboration was allowed: both Dutch *Secretarissen-Generaal* (Secretaries-General) and Belgian *secrétaires-généraux* practically fulfilled the functions of ministers, while the role of German occupation apparatus was merely to oversee (in the case of Holland) or direct (in the case of Belgium) these functionaries.[52] Then there were countries such as Vichy France and Denmark, which retained their governments. In such situations, according to Werner Röhr, "official state collaboration was developed even if it was not so named."[53] According to Nazi planners, both France (the northern and the southern parts) and Denmark were intended to be like Norway, "tightly bound to the 'Great Germanic Reich.'"[54] Furthermore, a group of countries in Europe, comprising Greece, Serbia, and a few other countries, was to be included in the "Great Economic Space" (*Großwirtschaftsraum*). The fate envisioned for these states was not annexation but German "political and economic supremacy."[55] Local collaboration was thus seen as an important factor, and following the invasion and occupation of these countries, new collaborationist governments were established. Later Northern Italy and Hungary, Germany's former allies, which had been seized and occupied after their attempt to leave the war, joined this group.

Finally, there were the Polish and Soviet territories, which from the beginning were seen as areas intended for colonization and exploitation (*Lebensraum*). Here collaboration was allowed only at the lowest possible level. In the occupied Soviet territories, however, one must differentiate between the Baltic area versus Byelorussia and Ukraine. The difference here was based foremost upon the "racial value." In the Baltic countries— Lithuania, Latvia, and Estonia—any attempts taken to create independent governments in the first days of the German invasion were nipped in the bud.[56] Yet, according to the Nazi racial scale, the Baltic people were considered superior to the Slavs, so the Germans permitted a higher level of collaboration in the Baltic region. Very early on, a number of local advisors were appointed to the German administration and given the title "country directors" (*Landesdirektoren*) in Estonia, "general directors" (*Generaldirektoren*) in Latvia, and "general councilors" (*Generalräte*) in Lithuania. In Lithuania there were Generalräte for the economy, agriculture, finance, education, justice, communications, work, and social security, all of whom were subordinate to the corresponding department in the Generalbezirk Litauen.[57] "Country directors," "general directors," or "general councilors" by no means acted as a collective body. Moreover, in the Baltic area, Germans also allowed the appointment of "advisors"—who became known as "local district elders" (*einheimische Kreisälteste*)—to *Gebietskommissare* as well as "city advisors" (*Stadträte*) and "community advisors" (*Gemeinderäte*) for the countryside.[58] The Lithuanians, for example, were eventually also permitted to administer their own order and security police, and all of this together created the illusion of *Lietuvos Savivalda* ("Lithuanian Self-Government"), existing parallel to the German administration.

In Byelorussia and the Ukraine, however, the Germans did not even bother to create such "illusions." They scarcely concealed that they had come there "to squeeze out of the country whatever economic capacities they could."[59] The interests and needs of the local population were of little or no importance to the Nazi rulers. Any sign of national independence was out of the question. A good illustration of this attitude is that of the German authorities toward the infamous Organization of Ukrainian Nationalists (OUN), whose members played a central role in the massacre of Lviv Jews in the first days of the German invasion into the Soviet Union. This organization, created in 1929, prior to the Nazi-Soviet war, had split into two factions: one was headed by the old OUN chief, Andrij Mel'nyk, and relied more heavily on cooperation with the Germans (OUN-M); the second faction was headed by Stephan Bandera (OUN-B), who supported the idea of an independent Ukraine that could carry on equal relations with Germany.[60] Immediately after the German occupation had started in different areas of the Ukraine, Bandera's faction began not only to openly promote the idea of an independent Ukraine but also to create Ukrainian organs of self-government and police, placing OUN members in key positions.[61] From the outset, the Germans, especially the SS, viewed these developments with a great deal of suspicion, as they did not quite correspond with their colonization and exploitation plans for the Ukraine. In September 1941, Germans stated explicitly that the national-political ideas propagated by Bandera's faction "represent an acute danger for German interests in the present and the future."[62] Ultimately, they did not hesitate to crack down on both Bandera's and Mel'nyk's adherents.[63]

Most often, the establishment of local self-administration followed quite soon after the occupation, under the aegis of military authorities both in Byelorussia and the Ukraine. It was allowed because of the shortage in German manpower, which was needed to administer the newly conquered territories; the Germans' lack of knowledge about the local conditions; and the German military's desire to concentrate on the fighting, along with its reluctance to get too deeply involved in the local political intrigues. Generally, both in Byelorussia and in the Ukraine, the initial creation of the so-called "local self-administration" was allowed to extend only to the prewar rayon level. At first, the occupying authorities did not bother to create the fictitious "advisory" bodies, as they did in the Baltic area. From the very beginning it was explicity stressed that local self-administration was merely intended to carry out German orders.

Finally, the personal attitudes of those who manned the German occupation apparatus also played an important role in defining the German position toward local collaboration. The following chapters review the position of Wilhelm Kube in Byelorussia; at this point, it is sufficient to provide examples of the two extremes of the Nazi approach: (1) the one held by the quasi-liberal head of the German civil administration in Holland, Arthur Seyss-Inquart, and (2) that of the notoriously brutal *Reichskommissar für Ukraine*, Erich Koch. Although Seyss-Inquart could hardly be described as "a liberal," as his sentence in Nuremberg might suggest, in July 1940 he spoke of binding "the Netherlands as closely as possible to the Reich economically, whilst keeping it independent, in order to preserve the Dutch Indies territories." He explicitly stated that this could be achieved, "if a political will can be created, such that would make the economic link with the Reich seem to be the will of the Dutch people."[64] At the other end of occupied Europe, Erich Koch proclaimed openly even before entering his office of Reichskommissar, "The Ukrainians are proto-Slavs (*Urslawen*). They will be ruled with makhorka, vodka and nagaika."[65]

The Collaboration and Collaborators

It would be wrong to attribute all collaboration during World War II to fascist and fascist-like parties, as did for example David Littlejohn, the British historian, in his early study *The Patriotic Traitors*.[66] Generally speaking, collaboration in German-occupied Europe transcended familiar classifications of ethnic groups, social class, and party alliances. Thus, in France we find collaborators such as the former member of Comintern's Executive Committee, Jacques Doriot; members of monarchist, chauvinist, and anti-Semitic Action Française; industrialists who made hefty profits from the contracts oiling the German war machine; and members of the working class.[67] According to Marxist historiography, workers constituted the backbone of the resistance to Nazi rule, despite the fact that some 59.000 of them volunteered for work in Germany.[68] Likewise in Belgium, both Flemish nationalists and Walloon Rex chose to side with the Germans.

It was not unusual to find left-wing politicians among the collaborators, especially in Western European countries. In Denmark, where collaboration operated at the state level, the Social Democrats, who during the period of German occupation continued to be an important element of Danish politics in general and of the Danish government in particular, also became supporters of collaboration with Nazi Germany. The Danish Social Democratic Prime Minister, Vilhelm Buhl, stated in 1942 that "the historic task of Denmark is to ensure and cement a close and peaceful collaboration with Germany."[69] In Belgium, we find among the most prominent collaborators a figure such as the president of the Belgian Labor Party (Parti Ouvrier Belge, POB), Henry De Man, who took seriously the socialist element of National Socialism and founded the Union of Manual Intellectual Workers. At a later stage of the occupation, this organization fulfilled the function of a trade union for those Belgian workers who were sent to work in Germany.[70]

The communists, too, were not immune to collaboration with the Nazis. The conclusion of the Soviet-German Non-Aggression Pact, signed at the end of August 1939, influenced the positions of communists toward Nazi Germany in various countries. Shortly before it was banned in May 1940, the communist press in Holland published articles impugning England and local capitalists for dragging Holland into the war on the side of the Allies, and demanded "peace and friendship with the German people";

it called upon the Dutch to display "an irreproachable attitude" to the occupying power and not to "allow themselves to be involved in the 'cause' of the Allies and their 'accomplices.'"[71] Although the Germans came to the Soviet territories supplied with the so-called Commissars' Order, which demanded the ruthless elimination of all Communist Party functionaries and rank-and-file party members, in reality some former members of the Communist Party, including those in high positions, found their way into the various collaborationist bodies there, too.

At least initially, fascist and fascist-like movements and parties played a less than prominent role in the occupation policies of their respective countries. The best examples of this are provided by Vichy France, Norway, Holland, and Denmark. In France, Pétain's Vichy government had full sovereignty over the so-called Free Zone, that is, the southern part of the country, which was unoccupied by German troops. Here, as Stanley Hoffmann has shown, collaboration was to a very large extent a matter of power struggles.[72] According to Hoffmann, the collaboration of the Vichy government was not necessarily voluntary, and he shows that the Pétain government was facing a dilemma: collaboration or "polonization." The threat of a German occupation of the Free Zone was always present (it was actually realized in November 1942, after the beginning of the Allies' Operation Torch in North Africa), while at the same time, the Germans also held a large number of French POWs, giving them the means to blackmail the Vichy government into supporting the German war effort.[73] American researcher Bertram Gordon also speaks of the Vichy government's limits regarding collaboration. His work states that "the Vichy government opposed ideological collaboration. Pétain fought tenaciously for a modicum of French independence in Hitler's New Europe, by attempting to keep communications open to the United States."[74] To be sure, under the conditions of Nazi-occupied Europe, the dividing line between voluntary and involuntary collaboration was very thin. In the case of Vichy, "attentiveness" to German demands was not rare, stemming from the belief that Germany would win the war and that this attentiveness would be rewarded by consideration and regard for French interests in the postwar New Europe.

The main aim of German occupation policies in both Western and Eastern Europe, it must be remembered, was to be able to exploit all the resources required for the German war effort. In areas such as Poland and the occupied Soviet territories, this goal could be achieved by sheer coercion; in Western Europe,

however, this aim required the existence of local administrations
with a minimal degree of authority throughout their countries,
at least enough to insure an uninterrupted supply of resources.
The Germans were well aware that the fascist organizations,
which were not very popular in the countries under discussion,
could not be relied on for these purposes. In Norway, Quisling's
Nasjonal Samling succeeded in recruiting a total of only 27,178
members toward the end of 1940, and this was with the support
of German Reichskommissar Terboven.[75] In Denmark, the local
Nazi party was too insignificant to play any role at all throughout the entire occupation period. In Holland, at least initially,
conditions were somewhat more favorable for the local Nationaal-Socialistische Beweging (National Socialist Movement, NSB)
headed by the engineer Anton Adriaan Mussert. From the very
beginning, the occupation authorities embarked on a course of
Nazification of the Netherlands and of the "bringing into line"
of Dutch society, creating various bodies there that were copies
of Nazi organizations in Germany, such as the Winterhulp Ned-
erland (Winter Aid Netherlands), or the Nederlandsche Arbeits-
dienst (Dutch Labor Service), which was analogous to RAD in
Germany. The benefits the NSB reaped from this process were
predictable, yet they were not unambiguous. As Gerhard
Hirschfeld remarks, most Dutch people regarded NSB party
leaders as "politically and morally corrupt."[76] Although membership in the organizations mentioned was compulsory, the
Dutch did not hurry to join, because the leadership was often in
the hands of NSB members. Moreover, according to the statistics
presented by Hirschfeld, in July 1943, only some thirty-five per
cent of all Dutch city mayors were NSB members, as opposed to
three per cent in October 1941, and some fifty per cent in the
summer of 1944.[77] In the ministries, the situation was even less
satisfactory for the NSB. A mere 16 of the 835 employees of the
Interior Ministry were members of the National Socialist Movement. Only the newly created Ministry for Propaganda and
Arts, a slavish copy of Goebbels' ministry in Germany, was an
undisputable domain of Dutch Nazis.[78] In France, Germans did
their utmost to keep out of power the half-dozen radical right-
wing parties and groups that considered themselves true collaborationists. Bertram Gordon writes that Germans feared the
disorder that might be created by the collaborationists' rise to
power, a situation that might be detrimental to the exploitation
of the country's resources. The Germans feared that the rule of
people who wanted a strong France would endanger any Ger-

man domination of the "New Europe" of the future.[79] To prevent the materialization of these dangers, Germans also created
a deliberate split among the French collaborationist groups, by
supporting—to a certain degree, of course—various groups at
alternate times. According to Bertram Gordon, "collaborationists were useful as a threat to induce official Vichy to toe the
line."[80]

Initially, even within the fascist or fascist-like movements
themselves, throughout Europe there were differences regarding the movements' attitude toward German occupation. The
Walloon Rexist movement in Belgium is a pertinent example. At
first, many members of this group were reluctant to collaborate
with the Germans, although their chief, Degrelle, presented
himself as a friend of Germany. It must be remembered that
Rex grew out of the extremist wing of the Belgian Catholic
Party, and as Catholics, many Rexists despised the neo-pagan-
ism displayed in Nazi Germany. Although already in the 1930s
Degrelle's movement received support from fascist Italy, its attitude toward the Third Reich was more than cool, since according to Martin Conway the latter was seen "as a combination of
Prussian militarism and pagan racism."[81] In Norway, too, there
were varying approaches, as evidenced by the fact that many
members of the Nasjonal Samling fought against the German
invaders in April 1940, and it is certainly an irony of history that
the shot that sank the *Blücher*, the flagship of the German
invading fleet in the Oslo fjord, was delivered by a certain Lieutenant August Bonsak, a member of Quisling's party.[82]

The role of the pro-Nazi movements in Western European
countries began to increase from about 1942–43. The deteriorating military situation of the Third Reich and the significant
increase in brutal force sanctioned by the occupation policies in
various countries led not only to a growing hostility toward the
occupation regime but also to a decline in the readiness to collaborate and in the number of collaborators. Even the traditional ruling elites, which as in Holland were initially prepared
"to cooperate with the German authorities in 'a most loyal'
way," exercised increasing reserve in their contacts with the
German authorities. In these circumstances, the Germans found
themselves compelled to rely more heavily on the local fascists.[83]
In Norway, Quisling, who had been kept out of power, became
the minister-president in February 1942, heading a "government" that consisted exclusively of Nazi members.[84] His
attempts, however, to Nazify Norwegian society are described as

a failure by David Littlejohn.[85] In France, toward the end of 1943, Marshal Pétain's attempts to adopt an independent or semi-independent course led to increased German pressure on his government to admit prominent collaborationists, such as the head of fascist Milice, Darnand, or the head of the Rassemblement National Populaire, Marcel Déat. In that way the Nazis ensured that the government maintained a pro-German course at a time when they were facing increasing resistance and the imminent Allied invasion of France.[86]

The spectrum of collaboration in various European countries was wide indeed. When speaking about different forms of collaboration, we must take into consideration the array of conditions prevailing in each of the occupied countries in various stages of the occupation. In Western Europe, however, the very motives for collaboration were more diverse than those in Eastern Europe, especially compared to those in the occupied Polish and Soviet territories, which in Nazi parlance were commonly defined as Ostgebieten. This difference stemmed chiefly from the fact that Nazi occupation policies were based to a great extent upon racial criteria. At least initially, the Dutchmen, Norwegians, or Danes, who were dubbed by people such as the SS head, Himmler, as "Germanic" people, were given more room to maneuver in their dealings with the occupation authorities than were the Poles, the Byelorussians, or the Ukrainians. The most radical Nazis, such as Hitler and Bormann, viewed the latter groups as no more than natural slaves of the Third Reich, and their lands were to be ruthlessly colonized and exploited. In John Armstrong's article on collaborationism in Eastern Europe, which concentrates particularly on the cases of Slovakia, Croatia, and the Ukraine, he stresses that collaborationism during the German occupation in Western Europe, and especially in France, sprang by and large out of ideological and social conflicts, while in Eastern Europe it was mostly "ethnic disaffection" that played a central role in the decision to collaborate with the occupying power.[87] Of course, this classification according to the East-West division is not entirely straightforward, as will be shown using the example of Byelorussia, an Eastern European country in which ideological considerations, first among them anti-communism, also played a role in the reactions of the occupied toward their occupiers. Nevertheless, it is hardly deniable that in the multiethnic societies of Eastern Europe, nationalism was a much more important factor than in the largely mono-ethnic societies of Western Europe.

Undoubtedly, at first, in most of the countries overrun by German forces, there existed among the populace at least some kind of readiness to adjust to the new conditions. British historian Martin Conway describes the atmosphere that reigned in Belgium in the aftermath of the German lightning-speed conquest of this country in the summer of 1940:

> [A]s the Belgian population returned to their homes, families and jobs, so they attempted to adjust to the circumstances of the German Occupation and to assess the position of their country. In doing so, almost all Belgians—regardless of their linguistic or political background—were agreed on one point: namely that the German military victory on the European continent was incontrovertible. While many hoped that Britain would fight off the expected German assault, only a very few rather foolhardy spirits were willing to predict that the British would prove able to challenge the Nazi hegemony on the European continent. For most Belgians, the overriding priority was therefore to preserve Belgian unity within a German dominated Europe.[88]

Of course, such sentiments were not unique to Belgium. In many European countries, the impression of German military superiority was palpable in the first weeks and months after the occupation, as was the feeling that it would be more expedient, so to speak, to adjust to and accommodate the new regime rather than oppose it. In the Soviet territories, the impression of apparent German invincibility was accompanied by a fervent hope that the German presence would bring a change for the better compared to the conditions that defined the Soviet era. Although in 1939, some people, such as the Byelorussian Christian Democrat priest Hadleŭski, were skeptical of the German ability to untangle existing problems, especially national ones (see the next chapter), various sections of the population still harbored expectations for social and economic improvements. In comparing collaboration in Western and Eastern European countries, we also should keep in mind that in the latter case, the occupation authorities from the very beginning did not hesitate to greet the populations of these countries with brutal terror. In Western Europe, in contrast, owing to ideological and political considerations, the Germans at first appeared more moderate, emphasizing the local populations' willing cooperation.

In general, the reaction of the various populations to Nazi occupation was defined to a very significant degree by their overall assessment of the situation of Nazi Germany. While in the summer of 1940, very few believed that Germany could ever be defeated, in 1943, after the US entered the war, and after El-Alamein and Stalingrad, very few thought that Germany would win. The ever-increasing need to access occupied Europe's resources to maintain the German war machine compelled the occupation authorities to introduce harsh policies. This in turn led to increased resistance in all of the occupied countries, even in the "model protectorate" of Denmark. If in the early stages of the occupation, the occupied populations (especially those in Western Europe) were prepared to do whatever it would take— excluding perhaps outright collaboration—or at the very least to take the necessary steps to accommodate themselves to the new conditions, toward the end of the occupation their attitude had switched to the opposite end of the spectrum. At that point, those still collaborating with the Nazis were clearly perceived as traitors. Yet, from the beginning through to the end of the occupation, a country's range of reactions between collaboration and resistance was defined chiefly in response to German policies. Thus, in Western Europe, where the Nazi aims were less rigorously pursued, people had more room to maneuver; therefore, the adoption of a "wait-and-see" strategy, which is neither collaboration nor resistance, was not exceptional. In Eastern Europe, in contrast, especially in Poland and the Soviet territories, which were openly and from the outset defined as German colonization space, the Germans dictated a policy of "whoever is not with us is against us," greatly narrowing the local inhabitants' range of possible responses.

Economic Collaboration

Local collaboration expressed itself in various spheres. In the case of virtually all of the occupied European countries, one may speak of forms of collaboration, such as political, ideological, and military; these were significant insofar as they reflected the aims of the Germans in the different countries. During the war, the chief goal of the Nazis was to pump out the war-important resources while maintaining "tranquility and order" (*Ruhe und Ordnung*), enabling the exploitation to be conducted in the quickest, most efficient manner possible. From the Nazi point of view, the two most important methods for attaining this goal were economic and political collaboration. Basically, economic collaboration implies mutual profit. Thus, while it is quite reasonable to speak of economic collaboration in Western Europe, it is difficult to do so in the case of the occupied Soviet territories, where German authorities, through their various agencies, exerted almost unlimited control over the flow of resources and the production process.

As stated by Werner Röhr, "although the agressor's hopes for booty were greatest with regard to Soviet Union ... the economic exploitation of resources and labor was nowhere as great as in France. It yielded the greatest participation in financing the war and made the greatest contribution to securing German military capacity economically."[89] Moreover, the gradual loss of territories in the East only increased the pressure on the economies of countries such as France, Belgium, and Holland.[90] Since in Western Europe the Germans left the management of day-to-day economic affairs in local hands and retained only supervisory and directorial functions, the French, Dutch, and Belgian industrialists were able to make healthy profits from supplying goods to the German Armed Forces.[91] As mentioned above, the total value of transactions between French industrialists and the Germans during the occupation reached several billion RM. In June 1940, shortly after the German occupation of Holland, the Dutch Metaalbond, which included metal industry firms, concluded an agreement with the German Netherlands Armaments Inspectorate. Although initially Dutch industrialists were reluctant to supply war equipment to the Wehrmacht, their reservations were rather quickly overcome, and Gerhard Hirschfeld characterizes the cooperation between the Dutch industry and the Wehrmacht's Armaments Inspectorate as "undisturbed and even harmonious."[92] The sums specified in these contracts certainly contributed to the compliance of Dutch industrialists. The German Heer (land armed forces), Kriegsmarine (navy) and Luftwaffe (air force) together provided the Dutch industry with contracts of around 740 million guilders in the autumn of 1940, while two years later, in the autumn of 1942, as many as 109 Dutch firms, employing 55,000 workers, were the sole suppliers of the German navy and merchant marine, delivering goods at a monthly value of about 27 million RM.[93] As in the political sphere, in the economic field there was some competition between various bodies, such as the Deutsche Bank and the Dresdner Bank, for "a share in the booty."[94] West European businessmen were able to use this competition to their own benefit. Similar rivalries, however, were found on the other side of the transaction between occupiers and the occupied, namely, among the West European businessmen, who competed for a greater portion of the profitable contracts, which in turn made it easier for the Germans to gain access to local resources.[95]

The work carried out for various German projects both inside and outside Western Europe, including Germany, should also fall under the rubric of economic collaboration. In contrast to the territories in the "East," where recruitments for the labor force almost from the beginning took the form of a manhunt, in countries such as Holland, Belgium, and France the conscription of labor, initially at least, proceeded on a voluntary basis. In Holland, cooperation was soon established among the construction divisions of the Wehrmacht, Organization Todt (OT), and the Dutch construction industry; in August 1941, as many as 120,000 Dutch workers labored in various airfields in Holland that were used by the German Luftwaffe. Many of these workers had previously been unemployed and were attracted by the good working conditions.[96] Local institutions in Western and Eastern Europe were involved in both voluntary and forced mobilization of workers for labor in Germany. On 21 June 1940, the Dutch Ministry of Labor issued an announcement directed primarily at local skilled workers, calling on them to volunteer for work in Germany, and promising them very good employment terms. When this appeal did not produce the necessary results, the same ministry did not shrink from exerting direct pressure, by denying social assistance not only to the workers who refused to go to Germany but also to their families.[97] Whether there was coercion or not, according to statistics provided by Gerhard Hirschfeld, in June 1940, "some 148,000 had responded to the calls of German and Dutch authorities and had taken up labor service in Germany."[98] According to German historian Ulrich Herbert, as many as 291,958 workers from four Western European countries alone (Holland, Belgium, Denmark, and France) were working in Germany in September 1941, many of whom had come voluntarily.[99]

As with political collaboration, in the economic sphere too Germans created an illusion of true partnership with Western European businessmen. The plan was to involve Western European firms and individual businessmen in the colonization process and in the exploitation of the resources in the occupied Soviet territories. In a number of countries, such as France, Denmark, and Holland, special "Eastern Societies" (*Ostgesellschaften*) or "Eastern Companies" were created.[100] The "Working Committee for the Promotion of Danish Initiatives in

Eastern and Southeastern Europe" was created in Copenhagen in December 1941; its members, according to Werner Rings, "toured the occupied Eastern territories and volunteered to help the Germans exploit the area with Danish capital and labor."[101] In Holland, the Nederlandsche Oost Compagnie (Netherlands Eastern Company) was created in 1942, with the purpose of settling three million—later this number was reduced to thirty thousand—Dutch farmers in the Ukraine and the Baltic area.[102] As might be expected, this project met with very little success.

Police Collaboration

The occupiers saw the most important form of collaboration— apart from the economic—as that which took place among the various police units, which also constituted one of the most sizable forms of collaboration. According to Werner Röhr, even in areas of lower racial status, such as the Protectorate of Bohemia and Moravia, and Poland, the total strength of the auxiliary local police forces was close to 25,000 people.[103] Although the occupiers considered local police forces in all of the occupied countries as no more than an auxiliary body for the German police, and even though the Germans spared no effort in both the West and the East to exert total control over these forces, differences still existed between the occupied Western European countries and the Eastern ones.

Beyond that, it is also possible to divide the local police formations in occupied Europe into three groups. First, in countries such as Vichy France, Norway, Holland, and even Poland, the Germans retained the police forces that had existed before the occupation, putting them practically or formally under German control, manifested in the person of a Higher SS and Police Leader (HSSPF). A second type is that of police forces created under the occupation, which included both the local police in the occupied Soviet territories and Darnand's Milice Française. And finally, the third group pertains only to Western European countries with fascist movements: the paramilitary units of these groups, too, were occasionally used for police duties.[104] So it was that in Belgium the Rexist Gardes Wallonnes were recruited in autumn 1941 for sentry duty in strategically important places, while members of Rex's militia, Formations de Combat, were included in 1942 in the German-controlled Hilfsfeldgendarmerie, "a part-time auxiliary police force."[105]

The German authorities in all of the occupied countries made every effort to exert extensive control over the local police forces. Yet, if in the Soviet territories the local police forces were seen as no more than an extended arm of the German police and were totally subordinate to the German police commanders, in the West the situation was somewhat different. In Holland, where on the eve of the German invasion there existed as many as five police organizations, the local Higher SS and Police Leader (HSSPF), Rauter, proceeded to unify the local police under his control. Dutch officials, namely, the presidents of police (*Politiepresident*), were appointed in five cities (Amsterdam, Rotterdam, Groningen, Arnheim, and Eindhoven), and as members of the Dutch Nazi party they were able to exert control over the local police at the municipal level.[106] Another example is that of France: in mid-1942, an agreement was established between the HSSPF of Belgium and Northern France, Oberg, and the secretary-general to the head of Vichy government for police affairs, René Bousquet. According to this document, the French police was granted independence both in the Unoccupied and in the Occupied Zone for dealing with "anarchism, terrorism, and communism" and with "all foreign actions susceptible of troubling order within France."[107] Given that the German police was supposed to deal exclusively with "enemies of the Reich," this agreement in effect turned the Bousquet-led French police into an important instrument for the persecution of French Jews.

In Poland and the occupied Soviet territories, the local administrations had no authority whatsoever over the local police forces. If in some cases, as in Lithuania, certain "national" police units began organizing very early after the German invasion, in a short time they were reassigned to work as German auxiliary forces (*Schutzmannschaften, schumas* for short).[108] The very term *Schutzmannschaften*, which referred to the local police units designated to serve the German goals, was introduced on Himmler's recommendations at the end of July 1941. Explicitly noted was that the members of Schutzmannschaften were not policemen in the proper sense of the word. They were defined rather as an "unofficial (*nicht beamtet*) support force for the German police in the occupied areas, and as such they were subject to its rules and jurisdiction."[109] Although German authorities tried hard to prevent local administrative bodies from exerting any kind of control over the local police, they were not opposed to the idea of shifting the responsibility for the pay and supply of the *schumas* to the local self-administration.[110]

In occupied countries of both Western and Eastern Europe, Germans did not hesitate to involve the local police in the most brutal aspects of occupation politics, and foremost among these was the genocide of Jews. In the West, the occupying authorities were apparently wary about the degree of this participation. While the policemen in Holland, France, or Belgium acted exclusively within the boundaries of their countries, the Baltic and Ukrainian police units were employed outside their own countries, despite the Germans' initial promise to use these units solely within their national borders. The activities of some of these units became especially notorious, as in the case of the 11th Lithuanian Police Battalion, which took an active part in the massacres of Byelorussian Jews. Similarly, the Ukrainian and Baltic policemen who participated in the quelling of the uprising in the Warsaw ghetto were also known for the cruelty they brought to their task.

Most often, growth of the resistance movement led the Germans to expand the local police forces in both the West and the East, which in turn led to the creation of new anti-resistance forces. In France, the significant increase in the Resistance movement in 1943 led the Germans to allow the creation of the French force known as Milice Française or simply Milice, headed by Joseph Darnand, which in mid-1943 in the southern zone alone counted 30,412 members, according to data quoted by Bertram M. Gordon.[111] The Milice became the major element of French collaboration in the later stages of the occupation, and contributed significantly to an atmosphere that many historians subsequently described as tantamount to a French civil war.[112] In Holland, too, the police system was expanded in the first year of the country's occupation (1940). According to Gerhard Hirschfeld, the number of officers in the Gemeentepolite, that is, the municipal police, alone rose from 11,000 men before occupation to 14,000 men afterwards.

In the occupied Soviet territories, the German authorities were reluctant to allow the local police forces to become too large. It appears that the size as well as the role of these forces was determined by the racial dogma. In the Baltic countries, where the populations were regarded as more "racially valuable," so to speak, the creation and expansion of the police forces was far more rapid than in areas such as Byelorussia and the Ukraine. According to data quoted by Romuald Misiunas and Rein Taagepera, in August 1941, in Lithuania alone there already existed as many as twenty *schuma* battalions with 8,388 members.[113]

Collaboration in the Persecution of Jews

One of the spheres in which the role of local collaborators was
most noticeable was the implementation of the "Final Solution
of the Jewish Question." Here, too, one may speak about a certain difference between the occupied East and the occupied
West. This difference stemmed to a very significant degree from
the situation that existed between the two World Wars.
Although anti-Semitism was quite rampant in both Western and
Eastern Europe, especially in the 1930s, it had a somewhat different nature in each case. In Western Europe, the Jewish emancipation of the nineteenth century was by and large an
acknowledged fact, whereas in those countries that only a quar-
ter-century before the Nazi invasion had been part of the Russian Empire, with its official anti-Semitism, Jews were still seen
as an "alien element," not an integral part of society. While
many of the Western European Jews in the middle of the twentieth century were assimilated and did not differ either in interests or appearance from their non-Jewish counterparts, the
Jews of Poland or the Baltic countries still retained much more
of their traditional way of life, and were often clearly distin-
guishable from the surrounding population both through their
behavior and their external garb. In the Soviet Union, despite
Soviet propaganda boasting of "friendship between nations,"
anti-Semitism did not disappear but rather continued to exist in
a somewhat suppressed form. Although formally equal, the
Soviet Jews were not necessarily seen by their non-Jewish
neighbors as full-fledged members of society.

From the end of the nineteenth century, many Western European countries witnessed waves of Jewish immigration from
Eastern and Central Europe. According to Renée Poznanski,
"just under one hundred thousand" Jews came to France
alone.[114] These Jews did not hasten to "be absorbed" into their
surrounding societies, but maintained their religion, their customs, and the use of Yiddish. Moreover, accustomed to see the
authorities of their native countries as a "hostile entity," they
were often confronted with a chilly attitude on the part of the
authorities in the new countries too.[115] In the 1930s, France
imposed rigid quotas on the employment of foreigners, and
xenophobic sentiments were quite widespread in French society
on the eve of the Nazi invasion.[116] The unassimilated Jews, some
of whom had been left-wing militants in their native countries,
came into a country that already had 350,000 unemployed in the

1930s. Not surprisingly, these Jews were considered by many of the French as "the very embodiment of the triple threat of economic, political, and cultural instability," to borrow Poznanski's words.[117] The distinction between "our own" and foreign Jews was not unique to France and was found in other Western European countries as well. Ultimately, it found expression there in the anti-Jewish policies during the Nazi occupation.

The chapter dealing with collaboration in the persecution of Byelorussian Jews will discuss the difference in the "extermination process" between Western and Eastern European countries; here it is sufficient to say that in most Western European countries, the process of deporting Jews to the death camps in the east was preceded by measures aimed at first stripping them of their rights so as to eliminate them from society. This was done under the guise of formal legislation. Because local administrations in Western Europe usually played more than a merely formal role in the countries' management, their "contribution" to the formulation of anti-Jewish measures cannot go unnoticed.

One of the most striking examples of such willing participation was that of the Vichy policy toward the Jews. All authors dealing with this topic agree that the anti-Semitic course of the Vichy regime was pursued without any pressure from the German side.[118] Robert O. Paxton even remarks that "[j]ust as France was not included in the 'Middle European Great Economic Region' of German peace plans, so it was not considered part of the area to be purified of Jews. In 1940, therefore, an indigenous French anti-Semitism was free to express its own venom."[119] The Jewish Statutes, worked out by Vichy's Justice Minister Alibert and signed on 3 October 1940, provided a definition of "Jew" based solely on racial tenets and foresaw the exclusion of Jews from French society.[120] To some extent, the Statutes were even more radical than the infamous Nuremberg laws in Germany which took into consideration factors such as adherence to the Jewish religion and belonging to a Jewish community.[121] In the French Statutes, however, race alone was the decisive factor in defining the person in question as a Jew. Moreover, *Mischlinge* ("half-breeds") with only two Jewish grandparents, for example, who even in Germany itself would have been considered somewhat ambiguous in terms of racial definition, were classified in Vichy France as Jews if they had a Jewish spouse.[122]

The "Jewish Statute" was merely one of many pieces of anti-Semitic legislation adopted by Pétain's government in the late

summer–early autumn of 1940. For example, the law of 27
August 1940 repealed that of 21 April 1939, which had called for
penalizing anti-Semitic publications in the press.[123] The French
law of 4 October also envisaged the internment of "foreign"
Jews (meaning Jewish immigrants from Eastern Europe and
those from Germany and Austria who arrived in the 1930s) in
camps, which according to Weisberg later became points of
departure toward Auschwitz.[124] Only a small step was required
then to move from this legislation to outright collaboration in
genocide. Robert Paxton is quite right in remarking that "the
French laws of 1940 and 1941 made the Final Solution much
easier."[125] The role of Vichy Prime-Minister Laval and his government in deporting Jews from France to the extermination
camps disclosed an important aspect of collaboration with the
Nazis during World War II, namely, it was practically impossible
to work with the Nazis and simultaneously preserve one's own
rules. If in September 1942, Laval had hoped to deport only "foreign" Jews and spare French-born Jews, in February 1943 he
was already prepared "to go further if France could get 'some
kind of political security' ... about French territory."[126]

The position of Secretaries-General in Holland was somewhat
different. Here, too, we can see their basic misunderstanding of
the general nature of the Nazi policies as well as their attempts to
draw a dividing line between Jews born in the Netherlands and
the immigrants. The picture presented by Gerhard Hirschfeld
gives the impression that the Dutch Secretaries-General, when
working out the anti-Jewish measures and implementing them,
acted with a great deal of reservation and, to a significant degree,
under German pressure.[127] The approach adopted by the heads of
the Dutch civil service toward anti-Jewish policies can be
described as technocratic and extremely formalistic. In 1937, the
Dutch government issued special "instructions" (*Aanwijzingen*),
which were supposed to outline the conduct of the civil service in
case of foreign occupation. These guidelines were based on the
assumption that the occupying power would respect The Hague
Land Warfare Convention, which, inter alia, obliged both the occupying power and the local administration to work jointly to maintain "public order and public life." So when occupation became a
reality, the local officials—chief among them the Secretaries-General—chose to believe that the Germans were indeed adhering to
the Hague Convention and that the measures imposed by the Germans were intended to serve solely for the "maintenance of public
order and public life."[128]

During the second half of 1940, when the process of expelling Jews from the civil service in Holland began, the Secretaries-General directed a letter to Seyss-Inquart, in which they "cautioned" the Reichskommissar about the repercussions of anti-Jewish measures in Dutch society, while making it clear that they would comply, seeing the German orders as a "temporary measure which ... served to maintain public order and security."[129] Although the letter was sent on 25 November 1940, on 1 October of the same year, the Secretary-General for Internal Affairs, Fredericks, had already instructed the municipal administration to cease the employment of Jewish civil servants. Likewise, on 4 and 5 October, various state and religious institutions were ordered to provide declarations on the employment of persons of the Jewish faith (the so-called Aryan Declaration, *Arierverklarung*).[130] In 1941, when the anti-Jewish measures in Holland escalated (a process that began in January 1941, with the separate registration of Dutch Jews), the Secretaries-General found themselves under pressure from various segments of Dutch society, among them the Catholic and Protestant Churches and the universities.

In this situation, the Secretaries-General continued to maintain their position, proclaiming their "understanding of the fact that from the German standpoint Jews are regarded as anti-German," while still stressing that "the sense of justice of the people and time-honored traditions [make it] 'distressing' for the council to cooperate."[131] One should remember that, in contrast to the local officials in occupied Soviet territories, the Dutch administration did have the option not to cooperate in the persecution of the Jews. In 1937, the above-mentioned Aanwijzingen, although vague, stated that when performing their duties under the occupation, civil servants must weigh very carefully the benefits or damage that occupation policies might cause their fellow countrymen and to resign immediately should they be disadvantageous to their own people.[132] The option of resignation was actually raised at meetings of Dutch General Secretaries, for example, after a German demand was issued to fire all Jewish civil servants; it was rejected on the pretext that such resignations would mean "general chaos in all areas."[133] The Dutch administration continued to cooperate loyally with the German authorities in the belief that by doing so they were protecting the interests of the Dutch people.[134]

In the occupied Soviet territories, the situation was different. While in countries such as Holland or France the deportations of

Jews were preceded by discriminatory legislation, in the Baltic area, Byelorussia, and the Ukraine, the anti-Jewish legislation either coincided with outright murder or was dispensed with altogether. In Lithuania, the local provisional government, which had been proclaimed at the beginning of the German invasion, adopted on 1 August 1941 the special "Jewish Statute," which was almost analogous to the Nuremberg laws.[135] Simultaneously, still in the early days of the German occupation, the Jews of Lithuania were murdered, both by the units of *Einsatzgruppe A* and by the Lithuanian militiamen. In Kaunas alone, according to the Israeli historian Yitzhak Arad, some 4000 Jews were butchered between 22 and 24 June 1941 by the Lithuanian nationalists.[136] The anti-Jewish pogroms staged by the local populations took place not only in the Baltic area but also in other Soviet territories. According to German historian Thomas Sandkühler, in the first part of July 1941, as many as 10,000 Jews fell victim "to the pogroms and the shootings" in the Western Ukraine (Galicia).[137] Recently, Polish historian Bogdan Musial connected this anti-Jewish violence to the NKVD (that is, the Soviet secret police) shootings and the torture of prisoners that occurred shortly before the arrival of the Germans, as well as to the general conduct of Jews during the Soviet period.[138] However, the German historian Dieter Pohl argues against such a connection, claiming that first, in many cases these pogroms were not preceded at all by the disclosure of sites of NKVD shootings; second, no NKVD member had been caught; and third, the violence was directed not only against Jews who had occupied a state office during Soviet rule, but rather against the entire adult Jewish male—and a large proportion of the female—population.[139]

Following the establishment of local self-administration, and of the auxiliary police in the occupied Soviet territories, these bodies became active participants in all stages of implementation of the "Final Solution," from the ghettoization of Jews to their murder and the misappropriation of Jewish property. Although the Germans as a rule did not take the local administrative apparatus in the occupied Soviet territories too seriously, they were ready to allow it extensive freedom of action in the persecution of Jews. Chapter VII deals with collaboration in the Holocaust in Byelorussia and reviews in greater detail the German authorities' attitude; at this point, suffice it to say that for the Nazis it was important to draw the local collaborators as deeply as possible into the murderous process, creating a tighter bond between the occupiers and the occupied. Moreover, the people manning the local administration and the police usually knew the location of the Jews and knew who was a Jew and who was not. We even know of cases in which the participation of the Germans in the murder of Jews was minimal. In the Lithuanian district of Shaki, according to the report of local district head Karalius and local police chief Vilčinskas, written on 16 September 1941, the German Gebietskommissar attended the massacre of 1,540 Jews, only to insure that the local policemen who carried out the murder would not rob the victims and take the loot for themselves.[140]

The local police was a very important element in the genocide of the Jewish people, both in Eastern and Western Europe, with relatively little notice taken of the degree to which the local police forces were Nazified. An apt example is the case of Holland. In his postwar testimony, the head of Security Police and SD in Amsterdam, Lages, acknowledged that "the main support of the German forces in the police sector and beyond came from the Dutch police. Without it ... it would have been practically impossible to seize even 10 percent of Dutch Jewry...."[141] The deportation of Dutch Jews began in 1942. In July and August 1942 alone, around 11,000 Dutch Jews were sent to the Westerbork transit camp, the first station on the road to Auschwitz. According to Hirschfeld, all Dutch police forces participated in the rounding up of the Jews. The most active however were the police training battalions, whose "performance" during these actions was characterized by HSSPF Rauter as "splendid."[142] The municipal police in small Dutch communities also acted alone, that is, on its own initiative, when rounding up the few Jews to the collection points set up on the orders of local mayors. In addition to the regular Dutch police forces that participated in collecting the Jews, in Holland there were special "commandos," created solely for "Jew-hunting,"such as the Henneicke Column, which consisted of thirty-five men. The eagerness of the Dutch police to persecute Jews cannot be explained by sheer anti-Semitism. According to Hirschfeld, both the possibility of becoming rich at the victims' expense, as well as the traditional conformism characteristic of police forces, must be taken into account.[143] It must also be acknowledged that, on the whole, the position of the Dutch Nazis in the police forces was not too strong, which explains their eagerness to identify with the occupiers' racial dogmatism.[144] The same can be said about French, Belgian, and Norwegian police, who also participated actively in the persecution of Jews in their respective countries.

In the east, wherever the murder of Jews took place, the local
police took more than an active part in it. Here, traditional anti-
Semitism, greed, the desire to prove loyalty to the Germans, and
sheer sadism produced the kind of conduct that met with the
aversion of the Germans themselves. The result of the Lithuanian policemen's avidness to persecute those who only a short
time earlier had been their neighbors was that, by the end of
1941, eighty per cent of Lithuanian Jews were already dead. In
his infamous report about the extermination of Lithuanian
Jews, Jäger, commander of the Security Police and SD (BdS) in
Lithuania and commander of the *Einsatzkommando* 3/A, explicitly "praised" the role played by the "Lithuanian partisans and
the appropriate civil institutions."[145]

Military Collaboration

Military collaboration in occupied Europe took place in various
frameworks: the Waffen SS, *Ostlegionen* (Eastern Legions), *Osttruppen* (Eastern troops), *Hilfswilligen* (auxiliary volunteers),
Organization Todt, and others.

The Waffen SS was one of the earliest and most sizable forms
of military collaboration throughout Europe. For people such as
Himmler, the Waffen SS were supposed to represent the elite
force and shock troops of the Aryan race. Since this force was
regarded from the very beginning with a great deal of hostility
by the Wehrmacht, the command of Waffen SS very early on
required the recruitment of people from outside the areas under
the Wehrmacht's jurisdiction. In 1938, Himmler approved the
recruitment of Germanics (*Germanen*), that is non-Germans of
"Nordic blood," into the SS *Verfügungstruppe* (literally "disposal
troops"), the forerunner of the Waffen SS. At that time, only
twenty non-German volunteers were serving in it; however,
within two years this number rose to one hundred and included
five US, three Swedish and forty-four Swiss citizens.[146] Ultimately, according to George H. Stein, as many as 500,000 foreigners served in the Waffen SS during the entire World War II
period.[147] In the case of citizens of Northern and Western
Europe, the impetus for joining the Waffen SS stemmed from a
desire to contribute to the Nazi attack against the Soviet Union.
Nazi propaganda depicted the Soviet campaign as an all-Euro-
pean anti-Bolshevist crusade. Yet, as shown by Stein, the role of
anti-communist feelings as a motivating factor for joining the
Waffen SS should not be overestimated. As he wrote, "if the

western volunteers ever had a strong idealistic conviction concerning the need to save Europe from the onslaught of 'Red Imperialism,' they acquired it after their enlistment into the SS."[148] To be sure, the members of various fascist movements, such as the NSB in Holland, NS in Norway or the Rex in Belgium, were an exception to this. However, although these movements' members played quite a significant role in recruiting people into various Waffen SS units, their numbers among the non-German Waffen SS soldiers were not particulary high, at least initially. According to the data provided by Gerhard Hirschfeld, the total number of Dutchmen who joined the various formations of the Waffen SS (such as *Standarte Westland, SS Viking Division, SS Netherlands Legion* among others) before 1945 was between 22,000 and 25,000, and of these, only about forty per cent were members of the Nationaal-Socialistische Beweging.[149] George Stein, who sought to destroy the image of the Waffen SS as a kind of European army, a sort of NATO forerunner, stated explicitly, "the majority of the west European volunteers enlisted in the Waffen SS for reasons other than those of political or ideological conviction."[150] He is quoting the Dutch psychologist van Hoesel, who in 1948 carried out a study of young Dutch collaborators, most of whom had belonged to the Waffen SS. According to van Hoesel, the majority of Waffen SS soldiers "had been motivated to volunteer by such factors as a desire for adventure, better food, the prestige of wearing an SS uniform, sheer boredom, desire to avoid the unglamorous compulsory labor service, and a variety of personal factors which included, in some instances, a wish to avoid prosecution for juvenile delinquency or petty criminality."[151]

Racial dogmatism permeated the whole structure of the Waffen SS. At first, neither French nor Francophone Walloons were deemed eligible to serve. Thus, the *Légion "Wallonie"* notwithstanding, the intention of the Rex Leadership was initially to be a Wehrmacht auxiliary unit, while the *Légion des volontaires Française contre le Bolshévisme* (The Counter-Bolshevist Legion of French volunteers, LVF for short) was registered as the 638th Wehrmacht regiment.[152] However, entry into Waffen SS units did not bestow equal status with the Germans. Even those defined as "Germanics" were often treated in a derogatory manner. In mid-1941, the leader of the Flemish Nazis, Staf de Clerq, complained to Himmler about the abusive treatment of Flemish volunteers by German personnel. According to de Clerq, Flemings serving in *Flandern* legion were beaten, threatened with pistols, publicly called "filthy people," a "nation of idiots," and a "race of Gypsies."[153] Moreover, Himmler and his men paid little attention to the desire of local Nazi leaders to see the Waffen SS units as "national" units. Despite strong protests from the leader of the Dutch Nazis, Mussert, to Hitler himself, Himmler decided to include the Netherlanders serving with the Netherlands Legion into the newly created 11th SS Volunteer *Panzer-Grenadier Division Nordland*, which also included Danes and Norwegians.[154]

As in other situations, reality eventually proved to be stronger than racial dogmatism, although the latter was never completely relinquished in favor of the former. Thus, in 1942, when the German military was on the decline, the Waffen SS opened its doors to recruits from the Soviet territories. The first to be accepted were the "racially more acceptable" Baltic people. In Estonia and Latvia, recruitment for the Waffen SS met with a certain degree of success; in Lithuania however, this process proved a failure. This resulted from German hesitance, as Himmler himself considered Lithuanians racially inferior, but also from the fact that in 1943, when the attempts were made to create a Lithuanian Legion in the framework of the Waffen SS, many Lithuanians were already deeply disappointed by the German policies in their country and were, therefore, in no rush to support the occupiers.[155] Ultimately, representatives of other nationalities of the former Soviet Union were also recruited, including Galician Ukrainians (actually Slavs) and even Moslems.

The Waffen SS was not the only form of military collaboration for Soviet nationals. Even before their entry into it, they were recruited as Hilfswillige (auxiliary volunteers), Ostlegionen (chiefly representatives of Caucasian and Central Asian peoples) and Osttruppen. According to Joachim Hoffmann, approximately one million Soviet citizens served in these frameworks.[156] More about these bodies will be said in Chapter VIII; of note here is that the recruitment proceeded not from any benevolent act by the Germans, but primarily in a response to the heavy losses suffered by German fighting troops during the Soviet offensive, along with the desire to spare "precious German blood." In summarizing his survey of military and police collaboration in various European countries, Werner Röhr reached the conclusion that the Germans had several reasons for recruiting foreign nationals to serve in various auxiliary police and military units: (1) they were seen as cannon fodder and as a means to save German blood; (2) drawing resources out of occupied countries for the German war effort not only strengthened the German fighting potential but also served to weaken potential resistance in those countries; (3) the use of these units (especially the police units) for measures such as the persecution of Jews and other "undesirables," as well as for other unpopular measures, was intended to turn these units into a kind of lightning-rod for the wrath of the local populations; (4) the employment of local auxiliary units in crimes associated with the Nazi regime served to compromise these units, binding them more closely to the occupation regime and making them an even more reliable instrument in carrying out occupation politics; and (5) those serving in various police and military units did indeed turn quite soon into mere executioners of the will of the occupying forces.[157]

Only the most salient forms of collaboration were discussed in this chapter. The following ones provide an analysis of the modus operandi of these and other forms of collaboration in occupied Byelorussia. In all countries, reaction to German occupation was to a significant degree a result of conditions that had developed in the interwar period, so the next chapter will examine the circumstances that evolved and led to the state of affairs that existed in Byelorussia on the eve of the Nazi occupation.

Notes

1. Hans Lemberg, "Kollaboration in Europa mit dem Dritten Reich um das Jahr 1941," in *Das Jahr 1941 in der europäischen Politik,* ed. K. Bosl (Munich and Vienna, 1972), 143, quoted in W. Röhr, "Einleitung," in *Europa unter Hakenkreuz,* vol. *Okkupation und Kollaboration,* ed. W. Röhr (Berlin and Heidelberg, 1994), 23.
2. Quoted in I. C. B. Dear and M. R. D. Foot (eds.), *The Oxford Companion to World War II* (Oxford, 2001), 192.
3. See Gerhard Hirschfeld, "Collaboration in Nazi-Occupied France," in *Collaboration in France,* ed. G. Hirschfeld and P. Marsh (Oxford, 1989), 2.
4. See Czesław Madajczyk, "Zwischen neutraler Zusammenarbeit der Bevölkerung okkupierter Gebiete und Kollaboration mit den Deutschen," in *Europa unter Hakenkreuz,* vol. *Okkupation und Kollaboration (1938–1945),* ed. W. Röhr, 51.
5. Ibid.
6. Ibid., 52. As early as 1940 and 1941 British propaganda attacked *Quislingism* as being loathsome and shameful.
7. See Armin Lang, "Zakhvat Norvegii s nemeckoj i norvezhskoj tochek zreniia," in *Vtoraja Mirovaja Vojna,* ed. W. Michalka, trans. N. Zakharchenko et al. (Moscow, 1997), 118.

8. Thus, Gerhard Hirschfeld quotes the article of Dutch scholar H. M. Rand-wijk, who maintained that "everyone who had participated in the resistance in some way, who was known to 'hate and abhor the Germans' was *goed* [good—L.R.]; everyone of whom this could not be said with certainty, with whom it was not known whether it was safe to discuss the transmissions of Radio Oranje, the exile station broadcasting from London, was *fout* [bad—L.R.]," see G. Hirschfeld, *Nazi Rule and Dutch Collaboration*, trans. L. Willmot (Oxford, 1988), 7n20.

9. Ibid., 2.

10. See C. Levy, *Le Nouveaux Temps et l'idéologie de la collaboration* (Paris, 1974); J. P. Azéma, *La Collaboration (1940–1944)* (Paris, 1975); P. Ory, *Les Collaborateurs, 1940–1945* (Paris, 1976); idem, *La France allemande: Paroles du collaborationisme français (1933–1945)* (Paris, 1977); Bertram M. Gordon, *Collaborationism in France during the Second World War* (Ithaca and London, 1980); Zeev Sternhall, *Ni droit ni gauche: L'idéologie fasciste en France* (Paris, 1983); J. F. Sweets, *Choices in Vichy France* (Oxford and New York, 1986); G. Hirschfeld and P. Marsh (eds.), *Collaboration in France* (Oxford, 1989).

11. See Hirschfeld, *Nazi Rule*.

12. Dear and Foot, *Oxford Companion to World War II*, 191.

13. Stanley Hoffmann, "Collaborationism in France during World War II," *Journal of Modern History*, 40, no. 3 (September 1968), 376 (the italics are in the original).

14. Gordon, *Collaborationism in France*, 17f.

15. Hirschfeld, *Nazi Rule*, 5.

16. Isaiah Trunk, *Judenrat* (Lincoln, 1996), 570–72.

17. Ibid., 572.

18. Dan Michman, *Holocaust Historiography* (London and Portland, OR, 2003), 238.

19. See Chapter V.

20. See Madajczyk, "Zwischen neutraler Zusammenarbeit," 46.

21. Quoted ibid., 50.

22. See Werner Rings, *Life with the Enemy* (New York, 1982), 73f.

23. Ibid., 107–8. According to Gerhard Hirschfeld who conducted in-depth research on Dutch collaboration, among the central aims of the Netherlands Union was the preservation of the Dutch Empire in Southeast Asia. See Hirschfeld, *Nazi Rule*, 66ff. It is also interesting to note that the Union's programme adopted in June 1940, along with condemning the political party system and speaking of the "organic structure of society," also explicitly proclaimed its loyalty to the House of Orange, which incidentally was headed by Queen Wilhelmina, who supported the idea of resistance to Nazi rule from her London exile during the Nazi occupation.

24. Rings, *Life with the Enemy*, 128.

25. Röhr, "Forschungsprobleme zur deutschen Okkupationspolitik im Spiegel der Reihe ,Europa unter Hakenkreuz," in *Europa unter Hakenkreuz*, vol. *Analysen-Quellen-Register*, ed. W. Röhr (Heidelberg, 1996), 148.

26. Röhr, "Okkupation und Kollaboration," in *Europa unter Hakenkreuz*, vol. *Okkupation und Kollaboration (1938–1945)*, ed. W. Röhr, 63.

27. To this day, this fact prevents Yad Vashem authorities from conferring on Szepticky the title of Righteous among the Nations. On Szepticky and his position regarding Nazi persecution of Jews, see Simon Redlich, "Metro-

politan Andrii Sheptyts'kyi and the Complexities of Ukrainian-Jewish Relations," in *Bitter Legacy*, ed. Z. Gitelman (Bloomington and Indianapolis, 1997), 61–76.

28. Hoffmann, "Collaborationism in France," 389.
29. For a more detailed analysis of the synthesis between socialism and nationalism as well as of Sorel's views, see Z. Sternhell, *Yesodot ha-Fashizm* (The Basics of Fascism) (Tel Aviv, 1996).
30. This aim was proclaimed by a special parliamentary act adopted on 20 March 1930.
31. Gordon, *Collaborationism in France*, 22.
32. James F. McMillan, *Twentieth-Century France* (London, 1992), 104.
33. Quoted in Littlejohn, *Patriotic Traitors*, 187.
34. Ibid., 136; Martin Conway, *Collaboration in Belgium* (New Haven and London, 1993), 7.
35. See, for example, Leonas Sabaliūnas, *Lithuania in Crisis* (Bloomington and London, 1972).
36. Dr. Franz Borkenau was initially active within the extreme left of the Labor movement in Germany. In 1929 he abandoned politics in favor of science, becoming a research fellow of the sociological institute at Frankfurt University and specializing in seventeenth-century science and philosophy and their interrelations. With the growth of the National Socialist movement in Germany, Borkenau began to study fascism closely. In 1934 he immigrated to England, where he engaged in research into politics, political science, and sociology. Apart from the work mentioned in the next note, his studies included *World Communism* as well as *Austria and After*, written a couple of months after the *Anschluß*, in May 1938, in which Borkenau predicted many events to come. Information about Franz Borkenau can be found in the book *The New German Empire*, cited below.
37. Franz Borkenau, *The New German Empire* (Paulton and London 1939), 11.
38. David Littlejohn is quite right in stating that "The defeat of 1940 had its roots not so much in military ineptitude, although that certainly played its part, as in public demoralization." See Littlejohn, *Patriotic Traitors*, 186.
39. Hermann Rauschning, *Hitler Speaks* (London, 1939), 17.
40. Quoted in Hirschfeld, *Nazi Rule*, 32.
41. Röhr, "Forschungsprobleme," in Röhr, *Europa unter Hakenkreuz*, vol. *Analysen-Quellen-Register*, 151.
42. Ibid.
43. Quoted ibid., 151.
44. Ibid.
45. Ibid.
46. Quoted by Madajczyk, "Zwischen Zusammenarbeit und Kollaboration," 53.
47. Röhr, "Forschungsprobleme," in Röhr, *Europa unter Hakenkreuz*, vol. *Analysen-Quellen-Register*, 152. Andreas Hillgruber, *Hitlers Strategie* (Frankfurt/Main, 1965), 77.
48. Röhr, "Forschungsprobleme," in Röhr, *Europa unter Hakenkreuz*, vol. *Analysen-Quellen-Register*, 151.
49. Ibid., 152.
50. In his study *Die Illusion*, Jürgen Thorwald publishes the map that may give a rough impression of the ideas of NS leadership regarding organization of "New Europe." See Thorwald, *Die Illusion*, 32–33. It should be kept in mind, however, that due to the polycratic nature of the Nazi regime, it is difficult to speak about any united picture of Europe after the projected

Nazi victory. The variety of views regarding Holland, for example, can be found in Hirschfeld, *Nazi Rule*, 27ff.

51. See Thorwald, *Die Illusion*, 32.
52. Hirschfeld, *Nazi Rule*, 19–20. In Belgium, the functions of the cabinet were fulfilled by the *secrétaires-généraux*, who headed ministerial departments after the ministers of the prewar Pierlot government left the country. See Conway, *Collaboration in Belgium*, 25.
53. Röhr, "Forschungsprobleme," in Röhr, *Europa unter Hakenkreuz*, vol. *Analysen-Quellen-Register*, 152.
54. Thorwald, *Die Illusion*, 32–33.
55. Röhr, "Forschungsprobleme," in *Europa unter Hakenkreuz*, vol. *Analysen-Quellen-Register*, 152.
56. Thus, for example, on 23 June 1941, merely one day after the Nazi invasion into the Soviet Union, the members of the Lithuanian Activist Front (LAF), the Lithuanian émigrés organization, proclaimed the creation of a Lithuanian provisional government headed by Ambrazeviãius. Although initially the German military authorities established some kind of *modus vivendi* with this government, it was disbanded in August 1941. See Romuald J. Misiunas and Rein Taagepera, *The Baltic States* (Berkeley and Los Angeles, 1993), 46–48.
57. Ibid.
58. Rafael Lemkin, *Axis Rule in Occupied Europe* (New York, 1973), 118.
59. Generalkommissar Kube,"Überblick über die politische Lage," in "Protokoll der Tagung der Gebietskommissare, Hauptabteilungsleiter und Abteilungsleiter des Generalkommissars in Minsk vom 8.April bis 10.April 1943," BA R93/20, 7.
60. John A. Armstrong, *Ukrainian Nationalism* (New York, 1963), 55ff.; "Tätigkeits- und Lagebericht Nr.1 der Einsatzgruppen der Sicherheitspolizei und des SD in der UdSSR und Verhalten der Kommunisten im Reich und in den besetzten Gebieten, 31.7.41," in *Die Einsatzgruppen in der besetzten Sowjetunion, 1941/1942*, ed. Peter Klein (Berlin, 1997), 128.
61. "TLB Nr. 1," in Klein, *Einsatzgruppen*, 129.
62. "TLB Nr. 4 (1.9–15.9.41)," ibid., 192.
63. "TLB Nr 7 (1.11.–30.11.41)"; "TLB Nr. 8 (1.12–31.12.41)"; "TLB Nr. 9 (1.1.–31.1.42)"; "TLB Nr. 11 (1.3–31.3.42)," all ibid., 262, 271–72, 285–87, 313; Armstrong, *Ukrainian Nationalism*, 106ff.
64. Quoted in Armstrong, *Ukrainian Nationalism*, 55.
65. Quoted in Thorwald, *Die Illusion*, 48. Makhorka is an inferior kind of tobacco and nagaika is a whip.
66. See Littlejohn, *Patriotic Traitors*.
67. In April 1942, the value of transactions between French and German industry reached 2.36 billion RM, while in the autumn of the same year it was already more than 4 billion RM. See Rings, *Life with the Enemy*, 76–77.
68. Ibid., 79.
69. Quoted in Littlejohn, *Patriotic Traitors*, 69.
70. About De Man and his views, see ibid., 150–51, Conway, *Collaboration in Belgium*, 30.
71. Quoted in Hirschfeld, *Nazi Rule*, 115.
72. See Hoffmann, "Collaborationism in France," 381–89.
73. Ibid., 377.
74. Gordon, *Collaborationism in France*, 23.
75. Littlejohn, *Patriotic Traitors*, 20.

76. Hirschfeld, *Nazi Rule*, 39.
77. Ibid., 42.
78. Ibid., 42–43.
79. Gordon, *Collaborationism in France*, 24.
80. Ibid., 25.
81. Conway, *Collaboration in Belgium*, 13.
82. Littlejohn, *Patriotic Traitors*, 13.
83. Hirschfeld, *Nazi Rule*, 133.
84. Littlejohn remarked caustically and aptly that in Germany itself Minister-President is no more than a head of *Land* (State) government. Littlejohn, *Patriotic Traitors*, 33.
85. Ibid., 34.
86. Gordon, *Collaborationism in France*, 289.
87. John A. Armstrong, "Collaborationism in World War II: The Integral Nationalist Variant in Eastern Europe," *Journal of Modern History* 40, no. 3 (September 1968), 397.
88. Conway, *Collaboration in Belgium*, 23.
89. Röhr, "Forschungsprobleme," in *Europa unter Hakenkreuz*, vol. *Analysen-Quellen-Register*, 156.
90. Ibid.
91. See Hirschfeld, *Nazi Rule*, 182.
92. Ibid., 184.
93. Ibid.
94. Röhr, "Forschungsprobleme," in Röhr, *Europa unter Hakenkreuz*, vol. *Analysen-Quellen-Register*, 156.
95. Ibid.
96. Ibid., 212.
97. Hirschfeld, *Nazi Rule*, 213.
98. Ibid., 220.
99. Ulrich Herbert, *Fremdarbeiter* (Berlin and Bonn, 1986), 99.
100. For more on these societies, see Dietrich Eichholz, "Wirtschaftskollaboration und 'Ostgesellschaften' in NS-besetzten Ländern," in Röhr, *Europa unter Hakenkreuz*, Supplement Volume 1 (Berlin and Heidelberg, 1994), 433ff.
101. Rings, *Life with the Enemy*, 78.
102. Littlejohn, *Patriotic Traitors*, 112.
103. Röhr, "Forschungsprobleme," in Röhr, *Europa unter Hakenkreuz*, vol. *Analysen-Quellen-Register*, 159.
104. Ibid., 157.
105. Conway, *Collaboration in Belgium*, 109, 151; Röhr, "Forschungsprobleme," in Röhr, *Europa unter Hakenkreuz*, vol. *Analysen-Quellen-Register*, 15.
106. Hirschfeld, *Nazi Rule*, 166.
107. Robert O. Paxton, *Vichy France* (New York, 1972), 295–96.
108. Already on 26 June 1941, the Supreme Command of Wehrmacht (OKW) issued a secret order demanding the disbandment of all paramilitary units in Lithuania that were smaller than a battalion. See Bronis J. Kaslas (ed.), *The USSR-German Aggression against Lithuania* (New York, 1973), 351–52.
109. Yehoshua Büchler, "Local Police Force Participation in the Extermination of Jews in Occupied Soviet Territory 1941–1942," *Shvut* 20, no. 4 (1996): 81.
110. Ibid., 83.

111. Gordon, *Collaborationism in France*, 28.
112. Röhr, "Forschungsprobleme," in Röhr, *Europa unter Hakenkreuz*, vol. *Analysen-Quellen-Register,* 162.
113. Misiunas and Taagepera, *Baltic States*, 57.
114. Renee Poznanski, *Jews in France during World War II*, trans. N. Bracher (Hanover and London, 2001), 2.
115. Ibid., 7.
116. Ibid., 8.
117. Ibid.
118. Richard H. Weisberg, *Vichy Law and the Holocaust in France* (Amsterdam, 1996), xix; U. Herbert, "The German Military Command in Paris and the Deportation of the French Jews," in *National Socialist Extermination Policies*, ed. U. Herbert (New York and Oxford 2000), 133; Paxton, *Vichy France*, 174; Poznanski, *Jews in France*.
119. Paxton, *Vichy France*, 174.
120. Weisberg, *Vichy Law*, 39–40; Poznanski, *Jews in France*, 42.
121. See Raul Hilberg, *Destruction of the European Jews* (New York and London, 1985), 1: 65-80.
122. Weisberg, *Vichy Law*, 39.
123. Paxton, *Vichy France*, 174.
124. Weisberg, *Vichy Law,* 56.
125. Paxton, *Vichy France*, 184.
126. "Report of BdS in Paris Knochen, 12.2.43," quoted in Paxton, *Vichy France*, 182.
127. Hirschfeld, *Nazi Rule*, 141ff.
128. Ibid., 141.
129. Quoted ibid., 140.
130. Ibid., 144.
131. Ibid., 146.
132. Ibid., 141.
133. Ibid., 144.
134. Thus, the Wehrmacht field commandant's office in The Hague, in its situational report on 18 February 1942, noted that "The mayors ... answer enquiries correctly and endeavor to obey quickly the instructions given them by the local commanders." Quoted ibid., 153.
135. The whole text of this statute in Russian translation can be found in Alexander Slavinas, *Gibel' Pompei* (Tel Aviv, 1997).
136. Yitzhak Arad, "'The Final Solution in Lithuania' in the Light of German Documentation," *Yad Vashem Studies* 11 (1976): 240.
137. Tomas Sandkühler, "Anti-Jewish Policy and the Murder of the Jews in the District of Galicia, 1941/1942," in Herbert, *National Socialist Extermination Policies* (New York and Oxford, 2000), 109.
138. Bogdan Musial, *"Konterrevolutionäre Elemente sind zu erschießen"* (Berlin and Munich, 2000).
139. Dieter Pohl, *Nationalsozialistische Judenverfolgung in Ostgalizien 1941–1944* (Munich, 1997), 55–56.
140. Azriel Shokhat, *"Helkam shel' ha-Litaim be-Hashmadat Yehudei Lita"* (Participation of Lithuanians in the extermination of Lithuanian Jews), in *Dapim le-Kheker Tekufat ha-Shoa*, issue 1 (1979), 83.
141. Hirschfeld, *Nazi Rule*, 173.
142. Ibid., 174.
143. Ibid., 177.

144. Ibid., 177–78.
145. Quoted in Slavinas, *Gibel' Pompei*, 296–305.
146. George H. Stein, *The Waffen SS* (London, 1966), 94.
147. Ibid., 138.
148. Ibid., 140.
149. Hirschfeld, *Nazi Rule*, 288.
150. Stein, *Waffen SS*, 141.
151. Ibid.
152. See Conway, *Collaboration in Belgium*, 96. Littlejohn, Patriotic Traitors, 242.
153. Ibid., 154.
154. Littlejohn, *Patriotic Traitors*, 119.
155. Misiunas and Taagepera, *Baltic States*, 58.
156. J. Hoffmann, Die Ostlegionen *1941–1943* (Freiburg im Breisgau, 1981), 11.
157. Röhr, "Forschungsprobleme," in Röhr, *Europa unter Hakenkreuz*, vol. *Analysen-Quellen-Register*, 171.

CHAPTER 2

HISTORICAL BACKGROUND

General Information

To understand the events of World War II in Byelorussia, it is worth casting a brief look at the period that preceded it. But first, we must provide some general information about Byelorussia, since, to this day, the country is still virtually *terra incognita* to most people outside its borders.

Today Byelorussia is an independent state in Eastern Europe, and a member of the Community of Independent States (CIS), the body formed after the dissolution of the Soviet Union. In the country's 207,600 square kilometers reside more than ten million inhabitants. On the west, Byelorussia is bordered by Poland; to the northwest, by Lithuania and Latvia; on the east it shares a border with the Russian Federation; and on the south with the Ukraine. The country's terrain is predominately flat with an extensive network of rivers. The longest rivers are the Western Dvina, the Neman and the Bug, with tributaries flowing to the Baltic Sea, and the Dnepr with tributaries flowing to the Black Sea. Byelorussia's forested areas are comparable to those of Germany, for example, and most of the Pripjat marshes in the south were drained after the war. Nevertheless, many people outside of Byelorussia still consider it "a country of large swamps, forests and plains."[1] Approximately sixty-five per cent

of the population consists of Byelorussians, while the rest are
Russians, Poles, Ukrainians, and Jews, whose number has
decreased significantly in recent decades, mainly due to emigration and repatriation.

Byelorussia did not gain independence until 1991; however,
Byelorussian historians, Vaclaŭ Lastoŭski, for example, considered past political entities such as the Polock principality, in the
tenth to thirteenth centuries, or the Great Duchy of Lithuania,
dating back to 1569 or even before 1385, to be the earliest manifestations of the Byelorussian state.[2] Until the fall of the Soviet
Union, the various territories that now comprise modern
Byelorussia were—most of the time—part of the neighboring
states, either the Great Duchy of Lithuania, the joint Polish-
Lithuanian State (*Rzezcpospolita*), the Russian Empire, the
Soviet Union or, as between the years 1921 and 1939, divided
between Poland and Soviet Union. Twice in Byelorussia's history, during both World War I and II, German forces were stationed on Byelorussian soil.

Byelorussia does not possess important natural resources.
Until the twentieth century, this meant that it was one of the
least developed regions in Europe economically. Until the 1920s,
it was an agrarian country, with most of the land concentrated
in the hands of a few families, such as the Princess of Hohenlohe
who held 1,729, 000 acres of arable land in the Minsk region
alone.[3] This situation left the majority of Byelorussian peasantry to experience an acute "land hunger," which continued
until the beginning of the twentieth century.

From a geo-political point of view, however, Byelorussia is
very strategically situated. Its location between the west and
the east, where it can serve as a kind of "springboard" to
Moscow, made it a natural arena for numerous invasions and
battles over the course of history. Both the battle of Lesnaya
(1708) between the Russians and the Swedes during the Great
Northern War, which was defined by Peter the Great as "the
mother of Poltava battle," as well as Napoleon's crossing of the
river Beresina after his unsuccessful Russian campaign took
place on Byelorussian territory.[4]

Nowhere else in the vast Russian Empire were the imperial
politics of Russification as successful as in Byelorussia at the
beginning of the last century, especially among its elite. The very
name *Byelorussia* was erased from the political parlance of the
period, and in the official Russian documents the country was
referred to as the "Northwestern Region" (*Severozapadnyj*

Kraj). The Byelorussian language was perceived as a dialect of "backward" peasants, rather than a language sui generis. The younger generation of Byelorussian society's upper classes went to study at the universities of Moscow and St. Petersburg, and many of them participated actively in the all-Russian liberation and revolutionary movements. One such St. Petersburg student, Ignacy Grinevitsky, was among the assassins of the Russian Emperor Alexander II in March 1881.[5]

Byelorussia between Two World Wars

The revival of nationalism that affected many European countries in the second half of the nineteenth century did not by-pass Byelorussia; however, due to the sweeping Russification of the local elite, it was only feebly manifested. Until the Russian Revolution of February 1917, this nationalist movement remained largely what Nicholas Vakar described as "cultural nationalism."[6] While it sought to demonstrate that the Byelorussian language was neither a Russian nor a Polish dialect but rather a language in its own right, it had no political pretensions whatsoever.[7] The February Revolution put an end to the Romanovs' tsarist rule in Russia and simultaneously gave new impetus to the development of national movements in various parts of the former empire; nevertheless, Byelorussian leaders such as the Luckevič brothers spoke chiefly in terms of either a revival of the medieval Grand Duchy of Lithuania or of some form of autonomy in the framework of a post-Imperial Russian State. After the October coup, it was only the Bolsheviks' stubborn opposition to any form of existence outside their direct control that finally brought about demands for an independent Byelorussian state.[8] Undoubtedly, the weakness of the Byelorussian national movement was also caused by the multinational character of Byelorussia, in which the Byelorussians themselves barely constituted a majority among the very strong Polish, Jewish, and Russian minorities.[9] To these minorities, Byelorussian nationalism was not a meaningful cause.

Yet, the very weakness of a Byelorussian national movement made it a useful tool in the hands of its more powerful neighbors, who sought to gain control over this strategically important area. Between 1915 and 1917, and later between 1917 and 1921, the Byelorussian inhabitants witnessed each of their subsequent rulers—Germans, Poles and Bolsheviks—attempt the

same strategy, namely, manipulating Byelorussian national aspirations to serve their own aims. A good example of this is the
short-lived Byelorussian People's Republic (Belaruskaja Narodnaja Respublika, BNR), proclaimed on 25 March 1918, which to
this day is celebrated as the first independent Byelorussian state
both by Byelorussian emigrants in the west and governmental
opposition in Byelorussia. Actually the BNR was allowed to exist
only because the Germans, who occupied almost all of Byelorussia as the result of the Brest-Litovsk treaty (1918), were at first
prepared to tolerate it and later, recognizing its usefulness to
their own interests, even to encourage it.[10] The same can be said
both about the Byelorussian Soviet Socialist Republic (BSSR)
that was proclaimed upon direct orders from Moscow on 1 January 1919 and about the short revival of the BNR in 1920, on
the territories occupied by Polish troops.[11] All of these attempts
to manipulate Byelorussian nationalism only enhanced the
indifference of the general public in Byelorussia toward the
nationalist idea. Thus, the Riga treaty between Poland and
Soviet Russia—concluded on 18 March 1921—according to
which about one quarter of the Byelorussian population found
itself under Polish rule and the rest under Soviet rule, was met
without any substantial protest in the country.[12]

Over the next twenty years, between 1921 and 1941, developments in Western (Polish) Byelorussia as well as in Eastern
(Soviet) Byelorussia created the socio-economic conditions that
were to have a direct bearing on the situation during the Nazi
occupation. Between the two world wars, the question of nationalism dominated European politics, and this was especially true
of Eastern and Central Europe. The states that arose on the
ruins of the Habsburg, Hohenzollern, and Romanov empires
were mostly multinational states, and a common feature of the
politics of these "succession states" was that they did not know
what to do with their national minorities. This failure proved to
be fatal at the end of the 1930s, when the Nazis were prompted
to manipulate the minorities' dissatisfactions to benefit their
own ambitions. This was, to be sure, an era before the term *multicultural* had been introduced, and national politics often meant
an aspiration to dissolve ethnic minorities within the titular
nation.[13] Perhaps the most striking example of this trend is interwar Poland and its relationship with the Byelorussian minority.

Poland emerged from the calamities of World War I and the
war with Soviet Russia as the state with the largest share of
national minorities. The Riga treaty provided it with a number

of territories inhabited predominantly by Byelorussians.[14] These territories were divided into several provinces (*wojewodstwa*): Wilno, Nowogrod (Byelorussian, Navahrudak), Białystok and Polesie as well as the northern part of Wołyn. All of these provinces, together with the predominantly Ukrainian territories to the south, came to be known under the common name *Kresy Wschodnie* (the eastern districts). German historian Bernhard Chiari characterizes *Kresy* as "the poorhouse of Poland," but it would not be a great exaggeration to say it was the poorhouse of the whole of Europe.[15] The Polish government was not interested in investing capital in the development of this border region, so during the entire interwar period, it remained predominantly an agricultural area, where the land produced meager crops for local consumption and the peasants' livelihood remained close to subsistence level.[16] Military installations, such as fortifications and barbed wire barriers, became an integral part of the landscape in this area. Another sign of the underdeveloped state of this region was the rampant increase in the number of predatory animals, such as wolves, which became a real threat to the local inhabitants.[17]

The social stratification in the Byelorussian part of the *Kresy* was determined according to nationality. The upper class, the landowners, included almost exclusively Poles, and was concentrated in the cities, while the Byelorussian peasants constituted a majority in the countryside. Ever since tsarist times, this area had been the heart of the Jewish Pale. It was characterized by a scattering of small towns (in Yiddish *shtetlach*) with a predominantly Jewish population. The way of life in the *shtetlach* differed very little from that of the surrounding countryside, as the majority of their inhabitants worked as craftsmen (shoemakers, tailors, blacksmiths) and peddlers supplying the local markets.

In the interwar period, almost no other country exhibited such a discriminatory, stereotype-based policy towards national minorities as did Poland, and this was perhaps especially true regarding the Byelorussian minority. Given that the Byelorussians lived in well-defined and densely populated areas, the majority of the Polish population never came in contact with them. Information about the Byelorussians was drawn from "informed" people, who came almost exclusively from the *Kresy* and were either the Polish landowners or their descendants. In their articles, travel guides, and even novels, these people depicted Byelorussian territory as a kind of "ethnographic museum," a country of extreme wilderness whose archetypal landscape was the Polesje marshland and whose population existed at a very low stage of civilization.[18] At the same time, these reports, which were based on the real or imagined conduct of the Byelorussian workers on the estates, emphasized the "reverence" of the Byelorussians towards high authority and their complete lack of political ambition. The Polish author Melchior Wańkowicz, for example, described the Byelorussians as follows: "The entire appearance, all the bows and smiles of the Belorussian, went to prove that he was overflowing with joy, that he was sufficiently rewarded by the sheer happiness entailed in serving 'his lordship.'"[19] Similar views were expressed by the publicist Władislaw Wydźga: "The Belorussian, good-hearted, with a gentle look in his eyes, quiet, stands on a very low rung of civilization ... It seems that [at the] foundation of his beliefs is a very conservative sentiment regarding respect for authority and to this end the need to maintain a proper hierarchy."[20]

Ultimately, the majority of the public in the Polish mainland came to believe that Byelorussians were not a distinct people at all but rather a kind of "lost Polish tribe," who under the influence of the Russian tsarist authorities had lost their ties to their Polish roots and now needed to be returned to the bosom of the mother nation.[21] This goal, however, created a dilemma for Warsaw. It would not oppose turning the Byelorussians into full-fledged Poles, although many Polish politicians, such as the Socialist, Pidulski, felt that such a process could be long and uncertain. Conversely, Poland was bound by the international agreements of the first post-1918 years, which—composed in the spirit of Woodrow Wilson's Fourteen Points—guaranteed extensive rights to national minorities.[22] These agreements, of course, also extended to the Byelorussian minority. Therefore Polish governments during the first period of independence were compelled to adopt tactics of caution and relative liberalism. Instead of outright Polonization in the Byelorussian territories, the policies of Byelorussification were encouraged, especially in education. Authorities in Warsaw believed that they could counteract the Russian influences from the other side of the border and still pave the first step on the road that would lead to converting the local population into "decent Poles." Consequently, they were prepared to allow the Byelorussians to send their representatives to the Polish Sejm (Parliament) in 1922.[23]

But this situation did not last long. If the Polish authorities had hoped that these concessions would earn them the thanks of the Byelorussians, they would very soon be disappointed. Instead of being full of gratitude, the Byelorussian Sejm delegates turned out to be a mouthpiece for the grievances of the Byelorussian population. Their speeches revealed that along with the so-called "Byelorussification" in *Kresy*, the Polish government was simultaneously implementing a colonization program in these territories. Hordes of Polish war veterans, the so-called *osadnicy* (literally "settlers") were being sent to these areas and were allotted lands from the large estates, while Byelorussian peasants were still suffering from land shortage. The Catholic Church began large-scale missionary work among the largely Orthodox population, in the firm belief that "Orthodox" and "Russian" were synonymous.[24] The Byelorussian delegates called upon the Polish government to respect the Minority Treaty that had been signed only a few years earlier.

The reaction of Warsaw to these calls and complaints was swift and harsh. At the end of 1924, the authorities closed 300 Byelorussian schools, suppressed the Byelorussian press, overburdened the Byelorussian villages with taxes, and forcefully dispersed any Byelorussian political meetings. In 1924 the Byelorussians even sent their complaints to the League of Nations, describing the multiple atrocities committed against the Byelorussian population.[25]

The Polish officials claimed that the protests arising from the Byelorussian quarter were the result of the Russian-Bolshevik influence, rather than a genuine Byelorussian phenomenon. But if they thought to block this influence by force, they achieved exactly the opposite. The relatively peaceful coexistence that had reigned in Soviet Byelorussia between the Soviet regime and Byelorussian nationalism in the 1920s now caused many Byelorussians in Poland to turn their eyes hopefully toward the east. In 1925, largely under the influence of the Communist Party of Western Byelorussia, some of the Byelorussian delegates to the Polish Sejm founded the Byelorussian Peasants and Workers Party (Belaruskaja syalyanska-rabotnickaja Hramada), whose very name revealed where its sympathies lay. In less than two years, this party mustered more than 125,000 members.[26] During the same period, the Communist Party of Western Byelorussia (KPZB) also increased its membership significantly, according to Nicholas Vakar.[27] In contrast, the number of Byelorussians who supported the Poles decreased significantly by the end of the 1920s. Among these was one of the founding fathers of Byelorussian political nationalism, Anton Luckevič, as well as the director of the Byelorussian gymnasium in Vilna (now Vilnius), Radaslaŭ Astroŭski, who would gain dubious prominence by the end of Nazi occupation of Byelorussia.[28] Some of the Byelorussian leaders in Poland, including former members of the short-lived BNR government, who only a few years earlier had fled westwards from the Bolshevist troops, were prepared to emigrate to the Soviet part of the country. They included the prime minister of the BNR government-in-exile, the historian Vaclaŭ Lastoŭski; Aljaksandar Cvikevič, who during the Russian revolution had been the deputy of another short-lived body, the All-Russian Constituent Assembly; the prominent Byelorussian writer Francišak Aliachnovič; and several delegates to the Polish Sejm, such as Symon Rak-Michajloŭski, Pjotr Miatla, and Branislaŭ Taraškevič.

In Soviet Byelorussia (BSSR), however, the conditions were not much better. In the early 1920s, the so-called New Economic Policy (NEP), which had been proclaimed in Lenin's lifetime and had been intended to shore up the country's economy after the calamities of the civil war, in fact led to liberalization in virtually all spheres of life. Thus, the so-called *prodrazvyorstka*, i.e., the policy of forceful confiscation of agricultural products from the peasants, practiced during the civil war, gave way to a policy of fixed taxation in kind, levied on the peasants. The Cheka (*Chrezvychajnaja Komissiya*, an extraordinary commission), the forerunner of the dreaded NKVD and KGB, relaxed its grip over the population. The former estates were parceled out, and during this period, the peasants in the Byelorussian territories increased their landownership by twenty-eight per cent compared to what they had owned under the Old Regime.[29]

The Bolshevist rulers knew very well that on the outskirts of the former Russian Empire, the nationalist repercussions of the post-revolutionary "spring of the nations" had not waned completely within a mere three years. Yet, they were also well aware that there were still people in these areas who placed nationalism above communist dogmas. Furthermore, the statesmen in the Kremlin knew that alienating these people would jeopardize the general process of the country's recovery. Thus, it was thought expedient to allow such local manifestations of nationalism, provided they did not threaten the very existence of Soviet rule.

In Soviet Byelorussia, the 1920s witnessed a flourishing of national culture. In 1921, an article by the prominent Byelorussian historian and the Peoples' Commissar (Minister) for Education, Ŭsevalad Ihnatoŭski, was published under the title "The

Byelorussian National Question and the Communist Party." In it Ihnatoŭski stated that "Byelorussian culture is a culture of the toiling masses," since the Byelorussian nation consisted almost exclusively of peasants and workers.[30] Thus, the author urged "to study and involve the Byelorussian semi-proletariat and proletariat of the Byelorussian village in Communism, using their native, comprehensible, everyday and domestic Byelorussian language."[31] In this way, in 1924, Byelorussian, along with Yiddish, the spoken language of the majority of the Byelorussian Jews, and Polish, was made an official language of the republic. It was to be used in all of the state's official bodies, political parties, trade unions, and cooperative groups as well as educational establishments. The population was encouraged to use Byelorussian in their daily life, and great effort was made to put an end to illiteracy in the country.[32] In 1926, a four-year elementary education became compulsory, and between 1925 and 1928, the number of schools for general education almost tripled (from 59 in 1925 to 161 in 1928); correspondingly, the number of students increased by almost 1.5 times (from 9,218 in 1925 to 13,437 in 1928).[33] Apart from general education, vocational education was also emphasized; for example, the number of what were called factory workshop schools (*Fabrichno-Zavodskije Uchilishcha*, FZU) almost doubled between 1925 and 1928 (from 7 to 13), and the number of students in them in those years more than doubled, from 441 in 1925 to 1,009 in 1928. In the BSSR in 1928, there were four institutes of higher education (Minsk State University, Minsk Communist University, the Byelorussian Agricultural Academy [Gorki], and the Vitebsk Veterinary Institute) with a total number of 4,632 students and 504 professors.[34] In 1927, the Soviet authorities were even prepared to create a Byelorussian infantry division in the Red Army and to rename the Western Military Region the Byelorussian Military Region.[35]

While all this was taking place, the numerous national minorities living in Byelorussia were not forgotten either. The Byelorussian State University created departments for training teachers for Jewish and Polish secondary schools, in addition to the three Jewish and one Polish teacher training facilities. The Institute of Byelorussian Culture encouraged research on Jewish and Polish cultures.[36]

The generosity of the concessions made on the part of Soviet rule was matched by a painful sobering at the end of the 1920s. For the local Communist Party leaders, these above-noted developments were the best way to achieve their ultimate goal, namely, the building of a truly socialist society. However, the Soviet leaders in Moscow, first among them the former Peoples Commissar for Nationalities, Josef Stalin, saw it differently. As early as 1923, Stalin acknowledged openly that all concessions to local nationalism were no more than a tactical step, the first one toward the suppression of any kind of "deviation towards nationalism."[37] Stalin's victory in the inner party struggle, in 1929, spelled doom for both NEP policies and the short-lived flirtation with regional nationalism.

There is almost nothing in the popular mindset that symbolizes Stalinism as much as collectivization policies and the great purges. Although in Byelorussia the process of collectivization was relatively slow (after all, Byelorussia did not possess such fertile soil as the neighboring Ukraine), it was still no less harsh than in other regions and led to significant tensions. The individual farms that had been supported by the authorities during the NEP period were the main target of the collectivization policies.[38] At the beginning of 1930, some 165,300 individual farms in Soviet Byelorussia were collectivized.[39] Many peasants were less than enthusiastic about this policy: they felt that the Soviet authorities, which only thirteen years earlier had proclaimed "The land for the peasants!", had deceived them. Some of them were even ready to use weapons to defend their right to work their own plot. In many places, spontaneous peasant revolts broke out. In the village of Zastaryn'ne, in the Vitebsk oblast, the peasants, armed with axes, pitchforks, and hunting rifles, almost lynched the chief of the local militia.[40]

The Soviet authorities responded with brutality against the so-called "kulaks."[41] Anyone who opposed the kolkhoz system was seen as a kulak, a member of the "class" hostile to Soviet rule. The GPU, the descendant of Cheka, opened a true war against such people. Many hundreds were arrested and sent together with their families to labor camps in the Arctic region. According to the American researcher of Byelorussian origin, Ivan Lubachko, between twelve and fifteen per cent of the Byelorussian peasants were deported during this period.[42]

These repressive measures, taken against the most efficient peasants, inevitably resulted in a sharp decline in the food supply. The "Great Hunger" of the 1930s in the Ukraine is well known; however, the situation in Byelorussia was no less severe. According to some estimates, between three and five per cent of the total Byelorussian population starved to death during those years.[43]

Collectivization also had severe social implications. Not only were fellow villagers encouraged to spy on their neighbors, who might be opposed to the state's policies, but even children, who underwent the Soviet school's "brainwashing," turned against their parents. One of these children, Pavlik Morozov, who denounced his own father and was eventually killed by relatives, was made a "pioneer-hero" and a martyr by the communist hagiography. In this period, one can already observe the development of the survival strategies that were implemented later during the German occupation.

The Stalinist regime was also resolute in its intention to eradicate any trace of what Stalin himself defined as "deviation toward nationalism." The waves of purges in Byelorussia were directed against communist leaders as well as prominent Byelorussian writers and artists. Even the official titles bestowed in the 1920s by Soviet authorities themselves did not protect anyone from the all-penetrating GPU-NKVD terror. For example, the famous Byelorussian poet Janka Kupala (Ivan Lucevič), who held the title "The People's Poet," could escape arrest only by stabbing himself in the stomach.[44] The local leaders who had taken seriously the slogans for building a society "national in form and socialist in content" were ruthlessly purged in 1929–30. Among the victims of the purges were the head of the Council of People's Commissars of BSSR, Mikalaj Haladzed, who committed suicide after his arrest by the NKVD, and the founding father of Soviet Byelorussia, Aljaksandar Čarviakoŭ, who was accused of anti-Soviet and counterrevolutionary activities and also committed suicide in order to avoid arrest.[45]

Byelorussia was also robbed of its intellectual elite. Among those shot in the NKVD cellars were Volfson and Vydra, directors of the Institute of Soviet Philosophy. People, who only a few years earlier had returned to Soviet Byelorussia—either fleeing from Polish persecution or in the belief that they would have the chance to build a Byelorussian national home—now, in the 1930s, underwent persecution for being "national-democrats" (*nacdems*), Polish spies (notwithstanding the fact that many of them sought protection from Polish persecution), who were supposedly seeking to tear Byelorussia away from the Soviet Union. Such accusations were also raised against the prominent historian, Vaclaŭ Lastoŭski; Jasep Lyosik, the poet and former president of the Rada of BNR in exile; and Sciapan Nekraševič. In 1933, the fictitious "Byelorussian National Center" was "discovered," and the members of this mythical center were accused of trying to establish a Byelorussian Democratic Republic. All of these "conspirators" had previously been victims of Polish repression. For example, former delegates to the Polish Sejm, Ihnat Dvarčanin and Jasep Haŭrylik, who had served terms in Polish prisons, were shot as "Polish spies."[46]

To make matters worse, the Soviet authorities accompanied this terror with wide-scale Russification policies. In 1938, teaching in Russian was made obligatory in all schools of the USSR. In the same year, the state authorities purged the Byelorussian language of all Polish elements. Eventually, not only was the Byelorussian language and its proponents proclaimed "enemies of the Soviet state," but also the symbols of Byelorussia were subjected to persecution. Thus, it was forbidden to mention the name of the fifteenth-century Byelorussian educator and publisher, Francysk Skaryna, or that of the Byelorussian national hero, Kastus' Kalinoŭski. The relics of St. Euphrosyne, the patron saint of Byelorussia, were taken away from the Polock Cathedral and placed in the Atheism Museum in Vitebsk.[47]

During the *perestroika* period opinion varied in Byelorussia regarding the exact number of Byelorussian victims of Stalinist terror. According to the researcher Boris Sachenko, for example, their number was equal to the number of those who perished during the Nazi occupation, i.e., approximately two million people.[48] For the purpose of the present work, however, it is more important to focus on the social implications of these events. The repressions robbed the Byelorussian society of its leaders who could have rallied and supported their people in the hard times to come. The Great Stalinist Purge destroyed the society's "immune system," that is, it stripped away the connections that transform a random group into a society: as well as denying the Byelorussians their identity, both cultural and national, it also destroyed the trust that defines any kind of relationship, whether among colleagues, neighbors, or members of one's family. All were encouraged to spy on and denounce one another in the name of some nebulous "bright future," a "communist paradise." The fact that these debilitating measures were enacted before the foreign invasion proved to be catastrophic during the German occupation. This created a widespread inertness in the society, which according to George Fisher was the most striking feature of Soviet society on the eve of World War II.[49] Yet, a new type of individual emerged, one who was able to live under any kind of totalitarian rule and who, for the sake of profit and survival, would turn against anyone designated by the authorities as the enemy.

"Reunification" of Byelorussia

Undoubtedly, the factor that augmented all of these existing tensions was the so-called "Reunification of Byelorussia," which was an outcome of the Molotov–Ribbentrop pact signed in August 1939. At first, the Soviet troops that entered Western Byelorussia on 17 September 1939 were greeted with joy by the Byelorussian as well as by the Jewish population, the two groups most discriminated against under Polish rule. In many places, triumphal arches were raised, and in others, the population expressed its joy by kissing passing Soviet tanks and even the boots of Soviet soldiers.[50] Even some Poles, believing that the Soviet soldiers had come to help their fellow Slavs in their struggle against the Germans, greeted them warmly.[51]

Nevertheless, there was a feeling in the air that the time had come for retaliating and settling old scores. The advance of Soviet troops into Eastern Poland was accompanied by Byelorussian outbursts of physical violence, the main victims of which were not only Poles but also Jews.[52] Not only did the Soviet soldiers refrain from intervening or preventing such attacks, they even encouraged them. Posters in Russian that explicitly called for violence against the Poles, "To Poles, Pans, and dogs—a dog's death" (*Polyakam, panam; sobakam-sobachya smert'*), were disseminated in some localities, for example, in Maladečna.[53] In other places, such as the village of Svislač (today Hrodna oblast), Soviet officers organized a meeting, where they said explicitly to the assembled peasants: "For twenty years you have lived under the yoke of the masters, who drank your blood, and now we have liberated you and we give you freedom to do with them as you please."[54] The primary targets of the attacks were Polish *osadnici*, military men, landlords, and priests. The families of these people, including women and children, were not spared.

One of the most striking features in the process of ensuring that newly acquired areas "join the Soviet family of nations" was the large-scale population movements. The new bosses in the "liberated" territories worked vigorously to bring them in line with the order prevailing in the Soviet Union. According to the Israeli historian, Ben-Cion Pinchuk, the people in these territories "had to travel in 21 months a road traversed by the Soviets in over 20 years."[55] The Soviet authorities were resolute in their decision to establish a stronghold here and to eliminate anyone who, from their point of view, might constitute an obstacle to their Sovietization policies. The Poles living in these areas, including those removed from the ruling positions they had previously enjoyed, were viewed as personae non gratae, from the very beginning up to the German invasion. According to the Polish government-in-exile, the Poles constituted fifty-two per cent of the total number of deportees cast out during the great deportations of 1940–41.[56] In Bialystok, the Soviet authorities were eager to create a Byelorussian majority artificially, by promoting the migration of Byelorussians from the countryside to the town and by expelling many Poles and Jews.[57] According to Soviet propaganda, the Byelorussians (and, in the Western Ukraine, the Ukrainians) were preferred when it came to filling various governmental jobs, so they were considered the main "beneficiaries" of the changes. However, here the Soviets were confronted with the same problem that the Germans would encounter a few years later, namely, the lack of Byelorussians with sufficient qualifications for the posts. Moreover, even the Byelorussians who had lived for a long period under "capitalist rule" were regarded with a certain degree of suspicion.[58] To solve these problems, the Soviets were compelled to appoint Jews and even some Poles to do the actual work, keeping Byelorussians as "figure-heads."[59] In addition, swarms of the so-called "Easterners" (*Vostochniki*), i.e., officials from the old Soviet territories, were sent out to the newly acquired areas.

Up to the beginning of 1940, those who suffered most from the new system were the Poles, but the economic policies introduced that year succeeded in disgruntling a wider segment of the population. The nationalization of middle-sized and small enterprises meant that many people ended up on the street. Some of them were able to find jobs in cooperatives, but others, considered "bourgeois elements," could not, and were thus left without a livelihood. The abolition of the zloty as the national currency, the high taxation, the cutting off of supply sources, and the "buying fever" of the Soviet soldiers and their family members very quickly emptied the shops in the former *Kresy*.

Although such repressive policies were exercised equally, regardless of nationality, many Byelorussians who had initially believed in the Soviet slogans of "national liberation" felt cheated and began to seek a scapegoat. The traditional scapegoat was the Jew. In the eyes of the non-Jew, it did not matter that Jews had been hit just as hard if not harder by the economic policies of the Soviets. All they saw was that under the new regime, the Jews received new—albeit small—opportunities, and had changed from being a traditionally despised minority to people with equal rights. In fact, quite a number of them even had become authority figures. This, combined with the policy of Sovietization in all its aspects, was enough to reignite anti-Semitism, which also expressed itself in restrained forms, such as throwing slips with the inscriptions "Death to the Bolsheviks and the Jews" and "Long live Hitler" into the ballot boxes during the election to the National Assembly.[60]

In his recent study "Konterrevolutionäre Elemente sind zu erschießen" (The counterrevolutionary elements are to be shot), the Polish historian Bogdan Musial ascribes the sharp rise in anti-Semitism in the territories annexed by the Soviet Union in September 1939 solely to the role that the Jews played during the period between September 1939 and June 1941.[61] He also describes the "abusive" attitude many Jews there allegedly adopted towards non-Jews, especially the Poles.[62] This author, however, ignores and even denies the existence of official Polish interwar anti-Semitism.[63] Jan Tomasz Gross, in his work *Neighbors*, expresses an interesting opinion regarding the constant accusations made about the Jews' support of the Soviets during the two years after the Soviet annexation of Western Byelorussia and Western Ukraine:

> [E]nthusiastic Jewish response to entering Red Army units was not a widespread phenomenon at all, and it is impossible to identify some innate, unique characteristics of Jewish collaboration with the Soviets during the period 1939–1941. On the other hand, it is manifest that the local non-Jewish population enthusiastically greeted entering Wehrmacht units in 1941 and broadly engaged in collaboration with the Germans, up to and including participation in the exterminatory war against the Jews. Thus, it appears that the local non-Jewish population projected its own attitude toward the Germans in 1941.[64]

Stalin knew very well that the population in the new territories was less than happy about Sovietization. He was also aware that a German invasion was more than probable, and he could not afford any unrest in the border areas. The result of all these calculations was not, however, the alleviation of the Sovietization process, but rather the implementation of harsher measures intended to rob the potential insurrections of their leadership. One must see the deportations of 1940–41, mentioned above, in this light. It is very difficult to say exactly how many people were deported to Siberia and Central Asia from Western

Byelorussia. The Byelorussian researcher, Janka Zaprudnik, suggests that a total number of 300,000 were exiled from this area (including the Vilna area).[65] One thing is certain: among the first to be deported were former civilian and government officials such as judges and policemen.[66]

In the work mentioned above, Musial put forward a thesis, according to which a correlation exists between what he calls "Soviet crimes," i.e., all the violence and terror that accompanied the Sovietization policies in the newly acquired West Byelorussian and West Ukrainian territories, and the radicalization of German policies in these and other occupied Soviet territories after 22 June 1941, especially in measures related to the persecution of Jews.[67] Musial's thesis has been criticized on numerous occasions by several historians. Dieter Pohl, for example, suggested quite rightly that Musial's portrayal of the entire Jewish population as the main beneficiary of Soviet rule had very little to do with objective historical analysis.[68] One claim that counters Musial's proposition is the fact that twenty-five per cent of the deportees from the annexed Polish territories were Jews, a percentage that was much higher than their weight in the entire population of these territories.[69] One must also remember that documents such as the infamous "commissars' order" or the "hunger plan" described in detail in the next chapter, to name only a couple, as well as various anti-Jewish decrees, were envisaged long before a single German soldier had stepped onto Soviet territory, and before the first mass graves of NKVD victims had ever been opened. It would seem that for the Germans, the Stalinist atrocities had more propagandistic than practical value, while simultaneously providing a kind of justification for the various measures of the occupation regime. They functioned as the pretext for—rather than the cause of—the ensuing events.

The Outbreak of the War

When, in the early morning of 22 June 1941, after heavy air raids on Soviet cities, the German forces crossed the USSR border, their invasion encountered a wide range of reactions, ranging from overt joy to fear and depression. The only thing that cannot be denied is that no one among the local population knew exactly what he or she could expect of this invasion. The rapid advance of German troops and the corresponding rapid retreat of the Soviet forces, despite the Soviet's prewar propaganda assurances that a future war would be waged "with little blood on foreign soil" (*maloj krov'yu, na chuzhoj zemle*), only added to the general confusion that reigned in the first weeks of the war.[70] The fact that the Soviet government was virtually paralyzed by the German attack as well as by the rapid advance of the enemy troops, while the local state apparatus collapsed like a house of cards, also added to the general chaos of these summer days of 1941.

Given that Stalin and his entourage did not believe in the probability of a German invasion before it really started, they had not considered any coherent plans for the evacuation of the civilian population. Only on 29 June, that is, when a significant part of Byelorussia was already in German hands, did a directive arrive from Moscow calling for the evacuation of the territories close to the frontline.[71] On 3 July, in other words, almost two weeks after the beginning of the war, Stalin addressed his people, calling them to implement a scorched earth policy before the advancing German troops:

> In case of forced retreat of Red Army units, all rolling stock must be evacuated, the enemy must not be left a single engine, a single railway car, not a single pound of grain, or a gallon of fuel. The collective farmers must drive off all their cattle, and turn over their grain to the safekeeping of state authorities for transportation to the rear. All valuable property, including non-ferrous metals, grain, and fuel which cannot be withdrawn, must be destroyed without fail.[72]

As all of these directives and demands indicate that in the entirety of measures related to the evacuation, top priority was given to war-important materials and enterprises. As for the people, the importance of their removal was defined by their social and economic status. So, according to some sources, priority in evacuation was given to members of the Communist Party.[73] Also among the first to be taken out were the employees of the military industrial plants. In some cases, as for example in Minsk, women and children too were included in this category, and were subject to immediate evacuation.[74] At the same time, the statement that the Soviet government undertook some special steps toward the evacuation or rescuing of the Jewish population must be discarded as a myth; hundreds of Jews, however, did try to flee the Germans on their own initiative.[75]

By focusing on the Soviet evacuation policies in the first weeks and months of the war, we frequently tend to overlook their impact on those who did not succeed in evacuating or fleeing and were compelled to stay behind. Only in recent years have voices been heard calling for an analysis to consider to what degree the execution of Stalin's "scorched earth" orders influenced the conditions that prevailed in the years of Nazi occupation. As early as the 1950s, the American scholar of Byelorussian origin, Nicholas Vakar, stated that in the course of the evacuation, "the damage to the civilian population," augmented by the destruction of anything that could have been of use to the Germans, "proved infinitely greater than that suffered by the Germans."[76] The same thought was repeated recently by the Polish-Byelorussian historian, Yerźy (Yuri) Turonak. He writes that the evacuation "played an important political role and was the destructive factor in the social life of occupied Byelorussia, worsening the everyday difficulties of its population."[77] This was especially the case in Eastern Byelorussia, where the Soviet authorities had more time to execute the scorched earth policy. Agriculture was hit particularly hard by these policies. Thus, according to the numbers given by Turonak, the total number of cattle in four oblasts, Vitebsk, Mogiljov, Gomel and Polesje, was reduced to thirty per cent of its original number, that of sheep to twenty-six per cent. Of the total amount of grain in Eastern Byelorussia (151.1 thousand tons), fifty-four per cent (81.2 thousand tons) was evacuated or "used otherwise," and twenty-eight per cent (42.5 thousand tons) was destroyed. Moreover, a significant portion of the agricultural machinery, including 5,000 tractors, was confiscated by the Red Army, as were a large number of horses, thus weakening the agricultural economy for years to come.[78]

Less clear is the situation regarding the destruction of many Byelorussian cities in the first weeks of the war. While most historians, including the Germans, tend to ascribe it chiefly to the German aerial bombings, as well as to ground warfare, Turonak sees it as a result of the Soviet-sponsored activities, of the "destructive battalions" (*istrebitel'nye batal'ony*), and he blames them for burning down cities such as Vitebsk and Polock.[79] It is interesting to note that in this case, Turonak relies on "Report of the Events" (*Ereignismeldung*) number 31 of the *Einsatzgruppe* (operational squad) B, which followed the Wehrmacht into Byelorussia. The main task of this and three other units that operated to the north and south of the *Einsatzgruppe B* was to kill all the elements deemed "undesirable" from the Nazi point of view: Jews, communists and Roma (Gypsies). To somehow justify all the mass murders in which they were engaged, the authors of these squads' reports accused Jews and communists of instigating sabotage and terror activities. Consequently, the data contained in these reports must be taken with great measure of caution. In this respect, it is noteworthy that at the beginning of 1942, the head of the working group "Weißruthenien" at the Reich's Ministry for the Occupied Eastern Territories spoke explicitly of the need to explain to the population that "it was not German pilots who, according to general opinion, demolished all the houses, but rather it was arson by Jews and communists that destroyed all the streets."[80]

The picture of the general chaos that reigned in the western part of the Soviet Union during the first days and weeks of the war would be incomplete without mentioning occurrences such as the looting of stores as well as the outbursts of violence against certain population groups, primarily against the Jews.[81] Although in Byelorussia the pogroms against the Jews in the first days of the German invasion did not reach the dimension of brutality exercised in the Baltic region and in Western Ukraine, they nevertheless did take place, accompanied by the murder of Jews and the looting of Jewish property, as happened, for example, in Hrodna, Navahrudak and Ivje, in Western Byelorussia.[82]

Moreover, the uncertainty about the German plans regarding Byelorussia undoubtedly contributed to the general chaos in the first days of the war. This insecurity gave rise to a whole range of rumors, gossip, speculations and conjectures. Some of them were based on the previous experience of the German occupation in World War I. Even though German politics in general, at the time, were anything but enlightened, as shown for example by the Israeli historian, Abba Strazhas, or by the American scholar of Lithuanian origin, Vejas Gabriel Liulevicius, by and large there existed a positive image of Germans among the population. Descriptions of characteristics such as "cultured, industrious, wonderful people" could be heard from many, including the Jews.[83] What none of these people knew at the time was that, from the German point of view, this war was primarily a racial one, in which peoples' right to live was determined by their "racial value" as well as by their usefulness for the German military effort.

As shown above, when German troops arrived in Byelorussia in June 1941, they found a complex tangle of socio-economic problems and, hence, fertile soil for collaboration for anyone who could help in solving these problems. But this readiness to collaborate was not something constant: to a very significant degree, willingness to engage in it depended on the behavior of the German occupation authorities themselves. In the next chapter we will see to what extent the occupation policies of 1941–44 encouraged or discouraged the cooperation of the local population in Byelorussia.

Notes

1. See Lee Ready, *The Forgotten Axis*, 143.
2. See Vaclaŭ Lastoŭski, *Karotkaja Historyja Belarusi* (Vilna 1910; repr., Minsk, 1993).
3. Ivan Lubachko, *Belorussia under Soviet Rule 1917–1957* (Lexington, 1972), 7.
4. See Vasilij Kljuchevskij, *Russkaja Istoriia*, vol. 2 (Moscow, 1995), 500.
5. In fact, it was Grinevitsky's bomb that mortally wounded the emperor. See, for example, Alan Moorehead, *The Russian Revolution* (New York, 1959). A short biographical note on Grinevitsky may be found in *Belaruski Nacyjanalizm. Davednik* available online: http://slounik.org/nac/.
6. See Vakar, *Belorussia*, 82.
7. One of the authors of classic Byelorussian literature, Francišak Bahuševič (1840–1900), wrote, "What is Belorussia? Belorussia is there, brothers, where our language is spoken and heard" (quoted in Vakar, *Belorussia*, 82).
8. See Vakar, *Belorussia*, 94–106; Lubachko, *Belorussia under Soviet Rule*, 12–30.
9. In tsarist Russia, Byelorussia was a center of the Jewish Pale.
10. The first steps toward the creation of the Byelorussian Republic were taken immediately after the February Revolution, when the Byelorussian National Committee was created. This committee was dominated by the Byelorussian Socialist Hramada (*party* in Byelorussian), which was founded by the brothers Anton and Ivan Luckevič in 1902, on the pattern of the Polish Socialist Party, and it demanded autonomy for Byelorussia together with social reforms. Later, in 1917, the committee was transformed into the Byelorussian Great Rada (Council). After the Bolshevik Revolution, on 14 December 1917, Rada called the First All-Byelorussian Convention in Minsk to discuss the future of Byelorussia following the new developments in Russia. The fate of this convention was similar to that of the Constituent Assembly in Petrograd in January 1918: both were dissolved by the Bolshevik troops. Only after the beginning of the German offensive in February 1918 and the retreat of the Soviet forces from Minsk could the Rada of the convention renew its activity. It proclaimed itself the temporary government of Byelorussia and created its executive organ, the People's Secretariat, headed by Jasep Varanok. The Rada directed an appeal to the German chancellor, in which it proclaimed the right of Byelorussians to independence, and refuted the claims of neighboring Ukraine, Lithuania, and Poland to parts of Byelorussian territory. Although

at the time of its proclamation the BNR included merely three governments of the former Russian Empire (Minsk, Mogiljov and Vitebsk) and
parts of Grodno (Hrodna) and Vilna (Vilnius), the Rada envisioned the res-
urrection of the medieval Grand Duchy of Lithuania, which would include
the territories that according to the Brest-Litovsk treaty had been incorporated into the Ukrainian and Lithuanian States and also part of the Polish
territory, the Bialystok area. German troops entering Minsk on 25 February 1918 "greeted" the Byelorussian national aspirations by tearing down
the white-red-white Byelorussian flag flying on the building of the People's
Secretariat and confiscating the treasury. The existence of the BNR after 25
March 1918 was largely due to the benevolent neutrality of the commander
of the German 10th Army, Erich von Falkenhayn, who, according to Turonak, saw in independent Byelorussia the possibility of liquidating the
Russian wedge, with the borders drawn according to the Brest-Litovsk
treaty, between independent Lithuania in the north and independent
Ukraine in the south. The German authorities made the People's Secretariat responsible for spheres such as trade, industry, social care, education,
and culture. Pursuing the line of bringing German culture to the peoples of
the East, Germans also encouraged the opening of Byelorussian schools.
The authorities in Berlin, however, did not hasten to recognize the BNR,
although the leading activists of the republic sent a telegram to Kaiser Wilhelm II stating that the bright future of Byelorussia would be possible only
"under the protection of German State." The German government did not
take Byelorussian nationalism seriously, seeing in the Byelorussians only
one of the "tribes" of the former Russian Empire and in Byelorussia, an
integral part of Russia. Moreover, Berlin was opposed to the claims of the
Byelorussian national movement to the territories that after the Brest-
Litovsk treaty had become parts of Germany's vassal states, Lithuania and
Ukraine. Still, the image of Germany as a champion of the Byelorussian
national cause outlived the Byelorussian National Republic. It was cherished and propagated by Byelorussian nationalists in the period between
the world wars, but especially during the Nazi occupation, as will be mentioned later. See Vakar, *Belorussia*, 98–105; Turonak, *Belarus' pad
nyameckaj Akupacyjaj*, 20–23. General information about the BNR can be
found in the encyclopedic dictionary *Belarus*. See Boris Sachenka (ed.),
Belarus. Encyklapedychny Davednik (Minsk, 1995), 90. For more on the
German attitude towards Byelorussian nationalism at the beginning of the
twentieth century, see an interesting article published in the 4 April 1918
issue of *Kölnische Volkszeitung und Handelsblatt*, Hauptstaatsarchiv
Stuttgart, E 40/72, 163.

11. See Lubachko, *Belorussia under Soviet Rule*, 27–28; Vakar, *Belorussia*,
    110–12.

12. The only objections to the new order came from the "corner" of the so-
    called Sluck Rada, the anti-Soviet body headed by a certain Prakulevič;
    from the self-appointed "government of Free Byelorussia" under the lead-
    ership of General Bulak-Balakhovič, which at one time controlled whole
    regions in southwestern Byelorussia; and from the "Byelorussian Popular
    Assembly" in Vitebsk. All of these bodies sprang up in 1918 and were the
    products of the general chaos created by the Russian civil war. All of them
    recognized no authority but their own, and spoke in no one's name but
    their own. See Vakar, *Belorussia*, 115–16.

13. See in this respect the discussion by Dan Diner, in D. Diner, *Das Jahrhundert verstehen* (Frankfurt/Main, 2001), 79ff., especially 109f.

14. It is extremely difficult to say how many Byelorussians lived in these territories. The Polish census does not provide an adequate picture, since it was heavily influenced by the Polonization trends. Thus, all Byelorussians of Catholic faith were registered as Poles and the 1921 census reduced the total number of Byelorussians from 3,700,000 to 1,041,760. In the 1931 census, these numbers were reduced still further, while the inhabitants of Polesje, the marshland on the Ukrainian border, were singled out as a separate "ethnic group," namely, the so-called *tutejšie* (literally "locals"). See Vakar, *Belorussia*, 121.

15. Chiari, *Alltag hinter der Front*, 33.

16. See Ben-Cion Pinchuk, *Shtetl Jews under Soviet Rule* (Cambridge, MA, 1991), 2.

17. Bernhard Chiari, "Geschichte als Gewalttat. Weißrussland als Kind zweier Weltkriege," in *Erster Weltkrieg. Zweiter Weltkrieg*, ed. B. Thoß and H.-E. Volkmann (Paderborn, 2002), 615–31.

18. Jerzy Tomaszewski, "Belorussians in the Eyes of the Poles, 1918–1939," *Acta Poloniae Historica* 51 (1985): 101–22.

19. Quoted in ibid., 104.

20. Ibid., 105.

21. Ibid., 120.

22. Thus, in 1920, Poland signed a treaty providing the right to education in their native language to "Polish nationals of other than Polish speech." See Vakar, *Belorussia*, 251n3.

23. Among these delegates was a member of the Byelorussian Peasants and Workers Party, Yury Sabaleŭski, who during the Nazi occupation of Byelorussia served as *Bürgermeister* (mayor) of Stoŭbcy, Nesviž and Baranaviči and who, in 1943, was appointed to the head of the "Byelorussian Self-Aid Organization" (BNS).

24. For more on the Church struggles in Polish Byelorussia between the world wars, see chapter 5.

25. So, for example, a four-family hamlet was taxed 726 zlotys. See Vakar, *Belorussia*, 123–24. The persecution of Byelorussians increased with the establishment of Pilsudski's dictatorship in Poland in 1925. This is somewhat ironic, since Pilsudski himself—although thoroughly polonized—was a descendant of a Byelorussian noble family.

26. See Janka Zaprudnik, *Belarus'. Na histarychnykh Skryzhavannjakh* (Minsk, 1996), 97.

27. According to Vakar, the total membership of KPZB in 1924 was around 1,500, whereas a year later 1,800 members were in jail, and some thousands were at large. See Vakar, *Belorussia*, 125.

28. Astroŭski was born in 1887 on the Zapol'e estate, Sluck rayon, Minsk oblast. At the beginning of the twentieth century, during his study at St. Petersburg University, he participated in the student unrest there. Up to the February Revolution he did not participate in political activities, concentrating rather on teaching. Only in April 1917 was he elected to the Commissar of the Russian provisional government in the Sluck district. During the Russian civil war he served with General Denikin's White Army. Between 1924 and 1936 he headed the Byelorussian gymnasium in Vilna. In February 1924, Astroŭski was one of the founders of propagandist Byelorussian-Polish society. After this was dissolved, according to Turonak,

he cooperated with the Communist Party of Byelorussia and in 1926 was even a member of the Communist Party of Western Byelorussia (KPZB). In 1924–25 he also supervised the work of a clandestine Komsomol (Communist Union of Youth) group in his gymnasium. From 1925 to 1926 Astroŭski was one of the leaders of Hramada and also directed the Vilna Cooperative Bank, through which Soviets financed this party. In December 1927, Astroŭski was arrested together with other Hramada members. After his release, he changed course and became an ardent adherent of close cooperation with the Polish government. On the eve of the German attack against the Soviet Union, he headed the Lodz branch of Byelorussian Representation, which will be discussed in the following chapter. See Turonak, *Belarus' pad nyameckaj Akupacyjaj*, 207. A very apologetic biography of Astroŭski, denying any connection with the communists, was written by Viktor Kalush (See V. Kalush, *In the Service of the People for a Free Byelorussia* (London, 1964)). For another version of Astroŭski's biography, see Alexej Solov'ev, *Belorusskaja Tsentral'naja Rada*, 164–67. According to Solov'ev, during his directorship of the Vilna gymnasium, Astroŭski was a vehement anti-communist.

29. See Lubachko, *Belorussia under Soviet Rule*, 64.
30. Note the strangely similar characterization of Byelorussians by Germans. See the following chapter.
31. Quoted in Zaprudnik, *Belarus'. Na histarychnykh Skryzhavannjakh*, 91. On promoting the national languages in various regions of the USSR in the 1920s as a means to facilitate their acquaintance with communist ideology, see Yuri Slezkine, "The USSR as a Communal Apartment, or How a Socialist State Promoted Ethnic Particularism," *Slavic Review* 53, no. 2 (Summer 1994): 414–52.
32. In 1905, some 63% of the total population in Byelorussia were illiterate, the highest rate in the entire Russian Empire. See Zaprudnik, *Belarus'. Na histarychnykh Skryzhavannjakh*, 7.
33. *Belorusskaia SSR v tsifrakh* (Minsk, 1929), 75, quoted in Lubachko, *Belorussia under Soviet Rule*, 87.
34. Ibid., 89.
35. Ibid., 85–86.
36. Ibid., 89–90.
37. See Stalin's speech at the Fourth Conference of the Central Committee of the Russian Communist Party in June 1923. Josef Stalin, *Sochineniia* (Moscow, 1952), 5:294, translated by Lubachko, *Belorussia under Soviet Rule*, 82.
38. According to the plan adopted in January 1930, the USSR was divided into three groups as to pace of collectivization. The ascription of a region to one of these groups was defined by its agricultural standing. The first group included the Lower and Middle Volga and the North Caucasus, where the collectivization was to be completed by the end of 1930–beginning of 1931. Byelorussia, as a "non-grain-growing region," was included in the third group, so the collectivization process was extended until 1933. In some aspects, this division is reminiscent of the Nazi plan dividing the regions of the Soviet Union into "subsidies-demanding regions" (*Zuschußgebiete*) and "surplus regions" (*Überschußgebiete*). See the next chapter for more on this.
39. This was still only 20.9% of the total number of individual farms. Lubachko, *Belorussia under Soviet Rule*, 97.

40. See ibid., 100.
41. Actually, one did not need to be rich to be defined as "kulak." Anyone who produced a surplus of food, had an "extra" cow or used outside help to work his plot was dubbed "kulak." It is somewhat ironic that under the NEP, many of those who later were labeled "kulaks" had been encouraged in their efforts to modernize their farms and were even rewarded for best achievements.
42. Lubachko, *Belorussia under Soviet Rule*, 103.
43. Here, Lubachko quotes a former Byelorussian collective farmer. It is difficult either to prove or disprove these data. See ibid., 104.
44. Vakar, *Belorussia*, 147.
45. Ibid., 149.
46. Dvarčanin came to Soviet Byelorussia as part of a political prisoner exchange between the Soviet Union and Poland. See the entry Dvarčanin in the encyclopedic dictionary *Belarus*, 265. Lubachko, *Belorussia under Soviet Rule*, 146.
47. Ibid., 148.
48. Quoted by Zaprudnik, *Belarus'. Na histarychnykh Skryzhavannjakh*, 101.
49. See Fisher, *Soviet Opposition to Stalin*, 6.
50. Such was the case in Baranaviči. In the Jewish shtetl Ružany, the dwellers celebrated the entering of Soviet troops as a religious holiday and greeted one another with the traditional Jewish greeting "Mazel tov!" See Evgenij Rosenblat, "Evrei v sisteme mezhnacional'nykh otnoshenij v zapadnykh oblastyakh Belarusi, 1939–1941," *Belaruski gistarychny sbornik* 13 (2000). The article was sent to me through the kind courtesy of Dr. Leonid Smilovitsky.
51. For example, in Równe (West Ukraine), the country prefect came out personally to greet the approaching Soviet troops, thanking them for bringing help in combat with the German invaders. See Jan Tomasz Gross, *The Revolution from Abroad* (Princeton, 1988), 23.
52. In the city of Hrodna, members of the local youth organization, together with the fire fighters and other elements, staged an anti-Jewish pogrom, in the course of which some thirty Jews were killed and their property looted and destroyed. See the testimony of Leib Reizer (in Yiddish), Yad Vashem Archive (YVA), O.33/296.
53. The word *pan* in Polish means "Mr." In Soviet parlance it was made the pejorative name for all Polish "capitalists" and "landlords." Gross, *The Revolution from Abroad*, 35.
54. Ibid., 36.
55. Pinchuk, *Shtetl Jews*, 11.
56. According to the Polish Government-in-Exile, the total number of deportees from Western Byelorussia and Western Ukraine was around 800,000. This number can be found in the Sikorski files, quoted by Pinchuk, *Shtetl Jews*, 10. In *Ne po svoej Vole* (Not on own Will), published in 2001, Pavel Poljan claims that the total number of deportees from the western regions of the USSR after the annexation of these regions, between 1939 and 1940, came to about 380,000–390,000 people. With this, Poljan quotes the older study by V. Parsadanova dealing with deportations from Western Byelorussia and Western Ukraine, according to which as many as 1,173,170 were deported only from these territories between the years 1939 and 1941. The question of why there are such discrepancies between the figures remains open (P. Poljan, *Ne po svoej Vole* (Moscow, 2001), 102). The most recent

data about the deportations were published by Russian scholar Alexander Gurjanov. According to him, the total number of deportees from the former Eastern Poland between September 1939 and June 1941 was approximately between 315,000 and 320,000 people. See Alexander Gur'janov, "Überblick über die Deportationen der Bevölkerung in der UdSSR in den Jahren 1930–1950," in *Vertreibung europäisch erinnern? Historische Erfahrungen. Vergangenheitspolitik – Zukunftskonzeptionen,* ed. Dieter Bingen et al. (Wiesbaden, 2003), 140.

57. Ibid., 7.
58. Even the Communist Party of Western Byelorussia, the undeniably pro-Soviet body, was dissolved; many of its members, accused of being "Polish agents," were arrested, deported, or shot.
59. See Pinchuk, *Shtetl Jews,* 7.
60. This was the case in the city David-Horodok. See Shalom Cholawski, *The Jews of Bielorussia during World War II* (Amsterdam, 1998), 13.
61. Bogdan Musial, *"Konterrevolutionäre Elemente sind zu erschießen"* (Berlin und Munich, 2000).
62. Ibid., 71f.
63. Ibid., 30.
64. Gross, *Neighbors,* 155.
65. See Zaprudnik, *Belarus'. Na histarychnykh Skryzhavannjakh,* 105.
66. Among the purged was the founding father of Byelorussian political nationalism, Anton Luckevič.
67. Musial, *"Konterrevolutionäre Elemente,"* 14.
68. See Dieter Pohl, "Der Mörderische Sommer von 1941 aus politischer Sicht," http://www.fritz-bauer-institut.de/rezensionen/nl20/pohl.htm.
69. According to Pavel Poljan, at the beginning of April 1941, Jews constituted 59,000 or 33.3% of the total number of the so-called Polish "special settlers" deported from the annexed Polish territories; this figure does not include the "settlers" deported to Kazakhstan, Krasnojarsk land, and Vologda oblast. See Poljan, *Ne po svoej Vole,* 98. According to an earlier study by Ben-Cion Pinchuk, who quotes the Polish government-in-exile, the Jews constituted 30% or approximately 250,000 of the total number of around 800,000 deportees from West Byelorussia and West Ukraine. See Pinchuk, *Shtetl Jews,* 39, and Pohl, "Der Mörderische Sommer" (see above, note 68).
70. Thus, in the first weeks of the invasion, German troops occupied Hrodna, Brest, Maladečna, Sluck, Baranaviči, Minsk, and Bobrujsk, i.e., almost all the areas of Western and Central Byelorussia. On 9 July they arrived at the river Dnepr; on 11 July they captured Vitebsk; on 13 July, Orsha; on 15 July, Polock; on 16 July, Smolensk; and on 22 July, Mogiljov. The rest of Byelorussia was in German hands until the end of August 1941; Gomel, until 19 August, and Mozyr, until 22 August. On the eve of the German invasion, the propagandistic film, *"Esli zavtra vojna"* (If tomorrow there is a war) was shown in Soviet cinemas. In this film, the ruling Soviet strategic conception was clearly expressed. The main idea behind this was that after the initial battles, the foreign invader would be pushed back behind the border and afterwards the war would be waged exclusively on the enemy's territory with minimal losses on the side of the Red Army. Some Soviet commanders, the most prominent among them Zhukov, then Chief of General Staff, had warned beforehand about the danger of relying too much on such concepts, but these warnings were not heeded. Only the battles of the first days and weeks of the real war proved the failure of this strategy.

71. See Turonak, *Belarus' pad nyameckaj Akupacyjaj*, 41.
72. See "The German Invasion of the Soviet Union," in Josef Stalin, *The Great Patriotic War of the Soviet Union* (New York, 1945; repr., 1969), 15.
73. See Solomon Schwarz, *Evrei v Sovetskom Soyuze* (New York, 1966), 45; Ben-Cion Pinchuk, *Yehudei Brit ha-Mo'atzot mul Pnei ha-Sho'a* (Soviet Jews in the Face of the Holocaust), (Tel Aviv, 1979), 79.
74. Pinchuk, *Yehudei*, 80.
75. The myth about the deliberate "Jewish evacuation" is dismissed both by Pinchuk and Schwarz. See Pinchuk, *Yehudei*, 85–97; Schwarz, *Evrei*, 47.
76. Vakar, *Belorussia*, 171.
77. Turonak, *Belarus' pad nyameckaj Akupacyjaj*, 47.
78. Ibid., 46.
79. See Gerlach, *Kalkulierte Morde*, 372–73. Turonak, *Belarus' pad nyameckaj Akupacyjaj*, 47.
80. "Politischer Lagebericht des Leiters der Arbeitsgruppe Weißruthenien, 10.2.42," *Bundesarchiv* (henceforth, BA) R6/308, Mikrofiche 2.
81. For mention of shop lootings in Hrodna as well as the looting of kolkhoz workshops by *Eisatzkommando (EK) 9/B*, see "Operational Situation Report USSR (henceforth, EM-L. R.) No. 13, 5.07.41," in *The Einsatzgruppen Reports*, ed. Yitzhak Arad and Shmuel Spector (New York, 1989), 9, "Operational Situation Report USSR No. 31, 23.07.41," ibid., 43. The lootings in Borisov are mentioned in "Stimmungsbericht des Abwehrs von Borisow, 12.7.41," BA R.90/126.
82. Andrzej Zbikowski, "Local Anti-Jewish Pogroms in the Occupied Territories of Eastern Poland, June–July 1941," in *The Holocaust in the Soviet Union*, ed. L. Dobroszycki and J. S. Gurok (New York and London, 1993), 177; Cholawski, *The Jews of Bielorussia*, 81–82. The Grodno pogrom is mentioned both in the testimonies of Jewish survivors and in the Nazi documents. See, e.g., "Testimony of Yehudit Gliksmann" (Hebrew), Yad Vashem Archive (YVA), O 33/314 and "Testimony of Leib Reizer," YVA, O 33/296; "Operational Situation Report USSR No. 13, 5.7.41," in Arad and Spector, *Einsatzgruppen Reports*, 9. For more on the pogrom in Ivje, see M. Kaganovich, *"Eikha Horava"* (How has it been destroyed), in Kaganovich (ed.), *Sefer Zikkaron li-Kehilat Ivje* (The Memorial Book of Ivje Community), (Tel Aviv, 1968), 499. When considering the pogroms in Byelorussia, one must remember that on 22 June 22 1941 the territory of Byelorussia differed from that of today. The Bialystok area, now belonging to Poland, was made part of BSSR in the aftermath of the Molotov–Ribbentrop pact, so technically Jedwabne, too, was part of Byelorussia. Moreover, Jedwabne was not an isolated case. The massacres of Jews carried out by the gentiles—with or without the minimal participation of the Germans—also occurred elsewhere, as for example in Radzilow (7 July 1941; 800–1,500 murdered), Grajewo (July 1941; some 100 victims), and Lomza. Moreover, all of these places belonged administratively to Byelorussia. The pogrom in Radzilow is described by Gross (*Neighbors*, 57–68).
83. Abba Strazhas, *Deutsche Ostpolitik im Ersten Weltkrieg* (Wiesbaden, 1993). This work deals mainly with German World War I occupation policies in Lithuania. See also Vejas Gabriel Liulevicius, *War Land on the Eastern Front* (Cambridge, 2000). See Fanja Skorokhod, *"Rimonim beli napatzim"* (Grenades without detonators), in *Minsk. Ir ve-Em* (Minsk. City and Mother), ed. Sh. Even-Shoshan, vol. 2 (Tel Aviv, 1988), 387.

CHAPTER 3

GERMAN POLICIES IN BYELORUSSIA (1941–1944)

The Eastern Policies of the Third Reich

The preparation of military plans for the German invasion of the Soviet Union began under the Supreme Command of the Army (*Oberkommando des Heeres*), during the period of general euphoria that followed the quick victory over France. Initiated in the summer of 1940, these plans received their final form at the end of that year. The campaign against the Soviet Union was codenamed after the medieval German Emperor Friedrich Barbarossa, who led the Third Crusade in the twelfth century but drowned in a river on his way to the Holy Land. The attack on the Soviet Union was to proceed in three directions: in the north, through the Baltic area towards Leningrad (now St. Petersburg); in the center, through Byelorussia towards Moscow; and in the south, in the direction of Kiev. The ultimate goal of "Barbarossa" was to reach the so-called "A-A line" (i.e., the line from Archangelsk in the north to Astrakhan in the south). Byelorussia, being the "corridor" to Moscow, was designated as a battle zone for the Army Group Center, the strongest of the three army groups participating in this invasion, led by Field Marshal Fedor von Bock, whose staff included three general field marshals.[1]

While the military aspects of the invasion were quite meticu-
lously planned, a dense fog was cast over the various echelons of
the Third Reich as to its outcome for the newly acquired territories. What would they look like after the conclusion of the fighting? Ultimately, any potential plans for the future political
organization of the conquered Soviet territories were replaced by
a mixture of racial dogmas, prejudices, stereotypical approaches,
and occasionally some lessons learned from World War I. Among
the Nazi rulers' ideas regarding the implementation of *Ostpolitik,*
several opinions can be discerned.[2]

Hitler's Vision of the East

The first and the most radical of these opinions was held by
Hitler, as well as by Bormann, Himmler, and Göring. For them,
the war against the Soviet Union was one of exploitation and
annihilation. Hitler had been obsessed for some time with the
idea of creating "a healthy, viable, natural relation between the
nation's population and growth on the one hand and the quantity and quality of its soil on the other hand."[3] He saw the realization of this idea in "the acquisition of a territory for
settlement, which will enhance the area of the mother country."[4] For this overgrown child, who in his forties was still an
enthusiastic reader of Karl May novels about cowboys and Indians, the so-called "Eastern territories"—primarily the Soviet
territories—were seen as a kind of new Wild West and El Dorado
that would provide ample space for German and Germanic colonization, while fueling the Nazi war machine with its seemingly
inexhaustible resources.[5] Thus, as early as 1924, during his
imprisonment in the Landsberg fortress after the abortive Beer
Hall Putsch, he clearly and unambiguously proclaimed in *Mein
Kampf,* the alleged Bible of National-Socialism, "And so we
National Socialists ... stop the endless German movement to the
south and west, and turn our gaze toward the land in the east.
At long last we break off the colonial and commercial policy of
the pre-War period and shift to the soil policy of the future. If we
speak of soil in Europe today, we can primarily have in mind
only *Russia* [the italics are in the English text–L. R.] and her
vassal border states."[6] He reiterated these views many times,
both before and after his rise to power. Already on 3 February
1933, merely a couple of days after his appointment as German
chancellor, Hitler outlined the future aims of German foreign

policy in his speech before the commanders of the Reichswehr. Among other things, he spoke of a "conquest of the new living space (*Lebensraum*) in the East and its ruthless Germanization" as the preferred aim of this policy.[7] The twenty-two month period (August 1939–June 1941) of the so-called *rapprochement* between Nazi Germany and the Soviet Union did not succeed in changing Hitler's intentions regarding the USSR. Likewise, he never regarded the Molotov–Ribbentrop non-aggression pact as binding. Again we find in *Mein Kampf* that he had stated explicitly that "the very fact of the conclusion of an alliance with Russia embodies a plan for the next war."[8]

The people living in the east were seen by Hitler as mere pawns in his game. The much advertised "crusade" against "Jewish Bolshevism" was by no means a campaign for the liberation of the Soviet national minorities. According to the Nazi Fuehrer, the primary purpose of the peoples of the "Eastern territories" was "to serve our economy."[9] Their very existence, according to Hitler, depended on the importance of their contribution to the Third Reich's war efforts as well as on their racial "value." Therefore, Hitler called for a "racial sifting" (*zu sieben*) of the local people in the "Eastern territories," considering them equivalent to the primitive "Indians" of North America (*als Indianer zu betrachten*).[10]

Hitler's ideas on what the "Eastern space" would look like after the victory over the Soviet Union were extremely vague and often contradictory. Thus, in July 1940, when he had decided on military action against the USSR, Hitler spoke of three state entities that would be created in the European part of the Soviet Union after the latter's destruction: Ukraine, Byelorussia, and the Federation of Baltic Republics. Later, he described these anticipated states as "buffer states" (*Pufferstaaten*), "those socialist entities dependent on us [i.e., on Germany–L. R.]," "which should be ... deprived of an intelligentsia of their own."[11] It is interesting to note that all of these statements were mentioned in the "war diaries" (*Kriegstagebücher*) as well as in memoirs of German generals. It is possible that these ideas were never a genuine expression of the Fuehrer's intentions, but rather were voiced before the Wehrmacht's high commanders only to persuade them that they were indeed informed of and sharing in Hitler's war plans and annihilation policies. Nevertheless, at the meeting of high Nazi functionaries that took place on 16 July 1941, at the Fuehrer's headquarters in Rastenburg, Hitler, while in a state of euphoria over the seem-

ingly imminent victory over the USSR, spoke of the "Eastern
space" as "a huge pie," which should be "cut in such way that
would make it possible firstly, to master it; secondly, to administer it; and thirdly, to exploit it."[12] According to Hitler, the
Crimean peninsula was to be cleansed of its inhabitants and
resettled by Germans; Galicia (West Ukraine), the Baltic area,
the "Volga colony," and "the area around Baku" were to become
the Reich's areas. Conversely, Finland, Germany's ally in the
war against the Soviet Union, was to be prepared for its new status as a Federal State of Germany. "The creation of military
power to the west of the Ural" was to be prevented by all means.
The "partisan war" (which at this stage was more of a phantom
then a reality) was for Hitler a welcome opportunity to "eradicate all that stands in our way."[13]

The Ostministerium and the Eastern Policy

Another point of view was expressed by Alfred Rosenberg, who in
April 1941 was appointed plenipotentiary for the main treatment
of the East European issues, the office that in July of the same
year would become the Reich's Ministry for the Occupied Eastern
Territories.[14] Rosenberg, a Baltic German, who in his youth had
studied in Moscow and spoke fluent Russian, was considered in
the Nazi party to be an expert on the Soviet Union.[15] In his two
works, *The Myth of the Twentieth Century* (1929), which even
Hitler found too boring to read, and *The Future Way of German
Foreign Policy* (1927), he outlined his political credos. As a
"decent" Nazi, he was a convinced anti-Semite; but in addition,
Rosenberg was also an outspoken anti-Russian. His hatred
towards everything Russian was equal to his hatred of communism. Rosenberg's *idée fixe* was to create a wall, a kind of *cordon
sanitaire* around Greater Russia (or Muscovy as he preferred to
call it), consisting of non-Russian nationalities, and to push Russia
back to its "natural borders." This should be done, according to
Rosenberg, by creating several blocks, which would include Great
Finland, remaining an independent state; "The Land of Baltic
Peoples" (*Baltenland*); Ukraine; and Caucasus (*Kaukasien*), the
latter three functioning as German Commissariats.[16] Russia
proper should be limited to the area between St. Petersburg,
Moscow and the Ural mountains.[17] The four blocks envisaged by
Rosenberg were supposed to both protect Germany from the
"Russian peril" and to "push the term and the reality of Europe

far into the East."[18] Rosenberg's view of the organization of the "Eastern space" was noticeably ambiguous and contradictory. He invoked the indignation of die-hard Nazis such as Martin Bormann with his proposal to encourage Ukrainian nationalism and build a Ukrainian university.[19] Yet, already in May 1941, he instructed the future plenipotentiary for the Baltic area and Byelorussia as follows: "The aim of the plenipotentiary of the Reich in Estonia, Latvia, Lithuania and *Weißruthenien* should be the creation of a German protectorate, and the future integration of these areas into the Great German Reich, through the Germanization of the racially suitable elements, bringing in racially pure Germans, and liquidation of the undesirables."[20]

The Wehrmacht and the East

Given the fact that more than half of Byelorussian territory remained under military rule until the very end of the German occupation, it is worth examining the Wehrmacht's position regarding the implementation of Eastern policies. Dallin contrasted the Wehrmacht's position with that of Hitler, since the former claimed to distinguish between the Bolshevist rule and the Russian people.[21] In light of recent research, however, Dallin's view must be corrected.[22] Although it is undeniable that there were officers in the Wehrmacht who remembered the cooperation practiced between the Reichswehr and the Red Army following the 1922 Rapallo treaty between Germany and Soviet Russia, it is also true that their working together was by no means a "romantic marriage." In fact, many German officers were prepared to accept not only Hitler's view of the war with the Soviet Union as an anti-Bolshevist campaign but also his *Lebensraum* theories. As early as 1915, Hans von Seeckt, the main representative of German-Russian post-Rapallo cooperation, wrote the following in one of his memoranda:

> Separate peace with France and Belgium, on the basis of the *status quo ante*. Then all land forces against Russia. Conquest of ten thousand miles, expelling the population, except of course Germans. Russia has a lot of room for them, particularly in magnificent south Siberia ... once there are two hundred millions of healthy and mostly German people on 200,000 square miles of soil, say in the year 2000, we shall at least be somewhat secure against this immense Russia that may one day give birth to another Peter the Great ... against this what does it mean to

expel a lot of riff-raff of Jews, Poles, Masurians, Lithuanians, Latvians, Estonians etc? We have the power to do it; and we have been plunged into conditions, which in terms of blood and destruction leave the *Voelkerwanderung* far behind; therefore let us behave according to the customs of the *Voelkerwanderung* period.[23]

Of course the high command of the Reichswehr and later that of the Wehrmacht were not opposed to the idea of milking the resources of Russia, since these resources would oil the Wehrmacht's gears. But the commanders in the field recognized—much earlier than the NS party bosses in Berlin—the fact that threats alone would not suffice to obtain access to these resources and that the preferred strategy would use both the carrot and the stick. This strategy, i.e., the efforts to recruit the local population's help in the exploitation (or plundering) of its own resources, was euphemistically named in the Wehrmacht's officers' memoranda "political warfare."

Furthermore, noting also the infamous orders of Generalfeldmarschall von Reichenau, which Hitler found "exemplary," or those of Generalfeldmarschall von Manstein, we may come to the conclusion that it is difficult to discern any difference between the aims of the commanders of the German Army and those of the political leadership of the Third Reich regarding the Soviet campaign. Only the means by which they hoped to achieve these aims might have been somewhat different.[24]

German Visions of Byelorussia

For three main reasons Byelorussia was of little interest to the Nazi decision-makers. First, it did not possess war-important natural resources, except possibly lumber and peat. Secondly, it was not part of the long-established German settlement tradition that existed in the neighboring Baltic region and in the Ukraine. And finally, Byelorussians were mostly deemed inappropriate for Germanization. The image of Byelorussia and Byelorussians in Germany was extremely obscure, and even three years of occupation did not succeed in clarifying this image. In part, the image dated back to the German occupation during World War I. As early as 1915, the German researcher of the Russian Empire's national minorities, Eckehard Ostmann, characterized Byelorussians as "peasants and workers without an intelligentsia ... of all the peoples [of the Russian Empire] the closest to the [ethnic] Russians."[25] The German observers were even not certain how to define the Byelorussians, as a people (*Volk*) or as a tribe (*Volksstamm*).[26] There existed in Germany a standard set of stereotypes that was applied to this country and its inhabitants. Byelorussia was usually depicted as a poor, backward country, "the only European country of which Baedeker knows nothing."[27] Some were even sure that here they had found the "original homeland of Slavs" (*Urheimat der Slawen*).[28] The Byelorussians were described as an extremely primitive people, "little and weak peasant people," "the most backward, the poorest, peasant people (*Bauernvolk*) this side of the Urals," people afflicted by sexual diseases, and so on.[29] Only in the second year of the occupation were the German officials "compelled" to acknowledge that "Byelorussians still are quick on the uptake (*einiges auf dem Kasten haben*) and cannot be approached with primitive tricks (*Kunststücken*)."[30]

In adhering to the stereotypes described, Nazis disregarded the development that Byelorussia had undergone since 1917. Although at the time of the German invasion into the Soviet Union in 1941, the majority of Byelorussians still lived in the countryside, urbanization and industrialization, especially in "old Soviet" part of Byelorussia, had already made progress. According to data supplied by Soviet authorities and quoted by Ivan Lubachko, during the New Economic Policy (NEP) period, the value of gross production of merely three industries—wood, food and paper—had risen here from 59.4 per cent to 60.7 per cent in 1925–1926, and fallen slightly (to 57 per cent) in 1926–1927.[31] The urban population of Eastern Byelorussia had increased from 847,830 (17 per cent of the total population) in 1926 to 1,372,522 (24.6 per cent of the total population) by 1939. The number of inhabitants in the five major cities, Minsk, Vitebsk, Gomel, Mogiljov, and Bobrujsk had increased in this period by approximately 305,000.[32] As was shown in Chapter 2, in the NEP period the educational level of the Byelorussian population also rose notably.

Owing to the almost complete loss of contact with reality, the stereotypes did not remain merely stereotypes, but were actually invoked as guidelines for policy making. Thus, among the definitions cited above, we can also find in various German documents descriptions of Byelorussians as "the most harmless and because of this the least dangerous (*ungefährlichste*) for us of all the peoples in the 'Eastern space,'" or even as "an ideal object of exploitation."[33] Definitions such as the last, as well as the statement that "Byelorussian peasantry does not strive to possess the homestead in German sense," could certainly provide hints of future German intentions.[34]

It is, in fact, impossible to discern any coherent prewar German plans regarding Byelorussia. As shown above, it was to be part of the *cordon sanitaire* around Russia, as envisaged by Rosenberg, and in this capacity its territory would even increase. Yet, various institutions, such as the Wansee-Institute, openly stressed the inability of Byelorussians to run their own state. The Byelorussians, according to this institute, were characterized by "folkish indifference" (*völkische Indifferenz*) and in its analyses, the institute emphasized the "fact" that "Byelorussians (*Weißruthenientum*) never acted out of their own 'popular force' (*Volkskraft*) and their own initiative as history makers. Their destiny from the very beginning of historic tradition to the present has been linked to other peoples and states."[35] It is little wonder then that the same Rosenberg also spoke of Byelorussia in terms of the future place of exile for all "undesirables" or "asocial elements" from the Baltic part of Ostland as well as from German-controlled Poland: "obviously many asocial people should be resettled from these Baltic lands and for these undesirable elements, including those from General Government and Wartheland, Byelorussia is a very appropriate reception area."[36] At some point, even the idea of turning Byelorussia into a huge nature reserve (*Naturschutzpark*), also proposed by the future minister for the Occupied Eastern Territories, was discussed.[37] Even as late as April 1943, that is, almost two years after the beginning of the occupation, the various German institutions were not sure what should be done with Byelorussia. Should it be involved firmly in German *Lebensraum*, or perhaps be "a foreground of the German Reich connected with the motherland solely through its strong points," or should it be viewed merely as an exploitable object?[38]

From the point of view of planners in Berlin, one—if not the major—function of the occupied Soviet territories was to supply food to Germany itself, to the German front as well as to the occupation forces stationed in these territories. As late as 1943, the Department for Food and Agriculture of the *Generalkommissariat Weißruthenien* (*GK Weißruthenien*) spoke of the occupied Eastern territories as a "source of food not only for the German Reich, but also for the whole of Western Europe."[39] For the Nazi rulers, the entire "Eastern space" was a huge breadbasket that had to be exploited ruthlessly, even at the cost of the needs of the local population. To this end, the plan as a whole was worked out on the eve of the Soviet campaign; it was one of the most terrible plans that history has ever known. The details of this plan, which envisaged the de-industrialization and de-urbanization of the Soviet territories and the deaths of millions of people, were recently analyzed in detail by the German historian, Christian Gerlach.[40] The guiding spirit behind this "hunger plan" was the state secretary (deputy minister) in the Reich's Ministry of Food and Agriculture, Herbert Backe. According to this plan, which was eventually integrated into Göring's signed *Grüne Mappe* (The Green Folder), the Soviet territories would produce a "surplus" of 8.7 million tons, mainly of grain and potatoes, through artificial lowering of the local population's consumption. This surplus should be used exclusively for the German war effort. The ultimate goal here was to prevent the repeat of what took place at the end of World War I, whereby the Entente's sea blockade of Germany led to food shortages, disorder, and rebellion, all of which culminated in the fall of the monarchy. Therefore, all Soviet territory under German control was designated as either "surplus areas" (*Überschußgebiete*), i.e., areas in the south and southeastern parts of the European section of the Soviet Union as well as the Caucasus, or as "subsidy areas" (*Zuschußgebiete*) lying in "the forest zone of the north." The former was seen as a predominantly agricultural zone, the latter as an industrial one. Both zones, according to this plan, should be hermetically separated, although its authors were conscious of the fact that such a separation would mean the "cease of supplies to the total forest zone, including the important industry centers of Moscow and Petersburg," inevitably resulting not only in the de-industrialization of this area but also in the deaths of a great many people. Basically, the idea was that "subsidy areas," including Byelorussia, would shift to the medieval "natural economy" (or "closed house economy," *geschloßene Hauswirtschaft* as it was so "elegantly" formulated in German documents).[41] Such an economy was supposed to satisfy only local subsistence needs, without engaging in any market activity, while at the same time the German occupation forces that were to be stationed in these territories would receive the right to loot whatever food they liked.

In his fundamental study dealing with German genocide politics in Byelorussia, *Kalkulierte Morde,* Christian Gerlach included a shocking document which revealed the German vision of Byelorussia's future to be devastatingly brutal and cruel. This text was first presented as part of the degree thesis prepared by Eugen von Engelhardt, titled "The Food Economy and Agriculture of the Byelorussian Socialist Soviet Republic" (*Die Ernährungs- und Landwirtschaft der Weissrussischen Sozialistischen Sowjetrepublik*), and was published before the invasion into the Soviet Union.[42] The study contains a series of marginal notes by an unknown author: according to Gerlach it may be a professor of agricultural studies from Berlin University, Waldemar von Poletika.[43] Based on these notes, the total urban population of Byelorussia, approximately two million people, as well as half the Byelorussian rural population, some 4,300,000 people, were to be starved to death to enable Hitler to realize his war plans.

It is undeniable that this "hunger plan" and the economic factor as a whole played an important role in the prewar Nazi plans regarding the *Ostraum*, as well as in the implementation of these designs during the occupation years. Nevertheless, it would be false to ascribe the responsibility for inhuman Nazi policies in the conquered territories to this factor alone, as does Christian Gerlach.

The ideological factor, too, is of paramount importance in understanding German policies. It must be remembered that along with the plans envisaging the deliberate starvation of many millions of people, there were also proposals for a forced population shift, of a size unknown since the Migration Period of the early Middle Ages. These plans were based not so much on economic calculations but rather on the racial principles of the Third Reich's ideology. From 1940 to 1942, under the patronage of *Reichsführer SS* Heinrich Himmler, the projects that came to be known by the title "General Plan East" (*Generalplan Ost*) were devised.[44] The most radical of these, developed by the Main Security Office of the Reich (RSHA), called for the removal of thirty-one million people living in the *Ostraum* (this term also included occupied Poland) to West Siberia, in order to make room for the settlers from Germany and "Germanic" countries. All these processes were to take place during the first thirty years after the war. In Byelorussia alone, seventy-five per cent of the population was deemed incapable of Germanization and was destined to be expelled or annihilated.

An alternative plan was suggested by Erhard Wetzel, who proposed to remove "racially valuable" Byelorussians from their native country into the Reich for "re-Germanization" and subsequent use in German agriculture and industry, or "at least" to "let them develop in Byelorussian space separately from the rest of the Byelorussians."[45] The same Wetzel also proposed to remove the Byelorussians "incapable of Germanization" into the Urals or to the North Caucasus, since "the Byelorussian population has a tendency to wander (*zur Wanderung neigt*)."[46] Thus we can see that the Eastern peoples were not regarded by the Nazi ruling circles as flesh and blood humans, but rather as pawns that could be moved and removed according to the will and caprice of the "player."

Little wonder then that in such circumstances, the very possibility of obtaining local cooperation in the administration of the occupied territories was never discussed seriously in Germany's prewar "Eastern campaign" plans. It was firmly believed that this campaign would be over in a matter of weeks, and then it would be time to proceed to the implementation phase of the racial and economic chimeras mentioned above.

Germans and Byelorussian Nationalists on the Eve of the Nazi Invasion into the USSR

In the various circles of the Third Reich, the "Eastern people" were generally seen as subhuman (*Untermenschen*) and therefore worthless. Nevertheless, the idea of using these people and their grievances to further the aggressive plans of Nazi Germany was not alien even to the most stubborn dogmatists. Hitler supported the idea of the destruction of a state targeted for attack by awakening from within any pre-existing conflicts, especially ethnic ones, as a preliminary step towards outright onslaught. Thus, the increased focus on issues of nationalism in central and east European countries in the 1930s created a fertile soil for the realization of such ideas. For example, before and during the German invasion of Poland, there were plans to provoke a Ukrainian rebellion in Galicia (West Ukraine), which had been discussed in the Abwehr (Army Intelligence and Counter-Intelligence Service) and the OKW (Supreme Command of Wehrmacht). The leading role in these plans was to be played by the Ukrainian emigrant organization OUN (Organization of Ukrainian Nationalists).[47]

Some efforts were made (chiefly on the part of Rosenberg's Foreign Organization of the Nazi Party, the Auslandsorganization) to provoke the Byelorussian minority in Poland, but the

attention this minority received cannot be compared to that
directed towards the Ukrainian minority in Poland. As early as
1933, Fabian Akinčyc initiated attempts to create a broad
Byelorussian National Socialist Movement in the West
Byelorussian territories, largely under the influence of Nazi
Auslandsorganization as well as of the Nazi-oriented Union of
Byelorussian Students in Berlin. The eventual failure of these
endeavors only enhanced the skepticism regarding the potential
use of Byelorussians in any future German expansionist plans.[48]

Although Nazi propaganda in the interwar period did not
spare any effort to present the Third Reich as the true defender
of the rights of small nations, many of the Byelorussian emigrants did not hurry to cast their lot unconditionally with Hitler.
The leader of the Byelorussian Christian-Democrats in emigration, priest Vincent Hadleŭski, wrote in 1939 after the occupation of Prague by Nazi Germany:

> Looking closely at all of these issues, we should note once again
> that the first problem, which fuels the agenda in European poli-
> tics, is a national one. Racist Germany is attempting to solve it,
> not out of principle, but out of tactics; taking advantage of the
> tangibility of national problems, Germany is hoping to expand
> her supremacy to the east. We must acknowledge that the tangi-
> bility of the national problems as well as Germany's desire to
> untangle these problems makes Germany a large and formidable
> force in the eyes of the Soviets and others. But will Germany
> untangle these problems? We are afraid that it might entangle
> them even more.[49]

After the Polish campaign, the number of Byelorussians living
in German-controlled territories increased. Polish POWs of
Byelorussian origin joined the veteran emigrants, those who had
escaped from Western Byelorussia and the Vilna (Vilnius) region
when annexed by the Soviets. Only then did the intelligence services of the Third Reich recognize the potential advantage that
these people held for German plans regarding the future Soviet
campaign. As early as July 1939, the "Byelorussian Confidence
Office" (*Weißruthenische Vertrauensstelle*), better known as "the
Byelorussian Representation" (Belorusskoje Predstavitel'stvo or
BP for short), was created in Berlin. Heading the organization
was the ardent Nazi-admirer Fabian Akinčyc who, as mentioned, was playing with the idea of creating a Byelorussian Nazi
Party in the early 1930s. However, Akinčyc's ability to exercise
authority was very limited, both among the Byelorussian emi-

grants as well as among the Germans themselves, so he was soon replaced by Anatol' Škutko.[50] The official aim of the BP, which was subordinate to the German Interior Ministry, was to register all the Byelorussians living in Germany, in the Protectorate of Bohemia and Moravia, and in German-occupied Poland; to organize relief services; and to assist these emigrants in finding jobs. In addition to its official objectives, the Byelorussian Representation served other aims too, as the former members of the BP, Bartkevič and Omeljanovič, testified before the Soviet investigators after the war. Its activities were monitored very closely by Section B "a" of the 4th Department of The Main Office for Reich Security (RSHA), i.e., the Gestapo. According to Omeljanovič's testimony, Škutko was even placed on the Gestapo payroll. The registration lists compiled by the Representation's officials were subsequently used for the selection of local administration personnel in occupied Byelorussia.[51]

It must be remembered that the chief principle guiding the Third Reich throughout its entire existence was divide and rule. In line with this tenet, the Byelorussian Self-Aid Committee (Belorusskij Komitet Samopomoshchi, BKS), an organization parallel to the BP, was founded in Berlin in the summer of 1940. At the head of this body stood Baroŭski, the former consul of the short-lived BNR in Berlin. The committee had its branches in Pozen (Poznan) and Litzmannstadt (Lodź) as well as in Munich, Leipzig, Prague, and a few other locations. Simultaneously, an organization with the same name, but independent of the Berlin Committee, was created in Warsaw for the General Government. This organization also had branches in Krakow and Bjeła-Podljaska. The Warsaw organization was headed most of the time by the young physician Mikalaj Ščors.[52] As with the BP, the BKS had the official aim of providing social aid, chiefly through the establishment of canteens for the needy as well as the organization of educational and cultural activities, such as lectures, amateur artistic ensembles, and libraries. However, as with the BP, the BKS both in Berlin and Warsaw was closely controlled by the Third Reich's security organs; this can be seen, inter alia, from the SD's interference in the appointment of the BKS head in Warsaw.

It seems that for the Germans the bodies mentioned above were merely tools to ensure constant control over the activities of the Byelorussian emigrants as well as their exploitation for German plans, but the Byelorussian emigrants saw in them a kind of lobby for the advancement of Byelorussian interests.

Although some Byelorussian emigration activists were very cautious with regard to the Third Reich's proclamations, others
were ready to accept Hitler's image as "defender of the small
nations." After all, the Slovaks had obtained their "independent" state! As early as 20 April 1939, that is, shortly after the
German occupation of Prague, two Byelorussian activists there,
Dr. Ivan Yermačenka, an ardent Germanophile and future head
of the Byelorussian National Self-Aid Organization in occupied
Byelorussia, and the elderly Vasil' Zakharka, the nominal presi-
dent-in-exile of the Byelorussian People's Republic, sent a sev-
enteen-page memorandum to Hitler personally asking him to
take into account the interests of Byelorussia in any "future
developments."[53] Contrary to expectations, this memorandum
drew attention in Berlin, in particular at Wilhelmstraße; on 3
August 1939, both Yermačenka and Zakharka were summoned
to the German Foreign Ministry, where the head of the Eastern
Department of this ministry, Professor Mayer, assured them
that "Germany is against a unified, indivisible Russia," but
refrained from making more specific promises.[54]

As the attack on the Soviet Union drew closer, the Byelorussian emigrants in Germany and in German-controlled territories
escalated their activities. Although the Non-Aggression Pact
signed between the Soviet Union and the Third Reich in August
1939 took many of them by surprise, as can be seen from
Zakharka's address of February 1940, the inevitability of a German-Soviet war forced Byelorussians who put their trust in Germany to make an attempt to consolidate their ranks, while
enhancing their cooperation with German secret services, in
particular with the Abwehr.[55] On 19 June 1941, a few days
before the German attack, the leaders of the Byelorussian emigration, such as the priest Hadleŭski, Mikalaj Škjaljonak, Anatol' Škutko and Vitaŭt Tumaš, created in Berlin the so-called
"Center." It was headed by Ščors and was destined to be turned
into a Byelorussian Provisional Government with the outbreak
of German-Soviet war. The example for such an organization
was apparently the "Front of Lithuanian Activists," which had
been created at approximately the same time and was notorious
for its proclamations to instigate pogroms against the Jewish
population; such calls were duly followed with the beginning of
the German advance into Lithuania. In the first days of German
occupation, the organization created a short-lived Lithuanian
provisional government.

At the same time, in the second half of 1940, the Warsaw Byelorussian Committee for Self-Aid began to cooperate with the Abwehr in the recruitment of Byelorussians for intelligence and sabotage activities inside the territory of Soviet Byelorussia. Near Warsaw, the Abwehr established a special center for training the agents, and in the spring of 1941, the special sabotage units were formed; their function was to execute acts of sabotage within Soviet territory before the advancing German troops. One of these groups, consisting of fifty men, was dropped over Soviet lines on 18 June 1941, merely four days before the beginning of the German invasion into the USSR. The group, whose task was to blow up the Stoŭbcy-Baranaviči railway, was ultimately arrested by Soviet border guards.[56] Towards the end of May 1941, the Abwehr's 2nd Department issued an order to use the sabotage units, consisting of Byelorussian (and Lithuanian) emigrants, to secure important bridges and sabotage railways in the first stage of Operation Barbarossa. These units were given a special password—*Minsk* for Byelorussian units— as well as special signs, a red handkerchief with the yellow patch in the middle.[57]

Those responsible for the planning of Operation Barbarossa were well aware of the fact that the German forces coming to the Soviet Union had only a very vague idea of the conditions reigning there. Local guides, as well as spies (elegantly named "trusted people," *Vertrauensmänner* or *V-Leute*) and those who simply were acquainted—whether more or less—with local realities, were badly needed in those hectic days of the spring and summer of 1941. Thus, each of the three Army Groups that participated in the invasion was allocated a sum of 30,000 roubles, specifically for the hiring and financing of *V-Leute*.[58]

The infamous *Einsatzgruppen* (literally "task forces"), which in the first days of the German invasion into the Soviet Union butchered many thousands of Jewish men, women, and children, including little babies, was also eager to make use of the services of those people who knew the "operational area." In the spring of 1941, the head of the Institute for Overseas Studies at Berlin University and the designated commander of the "vanguard force" (*Vorkommando*) of *Einsatzgruppe B,* Professor Franz Six, made contact with the Warsaw BKS and created a group of some thirty to forty Byelorussians who were to serve as guides and *V-Leute* for his unit.[59] Among these numerous recruits were people who later manned the local administration in occupied Byelorussia, such as Stanislaŭ Stankevič, the future "mayor" (*Bürgermeister*) of Borisov and Yury Sabaleŭski, who was a former Polish Sejm deputy, the future Bürgermeister of Baranaviči, and later head of the Self-Aid Organization.[60]

Once again, given their readiness to use the services of the Byelorussians, as well as the assistance of other emigrants, during the preparation stage of the Soviet campaign, the Germans refrained from making any far-reaching promises. The only assurance they gave the Byelorussian emigrants was of their intention to free Byelorussia from Polish as well as Russian influences, promises that later led to full-scale ethnic cleansings in the predominantly Polish areas of Western Byelorussia. Moreover, the Germans solemnly believed that the people in the Soviet territories targeted for invasion would be so grateful for their liberation from Bolshevism that they would gladly support the new rule; they felt, therefore, no need to make many extensive concessions.[61] Upon observation it becomes obvious that the reigning trend among the various Nazi institutions was to obtain maximum cooperation at a minimum price: a trend that continued well into the occupation period and even to its very end.

The Nazi Regime in Byelorussia: From Invasion to Occupation

During the first weeks and months of the German offensive, the whole of Byelorussia found itself under military rule. The military administration was generally divided into the front-line area, the Army's Rear Areas (*rückwärtige Armeegebiete*), and finally the Army Groups' Rear Areas (*rückwärtige Heeresgebiete*). The latter were supposed to separate the operational area and the civil administration, but the boundaries between these areas changed rapidly as the Wehrmacht advanced into Soviet territory. Even before September 1941, parts of Byelorussia were transferred to the authority of the civil administration, while the majority of Byelorussian territory was part of the Rear Area of Army Group Center. At the head of this body stood the aged General of Infantry Max von Schenckendorff, who was called back to service after eleven years in retirement.[62] The location of his headquarters shifted between Smolensk and Mogiljov. Formally, his position was subordinate to that of the supreme commander of the Army Group Center, but he enjoyed a large degree of independence. Even when the territories in Western Byelorussia were transferred to the civil administration (*GK Weißruthenien*), the Rear Area of the Army Group Center still encompassed a large part of Byelorussia (107,550 km²), which essentially coincided with the territory of the BSSR before September 1939.[63]

The entire Rear Area of the Army Group Center was divided into security divisions (*Sicherungsdivisionen*). These were both military and administrative units. As the borders of the whole Rear Area changed numerous times, especially in the first months of the German-Soviet war, so too did the borders of the security divisions. Between the end of August and mid-October 1941, the territory of *Rückwärtige Heeresgebiet Mitte* was divided into three security divisions: the 403rd in the north—which also included the Russian territories—with cities such as Vitebsk; the 286th in the middle, with Orsha and Borisov; and the 221st in the south, with cities such as Gomel and Bobrujsk. The key function of the security divisions was to fight any resistance in their areas, so they played a paramount role in the general barbarization of the occupation politics.

The area of each security division was divided in turn into several *Feldkommandanturen, i.e.,* field commandant office areas (two to four in every security division area). Each *Feldkommandantur* consisted of approximately 50 to 150 people. This office was responsible, inter alia, for controlling the local auxiliary police. The administration of everyday life was in the hands of the so-called *Ortskommandanturen* (local commandants), and they were also responsible for coordinating the local administration's activities.[64]

As was the case later with the civil administration, Hitler took care to ensure that the economic exploitation of the occupied territories was excluded from the authority of the military administration. Almost one month before the invasion, as early as 9 June 1941, the so-called *Wirtschaftsstab Ost* ("economic staff–East") was established and placed, not under the jurisdiction of the Wehrmacht's economic and supply department, but rather under the *Wirtschaftsführungsstab Ost* ("leading economic staff–East"), i.e., it was made part of Göring's economic empire.[65]

Strangely enough, while it was an official task of the military to "serve the pacification and securing of the occupied lands," de facto, even this was not within the military's monopoly.[66] Thus, the supreme leader of the SS and Police (*Höherer SS- und Polizeiführer, HSSPF*) for central Russia (*Rußland-Mitte*), Erich von dem Bach-Zelewski, the man whom even Hitler called "more tough and brutal" than RSHA chief Heydrich, the man who could "walk through a sea of blood," was appointed to Schenckendorff's staff.[67] Bach commanded the SS and police forces and was directly subordinate to SS chief Himmler.

The Germans took it for granted that the Russian campaign would be over in a matter of weeks; therefore, the military administration was considered merely a provisional form of government, which in a short time would give way to civil administration.[68] Consequently, the military authority's tasks were only vaguely defined: the military administration would pacify and secure the occupied territories, make their resources available for the continuation of warfare, and deal with the issues of tranquility, security and order (*Ruhe, Sicherheit und Ordnung*).[69] Hitler, who remembered for example the protests of the former German commander in Poland, General Blaskowitz, regarding the conduct of SS-men, now wanted to keep the military as far from politics as possible.[70] In fact, many of the Wehrmacht's high commanders preferred not to get involved in political controversies in the Soviet territories after the crumbling of Soviet rule and made efforts to rid themselves of all administrative functions as soon as possible. This trend expressed itself in attempts to hasten the transfer to civil administration rule, as well as in efforts to establish "local administration," which was manned by the local inhabitants.[71]

Local Self-Administration and Occupation

It will be left to the following chapters to show the exact modus operandi of the organs of the "local self-administration." Of note at this point, however, is that, in general the Germans lacked both the manpower and the necessary knowledge of local conditions to initiate any kind of structural reforms; instead, they simply took over the framework remaining from Soviet times, although only up to rayon level.[72] The highest local "authority" was the so-called "rayon leader" (*Rayonleiter*), who presided over the "rayon administration" (*Rayonverwaltung*) or *uprava* in Russian. He was generally appointed on the proposal of either *Feldkommandantur* or *Einsatzgruppe*. Subject to this leader's authority were a number of the so-called *Stadtbürgermeistern* (literally "city mayors") and *Landbürgermeistern* ("countryside mayors"). The former, appointed by the military authorities, headed a community with a maximum of 20,000 inhabitants, while the latter, named by the

Rayonleiter, headed the *Landgemeinde* (literally "countryside community"), the new incarnation of the old Soviet *sel'sovet*. The lowest level of "local self-administration" was held by the *Dorfälteste* ("village elder"), who in the old Soviet territories bore the name *starosta*; in predominantly Polish areas he was called *soltys*. These were usually appointed by *Landbürgermeistern*.[73]

The principles involved in the selection of personnel for the entire apparatus of "local self-administration" will be described in the next chapter; here it is sufficient to point out that, in general, the emphasis was on "political reliability" rather than on administrative skills, an approach that demonstrates the German authorities' true attitude towards local collaboration. From the very beginning, the "local self-administration" was not intended to be an independent body; its sole task, according to the Germans, was "to execute the orders of the responsible German offices" (*die Anordnungen der zuständigen deutschen Dienststellen durchzuführen*).[74] As early as July 1941, the commanders of *Einsatzgruppe B*, who closely followed the Wehrmacht units into Byelorussia, made it clear to Mikalaj Ščors, one of the leaders of Byelorussian prewar emigration who had come to Byelorussia at the start of the invasion, that the German authorities would not tolerate any kind of political ambition on the part of collaborators and that the chief task of the collaboration apparatus in German eyes was to cooperate "in the apprehension of communists, officials, commissars, intellectuals, Jews, etc."[75]

Actually, it was the military administration that already in the first stage of the occupation initiated and encouraged the creation and activities of the organs of "self-administration," a fact that gave birth not only to the legend about the "liberalism" of the military rule but also to its comparison with the "more cruel and brutal" civil administration. This legend was further fueled by the fact that the military authorities did not prevent the spontaneous dissolution of kolkhozes and the partition of their lands according to the number of heads in any particular homestead.[76] Several historians accepted this myth as an accurate reflection of war-time reality, and only recently has it been significantly revised.[77]

It is not easy to describe the period of military administration in Byelorussia, because, at least in the western part of the country, it was relatively short, lasting merely two months. Nevertheless, in this limited period, the local population was "treated" to a taste of what was in store. Occurrences such as unplanned and violent requisitions of food—especially poultry—products, the dragging of peasants out of their houses by passing German troops, and the senseless destruction of property were not rare incidents.[78] In addition, very strict limitations on movement from place to place were introduced. In October 1941, i.e., when the western part of Byelorussia was under the civil administration, Lieutenant-General von Unruh, commander of Rear Army Area 559, gave orders to shoot any civilians moving on the highways at night.[79]

The execution of the "Final Solution of the Jewish Question" began in the period of military rule, that is, when the role of the Wehrmacht authorities was not limited solely to supplying weapons and other materials to the infamous *Einsatzgruppen*. On the contrary, the military's involvement was expressed also in "preparatory measures," such as the creation of ghettos, the introduction of "Jewish patches," and even in direct participation in murder, as was the case in Bialystok.[80]

On 17 July 1941 Hitler came to the conclusion that the time was ripe to make the transition to civil administration in those areas of the former Soviet Union that were firmly in German hands. That day saw the creation, following the Nazi Fuehrer's order, of the Reich's Ministry for the Occupied Eastern Territories (*Reichsministerium für die besetzten Ostgebiete*), also called "the Eastern Ministry" (*Ostministerium* or OMi), administered by Rosenberg and recognized as the highest level of civilian rule. As had been planned earlier, Byelorussia—together with Lithuania, Latvia and Estonia—was included in the *Reichskommissariat Ostland,* and the *Gauleiter* of Schleswig-Holstein, Hinrich Lohse, was appointed as the head of this body. Later, the British historian Gerald Reitlinger would describe Lohse as a "comic satrap," who was once overheard shouting to Alfred Meyer, the deputy minister (*Staatssekretär*) of the Eastern Ministry, that his ultimate goal was to crown his son with the ducal crown (*Herzogskrone*).[81] His residence was in Riga, also the center of *Generalbezirk Lettland*.

According to the new order, the western part of Byelorussia, approximately the same territories that only two years earlier had been annexed by the Soviet Union as a result of the Molotov–Ribbentrop pact, was turned into *GK Weißruthenien*, the very name implying the intention to clear the country of any "Russian and Polish influences."[82] Appointed as chief of this body was the notorious anti-Semite, former head of the Nazi party faction in Prussian *Landtag* and the former *Gauleiter* of Kurmark (roughly the present-day territory of the Federal State of Brandenburg), Wilhelm Kube, who in the 1930s had been involved in a scandal within the Nazi party.[83] His appointment to this position was due chiefly to the personal involvement of Hitler, who wanted to find a good place for this "old fighter."[84] Kube came to Byelorussia without any knowledge of the country but with the ambitions of a lord. His pompous approach to this position was expressed in the extravagant employment of an entire staff of servants as well as in the huge inscription that read *"Generalkommissariat Weißruthenien"* upon his place of residence.[85] His definition of Byelorussians as "blond and blue-eyed Aryans," and his preference for Byelorussian bodyguards and valets, gave him the undeserved reputation as a "Byelorussophile," maintained to this day among Byelorussian nationalists. In reality, Kube openly declared his purpose: "to hold out with my men on the ruins of Minsk at least up to the end of the war" (*wenigstens bis zum Kriegsende mit meinen Männern auf den Trümmern von Minsk auszuharren.*).[86] He knew all too well that to achieve this purpose, the stick alone would not suffice; it must be used alternately with the carrot: "It is also worth appealing to the soul of this people," as he stated in 1942.[87] Thus, he was prepared to encourage Byelorussian nationalism, but only up to a certain point; only as far as this would help in the control and exploitation of the country, and as long as it would not endanger German interests. In one of his speeches, Kube proclaimed explicitly that "the White Ruthenians shall become a 'nation' only to the extent that they are capable of forming a wall against Muscovy and the eastern steppes."[88]

It must also be remembered that Kube, notwithstanding his desires, was not an absolute overlord in his "domain." Together with the order appointing Rosenberg as head of civil administration in the occupied territories, on 17 July 1941, Hitler also issued "The order regarding the police's role in securing the new occupied territories in the east." According to this order, SS-Reichsführer and Chief of German Police Heinrich Himmler received sole responsibility for pacifying and securing the Eastern territories.[89] There were a number of regional SS and police leaders (SSPF) subordinated to the supreme SS and police leaders (HSSPF) of every *Reichskommissariat.*[90] Within the framework of which it was supposed to act, the SS was virtually independent of the civil administration. Himmler enjoyed the right to issue directives on his own to all HSSPFs and regional SSPFs, as well as to all the levels of civil administration, on any question related to security and racial matters.

Another very important sphere was also removed from the authority of the civil administration, namely, economic issues. The exploitation of the occupied Soviet territories was entrusted to Hermann Göring's economic empire.[91] With the exception of the armament industry, the management of both industry and agriculture in the military administration area was controlled by the "Economic Inspection Center" (*Wirtschaftsinspektion Mitte*), which reported directly to Göring, the plenipotentiary for the Four Year Plan. The very important role of exploiting agricultural resources in the occupied Soviet territories was held by the Central Trade Society–East for Agricultural Marketing and Demand Ltd (*Zentralhandelsgesellschaft Ost für land-wirtschaftlichen Absatz und Bedarf mbH, Zentralhandelsge-sellschaft Ost* or ZHO for short). This body was nothing but an umbrella organization for various German enterprises that had come to the east and acted as trustees for the existing agricul-tural enterprises from the Soviet or even the Polish period. The ZHO personnel included 6,500 Germans and 800,000 local work-ers.[92]

The fact that both Lohse and his "subordinate" Kube reported directly to Hitler, in spite of their formal subordination to Rosenberg, reveals a picture of incessant power struggles. Indeed, the entire period of Kube's service as *Generalkommissar für Weißruthenien* may be described as a constant and almost obsessive defense of his authority against any encroachments, especially on the part of the SS. In this context, it becomes clear that his—albeit meager—encouragement of Byelorussian nationalism, as well as his protests against "anti-partisan actions" and occasionally even against Jewish actions, were merely attempts to protect his authority.

On 9 September 1941, Kube appealed to "the inhabitants of *Generalbezirk Weißruthenien*.[93] This address was a mixture of threats, calls to "help the German authorities in a ruthless per-secution and suppression of all instigators of disorder," and the standard promises of "security and order."[94] When we compare this "inauguration speech" with those made by the heads of other units of civil administration, e.g., that of Adrian von Renteln in neighboring Lithuania, we note similarities not only in style, but also in content.[95] This once again points to the fact that the Germans had come to the *Ostraum* with very obscure ideas; they saw it as something monolithic, and were unable to distinguish the individual characteristics of the various regions.

The administrative division of Byelorussia pointed to a lack of interest in the opinions and feelings of the Byelorussians themselves. Thus, the territory of *GK Weißruthenien* was divided into eleven *Kreisgebite*: Lida, Slonim, Navahrudak, Baranaviči, Hanceviči, Vilejka, Hlybokaje, the Minsk region, the city of Minsk, Borisov and Sluck. At the head of each one of them stood a *Gebietskommissar*. For the most part, the administration's menial work was in the hands of these people, who also controlled the activities of "local self-administration."

In addition to this division, the westernmost part of Byelorussia was turned into *Bezirk Bialystok*. This area, which encompassed the territories of present-day Hrodna and the Brest oblasts of Byelorussia, was placed under the authority of the "Supreme President of the Province of East Prussia," Erich Koch, who simultaneously headed *Reichskommissariat Ukraine*. Although formally the Bialystok region was not part of East Prussia, it became subordinated to the Königsberg's administration.[96] To create a territorial continuity between Koch's various "domains," the southern part of Byelorussia, mainly the Polesje region with cities such as Brest, Pinsk and Mozyr, was annexed to *Reichskommissariat Ukraine* and subsequently was divided into two *Generalkommissariate*: *Shitomir* and *Wolhynien-Podolien*. Simultaneously, in an attempt to compensate the Lithuanians in some form for the failure of their independence plans, a narrow strip of land in the northwest of Byelorussia was given by the Germans to *Generalbezirk Litauen*.

Although the German rulers in Byelorussia spoke officially about the rebirth of Byelorussia and its involvement in the New Europe, they did not really set any global goals for themselves.[97] The main tasks of those who controlled this country for almost three years were to extract whatever they could, both for the fueling of the Nazi war machine as well as for themselves, and to maintain "tranquility" in the country. Apparently, the fact that these two goals were quite contradictory bothered them very little. As German historian Bernhard Chiari has shown, very few of those who worked as personnel in the various administrative institutions in Byelorussia were dedicated Nazis. The majority were simply hoping to find personal promotion and new fortune, enjoy the fine-sounding titles and uniforms, or even escape active service at the front. They received hardly any training for their jobs.[98] No wonder, therefore, that German occupation politics in Byelorussia (as well as in other occupied territories) was an inconsistent assembly of ad hoc measures.

From the very beginning of German rule in Byelorussia, it was obvious that delicacy and humaneness would not be the guiding principles of the occupation authorities. As early as 23 August 1941, Rosenberg issued an order proclaiming that any sign of defiance as well as any dissemination of anti-German propaganda or gossip would be perceived as a most serious crime, punishable by death. According to the same order, SSPFs received special authority in all matters related to "security and order."[99] The so-called "Brown Folder" (*Braune Mappe*) that appeared on 3 September 1941 stated explicitly that Hague agreements did not extend to the "Eastern territories," thus making it clear that the sole law operating in these territories would be the "law of the jungle."[100]

As noted earlier, the general picture the Nazi invaders had of Byelorussia was extremely obscure, and there were no precise plans for ruling this country after its occupation. To consider the ever-repeated mantra of "liberation of Byelorussia from Polish and Russian influences" as indicative of a thought-out plan would be an outright exaggeration. Ultimately, the country was turned into a giant "laboratory," in which the Nazi regime experimented with its outrageous ideas. The idea of "political warfare", when stated clearly, meant the encouragement of local nationalism, or rather chauvinism on the most primitive level. Using this idea to taunt the local population; adhering to the *Herrenvolk* ideology; ruthlessly exploiting the country's natural and human resources; and annihilating entire population groups—beginning with Jews, Soviet POWs, and Gypsies, and ending with the burning down of whole villages in the course of what they termed "anti-partisan operations"—all these constituted the main features of Nazi occupation politics in Byelorussia.

The Germans installed in the occupation apparatus in Byelorussia knew only one thing: they belonged to the "race of lords" (*Herrenvolk*), which had come to the country (in Kube's own words) with a sole directive, "to administer this country, subordinate its economy to the German war in the East, and extract from it anything that could serve an economic capacity."[101] Yet, they had almost no knowledge of the country and its people. This information gap was filled by a generalized image of "the Eastern man." An example is the report issued in September 1943 by the *Sonderführer* Herlit from *GK Weißruthenien* entitled "On the Question of the Treatment of People." Although the report's author admitted that the "Russian is a rational person," he nevertheless saw in the Russian someone who had to rely on the leadership of others. In other words, in this report too, the *Herrenvolk* tenet prevailed.[102] The image of the "Russian" (this term refers both to ethnic Russians and Byelorussians) that emerges from the report is that of part child and part prehistoric man.

Agricultural Policies of the German Occupier

When speaking of the potential for collaboration during the occupation of Byelorussia, we must consider the degree to which the German authorities were ready or able to meet the local inhabitants' expectations. Chief among their expectations was a solution to the agrarian question. As mentioned above, immediately after the beginning of the German invasion into the Soviet Union, the kolkhoz system was spontaneously dissolved and in many places the lands were parceled out among the peasants. At first, the Germans neither encouraged nor discouraged this process, but they soon came to the conclusion that the preservation of the kolkhoz system would best serve their interests, since it would give them maximum control over agricultural production. Herbert Backe, the deputy minister in the Reich's Ministry for Food and Agriculture, was said to have claimed that "Germans should have introduced the kolkhozes, if the Bolsheviks had not supplied it before."[103] It is little wonder, therefore, that the much publicized so-called "agrarian reforms" satisfied nobody. According to the first of these reforms, which continued approximately until the beginning of 1942, the kolkhozes were renamed *Gemeinwirtschaften,* the literal translation of kolkhoz, and the peasant was able to slightly increase his own homestead's land (from 0.5 to 1 hectare). At the same time, the peasants were compelled to work nine hours a day at the *Gemeinwirtschaft.*[104] They were also warned not to take possession of land on their own.[105]

With far greater pomp, the "New Agrarian Order" (*Neues Agrarordnung*) was proclaimed. In reality, it too was anything but a reform. The manifesto that announced this New Order on 15 February 1942 stated explicitly that the kolkhoz system would not be abolished in the near future. It mentioned the renaming of the kolkhozes as a "transition" to new forms of working the land, although it specified neither the duration of this "transition" nor what form it would take. Although the peasants' homesteads were declared the "private property" of the peasant family (this was already the case de facto even before the manifesto was issued), German authorities had the absolute right to prescribe what the peasant could or could not build within the confines of his homestead.[106] Moreover, as early as November 1941, it was made clear that these homesteads would not be immune from German requisition of produce.[107] The lands of former kolkhozes were divided among a number of peasant families, not as a private property, but merely for the purpose of "work and exploitation" (*Bearbeitung und Nutzung*). In addition, a certain—and very considerable—amount of the produce was to be submitted to the German authorities.[108]

The economic significance of this so-called "agrarian reform" was much weaker than its social implications. It was made clear very early on that only those who actively supported the occupation regime could hope for certain benefits under the "New Agrarian Order." Thus, in April 1942, a few months after the documents cited were issued, the Supreme Command of the 16th Army (*Armeeoberkommando 16*) published a circular announcing that local "partisan-hunters" were promised extra land for their homestead as a reward.[109] This allotment would, however, take place only after the war, and as regards the source of the lands allocated for this purpose, these "would be free upon the exclusion of inappropriate elements."[110] It was a premise that, to say the least, did not help create an atmosphere of normality in the villages.

There was no doubt that the "New Agrarian Order" was to a very large degree a propagandistic strategy. In contrast to its pretentious slogan of "freeing the peasant from the kolkhoz system," which was extensively publicized in the press, both inside the "Eastern territories," in the Reich proper, and in other Nazi-occupied European countries, its real purpose was much more prosaic.[111] In the first place it was meant to facilitate the so-called "registering" (*Erfaßung*), or more bluntly stated, the exploitation of agricultural production, to ensure that the war efforts could continue. Moreover, the state of affairs was such that there was a significant shortage of agricultural machinery, resulting to a great extent from Soviet evacuation. The meting out of lands to a number of families as part of the New Agrarian Order would certainly alleviate the demand for this machinery, as Christian Gerlach has shown clearly.[112] Finally, as mentioned by Gerlach, the Germans perceived this system as a means of ensuring joint control over the individual members of these agricultural "teams."[113]

Although the Byelorussian soil could hardly be considered fertile, the Germans were still determined, in Kube's words, "to extract from this country whatever [they] could," and by any means. The peasants had to "transfer" (officially "sell") part of their agricultural produce to German authorities. By August 1941, norms had been established regarding the local peasants' delivery of food products to the Germans. Multiple notices posted all over Byelorussia claimed that submitting their crops was the peasants' "honorable duty" and an expression of their gratitude for being liberated from Bolshevism.[114] The propaganda also tried hard to persuade the Byelorussian peasant that handing over his food was actually a beneficial act. Thus, in his call to Byelorussian peasants, the chief of the Department of Food and Agriculture at the *GK Weißruthenien*, Wilhelm Freitag, promised a generous reward in return for deliveries of food products. According to Freitag, any peasant who submitted 100 kilograms of pork would receive in return 135 kilograms of animal fodder cereals and 400 kilograms of potatoes.[115] In reality, the situation was different. A peasant who submitted 100 kilograms of grain to the registration offices acting under the auspices of the Central Trade Society, i.e., the ZHO mentioned above, received in return 25 roubles (the rate of the rouble to Reichsmark was established as 10:1), while for a garden rake alone, for example, he was supposed to pay ZHO 40 roubles.[116]

One of the peculiarities of the produce delivery demanded of the peasants was that no ceiling was established, so the Germans were absolutely free to decide the amount of food to be delivered. Even when the economic situation in Byelorussia deteriorated significantly, the Germans continued to demand exorbitant amounts, set and calculated arbitrarily, and took no account of the actual conditions. In 1943, in the areas under civil administration, the approximate demands from one single peasant homestead were as follows: 300 liters milk per cow; 30 eggs per hen; approximately 197 kilograms grain per hectare of arable land (20 tons per village); approximately 655 kilograms of potatoes; and approximately 81 kilograms of vegetables. The following year, although farming conditions did not improve and the authorities themselves complained of significant production losses, caused mostly by partisan activities, the delivery quotas were increased.[117] Thus, for example, instead of 30 eggs per hen, 100 eggs were now demanded.[118]

Presumably, the German authorities knew better than the peasants themselves the latter's need for various food products.

The Food and Agriculture Department at the *GK Weißruthenien* "established" that in 1944/1945 the personal need of the "producer" for grain would be 432,132 tons and the difference between the yield and this need should be 192,268 tons, of which seventy per cent or 134,597 tons "can be registered."[119]

As the occupation proceeded, the peasants experienced more and more difficulties in keeping pace with the ever-increasing delivery quotas, and the Germans applied increasingly brutal measures to make the peasants fill these quotas. Thus, in May 1943, the Food and Agriculture Department at GKW demanded the use of police for the requisition of food in the villages.[120] Punishments for non-compliance with German demands were many and varied, beginning with the confiscation of land and cattle and concluding with the burning down of entire villages where "defiant" peasants resided.

Apart from these "naturally produced" taxes, Germans in many cases levied monetary taxes as well, including taxes on livestock and even on pets (dogs and cats). The owner of a dog was required to pay between 100 and 200 roubles, depending on the dog's breed.[121] In addition to these quasi "organized" requisitions, wild plundering, carried out by individual German soldiers as well as by entire units, was widespread. Letters written by German soldiers who participated in the so-called "anti-partisan operations," as well as their postwar memoirs, are abundant with descriptions of their "food trips" into the surrounding villages.[122]

Labor Policies under German Occupation

One of the most notorious symbols of Nazi rule in Byelorussia was the exploitation of the workforce, both inside Byelorussia, but even more so in the Reich. During the official conference of the *GK Weißruthenien* that took place in April 1943, the head of the Work Department in the GK, Freudenberg, stated clearly that "it [*Generalbezirk Weißruthenien*—L.R.] is of great importance as a reservoir of workforces, while the economic significance of *Generalbezirk*, in comparison to other occupied areas, such as the Ukraine, is of lesser value."[123] At first the mobilization for work in Germany proceeded largely on a voluntary basis. In the first months of the German invasion into the Soviet Union, special work-recruitment groups were sent into the Bialystok area as well as into the area of military administration.

By the end of 1941–early 1942, these recruitment groups had succeeded in bringing to the Reich 20,000 laborers; however, not all of these people had come to work in Germany voluntarily. Some of them had been forcefully "evacuated" during the combing of the Beloveža forests area.[124]

As early as November 1941, Hitler had stated unambiguously, "The area working directly for us embraces more than two hundred [and] fifty million people. Let no one doubt that we will succeed in involving every one of these millions in the labor process."[125] Of course, such numbers could not be achieved merely on a voluntary basis. In December 1941, Rosenberg had already issued an order demanding the registration of all able-bodied people between the ages of eighteen and forty-five. Refusal to comply with this order was punished by a fine of 1,000 RM (10,000 roubles) and three months of imprisonment.[126] To fulfill Hitler's wishes at the beginning of 1942, Fritz Sauckel, the NS party boss from Thuringia, was appointed as general-plenipotentiary for labor recruitment. Upon his appointment he proclaimed, "In order to provide the German housewife, above all mothers of many children ... with tangible relief from her burdens, the Fuehrer has commissioned me to bring into the Reich from the eastern territories some four to five hundred thousand select, healthy, and strong girls."[127]

It is very difficult to specify the exact number of Byelorussians who were sent to the Reich during the occupation period. The available data are fragmentary. We must rely heavily on the information contained in German documents, given that Soviet documents were also found lacking. Thus, for example, the intelligence reports of the Soviet partisan movement are silent on the phenomenon of forced labor. Perhaps this was due to the fact that the partisans officially considered those sent to work in Germany as traitors. At the end of September 1942, Sauckel "proudly" reported that up until 24 July 1942 approximately 1,080,000 workers had been brought to the Reich from the occupied Eastern territories.[128] According to the head of the Work and Social Administration Department at GKW, Helmut Freudenberg, in March of 1943 alone, 4,300 persons had been "mobilized" for work in the Reich, while in the entire year of 1942 and until April 1943, some 100,000 individuals from *Weißruthenien* alone were sent.[129] Even as late as May 1944, shortly before the collapse of the Army Group Center, its Supreme Command still reported that some 18,960 workers had been deported to Germany in that month alone.[130]

The rising number of people who were to be deported to the Reich is indicative of the fact that people could no longer be "mobilized," but only removed by force. Increasingly, the methods of Sauckel's men resembled manhunts: the soldiers would surround public places such as cinemas or churches, round up all those inside, and load them on trucks for deportation to Germany. Another method used for "registering" (*Erfaßung*) people to join the workforce in Germany was by means of the so-called "anti-partisan operations." Thus, the combing of the Naliboki forests, conducted within the framework of the "Hermann" "anti-partisan" operation, provided a "surpluswork-force" that was sent to Germany.[131] Generally, such forced recruitments to Germany were accompanied by wide-scale propaganda campaigns. According to them, the work in Germany was an expression of the Byelorussians' gratitude towards the Germans, for "liberating" them from Stalinism and also for "abolishing" the kolkhozes (although as was explained earlier, the kolkhozes were merely renamed). As touted by the propaganda, these two acts had transformed the Byelorussians into a "happy people."[132] Another very popular propaganda trick took the form of "letters from Germany," allegedly written by those who already were working there. These letters usually described the "undemanding work," the routine "evening dances," and other pleasures.[133]

In reality, those who found themselves among the so-called "Eastern workers" (*Ostarbeiter*) in Germany and German-controlled lands were virtually deprived of any rights and were subjected to the mercy of their employers. According to the "Directive regarding the labor legislation's treatment of laborers from the newly occupied Eastern areas," signed on 9 February 1942 by the Reich's minister for labor, Franz Seldte, German labor legislation did not extend to "Eastern workers." As foreign workers, they were not eligible to receive salary slips, which would have entitled them to services such as social aid. For the same reason they did not receive salary increments for working either additional hours or on holidays. The wage also could be decreased by the employer when the *Ostarbeiter*'s output fell below the average productivity rate of the German workers.[134] Generally, the *Ostarbeiter*'s wages were not to exceed 17 RM per week.[135] In this context too, the Nazis' racial dogmas were fully implemented. Thus, Byelorussians, together with Ukrainian and Russian workers, were submitted to the worst possible working conditions. Apart from receiving the lowest wages, their income was heavily taxed by their employers, as food and housing "expenses" were also deducted.[136] Eventually, these methods of forced labor recruitment and the treatment of laborers inside the Reich were among the main reasons that led Sauckel to the Nuremberg gallows after the war.[137]

But those who remained to work back in their homeland fared no better. The Soviet evacuation of war-important plants, on the one hand, and German air bombings on the first days of the invasion into the Soviet Union, on the other, left many Byelorussians unemployed. According to Christian Gerlach, in August 1941, in the area of *Wirtschaftsinspektion Mitte,* which still included the greater part of Byelorussia, there were 150,000 unemployed.[138] Although, as mentioned earlier, Rosenberg's order demanded the registration of anyone between the ages of eighteen and forty-five capable of working, in reality total employment in Byelorussia was not achieved until the end of the occupation period. So in October 1942, the Work and Social Administration Department of the *Generalkommissariat* in Minsk reported 4,400 unemployed.[139]

In hardly any other field of the occupation did the Janus-faced nature of the regime find such a clear expression as in that of labor policies. The Germans did not want to see anyone unemployed, yet they simply could not provide work for all the unemployed. As was noted earlier, Byelorussia was initially to be included in the "subsidiary zone" and was intended for de-industrialization. In practice, Byelorussia, together with other occupied territories, was expected to provide the German war-machine with all it required, a fact that postponed the projected de-industrialization to an undefined "postwar" future. In such circumstances, the Germans were compelled to allow local industries to function, assuming that they had managed to survive the Soviet evacuation and the heavy air bombings of the first days of the war. Preference was given to industrial branches related to agriculture, since all of the "Eastern territories"—regardless of the actual fertility of their soil—were treated as the breadbasket not only of the Reich but of all of Western Europe. Such preferential treatment also applied to those branches that were supposed to supply the needs of the Wehrmacht's front lines (although many of the previous Soviet armament plants were moved to the east). Many of these industrial enterprises, however, soon ran out of raw materials and were compelled either to close down or to change their original production line. Thus, for example, when the match factory in

Borisov ran out of chemical supplies, its workers were ordered to transfer to the weaving of bast shoes for German soldiers.[140]

The Germans used various techniques to reduce unemployment. Often they were strongly influenced by the Nazi ideology and dogmas that Germans brought into the country. One of the most "popular" measures was to evict the "undesirable" groups of the population, first the Jews followed by the Poles, and to replace them with Byelorussians. Christian Gerlach sees in this practice, especially in the eviction of the Jews, a measure that served "to satisfy or keep quiet the non-Jewish population."[141] In reality, this constitutes a clear example of the victory of ideological considerations over practical ones. Effectiveness was sacrificed in favor of some chimeras, in this case that of "Byelorussification," which the Nazis understood to mean liberation—in the most literal sense—freeing the Byelorussians from "foreign" influences. However, the Germans themselves complained repeatedly that "removing" Jews and Poles, especially specialists, hurt productivity, and that Byelorussians were not able to provide adequate replacements. Thus, the administrative department added the following comment to a report presented by the *Generalkommissar für Weißruthenien,* describing the "replacing" of Polish physicians and Jewish dentists by Byelorussians: "On the basis of experience, the Byelorussian physician works conscientiously only when under continuous control."[142] Moreover, the same report noted explicitly that "in some areas ... there is a shortage of manpower through the fallout (*Ausfall*) of Jews, which cannot be filled immediately everywhere."[143] Thus, if indeed as Christian Gerlach suggested, the practice of the "Byelorussification" of the workplace was no more than a tool in the struggle against unemployment, then—moral considerations aside—it was, to say the least, a very strange method, as more often than not its results were the exact opposite of what its initiators had expected.

Another typical Nazi method of "solving" the unemployment problem was work camps, which were run by various bodies, including the military, the SS, and the Todt organization. People lived there in appalling conditions. For example, in the camp situated in Minsk on Highway Street and run by the Todt organization, the inmates lived in small blockhouses with merely 1.3 m^2 for each person. Of the 200 men and 30 women who were imprisoned there in 1942, only 60 had a sleeping place.[144] They were assigned the most difficult work, including road building, the clearing of rubble, and the building of bridges. At the end of

1943, when the front was approaching the Rear Area of the Army Group Center, the inmates of such camps were used, inter alia, in the building of defensive structures on the so-called "Panther Line."[145] According to Christian Gerlach, the total number of the inmates of these camps in the Rear Area of the Army Group Center alone ranged between 60,000 and 95,000.[146]

Those working inside Byelorussia also suffered from difficult working conditions. The workers practically became the slaves of the enterprise at which they toiled. The employment conditions were defined by the German authorities, e.g., the *Gebietskommissare*. Any unauthorized change of workplace was out of the question.[147] The work day was usually ten to eighteen hours long, the pay was extremely low, and in many places workers were paid with food rather than priceless cash. In Polock, for example, the railroad workers received 3 kilograms of bread, 100 grams of grain, 100 grams of fat, and 10 grams of salt per week. Even when the salary was paid in cash, it was never enough to live on. A worker in Polock received 15–30 roubles a day (the rate of the rouble to RM was 10:1), while an office worker received 100–250 roubles. At the same time, the market price of butter was 350–400 roubles per (Russian) pound, equal to approximately 450 grams, and rye cost 1,000 roubles per pound.[148] In the area of *GK Weißruthenien,* the wages were even lower. There the non-skilled and menial laborers received between 0.80 and 1 rouble a day.[149]

It is little wonder that bartering flourished. Even the Germans themselves acknowledged the fact that the existing wages did "not secure the minimum existence;"[150] nevertheless, nothing or very little was done to alter the situation. Moreover, OKW Chief-of-Staff Keitel even criticized the Todt organization, as some of its offices paid their workers "the extravagant sum" of 25 roubles. Keitel demanded that they replace this sum with small portions of food.[151] Of course, in such a state of affairs, the productivity of the local workers could hardly increase. To solve this problem, in December 1941, Kube issued a directive regarding social insurance, which stated that the employer should pay compensation to an employee in the case of temporary loss of work capacity. From the outset, this payment was limited: single workers could take an absence of up to two weeks; married workers, up to four weeks; and, in the case of a work-related accident, up to ten weeks. Payment was limited to forty per cent of the wages earned during the last four weeks for singles, and sixty per cent of the same for married workers.[152] Rather than a practical step, this directive very soon became an occasion for political struggles inside Byelorussia. Although, formally, Poles were included in these regulations, attempts were made to exclude them from receiving social aid. According to the "compromise solution" reached after the foundation of the Byelorussian Central Council (a detailed description of this organization follows in the next chapter), only Byelorussians were eligible for the social security program, whereas Poles could press their claims only if their case matched some poorly defined "internal regulations."[153]

The Outcome and Shift in Occupation Politics

Not surprisingly, such occupation politics resulted in a growing resistance movement. Although this movement can hardly be called the "struggle of all people," as Soviet historiography claimed for many years, it still took on very considerable dimensions with the progress of German rule in Byelorussia. Both partisan and "anti-partisan" warfare will be described in detail in the next chapters. Nevertheless, the resistance undoubtedly lays claim to the bloodiest page in the history of the German occupation. Although Soviet historiography usually describes the partisan movement as surrounded by a halo of glory, and its participants as people "without fear or reproach," in reality, the fighting on both sides was characterized by excessive brutality. The death threats delivered to anyone believed to be collaborating with the Germans, as well as the killing of collaborators and their families by the partisans, were not a rarity. At the same time, on the other side, the Germans applied the most brutal methods, burning down entire villages with their inhabitants if they believed someone was cooperating with the partisans, and using people as living mine detectors. All the while, the Germans continued to make vague promises, mainly in the form of material benefits, to anyone willing to participate in the fight against the partisans.

Towards the end of the occupation, when the Germans de facto controlled only forty per cent of the Byelorussian territory and the partisan movement was consistently growing, even the occupiers understood that violence alone would not suffice, and that it was worth their while to try other methods. In fact, in 1942, the involvement of Byelorussian collaborators in the anti-partisan struggle increased. This involvement took various forms, for example, the number of the so-called *Wehrdörfer* ("defensive villages") and *Schutzmannschaftsdörfer* (auxiliary police villages) multiplied, and they were organized in the most important areas, especially along the roads. From the first half of 1943, they were posted in areas impassable for Germans. Another method of involvement was through the formation of the local mobile *Jagdkommandos* (hunting squads), members of which were promised an extra allotment of land, but only after the war. The toying with Byelorussian nationalism, which culminated in the creation of the Byelorussian Central Council at the end of the occupation, was also to a significant degree part of the German plans to increase local compliance and to dam the resistance movement.

The main principle guiding the Germans' actions in Byelorussia during all three years was their ideological dogma, together with the needs of the Reich. The local population with its needs and problems received only secondary attention. The confrontation with the realities of the population and its geography did nothing for the majority of occupation apparatus officials; it did not lead them either to a better understanding of this situation, nor to a revision of their preset stereotypes and prejudices. Rather, they chose to exhibit an even more fervent adherence to their dogmas. Many of the "final reports," compiled by former occupation officials after retreating from Byelorussia, clearly demonstrate this. Quite a number of these reports contain the lessons drawn from this period as well as proposals for implementing these lessons in case of a return to Byelorussia. (This belief in the eventual German victory, even when Allied bombs had reduced German cities to rubble is worthy of exclusive research.)[154] One must note, however, that the only lesson drawn was no lesson at all. These reports plainly reflect the adherence to the *Herrenvolk* tenet, and the view of Byelorussians as primitive people that can be moved and removed, not unlike chess figures manipulated by the will and whim of the "player."

Under these conditions, local collaboration was never perceived as a partnership, but rather as a tool for controlling, securing, and exploiting the country. The dominant trend among the German authorities was to obtain the local dwellers' help for the lowest possible price. In contrast, for many Byelorussians, collaboration—as well as resistance—gradually ceased to be a matter of choice: it became a means for survival in the abnormality of the situation.

The next chapters will analyze the exact role of the phenomenon called Byelorussian collaboration in its various aspects.

Notes

1. The Chief of Staff of the Army Group Center during the invasion was Gen-
   eralmajor (Major General) Hans von Greiffenberg. The Army Group consisted of the 4th Army (Commander-General Field Marshal Günther von
   Kluge) with the initially subordinate 2nd Panzer Group (Generaloberst
   Heinz Guderian); 9th Army (Generaloberst Adolph von Strauß) with 3rd
   Panzer Group (Generaloberst Hermann Hoth); and the 2nd Army (initially
   in reserve, under Commander-Generaloberst Maximilian Freiherr von
   Weichs) with the subordinate 2nd Air Fleet (Luftflotte), under the command of General Field Marshal Albert Kesselring.
2. The term *Ostpolitik* ("eastern politics") came into being during the Third
   Reich; it referred to the policies regarding the countries situated to the
   east of Germany, primarily towards the Soviet Union, but also towards
   Poland. After World War II and the creation of the two separate German
   states, this term was used in the field of German–German relations.
3. Adolf Hitler, *Mein Kampf*, trans. Ralph Manheim (Boston and Cambridge,
   1943), 2:643.
4. Ibid., 653.
5. The term "Germanic" in Nazi parlance designated the people of "German-
   related blood." This category included the Dutch, Norwegians, Danes, and
   several other nationalities.
6. Hitler, *Mein Kampf*, 654.
7. It is interesting to note that this meeting was held in the headquarters of
   OKH in Berlin. This building, known as the Bendler Block (after the
   Bendler, today Stauffenberg, Street), also sheltered the headquarters of the
   Home Army during World War II, and in July 1944 was a nerve center of
   the abortive "20 July coup" against Hitler and his regime. Moreover, in
   1933 Hitler made a speech in the very same room in which on the night of
   20/21 July 1944 the leaders of the plot, among them Stauffenberg, Ludwig
   Beck, the former Chief of General Staff, Olbricht and some others, were
   sentenced to death. Some of the plotters may have attended the meeting
   with the newly appointed chancellor eleven years previously, but we do not
   know of any kind of opposition on their part to what they heard. "Niederschrift der Rede Hitlers vor Befehlshabern der Reichswehr am 3. Februar
   1933 über innen- und außenpolitische Ziele," in *Dokumente des Verbrechens*, ed. Helma Kaden et al. (Berlin, 1993), 1:21.
8. Hitler, *Mein Kampf*, 660.
9. See Henry Picker, *Zastol'nye Razgovory Gitlera* (Smolensk, 1993), 198.
10. See "Monolog Adolf Hitlers über das deutsche Besiedlungsbild im Osten,
    aufgezeichent von Heinrich Heim, Führerhauptquartier, 17.10.41," in *Vom
    Generalplan Ost zum Generalsiedlungsplan*, ed. Czeslaw Madajczyk
    (Munich, 1994), 23–25.
11. Hans-Adolph Jacobsen (ed.), *Kriegstagebuch des Oberkommandos der
    Wehrmacht (Wehrmachtführungsstab)* (Franfurt/Main, 1965), 1:205. Walter
    Warlimont, *Im Hauptquartier der deutschen Wehrmacht* (Franfurt/Main,

1962), 168. See Franz Halder, *Kriegstagebuch*, 30 March 1941, see http://www.ns-archiv.de/krieg/sowjetunion/halder1941-30-03.shtml.

12. "Aktenvermerk vom 16. Juli 1941 über eine Besprechung Hitlers mit Rosenberg, Lammers, Keitel und Göring, aufgezeichnet von einem unbekannten Teilnehmer," Doument 221-L, *Der Prozess gegen die Hauptkriegsverbrecher vor dem Internationalen Militärgerichtshof* (IMT) (Nuremberg, 1949), 88.

13. Ibid., 87, 88, 90.

14. See "Ernennung des Reichsleiters Alfred Rosenberg zu Beauftragten für die zentrale Bearbeitung der Fragen des Osteuropäischen Raumes, 20.04.41," BA R6/4. "Ernennung des Reichsleiters Alfred Rosenberg zum Reichsminister für die besetzten Ostgebiete," ibid.

15. See the most recent biography of Rosenberg, E. Piper, *Alfred Rosenberg. Hitlers Chefideologe* (Munich, 2005).

16. The term *Balte* in German refers only to Baltic Germans. It should be noted, inter alia, that the term *kommissarisch* in German implies something provisionary.

17. See Piper, *Alfred Rosenberg*, 521.

18. Ibid.

19. "Aktenvermerk vom 16. Juli 1941," 221-L, *IMT*, 89.

20. "Document 1029 (USA-145)," in *Njurnbergskij Process*, ed. K. Gorshenin et al. (Moscow, 1955), 406.

21. Alexander Dallin, *German Rule in Russia* (Boulder, 1981), 56–57.

22. The Wehrmacht and its conduct during the Soviet campaign were for many years a "sacred cow" in German historiography. Only decades after the end of the war did historians such as Christian Streit, Manfred Messerschmidt, and a few others dare to slaughter this "cow" and revise the myth about the chivalrous Wehrmacht. In recent years, the major impetus for study of the Wehrmacht's role in the Russian campaign was provided by the controversial exhibition organized by Hannes Heer and Klaus Naumann, *The War of Extermination (Vernichtungskrieg. Verbrechen der Wehrmacht)*; this exhibition opened in 1995 and was subsequently displayed in many cities within and beyond Germany. Shortly afterwards, owing to the sharp criticism of its organizers regarding inaccuracies in the selection of materials, the exhibition was closed for revision and reopened in Berlin at the end of 2001. The materials from the first version of the exhibition were published as a book in German as well as in an English translation. For the latter, see Hannes Heer and Klaus Naumann (eds.), *War of Extermination* (New York, 2000).

23. Quoted in Reitlinger, *House Built on Sand*, 36.

24. See "Befehl des Generalfeldmarschalls Walter von Reichenau, Oberbefehlshaber der 6. Armee, vom 10. Oktober 1941 zum Verhalten der Truppe im Ostraum," in Kaden u.a., *Dokumente des Verbrechens*, 153–55.

25. See Eckehard Ostmann, *Russlands Fremdvölker: seine Stärke und Schwäche* (Munich, 1915), quoted in Turonak, *Belarus' pad nyameckaj Akupacyjaj*, 12.

26. See, for example, an article, "Die Weißruthenen," in *Schwäbischer Merkur* (Nr. 279, 18.6.1917), *Hauptsaatsarchiv Stuttgart*, E 40/72/758. Although the author describes Byelorussians as an "ancient people with [its] own culture and language," he also uses the *Volksstamm* definition.

27. Eugen Hollerbach, quoted in Gerlach, *Kalkulierte Morde*, 101. *Baedecker* is the famous German travel guide.

28. Denkschrift "'Weißruthenien' (Volkstum, Geschichte, Wirtschaft)," ausgearbeitet im Wansee-Institut, 1941, BA R93/18, 13. Eugen von Engelhardt, the author of the work *Weißruthenien: Volk und Land* that appeared in Berlin in 1943, preferred to see in Polesje (the southern part of Byelorussia) the land of origin of Slavs (see 24n).

29. Eugen von Engelhardt, *Weißruthenien: Volk und Land* (Berlin, 1943), 12. See Dienststelle Rosenberg, *Ostland,* quoted in Gerlach, *Kalkulierte Morde,* 101. See Generalkommissar Kube, "Überblick über die politische Lage," in "Protokoll der Tagung der Gebietskommissare, Hauptabteilungsleiter und Abteilungsleiter des Generalkommissars in Minsk vom 8.April bis 10.April 1943," BA R93/20, 7.

30. Abteilungsleiter Schröter über "Propaganda, Presse, Rundfunk und Film," ibid., 106.

31. Quoted in Lubachko, *Belorussia under Soviet Rule,* 77.

32. Gerlach, *Kalkulierte Morde,* 39. In his study, Gerlach relies upon the statistics of the Wansee-Institute. This had been established in Berlin in the interwar period, and to a significant degree consisted of the émigrés who fled from the Bolsheviks after November 1917. The Institute dealt with study of various aspects of life in the Soviet Union. During the Nazi period, it came under the aegis of the German intelligence and provided it with evaluations regarding the situation both in the occupied and unoccupied territories of the Soviet Union. A brief source of information regarding the Institute may be found in Walter Schellenberg's memoirs. See Walter Schellenberg, *The Schellenberg Memoirs,* ed. and transl. Louis Hagen (London, 1956), 318–19.

33. "Stellungnahme von Erhard Wetzel, Dezernent für Rassenpolitik im Reichsministerium für die besetzten Ostgebiete, vom 27. April 1943 zum im Reichsicherheitshauptamt der SS entwickelten 'Generalplan Ost'," in Kaden et al., *Dokumente des Verbrechens,* 1:209. See P.-H. Seraphim, *Das Judentum im osteuropäischen Raum* (Essen, 1938), 544.

34. Denkschrift "Weißruthenien" (see note 28), 59.

35. Ibid., 60.

36. Wartheland was a name given to the German-annexed part of Poland. See Document 1058-PS, IMT, vol. 26, 618.

37. "Byelorussia will be treated as the receiving point for many asocial elements as well as a natural reserve." See "Abschrift der Rede des Reichsleiters A. Rosenberg vor dem engsten Beteiligten am Ostproblem, 20.6.41," BA R 6/6, Mikrofiche 3.

38. "Unsere Verwaltungsaufgaben" (Bericht des Abteilungsleiter Verwaltung bei Generalkommissar für Weißruthenien Regierungsrat Jungwirth), "Protokoll der Tagung v. 8.-10. April 1943" (see note 29), 44.

39. See "Abschrift des Berichtes der Generalkommissar für Weißruthenien, Abt. Ernährung und Landwirtschaft-13.05.1943," BA R 93/7, 1.

40. See Gerlach, *Kalkulierte Morde,* 46–59, briefly also in idem., *Krieg, Ernährung, Völkermord* (Hamburg, 1998), 13–20.

41. See Gerlach, *Kalkulierte Morde,* 49.

42. This study was later reshaped into the book *Weißruthenien,* mentioned earlier.

43. It is interesting to note that this same von Poletika, former professor at Petrograd University and a member of the Russian Imperial Geographic Society, from 1950 on headed "the agricultural studies' research office for the eastern states" in Bonn. See Gerlach, *Kalkulierte Morde,* 58n.

44. Two of the three key documents related to the *Generalplan Ost* could not be found after the war: the plan worked out by Konrad Meyer, the head of the Main Department for Planning in the Staff Office of the Reich's Commissar for the Strengthening of the German People (*Reichskommissar für die Festigung deutschen Volkstums*); and the study of the 3rd Office (*Amt III-SD-Inland*) of the Main Office for the Reich's Security (*Reichssicherheitshauptamt* or *RSHA*). The reconstruction of the latter is possible from the Evaluation Letter written on 27 April 1943 by Erhard Wetzel, who was responsible for racial policies in the Reich's Ministry for the Occupied Eastern Territories. This document, presented in the course of the Nuremberg Trials, was also published in Kaden et al., *Dokumente des Verbrechens*, 1:186–228 as well as in Cz. Madajczyk, *Vom Generalplan Ost zum Generalsiedlungsplan*, 50–81.
45. It was believed in Nazi circles that these Byelorussians were actually of German origin. Wetzel himself noted, "I saw Byelorussians (*Weißruthenen*) that if they were Germans, their supposed homeland would have been Schleswig-Holstein." See Madajczyk, *Vom Generalplan*, 66 and 67.
46. Ibid., 68.
47. See Julius Mader, *Abver: Shchit i Mech' Tret'ego Reicha* (Rostov/Don, 1999), 105–9.
48. See Turonak, *Belarus' pad nyameckaj Akupacyjaj*, 26–27.
49. Quoted in Alexej Litvin, "Belorusskaja Krajovaja Oborona," in *Akupacyja Belarusi*, ed. A. Litvin (Minsk, 2000), 161.
50. Added to Akinčyc's low prestige among the Germans was not only the failure to create a Byelorussian National Socialist movement, but also the failure of the project to create Byelorussian sabotage forces in the Polish rear, during the Polish campaign.
51. See "Svidetel'stvo B. K. Bartkeviča o rabote Belorusskogo Predstavitel'stva v Berline" and "Svidetel'stvo I. V. Omeljanoviča o rabote Belorusskogo Predstavitel'stva v Berline," both in Solov'ev, *Belarusskaja Tsentral'naja Rada*, 100–103.
52. Between spring and mid-1940 BKS in Warsaw was headed by Akinčyc, who was transferred there from Berlin, pushing Ščors aside. Later, however, after the intervention of Warsaw SD, Ščors returned to his post. According to SD-men, "Ščors represented by himself something, while Akinčyc did nothing." See Turonak, *Belarus' pad nyameckaj Akupacyjaj*, 33.
53. The excerpts from this document were published by the Soviet historian Vasilij Romanovskij. See Vasilij Romanovskij, *Saudzel'niki ŭ zlachynstvakh* (Minsk, 1964), 21–22.
54. Ibid., 22.
55. See excerpts from it, ibid., 33.
56. See Erhard Moritz (ed.), *Fall Barbarossa* (Berlin, 1970), S. 260–61; Turonak, *Belarus' pad nyameckaj Akupacyjaj*, 35.
57. "Order V.O./Abwehr II regarding the securing of various objects during the first phase of operation *Barbarossa*, 31.5.41 (?)," "Anweisungen der Heeresgruppe B betreffend Kennworte und Erkennungszeichen für dem Einsatz der Angehörigen der 'Lehrregiments Brandenburg z. b. V. 800' sowie für weißrussischen und litauischen Nationalisten, 17.6.41," BA-MA RH 19 II/409.
58. "Schreiben Amts Ausland/Abwehr über die Belohnung der V-Leuten, 17.6.41," BA-MA RH 19 II/409.

59. The date is not quite certain. John Loftus, who mentioned the fact in his book, *The Belarus Secret* (New York, 1982), dates the first contacts between Prof. Six and Byelorussian emigrants back to spring 1940, but there must be a misprint as the plans for Operation Barbarossa began to be worked out only in July 1940, after the fall of France.

60. See ibid., 19–20.

61. Such a confident belief was expressed, for example, in the undated "Proposals for the questions of Eastern Politics," composed by the Eastern Ministry apparently on the eve of the invasion of the Soviet Union. See "Vorschläge zu Fragen der Ostpolitik," BA R 6/6, Mikrofiche 1–2.

62. Von Schenckendorff, who at the outbreak of the German-Soviet war was sixty-six years old, was sent into retirement in 1930 as a lieutenant general.

63. See Gerlach, *Kalkulierte Morde*, 135.

64. Regarding the division of the military administration area, see "Abschlußbericht über die Tätigkeit der Militärverwaltung im Operationsgebiet des Ostens," *Bindesarchiv-Militärarchiv* (in the following BA-MA) RH 22/215, 11.

65. Gerlach, *Kalkulierte Morde*, 143.

66. See "Abschlußbericht über die Tätigkeit der Militärverwaltung," RH 22/215, 12.

67. Quoted in Gerlach, *Kalkulierte Morde*, 182. It is interesting to note that after the war, von dem Bach was never tried and sentenced for the multiple crimes against humanity he committed as HSSPF Rußland-Mitte. In 1961, he was sentenced by a German court to four years and ten months imprisonment for the murder of three SA men during the "Night of the Long Knives" in 1934 and one year later to life imprisonment for the murder of three communists in 1933. See Ernst Klee, *Das Personenlexikon zum Dritten Reich* (Frankfurt/Main, 2005), 23.

68. The general euphoria that reigned in Germany during the first months of the Russian campaign expressed itself in many forms. For example, in the summer of 1941, the exhibition "The Sovereignty of Europe" was planned, as a result of the general belief that Soviet power had been crushed or that its defeat was at least near. See "Rosenbergs Schreiben an Göring v. 7.8.41," BA R 6/23, Mikrofiche 1.

69. See "Abschlußbericht über die Tätigkeit der Militärverwaltung," RH 22/215, 12.

70. Blaskowitz's complaints are quoted in Hilberg, *Destruction of the European Jews*, 1:190–91.

71. Thus, already at the beginning of July 1941, the Chief of Staff of the Supreme Command of the Wehrmacht (OKW), Fieldmarshal Wilhelm Keitel, turned to Hitler and personally proposed introducing the civil administration into the areas that were in German hands. See Yitzhak Arad, *Ghetto in Flames* (Jerusalem, 1980), 51.

72. The whole territory of the Soviet Union was divided into the so-called soyuz or "autonomous" republics, nominally federative bodies, which in turn were divided into oblasts, and then into rayons, "countryside councils" (*sel'sovety*), and single villages.

73. The general structure of the "indigenous self-administration" is described in "Abschlußbericht," 36–43.

74. "Bericht der Beauftragter d. Reichsm. f.d. bes. Ostgeb. b. Kommand. General d. Sich.-Tr. u. Befh. i. H. G. Mitte Major O. W. Müller an das Reichsmin-

isterium für die besetzten Ostgebiete Hauptabteilung I, 8.10.42," BA R6/76, Mikrofiche 1.

75. "Operational Situation Report USSR No. 27, 19.07.41," in Arad and Spector, *Einsatzgruppen Reports*, 37.

76. It is interesting to note the interpretation attributed to these occurrences by former Soviet historians. Thus, according to Alexander Zalesskij, the dissolution of the kolkhozes was not a result of the hatred toward the system, but rather "temporary transition to individual economy in order to get rid of the Hitlerian control over kolkhozes." See A. Zalesskij, *V Tylu Vraga* (Minsk, 1969), 29.

77. See, e.g., Vakar, *Belorussia*, 175. It must be remembered, for example, that the preparatory measures for genocide of the Jewish population, such as ghettoization and the marking of Jews with special signs in Byelorussia, were taken at the initiative of the local Wehrmacht commanders. The army also cooperated with the SD in the screening of the POW camps, knowing that all those "separated" as Jews, communists, and the like, were doomed to death. On the exact role of the military authorities in the annihilation and exploitation policies of military authorities in Byelorussia, see Gerlach, *Kalkulierte Morde*, 503ff.

78. So, for example, even as late as February 1942, complaints were heard about Minsk archival resources being used as burning materials by the German soldiers. See "Schreiben Hans Rolls an Staatsarchivdirektor Dr. Mommsen, 27.2.42," BA R 93/5. The wild orgy of looting and destruction by the Wehrmacht soldiers even led to the personal intervention of Göring, who in August 1941 issued an order aiming to replace the uncontrolled robbery of resources with organized exploitation. See "Schreiben OKH mit Wiedergabe des Befehls von Göring über Maßnahmen gegen Verschleuderung von Beute und Landesbeständen in den besetzten Ostgebieten, 28.08.41," BA R6/287, Mikrofiche 1. See also: Lubachko, *Belorussia under Soviet Rule*, 149.

79. See "Befehl des Kdt. r. A. Geb. 559 Generalleutnant von Unruh v. 10.10.41," BA-MA, RH 23/126.

80. See below, Chapter VII.

81. G. Reitlinger, *The Final Solution* (London, 1961), 215. Peter Kleist, *Zwischen Hitler und Stalin* (Bonn, 1950), 164.

82. Actually, the name *Weißruthenien* had already been used during World War I, when the German authorities toyed with local nationalisms in the German-occupied territories. See, for example, the article "Die Weißruthenen" in *Schwäbischer Merkur*, 18.6.1917, *Hauptstaatsarchiv Stuttgart* (HStAS), E 40/72/758. The obscurity of the status of Byelorussia in the German occupation apparatus during World War II expressed itself in its official definition: in some documents it appears as a *Generalbezirk*, while in some others as *Generalkommissariat*.

83. In May 1934, Kube wrote in *Cottbuser Anzeiger,* "What plague, dizziness (*Schwindsucht*) and syphilis are for the humanity, as far as health is concerned, the Jews are for the white peoples in terms of morality ... He who damages his race—and thereby the best heritage of our people—through mixed marriage (*Mischehe*) must be sterilized (*unfruchtbar gemacht werden*)". Quoted in Klee, *Das Personenlexikon zum Dritten Reich*, 346–47. Wilhelm Kube (1887–1943), the son of a sergeant in the Prussian army, was born in Glogau. He studied in Berlin at the prestigious gymnasium *Zum Grauen Kloster*, the most famous pupil of which was Bismarck. (The gym-

nasium, the oldest in Brandenburg, was attached to the Franciscan monastery that was heavily bombed by Allies during World War II. Today, only the ruins of the monastery are preserved near Alexanderplatz.) Subsequently he attended Berlin University where he studied history, political sciences, and theology. In 1909 he founded the extreme-nationalist students' union, which boasted a strong *völkische* ideology. Later, as a member of the German-Conservatives, he worked as a journalist for the party's various newspapers in Wismar and Breslau (today Wroclaw, Poland). Kube encountered World War I as the secretary-general of the party in Silesia, and in 1917 served a mere twenty-one garrison days as a militiaman (*Landssturmann*) in the reserve battalion of the 51st infantry regiment, after which he was recalled by his party. In 1919, he founded the "German Bismarck Union" (*Deutsche Bismarckbund*), which later gave birth to the Bismarck youth movement, which he headed from 1922 on. In 1920 Kube was also appointed secretary-general of the Berlin branch (*Landesverband*) of the German National People's Party (DNVP), the largest right-wing party in Weimar Germany before the rise of the Nazis. Between 1922 and 1923, he represented this party on the city council of Berlin. In 1923 Kube went over to the National Socialist Freedom Movement headed by Wilhelm Frick, later minister of the interior, and in the following year received a place in the Reichstag. In 1928 he entered the NSDAP and was made chief of its faction in the Prussian parliament (*Landtag*) and also head of the new Gau Ostmark, created from the former Niederlausitz area around Frankfurt on Oder and the Grenzmark. In 1932 he also became a church manager (*Kirchenvorsteher*) of the Gethsemane church community in Berlin and of the district synod of the 3rd Berlin district (Wagener). Kube was also initiator of the German Christians' movement. As the reward for "conquering" the Ostmark Gau for the Nazis, on 1 June 1933 Hitler appointed Kube as Gauleiter of the united *Großgau Kurmark,* with its center in the old garrison city of Potsdam. In the same year, he also became the supreme president (Oberpräsident) of Brandenburg-Berlin and also of Posen-West Prussia and entered the SS. On 26 April 1936 Kube sent an anonymous letter purporting to come from "a number of Berlin Jews" to the chief judge of the Nazi Party, Walter Buch, claiming that both the latter and his son-in-law Martin Bormann were married to Jewish women. Gestapo investigation disproved these "accusations" and also established Kube's authorship of the letter. As a result of this and also because of corruption, he was sent into retirement; two years later, however, he was sent once again into the Reichstag. In 1940, Kube volunteered for the Waffen-SS and for some time even served as a SS-Rottenführer (sergeant) in the concentration camp at Dachau. See Klee, *Das Personenlexikon zum Dritten Reich*, 346–47; Gerlach, *Kalkulierte Morde*, 161n; Helmut Heiber, "Aus den Akten des Gauleiters Kube," in *Vierteljahrshefte für Zeitgeschichte* (1956), H.1, 67–70; "Rundschreiben Nr. 99/36 von Stellvertreter des Führers R. Heß an alle Reichsleiter und Gauleiter, o. D.," in ibid., 77–78.

84. It is interesting to note that at the meeting on 16 July 1941 in Rastenburg, mentioned above, Hitler proposed Kube's candidature as future "Reich's Commissar for Moscow area," but this proposal encountered objections on the part of Rosenberg and Göring who claimed that "Kube had become too old for this." See "Aktenvermerk vom 16. Juli 1941," 221-L, IMT, 38:90.

85. Kleist, *Zwischen Hitler und Stalin*, 171.

86. Quoted by Gerlach, *Kalkulierte Morde*, 162.
87. Ibid.
88. Quoted by Dallin, *German Rule*, 204.
89. See "Erlaß des Führers über die Verwaltung der neu besetzten Ostgebiete, vom 17. Juli 1941," Document PS-1997, IMT 29: 234ff.
90. Acting in Byelorussia were the following: *HSSPF Rußland-Mitte* (Central Russia), responsible for the military administration area; *HSSPF Rußland-Nord* or *Ostland*, who was also responsible between September 1941 and November 1942 for *GK Weißruthenien*; *HSSPF Rußland-Süd* or *Ukraine*, with responsibility for the southern Byelorussian territories attached to RK Ukraine; and *HSSPF Nordost*, for the Bialystok area. Later on, the *HSSPF Rußland-Mitte* also took over the responsibilities of the *GK Weißruthenien* (changing its name to *HSSPF Rußland-Mitte und Weißruthenien*), and in 1944, after the attachment to *Weißruthenien* of the rest of the RK Ukraine, chiefly the Polesje area, it also took over these territories. Bach-Zelewski, who was *HSSPF Rußland-Mitte* at the beginning of the German occupation, continued to act in this capacity until autumn 1942. At this point, owing to his appointment as Himmler's plenipotentiary for "anti-partisan warfare," he passed his duties to SS and police leader (*SSPF*) *Weißruthenien* Curt von Gottberg.
91. See note 89.
92. See "ZHO-general information," BA R 33II/40.
93. About the confusion regarding the official name of the civil administration area in Byelorussia, see above, note 82.
94. "Aufruf des Generalkommissars Weißruthenien (Kube) vom 9. September 1941," in *Einsatz im "Reichskommissariat Ostland"*, ed. W. Benz et al. (Berlin, 1998), 21–22.
95. It can be found in Bronis Kaslas (ed.), *The USSR-German Aggression against Lithuania* (New York, 1973), 355.
96. Cz. Madajczyk, *Die Okkupationspolitik Nazideutschlands in Polen 1939–1945* (Berlin, 1987), 143–46.
97. See the publications in the largest "legal" Byelorussian language newspaper, *Belaruskaja Hazeta*, YVA C-762.
98. Until mid-October 1941 only two courses for so-called "eastern appointment" had taken place, both at the *Ordensburg Krössinsee* (Pomerania). See Chiari, *Alltag hinter der Front*, 59–72.
99. The order is quoted in Sh. Cholawski, *Be-Sufat ha-Kilayyon* [In the Eye of the Hurricane] (Tel Aviv, 1988), 58.
100. See ibid., 59.
101. See "Protokoll über die Tagung" (note 29), 7.
102. "Bericht des Sonderführers A. Herlit zu Fragen der Menschenbehandlung, 13.9.43," BA R 93/6, 1–5.
103. Quoted in Gerlach, *Kalkulierte Morde*, 342.
104. The cynical remark accompanying this directive is of note, "Since peasants anyway are used to working in the summer from sunrise to sunset, a couple of hours will be left for them to work on their own homestead farm." See "Neuordnung der Landwirtschaft in den besetzten Gebieten der Sowjetunion, aus den Handakten der Ministerialdirigenten Dr. Bräutigam, o. D.," BA R 6/71, Mikrofiche 1.
105. "Richtlinien zur Behandlung der Kollektivfrage, 15.8. 41," ibid.
106. "Die neue Agrar-Ordnung mit Präambel und Schlußwort des Reichsministers für die besetzten Ostgebiete, 15.02.42," BA R 6/71, Mikrofiche 3.

107. "Schreiben Dr. Meyers an Göring, November 1941," ibid., Mikrofiche 2.
108. "Die neue Agrar-Ordnung," see note 106.
109. The promise was for up to 50% more land than was foreseen otherwise. See "Abschrift des Schreibens Armeeoberkommando 16 betreffend Belohnung und Auszeichnung verdienter Partisanenjäger, 14.4.42," ibid.; "Durchführungsbestimmungen zu dem Befehl OKW Nr. 712/42 WFSt/Qu (Verw.) von 18.6.42," ibid., Mikrofiche 5.
110. "Schreiben des Vertreters des Chefs des Wirtschaftsstabes Ost Riecke an das OKH betreffend Durchführung der Agrarordnung, 9.06.42," ibid., Mikrofiche 4.
111. Thus, *Belaruskaja Hazeta* and *Baranavickaja Hazeta* were commanded to issue special commentaries on the directives related to "New Agrarian Order." See S. Zhumar, *Okkupacionnaja Periodicheskaja Pechat' na Territorii Belarusi v Gody Velikoj Otechestvennoj Vojny* (Minsk, 1996), 126; regarding the German press, see Dr. K. Schünnemann, "Die Neue Agrarordnung für den Osten," in *Der Alemanne* (Freiburg im Breisgau), 28 February 1942; "Neue Agrarordnung für die besetzten Ostgebiete," *Angriff (am Abend)*, 28 February 1942; "Das Ende des Kolchos," *Angriff*, 28 February 1942; "Neue Agrar-Ordnung für die Ostgebiete," *Berliner Allgemeine Zeitung*, 28 February 1942; "Neue Agrarordnung im Osten-Die Kolchose fällt," *Berliner Börsenzeitung*, 28 February 1942 ("The New Agrarian Order ... put the final line under the political and economic rape of country people through the Bolshevist collective system"), "Revolution im Osten," *NZ. am Abend* (Metz), BA R 90/74.
112. See Gerlach, *Kalkulierte Morde*, 353.
113. See ibid., 349.
114. One such poster was divided into two parts. On the left there was a picture of Byelorussian peasants at work while the head of a German soldier was shown in the background, and the inscription read: "German soldier protects both you and your better future." On the right side there was a happy-looking peasant holding high a "commodity card" with the inscription, "The commodity card informs you in time about the quantity of deliveries." The right part of this poster is furnished with the caption, "Conscientious fulfillment of deliveries is the honorable duty of every peasant." See Johannes Schlootz, *Deutsche Propaganda in Weißrussland, 1941–1944* (Berlin, 1996), 49.
115. In the same call, Freitag also stated that the peasant must deliver 75% of the slaughter weight of any pig weighing over 80 kg. See "Aufruf des Leiters der Abteilung Ernährung und Landwirtschaft bei GK Weißruthenien Freitags an die weißruthenische Bauern zur Erfüllung des Ablieferungssoll, o. D.," BA R 93/7, 9.
116. "Kritischer Erfahrungsbericht für die ganze Zeit der Zivilverwaltung von Gebietskommissar Slonim, 10.8.44," BA R 93/13.
117. Thus, according to the administrative department in GK Weißruthenien, already at the end of 1942 the losses in grain and straw alone accounted for 45,075 tons. See "Lagebericht der Abteilung II Verwaltung der Generalkommissar in Minsk, 15.10.42," BA R 93/3, 4f.
118. See "Testimony of the writer Mikhail Klimkovič before the Byelorussian Staff of Partisan Movement," YVA M 41/2445 (original- NARB 4-33a-250), 11.
119. "Getreidebilanz 1944/45, GKW," BA R 93/7, 10.

120. "Abschrift des Berichtes des Generalkommissars für Weißruthenien-Abt. Ernährung und Landwirtschaft, 13.05.43," BA R 93/7, 1.

121. See Klimkovič's testimony (note 118), 12.

122. Thus, after the war, the telephone operator of the 8th SS Cavalry Division "Florian Geyer" recalled the "anti-partisan warfare" in the Pripjat swamp area in south Byelorussia in May–June 1943, when the general situation regarding food went from bad to worse: "We lived there well, every day we used to go to surrounding villages to collect eggs [*Jeikas*, this word, distorted form of the Russian word *jajco*, "egg" has been preserved in Russian folklore to this day—L.R.]. In a short time we were so impudent that upon arriving at the edge of the locality we shot three times in the air and then went from house to house to collect the *Jeikas*. The people already knew us. In the evenings, we would feast on our findings." Quoted by Gerlach, *Kalkulierte Morde*, 262.

123. See "Abteilungsleiter Freudenberg über "Der Arbeitseinsatz"-Protokoll über die Tagung," 72.

124. See Gerlach, *Kalkulierte Morde*, 458.

125. Albert Speer, *Inside the Third Reich*, trans. R. and C. Winston (New York, 1970), 293.

126. The order is quoted, among other places, in Misiunas and Taagepera, *The Baltic States*, 55.

127. Quoted in Speer, *Inside the Third Reich*, 295.

128. "Bericht des Generalbevollmächtigten für den Arbeitseinsatz, Gauleiter Sauckel, über die Durchführung seines Auftrages und den beabichtigten weiteren Maßnahmen, Ende September 1942," BA R6/427.

129. "Abteilungsleiter Freudenberg," as in note 123, 75–76.

130. "Monatsbericht des Oberkommando der Heeresgruppe (Mitte) für Mai 1944," BA, R6/309, Mikrofiche 3.

131 "Auszüge aus der Berichterstattung des Gebietskommissars in Nowogrodek über Propagandamaßnahmen im Rahmen der Partisanenbekämpfungsaktion 'Hermann', vom 3. August 1943," in Schlootz, *Deutsche Propaganda*, 56–57.

132. "Propagandaflugblatt an die Bevölkerung," in ibid., 57–58.

133. "Propagandaaktion für den 'Arbeitseinsatz' mit Originalpostkarten von angeblich zufriedenen 'Ostarbeitern', vom 15. Mai 1944," in ibid., 60–61.

134. "Anordnung für die arbeitsrechliche Behandlung der Arbeitskräfte aus den neu besetzten Ostgebieten von 9. Februar 1942," *Deutscher Reichsanzeiger*, 13 February 1942, BA R 90/73.

135. "Arbeitskräfte aus den neubesetzten Ostgebieten," *Ostland* (Berlin), 15 February 1942, ibid.

136. "Arbeitskräfte aus dem neu besetzten Osten," *Der Freiheitskampf* (Dresden), 8 March 1942, R 90/76.

137. "Judgment of Fritz Sauckel at Nuremberg," published in *Avalon Project at Yale Law School, http://avalon.law.yale.edu/imt/judsauck.asp*; "Judgment: Sentences", ibid., *http://avalon.law.yale.edu/imt/judsent.asp*.

138. Gerlach, *Kalkulierte Morde*, 454.

139. "Lagebericht der Abteilung II Verwaltung der Generalkommissar in Minsk, 15.10.42-Arbeitspolitik und Sozialverwaltung," BA R 93/3, 4.

140. "Klimkovič's testimony" (note 118 above), 16.

141. Gerlach, *Kalkulierte Morde*, 454.

142. "Lagebericht der Abteilung II Verwaltung der Generalkommissar in Minsk: Gesundheitswesen und Volkspflege," see note 139.

143. Ibid.

144. Gerlach, *Kalkulierte Morde*, 495.

145. Ibid., 496.

146. Ibid.

147. See Rafael Lemkin, *Axis Rule in Occupied Europe* (New York, 1973), 123–24.

148. "The testimony of Major Alexander Shramko before the Vitebsk oblast Underground Communist Party Committee, 27.12.42," YVA M 41/2446, (NARB, 4-33a-263), 7.

149. "Lagebericht der Abteilung II Verwaltung der Generalkommissar in Minsk: Arbeitspolitik und Sozialverwaltung," note 140. It can at least be supposed that there is an error in this document; instead of roubles it should say RM.

150. See ibid.

151. See Cholawski, *Be-Sufat Ha-Kilayyon*, 61.

152. The original directive could not be found and is quoted by the head of social insurance department of the *Generalkommissariat für Weißruthenien* in his final report. See "Erfahrungs- und Abschlußbericht von Referent Sozialversicherung bei Generalkommissar für Weißruthenien über die Entwicklung der Sozialversicherung der einheimischen Arbeitskräfte im Generalbezirk Weißruthenien, 20.8.44," BA R 93/12.

153. Ibid.

154. See, for example, "Tätigkeits- und Lagebericht der Gebietskommissar Baranowitsche Werner, 11.8.44," BA R 93/13.

CHAPTER 4

BYELORUSSIAN "STATE-BUILDING": POLITICAL COLLABORATION IN BYELORUSSIA

When the Germans arrived in Byelorussia in 1941, they found the potential for collaboration. The Stalinist politics of forceful collectivization and repression only increased this potential. At the same time, the readiness to collaborate with the invaders was not something constant and, to a very large degree, it depended upon the fulfillment of expectations, which ranged from the dream of one's own piece of land to the creation of some form of statehood or, as was the case of the Poles, even returning to the status quo that existed before 1939. As shown in the previous chapter, on the eve of Operation Barbarossa, a group of Byelorussian émigrés living in Germany and in German-occupied Poland formed the so-called "Center," which was supposed to become the Byelorussian provisional government with the beginning of the German occupation of Byelorussia. The fact that leaders of the Center, such as Mikalaj Ščors, indeed believed that this plan would be realized is confirmed indirectly by the reports of the infamous *Einsatzgruppen*.[1] At the same time, a small group of Byelorussian National Socialists, headed by Fabian Akinčyc and Uladzislaŭ Kazloŭski, aped the German Nazi style and slogans, while dreaming of a National Socialist

Byelorussia.[2] The influence of this group was minimal, and Turonak, quoting a Nazi "specialist" on Byelorussia, Eugen von
Engelhardt, states explicitly that Byelorussian Nazis did not
play any significant role whatsoever, at least in the prewar
period.[3]

With regard to the Poles, an indication of their expectations
from the Germans and the basis for their cooperation can be
found in the letter to Rosenberg written by a certain Wenzel von
Gisbert Studnicki from Vilna (Vilnius). It stated that there were
people in Poland who not only expected the Germans to restore
Poland to its pre-1939 borders but also harbored thoughts of a
Greater Poland stretching from the Baltic to the Black Sea.[4]

From the very beginning of the occupation, the Germans
were not inclined to fulfill all of these expectations. Their a priori perception of the Byelorussians categorized them as a people
incapable of managing an independent state, owing to a "lack of
national consciousness." As regards Polish nationalism, the
Nazis were even less interested in promoting these national
ambitions. In general, the option of local collaboration did not
figure prominently in German prewar plans: it was firmly
believed that the Soviet campaign would be over in a couple of
weeks, after which it would be time to embark on the path to
ruthless colonization and exploitation of the newly conquered
territories. The interests of the peoples living in those territories
played no role in their plans. Only the failure of the Blitzkrieg
against the Soviet Union, the shortage of their own administrative personnel, and the almost complete lack of knowledge about
the conditions in the conquered areas compelled the Germans to
consider more seriously the use of the local inhabitants through
collaboration as opposed to exploitation.

Political collaboration in Byelorussia took on various manifestations, beginning with what was dubbed "local self-administration," which formed in the first days and weeks of the Nazi
occupation, and ending with the so-called "Byelorussian Central Council," convened only in the last months of Nazi rule. All
of these bodies, discussed in the following, were allowed to function only as far as the occupation authorities saw fit.

"Local Self-Administration"

The most basic form of political collaboration was the so-called
"local self-administration" or *landeseigene Verwaltung* in Ger-

man. It was this apparatus, with its figure of the *Bürgermeister*, and that of the auxiliary police, which over time became the very symbols of collaboration.

The establishment of this body began at the earliest stage of the German occupation, when the entire country was still under military rule. To a considerable extent its founding resulted from the reluctance of the Wehrmacht commanders to get involved in local political matters. Despite the Nazi's original intention to destroy the entire Soviet administrative apparatus along with its personnel, it soon became clear that they had neither the manpower nor the knowledge to carry out such far-reaching reforms. They were compelled, therefore, to take over the Soviet administrative structure, albeit only up to the rayon level.

The methods employed in manning this new-old administration soon revealed the true attitude of the occupation authorities toward this apparatus. The main criterion applied in selecting personnel was not administrative skills, but rather so-called "political reliability"; in the first place, this meant that non-Jewish (preferably also non-Polish) and non-communist candidates were selected. As might be expected, the first among the candidates for the highest posts in local self-administration were Byelorussian émigrés, some of whom had returend to Byelorussia as auxiliary personnel of *Einsatzgruppe B*, and others who arrived on their own. Thus, Vitaut Tumaš, the former head of the Lodz branch of Byelorussian Representation, was appointed *Bürgermeister* in Minsk; Yury Sabaleŭski, former deputy of the Polish Sejm, served as *Bürgermeister* in Stoŭbcy and later in Nesviž and Baranaviči; Stanislaŭ Stankevič, who worked with *Einsatzgruppe B*, was appointed as *Rayonbürgermeister* in Borisov.[5]

The appointing of former émigrés to senior posts in local administration revealed a somewhat schizophrenic aspect of the Nazi regime. On the one hand, the Germans found that the non-communist Byelorussian émigrés certainly fit their requirements; yet, on the other hand, they obsessively feared the political ambitions of such people. Little wonder then that the military authorities tried to keep the number of appointments conferred on Byelorussian émigrés as low as possible. In fact, in August 1941, the Supreme Command of the Army (OKH), acting on a personal initiative from Hitler, issued an order demanding the removal of émigrés from all leading positions, under the pretext that the latter "had ..., due to their long absence from their county, lost contact with the people and the area," and forbidding the entrance of the émigrés into the Eastern territories in the future.[6] The Germans made it clear to the representatives of the Byelorussian émigrés who had arrived in the country that their duty was solely to help to weed out "the enemies of the Reich" and that they should immediately abandon any dreams of state-building.

Given their mistrust of the émigrés and a general lack of administrators with experience—the majority of the officials from the Soviet period who were sufficiently experienced had been evacuated, had fled the country, or had gone under-ground—the Germans were compelled to turn to other sources to man the local self-administration. Therefore, they drew per-sonnel from among the local intelligentsia: teachers, lawyers, trade officials, physicians, and engineers. The Germans them-selves acknowledged that most of these people lacked the neces-sary professional skills; with the general perception, however, that the local administration was merely the mouthpiece and executor of German orders, such a shortcoming was certainly of little importance.[7] What mattered most was to demonstrate "great activity" (*großere Aktivität*) and "spiritual mobility" (*geistige Beweglichkeit*), that is, a readiness to comply with supreme German orders and the desire to carry these orders out as swiftly as possible.[8]

Officially, the communists were not wanted as personnel for the local administration; yet in reality, former members of the Communist party and of the Komsomol (the communist youth organization), as well as Soviet officials of various ranks, could find their way into this apparatus. A former member of the Communist party, Borovskij, was appointed as rayon chief (*Ray-onbürgermeister*) in the Senno rayon (today the Vitebsk oblast).[9] In Smolensk, a former Soviet lawyer, Menshagin, held the post of local Bürgermeister. The lack of professionalism was even more evident at the lowest level of the local self-administration, namely, at the level of the "village elder" (*starosta*). Any peasant who was prepared to accept the post could be appointed; in many cases, candidates barely knew how to read and write, but since the sole function of the "village elder" was to receive orders from above and ensure strict compliance with these orders, even individuals who had never had anything to do with administrative work, such as watchmen or members of the Pen-tecostalist sect, could be appointed.[10]

In Western Byelorussia, especially in areas such as Lida, Navahrudak and Bialystok, where Poles constituted a large part of the population, Germans were forced to rely considerably on the Polish population to man the local self-administration system. Here, too, the original anti-Polish dogmas and prejudices crumbled in the face of the harsh conditions of reality. In July 1941, the authors of the *Einsatzgruppen*'s monthly reports described their efforts to prevent the Poles from seizing leading positions in the local administration and to appoint Byelorussians instead.[11] At the beginning of August of the same year, the same authors had to acknowledge that "due to the lack of other suitable forces, German re-building in the cities still relies heavily on the Polish intelligentsia. The important posts are already held by Poles, and the initiative to replace them and create a stronger involvement of Byelorussian elements is only proceeding slowly."[12] Quoting various sources,Yerzy Turonak shows that in almost all of Western Byelorussia in the first weeks and months of the German occupation, the local self-administration was thoroughly "Polonized."[13] This situation led to incessant conflicts between Poles and Byelorussians, since the latter took seriously the German slogans calling for "freeing Byelorussia from Polish and Russian influences" and "Byelorussia for Byelorussians." Mutual accusations and denunciations became common occurrences, and toward the end of the occupation the Byelorussian-Polish conflicts became increasingly bloody.

The German military authorities played an important role in the appointment of virtually all levels of local self-administration. Although formally the *Landbürgermeister* and *Dorfälteste* were supposed to be appointed by the higher levels within the self-administration, the *Feld-* or *Ortskommandantur* could intervene at any time. At the very beginning of the occupation in the Soviet territories, when the military administration was almost completely ignorant of the situation there, local officials, especially *Rayonbürgermeistern,* had relative freedom in manning the lower posts. Once the establishment and stability of German rule increased, however, the *Feldkommandanturen* carried out whole-scale cleansing of the local administration, under the pretext that it was infected with nepotism and that the administrative apparatus had become overly inflated.[14] The most obvious reason for this purge was the prosaic desire to place the local self-administration under the rigid control of the German authorities.

In the initial stages of this apparatus's formation, its staffing proceeded, by and large, on a voluntary basis. A complete list of the motives of those who manned the organs of the local self-administration would be difficult to assemble. The tangle of problems that existed on the eve of the invasion, as briefly described in previous chapters, suggests that a great many Byelorussians believed that the Germans had entered the country with the intention of unraveling these knots, and that, therefore, it was worth cooperating with them in some form or other. The economic constraints should also be remembered in this context: since only those industries that catered to German needs were allowed to operate, the rate of unemployment was quite high and the option of serving in the local self-administration provided a relatively steady job.

As stated, collaboration with the Germans did not necessarily mean identification with their National Socialist ideology or its goals. The German historian Werner Röhr even maintains that "to speak reasonably of collaboration, at least two preconditions must be present: first, [the collaborative act] is a reaction to the occupation rule, and secondly, apart from the interests common to both sides, there are also divergent ones that the locals are striving to address through collaboration."[15] Undoubtedly, those in the occupied countries of Western Europe who decided to collaborate with Germans had more room to maneuver for the advancement of their particular interests than did the East European collaborators. For the latter, as time passed and the occupation became increasingly brutal, collaboration became more of a question of physical survival than adherence to pre-designated dreams and plans. In Byelorussia in particular, one may distinguish between various groups of people who, by collaboration, tried to achieve their own goals. Yerzy Turonak divides collaborators into three groups according to their aims. First, there were "Byelorussian public figures who strove for the creation of an independent Byelorussian State; second, there were Polish public figures, who strove to restore the situation existing before September 1939; and third, there were Soviet public figures of various nationalities, who carried out diversions and intelligence tasks in the hope of restoring the situation which had prevailed before June 1941."[16] This division is undoubtedly somewhat oversimplified, but it provides a partial picture of the state of affairs that existed in the organs of the so-called local self-administration. It proves the groundlessness of the approach followed in the Soviet period that depicts all collaborators as merely German accomplices who had no ideas or views of their own.

Byelorussian scholar Alexej Litvin also singles out three main groups of collaborators there.[17] First were those who were either "openly or secretly opposed to Bolshevism." They were mostly former émigrés, many of whom had pursued higher education outside of Byelorussia. Thus, for example, included among the collaborators who fit this group's definition is the second *Bürgermeister* of Minsk, Vaclaŭ Ivanoŭski, who from the 1920s until the beginning of the 1940s was a teacher, first in a Warsaw polytechnic high school and then as a professor in Vilna (Vilnius) University.[18] Many of those who could be identified with this category came from the Western—formerly Polish—part of Byelorussia, which meant that anti-Polish sentiments were quite rampant among them. Among the Byelorussian émigrés, those of the older generation still remembered the days of the so-called Byelorussian Popular Republic (BNR).[19] Although in 1918 the position of the Germans toward the BNR had been one of benevolent neutrality at best, at the time of the current German invasion, the myth of alleged German support for the BNR had become quite widespread among the Byelorussian nationalists. They hoped that this time, too, the Germans would support the creation of some form of Byelorussian statehood. Litvin speaks about this group as representing "political (ideological) collaboration." Before the war, however, many of the Byelorussian nationalists had belonged to Akinčyc's Party of Byelorussian National Socialists and were now prepared to identify completely with the Nazis' goals and slogans, with their aspirations ranging from the creation of a "New Europe" to the "Final Solution of the Jewish Question."

Another group mentioned by Litvin is that of non-émigrés, that is, those who "had lived in the territory of the BSSR before the war, and now, believing the Germans or their accomplices [*sic*], entered consciously into their service."[20] Litvin feels that this group, too, was motivated by anti-Soviet sentiments, since many among them had been victims of Soviet rule or had opposed the Soviet regime even before the war. Such a group classification is extremely limited, since, as will be shown later, this second group of non-émigrés also included former Communist party and Komsomol members. In this respect, of note is the report by an anonymous "Byelorussian from Latvia," compiled in August 1942, which mentions a group known as the *Vozvyshentsy* (literally "those on the rise"). The report states that these were people who had sought to preserve Byelorussia's national singularity in the framework of a Soviet state, during the period of the NEP. They subsequently suffered from the wave of Russification that swept Byelorussia at the end of 1920s

and during the 1930s, a fact which renders them a perfect fit
with the classification of this second group.[21]

Thirdly, Litvin mentions people who were drawn into collaboration by the generally grim state of affairs and were, by and
large, deprived of any choice in the matter.[22] Litvin describes the
first group as the "backbone" of collaboration in Byelorussia;
yet, in reality, as the occupation progressed and conditions
became increasingly harsh, people gradually came to consider
collaboration their only means of survival, rather than the fulfillment of their nationalist dreams. A statement made by the
same anonymous "Byelorussian from Latvia", suggests that, in
time, readiness to collaborate with the occupation authorities
dwindled as the public attitude toward collaborators became
more negative: "As soon as someone consciously puts himself on
the German side, he is perceived as a traitor to the nation and
severs connections with his compatriots (*Volksgenossen*)."[23] This
statement, however, is not easily substantiated.

As in other European countries, in Byelorussia too, the border between collaboration and resistance was often extremely
thin or even non-existent. There were Poles who combined work
in the institutions of local self-administration—and auxiliary
police— with membership in the clandestine Home Army
(Armija Krajowa; see the following chapters).[24] There were also
Byelorussians who combined their activities in various collaborationist bodies with membership in organizations such as the
clandestine Byelorussian Independent Party (Belaruskaja Neza-
ležnickaja Partyja, BNP), information about which is extremely
scarce. It was founded in 1942, by people such as the chief school
inspector at the *GK Weißruthenien*, Vincent Hadleŭski. Members of this party included people who held various posts in local
self-administration as well as in the auxiliary police, such as
Bürgermeister of Vitebsk, Ŭsevalad Rodz'ka (head of BNP's
Central Committee); Minsk police chief, Yuljan Sakovič; Nesviž
police chief, Ŭladzimir Sen'ka; and many others. The party
inscribed upon its banner "Against Germans and Bolsheviks,"
and in June 1944, it even planned the anti-German uprising,
intending to proclaim the founding of the Byelorussian People's
Republic. These plans were subsequently abandoned owing to
the speedy advance of the Soviet Army.[25]

Providing a reliable quantitative description of the participants in local self-administration is not easy, since precise numbers are not available. According to a mid-1943 evaluation
reported by the "Economic Inspection Center" (*Wirtschaftsin-*

spektion Mitte) and quoted by Christian Gerlach, within the inspection's activity area (that is, the area of military administration), there were approximately 60,000 local administration officials.[26] Information on *GK Weißruthenien* is fragmentary and can provide a picture only of particular regions. Nevertheless, some conclusions can be drawn as to the quantitative relationship between Germans and local personnel. In the *Gebietskommissariat* Baranaviči, in January 1943, there were 53 Germans and 161 local officials (a ratio of approximately 1:3); in *Gebietskommissariat* Lida, at the end of the German occupation, there were 86 Germans compared to 768 locals (a ratio of nearly 1:9).[27] Perhaps the most striking example of this was the *Gebietskommissariat* Hlybokaje, where, on the day of its creation, i.e. 20 September 1941, there were merely three German officials, and this in an area encompassing 400,000 inhabitants.[28]

The reason behind such ratios can be attributed chiefly to the fact that, from the very beginning, top Nazi echelons did not plan to dispatch large numbers of people to the "Eastern territories," in the belief that it would be possible to control such regions with a small number of "lords." Moreover, officials stationed in the occupied territories close to the frontline were seen as the primary reserve for the front's reinforcements.

The chief task of local self-administration was to maintain "peace and order," help the Germans establish control over the local population, and secure local natural and manpower resources and place them at the disposal of the German war machine. The Germans never concealed their aim in encouraging local collaboration. As late as February 1943, the Main Administrative Department of the Reich Ministry for the Occupied Eastern Territories wrote that "the essential task of German administration in the occupied eastern areas is to encourage the local population toward positive cooperation to achieve thereby maximal profit."[29] At various levels of German administration and in various stages of the occupation period, especially the later ones, calls were heard for granting additional flexibility to local self-administration and allowing it to exercise a greater degree of independence.[30] From its establishment through to the end of the occupation in Byelorussia, however, the indigenous self-administration was never perceived as an autonomous body. From the German point of view, "the local administration ha[d] one sole task, i.e., to execute the directives of responsible German offices."[31] Such a conception was based on the *Herrenvolk* tenet, which perceived the Slavs as incapable of taking an independent stance and therefore destined to be led by the superior Germans.[32]

In the area of military administration, the apparatus of the local self-administration was under the control of the *Feldkommandanturen*, while in the area of civil administration its activities were overseen by the *Gebietskommissar*. This control was more rigidly maintained at the level of rayon administration and became somewhat weaker at lower levels. The Germans did all they could to prevent the apparatus of the local self-administration from turning into a unified, cohesive body that could some day claim power of government. An official task at high levels of this apparatus was to "oversee" or, more plainly, to spy on the lower administrative levels.[33] Denunciations were quite rampant; personal scores were settled by mutual accusations of "political unreliability."[34] The situation was especially acute in the mixed Polish-Byelorussian areas. Here Byelorussian functionaries accused Polish officials of intending to create a Greater Poland, sabotaging German orders, and discriminating against the Byelorussian population.[35] Often even the deportation of Poles was demanded.[36] In some places, Polish inhabitants were expelled by sending them to Germany as forced labor. One example of this occurred in Nesviž, where the head of the labor department of the city's *uprava*, Ivan Kaloša, played an active role in implementing these measures.[37] In Stoŭbcy, too, the local *Bürgermeister*, Ivan Aŭdzej, participated in anti-Polish repressions. According to the postwar proceedings, in 1942 Aŭdzej "allegedly caused the arrest and execution of 120 Polish intellectuals" and was reportedly sentenced to death in absentia by the members of the Polish underground.[38] The local self-administration officials also played a prominent role in the persecution of Byelorussian Jews, especially in their ghettoization and in the requisition and disposal of the murdered Jews' property (see the following chapters).

With the rise of the partisan movement, local self-administration officials increasingly found themselves between a rock and a hard place. The village elders (*Dorfälteste*) and the *Bürgermeistern* of the cities, situated in the "partisan zones," were in an especially precarious position. As early as October 1941, the commander of the Rear Area of the Army Group "Center," Schenckendorff, explicitly demanded that "the *Bürgermeister* and the population be held wholly responsible for the peace, order and security of the highways, supplies and structures, both in the neighborhood and extending half the distance to the next community."[39] Particularly rigid demands were imposed on the local officials in places situated near strategically important railways. In such locations, administration heads were ordered to provide detailed information on the whereabouts of all local inhabitants and, if anything should go awry (at least from the German point of view), "the *Bürgermeister* would be called in to account for the aberration."[40] The fact that these people collaborated with the Germans did not guarantee them immunity from repressions inflicted by the latter. Proof of this can be found in the document issued by the *Kreislandwirt,* the German official responsible for managing agriculture in the occupied territories, in Valožyn, to the northwest of Minsk, at the end of July 1943. He complained of the activities of the infamous Dirlewanger unit, carried out as part of the "anti-partisan struggle" in Pirschaje area. In the course of this campaign, eleven localities were depopulated and burnt down, and all of the local administration officials (*Gemeindeverwaltung*) were deported to work in the Reich.[41]

From the very beginning, the officials of the local self-administration, became the favorite target of the partisans' assaults, regardless of the position they occupied. The leaflets distributed by partisans in various areas of Byelorussia, for example, in Košeleva, near Navahrudak, threatened to eliminate the "families of auxiliary policemen (*Schutzmännern*), *Bürgermeistern,* and village elders (*Dorfschulzen*)" together with "spies and partisan betrayers."[42] These threats were soon realized. Between 6 July and 6 August 1942, according to *Gebietskommissar* of Navahrudak, nine attacks were waged on community offices and auxiliary policemen in an area encompassing only four rayons (Navahrudak, Kareliči, Djatlava, and Ljubič).[43] Considering that the Germans did not have enough forces to protect the local officials from these assaults, the collaborators and their families found themselves in an extremely vulnerable position. In August 1942, the administrative department of the *Generalkommissariat für Weißruthenien* was compelled to acknowledge in despair that the partisans "are the masters of the situation. They proceed with especially violent terror against village elders and community chairmen, particularly through the use of extreme threats and the most terrible butchering of their family members. The community mayors (*Gemeindebürgermeistern*) and rayon mayors (*Rayonbürgermeistern*) have only one question: when will the Germans finally provide some protection against these Bolshevist bands?"[44] This question remained rhetorical.

Reports by various German institutions abound with entries about partisan assaults against collaborators and their families. On 5 October 1942, SSPF *Weißruthenien* reported a partisan attack on the homestead of an auxiliary policeman (*Schutzmann*) in the Vilejka area and the murder of his entire family— six persons—parents, siblings, and sister-in-law.[45] On 3 November 1942, the *Oberfeldkommandantur* 392 reported that partisans had murdered five persons of an auxiliary policeman's family in the village of Halica, northeast of Minsk, and eleven days later murdered eight people from a different family in the same village.[46] Whole villages could be suspected of collaborating with the Germans. In September 1942, the inhabitants of the village Orlja, situated in the territory of *GK Weißruthenien,* received a leaflet in which the partisans announced their intention to burn down the entire village, alleging that "90% of the inhabitants had proven to be traitors…, [since] on August 26, thirty men voluntarily joined the fascist units and took up fighting against the Soviet government and the partisans."[47]

Since the Germans were unable to protect those working with them, the collaborators sought out their own ways to cope with this situation. One was to create a kind of personal "army." Units of the "Byelorussian Free Corps of Self-Defense," known in short as Byelorussian Self-Defense, *Byelaruskaja Samaakhova* or BSA, were often used for this purpose.[48] The German authorities were slow in supplying the BSA units with weapons and uniforms, and these tasks eventually fell upon the shoulders of local officials. For their part, the latter were prompt to utilize the *Samaakhova* recruits for personal defense and "to enforce their will among the population," as was expressed somewhat vaguely by the *Gebietskommissar* of Slonim.[49]

Another survival strategy developed by the *starostas* of the villages situated in the epicenters of partisan activities was to cooperate with both sides. Thus, according to postwar testimony by one of the inhabitants of the village of Zasov'je (today the Lahojsk rayon, Minsk oblast), the village elder supplied both the partisans and the Germans with whatever they required: "When the partisans arrived, he collected for them what they needed and when the Germans arrived he did the same."[50] As early as May 1942, the department I c (Abwehr) of the commander of the Rear Area of the Army Group "Center" reported on the "double games" played by the local administration officials in Kasplja in the vicinity of Bobrujsk and in Bobrujsk itself.[51]

The desire to survive, in surroundings which Bernhard Chiari has described as lying between Scylla and Charybdis, led the local officials, especially the *starostas*, to cooperate more closely with the occupation authorities; interestingly, it also resulted in increased desertion rates in favor of the partisans' ranks.[52] Many *Dorfälteste* were quite ready to secure their own survival at the cost of their neighbors' lives, by denouncing them as partisans or pro-Soviets. The accused were then either sent to work in Germany, or publicly beaten, or punished in "retaliations" against those impugned as "partisan-supporters." The village elder of Ždanoviči, a released prisoner of war, collected winter clothes from the peasants to give to the Wehrmacht, and in the process also denounced a number of his neighbors as pro-Soviets. The *Bürgermeister* of Korolev-Stan, near Minsk, denounced three of his neighbors as "Soviet activists" and further accused them of the forbidden action of purchasing horses and agricultural products. During the arrest of those denounced, this *Bürgermeister* personally guided German policemen to his victims' homes and then participated in the house searches after the accused had been publicly executed. Moreover, he prohibited attempts to bury the executed in the local cemetery. The *starosta* of Malaja Slepjanka, also near Minsk, pummeled villagers who were slow to comply with demands made by him and the Germans. He beat one of the peasants who did not come immediately to extinguish a fire caused by the Soviet air bombing. He also kept the roads to and from the nearby Wehrmacht airfield open, using similar violent means.[53] The local village elder of Vasileviči (today Hrodna oblast in Western Byelorussia), during the "anti-partisan operation" of December 1942, protected the families of local collaborators who had suffered from partisan attacks by separating them from the rest of the villagers, among them women and children, who were going to be annihilated as "partisan-supporters."[54] In the Bobrujsk area, the local *starostas*, who received orders from the command of the German 9th Army via the *Rayonbürgermeister*, were instructed to select people from their villages to clear the mines in the area using their own harrows.[55]

The increased strength of the partisan movement and the weakness or even absence of German support led quite a number of local officials, especially at the lower levels, to contemplate changing sides. The situational reports of various German authorities repeatedly mention the disappearance of local officials and policemen, presumably "kidnapped" by the partisans.[56]

At the very least, it is possible that many of those "kidnapped" actually showed little—if any—effort to resist their "kidnappers'" and simply chose to desert.

While officials at the bottom levels of the local self-administration were constantly struggling for physical survival, the situation in the top echelons often looked radically different. According to the postwar testimony of the former *Gebietskommissar* of Minsk (*Minsk-Stadt*), Wilhelm Janetzke, submitted to the Soviet interrogators, the deputy *Bürgermeister* of Minsk, Demidovič-Demideckij, would arrange "little parties," renowned for the abundance of food and alcoholic beverages that came directly from SD stores. This custom was practiced by high-level officials, at a time when the general economic situation in occupied Byelorussia was extremely difficult and broad sections of the population were on the verge of starvation.[57]

As early as the first half of 1942, after the failure of both the German offensive against Moscow and the Blitzkrieg strategy in general, when German military forces had suffered significant losses, voices began to be heard inside the military administrations of the Eastern territories as well as among officials of the OMi, calling for a change in the methods of occupation politics, whereby the first step would be to provide local self-administration with a more active role in these politics. In the spring of 1942, the first attempts were undertaken to create a new level of self-administration above that of the rayon. The new level was called *Bezirksverwaltung* (district administration), and its area coincided with that of a single Feldkommandantur, encompassing approximately 8–10 rayons.[58] A *Bezirksverwaltung* was supposed to "oversee and support the *Rayonbürgermeister* and *Bürgermeister* in the FK area" as well as "deal with the precise organization of the local administration, and coordinate the economic and administrative interests of the rayon."[59] The creation of *Bezirksverwaltung* was by no means the result of some kind of benevolence toward the local population; rather, it reflected only the occupiers' harsh necessity and their search for maximum profit. Of course, the creation of the "district administration," not unlike other "indigenous administration" levels, was not the outcome of an overall plan, but merely a single arbitrary instance. According to an *Ostministerium* notice issued in February 1943, virtually all the directives and projects of the *Bezirksverwaltung*—among them budgets, staffing proposals for the position of department chief, and directives "concerning the Wehrmacht's interests"—required the approval of the *Feldkom-*

mandantur.[60] The fact that the "district administration" was subordinate both in the military and in the civil administration areas to the sole authority of the FK underscores the fact that the initiative for creating such a level came mainly from the military personnel, who due to their first-hand experience were more prone to "radical" measures.

The creation of the *Bezirkverwaltungen*, especially in the territory of the *GK Weißruthenien*, proceeded relatively slowly, at least at the beginning. By the end of May 1942, according to Rosenberg's report, there were only three districts with such a structure in the entire civil administration area.[61] In fact, from the very outset, the *Bezirkverwaltungen* were considered an "experimental" level of administration that could be easily abolished if anything went wrong. The Germans' attitude toward this "new administrative level" reflected the authority's general approach to the indigenous self-administration establishment. Specifically, the Germans aimed to make this administration the mouthpiece and mere transmitter and executor of their orders, on the one hand, and a kind of "lightning rod" that would absorb the outrage of the local population, on the other. In other words, the German strategy was to pay the lowest possible price for the local inhabitants' cooperation.

The Byelorussian Popular Self-Aid Organization

Another form of political collaboration was the Byelorussian Popular Self-Aid Organization or, in Byelorussian, *Belaruskaja Narodnaja Samapomač* (BNS). It was created in October 1941 on the initiative of *Generalkommissar für Weißruthenien* Kube, and its aims, at least officially, were quite innocent.[62] It was supposed to take over the functions of the Byelorussian Red Cross and also help homeless families, orphans, and children of working mothers, in short, anyone who was suffering as a result of the war.[63] Later, in 1943, the BNS was also entrusted to assist those who had fled the Soviet regime and preferred to live in Byelorussia under German occupation as well as those whom the Germans had forcefully resettled in Byelorussia.[64] In addition, the BNS also was supposed to "raise the cultural level of the Byelorussian population and ... present the local cultural values to the Germans."[65]

Under a direct order from Rosenberg, Dr. Ivan Yermačenka was appointed head of the BNS.[66] A man of great political ambition, Yermačenka was not a novice in politics. Born in 1894, in the village of Kapčoŭka in the Borisov district, he studied at a Moscow high school during World War I and graduated from officers' school. He went on to serve in the Russian Army and, at the close of the war, his position was aide-de-camp of General Wrangel, whose troops had fought bitterly against the Reds in south Russia during the civil war and were the last to leave the country after the defeat of the White movement. In the 1920s, after the evacuation of Wrangel's forces into Turkey, Yermačenka served as consul-general of the short-lived Byelorussian Popular Republic in the Balkans, and briefly as deputy minister of foreign affairs of the BNR in Lithuanian Kaunas. In 1922, he moved to Prague, where he graduated in 1929 from the local university and then practiced medicine. Earlier, in 1926, as an activist of the Byelorussian diaspora in the Czechoslovakian capital, he founded the Falcon Union, which was supposed to lobby on behalf of the interests of the Byelorussian minority in Czechoslovakia.[67] Married to an ethnic German, he was a sworn Germanophile, and as such was accused before World War II by many Byelorussian émigrés of "following the German lead too closely."[68] According to Yermačenka, the rebuilding of Byelorussia was possible only with German aid.[69] His appointment to the post of BNS leader derived—to a significant extent—from his connections to various circles in Germany. As early as 1940–41, he and Dr. Harald Waegener, future head of the department of public health and popular well-being (*Gesundheitswesen und Volkspflege*) of the *Ostministerium*, cooperated closely in an organization of Byelorussian physicians in Germany. Yermačenka also had numerous contacts with Professor Gerhard von Mende, who in the 1930s was engaged in Byelorussian studies at Berlin University and later headed a department for Caucasus in Rosenberg's ministry.[70]

As a result of his eagerness to cooperate very closely with the Germans, he was nicknamed "Herr-Jahwohl" by the Minsk populace; but Yermačenka saw himself as no less than the future leader of Byelorussia, and the BNS as the seed of a future Byelorussian government.[71] His appointment, in the summer of 1942, as one of Kube's advisors only strengthened Yermačenka's ambitions. His arrest in 1943 and the "special treatment" he received in the Minsk SD cellars, however, led to the sobering of those ambitions.[72]

Yermačenka's ideal was a Byelorussia without Russians or Poles (also, of course, without Jews, although *with* their property). He supported the idea of expelling Russians to the east, Poles into the General Gouvernement, and then transferring Byelorussian minorities from the border areas to the *GK Weißruthenien*.[73] To achieve this ideal of "Byelorussia for the Byelorussians," he was prepared to go far and was not deterred by the prospect of direct denunciations. In 1942, he sent a personal letter to Kube, which read as follows: "From the point of view of Byelorussian (*Weißruthene*) [*sic*], I propose that Mr. Sharski, who is currently deputy to Mr. Huzko, be appointed to replace Mr. Huzko. Regarding Mr. Panin, I must state that he is a Russian who ignores the Byelorussian language and by no means can remain as head of the art department, which should be purely Byelorussian. For this post I suggest Mr. Nikolajewitsch, the precentor of the Metropolitan choir."[74]

Little wonder then that the BNS attracted chauvinists and people with fascist or similar views, who saw their primary task not so much in assisting their needy compatriots as in liberating Byelorussia from her "sworn enemies," namely the Poles, Russian Bolsheviks, and "world Jewry" as well. A statute of the BNS, published coincidentally when the organization received official recognition from the German authorities, stated explicitly that "the BNS has an aim to liquidate in Byelorussia a misfortune ... raised by the Polish and Communist–Jewish dominion, and to create the possibility of a better cultural development for the Byelorussian people."[75] Only Byelorussians were considered for membership in the BNS.[76] The organization was subordinate to the department of public health and popular well-being at the *Generalkommissariat für Weißruthenien*.[77] Structurally, it was divided into eleven areas (*Gebiete*), to each of which a BNS "area head" (*Gebietsleiter*) was appointed: Baranaviči, Navahrudak, Slonim, Hlybokaje, Lida, the city of Minsk (Minsk-Stadt), Vilejka, the vicinity of Minsk (*Minsk-Land*), Sluck, Hanceviči, and Borisov. The area head, with a staff of ten people, was supposed to organize the BNS rayon, the community (*Gemeinde*), and village committees, which were entrusted with the collection of "donations" of cash, clothes and food.[78] Officially, these "donations" were later distributed in the following way: twenty-five per cent stayed in the rayon, another twenty-five per cent was transferred to the *Gebiet* level, and the remaining fifty per cent went to the Minsk central office of the BNS. According to the data in Yermačenka's personal letter to Rosenberg, it was redistributed from the central office in Minsk to the neediest *Gebiete*.[79]

As with the indigenous self-administration, it is almost impossible to provide exact quantitative data on the structure of the Self-Aid Organization. Its leadership reported almost 30,000 members at the end of 1942, but Bernhard Chiari justifiedly supposes that this number is exaggerated.[80] Even from the official data about BNS membership in particular areas, one may easily see that the organization was either strongly underrepresented or completely absent from predominantly Polish areas. In the Lida area, only 743 members were reported, while *Gebiet* Navahrudak could not claim a single member.[81] Moreover, in various areas, the center and the periphery differed considerably. According to a report compiled at the beginning of September 1942, in the Lahojsk rayon consisting of fourteen communities (*volosti* or *Gemeinde*, approximately analogous with Soviet-time *sel'sovet*), approximately 77.5% of the BNS members (232 out of 299) were from the city of Lahojsk itself, while the rest came from only three *volosti*: Lahojsk (17 members), Padonka (29), and Astražicki (21).[82]

Not infrequently, the local branches of the BNS were headed by people who simultaneously held high-ranking positions in the local self-administration and the local police. The BNS chief in the Minsk rayon, Kontaŭt, was also the local *Rayonbürgermeister*. A similar situation prevailed in Lahojsk rayon, where *Rayonbürgermeister* Kačan stood at the head of the rayon's BNS branch. In Vilejka, the BNS was led by Kalodka, who was also the chief of the police of the Ašmjany rayon.[83]

The BNS leaders might have considered their organization a prototype of a future Byelorussian government, but the Germans saw things differently. Yet, this organization could hardly be regarded as a blind tool manipulated by the German administration, as was claimed by Soviet and even a few post-Soviet researchers.[84] Up to a point, the Germans were prepared to tolerate the relative independence of BNS in matters of charity and culture. BNS also enjoyed extensive freedom of action concerning recruitment of people for work in Germany. The secret directive issued in July 1942 by Tulejka, who was the head of the Baranaviči rayon's BNS branch, noted that this labor recruitment was used for "cleansing" Byelorussia from Poles and other "undesirable elements."[85] At the same time, Germans were less than enthusiastic about the political ambitions of the Samapomač leadership and were eager to limit its activities to purely charitable ones. In this matter they were even ready to support BNS activities by allowing credit to the BNS central department; such credit, however, which reached the sum of 170,000 RM in the summer of 1943, became increasingly modest in the second half of that same year and nearly ceased to exist by the beginning of 1944.[86]

One might assume that in the difficult economic conditions reigning in occupied Byelorussia, public donations could hardly be a significant source of income for the BNS; however, during the Second Byelorussian Congress that took place in June 1944, the president of the Byelorussian Central Council, Astroŭski, spoke of 11,606,170 roubles collected in the fiscal year 1943/44 by Self-Aid, "through public donations and as a result of [the organization's] economic activities."[87] In reality, Samapomač's income came from a variety of sources: membership fees, earnings from the newspaper sales, and profits from various undertakings.[88] Along with these quasi-honest sources, the BNS also participated in one form or another in the income-generating repressive politics of the Germans. Thus, rayon BNS officials requested permission to divide among the needy peasants any "property in abeyance," which remained after the anti-partisan actions.[89] Bernhard Chiari quotes an interesting document from Byelorussian archives that indicates that the Self-Aid organization issued an order to the German *Gebietskommissare*, requesting the transfer of items that remained after the liquidation of the Jewish ghettos to the BNS authorities. Of course, German functionaries simply ignored this demand.[90]

It is very difficult to determine the extent of the BNS's influence throughout the country; *Gebietskommissar* of Slonim, Ehrenleitner, evaluated it as "equal to zero in the countryside."[91] Moreover, widespread corruption among the Self-Aid leaders certainly did not increase the organization's prestige. Even the "rosy" reports about Samapomač activities could not conceal the irregularities. Thus, the BNS reported that at the beginning of December 1943 it had at its disposal stores of donated cereals, potatoes, legumes, and fat totaling around 119,000 kilograms, of which 50,000 kilograms of foodstuffs and 1,835 kilograms of fat were distributed to the needy.[92] Even the simplest calculation shows that the needy received less than fifty per cent of the produce. The question of what happened to the rest remains open. That cases of corruption were not solitary instances is also learned from the head of the BNS, Yermačenka, turning in February 1942, together with the economic director of the organization, Schönemeier, to the managers of BNS warehouses and food stores through the newspaper *Belaruskaja*

Hazeta, threatening them with execution for the misappropriation of the collected goods and using them to make fraudulent
deals.[93] Eventually, corruption was one of the official reasons for
arresting Yermačenka and other BNS leaders at the beginning
of 1943. The head of the BNS did not conceal the fact that during his term as chief he had done whatever he pleased with the
organization's funds, including dispatching money to his family
in Prague and arranging parties.[94]

The atmosphere of mutual denunciations that prevailed
among the ranks of this organization certainly did not help to
increase its influence throughout the country. Tulejka, head of
the Baranaviči BNS area office, accused the BNS district head in
Novaja Myš, Jasep Žukovski, before the head of the political
department at the *Gebietskommissariat* Baranaviči, of lack of
initiative, corruption, squandering public donations as well as
favoring Polish nationalism. This document shows that the
work of the BNS encountered open hostility from the Polish as
well as the Byelorussian Catholic population in those areas
where such groups constituted a majority or at least a significant
part of the inhabitants.[95]

Three factors influenced the German attitude toward the
BNS and its place in the occupation landscape: the situation in
general, the personality of the man at the head of the German
civil administration in Byelorussia, and the power struggles
between Kube's administration and the SS. Wilhelm Kube, who
was *Generalkommissar für Weißruthenien* between 1941 and
1943, was certainly an ardent Nazi and, as such, demonstrated
the typical views of and prejudices toward all of the *Ostvölker*,
including the Byelorussians. Initially he was an unlikely candidate for championing Byelorussian interests. In 1942 he stated
that "White Ruthenians shall become a 'nation' only to the
extent that they are capable of forming a wall against Muscovy
and the Eastern steppe."[96] At the same time he was a pragmatic
man and, in contrast to his neighbor Erich Koch in Ukraine, he
quickly grasped that "makhorka, vodka and nagaika" alone
would not suffice to secure his dominion over the country.[97] At
the beginning of 1942, German security organs reported a sharp
deterioration of the general mood in Byelorussia as a result of
the worsening food situation and, simultaneously, the steady
growth of the partisan movement.[98] In light of this situation
Kube decided to back Byelorussian nationalism. The cautious
improvement in the status of the BNS, however, formally begun
on 29 June 1942 when Yermačenka was appointed personal

advisor (*muž daveru*, man of confidence) to Kube, cannot be explained only by the general situation in Byelorussia at the time. As noted, the third contributing factor to the growing role of Byelorussian nationalism was the constant power struggle between the civil administration and the SS apparatus. Actually, the BNS activists, in their euphoria over their "enhanced" status, failed to notice the moment when they became a pawn in these struggles. Yerzy (Yury) Turonak considers these conflicts to be one of the main features of the German occupation in *GK Weißruthenien*, at least until Kube's assassination in September 1943.[99]

The constellation of these three factors could explain what happened in the summer of 1942. Kube, who thought that "the so-called Byelorussian Self-Aid Organization should be reduced to the tasks fulfilled in [the] Reich by NSV," declared the BNS as "the representative of Byelorussian people" and ordered the creation of a central organ for this organization, the Supreme Council of the BNS (Haloŭnaja Rada BNS).[100] Demonstrating an even greater departure from his original approach, Kube further entrusted the BNS activists to issue an appeal to the population to join voluntarily the recently proclaimed "Free Corps of Self-Defense" (Vol'ny Korpus Samaakhovy, known simply as "Byelorussian Self-Defense," Belaruskaja Samaakhova or BSA), which was perceived by Byelorussian nationalists as the seed of the future Byelorussian army.[101]

At the same time as the Supreme Council of the BNS was created, the *Generalkommissariat* and the *Gebietskommissariate* established the institute of *Mužy Daveru* (men of confidence).[102] This institute, at least officially, was to assume the functions of an advisory body to the German civilian administrative organs; its creation was advertised in the German press as the "German administration's acknowledgment of the population's willing cooperation."[103] The apparatus of *Mužy Daveru* by *Generalkommissariat* consisted of four departments: politics, headed by Yermačenka himself; schools, headed by Yaŭkhim Skurat; culture, headed by Ivan Kasyak; and press and propaganda, headed by Anton Adamovič. This step, together with Kube's sanctioning of bodies such as the Byelorussian Scientific Society and the Women's League, succeeded in deceiving not only Kube's contemporaries, but also the historians who later dealt with the occupation period. For example, Turonak, in apparent disregard of Kube's views on Byelorussians as mentioned above, seriously suggests that "Kube appreciated and supported the Byeloruss-

ian question; he envisioned the creation of a separate Byelorussian state under the Reich's leadership."[104] In reality, an analysis
of Kube's expressions regarding Byelorussia made at different
times shows that he could hardly have been suspected of excessive Byelorussophilia.[105]

A discussion of the German attitude toward the BNS, as well
as toward other Byelorussian "national" bodies such as the
Union of Byelorussian Youth, should markedly differentiate
expressions made publicly, especially in front of Byelorussian
activists, from opinions reflected in the documents that circulated among the various Nazi institutions. Only an integration
of these two sources can provide the complete picture of the
Janus-like nature of German politics toward all or almost all of
the local bodies. While the German authorities had to make des-
perate attempts to bridge the gap between the National Socialist dogmas and reality, they were also trapped between the
dynamics developing from the local population that they governed and the directives they received from above.

Clearly neither Kube and his civil administration apparatus
nor any other German bodies were particularly interested in
promoting Byelorussian nationalism. The German authorities'
main fear was that "Dr Yermačenka with the help of the BNS ...
could become a Byelorussian popular leader (*Volksführer*) and
then would present a danger to us [i.e., Germans—L.R.]."[106] The
strengthening of BNS positions from mid-1942 onward was a
thorn in the flesh of many German organs, especially the SS.
The SSPF in *Weißruthenien*, Curt von Gottberg, destined to
become Kube's successor after the latter's assassination, wrote
very critically of the BNS and the practice of toying with
Byelorussian nationalism in general, in an undated letter to the
chief of the main SS office. According to Gottberg, "to date, the
BNS has caused only damage here in the country and has driven
the population mad ... these ideas of a national Byelorussia
(*Weißruthenien*), fabricated by the émigrés and Berlin armchair
politicians (*Salonpolitikern*) do not exist at all in the harsh reality."[107] The commander of the security police and SD in *GK
Weißruthenien*, Eduard Strauch, also accused Yermačenka of
having aspirations to become the prime minister of Byelorussia
and Kube of supporting him.[108]

Rosenberg's "Eastern Ministry" was not overly fond of
Kube's initiatives for the creation of local advisory bodies by the
German civil administration organs, since it saw in them "the
germ of the strivings for the autonomy in the whole *General-*

bezirk Weißruthenien."[109] In his August 1942 notice about the creation of the institute of *Mužy Daveru*, Rosenberg stated explicitly and unambiguously that "the appointment of the liaisons and men of confidence from some nation already means recognition of the organized form of this nation."[110]

Kube's own attitude toward the growing political role of the BNS was not unambiguous. In this case too, a distinction should be drawn between his public expressions and those intended for "internal use." Externally, he depicted the measures of the summer of 1942 as "recognition of the population's willing cooperation" and the activity of *Mužy Daveru* as "the service to its own people and to new Europe and Adolph Hitler," while in his official letters and speeches before German officials he expresses somewhat different views.[111] In his letter to Rosenberg, written in June 1943, Kube tried to downplay the importance of the "Confidence Council" (*Rada* or *Kamitet Daveru*), the advisory body created in June 1943, after dismissing Yermačenka from his post.[112] He depicted this institution as having "the task to assemble only upon my order and then inform my main department and department chiefs on all current questions. Furthermore, the German civil administration uses the confidence committee as a mouthpiece for necessary propaganda. Administratively, the confidence committee is merely a tool of the *Generalkommissar.*"[113] In his much-quoted speech before the *Gebietskommissare*, main departments (*Hauptabteilungen*), and department (*Abteilungen*) heads, delivered in April 1943, he stated: "I think it is wrong to have only one Byelorussian organization; instead we should have the possibility to play them one against the other according to the old tenet."[114]

The nationalists' ambition to create the basis for a future Byelorussian state came to an abrupt end at the beginning of 1943. The Reich's Main Security Office (RSHA) decided to stop playing games with Byelorussian statehood. A special RSHA emissary was dispatched to Minsk; he was supposed to investigate the accusation of "high treason" which was being brought against the BNS leader. Yermačenka, together with a number of other leaders of Samapomač, was placed under arrest, where he reportedly underwent torture.[115] Although the charge could not be proven, since the extension of Self-Aid authority was actually sanctioned by Kube himself, Yermačenka was still accused of financial machinations and was compelled to leave Minsk and return to Prague where he was forbidden from engaging in political activities. The former Polish Sejm deputy and former

Baranaviči *Bürgermeister*, Yury Sabaleŭski, was appointed as his successor. Before his departure, Yermačenka called a meeting of area BNS leaders, during which he announced that henceforth the activities of the Samapomač would be limited solely to healthcare and assistance to the needy.[116] In addition, the designation "popular" was excluded from the official name of the organization and it became the "Byelorussian Self-Aid Organization" (Belaruskaja Samapomach, BS).[117] Unofficially, the old abbreviation, BNS was also used (see Astroŭski's report at the Second All-Byelorussian Congress, quoted below).

Kube, who was not interested in too large an extension of BNS political influence, nevertheless saw in the SS assault on the BNS leader a threat to his own position: only this supposition makes sense of the "moral and spiritual"[118] support that Kube offered Yermačenka as well as his expression of thanks—extended also on Rosenberg's behalf—prior to Yermačenka's departure. Turonak points out quite rightly that this was supposed to hint that the repression against the BNS was solely a matter for the SS apparatus and was part of the power struggle between the civil administration and Himmler's empire.[119]

Summing up the description of the BNS activities and the German approach to it, it is evident that this attitude was more than ambiguous. The German authorities were certainly interested in the existence of an organization that would free them from the need to care about the hungry and the homeless and would thus improve the image of the Germans, which deteriorated significantly as the occupation progressed. Yet, the Germans also wanted to keep this organization within the framework of charitable activities, and they were sharply opposed to any sign of political ambitions. The tragedy of the Byelorussian Self-Aid Organization lay in the fact that it found itself at the center of power struggles between the civil administration and the security bodies. At first, the organization profited from these tussles, but ultimately, this precarious situation spelled doom for the organization in general and for its leaders' dreams of statehood in particular.

The Union of Byelorussian Youth (SBM)

Perhaps the most striking example of the German's manipulative and hypocritical attitude toward local collaboration is the Union of Byelorussian Youth or Sayuz Belaruskaj Moladzi, SBM for short in Byelorussian. Kube acknowledged the creation of this organization on 22 June 1943, in the Minsk State Theater, during the festivities dedicated to the second anniversary of the establishment of Nazi rule in Byelorussia (portrayed officially as the "liberation from the Bolshevism"). A statute issued at the same time described the aims and the tasks of the organization as well as its structure. The declared aim of the SBM was "to raise the youth to be idealistic, steadfast and consistent architects of the new Byelorussia (*Weißruthenien*) and to prepare these youths for their future tasks within the nation."[120] It also stated explicitly that the first mission of the new organization was to "free Byelorussian youths from hostile influences (Polish, Russian, Bolshevist and Jewish), renew their morals and raise them in the spirit of the new Byelorussia (*Weißruthenien*), under the strong leadership of the national-socialist Germany."[121]

The leading role in building this new organization was played by the youth department of the *GK Weißruthenien*, headed by Hitlerjugend's Bannführer Schultz; consequently, it is little wonder that the structural design of the Union of Byelorussian Youth was a near copy of the Hitlerjugend (HJ) in Germany. Its leadership was based on the *Führerprinzip*. At the head of the SBM stood the chief executive (*der Chef des Führungsstab*). The executive staff itself consisted of six departments: organization; propaganda, press, training and culture; social work and health care; physical fitness (*körperliche Ertüchtigung*); administration; and the task force Germany (*Einsatzgruppe "Deutschland"*).

Mikhas' Han'ko was appointed chief executive. Born in 1918 in the village Kaledzina, Maladečna rayon, Han'ko studied medicine at Vilnius University. At the outbreak of the German—Soviet War, he was recruited by the Soviet Army and was subsequently taken prisoner by the Germans. He was liberated at the personal request of Fabian Akinčyc, indicating that his political views coincided with—or at least were close to—those of the Byelorussian National Socialists. After completing the propagandist training courses at the German Wustrow, Han'ko served in the department of the press and censorship in GKW.

Like its German prototype, the SBM was divided into sections for boys and girls. The latter was headed by the former physician of the Minsk Isolation Hospital, Nadzeja (Nadezhda) Abramava. There was also a division into age groups: 10–14; 15–18 and 19–20 year olds.[122]

All Byelorussian boys and girls between the ages of 10 and 20 were accepted as members. From the data available, it is difficult to discern the organization's policy toward the various ethnic groups, such as Poles or Russians, but the information is clear as regards the Jews, who were excluded a priori. Moreover, according to the statute cited above, in some cases a certificate of ethnic origin would be demanded from a candidate before acceptance into the Union.[123]

The SBM was divided into *Akruhi* (*Gebiete*, circuits), *Pavety* (*Kreise*, districts), *Hramady* (parties for boys) and *Hurtki* (*Züge*, companies for girls), and finally into *Družiny* (*Kameradschaften*, comradeships). The chief executive, the department heads, and the heads of the SBM branches, called *Akruhovye kiraŭniki moladzi* (circuit youth leaders) in Byelorussian, were appointed directly by the *Generalkommissar für Weißruthenien*, while leaders at the lower levels were appointed by the chief executive, with the approval of the German *Gebietskommissare*. The latter were also supposed to control the activities of the circuit youth leaders. The executive staff itself was directly subordinate to the *Generalkommissar,* and all of its activities were supervised by the youth department of the *Generalkommissariat.*

To create the impression that the SBM was a truly Byelorussian national organization, it was allowed to have its own anthem, *Belarus' peradusim,* ("Byelorussia is above all") and its own emblem, a rhombus with the Byelorussian national white–red–white background, crossed sword and spade and double cross, termed the *Jarilo cross,* and the inscription SBM.[124] According to postwar testimony given by the younger brother of Han'ko, the SBM's chief executive, SBM members wore the green, *Ostarbeiter* uniforms.[125]

Researchers dealing with the SBM usually tend to overlook a very important aspect of this organization, namely, its division into two parts: the task force Byelorussia (*Einsatzgruppe "Weißruthenien"*); and the task force Germany (*Einsatzgruppe "Deutschland"*). The former included SBM members in Byelorussia itself, while the latter included "all Byelorussian boys and girls working in Germany as SBM members."[126] *Einsatzgruppe "Deutschland"* was supposed to help recruit young Byelorussians of working age to labor in Germany, and from the German perspective, this group was of greater importance than the *Einsatzgruppe "Weißruthenien."* This was stated clearly in the statute: "The Union of Byelorussian Youth sees the inclusion of Byelorussian boys and girls in the task force Germany as one of its chief duties. Fulfillment of this duty is equivalent to performing an active service for the war against Bolshevism."[127]

In their internal correspondence, the Germans were never surreptitious about their expectations of any of the youth organizations, either in the *Ostraum* in general or in Byelorussia in particular. In April 1943, i.e., two months before the SBM's actual establishment, Rosenberg's Eastern Ministry issued a paper dedicated to the prospective Union of Byelorussian Youth. In it, the OMi officials outlined three main purposes for youth-group work (*Jugendarbeit*) in Byelorussia: "The first aim ... should be to bring the youth to work ... The second is to overcome, as far as necessary, their indifference, which harbors not only the danger of passivity, but also that of a potentially explosive and thus very dangerous force; therefore, the aim is to activate the youth ... to activate it against Moscow ... The third mission is to get the youth off the streets (*Die Jugend muß von der Straße*)."[128] This document plainly demonstrates that what the Germans had in mind in announcing the Byelorussian youth organization was not to encourage an independent national youth body, but rather to create a reservoir for the workforce, as well as an anti-partisan force. As the Nazi occupation progressed, the Byelorussian youth became a pawn in the war between the German occupiers and the partisans, a war in which each side spared no effort to attract the youngsters to its side.

The SBM leadership itself strove to create the impression that the Union was genuinely a national and mass organization. Here, too, it is very difficult to establish the exact membership numbers. The only existing, reliable data are contained in the SBM's own documents, but not many of them survived the war; furthermore, the data must be assessed with a great degree of caution. Bernhard Chiari, quoting the Byelorussian historian Kavalenya, maintains that in June 1944 there were 4,127 boys and 3,974 girls in the SBM in *GK Weißruthenien* and 493 boys and 561 girls belonging to it in the Rear Area of the Army Group "Center".[129] Such a disparity between the two areas can be explained in part by a smaller percentage of the Byelorussian population in the eastern regions of Byelorussia, where Russians constituted a significant section of the population. Veronika Katkovič-Klentak, former head of the Minsk SBM organization, provided additional data. According to her report, the organization numbered no fewer than 45,000 members in the *Generalkommissariat* alone at the end of June 1944, but this number seems unlikely.[130] It is also difficult to obtain an exact picture of membership by age. In the Baranaviči district, for example, at the beginning of 1944, the majority of members belonged to the 10–14 and 15–17 age groups: 831 girls and 820 boys out of a total of 2,065 members, compared to a total of 414 boys and girls between the ages 18 and 20.[131] It is not clear, however, if a similar breakdown applied to the rest of occupied Byelorussia.

After the war, activists of the Union of Byelorussian Youth who found themselves in the West tried to present their organization as having had a significant degree of independence and as having pursued aims differing from those of the occupying regime, without shrinking from direct confrontation with it when necessary. Katkovič-Klentak expresses this in her recently published memoirs:

> The Germans, of course, had their own aim—the use of the youth—while our leadership was striving for a different goal. We were trying to arouse a national consciousness, patriotic feelings of responsibility for our homeland and an awareness of the need to struggle for her liberation. Due to these differences, a universal conflict existed between our leadership and the German representation, which complicated the work and created dangerous situations, including the arrests of officials of the executive staff and threats to dismiss the chief executive ... Despite all of the difficulties of the war and the dangers posed by the Bolshevist underground as well as from the chief occupiers, the Germans, the youth unexpectedly yet enthusiastically turned to the SBM.[132]

It is indeed undeniable that the SBM constituted a certain attraction for the young Byelorussians. Membership in the organization gave the youngsters a sense of social security, a feeling of involvement in a recognized organization, at a time when society in general was disintegrating at a rapid pace. The uniforms, too, provided no small attraction for the young boys. Both Bernhard Chiari and Lyavon Yurevič remarked quite rightly that in its organization and its style the SBM resembled not only the Hitlerjugend, but also the Soviet pioneer organization.[133] Thus, for many young Byelorussians, entering the Union did not represent a step into the unknown but rather something familiar, if not in content then at least in form.

Perhaps a special attraction for the young people was the possibility of a journey to Germany. These "journeys," in which the most prominent collaborators such as SBM activists and *Bürgermeistern* took part, were viewed from the German side as an almost a literal extension of Hitler's own idea that "once a year we will lead the group of Kyrgyzes through capital of the Reich, in order that they might fathom the might and greatness of its architectural monuments."[134] Undoubtedly, these trips were primarily a propagandistic affair: they received quite broad coverage in the German and local press and were used to mark various occasions, not least of these the recruitment of Byelorussians for work in Germany. During their stay there, the participants visited, inter alia, industrial and agricultural plants, where they would encounter "convincing proof" of the advantages of the German economic methods. The newspaper *Brüsseler Zeitung*, which dedicated an article to describing one such trip in the middle of 1942, noted that "the participants of the trip to Germany were most impressed by the management of the supply economy as well as by the measures for increasing productivity (*Leistungssteigerung*)."[135]

However, one should keep in mind that the progress of the occupation proved to many within the local population that German rule could scarcely provide a suitable alternative to the Soviet regime. Disappointment began to grow and readiness to collaborate was dwindling, even among those who initially had been prepared to cooperate in the sincere belief that the new authorities had come to liberate the country from Soviet rule and its "evildoings." The growth of the partisan movement, the loss of German control over significant parts of Byelorussia, and the Third Reich's military failures from the end of 1942 did nothing to further the local population's interest in collaborating with the Germans. In this context, the trips to Germany by prominent collaborators had the precise purpose of strengthening that interest and promoting the notion that only cooperation with Nazi Germany would secure the future of the Byelorussian people. The press in the occupied areas spared no effort in vividly describing the delight of the travelers and their eagerness to work with the German occupation authorities. On 19 January 1943 the *Deutsche Zeitung im Ostland* quoted the conclusions of one such participant, the *Kreisälteste* from the small town K. in the Minsk area. The conclusions were typical:

> After my German trip, I asked myself if and in what form the Byelorussian people would participate in the building of a new order in Europe. The Byelorussian nation, which in all spheres of life was terribly devastated by the Soviets, no longer has any possibility of building its future on its own: it has too little force for this. To achieve renewal, the first step should be to revive those

forces that can lead the nation. Now the Byelorussian people should be grateful to the Germans for their liberation from the Bolshevist yoke ... Our nation will be able to exist with dignity only when it pays attention to three points, which seem to me, from my experiences and observations, especially important: gratitude to the people that enlisted our Byelorussian people among the liberated European nations...; recognition that what has been a great source of strength for the German people, namely, National-Socialism, will be good for us, the Byelorussians, too; and working in the closest possible cooperation with the National-Socialists.[136]

Similar "conclusions" were drawn also by the members of the girls' section of the SBM, who traveled to Germany in the middle of 1943: "There is no future for the Byelorussian people, except through cooperation with Germany."[137] The timing of both of these expressions is also significant: they were produced in 1943, after the Battle of Stalingrad, and thus after the image of Germany as an invincible European superpower had declined considerably. This was a period when the Germans were striving harder than ever before to persuade the populations in the occupied countries that it was still worthwhile to stake their fortunes on the Third Reich, and—following the Soviet victories—a time when they could frighten these populations with the possibility of the "Soviet threat" replacing Nazi rule.

The illusion of the SBM as a truly Byelorussian organization was widespread not only among the Union's leaders; it also found its way into the studies of the historians dealing with the occupation in Byelorussia. Thus, Yerzy Turonak states, "[a]s a matter of fact, the SBM became the first and for the time being the only civil forum recognized in Berlin, which was able to carry out broad educational work according to the national spirit, practically unhindered by the slogans of the New Europe."[138] Yet, the Union of Byelorussian Youth did not act in a vacuum, but resulted from the conditions of the occupation. Berlin's "recognition" was not, of course, the result of any kind of benevolence. The last thing that either Rosenberg in Berlin or Kube in Minsk wanted was to create a reservoir for future Byelorussian leaders. Even if the organization did develop the possibility of carrying out "educational work according to the national spirit," as Turonak says–albeit with a strong admixture of anti-Semitism and anti-Polonism–and even though it was able to issue its own publications (monthly *Zhyve Belarus'*, "Long Live Byelorussia"; *Vuchebny Listok*, "Educational Leaflet"; and

Dzyonnik Zahadaǔ, "The Diary of Orders"), the limited scope of its activities were still defined by the Germans alone. True to their fashion, they did not spare any effort in instrumentalizing the SBM as far as possible for their own needs and goals. Although the German officials, as well as the SBM leaders, had presented the Union as "an independent organization," granted by the "Fuehrer as a gift to the Byelorussian people," a different tune could be heard in private circles, intended only for "internal use."[139] For example, the German leader of the *Einsatzgruppe "Weißruthenien,"* which oversaw the activities of Byelorussian children in Byelorussia, thought that from the German point of view "the most dangerous age is between 17 and 21. This age is undoubtedly 99% infected [by Bolshevist ideas–L. R.] and should be crossed off the list of the living."[140] Although such genocidal ideas may not have been shared by all Nazi officials, there can be no doubt that the general consensus was that the youth in Byelorussia should be put to the service of German military interests. Even Kube, contrary to Turonak's portrayal of him as surrogate patron saint of the Byelorussian youth movement in occupied Byelorussia, did not see in it anything more than a first step toward the creation of a Byelorussian "nation" that would serve as a wall against "Moscow and the eastern steppe."[141]

Strangely enough, most researchers who consider the activities of the Union of Byelorussian Youth and the youth policies of the German occupation authorities at large rarely mention that part of the SBM called "the task group" (*Einsatzgruppe*) or "work group" (*Arbeitsgruppe*) *Deutschland.* Surely the very existence of such a division does not suit the description of the SBM as an independent, national body, since the sole purpose of "task group Germany" was to supply the German war economy with young, able-bodied workers. It is not surprising, therefore, that this group's activity was given high priority by the German authorities themselves. In the same vein, the existence of the *Einsatzgruppe "Deutschland"* was—and still is—ignored by those researchers who see the collaborationists as no more than German accomplices, based on the notion that, at least officially, recruitment to work in Germany was supposed to proceed on a voluntary basis.

The *Einsatzgruppe "Deutschland"* was created simultaneously with the rest of the SBM and was sanctioned directly by the plenipotentiary for the work assignment, Fritz Sauckel. The "Additional Regulations for the organization of Union of

Byelorussian Youth" stated quite unambiguously that the main
task of the German task group was "to bring Byelorussian boys
and girls of ages 14–20 to work in Germany."[142] According to
these Regulations, the plan was to send a total of 10,000 girls
and 20,000 boys to work in the Reich, to Gau Thuringia and
Magdeburg. The boys were supposed to labor in the armament
industry, while the girls were to work in the clothing industry,
agriculture and "domestic economy."[143] Although the recruitment was to proceed on a voluntary basis, it is indeed very difficult to believe that all 30,000 youngsters could be recruited
voluntarily, especially if it is remembered that this was in 1943,
when, as was shown earlier, the readiness to cooperate with the
German authorities had diminished significantly and by which
time the recruitment for work in Germany in general took the
form of manhunts. Indeed, the Regulations document specifically allows for "recruitment of every kind" (*Werbung jeder Art*).
Given the context, it is more than likely that coercion was also
used. The Regulations envisaged a very broad recruitment campaign that included, apart from the SBM's functionaries, the
special staffs created by the *Generalkommissariat für
Weißruthenien*. All recruits were delivered to the special assembly camp (*Sammelpunkt*) in Slonim, where they could get a fore-
taste of what was expected in Germany. In Germany, too, the
employment proceeded on the basis of "closed camp societies"
(*geschlossenen Lagergemeinschaften*).[144] Although the propaganda office of the *GK Weißruthenien* would from time to time
publish leaflets with "original postcards" sent from the Reich
describing satisfaction with conditions in Germany, the "light
work" and the regular "evening dances," there is no reason to
assume that the youth recruited through the *Einsatzgruppe
"Deutschland"* fared any better than the rest of the *Ostarbeitern*
in the Reich.[145]

   Although the SBM was similar to the Hitlerjugend in its
structure, Germans themselves reacted very strongly to any
attempt to equate the two organizations. Thus Kube's successor
as *Generalkommissar für Weißruthenien*, Curt von Gottberg,
pointed out that the SBM "should avoid equating their tasks
and educational methods with those of the HJ."[146] One of the
German officials "elegantly" explained the reason for such opposition: the framework achieved by National Socialism following
a prolonged struggle of many years should not be applied freely
to Byelorussian youth.[147] Put more bluntly, it was unthinkable

to allow *Untermenschen* the same organizational structures as those that existed for the *Herrenvolk*.

The German authorities undoubtedly saw in the Union of Byelorussian Youth a very useful propaganda tool, as evidenced by the fact that the SBM's monthly publication, *Zhyve Belarus*, was controlled at the highest level. In other words, it was the Reich's Ministry for the Occupied Eastern Territories that decided on the prices, format, circulation, and of course, content of this periodical. Many publications were also well illustrated.[148] The messages conveyed in them were very similar to those produced after the organized trips to Germany, as mentioned above, and they more or less mirrored the general tendencies of the Nazi propaganda. Even the leader of the SBM, Mikhas' Han'ko, expressed his opinion on the links between the Byelorussian youth and the German fate. In January 1944, when the Germans were facing severe military difficulties, he wrote, "This war will bring both us and the German people either to a complete triumph over all enemies or ... to national death."[149] In October 1944, when a significant part of Byelorussia was already liberated from the Germans, the same Han'ko still called on the Byelorussian youth: "Help the German youth, who today is either guarding or working in factories that produce grenades, cartridges, tanks and planes, which are then deployed at the front. It is a great and honorable task. The more weapons and ammunition we have, the sooner Bolshevism will be destroyed (sic!). Whoever helps guard or works in the factories is helping destroy Bolshevism and saving his homeland from a deadly danger."[150]

Though a separate chapter in this volume deals with local collaboration in the Holocaust, it should be noted that anti-Semitism played an important part in the Union's propaganda. As mentioned above, Jews were excluded a priori from membership of the SBM. The leadership of the SBM, especially the organization's chief executive, Mikhas' Han'ko, who signed all his anti-Jewish articles with the nickname Ahanyok (small fire), persistently conveyed the message that Jews were not wanted in Byelorussia. As early as October 1941, he announced quite unambiguously, "In the land of Belarus, we, the Byelorussians, are the masters; the Jews are not welcome here."[151] In another article, he wrote that "a Jew [the author uses the pejorative term *zhid*–L. R.] was, is and will be a Jew; never will he change himself and turn into a better human being, never will he be a friend of the Byelorussian."[152] The numerous leaflets distrib-

uted by the SBM in large numbers called on the youth to participate in the anti-partisan struggle, while the partisans were usually depicted as either Jews or Jewish tools. The leaflet "To the
Byelorussian Boys and Girls," issued by the leading staff of the
Union of Byelorussian Youth, summoned the young people to
join the SBM and participate in defending Byelorussia "from
Jews, Bolshevists, and kolkhozes." The leaflet used particularly
violent anti-Semitic tones. The authors asked, among other
things, who were the true defenders of Byelorussia: "you, filthy
Jewish mugs, or we, the peasants' sons who work day and night
for liberation and the national, cultural and economic flourishing of our homeland?"[153]

One of the most striking examples of the manipulative attitude of the German authorities toward the youth organization
and youth work in general was the organization of SBM training
camps: Florianov (for girls), Al'bertin (for boys), and Drozdy
(today part of Minsk, defined officially as a "girls' agricultural
school"). The camps were intended chiefly for the district SBM
heads. Very little is known today about their exact educational
program. According to the postwar testimony of Valer Navicki,
who as local head of the SBM participated in the courses in
Al'bertin, the students learned chiefly "to walk, march and sing
the songs."[154] But apart from military drilling, a significant part
of the education in all of these camps was also to present pure
Nazi propaganda. Lectures on Hitler and other Nazi leaders, as
well as on the German Army, held a prominent place in their
educational program.[155] As was the case with the organized trips
to Germany, here too the message was clear: only reliance upon
the Third Reich could guarantee Byelorussia's national existence. The participants in the camp courses also heard lectures
on the history and culture of Byelorussia, but again, the bias
was more than obvious. The period of the short-lived Byelorussian People's Republic was one of the central themes in the
Byelorussian history lectures; however, this was only to show
that the Germans were traditionally benevolent toward the
national Byelorussian idea.[156]

According to Christian Gerlach, the camp in Al'bertin had an
additional role that was not widely known. In September 1943,
the orphanage, directed by the Standartenführer SS, Guntram
Pflaum, was transferred to Al'bertin from Bobrujsk. This
orphanage, established in 1942, was intended for children of
German origin and for Soviet children who, from the racial point
of view, were deemed suitable for Germanization. Not all of the

children, ages three to twelve, were orphans. In fact, this home served as a convenient front for Himmler's project, in which racially suitable children from the "eastern space" were selected and prepared for adoption in Germany. During the Bobrujsk period, the home was controlled directly by the HSSPF of Central Russia (*Rußland-Mitte*).[157] As Gerlach notes, the transfer of the orphanage from Bobrujsk to Al'bertin might indicate the integration and involvement of the SBM in the Germanization projects.[158] In other words, it is likely that the SBM also served Nazi aims that were in stark contrast to the officially proclaimed goals of educating the Byelorussian youth in a national spirit.

An extreme example of German attempts to exploit the youth movement in Byelorussia can be found in Drozdy camp, the "girls' agricultural school". Although this camp was defined officially as a girls' agricultural school, it was under the direct supervision of the SS and, as such, was part of the large-scale SS economic activities in the *Ostraum*. Assembled from all over the *GK Weißruthenien*, the girls at the camp participated in three-month courses, with the lion's share being agricultural work, whereas the training aimed at acquainting the students with the functioning of the SBM structures took place only on Saturdays. As Bernhard Chiari remarked, this SS establishment "served more as a means to increase agricultural production than as a school for SBM leaders."[159] The German authorities also made sure that any political education participants received during their training would not exceed the desired limits. In August 1943, Kube demanded that the *Gebietskommissare* should make clear to the girls assembled in Drozdy "the difference between political activity and their tasks in agriculture."[160]

At the very end of the occupation, the SBM was still being exploited for the recruitment of Byelorussian boys and girls. Above all, they were needed for work in armament plants. According to Dallin, about 10,000 boys and girls between the ages of fourteen and eighteen went to work in Germany, while Turonak claims that at the end of 1943, only the Junkers plant in Dessau received male youth workers aged fifteen to twenty, and these numbered no more than one thousand.[161] Later, the Byelorussian youth were also enlisted as anti-aircraft and Luftwaffe assistants, as well as so-called "SS pupils" (*SS-Zöglinge*). The recruitment for these purposes began following Himmler's direct orders issued at the end of April 1944.[162] Siegfried Nickel, the *Hauptbannführer* of the Hitlerjugend, was appointed head of the recruitment operation. The recruiting groups, termed *Krieg-*

seinsatzkommandos, operated not only in Byelorussia, but also
in the Baltic area and in the Ukraine. Recruitment proceeded on
a voluntary basis, and it is worth noting that the majority of
those enlisted were under military age (recruitment of Flak-
assistants and SS-pupils consisted primarily of boys between the
ages of fifteen and sixteen).[163] The recruitment of Byelorussian
girls as Luftwaffe assistants began on 15 July 1944, in line with
the agreement reached between the *Ostministerium* and the
Supreme Command of the Luftwaffe (OKL). According to this
agreement, the plan was to recruit throughout the whole Eastern space up to 25,000 "female members of tribes (*Volksstämme*)
(sic!) living there."[164] Curiously, this exaggerated plan to recruit
such huge numbers came at a time when almost half of
Byelorussian territory had already been liberated by the Soviet
army. The young women recruited were supposed to serve in
Flak-Artillery units, searchlight and air-barrier (*Luftsperr*) batteries, the military air force (general military service), and medical and logistics divisions.[165]

The recruitment campaign was supported by massive propaganda. The newspapers and the representatives of the Luftwaffe
who visited the schools sent out messages like the following:
"When Europe wins, the European youth of today will reap the
harvests of this victory, and future generations will be sure that
they will not need to fight ever again for their existence."[166] It is
difficult to establish the scope of the response to all of these calls.
According to Turonak, who quotes various sources, in June 1944,
some 5,000 youngsters volunteered for the Luftwaffe auxiliary service, 2,000 of whom came from the Hlybokaje area.[167] However, all
of these volunteers were SBM members and it is likely that many
of them simply chose to escape to Germany in the face of the great
Soviet offensive, knowing very well the fate that awaited them in
the Soviet Union as members of a pro-Nazi organization. At the
same time, it cannot be denied that the very possibility of serving
with the air force fascinated the young boys. After all, what young
boy does not dream of becoming a pilot? The Luftwaffe representatives who came to the schools, together with SBM members,
promised the schoolchildren that "some of you will be pilots; others will become navigators or flight engineers."[168]

In the course of this recruitment campaign, the old problem
of the German authorities' inability to bridge the gap between
practical necessity and racial dogmas again came to the fore. In
March 1944, the executive staff for politics (*Führungsstab Politik*) at OMi, headed by Himmler's man, the Obergruppenführer

SS Gottlob Berger, prohibited the use of the term "volunteers" (*Freiwillige*) regarding the SS and Flak auxiliaries recruited in the East, since this term was reserved exclusively for the members of the "Germanic" peoples.[169] Moreover, in the same month, when the Third Reich was little more than one year away from its collapse, Nazi functionaries still tried hard to impose strict criteria for the selection of recruits to the SS and Flak auxiliary service. According to the letter issued by the same staff, the candidates should be no shorter than 1.70 m, an unusual demand when dealing with boys aged fifteen or sixteen.[170] The recruitment, together with the ensuing *Heuaktion*, reveals once again the concurrence between the various German bodies. Very strong opposition to recruitment to the SS and Flak auxiliary service came from the side of Sauckel and his labor recruiting offices.[171] As Dallin pointed out, Sauckel's men were less than happy that at the last moment the potential workforce was slipping through their fingers. As it turned out, nobody paid attention to these protestations, despite the fact that at the time the Third Reich was literally fighting for its survival.

To summarize, it can be said that the very creation and encouragement—only to a certain extent—of the Union of Byelorussian Youth was by no means an expression of German sympathy for the Byelorussian national idea. From the outset, the Nazis primarily saw it as a propaganda tool as well as the means to establish better control over Byelorussian youth, by shielding them from Soviet propaganda and exploiting them for their own needs. For Curt von Gottberg, Kube's successor as the *Generalkommissar für Weißruthenien*, the Union was "the best means to approach the people."[172] Although publicly Germans spared no effort in expressing their sympathies toward SBM activities, during the entire period of the union's existence they did not hesitate to manipulate the organization. The creation of the *Einsatzgruppe "Deutschland"* clearly demonstrates that the Germans had a very precise idea of what they expected to gain from the SBM. In SBM training camps, especially in Drozdy, the education of a "new Byelorussian elite" was of secondary importance, while the greater part of the time was dedicated to physical work. In the case of the training camp at Al'bertin, the Germans did not shy away from subjecting the Byelorussian youngsters to their most dreadful project, namely, that of Germanization. In fact, even when the German authorities could have benefited from a more flexible approach in handling the SBM recruits, they still continued to cling to their racial dogmas and the *Herrenvolk* mentality. In short, the SBM serves as one of the best examples of the Nazi view of local collaboration in the occupied Soviet territories.

The Byelorussian Central Council

The creation of the Byelorussian Central Council, or Belaruskaja Central'nja Rada (BCR) in Byelorussian, can be seen as a high point in the development of political collaboration in Byelorussia. In retrospect, after World War II, the establishment and existence of this body was strongly mythologized, chiefly by Byelorussian émigrés. In the introduction to the collection of documents of the All-Byelorussian Second Congress (see below) issued in 1954, the BCR was described as the "national Byelorussian governing body of the country."[173] But can it indeed be considered "a government," or even a "puppet government," as Bernhard Chiari put it?[174]

The creation of the BCR was certainly not the result of some natural development, but rather of harsh necessity. The official acknowledgement of the creation of the Byelorussian Central Council came on 21 December 1943. At that time, the Soviet counter-offensive that began after the battle of Kursk was in full swing. At approximately the same time, the *Reichskommissariat Ukraine* ceased to exist. In Byelorussia, by mid-1943, the Soviet forces had liberated Gomel, Vitebsk, Kalinkoviči, and Mozyr. Whole areas of the country were proclaimed "partisan zones," free of German presence. Under these conditions, the acting *Generalkommissar für Weißruthenien*, Curt von Gottberg, who had succeeded Kube, called a meeting at which the BCR was officially proclaimed.[175]

Gottberg was an unlikely candidate to promote Byelorussian nationalism.[176] As a "Himmler man," he adhered to harsh occupation policies and believed in quelling resistance with iron and blood. In one of his operational orders, issued in December 1942, he maintained that "every bandit, Jew, and Gypsy should be seen as an enemy."[177] As noted, he felt that Byelorussian national ideas were the invention of émigrés and armchair, or desk, politicians.[178] One must keep in mind, however, that apart from being head of civil administration in occupied Byelorussia, he was also SSPF *Weißruthenien* and acting *HSSPF Rußland-Mitte,* after von dem Bach-Zelewski was appointed as the plenipotentiary for Anti-Partisan Warfare. This mean that it is

Gottberg who should be "credited" with the fact that Byelorussia was the first—and only—occupied country where the SS succeeded de facto in getting its hands on the reigns of government.

Gottberg's appointment as Kube's successor did not proceed smoothly. He was seen as a provisional figure appointed to restore calm in the country.[179] Rosenberg, who was less than happy about strengthening Himmler's positions, wanted Arno Schickendanz, one of his closest collaborators, to succeed Kube. Schickendanz was a Baltic German, a virulent anti-Semite, and the man previously designated to take over the never-created *Reichskommissariat Kaukasus*. Rosenberg even turned to Hitler personally to promote Schickendanz's candidature.[180] Hitler was also reluctant about Gottberg's candidature; not wanting to strengthen either of his potentates at the other's expense, he ultimately yielded to the intrigues of Gottlob Berger, the head of the political department in *Ostministerium* and Himmler's man.[181] He approved of Gottberg for this position, at least "until the state of hostilities in *Generalkommissariat [für Weißruthenien*–L. R.] would pass."[182] Thus, until the end of the occupation, formally at least, Gottberg's appointment was merely as "acting" *Generalkommissar*.

In his new position, Gottberg wanted two things: to be an absolute master in his domain and, as High SS and police leader, to maintain a state of tranquility in the area, using any means necessary. Although Soviet forces were already knocking at the door of *GK Weißruthenien*, Gottberg still harbored great ambitions of power. In April 1944, the *GK Weißruthenien* was excluded by Hitler's direct order from the *Reichskommissariat Ostland* and was instead subjected directly to the OMi.[183] A couple of months earlier, in February, Hitler granted Gottberg's request to place under his authority any areas that remained from the *Reichskommissariat Ukraine*, namely, the Brest, Pinsk, and Kobrin areas, and likewise, granted him civil authority over any military administration areas still held in German hands.[184] On 21 June 1944 merely a couple of days before the end of German occupation in Byelorussia, Gottberg became the *HSSPF Rußland-Mitte und Weißruthenien*.

But a more urgent task from Gottberg's point of view was to cope with the ever-increasing partisan movement. Since he could not depend on the German troops alone to both contain the Soviet offensive and suppress the partisans, Gottberg and the occupation authorities were compelled to rely heavily on local collaboration. Gottberg's flirting with Byelorussian nationalism must therefore be seen in light of these developments. In his speech dedicated to the creation of the BCR in December 1943, Gottberg made it clear that the chief purpose of the newly created body was to mobilize the local forces in the anti-partisan struggle.[185] Although in his appeal to Byelorussians made on 10 January, the newly appointed president of the Byelorussian Central Council, Radaslaŭ Astroŭski, spoke of the BCR as the "officially recognized, legitimate government of the Byelorussian nation," in reality, the BCR's independence was curtailed, as it pertained only to issues in the social, cultural, and educational spheres.[186] In all other areas, it was merely an advisory body to the German civil administration.[187] Gottberg preferred to see in the BCR no more than an "auxiliary administration" (*Hilfsverwaltung*).[188] An analysis of German internal correspondence reveals that German authorities saw in the BCR a rather provisional, ad hoc body and that there was uncertainty about its exact functions and structure. In March 1943 Gottberg expressed the following opinion:

> Today, for obvious reasons, nothing can be said yet about the final position of the Central Council, particularly whether it will remain an advisory (*Beratungsorgan*) and auxiliary organ (*Hilfsorgan*) or if it will develop to become a center for local administration: we must wait and see its performance (*Bewährung*) as well as the future formulation of its political tasks (*Zielsetzung*). I gave the Central Council certain hopes that in the case of good performance, it would acquire an independent position.[189]

Even the post of president of the BCR was seen as something provisional, as demonstrated in the note attached to Gottberg's letter to Rosenberg describing the structure of the newly created organization. Gottberg's note states that "the Central Council is headed *for the time being* (*zunächst*) by the president."[190]

It is possible that some historians, misled by the structure of the BCR, concluded that this organization functioned as a kind of a "puppet government." It consisted of a personal chancellery for the president; a general BCR chancellery with economic and financial sections; personnel and youth departments; an education department with sections for elementary, public, secondary and vocational schools, scientific societies, pre-school, and adult education as well as a methodology section; a cultural department with sections for culture and literature, professional art, music, and a local history and museums section; and a social department with sections for orphanages and homes for the disabled, social security and care. It also included a BNS section; a propaganda department that oversaw the propaganda, press, and film sections; a trade unions department, with production and food sections; a supply department, with sections for mobilization, allocation and care; and a department for the Byelorussian Home Guard (more will be said about this body in the following chapters). In other words, the organization was designed to address any need, managing issues pertaining to administration and municipal economy, finance, law, agriculture and forestry, health care, cooperatives and trade, industry and crafts, and buildings and highways.[191] Such a multibranched structure could really create an illusion of a serious, authoritative organization. However, from the picture presented above, it can be seen that the BCR was anything but a government with well-defined ministries. Gottberg himself hurried to assure his superiors in Berlin that the Germans still remained the masters of the situation in occupied Byelorussia and that "the most important sovereign rights, such as the supreme rights of defense, police duties, finance and economy still remain directly in the hands of *Generalkommissar*."[192]

Not even the BCR statute, issued on 21 December 1943 simultaneously with the announcement of the organization's establishment, could conceal the fact that the Byelorussian Central Council was a dependent body, subordinated to the German authorities. The fourth paragraph of the statute stated explicitly that the "Byelorussian Central Council is headed by a president who is appointed and dismissed by the *Generalkommissar*, while the remaining members are appointed by the *Generalkommissar* based on the president's recommendation." The fifth paragraph states that "the BCR issues its executive and administrative orders with the *Generalkommissar*'s consent."[193] The Central Council itself was subject to the direct control of the *Generalkommissar*, while the local BCR functionaries were under the control of the *Gebietskommissare*.[194]

The appointment of Radaslaŭ Astroŭski to the presidency of the Central Council revealed once again the schizophrenic nature of the Nazi regime. While Astroŭski had lived for a long time outside Byelorussia and was not widely known to the broad Byelorussian public, he was an ardent nationalist and could hardly serve as a blind tool of the German authorities. Astroŭski was a very controversial figure indeed. Like Yermačenka before him, he was not a novice in politics. His political career began after the February Revolution in Russia, when he was appointed

representative of the Russian provisional government in the
Sluck area; for a time he also occupied the post of education
minister in the government of the short-lived BNR. Astroŭski
was not too popular among the Byelorussian émigrés, who could
not forgive him his alleged cooperation with the Communists in
the 1920s. In the period between the world wars he was not considered a significant figure, and on the eve of the German invasion of the Soviet Union he occupied a secondary post as head of
the Litzmannstadt (Lodz) branch of Byelorussian Representation. At the beginning of the Nazi occupation of Byelorussia he
was entrusted with organizing district "self-administrations" in
the areas of Minsk, Bryansk, Smolensk, and Mogiljov. During
this time he made contacts with various German bodies, most
noticeably those related to security; these contacts certainly
later assisted him in becoming the head of the BCR. Although
for a very long time he had worked closely with the Germans,
Astroŭski was not as outspoken a Germanophile as Yermačenka.
At the end of 1943, during the secret meeting of members of the
Baranaviči *uprava* (city administration), it was alleged that he
even criticized the German authorities and demanded the right
to follow an independent course. He urged his audiences "to
adamantly come forth to issue a memorandum claiming that the
leaders of our homeland, Byelorussia, should themselves be
Byelorussians. We've had enough of asking for German permission or bribing them with fat, vodka, and whores until we
Byelorussians cannot find our own truth. The memorandum
must bring to the forefront the question of transferring authority to Byelorussians everywhere and in all sectors, to the police
and to all Byelorussian institutions."[195] In accepting the post of
BCR president, Astroŭski knew quite well that the Germans
needed the Byelorussian nationalists no less—if not more—than
the Byelorussians needed them. According to the biographer,
Viktor Kalush, Astroŭski even presented certain conditions
before accepting the post of president. He demanded from Gottberg "that a Byelorussian Home Guard (BKA) be created and
supplied with arms; that Byelorussians not be sent to the western front; and that facilities be provided for the Second All-
Byelorussian Congress."[196] It is not quite clear whether these
demands were stated as preconditions, given that the decisions
regarding the BKA and the All-Byelorussian Congress were
implemented much later. Based on both primary and secondary
sources, it is, however, quite apparent that to describe the history of the BCR is to relate an incessant series of attempts by

the Central Council to reduce the degree of its dependency on the German civil administration, and of the latter to curb these attempts.

Gottberg's personal attitude toward the BCR revealed once again that until the very end the Germans failed to come to grips with the reality that surrounded them. Instead of liberating themselves from their dogmas in favor of more pragmatic actions, they clung to their prejudiced doctrines. For the German civil authorities and for some of Rosenberg's officials in the Eastern Ministry, even the limited responsibilities assigned to the BCR were considered a dangerous deviation. Gottberg, in his conversation with Kienzlen, the *Ostministerium*'s official, made it plain that regarding school affairs, he did not intend to provide the BCR with too much authority. Accordingly, "only purely administrative tasks in the school that were already being supervised by the supreme authority, meaning the German civil administration, could be transferred to the Central Council and district school inspectors; the school policies, however, should remain directly in our hands."[197] In the same conversation, Gottberg further elucidated that the German civil authorities were reserving the right to intervene in the BCR's responsibilities in the fields of social security and "self-aid."[198] In February 1944, the Germans also rejected the BCR's demand to award it jurisdiction over the local populace, owing to the fear that "this [shift] would give [the BCR] supreme powers beyond the scope originally intended for it."[199]

At the same time the BCR, despite a precise understanding of its circumstances, tried to create the impression that it followed an independent course. Thus, in February 1943, Kienzlen compiled a list of complaints against the activities of the Central Council, accusing it of the following infringements: ignoring the order to introduce Latin script in Byelorussian; willfully striving to appoint local school inspectors; rejecting the candidature of Dr. Krupka (former "man of confidence" for school affairs) to the post of chief clerk for school affairs in the BCR; and finally attempting to sidestep the required approval of the civil authorities regarding the selection of textbooks and curricula.[200] For Kienzlen, all of these BCR breaches were on the brink of subversion. Bernhard Chiari also refers to the discussions held on the opening of the music school in Minsk. When one of the BCR officials suggested that the issue required additional consultations with the *Generalkommissar*, fearing that the school would be an attraction for draft-dodging youths, Astroŭski reacted sharply, "Send the Germans to hell! We are opening the music school in Minsk! The *Generalkommissar* acknowledges this fact and gives his approval."[201]

As can be seen from the documents, the Germans knew very well about the BCR's attempts to flirt with independence, but their reaction was relatively mild, especially taking into account the fact that only a few years later, such independent actions initiated by the leader of Byelorussian Christian-Democrats, who later also became the leader of the nationalist "Byelorussian Front," the priest Hadleŭski, resulted in his execution.[202] This unusual lenience in the case of the BCR might be explained by the fact that the Soviet Army was nearing the gates of *GK Weißruthenien* and the partisan war was raging throughout the country; the Germans, therefore, needed a local body that would have at least some degree of authority in the country. In this instance, a less severe reaction on the part of the Germans enabled them to use this organization to mobilize the local population to join the anti-partisan struggle, which was very much in line with their original rationale for establishing such a body.

The Germans were aware that it was highly unlikely that the BCR would be able to introduce and implement successfully an independent policy. They possessed a very powerful tool, namely financial leverage. The Central Council did not possess its own budget but was dependent upon subsidies from the German civil administration, which, of course, tried to keep these to a minimum. When Astroŭski presented Gottberg with a fiscal report of BCR's activities in May 1944, showing expenses amounting to no less than 140,305,559 RM but with income totaling only 3,824,650 RM,[203] the *Ostministerium*'s administrative department was prompt to "correct" these data, "establishing" the total expenses of the Rada at 7,155,695 RM.[204] This evidence demonstrates that while undoubtedly courting local collaboration, the German authorities were willing to pay only the lowest possible price.

The Central Council developed a broad anti-partisan propaganda campaign, directed not only at potential recruits for the anti-partisan struggle but also at the partisans themselves, calling on them to return from the forests and participate in the "building of a new Byelorussia." Astroŭski and other BCR activists issued numerous appeals to the partisans, which contained, in addition to general slogans, real or fictitious information, whose veracity is very difficult to ascertain today, about the mass desertions among the partisan units. In his appeal "To

Russian Partisans" issued in March 1944, Astroŭski spoke of 4,000 partisan deserters in the Sluck area.[205] Astroŭski also appeared at many meetings organized throughout occupied Byelorussia, urging the partisans to lay down their weapons and join the newly established and officially recognized Byelorussian Home Guard (see below). At one such meeting in Sluck, also attended by the local *Gebietskommissar*, Carl,[206] Astroŭski allegedly said to the partisans, "If you can convince me that by your actions you will bring happiness to our people and freedom to our country, then I myself will join you to fight both Stalin and the Germans."[207] This story, however, seems apocryphal.

On 23 February 1944 Gottberg issued an order to begin recruitment for the Byelorussian Home Guard (Belaruskaja Krajova Abarona or BKA), which was to be an integral part of the anti-partisan force in Byelorussia.[208] This body will be analyzed more closely in the chapter dealing with military–police collaboration in Byelorussia. The BCR was entrusted with the recruitment drive for this force.

The last action of the BCR in occupied Byelorussia was to summon the "Second All-Byelorussian Congress." The gathering took place in Minsk, in the Minsk City Theater (today Janka Kupala Academic Theater) on 27 June 1944 and was accompanied by the rumbling of Soviet artillery. The success, at least initially, of mobilizing the BKA gave the BCR's leaders the impression that the time had come to proclaim their own true BCR government, and perhaps to create a "second edition" of the BNR, which had failed twenty-six years earlier. However, these ideas did not match the Germans' aims. Despite the fact that Soviet troops had reached the outskirts of Minsk, the occupation authorities continued to uphold the tenets of the *Ostpolitik*, so that any mention of national independence was cause for alarm and outrage, like a red rag to a bull. Little wonder then that all preparations for the congress were under the control of the German security organs, while its program, its list of speakers and the texts of their speeches were handled by the BCR's political commission, headed by Mikalaj Škjaljonak, and required further approval by the head of the propaganda department of the *Generalkommissariat*, Fischer, as well as by the SD.[209]

To create the impression that the event was truly an *all-Byelorussian* undertaking, congress organizers invited Byelorussian émigrés from Lithuania, Latvia, the Reich's Protectorate Bohemia and Moravia, and *Bezirk Bialystok* to attend, as well as those in the General Government and the military administration areas. Of course, such a broad invitation needed the approval of the German authorities. Apparently the desired consent was issued by the *Ostministerium*, which considered the undertaking to be chiefly an extensive means of propaganda. Delegates to the congress were not elected; rather, the Congress mandate commission, headed by BNS chief Yury Sabaleŭski, requested that the local BCR representatives provide lists of candidates. It is hardly surprising, then, that the majority of those dispatched to the congress were activists in various collaborationist bodies. For example, all the delegates from the Hancevići district were either BNS or SBM activists.[210] The delegates living outside Byelorussia were notified of their participation by means of the local Gestapo. This led to somewhat tragicomic situations. These people, among them the physician from Prague, Ivan Heniuš, received Gestapo summons and expected their imminent arrest; instead they were told to go to Minsk.[211] Among the congress registrants were several deceased people, as was the case of Fabian Akinčyc, who was listed as a member of the congress's honorary presidium, despite the fact that he had been killed by resistance members almost a year earlier.[212] In the areas still under military administration, potential delegates were simply recruited by BCR representatives. As can be inferred from the monthly report of the Supreme Command of Army Group "Center", recruitment in this area led to certain tensions between the Byelorussian and Russian populations, since typically the BCR propaganda included not only anti-Semitic and anti-Polish but also anti-Russian slogans. To resolve the friction, the following accommodations were devised: the Byelorussian delegates from the military administration area would attend the congress merely as extras and not take part in the deliberations; their recruitment would proceed through the military authorities; and these delegates were to be prohibited from issuing instructions that might "chauvinistically offend the Russians."[213]

All in all, 1,039 delegates attended the congress.[214] According to official data, almost fifty per cent of them represented merely three administrative units of *GK Weißruthenien*, namely the city of Minsk (191), and the Slonim (159) and Baranavici (145) districts, while a total of seventy per cent of the delegates (695) represented the GKW at large.[215] Thus, it is somewhat difficult to speak of the congress as being truly "all-Byelorussian."

The organizers of the congress tried hard to create the impression that its fundamental issue was the continuation of the process that had begun in 1917 with the convocation of the First All-Byelorussian Congress, which had been dissolved by the Bolsheviks. Even the same building was used. The orators at the congress spared no effort in depicting the "sufferings" of the Byelorussian people under the Russian–Polish–Bolshevist yoke, and given the presence of Soviet forces at the gates of Minsk, they also hastened to deflect any Soviet claims to Byelorussian territory.[216] The vice-president of the BCR, Mikalaj Škjaljonak, even mentioned the Molotov–Ribbentrop pact as an example of Soviet imperialism, apparently forgetting that the Germans were also a party to this agreement.[217] Astroŭski himself unscrupulously depicted the German occupation as a period of Byelorussian rebirth and expressed his belief in the Germans' final victory.[218] The congress's delegates discussed plans for the future in various domains, such as education, social policy, and culture, as if the Soviet troops were not standing at the outskirts of Minsk.[219]

At the same time, the resolution issued by the congress was quite "moderate." Any mention of Byelorussian independence that might elicit a sharp reaction from the Germans was omitted altogether. The resolution merely declared that any and all connections between Byelorussia and the "Bolshevist Moscow and Russian State"–as well as any Soviet and Polish claims to Byelorussian territory–were null and void; furthermore, the resolution did not recognize the legitimacy of the BSSR; and finally, it proclaimed the Byelorussian Central Council with Astroŭski at its head as "the only legitimate representative of the Byelorussian people and its country."[220] Given the absence of any official recognition of an independent State of Byelorussia, the congress's intention when issuing this statement was to turn the BCR de facto into a Byelorussian government. The German reaction did not meet the congress's expectation, apparently for a very simple reason: Gottberg understood, certainly better than the BCR members, that in the current situation such a declaration would not change much.

In discussing the significance of the congress, a distinction must be drawn between the German and the BCR points of view. The BCR clearly recognized that its popularity among the broad masses of the Byelorussian population left much to be desired. Many of council's leaders were former émigrés who were not very well known in the country. In addition, the publication of the BCR-related statute in the "legal" newspapers made it very difficult to conceal from the public the fact of the BCR's limited authority and its role as a mere advisory body for the German administration. That meant that the congress was an important means by which Astroŭski and the BCR hoped to show that they were not merely puppets in German hands, but that they truly represented the Byelorussian people in standing up to the occupation authorities. Of course, as Turonak remarks, the personal ambitions of Astroŭski should not be ignored.[221]

For the Germans, the congress played chiefly a propaganda role. The image of the occupation authorities had suffered a great deal over the three years of the occupation, owing mainly to measures such as forced labor recruitment and brutal anti-partisan operations, and compounded by their inability to solve various problems, particularly the agrarian one. The German authorities' sanctioning of the Second All-Byelorussian Congress certainly demonstrates their eagerness to improve this image: they hoped to create the impression that they were truly anxious about the future of the Byelorussian people and that the Byelorussians could guarantee this future only by relying on Germany and supporting its struggle against the (partisan and regular) Soviet forces. Thus, in his address to the congress, Gottberg called upon Byelorussians once again to fight "together with the German people against the Bolshevist danger, for the liberation of Europe ... Then this difficult fight will bring a victory, which will give the Byelorussian people too a happy future."[222]

The congress came to a close on the evening of 27 June 1944; the next day saw the start of the evacuation of Rada's employees and members from Byelorussia that continued until 30 June.[223] This speedy evacuation certainly came as a surprise to many BCR members. In fact, large numbers of German officials were not precisely aware of what was going on at the front, including the city commissar (*Stadtskommissar*) of Minsk, Becher. His final report, written on 27 July, claimed that he was told by the military authorities that "the center [that is, front—L.R.] would not only be held by the Wehrmacht but, moreover, would already serve this year, as the basis for the German assault against Moscow, and that an offensive from there all the way to the Urals [*sic*] is possible and should be expected."[224]

Following their evacuation from Minsk, most of the BCR members arrived in Königsberg, where the *Gauleiter*, Koch, who in the past had also served as Ukrainian *Reichskommissar*, was quick to get rid of the uninvited guests and sent them on to Berlin through Pozen (present-day Poznan).[225] Astroŭski, however, found himself in Lodz, where he had headed the local office of the Byelorussian Representation prior to the German invasion of the Soviet Union. Later he was joined there by Francišak Kušal (of whom more will be said below).[226] On 12 July, all the members of the BCR were assembled by the Eastern Ministry in Berlin. The leaders of the council apparently took their role as representatives of a "Byelorussian government-in-exile" very seriously. Upon their arrival in Berlin, the deputy president of the BCR, Yury Sabaleŭsky, expressed his indignation that BCR members had not been greeted with an official reception at the railway station and that no hotel reservations had been made for them.[227] One of the first steps taken by the BCR in Germany was to issue a statement of protest, led by Astroŭski, on 20 July 1944, directed to all "governments and nations of the world," denouncing what they saw as the occupation of Byelorussia by Soviet forces.[228]

It is beyond the scope of the present work to examine the BCR activities in Germany. Of note, however, is that the discrepancies between the aims of the Germans and those of the BCR leadership, which had begun to appear earlier during the occupation, now came to the fore. The former, in the first place Rosenberg and his OMi, did not abandon their attempts to use the council to further their own interests, i.e., the defense of the Third Reich. The *Ostministerium* instruction issued on 9 October 1944 foresaw five main tasks for the BCR in Germany. The first was to aid in the struggle against Bolshevism through the formation of Byelorussian military units, participation in the creation of commando-like groups to be placed behind the Soviet lines, and dissemination of propaganda among Byelorussian workers. The second task was the unification of all Byelorussians in a future Union for the Liberation of Byelorussia (this union should be created by the BCR); the third task was to provide cultural, social, and legal care for Byelorussians living in Germany; and the fourth and fifth tasks were to recruit the youth and women's workforces, respectively.[229] Undoubtedly, the first of these tasks was deemed most urgent and, according to Turonak, the only real cause for the German support of the BCR.[230]

The old generation of BCR members, led by Astroŭski, sensing the overall situation and the imminent and inevitable defeat of the Third Reich, continued to pay lip service to the Nazis; however, they also sought ways to expand the BCR's maneuvering space so as to ultimately reach an agreement with the Western Allies. Thus, in January 1944, the new BCR statute was adopted, according to which Byelorussia would be a democratic parliamentary country with equal rights for all its citizens.[231] At the same time, Astroŭski was eager to avoid—as far as possible—any measures that might compromise him in the postwar period. Therefore, as Turonak observes, Astroŭski sought to hinder the establishment of Nazi-sponsored Byelorussian military units. He was particularly opposed to the inclusion of Byelorussians in Vlasov's movement, which will be examined more closely later.[232] This change in the position of the BCR leadership aroused opposition from those council members who wanted more than anything else to fight against the Soviets, under any conditions, even under German patronage, or as part of Vlasov's movement. The central figures in this camp included, among others, Ŭsevalad Rodz'ka and Mikhal Vituška. Rodz'ka was even appointed to head the special Abwehr saboteurs' school in East Prussian Dallwitz, where Byelorussian volunteers were trained to be saboteurs in the Soviet hinterland.[233] In the end, the controversy between the two groups of the BCR led to a fully-fledged split in the organization.

In summary, it must be said that the BCR could be considered to be the ultimate example of political collaboration, because here the differences between the goals of the collaborators and those of the German authorities were most obvious. The weakening of the German grip toward the end of the occupation enabled BCR members not only to proclaim their particular aims, but also to pursue them, albeit to a limited extent. The true tragedy for many—if not most—of those engaged in the many forms of political collaboration was that throughout the occupation, they continually entertained the illusion that one way or another they were participating in building the Byelorussian state. They did not understand that they would be allowed freedom of action only insofar as it suited German interests. Chapter 7, which deals with collaborating in Nazi annihilation policies, will show just how far many collaborators were willing to go in pursuit of their illusions.

On the other side of the occupational divide, the German authorities' attitude toward the BCR demonstrated clearly once again their true approach to the notion of local political collaboration. Even on the threshold of defeat, not only were they unable to view the local collaborators as partners, but they were also eager to put obstacles in their way. Dogmatism rather than

Realpolitik was the basis of both their general policy and their approach to local collaboration. Although the Germans recognized the practical need for securing local assistance, they were unable to liberate themselves from this dogmatism but still wanted to receive this assistance without paying a price, either literally or figuratively. Even as they faced their fall, any mention of the most restricted kind of independence for the local inhabitants of the occupied territories was absolute anathema to them. Political collaboration, then, serves as a perfect case study for examining the Janus-like nature of the Nazi regime. This regime spoke two different languages: one was intended for "internal" use only, while the other was for public dissemination. In short, this case study undoubtedly reveals the Germans' inability to bridge the gap between dogma and reality.

Notes

1. See, for example, "TLB Nr. 1, 31.7.41," "TLB Nr. 3, 15.–31.8. 41," in Klein, *Einsatzgruppen in der besetzten Sowjetunion*, 126, 173.
2. See Chapter VI dealing with the legal press in occupied Byelorussia.
3. Turonak, *Belarus' pad nyameckaj Akupacyjaj*, 27.
4. "Bittschrift an Rosenberg in politischer Angelegenheit (Ostlands- und polnische Angelegenheiten) von Wenzel von Gisbert Studnicki, o. D.," BA R 93/5.
5. See "Stanislaw Stankevich-short data," Simon Wiesenthal Center Archive (SWCA).
6. "Schreiben Oberkommandos des Heeres an Reichsminister für die besetzten Ostgebiete betreffend Einreise von Emigranten in die neu besetzten Ostgebiete, 5.8.41," BA R 6/339, Mikrofiche 1, "Abschlußbericht über die Tätigkeit der Militärverwaltung im Operationsgebiet des Ostens" (see ch. 3 n. 64), 39.
7. "Abschlußbericht über die Tätigkeit der Militärverwaltung im Operationsgebiet des Ostens," 39.
8. Ibid.
9. "Intelligence report No. 17, 24.8.42," Yad Vashem Archives (YVA) M 41/258 (National Archive, Minsk, 4-33a-69), 4.
10. Thus, for example, Anton Pantelej, a watchman before the war, was a *starosta* of Domžerick volost' in Begoml rayon (Minsk oblast), while Pentecostalist Kulbicki was *starosta* in the village Krasovščina near Maladečna (today Minsk oblast).
11. "TLB Nr.1, 31.7.41," in Klein, *Einsatzgruppen in der besetzten Sowjetunion*, 126.
12. "TLB Nr. 2, 29.7.–14.8.41," ibid., 146.
13. See Turonak, *Belarus' pad nyameckaj Akupacyjaj*, 53f.
14. "Abschlußbericht über die Tätigkeit der Militärverwaltung im Operationsgebiet des Ostens," 40.

15. Röhr, "Forschungsprobleme zur deutschen Okkupationspolitik im Spiegel der Reihe 'Europa unter Hakenkreuz,'" 148.

16. Turonak, *Belarus' pad nyameckaj Akupacyjaj*, 58.

17. Litvin, "Kalabaratsyjanizm na Terytorii Belarusi ŭ Hady Vjalikaj Ajchynnaj Vajny: Da Prablemy Vyvuchennja," in idem, *Akupacyja Belarusi*, 199.

18. See Ivanoŭski's biography in Turonak, *Belarus' pad nyameckaj Akupacyjaj*, 203n.

19. See Chapter II, note 10.

20. Litvin, "Kalabaratsyjanizm," 199.

21. See Chapter II; "Report on the moods of the population in Byelorussia, compiled by a Byelorussian from Latvia, August 1942," BA R90/126. The author speaks about the mutual enmity between the former émigrés and *Vozvyshentsy*.

22. Litvin, "Kalabaratsyjanizm," 199.

23. See "Report on the moods of the population in Byelorussia, compiled by a Byelorussian from Latvia."

24. See Martin Dean, "Polen in der einheimischer Hilfspolizei. Ein Aspekt der Besatzungsrealität in den deutsch besetzten ostpolnischen Gebieten," in *Die polnische Heimatarmee*, ed. Bernhard Chiari (Munich, 2003), 355–68.

25. For information about the Byelorussian Independent Party, see the dictionary *Belaruski Nacyjanalizm*, *http://slounik.org/nac/* as well as a short entry in the encyclopedic dictionary *Belarus*, 91.

26. Gerlach, *Kalkulierte Morde*, 199.

27. "Tätigkeits- und Erfahrungsbericht des Gebietskommissars Baranowitsche Werner, 11.08.44," BA R93/13. "Tätigkeits- Räumungs- und Erfahrungsbericht des Gebietskommissars Lida Hennig, 15.8.44," ibid.

28. "Tätigkeits-, Räumungs- und Erfahrungsbericht des Gebietskommissars Glebokie Hachmann, 16.08.44," BA R93/14.

29. "Schreiben der Abteilung II 1 bei Ostministerium, Februar 1943," BA R 6/35, Mikrofiche 5.

30. Ibid.

31. "Bericht der Beauftragter d. Reichsmin. f.d. bes. Ostgeb. b. Kommand. General d. Sich.-Tr. u. Befh. i. H. G. Mitte Major O. W. Müller an das Reichsministreium für die besetzten Ostgebiete, Hauptabteilung I, 8.10.42," BA R 6/76, Mikrofiche 1.

32. Such views on the "eastern people" were not limited to diehard Nazis but had roots in the period preceding the Nazi era and, moreover, were based on pseudo-scientific foundations. A psychotherapist, Gustav Richard Heyer, friend and pupil of Carl Gustav Jung, in his article "Zur Psychologie des Ostraumes," published around 1941 in the seventh issue of *Zeitschrift für Geopolitik*, describes the Slavs as natural slaves, living in a state of nature, close to animals, and presenting the Germans as a kind of a new Prometheus for these people. See BA R 6/8a.

33. See "Abschlußbericht über die Tätigkeit der Militärverwaltung im Operationsgebiet des Ostens," 38.

34. "Letters from the plenipotentiary for the saving of the possessions of the Minsk State Archive Menzhinskaja to the head of the archive department by Generalkommissar für Weißruthenien Dr. Korz from 28.11 and 3.12.41," BA R 93/5.

35. "Schreiben Gebietsleiters des WSW in Baranowitsche Tulejko an der Leiter der Abt. I Pol. in Gebietskommissar Baranowitsche Schmitt, o.D." (in Ger-

man and Byelorussian), BA R 90/158; "Report on the propagandistic work in Baranoviâi area during the July 1943, 6.8.43" (in Russian), ibid., "Schreiben Leiters der Propagandisten Bedrizki an Gebietskommissar in Baranowitsche Werner, 8.8.43," ibid.

36. "Report on the propagandistic work in Baranoviâi area ...," "Abrechnung des Leiters der Propagandisten Bedrizki über die Propagandaarbeit in Gebiet Baranowitsche für den August 1943, 6.9.43," ibid.

37. "Bedrizkis Schreiben an Schmitt, 10.11.43," ibid.

38. After the war Aŭdzej, who found refuge in the United States, vehemently denied that he had had anything to do with these repressions. See "File of Jan Awdziej," "Record of sworn statement made by Ivan Aŭdzej before the officials of the Immigration and Naturalization Service (US Department of Justice), 10.11.58," both in SWCA.

39. "Entwurf der Schreiben des Befehlshabers des rückw. Heeres-Gebietes Mitte betreffend Partisanenbekämpfung, 12.10.41," BA-MA RH 22/225.

40. "Bericht über die Besichtigung der Bahnsicherungen an Strecke Mogilew-Rogatschew, 7.10.42," BA-MA RH 22/233.

41. "Bericht des Kreislandwirt in Wolozyn über die Sonderaktion Dirlewanger in der Gemeinde Pirschaje, 25.7.43," BA R 93/7a.

42. The leaflet is quoted in "Abschrift des Ereignisberichtes des Generalkommissars (Gebietskommissars?) in Nowogrodek über das Auftreten von Banden im Gebiet Nowogrodek-Nachtrag für die Zeit vom 6.-12.7.42 und vom 13.7.-6.8.42, 6.8.42," BA R 6/348, Mikrofiche 1.

43. "Abschrift der statisticher Zusammenstellung des Gebietskommissars in Nowogrodek über das Auftreten von Banden im Gebiet Nowogrodek (Nachtrag für die Zeit vom 6.7.-12.7.42 und vom 13.7.-6.8.42," ibid.

44. "Schreiben der Abteilung II Verwaltung bei Generalkommissar für Weißruthenien an den Reichskommissar für das Ostland bezüglich Bandentätigkeit, 25.8.42," ibid.

45. "Ereignismeldung Nr. 35 des SS-und Polizeiführers Weißruthenien-Kommandeur der Ordnungspolizei, 5.10.42," BA R 6/348, Mikrofiche 4.

46. "Tagesmeldung des Ktdr der Sich.-Gebietes Weißruthenien (Oberfeldkommandantur 392), 3.11.42," ibid., Mikrofiche 5. "Tagesmeldung der Kdtr. d. Sich.-Gebietes Weißruthenien (Oberfeldkommandantur 392), 14.11.42," ibid., Mikrofiche 6.

47. "Flugblatt des Komitee zur Bekämpfung der deutschen Okkupanten, 9.42," (Übersetzung von Russisch), BA R 90/126.

48. Its formation will be discussed in following chapters.

49. "Schreiben des Gebietskommissars Slonim und Reg. Rat Dr. Ludwig Ehrenleitner an Generalkommissar für Weißruthenien Kube betreffend politischer Lagebericht Slonim, 21.3.43," BA R 90/126.

50. Ales Adamovich et al., *Ya iz ognennoj Derevni...* (Minsk, 1977), 71 (testimony of Emilia Partasjonok).

51. "Tätigkeitsbericht (April 1942) der Abteilung I c bei dem Befehlshaber des rückw. Heeresgebietes Mitte, 1.5.42," BA-MA RH 22/243.

52. Chiari, *Alltag hinter der Front*, 141.

53. Both cases are quoted by Chiari. See ibid., 143f., 145.

54. Adamovich et al., *Ya iz ognennoj Derevni*, 230, 234. There is a certain difference between the testimonies of the survivors. Thus, according to Marija Sosnovskaja, the *starosta* separated the families of local policemen from

the other villagers, while according to Tekļja Gerasimchik, only the family of the *starosta's* son-in-law was separated.

55. "Interrogation of the former commandant of Pariči Hauptmann Moll before the Soviet court, 24.1.46," YVA M.41/278II (National Archive, Minsk 4-29-113).
56. See, for example, "Lagebericht der Abteilung II Verwaltung der Generalkommissariat in Minsk: Kommunalwesen, 15.10.42," BA R 93/3.
57. "Excerpt from protocol of the testimony of prisoner of war Wilhelm Janetzke, written single-handed, 26.7.47," YVA M.41/277 (Archives of KGB Belarus, unsigned).
58. "Schreiben der Abteilung II 1 bei Ostministerium, Februar 1943," BA R 6/35, Mikrofiche 5.
59. "Bericht Nr. 8 über die militärische und politische Lage im Heeresgebiet Mitte, 15.05.42," BA R 6/51, Mikrofiche 1–2.
60. "Abschrift des Vermerks Abteilungs II in RMfdbO, Februar 1943," BA R 6/230, Mikrofiche 3.
61. "Besprechungspunkte Reichsminister Rosenberg, 29.5.42," BA R 6/51, Mikrofiche 2.
62. The announcement about the creation of the BNS was issued together by Kube and Yermačenka on 22 October 1941 and published in *Amtsblatt des Generalkommissars für Weißruthenien* on 4 November of the same year. It is quoted in Turonak, *Belarus' pad nyameckaj Akupacyjaj*, 85.
63. Ibid.
64. "Tatkräftige Hilfeleistung durch das WSW," *Minsker Zeitung*, 2–3 April 1944, BA R 6/289, Mikrofiche 2.
65. "Ermatschenkos Schreiben an Rosenberg, 17.1.44," BA R 6/106, Mikrofiche 1.
66. "Rosenbergs Schreiben an Dr. J. Ermatschenko, 26.09.41," photocopy published in Romanovskij, *Saudzel'niki ŭ zlachynstvakh*, 105.
67. The short biography of Yermačenka can be found in Turonak, *Belarus' pad nyameckaj Akupacyjaj*, 206n84. See also entry "Yermachenka" in Encyclopedic Dictionary *Belarus* (Minsk, 1995), 303.
68. "Entwurf des Schreibens der Ostministerium an Chef der Sicherheitspolizei und des SD betreffend Dr. Johann Ermatschenko, Leiter des BSW in Minsk, Mai 1943," BA R 6/106, Mikrofiche 1.
69. "Ermatschenko Schreiben an Rosenberg, 17.1.44," see above, note 65.
70. Turonak, *Belarus' pad nyameckaj Akupacyjaj*, 33.
71. Dallin, *German Rule*, 217.
72. "Vermerk von Abteilungsleiter II/2 beim Verbindungsoffizier des Chefs der Sichercheitspolizei und des SD beim Ostministerium Dr. Waegner betreffend Dr. Ermatschenko, 6.5.43," BA R 6/106, Mikrofiche 1.
73. "Ostministerium an Chef der Sicherheitspolizei und des SAID," see note 68 above.
74. Quoted in Chiari, *Alltag hinter der Front*, 115.
75. "Statute of Byelorussian Popular Self-Aid Organization in Minsk," in *Menskaja Hazeta*, 28 October 1941, copy in Solov'ev, *Belarusskaja Tsentral'naja Rada*, 105–7.
76. Ibid.
77. See "Rosenberg an Ermatschenko," in V. Romanovskij, *Saudzel'niki*, 105.
78. "Statute of Byelorussian Popular Self-Aid Organization in Minsk," see note 75 above. "Ermatschenko an Rosenberg, 17.1.44," see note 65 above.
79. Ibid.

80. "Mitgliederzahlen des Weißruthenischen Selbsthilfewerkes, Ende 1942," quoted in Chiari, *Alltag hinter der Front*, 117n.

81. The BNS's highest membership was, quite understandably, in the Minsk area (city of Minsk and the surrounding area), where a total of 9,628 members out of 29,605 were officially reported, approximately 33% of the total. See ibid.

82. The official designation of administrative units in Byelorussian was introduced by Kube in September 1942. According to this new designation, rayons were re-named as *povety*. The *Rayon-* and *Gemeindebürgermeistern* were called *nachal'nik* (head) *poveta*, *nachal'nik volosti* etc. See Turonak, *Belarus' pad nyameckaj Akupacyjaj*, 118. Quoted in Chiari, *Alltag hinter der Front*, 118.

83. V. Romanovskij, *Saudzel'niki*, 98.

84. Ibid., 96ff. Alexej Solov'ev, who issued his study about the Byelorussian Central Council in 1995, also defines BNS as "support of occupation administration of W. Kube," Solov'ev, *Belarusskaja*, 12.

85. A photocopy of the document is in Romanovskij, *Saudzel'niki*, 107.

86. The general list of credits given to the BNS central office is quoted in Chiari, *Alltag hinter der Front*, 119n.

87. R. Astroŭski (ed.), *Druhi Usebelaruski Kangres* (1954), SWCA.

88. Chiari, *Alltag hinter der Front*, 119, "Report of Byelorussian Popular Self-Aid Organization" (in Byelorussian), *Belaruskaja Hazeta* (BH) 18.6.42, 4, YVA, C-762.

89. "WSW an GebKomm Minsk, 30.7.42," quoted in Chiari, *Alltag hinter der Front*, 119.

90. Chiari, *Alltag hinter der Front*, 119f.

91. "Abschrift von politischer Lagebericht Slonim verfaßt von Ehrenleitner, 21.3.43," R 6/27, Mikrofiche 4.

92. "Tatkräftige Hilfeleistung durch das WSW," *Minsker Zeitung*, 2./3 April 1944, BA R 6/289, Mikrofiche 2.

93. "Za sumlennasc' ŭ pachesnaj pracy," BH, 5.2.42, YVA, C-762.

94. "Ermatschenko an Rosenberg, 17.1.44," see note 65 above.

95. "Schreiben des Gebietsleiters des WSW in Baranowitsche Tulejko an dem Leiter der Abt. I. Pol. im Gebietskommissariat Baranowitsche Schmitt (in Deutsch und Weißrußisch, o. D.," BA R 90/158.

96. This declaration was made on 7 July 1942 and quoted both in the letter of the *Ostministerium* regarding the Union of Byelorussian Youth as well as by Alexander Dallin. See "Abschrift der Schreiben der RMfdbO 'Das Weißruthenische Jugendwerk (WJW)', 19.4.43," BA R 6/186, Mikrofiche 1; Dallin, *German Rule*, 204.

97. See Chapter I, note 65.

98. "TLB Nr. 9 (1.1.–31.1.42), Nr. 10 (1.2–28.2.42), Nr.11 (1.3.–31.3.42)," in Klein, *Einsatzgruppen in der besetzten Sowjetunion*, 276–77, 283–84, 294, 300, 305–6, 311; "Operational Situation Reports USSR No. 172 (23.2.42), No. 175 (2.3.42), No. 178 (9.3.42), No. 182 (18.3.42)," in Arad and Spector, *Einsatzgruppen Reports*, 297, 301–2, 307–8, 314.

99. Even the assassination of Kube, which was officially an action of the Resistance movement, is depicted by Turonak as a result of SS intrigues. See Turonak, *Belarus' pad nyameckaj Akupacyjaj*, 124f.

100. "'Überblick über die politische Lage': Kubes Rede während der Tagung der Gebietskommissare, Hauptabteilungsleiter und Abteilungsleiter des Gen-

eralkommissars in Minsk vom 8. bis 10. April 1943," BA R 93/20, 11. NSV is an abbreviation of *Nationalsozialistische Volkswohlfahrt*, National Socialist Popular Welfare Organization. It was created in 1932, before the Nazi rise to power and in 1933 on Hitler's personal order was recognized as an organization inside the Nazi party. Its task, according to Ernst Klee, was "assistance to *Volksgenossen*, valuable exclusively from the NS point of view". See Klee, *Das Personenlexikon zum Dritten Reich*, 728.

101. Turonak, *Belarus' pad nyameckaj Akupacyjaj*, 117.

102. The "men of confidence" in *Gebietskommissariate* were Yuljan Sakovič (Minsk area), Yury Sabaleŭski (Baranaviči), Barys Rahulja (Navahrudak), Rygor Zymbajla (Lida), Aljaksandar Sivec (Slonim), Anton Sokal-Kutyloŭski (Hanceviči), Aljaxandar Kalodka (Vilejka), and Stanislaŭ Stankevič (Borisov). See BH, 12.7.42, YVA, C-762; Turonak, *Belarus' pad nyameckaj Akupacyjaj*, 118.

103. "Anerkennung der willigen Mitarbeit," *Stimme der Heimat*, 2 August 1942, BA R 90/85.

104. Turonak, *Belarus' pad nyameckaj Akupacyjaj*, 149.

105. See, for example: "The population of Byelorussia (*Weißruthenien*) owes the everlasting gratitude to Adolph Hitler, while the nations of Eastern Europe could not liberate themselves by their own forces from the Bolshevism" (Kube at the ceremony upon the *Gebietskommissar* Minsk-Stadt Janetzke entering office, quoted in "Gebietskommissar Minsk-Stadt," *Deutsche Zeitung im Ostland* (hereafter DZO), 10 December 1941, BA R 90/90); "You now belong to the Fuehrer" (Kube before the Byelorussian peasants during the so-called "disbandment of kolkhozes," "Endgültig befreit. Das Ende der Kolchosen in Weißruthenien," DZO, 10 June 1942, BA R 90/94); and also the quotations cited above.

106. "Vermerk des Ostministeriums betreffend Einheimische Selbsthilfewerk Weißruthenien, 8.1.43," BA R 6/106, Mikrofiche 1.

107. "Aus der Brief des SS- und Polizeiführers in Weißruthenien SS-Brigadeführer v. Gottberg an der Chef der SS-Hauptamt, o. D.," BA R 6/106, Mikrofiche 1.

108. "Schreiben des Kommandeurs der Sicherheitpolizei u.d. SD Weißruthenien Strauch an den Chef der Bandenkampfverbände SS-Obergruppenführer und General der Polizei von dem Bach betreffend Generalkommissar für Weißruthenien, Gauleiter Kube, 25.7.43," in Helmut Heiber, "Aus den Akten des Gauleiters Kube," *Vierteljahrshefte für Zeitgeschichte*, 1956, 1:80–92.

109. "Vermerk der RMfdbO betreffend Einbau weißruthenischer Kräfte in die deustche Verwaltung des Generalbezirks, 18.08.42," BA R 6/251.

110. Ibid.

111. W. Kube, "Zusammenarbeit für das neue Europa," *Minsker Zeitung* (MZ), 27/28 June 1943, BA R 90/107.

112. This body consisted of fifteen (according to Alexej Litvin, see Litvin's commentary to Turonak's study, Turonak, *Belarus' pad nyameckaj Akupacyjaj*, 138) or sixteen (according to Turonak, ibid.) members. Turonak gives the composition of the *Rada* as follows: Vaclaŭ Ivanoŭski (the head), Yermačenka's successor Sabaleŭski; the head of Central Bureau of Trade Unions Kanstancin Rabuška; leaders of SBM Han'ko and Abramava and Aŭgen Kalubovič, the head of Byelorussian scientific society. See Turonak, ibid.

113. "Abschrift Kubes Schreibens an Rosenberg, 28.6.43," BA R 6/289, Mikrofiche 1.

114 ."Überblick über die politische Lage," see ch 3. note 29.

115. "Vermerk vom Abteilungsleiter II/2 beim Verbindungsoffizier des Chefs der Sicherheitspolizei und des SD beim Ostministerium Dr. Waegner betreffend Dr. Ermatschenko, 6.05.43," BA R 6/106, Mikrofiche 1.

116. Turonak, *Belarus' pad nyameckaj Akupacyjaj*, 132.

117. A. Litvin, "Belorusskaja Krajovaja Oborona," in idem, *Akupacyja Belarusi (1941–1944)*, 180.

118 .'Strauchs Schreiben an von dem Bach, 25.7.43," see note 108.

119. Turonak, *Belarus' pad nyameckaj Akupacyjaj*, 132–33.

120. "Satzungen der Jugendorganization 'Weißruthenisches Jugendwerk', 1943," BA R 6/186, Mikrofiche 1.

121. Ibid.

122. Ibid.

123. Ibid.

124. The entire text of the SBM anthem appears in Yurevič, *Vyrvanaja Bachyny*, 15.

125. See ibid., 21.

126. "Satzungen der Jugendorganization 'Weißruthenisches Jugendwerk', 1943," see note 120.

127. Ibid.

128. "Abschrift 'Das Weißruthenische Jugendwerk'- Schreiben der RMfdbO, 19.4.43," BA R 6/186, Mikrofiche 1.

129. Chiari, *Alltag hinter der Front*, 223.

130. Quoted in Yurevič, *Vyrvanaja Bachyny*, 9.

131. Quoted in Chiari, *Alltag hinter der Front*, 224n. The *Gebietskommissar* of Baranaviči Werner reported that in August 1944 there were 5,000 members of SBM in his *Gebietskommissariat*, 2,500 of them uniformed. See "Tätigkeits- und Erfahrungsbericht des Gebietskommissars Baranowitsche Werner, 11.08.44," BA R 93/13. The military administration reported 1,139 SBM members in March 1944, in the areas of 4th and 9th Armies (AOK 9 and AOK 4) alone. See "Abschrift des Monatsberichts der Oberkommando der Heeresgruppe Mitte für März 1944, 12.4.44," BA R 6/281, Mikrofiche 4.

132. A. Katkovič and V. Katkovič-Klentak, *Uspaminy* (Bialystok, 1999), quoted in Yurevič, *Vyrvanaja Bachyny*, 7–8.

133. Chiari, *Alltag hinter der Front*, 228; Yurevič, *Vyrvanaja Bachyny*, 8. Pioneers were members of the children's communist organization.

134. Picker, *Zastol'nye Razgovory Gitlera*, 37.

135. "Bauernredner belehren Weißruthenien. Bericht von der Deutschlandsreise," *Brüsseler Zeitung*, 13 June 1942, BA R 90/85.

136. "Weißruthenien in neuen Europa," *Deutsche Zeitung in Ostland*, 19 January 1943, BA R 90/64.

137. "Weißruthenische Mädel auf Deutschlandfahrt," *Minsker Zeitung*, 15 July 1943, BA R 90/159.

138. Turonak, *Belarus' pad nyameckaj Akupacyjaj*, 136.

139. "Weißrutheniens Jugend führt sich selbst. Am 22. Juni: Gründung des Weißruthenischen Jugendwerkes," *Deutsche Zeitung im Ostland*, 25 June 1943, BA R 6/289, Mikrofiche 1. "'Bannführer Schulz über das weißruthenische Jugendwerk'-Protokoll über die Tagung der Gebietskommissare ...,, 8.-10.4.43," BA R 93/20, 67.

140. "Politische Lagebericht des Leiters der Arbeitsgruppe Weißruthenien, 10.2.42," BA R 6/308, Mikrofiche 2.

141. "Abschrift 'Das Weißruthenische Jugendwerk' (WJW)," see note 128.

142. "Zusatzbestimmungen zur Organisation 'Weißruthenisches Jugendwerk', Einsatzgruppe 'Deutschland,' o. D.," BA R 6/186, Mikrofiche 1.

143. Ibid.

144. Ibid.

145. "Propagandaaktion für den Arbeitseinsatz mit 'Originalpostkarten' von angeblich zufriedenen 'Ostarbeitern', vom 15. Mai 1944," in Schlootz, in *Deutsche Propaganda*, 60–61.

146. "Abschrift der Aufzeichnung des Generalkommissars von Weißruthenien v. Gottberg über die im weißruthenischen Raum zu treffenden politischen Maßnahmen, 1.12.43," BA R 6/281.

147. Quoted in Chiari, *Alltag hinter der Front*, 224–25.

148. S. Zhumar, *Okkupacionnaja Periodicheskaja Pechat' na Territorii Belarusi v Gody Velikoj Otechestvennoj Vojny* (Minsk, 1996), 75.

149. M. Han'ko, "Chamu tol'ki hety shlyakh?" *Zhyve Belarus'* 1 (1944): 44, quoted ibid., 139.

150. "Han'ko's call to Byelorussian youth," YVA M 41/112, 41 (original in Byelorussian State Museum for the History of Great Patriotic War (BGMIVOV), 5528–52).

151. *Menskaja Hazeta*, 5 October 1941, quoted by L. Smilovitsky, "Righteous Gentiles, the Partisans, and Jewish Survival in Belorussia, 1941–1944," *Holocaust and Genocide Studies* 11, no. 3 (1997): 303.

152. BH, 16.8.42, YVA, C-762.

153. "Belaruskije hlapcy i dzjaŭchaty!" leaflet issued by the leading staff of the Union of Byelorussian Youth, undated (1943/1944?), YVA M 41/112, 45–46 (BGMIVOV, 20-10a-4); see also BA R 90/156. A similar leaflet by the leading staff of the SBM was issued in 200,000 copies on 17 March 1944 and was supposed to be distributed in the schools of both *GK Weißruthenien* and of the Rear Area of Army Group "Center." See BA, ibid.

154. Quoted in Yurevič, *Vyrvanaja Bachyny*, 88.

155. Chiari, *Alltag hinter der Front*, 225.

156. Ibid.

157. Gerlach, *Kalkulierte Morde*, 1082.

158. Ibid., 1085.

159. Chiari, *Alltag hinter der Front*, 228.

160. Quoted in ibid.

161. Dallin, *German Rule*, 589. Turonak, *Belarus' pad nyameckaj Akupacyjaj*, 187.

162. See "Interrogation of Walter Kortmann, the member of the recruiting commando in the Baltic area by the officials of the Office of US Chief of Council for the War Crimes, 23.10.47," BA Microfilm 44. 832. The order itself, according to Dallin, was issued on 4 March 1944. See Dallin, *German Rule*, 589.

163. "Interrogation of Friedrich Kolvenbach, former member of *Kriegseinsatzkommando Mitte* by the Office of US Chief of Council for War Crimes, 24.2.48," BA Microfilm 44 832.

164. "Vereinbarung zwischen dem Reichsministerium für die besetzten Ostgebiete und dem Oberkommando der Luftwaffe über die Anwerbung und Einstellung von 25.000 Kampfhelferinnen aus den besetzten Ostgebieten in die Luftwaffe, o. D.," BA R 6/189, Mikrofiche 2.

165. Ibid.

166. "Der Ruf der europäischen Jugend," weißruthenische Zetung "Pahonia," zitiert bei *Deutsche Ost-Korrespondenz*, 1 June 1944, ibid. See also Turonak, *Belarus' pad nyameckaj Akupacyjaj*, 187.
167. Turonak, *Belarus' pad nyameckaj Akupacyjaj*, 187.
168. Quoted ibid.
169. "Vermerk des Führungsstabes Politik betreffend SS- und Flakhelfer, 16.3.44," BA R 6/189, Mikrofiche 1.
170. "Schreiben Führungsstab Politik und den Leiter der Führungsgruppe P 4 von der Milwe-Schröwen, 20.3.44," ibid.
171. *Heu* was an abbreviation of *"Heimatlos* (without a homeland), *Elternlos* (without parents), *Unterkunftslos* (homeless)". The aim of *Heuaktion* was to bring around 30,000–50,000 homeless and orphaned children between the ages of ten and fourteen to the work in the Reich. The campaign was controlled by the Reich youth leader (RJF) and *Ostministerium*. The speedy advance of Soviet forces prevented the carrying out of the *Heuaktion* on a wide scale, but according to the report of Supreme Command of Army Group Center, 4,000 children were deported to the Reich from the operational area of the 9th Army alone. See Gerlach, *Kalkulierte Morde*, 1087. See also "Erfahrungsbericht der Militärverwaltung beim Oberkommando der Heeresgruppe Mitte für die Zeit vom 22.6.41 bis August 1944," BA-MA RH 22/230; "Interrogation of Walter Kortmann," see note 162; Dallin, *German Rule*, 590.
172. "Vermerk über die Besprechung mit SS-Gruppenführer von Gottberg am 22. und 23. November 1943, 6.12.43," BA R 6/282, Mikrofiche 1.
173. Astroŭski, *Druhi Usebelaruski Kangres*, 8.
174. Chiari, *Alltag hinter der Front*, 98.
175. "Von Gottbergs Rede bezüglich Begründung des Weißruthenisches Zentralrats," in *Minsker Zeitung*, 21 December 1943, 1–2, BA R 93/5.
176. Curt von Gottberg (1896–1945), SS-Gruppenführer and Generalleutnant (Lt.-General) of the Police. Born in Prussian Wilten, he served as Oberleutnant (Lieutenant) during World War I, and was awarded the 1st and 2nd degree Iron Cross. After the war, Gottberg joined the notorious Ehrhardt Navy Brigade of the Free Corps. With this brigade, he took part in the Beer Hall Putsch in Munich in November 1923. In 1932, Gottberg joined the NSDAP and SS simultaneously. In 1937, he became chief of SS Main Race and Settlement Office (*SS-Rasse- und Siedlungsamt*). In 1939, Gottberg was appointed director of the Soil Office (*Bodenamt*) in Prague, but was subsequently forced to leave office because of a corruption scandal. In October 1940, Gottberg was made chief of Registration Department (*Erfassungsamt*) in the Main SS Office (*SS-Hauptamt*). In October 1942, he was appointed SS and police leader for *Weißruthenien*, and from March 1943, he also represented HSSPF *Rußland-Mitte*. From September 1943, he was Acting *Generalkommissar für Weißruthenien*, and from June 1944, HSSPF *Rußland-Mitte und Weißruthenien*. In May 1945, Gottberg was arrested by the Allies in Flensburg, where he committed suicide. See Gerlach, *Kalkulierte Morde*, 162n; Klee, *Personenlexikon*, 193.
177. Quoted in Klee, *Personenlexikon*, 193.
178. "The *Weißruthenen* are the invention of Berlin armchair politicians." Quoted in P. Kleist, *Zwischen Hitler und Stalin* (Bonn, 1950), 175.
179. "Abschrift des Schreibens des Reichsministers für die bestzten Ostgebiete Rosenberg an dem SS- und Polizeiführer beim Generalkommissar für

Weißruthenien SS-Gruppenführer von Gottberg, 24.9.43," BA R 6/492, Mikrofiche 1.

189. "Rosenbergs Schreiben an Lammers, 21.10.43," ibid.

181. See Dallin, *German Rule*, 221.

182. "Lammers Schreiben an Rosenberg bezüglich Neubesetzung der Stelle des Generalkommissars in Weißruthenien, 15.11.43," BA R 6/492, Mikrofiche 1.

183. "Schreiben des Reichsministers und Chefs der Reichskanzlei Lammers an Rosenberg bezüglich Erlaß des Führers über die Ausgliederung des Generalbezirks Weißruthenien aus dem Reichskommissariat Ostland, 4.4.44," ibid.; "Hitlers Erlaß über die Ausgliederung des Generalbezirks Weißruthenien aus dem Reichskommissariat Ostland, 1.4.44," ibid., Mikrofiche 2.

184. In the former case, Gottberg actually tried to face the decision makers in Berlin with a fait accompli: even before acquiring Hitler's formal agreement, he began to establish SS and police stations in Pinsk. For more on the discussions on the question of adding the remains of RKU to GKW and about the decision itself, see "Abschrift von Rosenbergs Fernschreiben an Bormann, 9.02.44," "Rosenbergs Fernschreiben an Bormann betreffend Verwaltung nordukrainischer Gebiete, 10.2.44," "Schreiben des Vertreters der Ostministerium von Allwörden an Gottberg, 14.2.44." All the documents are in BA R 6/263, Microfiche 1. See also Turonak, *Belarus' pad nyameckaj Akupacyjaj*, 163.

185. "Von Gottbergs Rede anläßlich der Begründung des Weißruthenisches Zentralrates," *Minsker Zeitung*, 21 December 1943, 1–2, BA R 93/5.

186. See "Vozzvanije R. K. Ostrovskogo, prezidenta BCR po povodu obrazovanija Rady," published in Solov'ev, *Belarusskaja*, 115–18. See 'Von Gottbergs Rede," see note 177. See also "Verordnung des Generalkommissars in Minsk v. Gottberg über das Statut des Weißruthenisches Zentralrates, 21.12.43," BA R 6/284.

187. Ibid.

188. "Entwurf des Gottbergs Schreibens an Rosenberg betreffend Errichtung und Organisation des weißruthenisches Zentralrates, 19.3.44," ibid.

189. "Vermerk über die Besprechung mit dem stellvertretenden Generalkommissar für Weißruthenien, SS-Gruppenführer v. Gottberg am 1.3.44. 10.3.44," BA R 6/263, Mikrofiche 2.

190. "Entwurf des Gottbergs Schreibens," see note 188.

191. See Solov'ev, *Belarusskaja*, 26–27.

192. "Entwurf des Gottbergs Schreibens," see note 188.

193. "Ustav BCR, 21.12.43," in Solov'ev, *Belarusskaja*, 111; "Verordnung des Generalkommissars in Minsk v. Gottbergs über das Statut des Weißruthenisches Zentralrates, 21.12.43," BA R 6/284, Mikrofiche 1.

194. "Entwurf des Gottbergs Schreibens," see note 188.

195. "Schreiben Jugendleiters Spak an den Leiter der Propaganda-Abt. Des Gebietes Baranowitsche Bedritzki, 13.12.43," BA R 90/158.

196. Kalush, *In the Service of the People*, 52.

197. "Auszugsweise Abschrift des Vermerks über die Besprechung mit dem stellvertretenden Generalkommissar von Weißruthenien, SS-Gruppenführer v. Gottberg am 1.3.44," BA R 6/284, Mikrofiche 1.

198. Ibid.

199. "Tätigkeits-, Räumungs- und Erfahrungsbericht der Gebietskommissare der Generalbezirks Weißruthenien, 8. 11.44," BA R 6/312.

200. "Schreiben des Leiters der Abteilung I/8 bei RMfdbO Kienzlen an Leiter der Hauptabteilung II von Allwörden betreffend Weißruthenisches Zentralrat, 10.2.44," BA R 6/284, Mikrofiche 1.
201. "Abteilung Politik an den GK, 31.5.44," quoted in Chiari, *Alltag hinter der Front*, 101.
202. See Vakar, *Belorussia*, 190; Lubachko, *Belorussia under Soviet Rule*, 161.
203. "Astrouskis Schreiben an Gottberg, 30.5.44," BA R 6/284, Mikrofiche 2.
204. "Vermerk der Abteilung II 6 beim RMfdbO, 9.6.44," ibid.
205. "Astrouski's Appeal to Russian Partisans (in Russian)," "Astrouski's appeal to partisans-Byelorussians, 15.3.44" (in Byelorussian), both in BA R 90/156, "Appeal of the deputy president of BCR in Navahrudak area B. Rahulja to the partisans, undated" (in Byelorussian), YVA M 41/112.
206. It was the same Carl who entered history because of his October 1941 report describing the atrocities committed in Sluck in the course of anti-Jewish *Aktion*. This document was presented at the Nuremberg Trials. See "Geheimer Bericht des Heinrich Carl, Gebietskommissar in Sluzk, an Wilhelm Kube, Generalkommissar für Weißruthenien, vom 30. Oktober 1941 über eine Vernichtungsaktion der Sicherheitspolizei und litauischer Kollaborateure gegen die jüdische Bevölkerung der Stadt Sluzk," in Kaden, *Dokumente des Verbrechens*, 3:57–61.
207. Kalush, *In the Service of the People*, 56.
208. According to Gottberg's order, areas such as the whole Lida district HSSPF Pripjat', Uzda, and Ivenec areas in Minsk district; Valožyn and Myadel areas in Vilejka district; Braslau area in Hlybokaje district; Kazlouščyna and part of Dereâin area in Slonim district; and part of Dyatlau area in Navahrudak district were excluded from the mobilization. See Solov'ev, *Belarusskaja*, 31, Litvin, "Belorusskaja Krajovaja Oborona: K voprosu o sozdanii belorusskogo natsional'nogo vojska v gody Vtoroj Mirovoj Vojny," in idem, *Akupacyja Belarusi*, 157, Turonak, *Belarus'*, 171. According to Turonak, the exclusion of these areas was connected to the secret agreements concluded between the German authorities and Polish Armija Krajova (Home Army), of which more will be said later.
209. See Solov'ev, *Belarusskaja*, 39–40; V. Romanovskij, *Saudzel'niki*, 167, Turonak, *Belarus' pad nyameckaj Akupacyjaj*, 182.
210. Solov'ev, *Belarusskaja*, 41.
211. See "Testimony of Larissa Geniush," quoted ibid, 43–44.
212. Solov'ev, *Belarusskaja*, 55.
213. "Monatsbericht des Oberkommanos der Heeresgruppe Mitte," BA R6/309, Mikrofiche 3. The interest of the military authorities in securing the interests of the Russians was not unselfish. Two organizations, the "Union for the Struggle against Bolshevism," headed by Mikhail Oktan, and the Russian Liberation People's Army (RONA), headed by engineer Kaminski, who stood out for his brutality during the suppression of the Warsaw uprising, consisted primarily of ethnic Russians and proved very useful in anti-partisan warfare. Thus, it may be assumed that the Wehrmacht simply could not afford to give up the support of these organizations in areas with predominantly Russian population.
214. Astrouski, *Druhi Usebelaruski Kangres*, 38.
215. This number also includes the delegates from the Pinsk and Kobrin districts, which were formerly part of *Reichskommissariat Ukraine* and, as was shown earlier, were officially under Gottberg's authority in February

1944. "Kopija Protokola 2-go Vsebelorusskogo Kongressa BCR," printed in Solov'ev, *Belarusskaja*, 123–34.

216. See "Pramova Prezydenta Kangresu Ja. Kipelja," "Spravazdacha Prezydenta BCR Praf. R. Astroŭskaga," "Dyskusija nad Spravazdachaj Prezydenta BCR: Pramova E. Jasjuka," "Pryvitanne ad Sayuzu Belaruskaj Moladzi," "Referat Vice-Prezydenta BCR M. Shkeljonka," "Referat Syabry BCR Aug. Kaluboviča" etc., all in Astroŭski, *Druhi Ŭsebelaruski Kangres*, 12, 16, 26, 33, 41–50, 52–64ff.

217. Ibid., 47.

218. Ibid., 16, 31.

219. Among other things, the opening of a number of high schools and theaters was planned as well as far-reaching measures in the social and political areas, such as creating special state funds for the social security of workers and their families. All this only stresses the congress delegates' inability to judge the reality in which they operated. See ibid., 21–22, 23.

220. "Rezaljucyja II Usebelaruskaga Kangresu," ibid., 67.

221. See Turonak, *Belarus' pad nyameckaj Akupacyjaj*, 175, 182. Turonak even calls the last paragraph of the congress's resolution, proclaiming BCR to be the representative of Byelorussian people, the "apotheosis of the Astroŭski's entire activity" (182).

222. "Pryvital'noje Pis'mo General'naga Kamisara Gen. von Gottberga," in Astroŭski, *Druhi Ŭsebelaruski Kangres*, 30.

223. We have various data regarding the exact date of the BCR evacuation from Minsk. Solov'ev (*Belarusskaja*, 61n) gives the period between 28 June and 30 June, while according to Turonak (*Belarus' pad nyameckaj Akupacyjaj*, 191), the evacuation occurred on 30 June. According to Kalush (*In the Service of the People*, 60), on the night of 28–29 June the BCR employees and their families were evacuated, while Astroŭski himself left on 30 June.

224. "Abschlußbericht des Stadtkommissars Minsk über die Räumung der Stadt Minsk, 27.7.44," BA R 93/14.

225. Ibid.

226. Kalush, *In the Service of the People*, 60; Turonak, *Belarus'*, 191; Solov'ev, *Belarusskaja*, 62.

227. "Abschlußbericht des Stadtkommissars Minsk."

228. Quoted by Turonak, *Belarus' pad nyameckaj Akupacyjaj*, 191f.

229. See Turonak, *Belarus' pad nyameckaj Akupacyjaj*, 192.

230. Ibid., 193.

231. Astroŭski, *Druhi Ŭsebelaruski Kangres*, 83–87.

232. See Turonak, *Belarus' pad nyameckaj Akupacyjaj*, 193–97. Astroŭski's negative attitude to Vlasov's movement was apparently shared by Rosenberg and his *Ostministerium*. As can be seen from various documents (see, for example, Rosenberg's letter to the head of Hitler's chancellery Lammers from 12 December 1944, BA R 6/492, Microfiche 5), Rosenberg saw in Vlasov's undertaking an attempt to build a "Russian State on German soil".

233. Turonak, *Belarus' pad nyameckaj Akupacyjaj*, 196–97.

CHAPTER 5

THE CROSS AND THE HOOKED
CROSS: THE CHURCH'S COLLABORA-
TION IN OCCUPIED BYELORUSSIA*

Background

The Church in Byelorussia, primarily the Orthodox one, constituted a potential source for collaboration. This collaborative
role was particularly pertinent given both the Polish and the
Soviet religious policies during the interwar period. The Orthodox Church in the Polish part of Byelorussia had become the
main object of the Polonization policies officially adopted by
Warsaw in the 1920s and 1930s. As was mentioned in Chapter 2,
the Polish State did not consider the Byelorussians to be a distinct nation, but rather a kind of "lost Polish tribe" that must be
restored to the bosom of the Polish nation. It is well known that
in Eastern Europe, national and religious allegiances were
strongly intermingled; therefore, the mission of turning
Byelorussians into "decent Poles" also meant turning them into
devout Catholics. To this end, the Catholic Church, with the
government's support, began its large-scale missionary work
among the Byelorussian population, which for the most part
belonged to the Orthodox Church. There were cases in which
Orthodox communities numbering less than 1,000 were simply

incorporated into the nearest Catholic parish.[1] Many Orthodox churches were converted into Catholic places of worship, while others were simply destroyed.[2] Byelorussian deputies in the Polish Sejm complained of Polish soldiers plundering their monasteries.[3]

In the Soviet part of Byelorussia, too, the Church—not only the Orthodox Church—was subject to pressure applied by the Soviet authorities. Actually, the situation of the Church in Eastern Byelorussia is inseparable from that of the Church in Soviet Russia and later in the Soviet Union. From the beginning of Bolshevist rule in Russia, the regime was in a state of a permanent conflict with the Church. One of the Lenin government's first decrees, adopted on 8 November 1917, i.e., on the day following the Bolshevist coup d'état, called for the nationalization of all the land in the country, making landownership by the Church illegal.[4] Further decrees by the new government stripped the Church of all its property and forbade religious teaching in schools. Already in the early 1920s, the mass closing of churches, many of which were converted into clubs, became widespread.[5] This was also the time when the Soviet authorities began to arrest, exile, and execute clergymen and parishioners who opposed the closing of the churches. According to data quoted by Church historian Dimitry Pospielovsky, from 1921 to 1923, 2,691 married priests, 1,962 monks and 3,447 nuns were exterminated in all of Soviet Russia.[6] It is impossible to establish how many of these victims were Byelorussian. In 1925, the League of Militant Atheists (Obshchestvo Voinstvujushchikh Ateistov) was established, headed by the Old Bolshevik Emeljan Yaroslavskij, who openly proclaimed the non-existence of God and proposed, at the end of 1939, that children be removed from parents who adhered to religious doctrines.[7] Among the steps that most offended the religious feelings of the Orthodox population in Byelorussia was the transfer of the relics of St. Euphrosyne, the patron saint of Byelorussia, from the St. Sophia Cathedral in Polock to the Atheism Museum in Vitebsk.[8] This move was carried out in accordance with the Soviet government order demanding "the complete liquidation of the cult of corpses and mummies."[9]

At the same time the Soviet rulers made use of the ancient tenet "divide and conquer." The Soviet authorities' support for the "Union for Church Renovation," which had formed at the beginning of the twentieth century following demands for radical reforms of the existing Church and whose members were prepared to come to terms with the Bolsheviks in 1923, was actually an attempt to weaken the much less obedient traditional clergy.[10]

After the reunion of Western Byelorussia with the rest of the country in 1939, the Soviet authorities initially proceeded with caution in their dealings with the Orthodox Church in the newly annexed territories. After all, the invasion of Soviet forces into eastern Poland in September 1939 was presented by Soviet propaganda as a step designed to protect the Byelorussian (and Ukrainian) minority. Therefore, it would be inopportune, from the Soviet point of view, to alienate this largely Orthodox minority from the start by introducing repressive measures. The Soviet authorities were aware that unlike in the "old Soviet" part of Byelorussia, where for decades the population had been exposed to vehement anti-religious propaganda, in the western part of the country the religiousness of the population remained largely intact. The new authorities were eager to use this religiousness to foster the integration of both parts of Byelorussia, which had been forced to separate some eighteen years earlier. The priests who had been opposed to separating from the Moscow Patriarchate during the Polish period were now favored by the new masters. Thus, the acting patriarch of Moscow, Sergij, appointed Pantelejmon, the former bishop of Navahrudak and Pinsk, as exarch of the Orthodox Church in Western Byelorussia and Western Ukraine, on 17 October 1939.[11]

Nevertheless, as noted in Chapter 2, the Soviet authorities viewed with considerable distrust anyone who had lived for a long time in a "capitalist" society.[12] The trend of replacing the native cadres with those from Eastern Byelorussia, called *Vostochniki*, also affected the Orthodox Church.[13] Thus, Pantelejmon, who only one year earlier had been elevated to head an Exarchy in the annexed territories, was replaced in July 1940 by Metropolitan Nikolaj from Moscow and exiled to the Žirovči monastery.[14]

Following these developments, as the Church in Byelorussia faced the Nazi invasion, it was rife with grievances toward past oppressors. Many—if not all—of the priests who had not been repressed during the Soviet time nevertheless felt no sympathy toward the Soviet regime. Also many of the Orthodox priests in Western Byelorussia harbored anti-Polish and anti-Catholic sentiments. Under these conditions, the Church certainly had motivation to serve as a potential source for collaboration with the

German invaders, who openly proclaimed their hatred both toward the "Bolsheviks" and the Poles.

It may be assumed that those in Germany engaged in planning the campaign against the Soviet Union were well aware of the Church's state of discontent. At the same time it is very difficult to point to religion as a major factor in Germany's prewar plans. Nazis were interested primarily in the resources of the Soviet Union as well as in winning those areas for colonization, while the peoples who inhabited the Eastern territories were seen as chess pieces, whose purpose would be to serve their German "lords." Their inner world and motivations were of little or no concern to these "lords." The American researcher Harvey Fireside, who dealt with Soviet and Nazi politics in relation to the Russian Orthodox Church, put it thus: "It was of little import to Nazi commissars whether laborers were loaded onto cattlecars bound for Germany willingly or not, or whether farmers yielded up their produce to armed squads with a smile."[15]

Relying on religion alone would not bring the Germans the dreamed of "riches" of the *Ostraum*. The only religious project underway on the eve of invasion was the one intended to build up the cadres of Orthodox priests in Germany, so that they would be prepared to take over the Church's affairs in the occupied Soviet territories. The origins of this project can be traced to the advice of Russian émigrés who surrounded Hitler in his Munich days and whose longing for the old pre-Bolshevist Russia revealed more wishful thinking than reality.[16] The realization of this project was assigned to the "Karlovcy Synod," the monarchist émigré Church group named after the town in Yugoslavia where it was formed, in the 1920s.[17] After their rise to power, the Nazis showed their open support for "Karlovcians" by transferring the responsibility for all Orthodox parishes in Germany to Berlin's Orthodox bishop Tikhon,[18] erecting a new Orthodox cathedral in Berlin, and providing financial assistance to maintain several Orthodox churches throughout Germany.[19]

From 1938 onward, the central figure in all of these developments was Archbishop Seraphim (Lade), a man of very obscure background. A German who had allegedly been converted to Orthodoxy in Russia, curiously enough he owed his bishopric investiture to the "Living Church of the Ukrainian Renovators," that is, to a group with a pro-Soviet orientation. Eventually, after his deportation from the Soviet Union, he came to Germany, presenting himself as a passionate anti-Bolshevist. In 1927, Seraphim presented the "Karlovcy Synod" with a document suggesting that the Ukrainian Renovationists were much less enthusiastic in their support of Soviets, a document that enabled Karlovcians to confirm Seraphim's bishopric title.[20] Later, he was named by Nazi authorities as the "Leader of all Orthodox" in the Third Reich and in all territories it controlled, and promoted to the title of Metropolitan.[21] The influence awarded to Seraphim, however, was in vain, as his only accomplishment—a temporary one, at that—was to subject the Warsaw Metropolitan Dionysius to his authority following the German occupation of this city in September 1939. This achievement was short-lived, as it was annulled only one year later by Hans Frank, Hitler's satrap in occupied Poland (General Government).[22]

Rosenberg's Influence

Rosenberg's appointment as head of the Reich's Ministry of the Occupied Eastern Territories in April 1941 demonstrates the attitude of Nazi rulers toward religious policies. Rosenberg was a sworn enemy of Christianity, especially of Catholicism. In his "opus magnum" *Der Mythos des 20. Jahrhunderts* (Myth of the twentieth century), of which Hitler himself allegedly said that he "could not read this nonsense (*Quatsch*)," Rosenberg described his "fantasies" about the "new religion," stating explicitly, "The idea of honor—national honor—is for us the beginning and end of our entire thinking and doing. It does not admit any equivalent center of power alongside it, neither Christian love nor Free-Masonic humanism, nor the Roman philosophy."[23] Seeing Christianity in its present form as "a Jewish invention," he proposed the creation of a new "people's religion" that would replace the "pimps' and cattle-traders' tales" of the Old Testament with "Nordic sagas."[24] In these, Jesus would be portrayed not as a crucified Lamb of God but as a "mighty preacher, angry in the Temple," and "well-proportioned, tall, blond, small-headed with a steep-forehead," a "spear-carrying God."[25] Even in this idea, Rosenberg was not original, since at the end of the nineteenth century the racist "guru" Houston Stewart Chamberlain had already denied Christ any Jewish origins.[26]

Rosenberg was not alone in his hostility toward Christianity. Hitler, and his "grey eminence," Bormann, shared similar views. For Hitler, the Christian Church was a "Christian-Jewish plague" (*christlich-jüdische Pest*).[27] In one of his "table talks"

Hitler harangued, "The heaviest blow that ever struck humanity was the coming of Christianity. Bolshevism is Christianity's
illegitimate child. Both are inventions of the Jew."[28] In a letter
to Rosenberg, Bormann stated, "The concepts of National-
Socialism and Christianity are irreconcilable ... Our National
Socialist ideology is far loftier than the tenets of Christianity
which, in their essential points, have been taken over from
Judaism. For this reason alone, we do not need Christianity."[29]

Nevertheless, the Germans were well aware of the propagandistic potential of the Church. Despite their aversion to Christianity, from their rise to power, the Nazis spared no effort in
exploiting the Churches (chiefly Protestant) in Germany for
their own needs and then turning them into mouthpieces for
their propaganda.[30] The same pattern also worked in the newly
conquered territories in the east. Here the Germans were in dire
need of "peace and order," and saw in the local priests (whom
they labeled with the derogatory term *Popen*, from the Russian
word *pop*, an Orthodox priest) the tool for achieving this. As
early as 1940, referring to the religious policies in occupied
Poland, Hitler said, "Polish priests will receive food from us and
will, for that very reason, direct their little sheep along the path
we favor... If any priest acts differently, we shall make short
work of him. The task of the priest is to keep the Poles quiet,
stupid, and dull-witted."[31] In the occupied Soviet territories, the
plan was the same. According to Hitler, "It is doubtful whether
anything at all can be done in Russia without the help of the
Orthodox priest. It's the priest who has been able to reconcile
the Russian to the fatal necessity of work—by promising him
more happiness in another world."[32] Again Nazism revealed its
schizophrenic nature: whereas it saw Christianity as a Jewish
invention, it was willing, nonetheless, to use this same Christianity for its own purposes.

This involvement in the field of religious policies gave people
such as Alfred Rosenberg free range to experiment with their
chimeras. It would not be an exaggeration to say that the
appointment of Rosenberg as Minister of Occupied Eastern Territories after a long period of virtual "oblivion" made his head
spin. He felt the time had come to implement his fantasies, primary among them his idea regarding a *cordon sanitaire* around
Russia. As shown by Alexander Dallin, Rosenberg's views on
implementing the religious policies in the *Ostraum* focused on
two of his favorite obsessions: anti-Catholicism and Russophobia.[33] The first of these led to the ruthless suppression of the

activities of the Catholic Church in the occupied Eastern territories and, theoretically at least, an acceptance of the Orthodox Church as the main "dialogue partner"; however, the second also implied a suspicious attitude to the Orthodox Church itself. Considering the Orthodox Church as no more than some "oriental custom with beautiful songs" and even "fetishisms," Rosenberg also thought that "The Orthodox Church has been a strong cohesive bond of the Russian *imperium*."[34] Once he was determined to root out "Russian imperialism," he was also intent on splitting the Orthodox Church in the conquered Soviet territories. As late as 1942, Rosenberg even proposed establishing three religious "boards" (*Vorstände*) in Byelorussia–Byelorussian-Orthodox, Russian-Orthodox, and Roman-Catholic–"in which the Byelorussians should receive priority."[35] Accordingly, the Russian Orthodox Church was supposed to be limited to the territories with a Russian majority.

Rosenberg believed, moreover, that the Ukrainians and Byelorussians, as well as other ethnic minorities of the Soviet Union, shared his own anti-Russian sentiments. The chief of the *Ostministerium* also believed that these feelings would be strengthened simply by the German's issuing some bombastic proclamations. On the eve of the invasion into the Soviet Union, one of his most cherished ideas was the issuing of what he termed a "tolerance edict," assuring the *Ostvölker* of German tolerance in matters of faith. In a draft—but deleted from the final version—of his speech given before the future *Reichskommissare* in May 1941, he expressed this notion as follows: "In the field of church policy, tolerance edicts may guarantee freedom of purely religious belief, although without any assumption of governmental responsibility for it. Here, too, we will have to take measures that reflect the varied conditions of each Reichskommissariat."[36] This idea, however, met with objections from both Bormann and Hitler, who mainly feared the implications that such declarations would have at home, where religious tolerance was non-existent.[37]

When speaking about both prewar and wartime Church policies of Nazi rulers, one must consider the principal concerns underlying these policies. In this, as in every other field, the German attitude was dictated by an obsessive, almost paranoiac fear of creating a strong, united opposition. Thus, Church-related politics were also affected by this fear. In one of his "table talks" in April 1942, Hitler stated that, "In all events, the creation of unified churches in more or less extensive Russian lands shall be avoided. It lies in our interests that every village should have its own sect with its own idea of God. Even if the inhabitants of particular villages will thus become the adherents of magic cults, like Negroes or Indians, we can only welcome this, since hereby the separatist tendencies in Russian space will be further strengthened."[38] The German authorities also wanted the activities of the Church in the occupied Eastern territories to be limited solely to charitable and spiritual duties, thus removing it as far as possible from political matters. In May 1942, Rosenberg expressed his "concern" before the *Reichskommissare* that "there should be no religious organizations in the occupied Eastern territories that, under certain conditions bypassing the spiritual work (*Seelesorge*), could create authorities (*politische Machtgebilde*) directed against the German administration."[39]

The Germans came to Byelorussia (and other Soviet territories) with either extremely vague ideas or none at all of the religious conditions reigning there. From the very beginning, various German authorities primarily saw the Church as a propaganda tool, which could be easily manipulated. Moreover, for Rosenberg personally, the Church was a kind of laboratory for his chimeras. It may be supposed that because the Church could not provide the Germans with the "riches" they expected of the *Ostraum*, the head of the "Eastern Ministry" was able to let loose his whims, unhindered by rivalries from other Nazi bodies.

From Theory to Practice

On their arrival in the Soviet territories, the Germans were somewhat surprised to discover that despite the repressive measures of the Soviet authorities, the religious feelings of the Soviet citizens had not withered away altogether.[40] In some places, cases of kneeling down before the crosses on the German tanks were reported.[41] The infamous *Einsatzgruppen* frequently reported "high attendance" at churches that were reopened by the passing German troops, where the priests, described by the same authors as "utterly primitive people" (*durchweg primitive Menschen*), usually offered thanksgivings services to the Germans.[42] The monthly report for the period between 1 and 15 September 1941 also noted that "There is present in the population a need for religion (*Religionsbedürfnis*). It does not matter to the population whether the divine service is held according to the Orthodox, Lutheran or Catholic rite. What is important is the fact that there is a divine service as such."[43] In October 1941, the *Einsatzgruppen* members even remarked that not only those of the older generation, but also young people, including former communists and komsomol members, were attending church. However, one may wonder precisely how the Germans were able to identify "former communists and komsomol members."[44] Today, it is difficult to ascertain to what extent these reports about religious zeal corresponded to reality or to decide whether they should be discarded as wishful thinking.

The Germans initially found fairly chaotic conditions reigning in the Church in the newly occupied territories. Except for the aged Metropolitan Pantelejmon and his deputy, Bishop Venedikt (Benedict), living in the Žiroviči monastery near Slonim, there were no active high-ranking Orthodox priests in Byelorussia. This situation was further aggravated after the transfer of the Polesje diocese headed by Archbishop Alexander to the *Reichskommissariat Ukraine*.[45] The Catholic Church was the first to take advantage of this situation and to resume its missionary work among the Byelorussian population; this had been interrupted by the Soviet annexation of Eastern Poland. Although the majority of Byelorussians belonged to the Orthodox Church, the Catholic Church, too, was strong there, especially in Western Byelorussia. As mentioned above, during the Polish period, the Catholic Church played an important role in the Polish authorities' assimilation policy toward Byelorussians.

In the power vacuum that resulted from the German invasion into the Soviet Union, Catholic priests tried to reinstate their missionary activities among the Byelorussian population. Although the first Wehrmacht units showed mere indifference toward the activities of the Catholic Church, and there were even cases when the Wehrmacht's Catholic chaplains assisted in organizing services in local churches, the *Einsatzgruppen*, who followed on the heels of the Wehrmacht troops, were much less tolerant in these matters.[46] They accused the Catholic priests of "Polish chauvinism" and were eager to suppress their activities, especially their missionary efforts, using the most brutal means.[47] The first "Operational and Situation Report," compiled on 31 July 1941, referred to a case in Slonim, where a local Catholic priest baptized children in the children's home according to Catholic rites, although the parents of some of the children were Orthodox. The report also mentions the "countermeasures" (*Gegenmaßnamen*) taken against such actions.[48] The Byelorussian nationalists, many of whom were natives of Western Byelorussia, also adopted a hostile stance toward the Catholic priests; like the Germans, they saw them as Polish agents.

At the beginning of the Nazi occupation, phenomena such as denunciations by Byelorussian nationalists against Catholics in general, and against their priests in particular (both Poles and Catholic Byelorussians), were quite widespread. These accusations resulted in the execution of a number of priests, such as Gliebovicz, who had been entrusted with missionary activities in the Minsk area by the Archbishop of Vilna (Vilnius). Two Byelorussian Catholic priests, Stanislav Glyakovski and Dionysius Malec, were also executed in Minsk after denunciations accusing them of pro-Polish activities.[49] The flow of such denouncements did not cease during the entire period of occupation. The head of the local propagandists in the Baranaviči area, Bedricky, accused the Catholic Byelorussians of sympathizing with the Poles in hopes of restoring a Polish state, and thought that they "d[id] not deserve to be taken into our political confidence."[50]

Such accusations fell upon the receptive ears of the German authorities. They retained a suspiciously hostile attitude toward the Catholic clergy and toward Catholics in general until the end of the occupation. The appointment of Vincent Hadleŭski, priest of Minsk Catholic Cathedral and founding father (and until 1936 leader) of Byelorussian Christian Democrats, to the position of chief school inspector in *GK Weißruthenien* only increased the suspicions that the Catholic Church was planning to expand its influence over Byelorussian youth.[51] It is not surprising then that Catholics such as Hadleŭski, who had come into Byelorussia at the same time as the Germans and who were initially prepared to cooperate with them, ultimately found their way into the underground, anti-communist "Byelorussian Central (People's) Front," whose banner was inscribed with the slogan "neither the Russians nor the Germans."[52] In the summer of 1942, Germans cracked down on this organization, arresting and executing its leaders, including Hadleŭski himself.[53]

But Catholics were not the only denomination that brought upon itself the outrage of the German authorities. Another religious group in Byelorussia that was viewed with considerable suspicion was the so-called Uniates (Greek Catholics). The origins of this group date to the sixteenth century, namely to the Brest Union, concluded in 1569. The main idea behind its creation was to alleviate the tensions existing in the Polish State at that time between the Polish Catholic elites and the Orthodox subjects.[54] Its rites combined both Orthodox and Catholic elements and acknowledged the supremacy of the Pope. At the time of the German invasion in 1941, the Uniates in Byelorussia numbered approximately 30,000.[55] They were formally subordinated to the Metropolitan of Lvov (today L'viv, Ukraine), Szepticky.[56] In 1942, Szepticky appointed Father Anton Nemancevič, who had spent some time in a Russian prison and had also studied in the Vatican, as the exarch of Byelorussia.[57] Although of minor importance, Uniates were regarded with suspicion by the German authorities. Their acknowledgement of Papal supremacy and the Catholic elements in the liturgy were reasons enough for the German authorities, and especially the enemies of Rome, such as Rosenberg, to cast a sidelong glance at the Uniates. In the second half of 1942, the Uniates, like the Catholics, were accused of pro-Polish sentiments as well as of wishing to promote the Uniate Church to the national Church of Byelorussia. Nemancevič himself was arrested and shot, and the congregation suppressed.[58]

The Catholics were not the only ones who tried to make the best of the situation in Byelorussia during the first weeks and months of the German invasion. The same was true of Metropolitan Dionysius, head of the Polish Autocephalous Orthodox Church, who enjoyed the support of the Nazi general governor, Frank. According to Alexeev and Stavrou, Dionysius wanted nothing less than to subordinate all the Orthodox Churches in the occupied Soviet territories to his authority. With the prospect of the seemingly inevitable capture of Moscow, it is alleged that he even issued blank forms with the heading "His Holiness Dionysius, Patriarch of Moscow and of all Russia."[59] He saw Byelorussia as his traditional field of jurisdiction; on the eve of the German invasion, he issued a memorandum maintaining that in 1939 Byelorussia had been withdrawn from his jurisdiction "only temporally, due to military conditions."[60]

The head of the Polish Autocephalous Church, however, did not limit himself to memoranda alone. He also undertook some practical preparatory steps with the intention of "recovering" his authority over Byelorussia. In September 1941, under his own chairmanship, he created the "Byelorussian Church Council" in Warsaw, which consisted of five men, among them Archimandrite Filafej (Narko) and Ivan Yermačenka, who was later appointed head of the "Byelorussian Self-Aid Organization." The council, among other things, proposed to the German authorities the candidatures of Archimandrites Feafan, Filafej, and Afanasij (Martos) as Episcopal chairs in Byelorussia. In September 1941, Dionysius also dispatched his agent to revamp the organizational structure of the Orthodox Church in Byelorussia.

For this mission Dionysius appointed as agent a very curious and rather mysterious figure named Vladimir Finkovski. The only information available about him comes from a short entry contained in the Operational Situation Report (*Ereignismeldung*) No. 90, compiled by the *Einsatzgruppe B* on 21 September 1941, as well as from Harvey Fireside's study.[61] It seems that Finkovski was, foremost, a very ambitious man. The authors of the report suggested that the chief motive behind his actions was the desire to become "bishop or archbishop of Byelorussia."[62] In any case, Finkovski was prepared to go quite far in his cooperation with the Germans: he performed "thanksgivings services for the Fuehrer," hung Hitler's picture in his room, and obliged his visitors to cross themselves in front of it.[63] In one of his sermons, Finkovski is said to have stated that "Byelorussia should never become an independent state but that it should remain forever under German sovereignty."[64] Although he succeeded in gaining the support of the Church Council of Minsk, he still provoked the sharp criticism of Byelorussian nationalists such as Ivan Kasyak, author of the postwar book on the Church struggles in Byelorussia during the Nazi occupation (see above, note 1). Kasyak, who shared Roseberg's separatist views, accused Finkovski of not being "an honest Byelorussian" and of harboring "Great Russian sympathies."[65]

These accusations ultimately found receptive listeners among the German authorities. As was the case with local self-administration, in Church matters the Germans viewed the activities of former émigrés with growing hostility, suspicious of their political ambitions. In fact, from the very beginning of the occupation, developments in the Church domain were carefully watched by the German authorities, especially the SS apparatus. In his directive to the HSSPFs in the occupied Soviet territories. issued on 2 July 1941, the head of RSHA Heydrich stated, "No action should be taken against the strivings of the Orthodox Church to influence the masses. On the contrary, these efforts should be encouraged as far as possible, while preserving the principle of separation of Church and State and avoiding the unity of the Church."[66] About a month and a half later, on 16 August 1941, Heydrich issued another "operational order" (*Einsatzbefehl*), No. 10, to the commanders of four *Einsatzgruppen* in the east. In it, relying upon Hitler's personal prohibition to assist in the "revival of religious life" in the newly occupied territories, he said that "The encouragement of Orthodox Church is ... almost out of the question."[67] The order also barred returning buildings and property nationalized during Soviet rule to the religious organizations, but it did allow for such buildings to be placed at their disposal for use (*zur Benutzung*) in religious services. Heydrich also prohibited the provision of any assistance for the organization of divine services.[68] Suspicious of the émigrés, the Germans did not trust the priests who remained in the occupied Soviet territories either. In his additional "operational order" (No. 13), issued on 15 October 1941 to *Einsatzgruppen* commanders, Heydrich expressed his "apprehension" that Soviets might "plant" their agents among the Orthodox priests and therefore demanded the establishment of strict control over these clergymen.[69] In accordance with this order, the priests of all denominations were allowed to carry out their activities only after a thorough examination conducted by the SD and the local commandos of the security police (*Kommando der Sicherheitspolizei*, KdS.[70]

The main problem with the Orthodox Church in Byelorussia from the German point of view was that it was too strongly "Moscow-oriented." The same *Einsatzgruppen* report that mentioned the religious enthusiasm of the population also expressed the fear that the Orthodox priests would use this fervor to preach "the holy indivisible mother Russia" and would strive for some unified form of Church organization.[71] In the second half of September 1941, moreover, the members of *Einsatzgruppe B* reported from Byelorussia, "The Orthodox Church is trying to increase its influence (*an Boden zu gewinnen*), especially in those territories that used to belong to the Soviet Union. There exists the risk that it would use the outbreak of emotionality (*Gefühlsbereitschaft*) of the heretofore oppressed population to feed a nationalist agenda."[72] This approach is similar to that which restricted the activities of the local self-administration: the main concern of the German authorities from the outset was to prevent any potential involvement of the Church in political activities. The SD plenipotentiary for Orthodox Church affairs in the east, Liebram, in his conversation with Rosenberg in September 1941 clearly explained the range of functions of the Orthodox Church in the *Ostgebieten*, "to keep Russians (*Russentum*) under control both from the Weltanschauung's point of view (*weltanschaulich*) and from the religious one."[73]

The attempts of Warsaw Metropolitan Dionysius to expand his jurisdiction eastward, although supported by Hans Frank, were not met with "proper understanding" in other Nazi institutions. In his *Einsatzbefehl Nr. 10*, Heydrich instructed *Einsatzgruppen'* commanders "to prevent autocephalous Orthodox Church under Metropolitan Dionysius from gaining special influence in the occupied areas that are annexed to the Gau of East Prussia and to the GG (General-Government)."[74] It is more than probable that the same approach also applied to the occupied territories to the east.

In such circumstances, the activities of Finkovski, who was connected to Dionysius, could not last long. Despite his submissiveness to the Germans, by the end of 1941, the German authorities yielded to the pressure of Byelorussian nationalists and gave reign to their own desire to prevent Dionysius from expanding his influence into Byelorussia; they arrested Finkovski and sent him to Warsaw.[75]

The next candidate selected to head the Orthodox Church in Byelorussia was the aged Metropolitan Pantelejmon (Rozhnovskij). Half-Pole and half-Russian, he began his church career at the beginning of the twentieth century. A graduate of the Nikolaev Engineering School and of the Kazan Theological Academy, he lived through the most tumultuous years of Russian history. If he had ever been asked what he did during these years, he certainly would have repeated the words said almost two hundred years earlier by his "colleague," one of the central figures of the French Revolution, Abbot Sieyès, "J'ai vécu" (I have survived). Until 1914 Pantelejmon was a bishop of Vitebsk and Polock in eastern Byelorussia; in 1913 he was in charge of transferring the relics of St. Euphrosynia, the patron saint of Byelorussia, from Kiev to Polock. In 1915 he became the bishop of Dvinsk (present-day Daugavpils in Latvia), but lived in Polock. After the Revolution and the Soviet-Polish war he found himself in the Polish part of Byelorussia, where he served initially as bishop of Navahrudak and Pinsk. His opposition to the idea of the independence of the Polish Orthodox Church from the Moscow Patriarchate, as well as to the aggressive missionary activities of the Catholic Church among the Byelorussian Orthodox population, brought him into conflict with the Polish authorities. They exiled him to the Žiroviči monastery, near Slonim, where he lived at the time of the Soviet annexation of Western Byelorussia in September 1939. His reluctance to break with the Moscow Patriarchate was rewarded, when Pantelejmon was appointed by the acting patriarch of Moscow, Sergij, on 17 October 1939, as exarch of the Orthodox Church in Western Byelorussia and Western Ukraine. Around a year later, however, in July 1940, Pantelejmon fell victim to the Soviets' general policy of replacing native personnel from the newly annexed territories with "Easterners."[76] He was replaced by Metropolitan Nikolaj, who was sent from Moscow. Pantelejmon encountered the German invasion once again in the Žiroviči monastery.[77]

The choice of Pantelejmon as the head of the Orthodox Church in Byelorussia was intimately connected with the German plans to organize an autocephalous church in Byelorussia, independent from the Moscow Patriarchate. These plans received a boost with the establishment of a civil administration in Byelorussian territory. On 3 October 1941 Kube sent a letter to Pantelejmon outlining the conditions for the organization of a Byelorussian autocephaly, as follows:[78]

1. The newly organized Orthodox Church [should] be completely independent of Moscow, Warsaw, Berlin, or others.
2. It [should] be named "The Byelorussian Autocephalous Orthodox National Church."
3. The church [will] be free of German interference in its internal life.
4. Church administration, religious instruction, and sermons [are to] be conducted in Byelorussian.
5. Bishops [will] be appointed with knowledge of the German authorities.
6. A legal statute of the "Byelorussian Orthodox Autocephalous National Church" [will] be drawn up and presented to the Germans.
7. the church [will] conduct its services in church-Slavonic.[79]

As can be seen, although proclaiming non-interference in the Church's internal life, German authorities actually intended to establish rigid control over the projected "Byelorussian Autocephalous Church" and, in their usual manner, were eager to carry through their plans with a blatant disregard of reality. The very choice of Pantelejmon, who, as noted, was opposed to the idea of severing ties with the Moscow Patriarchate during the Polish period, points to the trend characteristic of the Nazi rule

of following their predetermined illusions while ignoring existing conditions.

In Byelorussia, in contrast to neighboring Ukraine, there was
virtually no tradition of autocephaly, although the idea itself was
not new. It had been raised on several occasions in both the Polish and Soviet parts of Byelorussia in the 1920s and 1930s,
under various circumstances. In their attempts to combat the
influences from the east upon the Byelorussian minority, Polish
authorities strove to sever the ties between the Orthodox
Church in Poland and the Moscow Patriarchy, by creating the
autocephalous, i.e., independent, Orthodox Church in Poland.[80]
The pretext for this was the claim that the Moscow Patriarchy
found itself under the control of the Bolshevist rulers and was
therefore not independent in its decisions. According to Church
canons, however, the creation of an autocephalous Church
demanded the sanction of the Moscow Patriarchy, which functioned as the "mother Patriarchy" of the Orthodox Church in
Poland. However, the acting Moscow Patriarch, Metropolitan
Sergij, categorically refused to grant such a sanction. Although
ultimately the authorizatioin for the creation of an autocephaly
in Poland was obtained from the Constantinople Patriarchy,
thereby sidestepping the Patriarchy of Moscow, many Orthodox
priests in Poland did not accept this autocephaly. The then
Bishop of Navahrudak and Pinsk, Pantelejmon, was among the
most energetic opponents of autocephaly of the Orthodox
Church in Poland.[81] This struggle reached such a pitch that
Bishop Georgij, head of the autocephalous Orthodox Church in
Poland, was shot dead by Archimandrite (head of the Orthodox
monastery) Smaragd.[82]

Two modest attempts to further the idea of autocephaly in
Soviet Byelorussia were undertaken in the 1920s, and both
ended in overwhelming failure. The first was made in 1922 by
the bishop of Minsk and metropolitan of Byelorussia of that time,
Melchisedek. He was guided by religious rather than political
motives: he wanted to unite the so-called "old-believers"
(*starovery*), whose struggle with the Moscow Patriarchate dated
as far back as the seventeenth century.[83] Eventually Melchisedek
was persuaded by the Moscow metropolitan to both drop the
entire undertaking and renounce his title.[84] The idea of a
Byelorussian autocephalous Church was raised again during the
1927 Minsk conference of clergymen and lay supporters of the
Byelorussian national idea. This affair ended more brutally than

its precursor, as most participants were repressed during the
Stalinist purges.[85]

Although Pantelejmon formally accepted the conditions of the
German authorities with regard to the autocephaly, he adopted
the strategy rightly described by Harvey Fireside as "procrastination."[86] He made it clear to the Germans that the Byelorussian Orthodox Church must first mature for autocephaly. In the
meanwhile, he continued to mention the Moscow Patriarch
Sergij and, to the particular dismay of Byelorussian nationalists,
used Russian instead of Byelorussian in his sermons, claiming
with a considerable degree of justice that the population in the
towns and cities spoke only Russian.[87] Although upon his arrival
in Minsk in November 1941, Pantelejmon—together with
bishop Filafej, who was soon to become his deputy—was
received by Kube, he very soon found himself facing pressure
from the *Generalkommissariat* as well as from Byelorussian
nationalists, who demanded an immediate announcement of the
autocephaly of the Byelorussian Orthodox Church.

The extreme nationalists, who wanted "Byelorussia for
Byelorussians" and who shared Rosenberg's Russophobia,
spared no effort in abusing the Orthodox priests in Byelorussia
as "Moscow's agents." Thus, Ŭladzislaŭ Kazloŭski wrote in an
article published in *Belaruskaja Hazeta* on 6 June 1942, "Every
Orthodox priest was Moscow's missionary, the Russifier of
Byelorussia."[88] These people wanted a "national" Church with
priests solely of Byelorussian origin and with the Byelorussian
language as the only language of the liturgy.

As time passed, this joint German–nationalist pressure only
increased. Already in November 1941, Pantelejmon's former
deputy and proponent of the Moscow Patriarchate's orientation,
Venedikt (Benedict) was appointed archbishop of the Bialystok-
Hrodna diocese attached de facto to East Prussia. In 1942, the
bishop (later archbishop) Filafej (Narko) was appointed as Pantelejmon's deputy in Minsk in Venedikt's place.[89] In the characteristic manner of divide and rule, the German authorities tried
to play Filafej against Pantelejmon. In February 1942, Filafej
was summoned to Eger, the head of the main political department of *GK Weißruthenien*, who expressed his dissatisfaction
with Pantelejmon, especially since the latter continued to mention the Moscow Patriarch in his sermons. Eger informed Filafej
of his intention to ask Kube about the exile of the Metropolitan.
Later Pantelejmon himself was also summoned to the *Generalkommissariat*.[90]

All this pressure resulted in the convocation of the Council (*Sobor*) of Bishops of the Orthodox Church in Byelorussia in March 1942. Although autocephaly was not proclaimed, the Sobor decided to divide Byelorussia into six eparchies, four of which—Mogiljov, Vitebsk, Smolensk, and Baranaviči-Navahrudak—were supposed to be headed by bishops of Byelorussian origin.[91] This allowed the ardent nationalists to rejoice about the Byelorussification of the Orthodox Church. The subsequent consecration of the Byelorussian Afanasij Martos to the bishopric of Vitebsk and Polock, on 9 March 1942, was welcomed by the newspaper *Belaruskaja Hazeta*, the mouthpiece of the Byelorussian National Socialists (see Chapter 6).[92] Martos supported the idea of a Byelorussian "national" Church and soon after entering office, to the great joy of the nationalists, he issued directives for the use of the Byelorussian language in sermons, church services, and religious instruction in schools.[93]

Although nationalists, such as Kazloŭski, who was the leading proponent of Byelorussian Nazism (see Chapter 6), welcomed what they saw as the Byelorussification of the Byelorussian Orthodox Church, they did not ease their pressure on the hierarchs of this Church for a proclamation of autocephaly. This pressure reached its climax in the middle of 1942, when three Byelorussian bishops, Filafej, Afanasij Martos, and Stepan, the bishop of Smolensk, were compelled to send a joint address to *Generalkommissar* Kube. In their message, they spoke of an anonymous "dark force" that was "using the people who are completely ignorant of church affairs but think falsely that intervention in these affairs serves the people. In reality, however, this attempted intervention with its accompanying complaints against the Church's administration creates an unhealthy atmosphere of mistrust on the part of the German authorities toward the Orthodox Byelorussian hierarchy."[94]

Kube, however, was hardly the right person to approach with such petitions. In his desire "to hold out on the ruins of Minsk" and given his own struggles with the Himmler-controlled SS apparatus, he was quite eager to enlist the support of Byelorussian nationalists on the one hand, but was not opposed to the idea of making the Orthodox Church a tool for his propaganda, on the other. In these circumstances, the *Generalkommissariat* became yet another source of constant pressure on the heads of the Byelorussian Orthodoxy, a pressure that was supposed to lead to the proclamation of a Byelorussian Autocephalous Church.

In June 1942, the German authorities had had quite enough of Pantelejmon's reluctance to proclaim the autocephaly, as well as of his "pro-Moscow" mood.[95] His delay in the consecration of Protoierei Simeon as bishop of Smolensk—though the consecration eventually did take place—was the final straw.[96] On 1 June 1942 the Germans issued an order exiling Pantelejmon "in view of his advanced age," which was formally true since Pantelejmon was then seventy-five years old, to the "abolished and half-demolished monastery in the village of Liady, forty kilometers from Minsk," according to Archbishop Venedikt.[97] Although Pantelejmon retained his title of metropolitan, he became a mere figurehead, while the administration of the Metropolis was transferred to his vicar, Filafej.

Hermann Weidhaas, a research assistant of the publishing office in *Reichskommissariat Ostland*, who met Filafej during his visit to the *GK Weißruthenien* in April 1944, described Filafej as a perfect executioner of the German will, who knew exactly what the authorities expected of him.[98] Nevertheless, it would be wrong to portray Filafej as a puppet of the Germans. If the Germans and the Byelorussian nationalists had both hoped that the breakthrough for autocephaly would finally be achieved with Filafej's appointment as acting metropolitan, they were disappointed. Filafej was not ignorant of the reality of the situation. First, he was aware that a unilateral proclamation of a Byelorussian Autocephalous Orthodox Church would constitute a violation of the Church canon, according to which an autocephaly required the permission of the "Mother Church," namely, the Moscow Patriarchy, as well as that of other Orthodox Churches, some of which were even outside the German occupation zone. Secondly, Filafej knew that the idea of autocephaly had virtually no basis throughout the country. Finally, there simply were not enough clergymen ready to carry out this idea. Under these conditions, Filafej adopted a course that was a mixture of procrastination and concessions to the joint German–Byelorussian nationalist pressure. On 5 August 1942 Filafej issued a directive for the convocation of a Sobor of hierarchs, clergymen, and believers to open in Minsk on 28 August 1942. According to the directive, the purpose of the Sobor, which was supposed to consist only of people of the Orthodox faith and Byelorussian nationality, was to provide the Byelorussian autocephaly with "canonical legalization."[99] It stands to reason that Filafej was compelled to issue this directive by the German authorities and by local collaborationist bodies such as the "Self-

Aid Organization." Kazloŭski, in an article published in *Belaruskaja Hazeta* on 30 August 1942, wrote about the Sobor that was due to convene that very day:

> It should be remembered that the acknowledgement of an auto-
> cephaly alone would not Byelorussify the Church and would not
> make it nationally conscious. This would require the fundamen-
> tal reeducation of the entire clergy, which to a significant degree
> is imbued with sympathy to everything Russian. The Sobor in
> Minsk will show what the representatives of Orthodox clergy
> want: either to march shoulder to shoulder with the Byelorussian
> people, their aspirations and the strivings of a new Europe, or be
> further cut off from the people and continue to direct their eyes
> toward Moscow. In the latter case, a ruthless struggle would arise
> between nationally conscious Byelorussian people and Moscow
> advocates, who might be wearing either tsarist shoulder straps,
> Bolshevist stars, or church cassocks.[100]

The Sobor itself, which opened on 30 August instead of 28 August 1942, proceeded according to the German scenario, with participants speaking of the identical interests shared by the German authorities and the Church hierarchy, and of the "historical mission" of the German Army, restoring religious life after years of Polish and Bolshevist oppression, and so on.[101] The Sobor closed with an address directed to Hitler, thanking him for the "liberation of Byelorussia from the Moscow–Bolshevist yoke," and with a thanksgiving service.[102] As to the question of establishing an autocephaly, supposedly the main issue, the participants—aware of the idea's lack of popularity—found a way to slow down the whole matter. The statute adopted at the Sobor insured that autocephaly would be proclaimed officially only after its ratification by "all other Christian Orthodox Churches," i.e., including the Moscow Patriarchy.[103] On 17 April 1943, the bishops in Byelorussia signed the "Epistles to the Eastern Patriarchs" on this matter and handed it to *Generalkommissariat*. The final fate of these "Epistles" is mysterious, and until the end of the occupation the Byelorussian Orthodox Autocephalous Church remained a fictional entity on paper.[104]

Although the nationalists proclaimed the Sobor as "All-Byelorussian," in reality, only two bishoprics, Minsk and Navahrudak, were represented there. The Germans did not allow Metropolitan Pantelejmon to participate, while the Archbishop of Bialystok-Hrodna Venedikt, already on his way to Minsk, was removed from the train by German soldiers and sent back home.[105]

The statute adopted at the council did proclaim in principle the possibility of turning the Orthodox Church in Byelorussia into an autocephalous one; the majority of the Orthodox clergy, however, still remained indifferent to the idea of autocephaly. Even as late as June 1944 an official in Rosenberg's Eastern Ministry, von der Milwe-Schröwen, remarked, "the predominant part of Byelorussian orthodox clergy is in a pro-Russian mood (*russisch gesinnt ist*). The training of a nationally conscious hierarchy encounters some difficulties; it would be possible only on the condition that the Germans develop an initiative related to Church matters."[106] The German repressions carried out in the early part of 1943 against the BNS leadership, and particularly against the organization's leader Yermačenka (see Chapter 4), were in some respect beneficial for the Orthodox Church in Byelorussia. The shifting of the Germans' negative focus onto the BNS also reduced the pressure exerted on the Church hierarchs by the separatists who constituted the backbone of the "Self-Aid Organization." In the second half of 1943, the Orthodox Church in Byelorussia even conducted a number of consecrations that could be viewed as contradicting the principle of the Byelorussification of the Church. These included the consecration of the bishop of Bryansk Pavel, who was of Russian origin, on 11 July 1943, and the bishop of Gomel and Mozyr Grigorij, an ethnic Ukrainian, on 19 September 1943.[107]

Although the majority of Byelorussian Orthodox clergy continuted to be largely unenthusiastic about the autocephaly of the Church, until the conclusion of the occupation it was not opposed to collaborating with the authorities in other "less global" matters, especially those it considered to be a "contribution to the fight against godless Bolshevism." As a rule, until the very end the *Gebietskommissare* noted in their reports the "loyal and reliable" behavior of the Orthodox Church.[108] The Metropolitan Pantelejmon, who was later portrayed by researchers such as Alexeev and Stavrou as no less than an adamant opponent of the German authorities,[109] issued in May 1942, shortly before being banished to Liady, an anti-partisan pastoral epistle which stated, inter alia:

> We, Byelorussians, did not liberate our own homeland from the unbearable Bolshevist yoke by our own forces. The Almighty heard our moans and our prayers and, when we had lost any hope, performed a great miracle: Our neighbors in the West, German brothers, sent with God's help their brave sons, the great

Christian Army, and it threw off from our shoulders the cruel
Bolshevist yoke, pulled us out from the communist slave chains,
and restored Byelorussia once again to a new life.

In the same epistle, the Metropolitan also characterized the partisans as "ordinary thieves and rogues, who conceal their rob-
beries of the peaceful population by patriotic justifications."[110]
Pantelejmon's former deputy, the Archbishop of Bialystok and
Hrodna Venedikt, also issued an epistle "To the Orthodox
Byelorussian people" on 27 April 1943, which said, inter alia, the
following: "The best peoples of the world ... are sending hundreds
and thousands of their children to the front and, under the command of heroic Germany, are defending the freedom of Europe.
We are lucky that our country is protected by this people."[111]

Yet it would be wrong to portray the position of the Orthodox
clergy during the Nazi occupation as one of total submission to
German demands. This was the view advanced for many years
by Soviet historiography and is still espoused today by modern
researchers such as Bernhard Chiari.[112] Indisputably, the Germans' attitude toward the Orthodox Church in Byelorussia, as
in other occupied territories, was characterized by a desire to
control and use it. In the so-called "Tolerance Edict," Rosenberg, moved by a zeal for reform, had intended to proclaim "freedom of faith" in the occupied Eastern territories (this, of course,
did not apply to Judaism). Ultimately, however, this initiative
degenerated into a half-hearted "Directive regarding the Freedom of Religion in the Occupied Eastern Territories" (*Verordnung über die Religionsfreiheit in den besetzten Ostgebieten*),
issued by both *Reichskommissare* Lohse and Koch, in June
1942.[113] The document called "Directive regarding the Legal
Status of Religious Organizations" (*Verordnung über die
Rechtsverhältnisse religiöser Organisationen*), issued simultaneously with the "Freedom of Religion Directive," rather than
touching upon the liberalization of religious life, imposed very
rigid frameworks for the activities of any kind of religious body,
allowing the unceremonious interference of the Germans in
them, thus insuring that any sign of possible opposition would
be thwarted from the outset.[114]

According to these directives, the life of any particular religious organization in the occupied Eastern territories had to
evolve, from its very beginning, under the scrutiny of the Germans. The establishment of any new religious organization, such
as a new monastery, demanded the authorization of the German

civil administration. Furthermore, the Germans awarded themselves the right to control the appointment of people into the "governing bodies" of religious organizations. Based on the second of the directives mentioned above, the *Generalkommissar* could reject a candidate owing to "objections of a general-political nature."[115] Even financial matters did not remain beyond the reach of German control. Thus, according to the "Directive regarding the Freedom of Religion," gifts and mortgages made to religious organizations and exceeding the sum of 1,000 RM required the approval of the *Generalkommissar.*[116]

A directive proclaiming freedom of religion did not necessarily preclude persecution of the Jews. The "Freedom of Religion Directive" also required religious organizations to report the nationality (*Volkszugehörigkeit*) of its members to the Germans.[117] One may assume that the underlying purpose of this demand was to prevent the concealment of Jews, a phenomenon quite widespread among religious bodies in Western Europe, particularly in France.

These demands and directives were not relegated to the theoretical level but were actively implemented. German officials had the right to interfere in the religious life of the occupied territories, and they used and abused this right quite freely. When Metropolitan Pantelejmon allowed one of the priests to return to his parish in Sluck after serving a prison term owing to corruption as well as maiming and offending an official, the Sluck *Gebietskommissar* Carl revoked the metropolitan's decision, maintaining that "the confidence of the local population in such a priest had been lost."[118]

In Byelorussia, the Germans created the impression, at least outwardly, that the Orthodox Church enjoyed a privileged position. This notion was strengthened when buildings belonging to the Catholic Church were transferred to the Orthodox Church, for example in the area of Hanceviči, in Lahojsk, and elsewhere, too.[119] At the same time, the Germans did not hesitate to ignore this so-called "privileged position" when it concerned their own interests. As soon as the Germans realized that priests were receiving "payment" in the form of various foodstuffs in exchange for performing baptisms, weddings, and funeral ceremonies, they were quick "to recognize" rivalry in the appropriation of these food products and demanded the establishment of strict tariffs and general regulations imposing taxes on the priests.[120]

Operating under these restrictions, the Orthodox Church in Byelorussia was left with very little room to maneuver. Nevertheless, this study seeks to understand whether the Church served as a blind tool in German hands or whether it found a formula allowing it some degree of independence in the face of the occupiers. To evaluate correctly the position of the Church in a society under occupation, it must be assumed that priests did not act in a vacuum; they had to take into account not only the demands of the Germans but also the interests of their parishioners. A good example in this respect is the bishop of Bialystok and Hrodna, Venedikt, who was at one time the deputy of Metropolitan Pantelejmon. Documents published in the 1960s by the Soviet historians Zalesskij and Azarov intended to demonstrate the reactionary role of the Orthodox clergy, including Venedikt, during the Nazi occupation of Byelorussia. In reality, careful examination of these documents reveals to the attentive historian the ambiguous situation of the Orthodox clergy during this period. It is true that Venedikt, like his superior Metropolitan Pantelejmon, issued epistles containing thanks to Hitler and the German army. It is equally incontestable that he was opposed to the partisans, calling them "so-called bandits."[121] He also provided a propagandistic cover for the recruitment of a labor force to work in Germany.[122] Yet, a closer look at the same documents reveals a more complex picture. In an appeal to the clergy of his eparchy regarding the German demand to provide labor for work in Germany, Venedikt says, "The authorities have issued the directive about the recruiting of young men and women of our district [the district of Bialystok—L. R.] for a compulsory two-year work period that simultaneously leads to the release from compulsory work for the rest of the local population outside the district ... It [the directive—L. R.] is favorable for the masses of your parishioners and creates a calm atmosphere for peaceful work of those who according to this directive would not be liable for compulsory work outside our district."[123] In other words, while complying with German demands, he is also responding to an ulterior motive.

These words may possibly be dismissed as utter cynicism, but before doing so one should consider that Venedikt did not know exactly how many workers the Germans planned to pull out of the occupied territories, figures that are known to modern researchers. However, he certainly knew what the Germans were capable of doing. One must keep in mind that at the time the appeal was issued, the so-called "anti-partisan undertakings" were underway, encompassing not only eastern and central Byelorussia, but also the western part (including Hrodna region).[124] In the course of these "undertakings," whole villages were depopulated and burned down, their inhabitants either killed or deported to work in Germany.[125] In this context, the Venedikt's position, as well as that of some other priests, could be described as attempting to avoid the worst scenario; that is, by fulfilling some of the Germans' demands he hoped to prevent full-scale repressions against his entire flock. This approach was not unique to the Orthodox clergy nor to the clergy in general, as it was shared by other bodies in the occupied territories, even by some of the Jewish *Judenräte*, although this example is not without its own complexities. Not all of these bodies and individuals had heard about schemes such as *Generalplan Ost*, or Backe's "hunger plan." They were under the illusion that they could somehow sate the Nazi Moloch.[126]

Also of note is the participation of the Church in the "collecting campaigns" (*Sammelaktionen*). During the occupation, the German authorities turned a number of times to the Byelorussian population with an appeal to submit various materials, such as metals, needed by the Wehrmacht.[127] For example, when it became clear that the war against the Soviet Union would not end before the beginning of the winter, and the German soldiers were poorly equipped for warfare in winter conditions, the population in the occupied territories was called upon to submit winter clothes. Nazi propaganda then reported on the "grandiose" successes of such "campaigns."[128] From the documents available, it seems that the Church participated quite actively in these *Sammelaktionen*. The *Gebietskommissar* of Hlybokaje, Hachmann, noted in his final report, composed on 16 August 1944, "I used chiefly the priests of the Orthodox Church in the *Sammelaktionen* carried out on the Wehrmacht's behalf, such as collections of furs, metals and carts (*Panjewagen*)."[129] According to the German press, in early June 1942, shortly before his banishment to Liady, Pantelejmon even called on "archpriests (*Pröbste*), priests and churchwardens" to submit "all the non-ferrous metals, especially church bells, unnecessary for the divine services, the numbers of which can be reduced for the time being."[130] There would seem to be nothing unique about this appeal, if it were not for the fact that Pantelejmon's predecessors some two hundred years previously had allegedly demonstrated much less understanding when, during the North War between Russia and Sweden, Peter the Great tried to smelt church bells for cannons.

Apparently in 1942, Pantelejmon, as well as many other Orthodox priests in the occupied Eastern territories, still believed that the German army was primarily struggling against the "godless" Soviet regime. Many of them certainly did not want to encounter the Soviets again, who still had the image of anti-religious persecutors.[131] Simply put, the Orthodox clergy was ready to transfer the church bells to the Germans rather than see the same church reduced to rubble by "the Bolsheviks." An additional point, however, must also be considered. Even if the German policy toward the Church could hardly be defined as enlightened, the ambiguous position of the Nazis toward the Orthodox Church still contrasted with outright Soviet hostility. It is beyond any doubt that the Germans tended to control the Church, to manipulate it, to treat the priests with disregard whenever they deemed it suitable, and to distance the Orthodox Church as far as possible from political matters. Yet the indifferent position adopted from the outset by the Germans toward everyday religious practices was regarded as support by quite a number of higher and lower Church hierarchs.[132] Despite various limitations, many churches were reopened during the occupation: according to Pospielovsky in six cities of eastern Byelorussia, Borisov, Mogiljov, Orsha, Škloŭ, Vitebsk with its suburbs, and Polock, as many as fifty-three churches reopened, while in Borisov alone twenty-one churches resumed their services.[133] According to Alexeev and Stavrou, in the Smolensk area, which after the hoped-for future victory over the Soviet Union was supposed to be added to *GK Weißruthenien*, the priests performed 150 to 200 baptisms daily.[134] In January 1944, Gottberg reported that some 25,000 people participated in the Epiphany ceremony in Minsk. It may be conjectured, however, that (a) this number is exaggerated, and (b) people simply used the opportunity to get out of work.[135] While the developments in the Church sphere in the occupied Soviet territories during the war may be cautiously referred to as a "religious revival," they nonetheless constituted a stark contrast with the practices of the Soviet regime that turned the churches into dance clubs and engaged in outright suppression of the clergy.[136] Such an assessment certainly could provide a sufficient basis for cooperation between the Orthodox Church and the occupation authorities.

The role of the Orthodox Church as a propagandist tool against Bolshevism increased further in the final stage of the occupation. This was caused not only by the approach of the Red Army but also by the developments in the Soviet rear. The reinstating of the Church in the German-occupied territories showed Stalin that all the proclamations about the non-existence of God and all the terror against the Church had not succeeded in eliminating the people's religious faith. Moreover, the Soviets could not simply close again the many churches in the liberated territories that had been reopened during the Nazi occupation without provoking the outrage of the believers, certainly an undesirable measure during the war. Thus, the Soviet government came to the conclusion that some kind of reconciliation with the Church would be more appropriate for the moment. This gesture was carried out with the help of the acting Moscow patriarch, Sergij, who on the first day of the Nazi-Soviet war had issued a proclamation "To the Whole Church," in which he damned "the fascist bandits" and blessed "with heavenly grace the people for their heroic battle."[137] In August 1943, Stalin himself received the patriarch and allowed him to convoke a Sobor of bishops to "elect" a new patriarch, or rather to proclaim the acting Patriarch Sergij as patriarch with all rights.[138] The authorities also allowed the reopening of a number of churches throughout the Soviet Union, although the majority of attendants belonged to the older generation.[139]

For their part, the Germans reacted with counter-measures in the territories still under their control. Although they were highly suspicious of the Sobors, conferences, and the like, fearing that germs of opposition would take hold at such events, in early 1944 Gottberg nevertheless initiated the bishops' council, which was set to take place in Minsk in May that year. For this event, even Pantelejmon was allowed to return from exile, and he subsequently issued an anti-Bolshevist Christmas epistle.[140] The Sobor, which took place on 12 May 1944, formally reaffirmed the intention to initiate the Byelorussification of the Church, but most of the council's practical decisions, such as the plan to open a new seminary, were actually of little significance, since the German occupation was coming to an end. This Sobor showed once again that the tension between the church authorities and the Byelorussian "lay" collaborators—this time in the form of the BCR—who adhered to the notion of a thorough Byelorussification in all spheres of life, did not cease until the very end of the occupation.[141]

The story of collaboration on the part of the Orthodox Church would not be complete without some reference to the Church's position toward the Holocaust. It is indeed very difficult on the basis of the scanty documents available to create a coherent picture. The German authorities' main concern, however, was that the Church should not provide shelter for persecuted Jews. As stated above, the "Directive regarding the Freedom of Religion" demanded that religious organizations provide information about "the national origin" of its members. Moreover, shortly before his exile to Liady, Pantelejmon issued a decree which, inter alia, prohibited the baptizing of Jews, as that might help them to hide. The statement by Alexeev and Stavrou that the decree was a result of pressure exerted by the German authorities is extremely difficult to either prove or disprove.[142] With some degree of caution, we can state that the stance of the Orthodox Church in Byelorussia toward the Jews was less aggressive than that of the Catholic Church in neighboring Lithuania, where in the first days and weeks of the war there were a number of Catholic priests who not only incited their flock against the Jews but who also personally led the gangs that carried out the massacres of the Jews.[143] In Byelorussia we have no evidence of such actions, although anti-Semitic sermons were not unknown there, as will be shown in the chapter dealing with the collaboration in the persecution of Jews.

To sum up, one may note that not only was the position of the German occupation authorities toward the Orthodox Church in Byelorussia ambiguous but also vice versa. Although a significant number of high Church hierarchs and lower-rank clergy shared anti-Soviet sentiments, their collaboration with the German authorities was never blind. Many of them were quite eager to participate in activities initiated by the authorities, such as the *Sammelaktionen*; apparently, they genuinely believed that by doing so they were contributing to the war against the "godless Bolsheviks." The clergy also played a not unimportant role in the recruitment of labor for work in Germany. Yet, it must be asked: is it possible to define the role of the Orthodox Church as simply "aiding and abetting" the Germans, as Soviet researchers did for many years?

A close analysis of the available sources proves that at least in Byelorussia the Orthodox Church's willingness to collaborate with the Germans had its limits. This willingness ended or at least was weakened when the requested collaboration contradicted the Church's canons, traditions, and public opinion. The Soviet historians spared no effort in demonstrating the "antinational" (*antinarodnyj*) character of the Church activities, but, in reality, the clergy was by no means deaf to the mood prevailing among its parishioners. Many priests were "sandwiched" between German demands and their parishioners, whose interests they were supposed to defend. As the case of Archbishop Venedikt shows, at least some of them sincerely believed that by complying with certain German demands, they could spare their parishioners even worse troubles.

The problem of Byelorussian autocephaly demonstrated once again that the Germans were unable to rise above dogmatism and to see the real situation reigning in the occupied country. Supported by the Byelorussian chauvinists who saw themselves as the sole and true representatives of the Byelorussian people, the occupiers pushed for the proclamation of a Byelorussian Autocephalous Church, thereby completely ignoring the idea's unpopularity in Byelorussia as well as the lack of an autocephalous tradition in that country. Even the fact that a unilateral proclamation of autocephaly would contradict the Church canons did not deter people such as *Generalkommissar* Kube, whose personal dreams and aspirations, like those of his formal superior Lohse, included having the Church at his beck and call.

The fact remains that even measures such as the issuing of the "Toleration Edict," which perhaps was thought of as a positive step, ultimately degenerated into a directive which, contrary to its title, resulted in yet further tightening of German control over religious life in the occupied territories. Issuing this directive almost simultaneously with the proclamation of the so-called "New Agrarian Order" (see Chapter 3) clearly shows that the Germans were guided by considerations of expediency, rather than by the interests of the people they wanted to rule or by the actual conditions.

Notes

* This chapter is based primarily on the following studies (in chronological order): H. Fireside, *Icon and Swastika* (Cambridge, MA, 1971); V. Alexeev and Th. Stavrou, *The Great Revival* (Minneapolis, 1976); A. Dallin, *German Rule in Russia, 1941–1945* (Boulder, 1981); and D. Pospielovsky, *The Russian Church under the Soviet Regime, 1917–1982* (New York, 1984), vol. 1. In addition to the paucity of more recent research on the subject, the state of primary sources also leaves much to be desired. Among the studies mentioned, the most extensive account of Church-related developments in occupied Byelorussia is contained in Alexeev and Stavrou's book, which draws heavily upon both German and local sources. Unfortunately, the current author was unable to obtain a copy of Ivan Kasyak's book *Z Historyi Pravaslaŭnaj Tsarkvy Belaruskago Narodu*. During the occupation period, Kasyak was one of the most prominent collaborators and was also directly involved in the Church's struggles in occupied Byelorussia. His

book is quoted, however, by the authors mentioned above. This chapter was published in a somewhat altered form in the *East European Quarterly*: "The Orthodox Church in Byelorussia under Nazi Occupation (1941–1944)," *East European Quarterly* 39, no. 1 (Spring 2005): 13–46.

1. Eugen von Engelhard, *Weißruthenien* (Berlin, 1943), 144. Von Engelhard's work must be read with a great deal of caution. He was an official in the Reich's Ministry for the Occupied Eastern Territories and fully concurred with the Nazis' stereotype of Poles and their animosity toward them. Still, his work, *Weißruthenien*, published during the Third Reich, contains some valuable information otherwise inaccessible to the modern researcher.
2. Ibid.
3. Vakar, *Belorussia*, 122.
4. Pospielovsky, *Russian Church*, 1:31.
5. Ibid., 32.
6. Ibid., 99.
7. Fireside, *Icon and Swastika*, 43.
8. Vakar, *Belorussia*, 148.
9. Pospielovsky, *Russian Church*, 39.
10. The Renovationist Council (*Sobor*) assembled in April 1923 praised the Soviet system and greeted Lenin as a fighter "for the great social truth." See ibid., 56. For more on the Renovationists and their relations with the Soviet regime, see ibid., 43ff.
11. The *exarch* is the head of an Orthodox Church district consisting of several dioceses, and enjoys some degree of independence.
12. See chapter 2, 000.
13. See ibid.
14. Alexeev and Stavrou, *Revival*, 115–16.
15. Fireside, *Icon and Swastika*, 75.
16. Ibid., 77; Pospielovsky, *Russian Church*, 222.
17. On the history of "Karlovcy Synod," see Pospielovsky, *Russian Church*, 113ff.
18. Ibid., 222f.
19. Fireside, *Icon and Swastika*, 77; Pospielovsky, *Russian Church*, 223.
20. Pospielovsky, *Russian Church*, 223.
21. Ibid.
22. Fireside, *Icon and Swastika*, 77.
23. Thorwald, *Die Illusion*, 24. Alfred Rosenberg, *Der Mythos des 20. Jahrhunderts* (Munich, 1935), 514.
24. Ibid., 614.
25. Ibid., 616; ibid., 617.
26. Chamberlain wrote, "Only one assertion can therefore be made on a sound historical basis: in that whole region [i.e., the Galilee–L.R.] there was only one single pure race, a race which by painfully scrupulous measures protected itself from all mingling with other nations—the Jewish; that Jesus Christ did not belong to it can be regarded as certain," Houston Stewart Chamberlain, *The Foundations of the Nineteenth Century*, trans. J. Lees (London and New York, 1911), 1:212.
27. Hans-Günther Seraphim (ed.), *Das Politische Tagebuch Alfred Rosenbergs* (Göttingen, 1956), 97.
28. *Hitler's Table Talk 1941–1944*, trans. N. Cameron and R. H. Stevens (London, 1973), 7.

29. Quoted in Dallin, *German Rule*, 472.
30. The church struggles relating to these efforts in the first years of the Nazi regime are described inter alia in the biography of Dietrich Bonhoffer, written by Eberhard Bethge. See Eberhard Bethge, *Dietrich Bonhoffer*, trans. E. Mosbacher et al. (New York and London, 1970).
31. Quoted in Fireside, *Icon and Swastika*, 73.
32. *Hitler's Table Talk*, 3.
33. Dallin, *German Rule*, 474.
34. Seraphim, *Politische Tagebuch*, 97. Quoted in Dallin, *German Rule*, 474.
35. "Abschrift des Schreibens des Reichsministers für die besetzten Ostgebieten an Reichskommissare für das Ostland und Ukraine bezüglich Religionsgesellschaften in den besetzten Ostgebieten, 13.05.42," BA R 6/18, Mikrofiche 3.
36. See "General Instructions, 8 May 1941, found in Rosenberg's files on Russia, for Reich Commissioners in the occupied eastern territories," Document 1030-PS, *IMT* (Nuremberg, 1947), vol. 26, 576–80, esp. 579.
37. Fireside, *Icon and Swastika*, 81; Dallin, *German Rule*, 480.
38. Picker, *Zastol'nye Razgovory Gitlera*, 198.
39. "Abschrift des Schreibens des Reichsministers für die besetzten Ostgebieten an Reichskommissare für das Ostland und Ukraine bezüglich Religionsgesellschaften in den besetzten Ostgebieten, 13.05.42," BA R 6/18, Mikrofiche 3.
40. According to Alexeev and Stavrou, 57% of the Soviet citizens declared themselves believers during the census that was carried out in 1937, that is, at the high point of the religious persecution by the Soviet authorities. See Alexeev and Stavrou, *Revival*, 26.
41. "Organization of propaganda in the 'Eastern-instructions' proposed by the press-chief in the 'eastern ministry' dealing with 'New Agrarian Order,' local self-government, religious matters, and military formations of Soviet minorities, January 1942," BA R 90/31.
42. In some cases, for example in Borisov, the Wehrmacht allegedly assisted in the restoration of church buildings. See Wilfried Strik-Strikfeldt, *Gegen Stalin und Hitler* (Mainz, 1970), 23. "TLB Nr. 3, 15.8–31.8.41," in Klein, *Einsatzgruppen*, 164. See, for example, "Operational Situation Report USSR No. 13," in Arad and Spector, *The Einsatzgruppen Reports*, 8–9.
43. "TLB Nr. 4 (1.9–15.9.1941)," in Klein, *Einsatzgruppen*, 187.
44. "TLB Nr. 6, 1.10–31.10.41," ibid., 234.
45. Alexeev and Stavrou, *Revival*, 111–12.
46. "TLB Nr. 2, 29.7–14.8.41," in Klein, *Einsatzgruppen*, 149. The fact that such activities were not a rarity can be inferred from the official request directed by *Einsatzgruppen* command to Wehrmacht offices to stop it (see ibid.).
47. Ibid.
48. "TLB Nr. 1, 31.7.41," ibid., 127.
49. Turonak, *Belarus' pad nyameckaj Akupacyjaj*, 83.
50. "Bedritzki an Propaganda-Referenten Lauch, 29.9.43," BA R 90/158.
51. "Report on the moods of the population in *Weißruthenien*, written by a Byelorussian from Latvia, August 1942," BA R 90/126. The text of the document leads to the conclusion that this report was actually written by the German security organs and not by an anonymous "Byelorussian from Latvia."
52. Vakar, *Belorussia*, 189–90.
53. Ibid. 190.

54. See, for example, Lastoŭski, *Karotkaja Historyja Belarusi*, 63.

55. Fireside, *Icon and Swastika*, 140.

56. Szepticky is considered a controversial figure, as he both blessed the creation of the Ukrainian Waffen-SS Division "Halychyna" and also assisted persecuted Jews. The first fact to this day prevents Yad Vashem authorities from conferring on Szepticky the title "Righteous among the Nations." On Szepticky and his position regarding the Holocaust, see S. Redlich, "Metropolitan Andrii Sheptyts'kyi, and the Complexities of Ukrianinian-Jewish Relations," in Gitelman, *Bitter Legacy*, 61–76.

57. Fireside, *Icon and Swastika*, 140.

58. Vakar, *Belorussia*, 278.

59. Alexeev and Stavrou, *Revival*, 113–15.

60. Quoted ibid., 113.

61. "Operational Situation Report USSR No. 90, 21.9.41," in Arad and Spector, *The Einsatzgruppen Reports*, 146; Fireside, *Icon and Swastika*, 141.

62. "Operational Situation Report USSR No. 90," see note 61.

63. Ibid.

64. Ibid.

65. Ibid.

66. "Heydrichs nachträgliche schriftliche Einweisung der vier Höheren SS- und Polizeiführer im Osten vom 2.7.1941," in Klein, *Einsatzgruppen*, 328.

67. Hitler's directives on this matter, if they existed at all, could not be located, so the author was compelled to rely on Heydrich's rendition of their content. "Einsatzbefehl Heydrichs Nr. 10 vom 16.8.1941," in Klein, *Einsatzgruppen*, 346. See also "Einsatzbefehl Nr. 13 des Chefs der Sicherheitspolizei und des SD vom 15.10.1941," ibid., 354.

68. "Einsatzbefehl Nr. 10," ibid., 346–47.

69. Einsatzbefehl Nr. 13," see note 68.

70. These were the parts of *Einsatzgruppen* who remained in place and did not follow the Wehrmacht units in their advance to Moscow. "TLB Nr. 5, (15.9–30.9.41)," in Klein, *Einsatzgruppen*, 212; "TLB Nr. 6 (1.10–31.10.41)," ibid., 235.

71. "TLB Nr. 4," ibid., 187.

72. "TLB Nr. 5 (15.9–30.9.41)," ibid., 220.

73. "Akten-Notiz von Rosenberg über die Unterredung mit SS-Obersturm- führer Liebram (Ensatzkommando Ostland, SD)in Riga am 8.9.41," BA R 6/179, Mikrofiche 1.

74. "Einsatzbefehl Heydrichs Nr. 10," in Klein, *Einsatzgruppen*, 346.

75. Fireside, *Icon and Swastika*, 141.

76. For more on the practice of replacing local cadres by *Vostochniki*, see Pinchuk, *Shtetl Jews*, 48.

77. The information on Pantelejmon can be found in Alexeev and Stavrou, *Revival*, 115–16. See also: "Vertraulicher Bericht des wissenschaftlichen Referents der Publikationsstelle Dr. Hermann Weidhaas über seine Erfahrungen und Tätigkeit während der nach Weißruthenien unter- nommenen Reise im April 1944," BA R 90/127 and Vakar, *Belorussia*, 122.

78. Alexeev and Stavrou, *Revival*, 112.

79. Vakar also mentions Kube's letter to Pantelejmon (*Belorussia*, 278), but not its content.

80. According to the hierarchy existing in the Orthodox Church, the Church in Poland was subordinate to the Moscow Patriarchy, which in turn, formally

at least, was subordinate to the Constantinople (Istanbul) Patriarchy as a "Mother Church."

81. Von Engelhard, *Weißruthenien*, 145.
82. Ibid., 145f.
83. For more on the origins of the *starovery* movement, see Kljuchevskij, *Russkaja Istoriia*, 2:380ff.
84. Fireside, *Icon and Swastika*, 140.
85. Ibid., 141.
86. Ibid., 142.
87. Alexeev and Stavrou, *Revival*, 119.
88. "Nazaŭsjody spynic' rusyfikacyju Belarusi," *Belaruskaja Hazeta*, 6 June 1942, 1, YVA, C-762.
89. Alexeev and Stavrou, *Revival*, 116.
90. Ibid., 117–18.
91. Minsk-Vilna (Vilnius), without Vilna itself (headed by Pantelejmon); Hrodna-Bialystok (bishop, later archbishop Venedikt), Mogiljov (Filafej received the title of bishop of Mogiljov and Mstislavl); Vitebsk (bishop Afanasij Martos); Smolensk (bishop Stepan); and Baranaviči-Navahrudak (headed by bishop Veniamin, Byelorussian by origin, who at the time of the Sobor was bishop of the Autonomous Ukrainian Church in Poltava, RKU). See ibid., 118. Dallin's statement about the new eparchies' borders coinciding with those of the *Gebietskommissariate* is not correct. See Dallin, *German Rule*, 486.
92. "Novy Belaruski Episkap," BH, 11.3.42, 4, YVA C-762.
93. These directives were quoted in BH, 21.5.42, 3, YVA, C-762.
94. "Iz Otnoshenija Zamestitelja Metropolita Belorusskoj Pravoslavnoj Tserkvi i Episkopov General'nomu Komissaru Bjelorussii o zadachakh tserkvi po bor'be sovmestno s fashistami protiv kommunizma i ob okazanii dukhovenstvu material'noj pomoshchi za vernuju sluzhbu gitlerovtsam," in A. Zalesskij and A. Azarov (eds.), *Dokumenty Oblichajut* (Minsk, 1964), 82. The collection of documents *Dokumenty Oblichajut* ("The Revealing Documents") intended to show the "reactionary" role of the Church during the German occupation of Byelorussia and was therefore compiled in the best tradition of Soviet propagandistic historiography.
95. Alexeev and Stavrou (*Revival*, 119–20), Pospielovsky (*Russian Church*, 233), and Dallin (*German Rule*, 487) relate the exile of Pantelejmon to the intrigues of Byelorussian separatists.
96. The senior post in the Orthodox Church's hierarchy. Simeon was due to change his name to Stepan (Stefan). According to Alexeev and Stavrou, the opposition of Pantelejmon to Simeon's appointment was caused by the fear of an increase of Byelorussian influence in the Orthodox Church. See Alexeev and Stavrou, *Revival*, 118; Dallin, *German Rule*, 486.
97. Quoted by Alexeev and Stavrou, *Revival*, 116–17, 119.
98. "Vertraulicher Bericht des wissenschaftlichen Referenten der Publikationsstelle Dr. Hermann Weidhaas über seine Erfahrungen und Tätigkeit während der nach Weißruthenien unternomenen Reise im April 1944," BA R 90/127.
99. "Rasporjazhenije zamestitelja mitropolita belorusskoj pravoslavnoj tserkvi o sozyve po soglasovaniju okkupatsionnymi vlastjami tserkovnogo sobora dlya ofitsial'nogo provozglashenija otdelenija belorusskoj tserkvi ot russkoj pravoslvanoj tserkvi," in Zalesskij and Azarov, *Dokumenty Oblichajut*, 83–86.

100. "Sabor pravalsaŭnaje tsarkvy ŭ Mensku," BH, 30.8.42, 1, YVA C-762.
101. Quoted in Chiari, *Alltag hinter der Front*, 105.
102. "Telegrama ot imeni I Vsebelorusskogo pravoslavnogo tserkovnogo sobora Gitleru s vyrazhenijem blagodarnosti za avtokefaliju beloruskoj tserkvi i pozhelanijami skoroj i polnoj pobedy fashistskoj armii v bor'be protiv SSSR, 30.8.42," Zalesskij and Azarov, *Dokumenty Oblichajut*, 86–87. Chiari, *Alltag hinter der Front*, 105; Pospielovsky, *Russian Church*, 1:233; Fireside, *Icon and Swastika*, 143.
103. Vakar, *Belorussia*, 278.
104. Ibid.
105. Alexeev and Stavrou, *Revival*, 122.
106. "Schreiben des Leiters der Führungsgruppe P 4 in RMfdbO an den Leiter der Führungsgruppe P 3 betreffend Aktenvermerk Thurmanns vom 16. Mai 1944, 1.06.44," BA R 6/179, Mikrofiche 4.
107. Alexeev and Stavrou, *Revival*, 128–29.
108. See, for example, "Tätigkeits-, Räumings- und Erfahrungsbericht des Gebietskommissars für Nowogrodek, 3.08.44"; "Tätigkeits-, Räumungs- und Erfahrungsbericht des Gebietskommissars Glebokie Hachmann, 16.8.44"; "Tätigkeits-, Räumings- und Erfahrungsbericht des Gebietskommissars in Kobryn Panzer, 21.8.44," all in BA R 93/13.
109. See Alexeev and Stavrou, *Revival*, 116.
110. "Deutschland hat uns befreit," *Minsker Zeitung*, 24/25.5. 42, BA R 90/107. The Byelorussian version of the same epistle was published in BH, 31.5.41, 4, YVA, C-762.
111. "Iz poslanija arkhijepiskopa Belostokskoj i Grodnenskoj eparchij belorusskomu narodu," in Zalesskij and Azarov, *Dokumenty Oblichajut*, 91–92.
112. Ibid. Thus, according to Chiari, "The Byelorussian Orthodox Church remained, cut from its spiritual center, the instrument in the hands of German occupants." See Chiari, *Alltag hinter der Front*, 107.
113. Unfortunately, the only version of the document available to this author is the so-called "First Instruction for the Execution of Directive regarding the Freedom of Religion in the Occupied Eastern Territories" dated March 1942. See "Erste Durchführungsverordnung für das Reichskommissariat Ostland zu den Verordnung über die Religionsfreiheit in den besetzten Ostgebieten vom März 1942" (in the following, "Verordnung über die Religionsfreiheit"), BA R 6/18, Mikrofiche 2.
114. "Verordnung über die Rechtsverhältnisse religiöser Organisationen, 1.6.42," BA R 6/178, Mikrofiche 1.
115. Ibid.
116. Ibid.
117. Ibid.
118. The case is quoted by Chiari, *Alltag hinter der Front*, 107.
119. "Tätigkeitsbericht von Gebietskommissar für Hansewitsche Hördt für die gesamte Zeit seit Übernahme des Gebietes in die Ziwilverwaltung, 23.8.44," BA R 93/13. "Vypiska iz otcheta nachal'nika policii i vojsk SS Belorussii ob aktivnom sotrudnichestve logojskogo svajshchennika s okkupantami i karatel'nym batal'onom SS palacha Dirlevangera," in Zalesskij and Azarov, *Dokumenty Oblichajut*, 92.
120. Chiari, *Alltag hinter der Front*, 106.
121. "Iz poslanija archiepiskopa Belostokskoj i Grodnenskoj eparkhij k dukhovenstvu, 22.1.43," Zalesskij and Azarov, *Dokumenty Oblichajut*, 88.

122. "Iz obrashchenija archiepiskopa Belostokskoj i Grodnenskoj eparkhij k dukhovenstvu, 15.4.43," ibid., 90–91.
123. Ibid., 90.
124. See the testimonies in Adamovich et al, *Ya iz ognennoj Derevni...*
125. A more detailed description of these "operations" will be provided in the chapter dealing with repressive politics of the Nazi occupation regime.
126. For a recent discussion about the precarious position of Jewish Councils (*Judenräte*), see D. Diner, "Beyond the Conceivable. The Judenrat as Borderline Experience," in idem, *Beyond the Conceivable* (Berkley, 2000), 117–29.
127. See, for example, an appeal by Kube published in *Belaruskaja Hazeta* on 2 April 1942 in which the submitting of metals and metal wares is presented as a "contribution for the struggle for the new Europe." See BH, 2.4.1942, 1, YVA, C-762.
128. *Deutsche Zeitung im Ostland* on 20 February 1942 published an article about the "enthusiastic" donations of furs and fur coats for the German army by the population of occupied Byelorussia, which, among other parts, read as follows, "What nobody thought possible, in the wretched economic situation, has came true: more than 100 000 fur coats and furs were presented (*dargebracht*) [*sic*] to the German soldiers" (H.-J. Schröter, "Spenden eines verarmten Landes," *Deutsche Zeitung im Ostland*, 20 February 1942). Of course, the number itself should be considered an exaggeration.
129. "Tätigkeits-, Räumungs- und Erfahrungsbericht des Gebietskommissars Glebokie Hachmann, 16.08.44," BA R 93/14.
130. "Weißrutheniens Metropolit wirbt für die Metallsammlung," *Minsker Zeitung*, 3 June 1942, BA R 90/107.
131. It was only some years later, in 1943, that Stalin was ready to reconcile himself with the Orthodox Church, mainly due to his impression of the events in the German-occupied territories as well as his understanding that communist slogans alone would not suffice to induce many of the Soviet people to fight against the Germans. See Fireside, *Icon and Swastika*, 166.
132. Thus, Heydrich in his "operation order No. 10" (16 August 1941) instructed the commanders of *Einsatzgruppen* as follows, "The support of the Orthodox Church is also almost out of the question. In the places where the population of the occupied territories of Soviet Russia expresses the wish about religious service and where there is a clergyman without the support of occupation authorities, the resumption of religious activities can be tolerated" (Klein, *Einsatzgruppen*, 346).
133. Pospielovsky, *Russian Church*, 235.
134. Alexeev and Stavrou, *Revival.*
135. See "Schreiben an den Leiter der Führungsgruppe P 4 in RMfdbO von der Milwe-Schröwen, 18.5.44," BA R 6/179, Mikrofiche 2. Alexeev and Stavrou claim that between 80,000 and 100,000 people took part in the ceremony. It is extremely difficult to confirm or disprove these numbers empirically. Alexeev and Stavrou, *Revival*, 134.
136. Conservative Western historians such as Alexeev and Stavrou, as well as Pospielovsky, see the situation in this way (ibid., Pospielovsky, *Russian Church*, 234).
137. See Fireside, *Icon and Swastika*, 172.
138. Ibid., 166, 178.

139. The Moscow *New York Times'* correspondent described the people assembled for the 1944 Christmas services in the Soviet capital as being "a normal sample of Moscow's housewives and middle-aged men." Only a few soldiers belonged to the younger generation. Ibid., 181.

140. "Von Gottbergs Fernschreiben an Ostministerium-Führungsstab betreffend Mobilisierung aller Kräfte gegen dem Bolschewismus, 5.2.44," BA R 6/179, Mikrofiche 5.

141. Alexeev and Stavrou, *Revival*, 131.

142. Ibid., 120.

143. See Sara Neshamit, *"Bein Shittuf Pe'ula le-Meri"* [Between collaboration and resistance], *Dappim le Heker ha-Shoa ve ha-Mered*, 2nd series, 1st supplement (1970), 163.

CHAPTER 6

IDEOLOGICAL COLLABORATION IN BYELORUSSIA: THE "LEGAL" PRESS AS A PROPAGANDIST TOOL OF THE NAZIS' "NEW EUROPE"*

When Nazi Germany started the war against the Soviet Union, it already had a very powerful propaganda machine, created by Josef Goebbels, that applied the newest achievements of technological progress.[1] Upon arriving in the Soviet territories, the Germans understood fairly quickly that the stick alone would not suffice to rule the peoples there and that some explanatory work would also be needed. As time passed, propaganda became one of the most important elements of occupation policies. The occupation authorities also soon came to the conclusion that their aimes would be best achieved if the propaganda were carried out in the native language. The head of the propaganda department in *GK Weißruthenien*, Schröter, in his report at the conference of GKW high officials in April 1943, described the main objectives of the propaganda in occupied Byelorussia thus:

1. To struggle against Bolshevism
2. To struggle against banditry [partisans–L. R.]
3. To recruit locals for voluntary work in Germany

4. To pursue the "struggle for production" (*Erzeugungss-chlacht*) of local agriculture.[2]

As these issues demonstrate, the Germans perceived local propaganda chiefly as a tool for pacifying and exploiting the country. Its importance in the occupied territories can be deduced from the variety of media through which it was carried out—newspapers, radio, movies—the number and circulation of the various newspapers, the number of radio transmitters connected to the main line, and the number of cinemas allowed to open. Thus, according to the same Schröter, in five districts (*Gebiete*) alone of *GK Weißruthenien* (Minsk, Baranaviči, Vilejka, Sluck, and Slonim) as many as 7,637 radio transmitters were allowed to be connected to the main line, although some eighty-four per cent of these (6,385) operated in two districts, Minsk and Baranaviči.[3] Also from Schröter's report, we learn that thirty-six movie theaters were open in the territory of GKW, with the total number of theater-goers reaching as high as 100,000.[4] Of course, as with all the data provided by German officials, it is difficult to establish the extent to which these data reflect reality or merely German aspirations.

However, it was the press that occupied a central place in the propaganda of the occupied Soviet territories. It is not easy to assess accurately the circulation size or the number of newspapers and magazines published during the German occupation in the Eastern territories. The Byelorussian researcher Sergej Zhumar, who in the 1990s published a study dealing with periodicals in Byelorussia during the Nazi occupation, pointed out the great differences in data regarding the number of newspapers published in the Byelorussian language.[5] According to the *Ostministerium,* in May 1942 out of a total number of 130 newspapers in various languages published in the Occupied Eastern Territories, six appeared in Byelorussian.[6] In his report, however, Schröter spoke of thirty-three periodicals published in the *GK Weißruthenien* alone, while a bulletin titled *Die Ostkartei* and published by the *Reichskommissariat Ostland* referred to a mere four periodicals published in Byelorussian in the years 1942–1943: *Baranavickaja Hazeta, Belaruskaja Hazeta, Holas Vjoski,* and *Belaruskaja Škola.*[7] In the appendix to his work, Zhumar cites a bibliography of the periodicals published in Byelorussian between 1941 and 1945 in Byelorussia itself as well as in other occupied territories and in Germany. According to this list, the total number of Byelorussian-language periodicals published only in the territories of *GK Weißruthenien* and in the Rear Area of the Army Group Center, that is, more or less within the present borders of Byelorussia, came to approximately forty titles. Of these, only about fifteen appeared more or less regularly, while the rest had published only a very small number of issues.[8] The minimum circulation of these periodicals came to about 175,800 copies.[9] At the same time, nearly fifty Russian-language periodicals circulated in the territories of *GK Weißruthenien* and in the Byelorussian part of the Rear Area of the Army Group Center, the majority of them in the latter, since the greater part of the Russian population was concentrated there.[10]

Of course, there was no such thing as an independent press. Both in the civil and military administration areas, the Germans established and maintained rigid control over all mass media, including periodicals. In the *GK Weißruthenien* a subdivision of the press existed inside the political department, which controlled the activities of the press in the civil administration area. Every *Gebietskommissariat* also had either a department or a subdivision for the press, which oversaw the periodicals issued at the local level. To ensure that the press did not deviate from the ideological lines established by the authorities, the "Press Publishing House 'Minsk' Ltd." was created in March 1942. The head of the propaganda department in the *GK Weißruthenien*, Schröter, became the head of this body; according to Zhumar, around mid-1943 it was renamed the "Publishing and Typographical Society Minsk Ltd."[11]

In the part of Byelorussia under the military administration, all propaganda work was controlled by the military propaganda department, designated *Propaganda-Abteilung Wehrmacht* (PAW), with its seat in Smolensk. The PAW had its own subordinate bodies, named "operational units" (*Einsatzstaffeln* or *Einsatzzüge*), which controlled the propaganda in various places.[12]

As in other collaborationist bodies, the people engaged in propaganda represented various views and were guided by a variety of motives. Alongside people such as Aljaxej Syankevič and Ŭladzislaŭ Kazloŭski, who identified themselves with the National Socialist ideology, there could also be found figures such as Francišak Aljakhnovič, one of the veterans of the Byelorussian national movement, who began his career at the beginning of the twentieth century, as well as others who continued their journalistic work from the Soviet period. Among the latter were Nina Glebko, the wife of the Byelorussian national poet Petrus Glebko; Sovenok; Nikolaj Baykov, whose articles had appeared before the war in periodicals such as *Saveckaja Belarus*; and Mikhail Golubovskij (Bobrov), previously a journalist for the Soviet newspaper *Izvestija*, the second largest Soviet newspaper after *Pravda*.[13]

Some of the Soviet-period journalists who contributed to the legal press during the Nazi occupation had been through the Stalinist repressions. For example, Viktor Gut'ko, one of the writers for the *Menskaja Hazeta*, a predecessor of the *Belaruskaja Hazeta*, had worked before the war as copyeditor of both *Saveckaja Belarus* and *Vicebski Praletary* (Vitebsk Proletarian) and had contributed to the *Fizkul'turnik Uzbekistana* (the Uzbekistan Athlete). In the 1930s he spent three years in the camps in Siberia. The same can be said of Sovenok, mentioned above, who spent six years in Stalin's camps and prisons.[14] Yet, there were also people such as Mikhail Golubovskij (Bobrov), also mentioned above, whose contribution to periodicals such as *Izvestija* almost certainly presupposed membership in the Communist Party as well as some degree of loyalty to the Soviet regime.

The degree of influence that the periodical press and other legal mass media had upon the population is not immediately discernable. However, it can be safely stated that, in general, the newspapers' income did not exceed their expenses. Without overburdening the present work with numbers, it is known that a monthly newspaper subscription cost approximately 2,560 RM, while newspapers like the *Belaruskaja Hazeta*, which published about eight issues per month, spent a minimum yearly sum of 3,600 RM for the newsprint alone.[15]

An additional problem in the mass media sphere was that, the Byelorussification trend, propelled both by the German authorities and the Byelorussian nationalists, found relatively little understanding among the general public. Bedritzki, already mentioned on several occasions in this work, complained at the beginning of 1944 that in Baranaviči, the Russian-language newspaper *Novyj Put* enjoyed much greater popularity than the Byelorussian-language *Baranavickaja Hazeta*. The circulation of the latter decreased in 1944 from 4,000 to 2,000 copies (in a city of 300,000 inhabitants), and sellers attempted to encourage its distribution by giving it as a makeweight with other newspapers.[16]

What content filled the newspapers and other mass media under the occupation? For the purposes of the current work, the

Belaruskaja Hazeta (The Byelorussian Newspaper, henceforth BH) will serve as a case study, since it was arguably the most widely disseminated Byelorussian-language newspaper, with a circulation of between 10,000 and 80,000 copies. Between 7 July 1941 and February 1942, it was issued in Minsk under the title *Menskaja Hazeta* and from February 1942 until the end of the occupation as the *Belaruskaja Hazeta*. It was published once or twice a week, and contained four pages.[17] The main positions on the editorial staff were occupied by members of the Party of Byelorussian National Socialists (PBNS), such as Syankevič and Kazloŭski. This relatively small group formed in Eastern Poland in the 1930s, shortly after Hitler's rise to power. It was headed by Fabian Akinčyc who was described by Alexander Dallin as "a pathological fanatic, ex-Bolshevik, turned fascist."[18]

In reality, Akinčyc never belonged to the Bolshevist party; rather, he followed a very twisted political career. Born in 1886 in the village of Akinčycy in Minsk district (today Akinčycy is part of the city of Stoŭbcy), he was a member until 1917 of the Social-Revolutionary Party (*PSR*), which focused its activities on the Russian peasantry and gained notoriety through the numerous acts of terror its members perpetrated against Russ-ian State officials. In the 1920s, Akinčyc was among the leaders of the Byelorussian Peasants-and-Workers Party (*Hramada*) in Poland (see Chapter 2) and headed the Vilna (Vilnius) city com-mittee of this party. He was arrested during the Polish crack-down upon the *Hramada* at the end of the 1920s, but after his release in 1930, he did a turnabout in his political stance and accepted the proposition "better the Poles than the Soviets." In 1933, after the Nazi's rise to power in Germany, Akinčyc once again changed his views, becoming an ardent admirer of Hitler and of the National Socialist ideology. In 1937, after the Polish authorities banned the Party of Byelorussian National Socialists (PBNS) and its official paper, the *Novy Shlyakh* (The New Way), Akinčyc, together with other party members, left for Germany. Another group of party members, with Ŭladislaŭ Kazloŭski at the helm, continued their activities illegally in Vilna. As shown in Chapter 3, the Germans never took Akinčyc and his "Nazi Party" too seriously. In 1939, Akinčyc was appointed head of the Byelorussian Representation in Berlin, which issued the news-paper *Ranica* (The Morning) and worked with Polish POWs of Byelorussian extraction.[19] Very soon afterwards, however, he was robbed of his post.[20] Generally speaking, the influence of the Byelorussian Nazis inside Byelorussia was extremely modest.

After all, they were émigrés, unknown to most of the Byelorussian population, so for them, the *Menskaja* and then the
Belaruskaja Hazeta, issued in many thousands of copies, provided an opportunity to emerge from oblivion and make their
views more widely known.

As the items in the BH indicate, their views did not differ
much from those of like-minded persons in Germany. A good
example is the report on the "Germany trip" of Byelorussian
peasants that took place in the second half of April 1942. The
report, published in the BH on 7 May 1942 and signed by its
author with the pseudonym "Padarozhny" (a traveler), quotes a
letter addressed by the junket's participants to Rosenberg. It
reads, inter alia, as follows, "We have seen ... that racially pure
Aryan blood in union with the soil created a culture, created a
nation, and its well-being is so strong and unshakable that it
seems totally free of any external challenges. We wish this to be
an example for ourselves."[21] It is more than likely that the word-
ing of this address also expressed the position of the *Belaruskaja
Hazeta* editorial staff itself; indeed, many of its members readily
accepted the theories about Aryan origins of the Byelorussian
people and the "blood-and-soil" ("Blubo") ideology. Those who
published in the BH also believed sincerely in the Nazi myth of
a "new Europe" established under German hegemony, where
small nations such as Byelorussia would be secured an appropriate place. This myth was propagated widely both in the articles published by the newpaper's chief contributors, such as
Kazloŭski, and in the speeches of Nazi leaders, such as Hitler
and Rosenberg. Although the latter never mentioned Byelorussia and Byelorussians in their speeches, usually confining themselves to general phrases, the BH editors tried hard to persuade
their readers that the Third Reich leadership was constantly
thinking about Byelorussia too.[22]

General information about Akinčyc's group is scarce indeed.
From various sources, one may discern that the Byelorussian
Nazis basically rejected the idea of the immediate creation of a
Byelorussian State, claiming that the Byelorussian people were
not mature enough for such a step.[23] In the rough draft of his
memorandum compiled in October 1942, Akinčyc spoke of the
"reeducation" of Byelorussian society "according to the political
line."[24] The leader of the Byelorussian Nazis argued that only
Byelorussians sharing a National Socialist ideology should be
accepted into the administrative system throughout the country.[25] In the same document, Akinčyc even called for the segre-

gation of Byelorussian society in line with political views, while all the "hostile elements should be either rendered harmless or eliminated."[26] He concluded this proposal with a call to create a Byelorussian political organization "with which German authorities would be able to cooperate."[27]

One of the main features of the Byelorussian Nazis, not unlike Nazis in other European countries, was the constant and obsessive search for real or imagined enemies. This paranoiac trend also found expression in the pages of the *Belaruskaja Hazeta*, which constantly castigated the "enemies of Byelorussian people"; the first assigned as such were the Jews, followed by the Poles, Russians, and those who were descriptively dubbed "Moscow's agents." In the leading article published in BH on 18 July 1942 and entitled "Praca i Zmaganne" (Work and Struggle), Kazloŭski stated that the "hidden" enemies of the Byelorussians were not only the "Judeo-Communists," Poles, and Russians, but also anyone who spoke Russian. In the same article, Kazloŭski proposed to expel all Russians and Russian-speaking people living in Byelorussian territory to the ethnic Russian territories.[28] The author was not bothered by the idea that such plans would involve resettling large sections of the Byelorussian population, given that the majority of Byelorussia's urban population at that time was Russian-speaking.[29]

As can be gathered from *Einsatzgruppen* reports, from the German perspective the cooperativeness of the local population in Byelorussia left much to be desired.[30] The authors of these reports blamed the population's "passivity" on the steadily deteriorating situation in general, as well as on the supposed fear of—or perhaps hope for—the return of the Soviets. Given these circumstances, periodicals such as the *Belaruskaja Hazeta* were supposed to encourage an overall readiness on the part of the population to collaborate with the Germans. The most popular method for doing this was by underscoring the contrast between German and Soviet politics and by refuting any rumors about a possible return of Soviet rule. Little wonder then that information about the situation on all fronts of World War II was limited, while bombastic reports about successful maneuvers by the Axis forces, real or imagined, took up a great deal of space in the press. Moreover, there were also articles such as "Z Drugoga Boku Saveckaha Frontu" (From the other side of Soviet front, 23 April 1942), which were supposed to prove beyond a doubt not only that the Soviet forces posed no threat, but also that the Soviet rear was on the verge of disintegration.[31]

Another favorite topic frequently appearing on the pages of the *Belaruskaja Hazeta* was the "atrocities" of the Stalinist regime. The BH correspondents made liberal use of their blackest ink to describe in great detail the "horrors" of Stalinist terror. Aljakhnovič's memoirs, published in several issues under the title "Ŭ kapcjurokh GPU" (In the GPU's Clutches), described the situation in the Soviet prisons and labor camps.[32] While widely touting the "agrarian reform"—which, in fact, produced less than modest results in the Byelorussian territory— the *Belaruskaja Hazeta* did not fail to highlight the contrast between German agrarian policies, depicted as friendly to Byelorussian peasants, and those of the Soviet period. The issue of 26 October 1942 makes for an interesting example. Two articles were published on the same page: "Shchaslivyja Sjaljane na Ŭlasnaj zjamli" (The happy peasants on their own soil) and "Znachan'nje samastojnaha sjaljanstva na ŭskhodze" (The significance of independent peasantry in the East). The first depicted "the enthusiasm" of the Byelorussian peasants in welcomng the "agrarian reform", while the second mentioned, among other things, "the evils" wrought by the Soviet authorities on Byelorussian agriculture.[33]

Although all of these materials served the Germans' well-defined purpose, an important point should be considered: not all of these materials necessarily provided a distorted presentation of reality. In many cases, the information about Soviet foreign and internal politics was based on real facts known in the West at that time, but which remained—until the 1990s—concealed from the public in the Soviet Union. For example, in the 12 April 1942 issue of the *Belaruskaja Hazeta,* an article appeared entitled "Tak insceniravala Maskva vajnu suproc' Finljandyi" (So Moscow has staged the war against Finland). The article described quite accurately the border incidents provoked by the Soviets, which led to the Soviet–Finnish war, also known as the "Winter War" of 1939–1940. Of course, even the exposure of "Soviet crimes" had its limits. Thus, "delicate" themes, such as the German role in the Soviet annexation of Western Byelorussia, were carefully omitted. On 9 March 1942 the newspaper also published, albeit in distorted form, the famous document "Lenin's political testament," which contained a critique of many leading Bolsheviks, including Stalin. Only at the end of the 1980s, with the beginning of Gorbachov's *perestroika,* did this document become widely known in the Soviet Union.[34]

The "anti-Bolshevist" propaganda of the legal mass media, such as that expressed in the *Belaruskaja Hazeta*, was closely connected to the anti-partisan propaganda. On 11 November 1942, the Supreme Command of the Wehrmacht (OKW) issued instructions for the organization of such propaganda in the occupied territories, which read as follows:

> It must be made clear to the population that its life and property will be secure only in a land free of partisans. The partisans should be shown as promoters of the war and the enemies of peaceful work. The population should know that it brings ruin upon itself through its support of partisan detachments, since this in turn leads to the annihilation of entire villages; in contrast, cooperation with Germans in the struggle against the partisan detachments brings it great advantage.[35]

Actually the number of "anti-partisan" articles in BH was closely related to the development of the partisan movement in Byelorussia. Until approximately mid-1942 the partisan movement was still relatively weak, which is reflected in the fact that until the summer of 1942, articles about the partisans were relatively rare. Only at the beginning of May did the newspaper publish a very laconic article informing its readers about the exposure and execution of a "band" in Minsk. No names were ever mentioned.[36] Informing the readers about the hanging of twenty members of this "band" and the execution by firing squad of 120 others, the publication delivered the following message, "Anyone working against rebuilding, anyone stealing, killing, robbing or sabotaging will be ruthlessly eliminated."[37] Usually the Byelorussian legal periodicals, including the *Belaruskaja Hazeta*, strove to create the impression that Byelorussians had nothing whatsoever to do with the partisan movement. Although, as will be shown later, the partisan detachments that identified themselves with the communist ideology were a minority, the collaborationist mass media portrayed them all as exclusively Jewish-Bolshevist-Russian "hirelings." For example, in March 1944, the *Belaruskaja Hazeta* published an article about one of the partisan detachments commanded by Tikhon Bumazhkov.[38] Borrowing from a 1941 item in the main Soviet newspaper, *Pravda*, the authors of the *Belaruskaja Hazeta* articles wanted to show that all the members of Bumazhkov's detachment, including the commander himself, were ethnic Russians.[39]

Among other things the collaborationist press accused partisans of setting out to damage the "friendly relations" between Germans and Byelorussians: "They [the partisans—L.R.] want to start quarrels between the Byelorussian people and the Germans—German authorities and soldiers—to put a dark stain upon the conscientious Byelorussian people."[40] However, even the legal mass media were not able to completely conceal the fact that there were Byelorussians among the partisans. This fact demanded an "explanation," and one was provided by the Vitebsk *Belaruskaje Slova* (Byelorussian Word), on 31 March 1943, "We should not forget that there are Byelorussians who reached the forest for various reasons and who have nothing in common with bandits. They should return home ... they will not meet with punishment."[41]

Usually the legal periodicals spared no effort to discredit the partisan movement. So in a number of issues in 1944, *Belarus na Varce*, the organ of the Byelorussian auxiliary police, published the testimonies of a captured Soviet Army captain, Rusanov, a former member of the Ukrainian Staff of the partisan movement. Rusanov told of the deliberate organization of the partisan movement by the Soviet authorities, of the partisans' provocative activities, of NKVD control over partisan detachments, of mistrust on the part of the Soviet authorities toward all those remaining in the German-occupied territories, and he gave disparaging descriptions of the central figures in the partisan movement.[42] Basically, Rusanov's testimonies were a mixture of truth, half-truths, and propagandistic inventions. It stands to reason that the effect of all these "disclosures" was dubious, since until 1944 the Germans had done their utmost to enhance the prestige of the resistance movement in the eyes of broad sections of the population.

In his analysis of the legal press in Byelorussian territories during the occupation, Sergej Zhumar remarks quite correctly that a "quantitative increase in anti-partisan publications was proportionate to the increase in the activities of the partisan movement."[43] This is certainly correct; furthermore, one additional factor should take be taken into consideration, namely, the infamous "large undertakings" (*Großunternehmen*) against the partisans that were carried out by the Germans from 1942. According to the data provided by German historian Christian Gerlach, the number of such operations rose from nine in 1942 to twenty-eight in 1943.[44] These undertakings, usually accompanied by excessive brutality, left behind many hundreds of innocent people, who had nothing to do with the partisans, murdered; entire villages were burned down, and the cattle driven away (see Chapter 7). All this demanded at least some kind of justification, and the collaborationist mass media were mobilized to provide such justifications. So, for example, according to the *Hazeta Sluččyny* (The newspaper of the Sluck area) on 30 January 1944, "The bandits arranged the matter in such a way that some of our villages were burned down."[45] *Belaruskaja Hazeta* was more explicit. On 16 August 1942, that is, at the peak of the "anti-partisan operation *Greif* (Griffin)," carried out between 14 and 20 August in the area between Orsha and Vitebsk (Eastern Byelorussia), which claimed 1,395 victims, it stated, "[I]n the places where the population supports these partisan bands or hides them or provides shelter for their individual members, it signs its own death sentence, since not the partisans but the German army is in charge in the country. The latter has the power in its hands and this will be used everywhere, wherever there is a need to break down the opposition."[46]

Another main task of local propaganda, as evidenced in Schröter's report at the conference of GKW officials in April 1943, was to assist in the recruitment of labor for work in Germany. The local legal mass media in Byelorussia began its propaganda to recruit workers for the Reich fairly early. In February 1942, the *Belaruskaja Hazeta* began publishimg materials that can be considered as preparation for this campaign. Numerous articles published from the end of February onward described the "ideal" working and living conditions in Germany. The issue of 22 February 1942 discussed the conditions in the boarding houses of the German Labor Front (Deutsche Arbeiterfront, DAF), while the next BH issue (26 February 1942) informed its readers about the rational use of labor in Germany.[47] The notion of advantageous working conditions in Germany compared to those in Byelorussia appeared repeatedly in later issues of the newspaper.[48] The "advertisements" for working in Germany were not limited to abstract phrases: both the periodical press and the radio regularly transmitted stories of the "happy" *Ostarbeitern*. Even the obvious absurdity of such stories did not deter their authors. Thus, on 21 May 1942, the *Belaruskaja Hazeta* published the story of a man who had lost four fingers on one hand during his stay in Germany and was sent back to Byelorussia; however, according to the article, he volunteered yet again to go to work in the Reich.[49] As previously noted, one of the most popular devices in this recruitment campaign was quoting letters by those already working in Germany. In May 1944, the propaganda department of the *GK Weißruthenien* issued an order to distribute 1,600,000 copies of these letters as leaflets throughout the country.[50] Moreover, these texts, which described the work as "not difficult" and told of "regular evening dances," were also transmitted over the radio as early as 1942.[51] The "Germany trips" mentioned before also served to demonstrate the "superior" economic methods existing in Germany, as the majority of the participants' time on these trips was dedicated to visits to various industrial and agricultural sites. The propagandistic importance of these trips is highlighted by the fact that they were accompanied by journalists from both the German-speaking and local press, who described them in great detail.[52] Generally, volunteering to work in Germany was presented by the collaborationist mass media as an "honorable duty," an expression of gratitude to Germany for "liberating" Byelorussia from the Bolshevist yoke; thus, it was also considered a service to Byelorussia and a contribution to the war against Bolshevism.[53]

The Germans considered the legal mass media quite an important tool in the exploitation of the economic resources of the country. The periodical press, as well as other media, was supposed to make measures imposed by the occupation authorities, such as product delivery duty, palatable to broad sectors of the Byelorussian population. As with the mobilization of labor for work in Germany, here too the provision of products to the Germans was portrayed by the press and the propaganda posters as a contribution to the war against Bolshevism, a sign of gratitude for the "liberation" of Byelorussia from the Soviets, and even as an "honorable duty" of the peasants.[54] It was difficult, however, to explain to the peasants why there was no upper limit on these deliveries. Even the most energetic propaganda could not conceal the fact that the recompense the peasants were supposed to receive from the Central Trade Society "East" (ZHO) was less than modest.[55] An article in the May 1942 *Belaruskaja Hazeta* stated that the peasant was supposed to receive 25 roubles (2.50 RM) for 100 kg of grain, 12 roubles (1.20 RM) for 100 kg potatoes, and between 70 and 200 roubles (7–20 RM) for a head of cattle.[56] These prices were supposed to appear quite "solid", but even the Germans were compelled to acknowledge that such prices barely covered the peasants' expenses for agricultural equipment.[57]

At the beginning of 1942, one of the most important topics in the local periodical press was the so-called "New Agrarian Order," proclaimed on 16 February 1942. Christian Gerlach, who claimed that its main purpose was "to urgently increase agricultural production in Byelorussia despite the war conditions," has described it in detail.[58] The interests of the local peasants and their traditional dreams of owning their own piece of land were of secondary importance, at best. The plan to dissolve the kolkhozes was scheduled for some obscure date in the future; for the time being, all the kolkhoz land was to be distributed among the homesteads only for the peasants' use, not as private property. Presumably every peasant farm would work on a land strip of the same size; the German authorities had the right to decide what should be sown and built on these strips. A number of homesteads were supposed to be united into what was called "agricultural cooperatives" (*Landbaugenossenschaften*) or "collective economies" (*Gemeinwirtschaften*) and to sow crops jointly.[59]

Such a "reform" was much less than the average peasant expected and, as usual, the propaganda tools were supposed to sweeten the bitter pill. Periodicals such as the *Belaruskaja Hazeta* were supposed to show that this did constitute a reform and not merely a cosmetic change. The front pages of the newspapers were allocated to this purpose, and the headlines dedicated to this theme were set in large letters. Moreover, the newspapers did not limit themselves to formal announcements about the "New Agrarian Order," but published a series of (translated) commentaries, written by high-ranking German officials such as Kube himself, on this new "order."[60] All of these articles described the German "agrarian reform" as "a gift to the peasantry."[61] They also bore an additional message: only cooperation with the Germans could ensure profits. The same article in the *Belaruskaja Hazeta* that informed the readers about the main tenets of the "reform" also contained an explicit call to "cooperate with us—the more the better for you!"[62] Such articles made it clear that the main beneficiaries from the "New Agrarian Order" would be the local collaborators.

The German authorities announcing the "reforms" apparently knew very well that the extremely obscure formulation of the "Order" would lead to certain misunderstandings throughout the country. The legal mass media were supposed to forestall these potential misunderstandings. A particularly delicate subject in this respect was the non-abolition of the kolkhozes. In reality they were only renamed, using the term "collective economy" (*Gemeinwirtschaft*), a more or less literal translation of the word *kolkhoz*, or "agricultural cooperatives"; nevertheless, this was presented to the public as the necessary transitional step towards private economy, which the German authorities planned to introduce some day in the future.[63] The *Belaruskaja Hazeta* explained to its readers that owing to the destructive policies of the Soviets, the immediate dissolution of the kolkhozes would result in empty lands, which would inevitably lead to hunger.[64] In his article published in March 1942, Kazloŭski even promised that in *GK Weißruthenien* the stage of collective cultivation of the land would be bypassed and the peasants would receive the land directly for individual use.[65]

The New Agrarian Order presents a very good example of the disparity between propaganda and reality. Clearly, the Germans never thought seriously about a transition that would culminate in the local peasants' ownership of the land. The paucity of agricultural machinery and draft animals (in some cases, between three and eight homesteads had one horse, and eighty homesteads had five carts, five plows, and sixteen harrows), together with the heavy taxation in kind and the desire to control the peasants, led to the spread of collective forms of land cultivation throughout Byelorussia.[66] In the areas of *GK Weißruthenien* that had belonged to the Soviet Union before 1939, namely Minsk, Sluck, and the Borisov areas, in 1942 all of the former kolkhozes were turned into *Landbaugenossenschaften* (1,400 kolkhozes were turned into 5,300 "agricultural cooperatives," which included between 117,000 and 123,000 homesteads).[67] In the former Polish areas, where the kolkhoz system was still in its infancy, the situation was more complex. In some cases the authorities were even prepared to return lands to their former Polish landowners, who only two years earlier had been dispossessed of them by the Soviets.[68] Even the smallest farmsteads (usually of no more than five hectares of land) were allowed to continue to exist there throughout the occupation period.[69]

Although both the Byelorussian- and the German-language press constantly stressed the contrast between the agricultural conditions that characterized the Soviet period and those dictated by the German authorities, the difference was virtually non-existent. Even the conferences for the functionaries of the new "cooperatives"' were almost exact copies of the conferences from the Soviet period, except "that at the seats formerly occupied by communist functionaries now sit our own agricultural leaders (*Landwirtschafts-Führer*)," as one of the officials of Berlin Wansee-Institute put it.[70] The Byelorussian peasants themselves racked their brains over the question of how to meet the Germans' demands for agricultural products with virtually no horses, no fertilizer and no machinery, while the German and local press constantly depicted rosy pictures of "happy peasants" going to Germany to thank Rosenberg personally for the reforms and sending letters of thanks to "Hitler the liberator."[71]

Anti-Semitism also occupied quite an important place on the pages of the legal press in Byelorussia. The newspapers and magazines both for adults and children spread the idea that the Jew is an enemy of humankind in general and of Byelorussians in particular. The collaborationist periodicals actually supported not only the "removal" of Jews from Byelorussian society but also their physical extermination. German anti-Jewish policies were presented as examples to be followed by Byelorussians. Reporting on the school teachers' courses that took place in Minsk in March 1942, the *Belaruskaja Hazeta* noted that during these courses, films such as Fritz Hippler's *Der Ewige Jude* (The Eternal Jew), were shown, remarking that "Germans have shown the Jews their proper place, –the ghetto."[72] One of the contributors to the *Belaruskaja Hazeta* was M. Buzuk, whose style is reminiscent of that of Julius Streicher. In an article dedicated to anti-Semitism in Byelorussian folklore, M. Buzuk surveyed the strong anti-Semitic tradition existing in Byelorussia. He wrote in the résumé, "The present expelling of Jews (*zhids*) from our public life must be taken with great joy by the Byelorussian masses."[73] The BH's predecessor, the *Menskaja Hazeta*, expressed full support for the ghettoization of Byelorussian Jews, and in September 1941, it stated: "Previously, Jews were more than 60% of the population in Vitebsk. Many of them fled during the Bolshevists withdrawal. Now the Jews are locked in the 'ghetto' and are deprived of the opportunity to demoralize the soul of Byelorussian people."[74]

The magazine *Belaruskaja Škola* (Byelorussian school), intended for schoolchildren, was issued by the Byelorussian schools inspectorate of *GK Weißruthenien* during 1942. In several of its essays on German history, the "domination of the Jews" was presented as the main problem of the Weimar Republic, and Hitler was shown as the man who would solve this problem. In the essays published under the general title "National Socialist Germany," appearing in April and May 1942, readers were told that "a Jew cannot be a friend of the German nation, regardless of whether he spoke German, since it is not the language–often an incidental phenomenon in human life–that unites people but the blood that flows in their veins."[75] In September 1941, the *Menskaja Hazeta* wrote that "the interests of Jews and non-Jews are incompatible; Jewish ethics and moral codes should not poison other nations ... there is no room for the Jews among us at all."[76]

As the next chapter shows, the confrontation with the mass murder of Jews led to a certain "sobering" of the population in Byelorussia with regard to the "Jewish question." This however was not the case with the collaborationist periodicals. Here, the physical extermination of Jews was met with complete understanding. On 12 May 1943, Kazloŭski, writing in the *Belaruskaja Hazeta* about the bombing of Minsk by the Soviet air force on the night between 2–3 May of the same year, expressed his "regret" that not one of the bombs had hit the Jewish ghetto.[77] Another issue of the same newspaper quoted a letter by a Byelorussian *Ostarbeiter*, Yulia Dzejkina, who was employed in Saarland. Part of the letter read as follows: "When I see how people are living in Germany, I wish [the German army–L. R.] the greatest success, not only in taking Moscow but the whole of Russia, and extinguishing the entire pest that was created there by Stalin ... Do not spare Jews; they deserve it! [that is, deserve death—L. R.]."[78] An especially violent anti-Semitic tone was adopted by the head of the Union of Byelorussian Youth (SBM), Mikhas' Han'ko, whose writing (under the pseudonym Ahanyok, i.e., small light) promoted the idea of "removing" Jews from Byelorussian society. In various publications he constantly referred to Jews as "the enemies of the Byelorussian people."[79]

Generally, the Nazi authorities attached great importance to the anti-Semitic propaganda in the occupied Eastern territories. It was not only printed media that took part in this. The movie theaters allowed to open in the occupied territories frequently showed films such as *Der Ewige Jude* and *Jud Züss*, the two most infamous pieces of National Socialist anti-Jewish visual propaganda. The American historian Robert Herzstein rightfully pointed out that the main purpose of screening these films was to prepare ... the populations of the occupied European countries for the "Final Solution of the Jewish Question."[80] In fact, the purpose of all the anti-Semitic propaganda was to persuade the people both in Germany and in the occupied countries that Jews were not part of society, that they were not even part of mankind.

Newspapers, such as the *Belaruskaja Hazeta*, readily accepted all the anti-Jewish slogans and stereotypes envisaged by the Nazi propaganda. Consequently, their portrayal of Jews as "national parasites" and the main beneficiaries of Soviet rule contributed to the "legitimization" of the extermination process.[81]

The publications in the Byelorussian collaborationist press reflected the general policies of the Germans toward Byelorussian nationalism. Although the Germans' habit of toying with Byelorussian nationalism had its limits and served very specific purposes (foremost the strengthening of Kube's position vis-à-vis the SS-apparatus), such faux gestures were taken too seriously by many of the Byelorussian nationalists. The illusion that the Germans were intending to provide Byelorussians with at least some kind of statehood, even if only in the form such as that seen in Slovakia, was shared by many collaborationists and found its expression in the legal periodical press, especially during 1942. In February of that year, Kazloŭski wrote in the *Belaruskaja Hazeta* that in contrast to the Soviet and Polish period, under German occupation "schools, self-government, police, cultural and artistic life are the outposts of the Byelorussian people's guard."[82] In this respect, the Byelorussian Self-Aid Organization (BNS) was seen as the seed of a future Byelorussian government, and as such, it became a favorite of various Byelorussian publications, such as the *Belaruskaja Hazeta* in which the BNS was unambiguously presented as the hub of Byelorussian intelligentsia and Byelorussian leadership.[83] Although time and again, reports about cases of corruption in the organization penetrated the mass media, they were the exception rather than the rule. BH, for example, constantly published rosy reports about the BNS's charitable activities among the needy Byelorussian population.[84]

As this study progresses, it becomes increasingly evident that the essence of the propaganda was to promote the notion that only by depending upon Germany could Byelorussia ensure its future. The local legal mass media tirelessly put forward this idea, sincerely believing in the slogans promoting the "New Europe," where "small nations" (such as Byelorussia) could find their rightful place. In the article dedicated to the memory of Kastus Kalinoŭsky, who led the anti-Russian rebellion in the nineteenth century, *Belaruskaja Hazeta* stated, "And we are proud … that we are a nation of 20 million people, which will be granted its place in the new Europe."[85] Examples from the past, which were supposed to demonstrate the "traditional benevolence" of Germany and its government toward the Byelorussian national movement, were frequently invoked. An especially popular theme in this respect was the mythical support provided by the Germans to the short-lived BNR during World War I, although this "support" actually amounted to no more than benevolent toleration, which existed largely due to strategic considerations.[86]

For the Germans, the local press also served as a tool to conceal their true intentions regarding both Byelorussia and other occupied territories. In the first half of 1942, the *Belaruskaja Hazeta* published a number of articles in which the authors, both local collaborators and German officials—such as the head of the propaganda department at *GK Weißruthenien* of that time, Heinrich Kurz—assured readers that the Germans were truly friends and allies of Byelorussia and that they did not harbor any assimilatory intentions towards the Byelorussians. In his speech of 1 May 1942, published in BH, Heinrich Kurz remarked, "The Germans do not want the Byelorussians to be Germans. They want Byelorussians to develop their nation, their own culture."[87] One could question exactly how much the German officials in Minsk knew about the processes in Berlin; regardless, it should be noted that all of these "assurances" were given just when the details of the infamous *Generalplan Ost* (GPO) were being planned.[88] According to this scheme, which was worked out under Himmler's personal patronage, Byelorussia, together with some other occupied Soviet territories, was destined for colonization by German and "Germanic" settlers.[89] According to the RSHA version of the GPO, seventy-five per cent of the Byelorussians, that is, between five and six million people, were deemed "ineligible for Germanization" (*Eindeutschungsunfähig*) and were to be expelled or physically exterminated.[90] Moreover, in 1941, the establishment of the special children's home in Bobrujsk marked the beginning of one of the most infamous projects envisaged by Heinrich Himmler, namely, the selection of "racially suitable" children from the occupied Soviet territories and their preparation for subsequent adoption by families in Germany.[91]

Nazi propaganda, from the very beginning of National Socialist rule in Germany, was directed not only at the adult population but at children as well. Children and youth, whose world of ideas was still in the process of formation, were more susceptible to such propaganda. Although the opinion of the *Untermenschen* was much less important than the German point of view, the children, by means of the various media, were also brainwashed with the ideas outlined by the occupation authorities. In

Byelorussia, for example, a truly diverse range of media were available for these purposes. The most basic of these was, of course, the school. Here, the distinction between public proclamations and expressions "intended for internal use" becomes clear. Thus, the German-language *Minsker Zeitung* wrote in September 1942, "The aim of the school policy is to grant the Byelorussian youth a basic European education. The German administration promotes national originality and development. Therefore, this task is not limited only to professional education (*nicht allein auf das Fachliche begrenzt*), but is also of political importance."[92] In their internal correspondence, however, the Germans were much more explicit. Almost a year after the article in *Minsker Zeitung,* Otto Bräutigam, the head of general political department in *Ostministerium*, in his letter to Kube, explained the tasks of Byelorussian schools: "The Byelorussian schools are charged with the task of professionally training the younger generation (*die berufliche Nachwuchs*), striving for a positive attitude among the Byelorussian population in regard to cooperation [with Germany—L. R.] and keeping this area quiet."[93] The issue of the organization of the Byelorussian schools as such is beyond the framework of the present study and has been described in some detail by German researcher Bernhard Chiari in *Alltag hinter der Front.*[94] Suffice it to say that education in Byelorussia at that time was offered through the four-class public schools (*Volksschule*), in which the main emphasis was on delivering professional education that would provide the German war economy with the "necessary" workforce. The subjects considered most important were arithmetic, Byelorussian, and German: "After all," according to von Gottberg, "the Byelorussian population should certainly learn to speak a little German, if only to understand the universal language of commands."[95] Education was compulsory; the parents of children who missed lessons were even threatened with punishment.[96]

However, the most important issue in this instance is not how subjects were studied in Byelorussian schools, but rather what was studied there, that is, what kind of messages were conveyed to the schoolchildren. The main idea received was clear: only cooperation with Germany could guarantee Byelorussia's future. So, for example, in Baranaviči, an order was issued, mandating that the first lesson of every day had to begin with a five-minute lecture given by the teacher about the role of Germany as the "liberator" of Byelorussia. According to Chiari, the daily repetition of such a ritual caused some children to simply avoid the lessons entirely.[97] To show that Germany was indeed encouraging the Byelorussification of the schools, the children were also supposed to greet the teacher entering the classroom with their hands raised in the Nazi salute, to exclaim "Zhyve Belarus'!" (Long live Byelorussia), and only then take their seats.[98]

Although the Germans constantly stressed the contrast between education in the occupation period and under the Soviet regime, there were really more similarities than differences. Instead of tales about Lenin's childhood, the school children now learned about the childhood of the Nazi Fuehrer. These stories were also conveyed by the legal periodical press. In October 1943, the *Belaruskaja Hazeta* published the first chapter of *Mein Kampf*, describing Hitler's childhood, in the "For our children" column.[99]

As shown above, anti-Semitism also played a prominent role in the propaganda targeted at children. Lessons and articles on the history of Germany contained messages, including one which claimed that during the Weimar period, Jews, especially Jewish Reichstag deputies, were hostile to the interests of the German people and that only Hitler "succeeded in solving the problem."[100] Evidence of the importance that the Germans attributed to propaganda directed at children may also be seen in the variety of means used: schools, newspapers and magazines, as well as the radio were all recruited in order to target the younger audiences.[101]

In conclusion, it is possible to say that from the German point of view, the collaborationist "mass media" were foremost used as tools to convey the desired ideas, and more specifically, to encourage the cooperativeness of the local population, which had been undermined as a result of reckless occupation politics. Thus, the legal mass media were also recruited, in an attempt to justify various unpopular measures imposed by the authorities, such as brutal anti-partisan warfare, recruitment of labor for work in Germany, and exploitation of the local economy.

As with other forms of collaboration, journalists had a variety of motives for working within the framework of the legal press and other mass media. Such motives ranged from the desire to continue a journalistic career that had begun during the Soviet period, to unconditional identification with the Nazi ideology. For members of the Party of Byelorussian National Socialists, a group which prior to the German attack against the Soviet

Union had enjoyed only minimal influence, the prospect of being published in a newspaper such as the *Belaruskaja Hazeta*, with a circulation of tens of thousands, certainly presented an appealing opportunity to make their voice heard.

Of course, political and ideological collaboration were not the only forms and methods of local collaboration. The next chapter will analyze the part played by the local collaborationist bodies in the repressive politics of the Nazis. The first part of the chapter will deal with the most infamous and most repulsive aspect of German occupation policies, namely, the persecution and extermination of the Jewish population of Byelorussia and the role local collaborators played in it.

Notes

* "Legal" press refers to the press that the German authorities allowed to be published, as opposed to the clandestine press. Subsequent references in this book will use the term *legal* without quotations.

1. See R. Herzstein, *Vojna kotoruju vyigral Gitler*, trans. A. Utkin et al. (Smolensk, 1996).
2. "Abteilungsleiter Schröter über 'Propaganda, Presse, Rundfunk und Film'"; "Protokoll über die Tagung," BA R 93/20, 109.
3. Ibid, 112.
4. Ibid., 115.
5. Sergej Zhumar, *Okkupatsionnaja Periodicheskaja Pechat' na Territorii Belarusi v Gody Velikoj Otechestvennoj Vojny* (Minsk, 1996).
6. Quoted ibid., 9.
7. BA R 93/20. Zhumar, *Okkupatsionnaja Periodicheskaja Pechat'*, 9–10.
8. For example, the newspaper *Belaruskaja Staronka* (The Byelorussian Country), which appeared in June 1943 in Orsha, a military administration area, numbered only two issues. Ibid., 198.
9. Ibid., 197–206.
10. Ibid., 207–15.
11. Ibid., 26.
12. Ibid., 66.
13. Petrus Glebko was a member of the partisan movement. Baykov was a veteran contributor to the Byelorussian press. He was a famous linguist and literary critic, whose articles were published before the war in the magazine *Polymja* [The Flame] and the newspapers *Literatura i Mastactva* [Literature and Art] and *Saveckaja Belarus'*, mentioned above. It is interesting to note that the encyclopedic dictionary *Belarus'* (66f.) cited 1941 as the year of Baykov's death; however, according to Zhumar, he lived through the occupation period and was one of the most active contributors to periodicals such as *Belaruskaja Hazeta* and *Holas Vjoski* [The Voice of the Village]. In 1944, Baykov assisted in the publication of the magazine *Malady Zmahar* [The Young Fighter], issued by the *Einsatzgruppe "Deutschland"* of the SBM (see Chapter IV) in Germany. Ibid., 30. According to Zhumar, at the

beginning of the Nazi-Soviet war, Golubovskij was at the front with a rank of lieutenant-colonel, when he was taken prisoner and decided to collaborate with the Germans. For some time he even served as a commandant of Bobrujsk camp for female POWs. Subsequently, he edited a number of Russian-language legal periodicals, such as *Novyj Put'* (Bobrujsk), where he was editor-in-chief, *Na Strazhe Rodiny* [At the Homeland's Guard] under the pseudonym Beresov, and *Tserkovnyj Blagovest* [The Ringing of the Church Bell] under the pseudonym Simonov. Ibid., 31.

14. Ibid., 29–30.
15. Ibid., 27.
16. "Schreiben des Leiters der Propagandisten Bedritzki an Gebietskommissar für Baranowitsche, 14.1.44," BA R 90/159.
17. Zhumar, *Okkupatsionnaja Periodicheskaja Pechat'*, 197–98. Sometimes the number of pages was larger. For example, the 19 April 1942 issue, which was dedicated almost entirely to Hitler's coming birthday, consisted of five pages. *Belaruskaja Hazeta* (BH), 19 April 1942, YVA C-762.
18. According to Alexej Litvin, they gathered in Vilna (Vilnius), then part of Poland. See Litvin's entry "Belaruskaja Nacyjanal-Sacyjalistychnaja Partyja" in the encyclopedic dictionary *Belarus'*, 91. Dallin, *German Rule*, 213n. See also Solov'ev, *Belarusskaja Tsentral'naja Rada*, 145–46.
19. Ŭ. Kazloŭski, "Byelaruskaja Emigracija ŭ Njamechchyne," BH, 5 February 1942.
20. See the entries "Akinčyc" and "Belaruskaja Nacyjanal-Sacyjalistychnaja Partyja" in *Belaruski Nacyjanalizm*, http://sounik.org/nac/
21. "Delehatsiia belaruskikh sjaljan ŭ Njamechchyne," BH, 7 May 1942.
22. The publishing of Hitler's speech in the very first issue of *Belaruskaja Hazeta* can serve as an example. BH, 5 February 1942, 1.
23. Turonak, *Belarus' pad nyameckaj Akupacyjaj*, 85.
24. Photocopied excerpts of the memorandum appear in Romanovskij, *Saudzel'niki*, 199.
25. Ibid.
26. Ibid.
27. Ibid.
28. "Praca i Zmaganne," BH, 18 July 1942, 1.
29. See "Report on the moods of the population in Byelorussia compiled by a Byelorussian from Latvia, August 1942," BA R 90/126.
30. "TLB Nr. 3 (15.8–31.8.41)," "TLB Nr. 4 (1.9.–15.9.41)," "TLB Nr. 5 (15.9–30.9.41)," "TLB Nr. 9 (1.1–31.1.42)," "TLB Nr. 10 (1.2–28.2.42)," "TLB Nr. 11 (1.3–31.3.42)," in Klein, *Einsatzgruppen*, 173, 190, 213–14, 283–84, 300, 311. "Operational Situation Report USSR (OSR) Nr. 20, 12.7.41," "OSR Nr. 27, 19.7.41," "OSR Nr. 36, 28.7.41," "OSR Nr. 43, 5.08.41," "OSR Nr. 90, 21.9.41," "OSR Nr. 106, 7.10.41," in Arad and Spector, *Einsatzgruppen Reports*, 20, 37, 53–54, 69–70, 145–46, 171.
31. "Z Druhoha Boku Saveckaga Frontu," BH, 23 April 1942, 3.
32. *Gosudarstvennoje Politicheskoje Upravlenije* (The State Political Department, GPU for short) was created in 1922 as the successor of the dreaded CHK (*Chrezvychajnaja Kommissija*), the main instrument of Red terror after the Bolsheviks' seizure of power. In 1923 it was renamed OGPU (*Objedinjonnoje Gosudarstvennoje Politicheskoje Upravlenije*, Joint State Political Department). OGPU was part of the infamous NKVD apparatus and played an active role in the Stalinist terror. F. Aljakhnovič, "Ŭ Kapcjurokh GPU," BH, 5 February 1942 ff. The publication of

Aljakhnovič's memoirs had begun earlier in *Menskaja Hazeta*, the predecessor of *Belaruskaja Hazeta* (issues 7–25), but unfortunately I could not
obtain access to its copies.

33. "Shchaslivyja Syalyane na ŭlasnaj zjamli," "Znachan'nje samastojnaha
    sjaljanstva na ŭskhodze," BH, 26 October 1942, 3.
34. "Shto kazaŭ Lenin pra svaikh paplechnikaŭ," BH, 9 March 1942, 1.
35. Quoted in Zhumar, *Okkupacionnaja Periodicheskaja Pechat'*, 109.
36. Apparently the reference here is to the members of the Minsk clandestine
    organization led by Isaj Kozinets. At the beginning of February 1942, some
    300 members of this organization were arrested, including Kozinets him-
    self. Their arrests were a heavy blow for the resistance movement. See
    "TLB Nr. 11," (1 to 31 March 1942), in Klein, *Einsatzgruppen*, 305–6, 314n;
    "Reports from the Occupied Eastern Territories No. 2, 8.5.42," "Reports
    from the Occupied Eastern Territories No. 5, 29.5.42," in Arad and Spector,
    Einsatzgruppen Reports, 339–41, 346.
37. According to the RSHA report compiled on 29 May 1942, twenty-eight
    "members of the Byelorussian partisan organization were hanged in public
    in Minsk; 251 people were shot on the same day" (that is, on 5 May 1942),
    see previous note. "Khto sabatuec' adbudovu, budze z'nichtozhany," BH, 10
    May 1942, 1.
38. Bumazhkov's detachment operated in Polesje area, in southern Byelorus-
    sia, from 1941 and was celebrated by Soviet propaganda as one of the very
    first partisan units.
39. "Jany iznoŭ na Belaruskaj zjamli," BH, 22 March 1944, 2.
40. Quoted in Zhumar, *Okkupacionnaja Periodicheskaja Pechat'*, 111.
41. Quoted ibid.
42. Quoted ibid., 115–16.
43. Ibid., 117.
44. Gerlach, *Kalkulierte Morde*, 899–904.
45. Quoted in Zhumar, *Okkupacionnaja Periodicheskaja Pechat'*, 112.
46. "Perad rasplataj," BH, 16 August 1942, 1.
47. "Internaty dlja moladzi," *Belaruskaja Hazeta*, 22 February 1942, 2;
    "Razmerkavanne rabochaje sily," BH, 26 February 1942, 2.
48. See, for example, "Praca i khleb ŭ Njamechchyne," BH, 9 March 1942, 4;
    "Na pracu ŭ Njamechchynu," BH, 21 May 1942, 1, etc.
49. Ibid.
50. "Propagandaaktion für den 'Arbeitseinsatz' mit 'Originalpostkarten' von
    angeblich zufriedenen 'Ostarbeitern', vom 15. Mai 1944," in Schlootz,
    Deutsche Propaganda, 60–61.
51. Ibid. "Praca i khleb ŭ Njamechchyne," see note 48 above.
52. See, for example, the report about the April 1942 trip, mentioned previ-
    ously in this chapter.
53. "Na pracu ŭ Njamechchynu," see note 48 above.
54. See Schlootz, *Deutsche Propaganda*, 49. See also "Zdacha pavinna byc'
    abavjazkavaj," BH, 27 May 1942, 4.
55. The whole name of the organization was "Central Trade Society 'East' for
    Sale and Demand Ltd" (Zentralhandelsgesellschaft Ost für Absatz und
    Bedarf mBH, ZHO). It was founded in July 1941, at Göring's personal ini-
    tiative, to fulfill the following functions: "central procurement, storage and
    transportation of agricultural products, the trusteeship (*Betreuung*) over
    the processing works of the food industry as well as supplying of agriculture
    with the means of production and necessities." In the civil administration

area, it was subordinate, at least formally, to the economic department of *Ostministerium*, while in military administration area it was subordinate to the "economic staff 'East'" (*Wirtschaftsstab Ost*), which was responsible for supplying the Wehrmacht. The ZHO was not an organization in the proper sense, but rather a kind of "umbrella" which took under its trusteeship the industries existing from the Soviet time. This explains the fact that it was also one of the major employers—if not the only significant employer—of local labor inside the occupied Soviet territories. At various times, within the whole Eastern territories the ZHO employed some 6,500 Germans and as many as 800,000 locals. See "ZHO-General Information," which can be found in the index of documents stored at the *Bundesarchiv* branch in Berlin suburb Dallwitz-Hoppegarten.

56. "Novy paradak tsenaŭ na sel'ska-haspadarskija pradukty," BH, 21 May 1942, 1.
57. Even such a "diehard" Nazi as the *Gebietskommissar* of Slonim, Gerhard Erren, in his concluding report, composed in August 1944, pointed out this disparity. According to him, it was wrong when the peasant who received 2.50 RM (25 roubles) for 100 kg of grain was supposed to pay 4 RM (40 roubles) for the garden rakes alone. See "Kritische Erfahrungsbericht für die ganze Zeit der Zivilverwaltung von Gebietskommissar Slonim, 10.8.44," BA R 93/13.
58. Gerlach, *Kalkulierte Morde*, 342f. See the text of the "Order": "Die Neue Agrarordnung mit Präambel und Schlußwort Rosenbergs, 15.2.42," BA R 6/71, Mikrofiche 3.
59. Ibid., 347–48.
60. See, for example, "Ŭ Belarusi Ŭzdykhnuli," BH, 16 March 1942, 1–2.
61. "Novy agrarny paradak-dar sjaljanstvu," BH, 1 March 1942, 1. At almost the same time, the economic inspector Weigand wrote to the commander of the Rear Area of Army Group "Center," von Schenckendorff: "the new agrarian order does not pursue a goal to make the Russian peasant happy, but to create a basis for utilization of the agricultural production of the occupied Russian space for further waging of war." Quoted in Gerlach, *Kalkulierte Morde*, 352.
62. Ibid.
63. Ibid.
64. Ibid.
65. "Zjamlja i Volja," BH, 16 March 1942, 1.
66. This was, for example, the case in the village of Selitrepniki, Borisov area. See "Klimkovič's testimony before the Byelorussian Staff of the Partisan Movement," YVA M 41/2445 (NARB 4-33a-250), 10.
67. Gerlach, *Kalkulierte Morde*, S. 358; Chiari, *Alltag hinter der Front*, 135.
68. Sometimes, upon their return, the Polish landowners used physical violence to "punish" those peasants who, from their point of view, had "seized" their property "illegally." Occasionally, they even turned to the Germans for assistance. See Turonak, *Belarus' pad nyameckaj Akupacyjaj*, 59–60; Chiari, *Alltag hinter der Front*, 133.
69. Gerlach, *Kalkulierte Morde*, 364.
70. Quoted in Chiari, *Alltag hinter der Front*, 137.
71. The publications in the German-language press that appeared both in Germany and in the occupied territories can be found in the *Bundesarchiv*, under the common signature R 90/74 as well as R 90/76–80. The materials of the *Minsker Zeitung*, the German-language version of *Menskaja Hazeta*,

are found in the same archive under the signature R 90/107. See also the publications in *Belaruskaja Hazeta* quoted above.

72. The premiere of Fritz Hippler's film *Der Ewige Jude* took place in Germany in November 1940. Together with Veit Harlan's feature film *Jud Züss*, produced two months earlier, this movie was an integral part of the Nazi anti-Semitic propaganda. It was a milestone on the road to the Holocaust. The American researcher of Nazi propaganda, Robert Herzstein, wrote about *Der Ewige Jude*, "The main task of the film was both ideological and psychological preparation of the German people, its allies as well as the population of the occupied countries, for the 'final solution of the Jewish question.' Those who saw *Der Ewige Jude* in 1941 and who occasionally had knowledge of Auschwitz in 1943 were more easily held in subordination and it was not the matter of realization of [their] own guilt as accomplices. Simply, these people were convinced that German authorities had no another choice," Herzstein, *Vojna kotoruju vyigral Gitler*, 374–75. "Byc' vartymi Ŭzgadaval'nikami narodu," BH, 29 March 1942, 6.

73. "Zhidy ŭ Belaruskaj Narodnaj Tvorchastsi," BH, 8 July 1942, 3.

74. In collaborationist circles, it was usual to refer to the Jews using the derogatory word *zhid*. Quoted in Zhumar, *Okkupacionnaja Periodicheskaja Pechat'*, 170.

75. "Nacyjanal-sacyalistychnaja Nyamechchyna," *Belaruskaja Shkola*, 3 April 1942, 5, quoted ibid., 166.

76. *Menskaja Hazeta*, 2 September 1941, quoted in ibid., 167.

77. "Zhydoŭski teror," BH, 12 May 1943, 1.

78. "Listy na Batskaŭshchynu," BH, 27 June 1942.

79. See Chapter IV.

80. Herzstein, *Vojna kotoruju vyigral Gitler*, 375.

81. BH, 10 June 1942, 2. See, for example, "Zhidy-valadary Savetskaga Sajuzu" (BH, 18 June 1942), in which the Soviet Union was defined as a "Jewish paradise."

82. Kazloŭski, "Belarus na svajoj varce," BH, 26 February 1942, 1. It should be remembered, however, that when this article was published many of the positions mentioned were still occupied by non-Byelorussians, mostly Poles, especially in the predominantly Polish regions.

83. See, for example, N. Shchyraja, "Da Kiraŭnikoŭ," BH, 5 April 1942, 3.

84. See Chapter IV, note 92, and E. B., "Patreben idejovy Ŭzdym da pracy," BH, 6 March 1942, 3.

85. "Vyaliki zmagar za Maci-Belarus," BH, 23 April 1942, 1.

86. See Chapter II, note 10.

87. "Svjata Pracy ŭ Mensku," BH, 7 May 1942, 1. See also "Buduchynja Belarusi," ibid., 6 March 1942, 1.

88. The first version of the plan was worked out on 15 June 1941, that is, a couple of days before the attack against the Soviet Union, by the SS-Standartenführer Prof. Konrad Meyer, chief of the main planning department in the main staff office of the Reich's Commissioner for the strengthening of German nation (*Reichskommissar für die Festigung deutschen Volkstum*), which was occupied by Himmler himself.

89. As well as Byelorussia, these also included the Baltic region, "Ingermanland" (that is the area around Leningrad), together with the Crimean peninsula and the South Ukrainian area (so-called Taurida). See "Schreiben des Reichsführer SS an Prof. Dr. Konrad Meyer mit der

Weisung, Litauen, Lettland, Estland, Weißrußland und das Gebiet von Leningrad bei der Ausarbeitung des Generalsiedlungsplanes in den Ostsiedlungsraum einzubeziehen, 12.1.43," in Madajczyk, *Vom Generalplan Ost zum Generalsiedlungsplan*, 256. Thus, Gerlach's statement that the greater part of Byelorussia played no part in German colonization plans must be corrected. See Gerlach, *Kalkulierte Morde*, 111f.

90. "Stellungnahme von Erhard Wetzel, Dezernent für Rassenpolitik im Reichsministerium für die besetzten Ostgebiete, vom 27. April 1943 zum in Reichssicherheitshauptamt entwikelten 'Generalplan Ost'," in Kaden et al., *Dokumente des Verbrechens*, vol. 1, 186f, especially 207f.

91. As shown by Christian Gerlach, at first this project was supposed to include only the children of ethnic Germans (*Volksdeutsche*). Very soon, however, the practices were also extended to non-German children. As noted previously, not all these children were orphans. See Gerlach, *Kalkulierte Morde*, 1082.

92. Quoted in Chiari, *Alltag hinter der Front*, 207.

93. "Schreiben Bräutigams an Generalkommissar für Weißruthenien bezüglich die Richtlinien für das einheimische Schulwesen in Generalbezirk Weißruthenien, 5.8.43," BA R 6/289, Mikrofiche 1.

94. Chiari, *Alltag hinter der Front*, 206f.

95. "Auszugsweise Abschrift des Vermerks über die Besprechung mit dem stellvertretenden Generalkommissar von Weißruthenien v. Gottberg am 1.3.44," BA R 6/284, Mikrofiche 1. See "Schreiben Bräutigams an Kube," note 93, and "Kali skonchycca shkol'ny god," BH, 26 April 1942, 3.

96. "Da vedama bac'koŭ," BH, 26 April 1942, 3.

97. Chiari, *Alltag hinter der Front*, 217.

98. Ibid., 217–18.

99. BH, 20 April 1943 (p. 3) and 24 April 1943 (p. 2).

100. Quoted in Zhumar, *Okkupacionnaja Periodicheskaja Pechat'*, 166.

101. There were special radio programs for children such as "Children's Radio," and "Byelorussian fairy tales." See "Abteilungsleiter Schröter über 'Propaganda, Presse, Rundfunk und Film'"; see also note 2 above.

CHAPTER 7

COLLABORATION IN THE
POLITICS OF REPRESSION

This chapter deals mainly with the repressive politics of the Nazi regime in Byelorussia and the role that the local collaborationist bodies played in it. Since Byelorussian Jewry was the main target of such politics, a substantial part of this chapter will focus on the genocide of the Jewish people. Other categories of people were also defined by the Nazis as "undesirables": Soviet soldiers straggling through the countryside, communists, Roma and *Ortsfremde* ("strangers"). In this context it is impossible not to mention other phenomena, such as the "anti-partisan warfare" and the atrocities committed in its course, which became one of the main symbols of German rule in Byelorussia. The aim here is to treat all of these topics thoroughly, with the degree of detail varying, according to the availability of sources.

The theme of persecution of the Jews must be tackled first, for a number of reasons. This is primarily because this topic is well documented. Second, the annihilation of the Jews was one of the areas in which the local collaborators were expected to participate from the outset, and indeed they played a paramount role. Finally, the involvement of local collaborationist forces in the most horrible crimes provided the Germans with the opportunity to entangle these forces in their activities, reinforcing their loyalty.

Collaboration in the Holocaust*

In October 1941, two officials from Rosenberg's Ministry for the Occupied Eastern Territories, Eugen von Engelhardt, the author of the book *Weißruthenien: Volk und Land,* which appeared in Berlin in 1943, and a young jurist from the Department for Lithuania and Byelorussia, made a trip through the occupied Soviet territories to gain information. On their way to Smolensk, the two stopped to spend the night in a locality near Lake Naroč, in northwestern Byelorussia. The following morning they decided to enjoy the wonderful weather and to walk to the lake. Partisan activity at this time was still insignificant, so the two expected a pleasant trip. On the way to Naroč, the two men came across a small village, where one of the local peasants volunteered to show the Germans the way to the lake. Both Germans spoke fluent Russian and could converse freely with their guide. Upon arriving at the edge of the forest, the peasant pointed to an almost invisible little hill and said quite joyfully, "Our Jews are lying over there." Then the peasant told how the residents of the surrounding villages drove "their" Jews to this gathering place where they were subsequently shot by either Lithuanian or Byelorussian policemen (the guide did not know their exact origin). The peasant followed this by complaining to the two travelers about the "damages" inflicted on the local inhabitants by the Jews. The visitors then continued on their way.[1]

Often, when dealing with the Holocaust of European Jewry, we receive a somewhat distorted picture, which portrays the Germans as the sole executioners and the Jews as the victims. Yet, as the above story shows us, the extermination of the Jews did not occur in a vacuum or on a desert island but frequently—especially in the case of the occupied Soviet territories—before the eyes of the non-Jewish population. The question then arises: what role did this population play in the extermination process? Was the Holocaust indeed, as Goldhagen put it over a decade ago, a purely "German undertaking"?[2] Were the local residents merely extras, observers, or bystanders or did they have a more active part in the extermination of people who shortly before had been their neighbors, acquaintances, business partners, and sometimes even family members?

The whole problem recently came into the limelight after the publication of Jan Tomasz Gross's study *Neighbors,* which dealt with the massacre of the Jewish population of the Polish town Jedwabne by their Polish neighbors. For many years, the Poles had presented this massacre as a purely German crime.[3] Gross's book, however, led to a reevaluation of the theme of the interethnic relations within Polish society, a reconsideration that culminated, among other things, in public apologies by the former Polish President, Kwasniewski, to the Jewish people. In other East European countries, however, such a reassessment has been somewhat slow to come, although the leaders of the "successor states" of the former Soviet Union, such as Lithuania, Latvia, and Ukraine, also made official declarations expressing their deep regret to the Jews for the role played by the Christian populations in these countries during the Holocaust.

Undoubtedly, the German authorities were the driving force behind the "Final Solution of the Jewish Question." The German historian Gert Robel stated that "both the legal and the moral responsibility for the murder of the Jewish citizens of the Soviet Union are exclusively on the German side."[4] Yet, the sheer number of victims leads us to the obvious conclusion that the Germans alone, without local assistance in every occupied country, could not have accomplished murder on such a scale.

In the case of Byelorussia, two opposing views were presented. In one the murder of Byelorussian Jews was portrayed, by and large, as a German matter. We find that Nikolas Vakar wrote

> Disheartened and appalled, the common people assumed the position, outwardly at least, that the Jewish problem was a German one, and not their concern. With all their compassion for the victims, how indeed could they help? On the other hand, a few nationalists collaborating with the occupants had overtly taken the German stand. They joined hands with the Nazis in the persecution—sometimes in the execution, as at Borisov—of the Jew as if hastily to cement with his blood their position of henchmen.[5]

A radically different statement was made by John Loftus, who served in the 1980s as the federal prosecutor in the Office of Special Investigations (OSI) of the Criminal Division of the US Justice Department. According to Loftus, "the Holocaust in Byelorussia was unique. In no other nation under German occupation did the inhabitants so willingly and enthusiastically visit such a degree of inhumanity upon their neighbors."[6] In this chapter we shall see if it is possible to bridge these two points of view and consider what measure of truth is in each of them.

When discussing collaboration in Byelorussia during the Holocaust, the question is often typically limited in terms of its

location and executioners. The former refers only to the Western
area, i.e., the territories that were part of *GK Weißruthenien*,
while the latter takes into account only the local auxiliary police
and the local self-administration,[7] two bodies that were directly
involved in the extermination process. The case of Eastern
Byelorussia is of no less interest for the historian dealing with
interethnic relations during the World War II, particularly since
in this area, which belonged to the Soviet Union, an entire generation had been raised on slogans of internationalism and
"friendship among nations." Similarly, to limit the discussion
only to the so-called "official collaboration" merely touches the
tip of the iceberg and focuses only on an invariable factor. As historians, however, it is more interesting to examine the general
public's attitudes towards the mass murder that took place
before its eyes: such a discussion concentrates on a variable that
is highly dependent on a number of factors, not least of these the
affect of German politics.

On the eve of the German invasion, Byelorussian Jewry numbered about one million people; it was largely exterminated in
two major waves: between the late summer and winter of 1941,
and during 1942. The number of Jews who perished in the Holocaust in Byelorussian territory is among the highest in Europe
and, according to various data, amounts to approximately eighty
per cent of the prewar Jewish population.[8] Byelorussian land
became a huge graveyard not only for the Jews who lived there
but also for the Jews brought there from all over Europe, primarily from Germany, Austria, the Protectorate of Bohemia and
Moravia (the present-day Czech Republic), General Government, and Warthegau (the Polish territory annexed by the Third
Reich). It was in Byelorussia that the new killing techniques,
primarily the infamous *Gaswagens* (mobile gas chambers)—
nicknamed by the population *dushegubki* (murderers)—were
first tried out.[9] And finally, it was in Byelorussian territory that
the shift to systematic extermination of entire Jewish populations took place.

The Extermination Process in Byelorussia

When dealing with the Holocaust in the occupied Soviet territories, one cannot fail to note the lightning speed of the extermination process. In Western Europe, including Germany itself,
the extermination process, as depicted by Raul Hilberg in his
classical and controversial work *The Destruction of European*

Jews, developed over a long period of time. This allowed for an interlude of several years between the various stages of the process, which began with robbing Jews of their civil rights and ended with deporting them to the extermination camps in the East.[10] In the occupied Soviet territories this process was much "shorter": the time that passed between "the removal" of the Jews from society and their murder was only a few months at most, and at other times it was only a matter of weeks or days. The question then arises as to whether this difference might be related to the general attitude prevailing in the environment in which the Jews lived. As we know, in Western Europe, including Germany, the Jews' emancipation had begun as early as the nineteenth century, and at the time of the Nazi rise to power their civil rights were an accepted fact. In Eastern Europe, especially in territories which only a quarter of a century earlier had been part of the Russian Empire, anti-Semitism was an integral part of official policy and pogroms occurred quite frequently. Thus, in these areas, the Jews were still perceived by many non-Jews as second-class citizens, a humiliated minority. Officially, after 1917, the Soviet authorities did condemn anti-Semitism as "a vestige of the bourgeois past" (*perezhitok burzhuaznogo proshlogo*).[11] This meant that in Western Europe, prior to the extermination of Jews, the Nazi rulers were compelled to persuade the general public that Jews were not actually part of society; in *Ostraum* they could safely skip that step and proceed directly to the stage of mass murder. This offers a partial explanation for the different pace of the annihilation process in Western and Eastern Europe.

The Nazis regarded the peoples living in the East, especially the Slavs, as "subhuman" (*Untermenschen*), but they were also aware of the rampant anti-Semitic feeling among these populace and were eager to exploit these sentiments for their own goals.

For the German anti-Jewish plans, the participation of the local population in the persecution of Jews had dual significance: for propaganda and for practical purposes. From the moment the National Socialists rose to power, they strove to present every step against the Jews, beginning with the anti-Jewish boycott of 1 April 1933, as spontaneous, the expression of "a popular desire for self-cleansing." The same pattern was applied successfully in the occupied Soviet territories, including Byelorussia, although there, of course, "the popular will" was less important. It was not by chance that the infamous *Einsatzgruppen*, which followed on the heels of the Wehrmacht units into the Soviet Union in June

1941, received Heydrich's instruction that read, among other things, "No obstacles should be put before attempts at the self-cleansing (*Selbstbereinigungsbestrebungen*) of anti-communist or anti-Jewish circles in the newly occupied territories. On the contrary, these efforts should be encouraged, imperceptibly, of course, and intensified and directed toward the right course of action (*in die richtigen Bahnen zu lenken*)."[12] These "self-cleansing efforts" were intended to ensure that their policies would be indulged by the local population.

During the entire occupation period, the German bodies responsible for executing the "Final Solution of the Jewish Question" faced the problem of lack of manpower.[13] The German army's heavy losses on the eastern front, which increased drastically after the failure of the battle of Moscow in the winter of 1941/1942, led to an increasing demand for reinforcements, and the units stationed in the occupied territories close to the front were considered the obvious reserve from which to draw on. In summer 1941, the commander of the Rear Area of the Army Group "Center" had at his disposal up to six divisions for the so-called "cleansing operations" (*Sauberungsaktionen*); by the autumn, the number of available divisions had been reduced to four.[14] Moreover, from the very outset the *Einsatzgruppen*, responsible for "cleansing" Soviet territories from all "undesirables," primarily Jews and Communists, had been very small units. For example, *Einsatzgruppe B* under the command of Brigadeführer SS (Major General) Artur Nebe, whose activity covered a large part of Byelorussian territory, consisted of only 655 people.[15] Another important factor to consider is that the German bodies responsible for the so-called "cleansing operations" operated in an area that was for the most part unfamiliar, and at first they did not know who was Jewish and who was not. Jews of "Aryan appearance" could easily avoid these bodies, while situations occurred, such as in Baranaviči, a city to the southwest of Minsk, where the Germans executed all the inhabitants of one of the city's streets, both Jews and non-Jews, simply because they thought they all looked Jewish.[16]

It is very difficult to measure empirically the initial readiness of the Byelorussian population to collaborate with the Germans in the persecution of the Jews. The fact that in Byelorussia the German invasion was not accompanied by outbursts of violence, as happened in Lithuania and West Ukraine, still does not indicate their unwillingness to cooperate in the mistreatment of Jews. In some locations, especially in West Byelorussia, such as

Hrodna, Navahrudak, and Ivje, anti-Jewish pogroms—along with looting of Jewish property—did take place.[17] The pogroms that occurred in predominantly Polish areas can be seen as outbursts of the anti-Semitism that had been brewing there over the previous decades and which merely intensified after September 1939. It would be wrong to attribute the pogroms to some alleged "collaboration" between the Jews and the Soviet regime or to portray them as a reaction to "NKVD crimes" committed after September 1939 in the annexed territories.[18]

The first *Einsatzgruppen* reports provide conflicting views on the initial popular Byelorussian attitudes toward the anti-Jewish policies. On the one hand, they speak of the friendly attitude of Byelorussians toward the Germans and of the intensification of collaboration in searching after people who were defined "undesirable" by the occupiers.[19] Thus, the authors of these reports mentioned, inter alia, the "kolkhozes' chairmen and *Dorfälteste*," who came "from a distance of forty to fifty km to request that their communities be cleansed from Bolshevist and Jewish elements."[20] At the same time, these reports also speak of the Byelorussian population's lack of readiness to commit acts of physical violence against the Jews. Thus, the daily report dated 5 August 1941 notes that "There is practically no Byelorussian national consciousness left in that area. A pronounced anti-Semitism is also missing ... In general the population harbors a feeling of hatred and rage toward the Jews and approves of the German measures ... but it is not able by itself to take the initiative in regard to the treatment of the Jews."[21] The last phrase, together with the actual active participation of Lithuanian and Ukrainian rather than Byelorussian police battalions in the massacres of the first wave of extermination, gave birth to apologetic views regarding the role of the Byelorussian population in the Holocaust.[22]

In Byelorussia, the extermination process did not differ greatly from that in other occupied Soviet territories. This counters suggestions found, in the main, in some German research of the 1990s.[23] Enough evidence exists, however, to speak about a pre-designed plan rather than local improvisation. Yet, some difference is evident in the pace of extermination between the western and eastern parts of the country. Whereas most of the Jews in Eastern Byelorussia had already been murdered before the end of 1941, in Western Byelorussia at the end of 1942, some 30,000 Jews were still alive.[24] In explaining this, it should be highlighted that in Eastern Byelorussia the Jews had more time to flee, so there were fewer Jews there when the Germans arrived, which in itself facilitated the work of the Nazi killing machine.[25] Additional motivation for extermination in Eastern Byelorussia—areas that had been part of the Soviet Union before 1939—may have derived from the Jews who lived there being precisely those whom the Nazis considered to be the embodiment of "Jewish Bolshevism," as so frequently touted in their propaganda. Finally, the economic factor played a role. The economy in the "old Soviet" part of Byelorussia was completely Sovietized and based on large industries, making it easier to dispense with the Jews. By contrast, in Western Byelorussia, annexed only two years before the German invasion, Sovietization of industry was still in its early stages, and there were still small undertakings where Jews played an important role. At first many of them could be exploited for the German military effort, although, as we shall see, the Nazis incessantly strove to replace the Jews with others, even when this was detrimental to their economic aims.

Actually, the killings of the Jews began immediately upon the arrival of the Germans. As previously noted, in Western Europe the stages of deterioration in Jewish status are clearly discernable, beginning with depriving Jews of their civil rights and ending with their subsequent elimination. By contrast, in Byelorussia, as in other occupied Soviet territories, it is impossible or at least difficult to distinguish such a process. The first "wild" killings were often committed by the Wehrmacht units or police formations that were merely passing through the area. In Bialystok (today in Poland) as early as 27 June 1941, that is, only a few days after the outbreak of the German–Soviet war, the massacre of the Jews was organized by the 221st security division together with the 309th police battalion. Of the 1000 people murdered on this occasion, at least 800 had been locked in the local synagogue and burned alive.[26] In Rečica, a small town near Gomel in southeastern Byelorussia, the local military commandant refused to take the city under his authority until it was "cleared" of the Jews.[27] The well-known "Order No. 24" issued on 24 November 1941 by Gustav von Bechtolsheim, the military commander of *Ostland*, allowed for the participation of the Wehrmacht units in anti-Jewish massacres. It stated explicitly, "Jews must disappear from the countryside and the gypsies should be eliminated as well."[28] Generally speaking, the Wehrmacht's role in the Holocaust is a theme apart and cannot be dealt with extensively within the framework of this book.

As noted, a particularly ominous role in the murder of Jews in June and July 1941 was played *by the Einsatzgruppe B*, especially *Sonderkommando 7a*, commanded by Walter Blume; *7b*, commanded by Günther Rausch; *Einsatzkommandos 8*, commanded by Otto Bradfisch; and *9*, commanded by Alfred Filbert. The same applies to the "advanced group" (*Vorkommando*), which was later renamed *Vorkommando Moskau* under the command of former Berlin university professor Franz Six. Every one of these units numbered merely 100 to 150 people. Yet, within a few months the number of their victims was enormous. As of 4 September 1941, the commander of *Einsatzgruppe B* Nebe reported to Berlin that 16,964 people had been killed by his group by 20 August 1941, while during this period *Einsatzkommando 9* alone had massacred 8,096 people, most of them Jews. Furthermore, during this period, all of these units covered quite a large territory. For example, *Einsatzkommando 9* operated in July 1941 in the Vilejka area in central Byelorussia and in August 1941 in the Vitebsk area, in the eastern part of the country, many miles away.[29]

Recently, especially in German historiography, a discussion has developed regarding the exact process of extermination and its scope at various stages. The two chief resources informing this discussion were Heydrich's directive to four HSSPFs in the east, issued on 2 July 1941, with precise definitions of the categories of people that should be executed immediately, namely, "Jews in party and state positions", and the *Einsatzgruppen'* reports. Scholars such as Christoph Dieckmann and Christian Gerlach maintained that it was impossible to speak about the total extermination of the Jewish population before the late summer and early autumn of 1941.[30] In reality, as demonstrated by Peter Longerich, as early as July 1941, the murderous activities of *Einsatzgruppe B* units operating in Byelorussia were not limited to "the Jewish-communist functionaries" nor to "NKVD agents," but were indiscriminately extended to the annihilation of not only the entire Jewish intelligentsia but also all able-bodied Jewish males.[31] At the end of July 1941, the units responsible for "pacifying" the conquered Soviet territories went over to the systematic extermination of the entire Jewish population, including women and children.

The "first shot" in the extended process was fired in the Polesje region, southern Byelorussia and northern Ukraine, by the 2nd Cavalry-Brigade of the SS, commanded by Hermann Fegelein, also nicknamed "Hitler's brother-in-law." Supplied with Himmler's order from 30 July or 1 August 1941, dictating that "all Jews should be shot; Jewish women (*Judenweiber*) should be driven into the swamps,"[32] this brigade by its own report killed 15,878 people in only two weeks (29 July–12 August 1941).[33] Although the report describes the victims as "looters," "partisans," and "Red Army soldiers," in reality the majority of those killed during the Polesje raid were Jews.[34]

The massacres of late summer–early fall 1941 were concentrated mainly in Eastern Byelorussia. By the end of 1941, when the extermination wave was halted temporarily, owing mainly to weather conditions, various data indicate that only 30,000 Jews remained in the ghettos of Rear Area of Army Group "Center," i.e., in Eastern Byelorussia, while another 140,000 had become victims of the Nazi killing machine. The Jewish communities of Mogiljov, Vitebsk, Bobrujsk, and Gomel had virtually ceased to exist.[35] At the same time, some 60,000 Jews were murdered in the territory of *GK Weißruthenien* between October and December 1941. Here the main foci of massacres were the Minsk and Borisov areas as well as the countryside.[36] Other prominent players in the massacres in the GKW territory, apart from the *Einsatzgruppe B*, were the 707th Wehrmacht Infantry Division, commanded by Generalmajor Gustav von Bechtolsheim; the 11th Reserve Police Battalion under the command of Franz Lechthaler, to which two Lithuanian Auxiliary Police (*Schutzmannschaft*) battalions were subordinated; and the 322nd police batallion.[37]

Fall 1941 also marked the beginning of the deportations of German, Austrian, and Czech Jews to the Minsk ghetto. The majority of those who survived the trip were murdered directly upon their arrival, either in gas vans or by shooting in the Blagovščina forest, some thirteen kilometers to the southeast of Minsk. Only artisans or able-bodied people who could work were allowed into the "special" or "Hamburg" ghetto, as it was known by the Minsk Jews.[38] The majority of these ghetto dwellers were murdered, in the course of 1942 and 1943. Only seven out of some 7,300 inmates of the Minsk "Hamburg ghetto" survived the war.[39]

The second wave of mass murder in Byelorussia began early in 1942 and continued into 1943. It reached its peak in the summer of 1942. On 31 July 1942, Kube reported to his superior, *Reichskommissar* of Ostland Lohse, that 55,000 Jews had been killed in GKW during the preceding ten weeks.[40] The Minsk ghetto was one of the largest in the occupied Soviet territories:

at the time of its establishment in 1941, between 75,000 and 85,000 Jews were incarcerated there.[41] During the series of *Aktionen* that took place between the fall of 1941 and October 1943, the entire population of the ghetto was exterminated.[42] This second wave of massacres in Byelorussia coincided with two significant developments: the growth of the partisan movement, which became massive and much better coordinated in the course of 1942, and the Germans' anti-partisan "large undertakings" (*Großunternehmen*), which began in the spring of the same year (see below). German propaganda was quick to portray Jews as the main "instigators" of the partisan movement and thus to use the image of "Jewish bandits" as a kind of legitimization for the massacres.[43] This pretext was supported by the fact that, knowing the fate that awaited them, the Jews in many ghettos revolted and in part succeeded in escaping to the forests. This was the case in Ljakhaviči, July 1942; Mir, August 1942; Baranaviči, summer 1942; Ljakhviči, September 1942; and a few other places.[44]

Local Attitudes toward the Persecution of Jews

The testimonies of Holocaust survivors depict the general change in the atmosphere around the Jews at the very beginning of the Nazi occupation: the shift occurred in a matter of days, giving them a sense of helplessness and a feeling of hostility from the surrounding world.[45] Frida Raisman from Minsk noted in her recently published testimony that "With the transfer into the ghetto, all had changed literally in the matter of one day. We were isolated from the majority of the population, and at that moment, all that perhaps had been deeply concealed came to light. Friends no longer recognized us; in mixed families, it was not unusual for wives to suddenly denounce their husbands, or vice versa."[46]

When talking about the reactions of the local population in Byelorussia toward German anti-Jewish policies, one must differentiate between two stages: the expulsion of the Jews from society and their physical elimination. It is likely that a significant number of non-Jews, who still thought in line with the conceptions of the Pale, did not oppose—or, for that matter, actively supported—the isolation of the Jews.

The various discriminatory measures carried out against the Jews in the first days and weeks of the occupation were but a preliminary step to their murder. Such moves included forbid-

ding the Jews to step on sidewalks, prohibiting them from using
public transport, marking them with yellow patches, and ultimately confining them to the ghettos. All these measures
together did not arouse much opposition from the non-Jewish
population. Thus, the patches, which in many places were worn
both on the breast and on the back, were cynically nicknamed
"The Order of Stalin" and "The Order of Lenin."[47] Complaints
about the "troubles" the Jews caused the local residents were
not a rarity either. In some places, such as Borisov, non-Jews
said quite openly, "Let them die, they did us a lot of harm!"[48]
Undoubtedly, the initial attitude of the non-Jewish population
toward the persecution of Jews presented a mixture of traditional anti-Semitism and fear of opposing the authorities. Yet, it
is not unlikely that the dividing line the Germans drew between
Jews and non-Jews was perceived by many as a step by which to
return the Jews to their "natural state," i.e., that of a humbled
and persecuted minority, familiar to both Jews and non-Jews
from the days of the Pale.

At the same time, it is also possible that to complete the
bloody work, all units engaged in the killing of Jews were compelled to rely on the assistance of the local inhabitants, who not
only knew the territory, but also knew who was a Jew and who
was not. From the documents available, it appears that it was
not unusual for the locals to extend such help. The denouncing
of Jews by their non-Jewish neighbors was frequently encountered during the first months of the occupation. This can be
deduced indirectly from the establishment of an entire series of
"information posts" (*Anzeigestellen*) where the local non-Jewish
residents were encouraged to go to submit information on the
whereabouts of Jews and communists—"to reveal the concealment of their former oppressors" in Nazi parlance.[49]

There were various reasons for the denunciation of Jews.
Sometimes, a conflict between neighbors was reason enough to
hand a Jew over to the German authorities.[50] Even family bonds
did not always protect Jews from condemnation to the German
authorities or to the local police. For example, Miriam Paperno
from the village of Davidovka was denounced by her Byelorussian mother-in-law.[51] In Minsk, a non-Jewish wife who saw that
her Jewish husband had succeeded in escaping the German
encirclement and had returned safely to the city shouted "Catch
the *zhid*!"[52]

Israeli researcher Daniel Romanovsky has voiced an interesting opinion on the readiness of the non-Jewish population in

Byelorussia to hand over to the Germans those people with whom they had lived for generations. He feels that many of the Byelorussian residents, especially in Eastern Byelorussia, who were mainly peasants, considered the war between Germany and the Soviet Union to be a continuation of the Russian civil war of the 1920s. One of the most striking features of this war was the frequent change of power. In this context, the Germans were seen by many as merely new authorities. Moreover, the entire Soviet period was characterized by an almost incessant struggle against the "anti-popular elements", i.e., real or imagined enemies of the Soviet regime, such as "bourgeois elements," "deviationists" (*uklonisty*), Trotskyites or "kulaks." Now the new authorities arrived with a fresh list of "enemies," in which the Jews figured prominently; it is no wonder that the same people, who only a few years earlier had participated in ousting the "kulaks" from their villages, were now eager to harness themselves to a similar cause: casting Jews out from their midst.[53] Furthermore, in the last years before the Nazi invasion of the Soviet Union, particularly after the annexation of the eastern Polish territories, the persecution of "counterrevolutionary elements" proceeded not only along class lines but along national lines as well, as was the case with the Polish population.[54] This means that there are grounds for Romanovsky's conclusion that the "Soviet regime created a kind of citizen that was well suited to live under the totalitarian regime, especially under one established by the Nazis."[55] It is worth noting that, at least in the first stages of the extermination process, economic considerations did not play an important role in the decision to participate in the persecution of Jews. This can be seen, inter alia, from the size of the "reward" that people received for denouncing Jews. Often this "reward" amounted to one kilogram of sugar, a small amount of *makhorka* (cheap tobacco), or a kerchief, that is, items that were of no great value.[56]

Undoubtedly, the lack of almost any opposition on the part of the general public to the first anti-Jewish steps led to the significant escalation in the extermination policies, which began in the late summer–early autumn 1941. It can also be assumed that this escalation, which expressed itself in a wave of murderous *Aktionen* in Byelorussia as well as in other occupied Soviet territories in the second part of 1941, was related to the general sense of "euphoria" that reigned in top Nazi echelons after their initial victories on the eastern front.[57] This sensation, which was created by many, both in the civil and the military administration, led to the feeling that the war against the Soviet Union was drawing to a close and that the time was ripe to implement Hitler's "prophecy" regarding the end of Jewry.[58]

As mentioned previously, in their murderous activities, the Germans increasingly depended on local collaborationist bodies, chief among them the so-called local self-administration and the auxiliary police. The local *Bürgermeistern* were often key figures in the various stages of the genocide process, although after the war, many of those who found their way west maintained that they were no more than pawns in German hands and had nothing to do with the "Final Solution."[59]

Such statements, however, contradicts evidence found in various sources. The "local self-administration" bodies were of paramount importance during the preparatory stages leading to the mass killings. Many of those appointed to key positions in this apparatus were natives of the area in which they acted, and the German authorities relied not only on their knowledge of the people and the terrain but also on their willingness to divulge this knowledge. It is little wonder then that in the summer of 1941, when the German authorities decided to create the first Judenräte with the initial purpose of registering all local Jews, these councils were often under the control of the provisional "town commissar," a forerunner of the *Bürgermeister*.[60] Also, the local officials' knowledge of which city neighborhoods had the poorest living conditions and should therefore be assigned to the Jews gave them an important role in the ghettoization process.

In many places, such as Minsk, Borisov, and Stoŭbcy to the southwest of Minsk, Jewish ghettos were under the direct control of the local city councils (*upravas*).[61] The local *uprava* in Minsk, for example, established early on a special "department for Jewish affairs" (*adzel pa žydoŭskim spravam*), which was responsible, inter alia, for supplying the ghetto with food and medicines as well as allocating work to the ghetto inmates.[62] Among other things, the local "mayors" were responsible for hermetically closing the ghetto, preventing any possibility of contact by ghetto inmates with the non-Jewish population. Such contact was not rare and had taken on various forms, especially that of bartering, which can be deduced from the order issued in 1941 by the Stoŭbcy *Bürgermeister* Ivan Aŭdzej (Jan Awdziej) that the non-Jewish population should "stop smuggling food to the Jews."[63] The rapid ghettoization process in Byelorussia, with most of them being established between summer and autumn 1941, also indicates the active role of the local self-administration in this development. During the ghettoization process, local bodies acted in close cooperation with the German military authorities, as was the case in Minsk, where the order for the establishment of the ghetto was signed jointly by the military commandant of the city and by the city's *Bürgermeister* Vitaŭt Tumaš.[64] In Mogiljov, the signature of the "city management" appears beneath the order to establish the ghetto.[65]

Since the ghettos were subjected to the authority of local *upravas,* the officials of these councils enjoyed a sense of power, operating as "overlords" controlling the life and death of the ghetto inmates. For example, the person responsible for the Minsk ghetto was Vladimir Gorodetskij, a drunkard who according to his own boastings had taught the history of the Communist party in one of Leningrad's institutions before the war. He would enter the ghetto whenever he pleased, participate in the robbing of its inmates and, allegedly, even murder Jews "just for his personal fun."[66] Two of the most striking illustrations of the ominous role played by the local collaborationist bodies in the extermination process are the mayor of Borisov, Stanislaŭ Stankevič, and the head of the Borisov police, an ethnic German by the name of David Egof. Stankevič was active in all stages of the extermination process, issuing orders for the ghettoization of local Jews, taking steps against those Jews who tried to defy ghettoization orders, "taxing" ghetto inmates with requisitions of cash and valuables and, ultimately together with Egof, bearing direct responsibility for the massacre of between 6,500 and 7,000 members of the Jewish community in October 1941.[67] In addition, Egof played an active role in the misappropriation of the property left after the Jews were murdered. At the time of his arrest, in January 1942, many valuables were found in his office.[68] Of note regarding both Stankevič and Egof is that they both had lived and worked in Soviet territory prior to the Nazi invasion—Stankevič had been a teacher in Navahrudak and Egof in the locality of Zembin.[69] When trying to explain the motives for their conduct, we may assume that both traditional anti-Semitism as well as a strong desire to prove their loyalty to German authorities played a part in their decision. Beyond those combined motives, it is likely that "the intoxication of power" also influenced their actions, a factor that stemmed directly from the ghetto being subject to the local administration's control.

Generally, the role of both local self-administration and especially that of the auxiliary police in the persecution of Jews
became increasingly noticeable as the extermination process
progressed. It was during the second wave of mass murders,
which began in the spring 1942 and reached its peak in that
summer that the involvement of the local policemen became
most salient. This can be attributed to the general increase in
local police forces that occurred from the end of 1941, as discussed in the next chapter. The expansion of local police forces
was connected to the rise of the resistance movement in
Byelorussia, especially from mid-1942, but also to the shifting of
the German forces at the Eastern Front. At the conference of
the functionaries of *GK Weißruthenien,* in Minsk on 29 January
1942, in the presence of Wilhelm Kube, the participants agreed
that although "the complete expunging (*Ausmerzung*) of the
Jews" is temporarily impossible due to the need for their workforce, nevertheless the process should be launched "starting
with large executions" in the coming spring.[70] At the same conference, the SS and Police Leader in *Weißruthenien,* Zenner, and
SD representative *SS-Sturmbannführer* Hofmann pointed to
the insufficient police forces and the resulting difficulties in proceeding with large-scale executions.[71] At least, it may be
assumed that the expansion of the local auxiliary police formations in 1942 in Byelorussia was closely connected to the extension of the extermination process there.

For the Germans, the active participation of the local auxiliary police units in the massacres was desirable for at least three
reasons: first, lack of German forces; second, the desire to
involve indigenous collaborators as thoroughly as possible in the
crimes, increasing thereby their loyalty and readiness to collaborate; and third, the sense of "moral relief" that the participation of the local policemen provided the German perpetrators.
Wherever the mass murder of the Jewish populations took
place, the active participation of the local police forces is apparent. In Borisov, the local policemen controlled the implementation of the "yellow patch" orders, and oversaw the resettlement
of the Jews into the ghettos.[72] During the so-called *Aktionen,* it
was the local policemen who removed the Jews from their
homes, gathered the victims to the designated killing spots, cor-
doned the execution areas, and finally pulled the triggers of their
guns for the execution itself.[73] Occasionally, the local police carried out the executions on its own initiative, even without German supervision, as was the case in Chaussy, to the southeast of

Mogiljov. There the commander of the local police, Danilov, personally commanded the extermination of Jewish families of the locality.[74] The conduct of the policemen, many of whom were in a state of alcoholic intoxication during the executions, aroused even the loathing of the Germans.[75]

In many cases, survivors have described the conduct of the auxiliary policemen as even more brutal than that of the Germans themselves. Oswald Rufeisen, a Jewish boy who during the German occupation posed as a Pole and worked for a time as a secretary and translator for the Mir police in Western Byelorussia, delineated a certain difference in the attitudes of German and Byelorussian policemen toward their respective participation in the *Aktionen*. According to him, many German policemen perceived the killing of Jews as a "dirty business," from which they preferred to abstain whenever possible.[76] Moreover, the inclusion of women and children in the list of victims, especially in the late summer of 1941, demanded that some kind of "justification" be provided. For example, the commander of 101st Reserve Police Battalion, Major Wilhelm Trapp, tried to "justify" the impending massacre of the Jews of the Polish locality of Józefów by referring first to the alleged Jewish instigation of an anti-German boycott in the USA, then to the alleged involvement of the Jews with the partisans, and finally to the Jewish involvement in the Allied bombings of German cities.[77] It is not surprising that by 1942, the rumor about the intimate connection between Jews and partisans had spread among the German authorities in both Western and Eastern Byelorussia.[78]

The local policemen, however, needed no such justifications, as they perceived the anti-Jewish *Aktionen* as a kind of amusement.[79] It appears that had they wished to do so, the local policemen could have tried to evade participation in the murders, as seen in the example of Polish policeman P., from Western Byelorussia. He claimed that his physical condition did not allow him to participate in the shootings, since in such cases he lost consciousness.[80] Yet very few policemen attempted to exploit these opportunities. On the contrary, the local policemen often participated enthusiastically in the persecution of the Jews.[81] Rufeisen's observation is also corroborated in archive documents. When the rayon chief of Borisov *Ordnungsdienst*, Kovalevskij, ordered the *OD* commander in Novo-Borisov, Bakhanovich, to dispatch fifteen policemen to oversee the resettlement of the Jews into the Borisov ghetto, seventeen appeared instead.[82] This difference may be explained, at least partly, by the fact that this was a perverted world, in which murder was a routine job, and the application of excessive brutality to this task was considered a top performance meriting a "distinction," which in turn might lead to the murderer's promotion, or to benefits, especially material ones. This possibility was indeed significant in the ever-worsening economic situation resulting from the Nazi occupation policies. The killing of unarmed people was recognized as an easy way to improve economic conditions for the policeman and his entire family.

The role of "pure" anti-Semitism in the readiness of the local policemen to participate in the murder of Jews is difficult to ascertain. Before the war, Jews lived in relative harmony with their Byelorussian and Polish neighbors in the locality of Mir, for example, while after the start of the German occupation it was the local police who were noticed for their conspicuous brutality in the persecution of Jews, the very same people who before the Nazi occupation had not shown themselves to be outspoken anti-Semites.[83] Moreover, many policemen, especially in the eastern part of Byelorussia, belonged to a generation that had grown up during the Soviet period and been educated on the tenets of "friendship among nations." As the next chapter will show, it was also not unusual to find former communists and Komsomol members now functioning not only as rank-and-file policemen but as police commanders as well. It may be assumed, therefore, that beyond pure anti-Semitism, there was a desire to prove one's loyalty to the Germans, which might lead to benefits of economic gain. And, as mentioned, there was the "intoxication of power," which also played a part in motivating the auxiliary policemen to treat the Jews, as well as other "undesirables" such as Communists and Roma, with exceptional brutality. British researcher Martin Dean quotes the former police secretary of Mir, who described the conduct of local policemen as follows: "The policemen could kill or beat anyone without any reason ... It was enough to say that the future victim was a partisan or a communist to justify themselves in the eyes of the *Gendarmerie*. They killed people to prove their loyalty to the German authorities. That group was very enthusiastic about the murders..."[84]

An additional tragic aspect was that often among the persecutors of the Jews were people who before the war had been friends, acquaintances, business partners, colleagues, clients, or patients of the persecuted. Shalom Cholawski, in his study dealing with the Holocaust in Eastern Byelorussia, gives the following example. In Minsk, a Jewish woman, who had worked as a pediatrician before the war, on her return to the ghetto with the working column, recognized among the local policemen standing on the sidewalk a former patient whose life she had saved. When she approached him and asked for assistance, the man threw her to the ground and kicked her with such cruelty that she was brought back to the ghetto on the verge of unconsciousness.[85] As shown in previous examples, even family ties did not always guarantee survival. A peasant, Ivan Menz, from the village of Pariči, killed his Jewish wife, Frejdl Nisman, and their two children with his own hands when he joined the local auxiliary police.[86]

The question that must be asked is: What exactly did the non-Jews know about the fate of the Jews? As may be gleaned from the incidents described above, they knew quite enough and certainly more than the Germans themselves wanted them to know. Indeed, the German authorities did their utmost not to attract the attention of the local residents to the mass executions. As can be seen from the often cited report by the Sluck *Gebietskommissar* Carl, this, of course, was not due to any humanitarian reason, but rather due to a fear that "excesses" during these executions would damage the image of the Germans as perceived by the local population.[87] On 30 August 1941, the head of the Gestapo, Heinrich Müller, even sent a telegram to all *Einsatzgruppen* demanding explicitly that they "prevent the crowding of spectators during the mass-executions" (*bei Massen-Exekutionen das Ansammeln von Zuschauern ... zu verhindern*).[88] Several statistical tables published by scholars dealing with the Holocaust in Byelorussia and in the Soviet territories as a whole show that in most cases the mass shootings of Jews took place either on the outskirts of or outside the localities.[89]

It was, however, very difficult to conceal the mass executions. In many places, the local inhabitants were sent to dig the ditches in preparation for the killings and they were the first to spread the word about the forthcoming executions.[90] Moreover, the Jews were usually led to the execution sites in full view of the local non-Jews and, in some cases, the local inhabitants even participated actively in rounding up their Jewish neighbors. Just before the liquidation of the Krinek (Krynki) ghetto (Hrodna area) in November 1942, the Germans even invited Poles from the vicinity to take part in the "celebrations" of the *Juden-Aktion.* On the day of the *Aktion,* the Poles assembled just outside the ghetto's gates armed with clubs, beating Jews as

they were led out of the ghetto to the execution site.[91] The police
cordons set up around the designated killing places may also
have provided a hint as to what was going on behind these barriers. The perpetrators themselves often spoke quite openly
about the "ghetto cleansings" and were not ashamed to describe
in detail all of the atrocities they committed during the *Aktionen*. Thus, when drunk the commander of the Nesviž police,
Sen'ko, told the inhabitants of the village of Snov about his participation in the massacre of Baranaviči Jews in June 1943, and
how during this massacre he personally threw Jews off balconies
on the second and third floors of the houses.[92]

At the same time, the growing scale of mass murders led to a
certain change in the attitude of the non-Jewish population to
what they witnessed and to a more sober exercise of judgment.
So, while the attitude of the non-Jews toward the measures
intended to rob the Jews of their civil rights could be described
as neutral-affirmative, the mass executions which claimed the
lives of hundreds and thousands were sometimes met with condemnation. In Borisov, for example, those same people who
before the *Aktion* had been quite eager to get rid of the "Jewish
trouble-makers," when confronted after the massacre with the
atrocities committed in its course, expressed quite a different
opinion: "Who ordered such a thing? How could 6,500 Jews be
killed in one go? It is the Jews now, when will our turn come?
What have these poor Jews done? All they did was work! Those
who are really guilty are safe!"[93] Perhaps the anxiety regarding
questions such as "when will our turn come?" and "who will be
the next target of Nazi terror?" played a more dominant role in
these condemnations than any actual indignation about the
atrocities or sympathy for the victims. In November 1942, the
district Gendarmerie head (*Gendarmerie-Gebietsführer*) of Brest
reported on rumors circulating there that claimed that "after
the 'Jewish actions,' first the Poles, then the Russians, and then
the Ukrainians will be shot."[94]

Although public opinion in the occupied Eastern territories
was of little consequence to the German occupation authorities,
nevertheless a certain effort was made to make anti-Jewish policies "plausible" in the eyes of the general public. Here an especially significant role was ascribed to the Orthodox Church and
the legal mass media. As shown in previous chapters, the role of
the Church in Byelorussia regarding the persecution of Jews
was rather ambiguous, whereas the legal press in Byelorussia
became a true mouthpiece for anti-Jewish policies.

Misappropriation of Jewish Property as a Form of Collaboration

Collaboration in the persecution of Jews refers not only to denunciation and murder, but also to the misappropriation of the property of those killed. To date, historiographic studies have afforded only cursory treatment to the issue of the misappropriation of goods and property belonging to Holocaust victims as part of "collaboration in the Holocaust" in Byelorussia.[95] One of the traditional stereotypes regarding the Jews, widespread in Byelorussia as well as in other Eastern territories, was that of the Jews' "fabulous wealth." The desire to take possession of the Jews' property undoubtedly influenced the attitude of the local population to various anti-Jewish measures. The Germans did their utmost to reinforce the stereotype regarding Jewish wealth. For example, according to the *Einsatzgruppen'* monthly report for March 1942, immediately after the mass murders of Jews in Minsk, Vilejka, and Baranaviči, the Germans organized for the local non-Jewish population "inspections" of the houses of the murder victims. The Germans sought to convince the local inhabitants that "the Jews still possess large stores of food products, while their own supply situation is extraordinarily bad."[96] According to various testimonies, the misappropriation of Jewish property took place on a large scale and manifested itself in the ugliest of forms. In various places, on the eve of an *Aktion,* local residents assembled with their wheelbarrows in the streets leading to the ghetto in anticipation of the moment when the massacre would be over and it would be possible to begin the wild orgy of pillaging the victims' property.[97] The German officials complained that there were not enough police "to stop the local population's thirst for plunder" (*der Plünderungsgier der einheimischen Bevölkerung Einhalt gebieten zu können*).[98] In many places the property of the murdered Jews became a point of issue between the officials of the local self-administration and the Germans. Thus, Vasil'ev, the *Bürgermeister* of the small locality of Samakhvalaviči in the Minsk area, complained to the Minsk rayon administration about the conduct of the Wehrmacht soldiers, who took possession of the cattle, poultry, and other property left behind by the victims, while threatening to shoot the local officials and policemen who were trying to prevent them from doing so.[99] Sometimes the misappropriation of Jewish property began while the Jews were still alive. In the locality of Usvjaty, in the south of the Pskov oblast (today northwestern Russia), one of the local non-Jews turned to an elderly Jew

named Zalmanson, whose son had been killed shortly before-
hand, with the following words: "Give me your cow—they [the
Germans—L. R.) are going to shoot you anyway and then the
Germans will get your cow."[100]

The local police officers and the members of the local administration were the first to profit from the Jewish property. Entering the ghetto after the *Aktionen* in search of hidden Jews
enabled the indigenous police officers to loot Jewish houses.
According to the testimony of former Karsakoviči *Gemeinde-*
bürgermeister, Konstantin Mozolevsky, submitted to the Soviet
interrogators after the war, the policemen who participated in
the massacre of Borisov Jews returned with "watches and other
items that they received as a reward, from the property of the
executed Jews."[101] According to the order of *Generalkommissar*
für Weißruthenien, Wilhelm Kube, the police officers, together
with their families, were supposed to enter "the better" apartments of the exterminated Jews.[102] Those guarding the ghetto
perimeters could also profit from the illegal barter trade organized near the fences between Jews and non-Jews.[103] In many
cases, the policemen entered the ghetto whenever they pleased,
violating its inmates, raping, killing and looting indiscriminately. In Minsk, such "visits" were quite regular and claimed
scores of victims.[104]

In some situations, the Germans, as noted, competed against
the local population for the misappropriation of Jewish property,
while on other occasions they were quite eager to involve the
local population directly or indirectly in this process. Given their
position as an occupying authority, the dispensation of the property of the murdered Jews was an easy and cheap way to buy the
endorsement of the local population and solve, at least partially,
their economic problems. Illustrative of this is the directive
issued by the *Ostministerium* on 13 April 1942, according to
which the native employees of the German war industry enterprises working in the occupied Eastern territories were supposed
to be supplied with textile goods from Jewish property.[105]

Apart from the "wild" misappropriations, there were also
"organized" or "quasi-organized" misappropriations. Thus, the
local *uprava* was supposed to register Jewish property immediately after the *Aktionen* took place. Part of it was supposed to be
transferred to German authorities, while another part was distributed to the local inhabitants. In Bobrujsk, the local *Kom-*
mandantur even issued special instructions regarding Jewish
property, stating explicitly that "all cash, securities, precious

metals, necklaces and other valuables must be transferred immediately to the *Feldkommandantur*," while "the items that are not new and that did not possess a special value" should be released to the population.[106] The sales of Jewish houses were one of the most profitable businesses for the local *upravas*. According to the report of the financial department of the Mogiljov *uprava* from the beginning of May 1942, the income from the sale of Jewish houses amounted to 812,478 roubles, out of a total income of 1,584,211 roubles and 9 kopecks, that is, approximately fifty-one per cent, while at the beginning of June of the same year, the share of the income from the sale of Jewish houses reached more than sixty-five per cent of the total income of the *uprava*—975,043 roubles out of 1,489,498 roubles and 99 kopecks.[107] Although officially, priority in the sale of the Jewish houses and apartments was given to people who had lost their houses as a result of fire, whose houses had been requisitioned by the German authorities, or who had lost their homes in the Soviet period, and to refugees, in reality, protectionism and nepotism were often the only criteria for the allocation of the living quarters.[108] In Novo-Borisov, a refugee from Minsk, Marija Mokraja, was denied the apartment allocated to her by the city's *uprava*, when the man in charge of the neighborhood in which the apartment was situated, Sarapajev, decided to transfer it to one of his acquaintances. The woman complained to the head of the Borisov OD, but to no avail; Sarapajev refused to provide explanations, stating solely that he relied on his own authority. This is a most revealing case of the relations between various levels of the local self-administration.[109]

The organs of local self-administration and the police were meticulous in making sure that not even the smallest item of Jewish property would get lost. Thus, Bakhanovich from Novo-Borisov asked Stankevič, the *Rayonbürgermeister* of Borisov, what should be done with those Jews who, in his words, "were squandering" (*razbazarivajut*) their property, i.e., transferring or selling it secretly before resettling into the ghetto, as well as with the non-Jews who were acquiring this property.[110] In July 1942, Stankevič demanded from the heads of the Borisov and Novo-Borisov police (*Ordnungsdienst*) a report on the people who had seized the Jews' cows without paying.[111]

The expropriated Jewish property was often sold in special stores and found its way onto the black market.[112] In Minsk, this material was stored "up to a man's height (*mannshoch*)" in the local opera house.[113] Once money had lost its value as a means of payment, this seized property acquired the value of currency. One of the archive documents tells of a woman who exchanged chickens and eggs for the clothes of murdered Jews stockpiled in the special storehouse near Minsk, and then turned around and exchanged the newly acquired clothes for food in Western Byelorussia.[114]

Indeed, it is very difficult to name any bodies which did not profit in one way or another from the annihilation of the Jews. A prominent place among the main profiteers was held by the "Byelorussian Self-Aid Organization" (BNS), which was officially supposed to help all those suffering as a result of the war and take over the functions of the Byelorussian Red Cross. In his report before the delegates of the Second All-Byelorussian Congress, mentioned in Chapter 4, the president of the Byelorussian Central Council (BCR), Astroŭski, spoke of 11,606,170 roubles collected by the BNS "through public donations and as a result of its economic activity" in the financial year of 1943.[115] The sum quoted by Astroŭski is indeed very impressive, even more so as this was toward the end of the occupation period, when economic conditions had worsened considerably for the majority of Byelorussians. Apparently, additional sources, about which Astroŭski preferred to keep silent, fed into the BNS income. This is indeed curious, especially since this report, submitted in 1944 to the Byelorussian congress, was edited in the 1950s, after the defeat of the Third Reich. Actually, misappropriated Jewish property was one of the sources of the BNS's prosperity that year, as shown by Bernhard Chiari, who quotes documents indicating that the BNS had used Jewish property to replenish its supplies and in 1942 even issued an instruction to the German *Gebietskommissare*, demanding the transfer to the BNS authorities of the items remaining after the liquidation of the Jewish ghettos.[116] Of course, German functionaries simply ignored this instruction.[117]

Even establishments such as hospitals turned a profit, directly or indirectly, from the murder of the Jews. In September 1942, the *Stadtskommissar* of Minsk, Janetzke, made a plea to the health department of *Generalkommissariat für Weißruthenien*, on behalf of the city's First Hospital, for hospital items such as bedclothes from the Jewish property stored in the opera house.[118]

To sum up this section, it appears that local collaboration in the Holocaust had many faces; traditional anti-Semitism alone, however, does not suffice to explain this collaboration. The desire to take possession of Jewish property and to demonstrate loyalty to the occupation regime also played quite a prominent part in the decision to turn against those people who only recently had been neighbors, friends, and sometimes even relatives. The general context in which the Holocaust took place cannot be overlooked either. Bernhard Chiari aptly likened Byelorussian society during the German occupation to a raft drifting in stormy waters, where the passengers in their struggle for their physical survival are ready to toss into the water all those seen as "unnecessary ballast."[119] The Jews, traditionally perceived as outcasts, were the first "candidates" for this role.

From the German point of view, local collaboration in the persecution of Jews also provided a kind of "alibi," enabling them to portray the whole process of the "Final Solution" as something spontaneous, an expression of the popular desire to "self-cleanse." Even if this collaboration was of a smaller scope than hoped for by the Germans, it still presented a factor of paramount importance in the greatest tragedy of the twentieth century.

The Collaboration in a War against "Undesirable Elements"

Collaboration in the "Anti-Partisan Operations"

Khatyn is located sixty km to the northeast of Minsk, about one hour's journey from the Byelorussian capital. Until 22 March 1943, it was a small village with 26 houses and 156 inhabitants.[120] On 24 March 1943, German *Oberfeldkommandantur* 392 reported the following: "On 22.3., the security patrol of urban police (*Schutzpolizei*) was attacked by bandits near Huba (fourteen km to the north of Logojsk). One captain (*Hauptmann*) of *Schutzpolizei* and three Ukrainians were killed, one Ukrainian was wounded.[121] The band was revealed during the pursuit. Thirty enemies killed. The bandits' village (*Bandendorf*) of Khatyn (twelve km to the southeast of Pleshchenice) was hereby destroyed together with ninety inhabitants."[122] A more detailed report of what happened in Khatyn was provided by the 118th auxiliary police battalion (*Schutzmannschaftbataillon*) in its letter to the SSPGF (*SS- und Polizei Gebietsführer*) in Borisov. According to this report, the village was encircled by various German units, including parts of the infamous Dirlewanger's unit (discussed below), and attacked from all sides.[123] The authors of the report spoke about strong resis-

tance encountered in the village, but in reality, the villagers
were simply driven together into the barn in the center of the
village and burned alive. Only three children and one old man
were able to save themselves.[124]

Today Khatyn is a memorial for some 628 Byelorussian villages that were burned down along with their inhabitants during the so-called "anti-partisan operations," which ultimately
became the very symbol of Nazi occupation politics. The majority of the victims of these operations were innocent people
accused of supporting partisans.

Before discussing "anti-partisan warfare" in greater depth, a
brief treatment of the partisan movement itself is called for.
This movement, which in the popular mind became a symbol of
Byelorussia during the war, had small beginnings.[125] From the
very outset of their activities inside Byelorussia, the infamous
Einsatzkommandos of *Einsatzgruppe B* cited the "struggle
against the bands" as one of their most important activities;
nevertheless, even from these reports, it can be surmised that
before 1942 the partisan movement was a rather marginal phenomenon.[126] The Soviets initially had no coherent plan to create
a wide guerilla movement. Despite Stalin's call to form partisan
units that would "blow up bridges and roads, damage telephone
and telegraph lines, set fire to forests, stores, transports," voiced
in his "scorched earth" speech of 3 July 1941, little was actually
done.[127] Although a day earlier, on 2 July 1941, the first secretary of the Central Committee of the Communist Party of
Byelorussia, Pantelejmon Ponomarenko, had already reported
to Moscow on "the unfolding of a partisan movement," the
movement's actual evolvement took longer.[128] The party functionaries, who were originally entrusted with the organization
of the resistance movement in various regions, often simply fled
without doing a thing. Byelorussian historian Alexej Litvin
recently published some previously inaccessible documents from
the Byelorussian archives. They revealed that on 21 July 1941
the Central Committee of the Byelorussian Communist Party
decided to punish a number of functionaries who, after taking
flight, refused to return to the rear to organize the partisan
movement.[129] Under those circumstances, the first partisan
detachments consisted mainly of Red Army soldiers who had
succeeded in escaping the German pockets and had lost contact
with their military units. Originally, these detachments resembled bands of rogues rather than military or even paramilitary
troops. Their discipline left much to be desired. As late as 1942,

for example, one such "detachment," deployed near Sukhoj Ostrov, used their explosives to "stun" the fish. In addition, the use of physical violence by partisan unit members against their commanders was not uncommon.[130] Arms' supplies were very scarce. As late as January 1942, only ten of the twelve members of the Chkalov detachment of the Sverdlov brigade were armed with modern weapons, while the two remaining men had axes.[131] Food reserves, too, were extremely scarce. To obtain food, the partisans were compelled to raid the surrounding villages, a fact that made the peasants hate the partisans. It is no surprise, therefore, that the peasants, who originally nicknamed the partisans *lesaviki* (wood demons), were quite ready to inform the German authorities about these raiders.[132] In such a state of affairs, the Germans at first had little problem fighting the partisans.

The situation began to change at the beginning of 1942. The second wave of the liquidation of Jewish ghettos and the increase in the deportation of forced workers to Germany resulted in growing numbers of people fleeing into the woods. There they joined the Soviet POWs who had escaped the appalling conditions of the POW camps. (Nevertheless, a significant number of the POWs preferred to join the German side and "volunteered" for the various auxiliary police structures; see below.) The unifying concept for all these people was not some lofty motive, such as "Soviet patriotism," as suggested repeatedly by Soviet historians, but chiefly an entirely prosaic desire for survival.

The increase in the number of partisans attracted the attention of both the Soviets and the Germans. The Soviets were eager to bring this movement under its control and at least, at this point, to assume a leading role in encouraging a mass partisan movement. Although many historians, even non-Soviet ones such as Polish historian Yerzy Turonak, see the situation slightly differently, not all partisan units active in Byelorussian territory were Soviet ones.[133] In both the western and the eastern parts of Byelorussia there were national units, for example, Jewish units, which according to some sources, such as Nikolas Vakar, numbered between 10,000 and 11,000 people.[134] Many of these units, such as the Jewish detachment headed by the Belski brothers, recognized the Soviets' authority only formally. In the territories annexed by the Soviet Union in 1939 in accordance with the Molotov–Ribbentrop pact, there existed an entire network of clandestine Polish units, known as Armija Krajowa

(AK for short, literally the Home Army), which was directly subordinate to the Polish government-in-exile in London. There was also a network of Byelorussian national partisan detachments, united with the Byelorussian People's Partisan Movement (Belaruskaja Narodnaja Partyzanka, BNP), that fought primarily against Soviet and Polish partisans.[135]

In the spring of 1942, the Central Staff of the Partisan Movement was created in Moscow, headed by Kliment Voroshilov, who had been considered an expert on partisan warfare since the days of civil war in Russia. In September 1942, the Byelorussian Staff of the Partisan Movement was founded, headed by Pjotr Kalinin, Second Secretary of the Central Committee of the Byelorussian Communist Party.[136] As mentioned earlier, these bodies were created not only to coordinate a growing, battleworthy resistance movement in the occupied territories, but also to ensure that this resistance would be under a central control and directed in the right way. To accomplish these objectives, special training schools were opened in the Soviet hinterland and their graduates were parachuted behind German lines. In many cases, they were appalled by the state of the various partisan units they encountered in Byelorussia, especially by their preference for defensive tactics with sporadic counterstrikes over offensive ones, as well as by the virtual lack of "party komsomol" work.[137]

Although the Germans might have been surprised to find that the Byelorussians, whom they had considered a "submissive people," dared to resist them, this unexpected development served them well. As early as July 1941, when there was virtually no resistance movement in the occupied territories, Hitler proclaimed the following: "a partisans' war also has its advantage; it enables us to eradicate what is against us."[138] This view was reiterated by the chief of the operational department in OKH, Generalleutnant (Lt. General) Adolf Heusinger: "The treatment of the civilian population and the methods of antipartisan warfare in operational areas presented the highest political and military leaders with a welcome opportunity to carry out their plans, namely, the systematic extermination of Slavism and Jewry."[139]

In general, the German "anti-partisan struggle" was riddled with errors. Although in the occupied Eastern territories the German response was intensified with the addition of racial dogmas and prejudices, such conduct was hardly unique. Dating back to the days of the Franco-Prussian War (1870–71), the German military was obsessed with the theme of civilian resistance, of *franc-tireurs*.[140] In her classic work, *August 1914*, Barbara Tuchman describes the German attitude to civilian resistance as follows:

> Fear and horror of the *franc-tireur* sprang from the German feeling that civilian resistance was essentially disorderly. If there has to be a choice between injustice and disorder, says Goethe, the German prefers injustice. Schooled in a state in which the relation of the subject to the sovereign has no basis other than obedience, he is unable to understand a state organized upon any other foundation, and when he enters one he is inspired by an intense uneasiness. Comfortable only in the presence of authority, he regards the civilian sniper as something peculiarly sinister. To the western mind the *franc-tireur* is a hero; to the German he is a heretic who threatens the existence of the state.[141]

Even before World War II, this *franc-tireurs* complex led to the most brutal methods of quelling civilian resistance. During the Herero uprising in German South West Africa, in 1904–5, German General Lothar von Trotha proclaimed his intention to "annihilate the revolting tribes with streams of blood and streams of gold."[142] And this did not remain a mere declaration. By 1911, 81.25 per cent (65,000 out of an original 80,000) of the Herero tribe had been exterminated.[143] The memoirs of German soldiers and officers who served during World War I in Belgium and France are dotted with mentions of repressions against the localities whose inhabitants showed even the slightest sign of resistance to the Germans.[144] In August 1914, after a German officer was shot at in the Belgian city of Louvain, German troops subjected the city to an "orgy of killing, pillage, and pyromania."[145]

During World War II in the occupied Soviet territories, this traditional fear of *franc-tireurs*, together with the racial dogmas that were common then, resulted in the most terrible methods of suppressing resistance, which will be described in the following.[146] These methods, however, were neither an improvisation nor an overreaction produced by the anxiety associated with "besieged fortress" mentality. Rather, they were planned in advance, even before the invasion into the Soviet Union, when it was by no means clear what the actual conditions would be. In fact, the means used as a reaction to resistance relied on the series of orders developed in the spring and summer of 1941, which provided the basis for the atrocities committed in the course of the war against the USSR.[147] On 3 April 1941, the chief of staff of the Army's Supreme Command (OKH), Franz Halder, signed the order which stated, "The active or the passive resistance of the civilian population should be nipped in the bud through severe punitive measures (*Strafmaßnahmen*)."[148] The infamous "Barbarossa Order," which established the rules for military justice in the operative area (or rather perverted them), was signed by the chief of staff of the Wehrmacht's Supreme Command (OKW), Keitel, on 13 May 1941. This order demanded quite unambiguously, "*Franc-tireurs* (*Freischärler*) will be liquidated ruthlessly (*zu erledigen*) by the troops in combat or while fleeing. Also all other attacks by enemy civilians against the Armed Forces, its members and auxiliaries (*Gefolge*) will be suppressed on the spot by the troops, with the most rigorous methods until the assailants are finished."[149] Even phenomena such as repressions against entire localities were not "invented" during the occupation period. In the course of implementing the cited "military justice order," the General for Special Assignments by the Army's Supreme Commander (*Oberbefehlshaber des Heeres*), Generalleutnant Müller, presented a draft which said, inter alia, "Against localities from which troops have been attacked in a deceitful or treacherous manner, collective coercive measures (*Gewaltmaßnahmen*) will be applied immediately upon the order of an officer of the rank of at least battalion, etc., commander, if the circumstances do not permit a quick identification of individual perpetrators."[150] Little wonder then that when faced with the partisan movement in occupied Byelorussia, the Germans were hardly interested in the real causes of this movement. Although the more pragmatic among the Germans were compelled to acknowledge that various "excesses" of Nazi occupation politics were doing no good for the German cause, the German authorities by and large preferred to rely upon dogmatism and brutal force.[151] Characteristically enough, those responsible for the anti-partisan struggle looked for "inspiration" in the memoirs of Lawrence of Arabia rather than in the real situation.[152]

Although those living in the "Eastern area" were originally seen as *Untermenschen*, the Germans were soon compelled to acknowledge the fact that some kind of local cooperation would be useful in quelling the resistance movement. As well as calling for repressions against real or potential resistance in the Soviet territories that were to be occupied, Halder's order, quoted above, also stated: "It should be made clear early on, which parts of the population could be relied on by German troops. Those populations hostile to the Soviet Russian government and state should be utilized for German interests, by allowing them to enjoy certain liberties and material benefits."[153] The desire to use local collaboration in the occupied Eastern territories stemmed both from the inadequacy of German forces to put down the growing resistance movement and the desire to spare "precious" German blood.[154] The fact that using one part of the population in the occupied Soviet territories against another could unleash a civil war did not bother the German authorities. Such a development was even desirable from their point of view. At the beginning of 1942, the department of war administration at the office of the General-Quartermaster in OKH issued a document titled "Suggestions for the disintegration of the Soviet capacity to resist (*Widerstandskraft*)." This document spoke openly of provoking a civil war in the Soviet territories.[155]

Supplied with orders such as the above, it is little wonder that the Germans coming into the *Ostraum* were ready to translate them into reality and crack down on anyone they deemed "dangerous." Although after the war, many former Wehrmacht soldiers and officers tried to create the impression that they had nothing to do with the atrocities committed in the occupied Soviet territories and to dump sole responsibility upon the SS-apparatus, things were actually quite different. In October 1941, Generalleutnant Walter von Unruh, commander of the rear Army area (Korück) 559, issued an order directed at the 137th infantry division, making it clear that "whoever causes harm to the Wehrmacht should be eliminated."[156] In the same order, von Unruh called for fighting and ruthlessly doing away with partisans as well as for "cleansing localities from all suspicious and alien (*Ortsfremde*) elements, and preventing the population from wandering at night ... Troublemakers, instigators (*Aufwiegler*), partisans in civilian clothes should be hanged or shot immediately."[157] The orders issued at lower levels were no less drastic. Thus, divisional order No. 29 for the 8th infantry division also stated that "one should proceed with the most severe means against the beginning of the creation of partisan groups. Anyone from these groups who is captured alive and falls into the troops' hands must not be shot, but hanged. Their corpses should remain hanging for at least one week as a deterrent."[158]

From the very outset, the German authorities in their "anti-partisan warfare" adopted the principle known to local inhabitants from Soviet times, namely "anyone who is not with us is against us" (*Kto ne s nami-tot protiv nas*). Thus, in "Operational

Order Nr. 12" (*Einsatzbefehl 12*) issued on 18 September 1941, regarding the "cleansing operations" in the Polesje area (the main victims of these operations were Jews, mostly women and children), Himmler stated explicitly that all the villages there should be seen "either as strong points for us or as strong points for the enemy."[159] This attitude, extended to include the whole territory of Byelorussia, was only reinforced with the growth of the partisan movement. All over Byelorussia posters in the Byelorussian language were hung calling on the population to join the anti-partisan struggle. They stated unambiguously: "Whoever does not hinder the activities of bandits is their accomplice."[160] Under such conditions the population in occupied Byelorussia, as well as in other occupied Soviet territories, had very little choice; any neutral stance was excluded almost from the beginning.

In the first weeks and months following the German invasion, "straggling" Soviet soldiers brought upon themselves an intense outpouring of rage from both the German field troops and the security organs. Usually these "stragglers," who were called by the local population *okruzhentsy*—that is, "the surrounded," those who, encircled by enemy troops, were cut off from the front and were forced to live illegally in the occupied territories—were people who had succeeded either in breaking through the German pockets or had escaped from the POW camps and had lost contact with their units. Some of them went into the forests, creating the first partisan groups; others came to various villages, exchanged their uniforms for civilian clothes, and "vanished" among the local population. They, as well as the "strangers" (*Ortsfremde*) and the so-called "wanderers," were from the outset the target of German persecution. From the German point of view, the assistance of the local inhabitants in these persecutions was of paramount importance. The key role was played by the newly appointed organs of "self-administration." The *Bürgermeistern* and other officials were ordered by the German authorities to deliver into their hands "commissars, trouble-makers and *Ortsfremde*."[161] In the summer of 1941, the commander of the 3rd company of the infamous 309th police battalion stated before the assembled *Bürgermeistern* in the Ivaceviči district (today the Brest oblast) that it was their duty, "apart from harvesting the crops, also to hand over (*Ablieferung*) the straggling Russians."[162] The same source that mentions such "clarifications" also reports "with satisfaction" that "in a number of days, 120 soldiers, followed by 60 more straggling (*Versprengte*) soldiers in five additional days were handed over by the *Bürgermeistern*."[163] In October 1941, the 137th infantry division carried out a so-called "pacification" operation in the Jukhnov-Vjaz'ma-Dorogobush-Jelnja-Kirov area (today western Russia), the main aim of which was to hunt down the straggling Soviet soldiers. Its final report on this mission read as follows: "Almost in all of the localities, it was good to work with the appointed *Bürgermeistern*."[164]

Assistance in spotting "straggling" Soviet soldiers, however, did not come only from "indigenous self-administration." As noted, many of these soldiers who roamed the forests raided the surrounding villages for food, which did not make them particularly popular with the local inhabitants. Initially, the latter were quite eager to inform the occupation authorities about these soldiers. As early as July 1941, the office of the commander of the Rear Area of the Army Group "Center" reported that during the "police operation" in the area of the railway Baranaviči-Luninec, 88 "Russians" (that is, stragglers) and 200 Jews who "were engaged in assisting the Russians" were captured "through the active assistance of the inhabitants."[165] Daniel Romanovsky, comparing the attitude of the local population in Northeastern Byelorussia and Western Russia toward the Jews and the stragglers, notes: "The same people who had refused to give refuge to Jews gave it freely to escaped prisoners of war and *okruzhentsy* ... although the punishment for this was no less severe than that for harboring Jews. This was because in the eyes of the local population the *okruzhentsy* were 'our boys'."[166] In reality, however, the attitude of the local dwellers toward the *okruzhentsy* was not as idyllic as that depicted by Romanovsky. The readiness of the locals to inform Germans of the stragglers stemmed partly from the fact that initially these groups of soldiers were no more than bands of ruffians causing trouble to villagers. Another part of the explanation relates to the theory that Daniel Romanovsky presents in the section of his chapter dealing with collaboration in the persecution of the Jews, namely, the ability of *homo Sovieticus* to adjust to any kind of totalitarian regime and its demands. In 1952, the American researcher George Fisher spoke of political inertness as a striking feature of the Soviet people. He described this inertness as "the nearly perfect ability of the Soviet citizen to adjust instantaneously to what he guesses instinctively, through senses perfected to the nth degree for this pathetic yet all-important task, to be the 'party line', the policy, or the official wish, of the moment."[167] It was precisely this political inertness that ultimately led the people to act against all those whom the new authorities (in this case the Germans) marked as undesirable, dangerous elements, be they Jews, Communists, straggling Soviet soldiers, or *Orts-fremde*.

As previously noted, in the beginning the Germans had little trouble suppressing the beginnings of resistance. This was due to the cooperation of the local inhabitants. Early attempts to create partisan units did not meet with the understanding of the locals. The American historian Mathew Cooper, in his standard study *The Nazi War against Soviet Partisans*, quotes the commander of one of the partisan detachments, Linkov, who recounted his difficulties in gathering his men who had been parachuted into Byelorussia from the Soviet rear in 1941. According to Linkov, these problems related directly to the indifference—if not hostility—of the local population. In fact, the residents even provided the Germans with a detailed description of Linkov himself.[168] Additional Soviet sources confirm the information about the initial hostile attitude on the part of local population toward the nascent partisan movement.[169]

The situation began to change toward the end of 1941, and even more so in 1942. At the end of May 1942, the commander of the Rear Area of the Army Group "Center," general of infantry Max von Schenckendorff, was compelled to state in desperation that "at present partisans are dominating the great parts of the Army area (*Heeresgebiet*) 'Center', since it is currently impossible to pursue their annihilation through offensive action, due to insufficient troops."[170]

The Moscow offensive and later Hitler's decision to shift the main thrust of the war against the Soviet Union to the south, led to the withdrawal of a considerable part of the forces from the Rear Area of the Army Group "Center."[171] This compelled the commanders operating in the area to draw upon the available troops and to rely extensively on local forces. The more pragmatic among the Wehrmacht field commanders also understood that such use also demanded certain amendments to the *Ost-politik*. Such amendments did not taint the ultimate goal of Nazi occupation politics in the Eastern area, especially the exploitation of the economic resources, chief among them the raw materials—after all, the greater part of these materials was supposed to oil Wehrmacht's gears.[172] Nevertheless, these changes envisaged a greater degree of self-government for the local inhabitants as well as the creation of a "Russian" anti-Communist military force with a "Russian de Gaulle" at its head. In March 1942, von Schenckendorff issued another communiqué, proposing some ways in which to cope with the ever-growing partisan movement.[173] One recommendation was to promise the *Ostvölker* the creation of an "independent national Russia." According to Schenckendorff, this state would be dependent on Germany, and its western borders would take into account the settlement interests of Germany. He also suggested instituting several new policies, such as immediate agrarian reform; care for the religious needs of the native inhabitants; support for the organs of indigenous "self-administration," which were nevertheless supposed to be under strict German control; reduction of peasants' delivery duties; and preferential treatment for collaborators. As can be seen here, the idea of involving local forces in the anti-partisan struggle was—from beginning to end—a matter of expediency and not an expression of inherent "liberalism" on the part of the German military. Schenckendorff's letter shows once again that the Wehrmacht commanders, at various levels, usually shared the *Lebensraum* views of the Nazi leadership. In May 1943, Oberstleutnant (Lt. Colonel) Harteneck, the chief of staff of the 2nd Army (AOK 2), also issued a memorandum stating that "we can master the wide Russian expanse that we have conquered only *with* the Russians and Ukrainians who live in it, never against their will." For Harteneck, like other German commanders who supported a quasi-"liberalized" approach to politics in occupied Soviet territories, involving the local population in the occupation politics was only a means for a more effective exploitation of the economic resources as well as for sparing German blood.[174]

"Autonomous District Lokot" and Anti-Guerilla Warfare in Western Russia and Eastern Byelorussia

In their desire to cope effectively with the resistance movement, some Wehrmacht commanders were prepared to go very far. At the end of 1941, the commander of the 2nd Panzer army, Generaloberst Rudolf Schmidt, gave permission to create the autonomous district Lokot in the Kursk-Orjol region near the Bryansk forest, as it had become the focal point of partisan activities quite early on.[175] It is not clear if Schmidt was acting on his own initiative or if he had received sanction from above. The district, defined in German documents as the "autonomous district Lokot" (*Selbstverwaltungsbezirk Lokotj*), initially encompassed some 581,000 people, but in time it expanded to include around 1,700,000 people, and it was headed by the engineer Voskobojnikov.[176] He was killed by partisans in early 1942, and was succeeded by another engineer, Bronislav Kaminski, a brutal figure with an obscure background, who came to Lokot after spending five years of exile in the Urals area.[177] Both Voskobojnikov and Kaminski were enthusiastic admirers of German National Socialism and founded a dwarf party called the National Socialist Russian Labor Party. To fight the partisans, both men organized their private armed forces, known as the Russian Liberation People's Army (Russkaja Osvoboditel'naja Narodnaja Armija, or RONA for short), which according to German documents was some 8,000–9,000 men strong in 1943 and consisted of thirteen battalions organized in four regiments.[178] Already from the fall of 1941, these forces waged heavy fights against partisans, initially without any coordination with the Germans. The Germans were slow to supply the various collaborationist units with weapons, so RONA was equipped with weapons that its soldiers captured from partisans. It had at its disposal heavy cannons, heavy grenade launchers, and heavy machine guns.[179] According to Mathew Cooper, Kaminski's army even had a unit of twenty-four legendary T-34 Soviet tanks.[180]

The undertaking was evaluated by the German authorities as an unambiguous success. According to the Germans, Kaminski's forces were able not only to fight partisans effectively in their district, but also to produce enough food to feed both the district's own population and to deliver surplus to the German authorities.[181] Kaminski's private army, RONA, survived the Lokot project. After the liberation of the Lokot area by the Soviet Army in mid-1943, RONA was transferred to neighboring Byelorussia, where its units participated in anti-partisan struggles. By then it had been renamed the 29th Waffen-Grenadier Division der SS "RONA" (Russian No.1) and had gained special notoriety during the quelling of the Warsaw Uprising of 1944, for "competing" successfully against Dirlewanger's brigade for the highest degree of brutality. The atrocities committed by Kaminski's men in Warsaw were too much even for the Germans.[182] Ultimately, Kaminski was summoned to Litzmannstadt (today Lodz), where he, together with his driver, his chief of staff, and the division's physician, was executed by an SS squad;[183] his troops were withdrawn from the fight.[184]

Although it was praised at various levels of German administration, the Lokot project remained the only undertaking of its kind; but the Germans did launch a number of other projects in Byelorussian territory between 1941 and 1942, to hold the growing partisan movement in check. In April 1942, Schenckendorff ordered the creation of two units, called "combat battalions" (*Kampfbataillone*), "Dnepr" and "Beresina," consisting of Soviet POWs.[185] By August 1942, three more units of a similar kind were added, namely "combat battalions" "Volga" and "Dvina" (*Düna*), as well as the 102nd Cossack detachment (*Abteilung*).[186] In September came the establishment of three new units: a combat battalion "Pripjat'" (*Pripet*); an experimental unit *Graukopf* (that is grey hair), named after its commander, former Soviet colonel Bojarskij; and a "volunteers' reserve regiment 'Center'" (*Freiwilligen-Ersatz-Regiment Mitte*).[187]

Though the next chapter will examine, as far as possible, the exact modus operandi of all of these units, it is worth noting here that the attitude of the German military authorities towards these units was quite ambiguous. Despite their announcement about the importance of the use of local forces in anti-partisan warfare, the German commanders regarded the personnel recruited into these units with a considerable degree of suspicion. Schenckendorff's order from 29 April 1941, regarding the formation of the "Dnepr" and "Beresina" units, is very revealing on this point.[188] According to this order, both units were supposed to be led by "Russian" officers; nevertheless, German "framework personnel" (*Ramenpersonal*) were appointed to accompany the units. Officially, the "framework personnel" was supposed to fulfill mainly logistic duties, yet it is possible that they were intended to control the conduct of the units' soldiers. Moreover, in the same order the soldiers in the "combat battalions" were defined as POWs until "after the final examination and trial (*Bewährung*)," at which point they would "be released, in order to become Wehrmacht escorts (*Wehrmachtgefolge*)."[189] The inferior status of these soldiers was further underscored by Schenckendorff's conditions, which explicitly stated that they should be armed only with captured weapons, and that their allowance should be rationed according to the norms for deserters.[190]

In the anti-partisan struggle, as well as the local units formed in Byelorussian territory, the Germans also used various formations from other occupied territories, primarily from the Baltic region—foremost from Lithuania and Latvia—and the Ukraine.[191] As it provides a good case study of the German authorities' attitude to various "eastern formations," and their stubborn adherence to racist dogmas, this topic will be discussed in greater detail in the next chapter.

Cossacks and Anti-Partisan Fighting in Byelorussia

Another project greatly favored by Nazi decision-makers at various levels was the use of Cossacks in the anti-partisan struggle. For a number of reasons the German attitude towards the Cossacks was fairly benevolent. First among these was a racial motive: based on the conviction that the Cossacks were actually descendants of the Goths who once roamed the South Russian steppes, Hitler, as well as some of the other Nazi leaders, considered them to be of Germanic blood.[192] Secondly, the Cossacks had a long tradition of struggle against Soviet rule, which was to their favor. The "veterans" of this fight, who were émigrés during the interwar period, such as the ataman (chieftain) of the Kuban Cossacks, Vjacheslav Naumenko, and the ataman of the Don Cossacks, Pjotr Krasnov, were among the Nazis' early supporters.[193] Finally, it can be surmised that Hitler, who, as we know was still a passionate reader of Karl May's Westerns even in his forties, saw the Cossacks as the embodiment of the modern cowboys. Whatever the reason, the creation of Cossack units, named initially "hundreds" (*sotni* in Russian or *Kosaken-Hundertschaften* in German), began quite early on. In October 1941, Schenckendorff reported the existence of such units recruited primarily from among the Soviet POWs; not all of them were Cossacks by origin, but they posed as such to escape the appalling conditions of the POW camps. From the very beginning, these units were recruited to serve as anti-partisan, as well as scouting, units.

Among these units, the 102nd Cossack regiment, renamed later the 600th Cossack battalion and then the 600th Cossack regiment, played a central role in the anti-partisan struggle in Eastern Byelorussia. It was commanded by former Soviet Major Kononov. According to the brief information provided in Alexej Litvin's article, at the beginning of the German invasion into the Soviet Union Kononov commanded the Soviet 436th infantry regiment stationed near Baranaviči.[194] His father was an *esaul* (a Cossack military rank equal to an army captain) in the "Greatest Don Army," which, led by Krasnov, waged a bitter struggle against the Red Army during the Russian civil war. In 1918, Kononov the elder was hanged by the Bolsheviks. Kononov's eldest brother perished during the civil war, and two of his other brothers were repressed during the Stalinist purges. He succeeded in concealing his background, and enjoyed a splendid career in the Red Army, which he entered as early as 1922. In 1938, Kononov completed his training in the military academy and was awarded the Order of the Red Star for his participation in the Soviet–Finnish ("Winter") war. At the beginning of the German invasion, Kononov's regiment covered the retreat of the Soviet 155th division, but on 22 August 1941, it deserted en masse to the Germans. Taking into account Kononov's background, it must be said that in his case the decision to join the German side stemmed most probably from a genuine hatred of the Soviet regime.

It is not easy to determine the exact date of the creation of the 102nd Cossack regiment. Litvin sets it as 22 October 1941, but the author of this work found a document written by Schenckendorff, dated 25 April 1942, which speaks about the regiment's creation.[195] The main stock of the regiment's soldiers consisted of deserters who joined the Germans together with Kononov. Additional recruitment was carried out in a number of POW camps in Eastern Byelorussia and in Western Russia, providing 542 new soldiers, only 400 of whom were Cossacks by birth. According to Litvin, at the end of 1941 there were 77 officers, 201 *urjadniks* (Cossack NCOs) and 1,521 rank-and-file Cossacks in the regiment.[196] Clearly not all those recruited in the POW camps joined the unit out of loathing for Soviet rule. For many, it was simply an opportunity to escape the inhuman conditions of these camps and to eat relatively well.[197] As early as November 1941 "special directive No. 64" was issued; it regulated the food supplies for various local auxiliary troops, including the Cossack hundreds operating in the "eastern area." According to this directive, during and following operational activities, these troops were supposed to receive a maximum weekly ration of 2,100 g of bread; 100 g of meat; 70 g of fat; 140 g of jam; 160 g of sugar; 400 g of fruit and legumes; 6 kg of potatoes; 120 g [*sic*] of coffee beans; and fresh vegetables.[198] Of course, such amounts could not be considered sufficient by any standard, and it is difficult to confirm whether they were actually applied. Nevertheless, such levels were still somewhat higher than the "hunger norms" rationed out to the Soviet POWs in the camps and those marching in the rear. According to data quoted by Christian Streit, prisoners who were supposed to be transferred to the Rear Area of the Army Group "Center" received a daily ration of 20 g of millet and 100 g of bread without meat, or 100 g of millet without bread, or "according to the work (*Arbeitseinsatz*) up to 50 g millet, 200 g bread, and fresh meat if any could be obtained."[199] Given these rations, there can be little wonder that cannibalism was rampant in the Soviet POW camps or that the recruitment campaigns for the *Osttruppen* found a ready response among the prisoners.[200]

In April 1942, the regiment consisted of four squadrons (two mounted, 1st and 2nd; and two unmounted due to a lack of horses, 3rd and 4th), a half-battery of 7.62 cm guns, a half-platoon of captured "Russian" anti-tank guns, and a half-platoon of regimental reconnaissance (*Staffel*). In addition, one platoon from each of the 3rd and 4th squadrons was supplied with bicycles.[201] From the German perspective, Cossacks proved to be effective "partisan-hunters." In an undated letter to Rosenberg, the head of Economic Staff East (*Wirtschaftsstab Ost*) stated that "our troops ... could make good use of such 'anti-Comintern Cossacks' [*sic*]."[202] The 102nd Cossack regiment (later the 600th Cossack regiment) participated in many of the so-called "great undertakings" carried out from 1942 on in the area of Eastern Byelorussia: "Bamberg," 26 March–6 April 1942, north and south of Bobrujsk; "Adler" (Eagle), July–August 1942, in the Bobrujsk-Mogiljov-Beresino area; "Blitz" (Lightning), 23 September–3 October 1942, in an area between Polock and Vitebsk; and apparently in several other undertakings as well.[203] During these undertakings, soldiers of the 102nd regiment committed multiple atrocities. The regiment's chief, Lieutenant von Rittberg, interrogated by Soviet investigators after the war, acknowledged that "we [i.e., the 102nd Cossack Regiment] burned down the settlements, shot as partisans those persons discovered in the forests, and arrested and partly [*sic*] eliminated any persons suspected of connections to the partisans."[204] These data are corroborated in German documents. During operation "Bamberg," the Cossacks actively participated in the murder of Jews and those whom they accused of supporting partisans. On 1 April 1942 they killed ten Jews in the forest near the locality of Ozemlja and handed over two Jewish women to the German troops. In the village of Protasy, Cossacks organized the massacre of the members of "partisan" families and burned down their houses.[205] In July 1942, the commander of the 3rd company of the 51st reserve police battalion also reported the practice by the Cossacks of burning villages in the Mogiljov area, remarking that the majority of the population executed in these villages were women and children.[206] Although Sonderführer

Kuhr, who compiled the report on the Cossacks' role in the "Bamberg" operation, criticized the Cossacks' tendency to loot, he nevertheless defined them as very useful for "anti-partisan operations."[207]

Indeed, although German authorities viewed the "eastern" auxiliary units with a great deal of suspicion, the 102nd Cossack Regiment enjoyed a considerable degree of confidence from the Germans. Thus, after the mutiny that occurred on 18 September 1942 in the combat battalion "Beresina," all the combat battalions were subordinated to German security divisions, and the "Beresina" companies dismantled and dispersed among various German troops, while the status of the 102nd Cossack regiment remained intact.[208]

From the German point of view, one of the main advantages of the various Cossack units was that, at least initially, they were virtually immune to Soviet propaganda. With time, the Soviet partisans began to exchange their practice of assaulting individual collaborators and collaborationist bodies with a policy that sought their enemy's "disintegration." In 1942, various partisan commanders suggested several ways in which the clandestine organs of the communist party could operate to bring about the collapse of the collaborationist units.[209] One of the most popular methods was through the distribution of leaflets containing the following message: "Anyone who mistakenly entered the police service and will lay down his weapons need not be afraid of the partisans."[210] Among the Cossack units, however, such appeals initially had little effect. There is an undated document (probably from 1942) that shows the reaction of members of a Cossack formation to the partisans' propaganda. In one written response to such leaflets, the Cossacks cursed the partisans extensively, calling them the tools of world Jewry.[211] Only in 1943 did this situation begin to change. In March 1943, the 600th (former 102nd) Cossack regiment received new recruits from POW camps in Germany. These newcomers, the majority of whom had spent more than a year in these camps and had apparently heard about Stalingrad, were less than eager to fight for the German cause.[212] Of the first thousand new recruits, two hundred refused outright to join the regiment, and in April 1943, two squadrons, the 3rd and 4th, as well as a battalion of artillery, deserted en masse to join the partisans.[213] Later that same year, the remnants of the 600th regiment were transferred to Poland, where they became part of the newly formed von Pannwitz's Cossack division.[214]

Despite this change in 1943, even when many Germans were sure that Germany had lost the war, the Cossacks generally still enjoyed the confidence of the German authorities they had previously garnered. In 1942, Schenckendorff ordered to double the number of Cossack and Ukrainian auxiliary units.[215] Even Hitler, who on 16 July 1941 had proclaimed that "only a German is allowed to bear weapons ... not a Cossack," approved the creation of additional Cossack hundreds less than one year later, but only after he was assured that the Cossacks were Gothic descendants.[216] An additional sign of German confidence in the Cossacks was that the number of German personnel in these units was reduced to a minimum, consisting chiefly of "framework personnel" and liaison officers.[217] Toward the end of the German occupation of Byelorussia, the entire Cossack army, headed by the field ataman and chief of staff, Sergej Pavlov, was transferred to the Navahrudak area, where the Cossacks were entrusted, inter alia, with securing the Haradišče-Navahrudak-Berozaŭka highway, an important route for bringing German supplies.[218]

Local Collaboration in Anti-Partisan Fighting in Generalkommissariat Weißruthenien: Byelorussian Self-Defense Corps

In the part of Byelorussia under civil administration, the German authorities were not the only ones eager to involve the local population in the anti-partisan warfare. In the middle of 1942, Kube, who wanted to strengthen his position chiefly vis-à-vis the SS apparatus while facing a growing partisan movement, decided to enhance the status of the "Byelorussian Self-Aid Organization" by creating its Supreme Council (see Chapter 4). At the same time, he also resolved to create a Byelorussian force that would take an active part in the anti-partisan struggle. That the partisan movement was a serious presence in the *GK Weißruthenien* at this time can be deduced from Kube, together with SSPF *Weißruthenien*, Carl Zenner, appealing on 1 July 1942 to the Byelorussian population to help the Germans in their struggle against the partisans. In return, he promised that anyone who informed the occupation authorities about partisan activities would win the "protection of Germany" (in most cases, this promise proved to be hollow). Other promised rewards included cash, vodka, cigarettes and *makhorka*, and even ownership of their own farms for "those who excelled especially in the struggle against Bolshevist bands."[219]

Under these conditions, on 29 June 1942 Kube published a notice for a project to establish a body named "Free Corps of Byelorussian Self Defense" (Vol'ny Korpus Belaruskaj Samaakhovy), known also in brief as "Byelorussian Self-Defense" (Belaruskaja Samaakhova, or BSA), whose sole purpose was to fight partisans.[220] As noted by Turonak, the very name "Free Corps" was not incidental. Traditionally, the German "Free Corps" (*Freikors*) were irregular units of volunteers without a firm structure and without a well-established membership.[221] The BNS leaders, however, interpreted the creation of the BSA as an indication of the German authorities' intention to create a body of army corps size, which would ultimately serve as the nucleus of a future Byelorussian army. This impression was further reinforced by the fact that while officially BSA units were supposed to be subordinate to SSPF *Weißruthenien,* the BNS was actually left to bear sole responsibility for the recruitment of soldiers as well as for the latter's supply of food, living quarters, and uniforms.[222] Moreover, the head of the "Self-Aid Organization," Yermačenka, who already held the rank of colonel in the Russian White Army, became the supreme commandant of the BSA (*Oberkommandant des weißruthenischen Selbstschutzes,* as it was called in German), while in the Supreme Council of the BNS, a special department for the "Self-Defense Organization" was created.[223] Those responsible for mobilization into the BSA, for example Francišak (Franz) Kušal and Kanstancin Ezavitaŭ, announced their great successes, while Kube reported the recruitment of some 15,000 volunteers.[224] At the same time, members of the Polish underground reported on the forced mobilization in the Hancevǐci area.[225] It is obvious that a significant number of people saw the BSA as the kernel of a future Byelorussian army.

The Germans viewed things quite differently. Not opposed to the idea of shifting the main burden of anti-partisan warfare to the shoulders of BSA men, some people, for example Ludwig Ehrenleitner, who in 1943 was the acting *Gebietskommissar* of Slonim, saw the establishment of the "Self-Defense" units as "the opportunity on the whole to involve the Byelorussian people politically (*politisch zu erfassen*)."[226] As in many cases before and after, the tendency of the German authorities to obtain local collaboration at the lowest possible price is clearly seen here. According to Zenner's order regarding the creation of the BSA, the German police was supposed to supply these units with weapons.[227] In October 1942, the commander of the security police (BdS) in Ostland, the infamous Walter Stahlecker, had to admit that the "Byelorussian public to its great amazement [*sic*] was compelled to acknowledge the fact that the matter of Byelorussian Self-Defense had not been clearly approached and that the Self-Defense men standing ready had not been given any weapons."[228] Despite Kube's fine speeches, which claimed that the BSA would contribute to making "Byelorussia … the indisputable space of the Byelorussian people, in which everyone could speak his own language freely, perform his work, cultivate his land and, above all, enjoy the fruits of his labor without any cares," the reality was quite different.[229] In March 1943, Ehrenleitner reported to Kube about the lamentable situation of the BSA units in the Slonim area.[230] According to Ehrenleitner's statement, no one knew the exact deployment location nor the size of the individual BSA units. Moreover, the same document shows that in their desire to spend as little as possible on local collaboration, the German authorities simply transferred the responsibility for supplying the BSA units with food, uniforms, and weapons to the officials of the local self-administration.

This had two consequences. First, as seen in the chapter on political collaboration, those officials who often found themselves between the anvil and the hammer were quick to turn the "Self-Defense" units into their private army. Second, the fact that the burden of providing supplies to BSA soldiers was thrust upon peasants, forcing them to deliver a significant part of their food to the occupation authorities, did not contribute to either a healthy atmosphere in the villages nor to the popularity of the BSA as a whole in the view of the population. So it is not surprising that when the Germans cracked down upon Yermačenka and the BNS in May 1943, and dissolved the "Self-Defense Organization," there was no outcry of any kind from the Byelorussian population. The fact that the Germans were slow to supply the BSA and other auxiliary units with all necessary goods was utilized by the partisans in their propaganda, which sought the disintegration of these units. One of the partisan commanders, Major Shramko, whose detachment operated in the Polock area, suggested that the soldiers of the voluntary units be informed that partisans were provided with food, clothes, and ammunition as an incentive for them to desert their ranks and join the partisans.[231] Little wonder then that instead of being a tool in the anti-partisan struggle, the BSA units ultimately became a source for reinforcements for partisan units. For example, the Wehrmacht commander in Ostland reported that in one single day, 17 January 1943, seventy-seven BSA men deserted to the partisans.[232]

Defensive and Auxiliary Police Villages

As the occupation progressed and the partisan movement in Byelorussia grew increasingly stronger, the lack of German forces to quell this movement also became all the more evident. Whole areas in the occupied territory were turned into "dead zones," only because the German authorities did not have enough forces to control these areas.[233] An additional result of the growing partisan activity was a significant decline in the Germans' ability to exploit the country's resources effectively. All this led the German authorities to seek new ways in which to solve these problems. The occupation authorities continued to experiment with the notion of increased involvement of local collaborators in their anti-partisan warfare. One of the most notorious experiments, carried out in the later stages of occupation, was the "defensive villages" (*Wehrdörfer*) and "auxiliary police villages" (*Schutzmannschaft-, Ordnungsdienstsdörfer*). The main purpose of these newly established occupation bodies was to assist in "pacifying" the country as well as to be a basis for the procurement (*Erfassung*) of agricultural products in the countryside.[234] Although the *Wehrdörfer* project was a favorite of Kube's successor, von Gottberg, these defensive villages were created not only in the civil administration but in the military administration area as well. Gottberg announced his intention to establish this defensive village network simultaneously with the proclamation of the Byelorussian Central Council, in December 1943. These villages were supposed to be strongholds situated in strategically important areas, initially along the roads and mainly in those areas which in time became virtually inaccessible to the Germans, meaning some forty-one per cent of Byelorussian territory towards the end of the occupation. To facilitate control over these villages and enhance their defensive capability, the villages were organized in groups of ten or twenty.[235] The creation of these villages per se was not an expression of moderation in German *Ostpolitik*. It was rather a result of the harsh reality that the German authorities faced, in particular the realization that not only were the anti-partisan warfare methods implemented until that point unsuccessful in eliminating the partisan movement, they were actually driving many of the local inhabitants to join the partisans. For example, a letter directed from the leading political staff in the *Ostminis-terium* to the personal secretary of the chief of the SS leading staff, Hauptsturmführer Brandenburg, expressed the hope that the organization of the *Wehrdörfer* would bring "much more success than the so-called 'big actions' (*Großaktionen*), which in many cases encouraged the bands, rather than eliminating them (*nicht bandenvernichtend, sondern bandenfördernd gewirkt haben*)."[236]

The difference between the *Schutzmannschaftsdorf* and the *Wehrdorf* was that the former was a settlement composed solely of auxiliary policemen and their families, whereas in the latter, the original inhabitants constituted the majority of the village population; the remainder were a number of the so-called "order service hunt commandos" (*OD-Jagdkommandos*), consisting of local auxiliary policemen brought in from outside to strengthen the villages' defense.[237] The *Schutzmannschaftsdörfer* were supposed to consist of 50 to 100 armed men accompanied by German "framework personnel" from the Gendarmerie units. In some cases, they also had a German "agricultural leader" (*La-Führer*), since a village defined as a "stronghold" was to be the "political and economic center of its area."[238] Every *schuma*-village was allocated a special operation area, called *Feldmark*, which it was supposed to secure and also use for food supplies.[239]

The proclamation of an individual village as a *Wehr-* or *Schutzmannschaftsdorf* was preceded by the "cleansing" of the village of all "undesirables."[240] Afterward, a special ceremony took place, in the course of which "consumer goods" were distributed among the villages; these included alcoholic beverages, *makhorka*, sweets, and decorative items.[241] The newly "initiated" defensive village was supposed to be both a stronghold and a kind of military unit. Although the creation of such villages demonstrated the German occupation authorities' difficulty in controlling a particular region, the idea of making these villages autonomous or even semi-autonomous bodies was nevertheless out of the question. According to the Schenckendorff order issued on 29 January 1944, *Wehrdörfer* were supposed to be supervised (*betreut*) by the local civilian or military authority.[242] To control the defensive villages or groups of such villages, special German commandants were appointed. The criteria for such an appointment is revealed by the case of the group of defensive villages called Chidra, in Eastern Byelorussia, located along the road from Mar'ina Gorka to Bobrujsk. Here, a Baltic

German was appointed as commander of the group of defensive villages (*Wehrdorfgruppenkommandant*); his intention was to establish "direct German rule without the self-administration of the Russians."[243] It is informative that even towards the end of the occupation period, the Germans authorized people with such views to control their most "promising" projects.

The German attitude to the *Wehrdörfer* project showed once again the schizophrenic nature of the German occupation regime. During the ceremonies at which villages were proclaimed as "defensive villages," a rosy picture of the future was depicted. The head of the political department in the Eastern Ministry, Otto Bräutigam, looked on with enthusiasm, as he considered the *entire Wehrdörfer* project a return to "the medieval system of fortresses and castles." He rejoiced that "the system of *Wehrdörfer* [was] really excellently planned and designed."[244] Yet in contrast, Gottberg, who was one of the principal initiators of the project, was quite skeptical. In March 1943, in one of his private conversations he claimed "that the villagers in the defensive villages (*Wehrbauern*) are, of course, no idealists and one should guarantee them some privileges in order to keep them ready for action. This means vodka as well as exemption from the duties of delivering cartloads of firewood and timber."[245] Gottberg also rejected the idea of instituting land re-privatization measures in the *Wehrdörfer*, although he promised to award land to "especially outstanding leaders of defensive villages."[246] According to Gottberg, the villagers of the *Wehrdörfer* were supplied with "safe-conduct passes" which freed them from various Wehrmacht duties, "excluding of course the duty of procurement of taxes" (*Aufbringung der Umlagen*).[247] All of this was nonetheless much less than the members of the defensive villages had expected. As was the case with the BSA, here too the Germans were slow to supply the peasants with weapons, so that initially, in places such as Chidra, the villagers were armed with "Russian" weapons that they had "organized" for themselves.[248]

It is difficult to determine the pace at which the *Wehrdörfer* or *Schutzmannschaftsdörfer* were established. The command of the Army Group Center reported in January 1944 that in the spring of the previous year, as many as sixty strongholds had existed on its operational territory, although they had not yet been named *Wehrdörfer*.[249] In May 1944, the supreme command of the Army Group Center reported twenty-seven villages in the territory of various armies, which were to be proclaimed

Wehrdörfer in the very near future.[250] The same report also
spoke of fifty-five *Wehrdörfer* in civil administration areas.[251] In
his final report, composed in August 1944, the *Gebietskommissar* of Baranaviči, Werner, told of fourteen *Wehr-* and *OD-Dörfer*
created in his district since autumn 1943.[252] If by creating these
defensive villages the Germans sought to gain the sympathy of
the local population, they were quickly disappointed. According
to the July 1944 report by the same Werner, only fifty per cent of
the *Wehrdörfer'* peasants in the Baranaviči area decided to leave
Byelorussia together with the Germans; the other half decided
to stay, although they could safely assume that their lot under
the Soviets would not be an easy one.[253]

Terror as a Means of Anti-Guerilla Fighting

Eventually the anti-partisan struggle became more and more
brutal, as whole villages were burned down, together with their
inhabitants.[254] A number of concentration camps were created
in Byelorussian territory too, the most infamous of which were
the camps of Malyj Trostenec, termed the Byelorussian
Auschwitz, near Minsk, where—according to Soviet data—about
150,000 people were exterminated, and that of Koldychevo, near
Baranaviči, where approximately 22,000 people were put to
death during the two years of its existence.[255] It can be assumed
that the anti-partisan warfare provided the Germans with an
opportunity to begin implementing their plans to turn the Eastern territories, including Byelorussia, into a settlement space
for German and Germanic colonists, as foreseen by the *Generalplan Ost.*

The main method adopted by the Germans in their anti-partisan struggle was brute force and terror; an example of this is
the use of the "device for search after mines No. 42" (*Minen-
suchgerät 42*).[256] The main victims of this struggle were a large
number of innocent peasants, who were "suspected of partisan
activities" (*Bandenverdächtige*). The so-called "anti-partisan
undertakings," which began in early 1942, encompassed more
and more people.[257] Operation Cottbus, which was carried out
between 20 May and 23 June 1942, in the Lepel'-Begoml-Ušači-
Novo-Borisov area in Eastern Byelorussia, alone accounted for
9,796 victims, in addition to 2,000–3,000 people killed in the
"deactivation of mines."[258] That the majority of the victims in all
these operations were non-combatants can be deduced from two
indicators: first, the low number of German losses reported, and

secondly, the relatively small amount of weapons captured during the course of these undertakings. The Germans reported 128 dead among the German and "allied" units as well as 1,009 weapons captured during Operation Cottbus. Commander of the Army Group "Center" Schenckendorff reported about 191 skirmishes and battles with partisans in November 1942 alone, as a result of which 1,977 "enemy deaths" were registered as well as 142 casualties on the German side and 53 weapons captured, the great majority of which (42) were machine guns. There were also two hunting rifles.[259] The "Jollasse Group" mentioned that Operation Dreieck and Viereck resulted in 1,064 enemy deaths, 45 casualties of their own and merely thirteen weapons captured (five of them 12.2 cm guns).[260]

As was demonstrated to some degree in the chapter on political collaboration, local collaborationist bodies, especially local auxiliary police, were strongly involved in this circle of violence, playing a prominent part in a process of increasing brutalization. At the beginning of 1942, the infamous *SS-Sonderkommando* led by Oskar Dirlewanger made its appearance in Byelorussia, to take part in suppressing the partisans.[261] The "trademark" of this unit, which consisted mostly of criminals from various concentration camps, was the brutal methods of the anti-partisan struggle. The Khatyn case cited earlier was indeed characteristic in this respect. As previously noted, even the officials of the local self-administration were not spared by Dirlewanger's men.[262] At the same time, almost from the very outset, the *Sonderkommando* made use of the local auxiliaries from various nationalities of the former Soviet Union. According to the data provided by American researcher French MacLean regarding Dirlewanger's unit, the ratio of the "foreign troops" in the unit, that is, the local auxiliaries, doubled from fifteen per cent (between July 1942 and June 1943) to thirty per cent (between July 1943 and June 1944).[263]

One of the most striking examples of the involvement of the local Byelorussian police forces in the reign of terror was that of the Koldychevo camp.[264] It was established in the spring of 1942, on the territory of a former estate some seventeen kilometers from Baranaviči.[265] The leading role in the camp's organization was played by the commander of the Baranaviči security police department, Woldemar Amelung. Koldychevo was a unique case in that the majority of its personnel consisted of Byelorussian policemen, members of the 13th SD battalion. The number of victims of the camp was great. According to both Galina Paromchyk and Christian Gerlach, the total number of victims came to approximately 22,000 people.[266] Both Jews and non-Jews, all those defined as "undesirables," had been gathered there. The camp's guards were involved in numerous and unspeakable atrocities. It seems that especially sadistic behavior was exhibited by the Byelorussian policeman Nikolaj Kal'ko, who later became the commander of the guards. The indigenous guards' wild and violent actions in Koldychevo are illustrated in numerous examples quoted by both Bernhard Chiari and Galina Paromchyk. One night, for example, a number of jailers "amused" themselves by forcing the male and female prisoners to have sexual intercourse in the camp dining room. During this, inmates were beaten mercilessly with sticks and then killed. On Kal'ko's order, the corpses were thrown out of the window.[267]

The German authorities closed their eyes upon such excesses, ascribing them to the nature of *Untermenschen*. Yet, the Germans themselves created the conditions under which all of those described as "undesirables," whether Jews or non-Jews, were constantly dehumanized, thus offering them as prey for the worst atrocities. Once again it becomes clear that all of the bestial behavior described above cannot be explained by suggesting that the guards were merely over-anxious due to the nature of the anti-partisan warfare. In cases such as that of Koldychevo, most of the policemen acted on their own accord: they had simply become intoxicated with their power over the life and death of the inmates. It is also reasonable to assume that many people who were sadists by nature must have found their way into the local police force.

Against the Strangers

One of the main effects that Nazi occupation had on Byelorussian society was that it heightened all of the old anxieties and animosities. The villagers' traditional suspicion towards all strangers was transformed into the genuine persecution of the *Ortsfremde*. The treatment of the *Ortsfremde* worsened further in the later stages of the occupation period, when the Germans' retreat from the areas to the east of Byelorussia was accompanied by the arrival of those who had chosen to leave their homes together with the Germans. The difficult economic conditions in Byelorussia at that time only aggravated the problem. Knowing that the Jews and the partisans were a priori singled out as "undesirables," the locals often accused the newcomers of being both. The villagers' long-held wariness of strangers was quite sufficient to compel the organs of local self-administration, especially the *Dorfälteste* and the auxiliary police, to proceed against such people on their own behalf, without specific instructions from the German authorities. In June 1943, the auxiliary police (OD) of the Krupki rayon in Eastern Byelorussia persecuted a female refugee named Vera Parinskaja, after she was accused by the *starosta* of the village of Smorodinka, Mavgonets, of being not only Jewish but also in contact with the partisans.[268]

One of the most "popular" methods of persecution of the *Ortsfremde* (and also of the Poles) by local self-administration officials was to send their victims to work in Germany. Thus, for example, in May 1942, the Borisov *Rayonbürgermeister*, Stankevič, issued a directive to the *Bürgermeister* of Borisov as well as to the chiefs of the OD in Borisov and Novo-Borisov, in which he stated that "by sending a certain number of people to Germany, we are providing a better chance to feed the remainder, since we do not have enough produce for the population. Thus those products that otherwise would be used by those exiled [*sic*] to Germany will be saved for those who remain."[269] Stankevič explicitly demanded that the "non locals (refugees)" be the first to be sent to Germany.[270]

Collaboration in the Anti-Polish Campaign in Byelorussia

As has been mentioned on several occasions in this work, the German occupation intensified the tension that characterized the Byelorussian-Polish relationship. Although, as shown, the Germans were compelled to draw on the Poles to man positions in local self-administration and in the local auxiliary police during the earlier stages of the occupation. In their characteristic manner of divide and rule, however, they created the impression that they had a preference for the Byelorussian section of the population. The Byelorussian legal mass media were allowed to wage anti-Polish propaganda, so one finds that the Byelorussian-language *Novaja Daroha* (The New Road), published in Bialystok, wrote in May 1942 about the "domination" of Poles in various collaborationist bodies: "These *Pans*, who up to 1939 occupied these or other posts in the administration, apparently are forgetting whose bread they are eating and imagine themselves in the old role ... Anyplace where there are active Byelorussians these relations are very quickly corrected and justly settled by the German authorities."[271] Turonak, in his

apologetic stance toward Kube, described the "Polish-Byelorussian" relations created by the *Generalkommissar für Weißruthenien* up to mid-1942 as a "system of fragile balance,"[272] but it
appears that this view must now be corrected.

In mid-1942 the Germans began an open anti-Polish campaign. A particularly tough position was adopted by Slonim
Gebietskommissar Erren. In June 1942, a special fine was introduced in the Slonim district, imposed as a penalty for the use of
"another language," that is, other than Byelorussian or German.[273] As early as the autumn of 1942, eighty-four members of
the Polish intelligentsia were shot by the occupation authorities,
and one thousand Poles were ejected from their workplaces and
replaced by Byelorussians. In April 1943, the *Gebietskommissar*
of Vilejka Haase thought that "the removal of the Poles from
Byelorussia is necessary."[274] The various Byelorussian collaborationist bodies did not hide behind the German authorities in
inciting the population against the Poles and in carrying out
various anti-Polish measures. An especially active role in this
respect was played by bodies such as the BNS, the BCR, and the
local self-administration. According to Polish historian Kazimierz Krajewski, the functionaries of the "Byelorussian Popular Self-Aid Organization" compiled the lists of the Poles who
were to be arrested or executed.[275] The Byelorussian auxiliary
police units also participated in the repressive measures against
the Poles in various areas of Western Byelorussia.[276] In the chapter dealing with political collaboration, mention was made of the
violent anti-Polish philippics of the head of local propagandists
in Baranaviči area, Bedritzki. The latter not only accused the
Poles of political unreliability, but also explicitly demanded the
deportation of the Poles (see p. 138). In February 1944, under
the influence of the Byelorussian Central Council, Gottberg
issued a regulation that excluded Poles from provisions regarding illnesses, accidents, and the special security program for
indigenous workers, which had been established by Kube a year
earlier.[277] As noted, Poles were excluded a priori from membership in organizations such as "Byelorussian Self-Aid" and the
"Union of Byelorussian Youth." Like *Ortsfremde*, Poles were
also the first "candidates" for deportation to work in Germany.
It was, in fact, one of the most "popular" methods implemented
by the officials of local self-administration in Byelorussia for
eliminating Polish influence.

The response of organizations such as Armija Krajowa to all
of these measures was harsh indeed. Turonak, who quotes

Byelorussian sources, relates that anti-Byelorussian measures increased significantly in the Lida area, where Poles constituted a significant part of the population, and that some 1,200 Byelorussians were killed there by AK units.[278] The Soviet partisans also reported occasionally on attacks conducted by Polish Home Army units against Byelorussian villages in Western Byelorussia. According to the account by the "Leninskij Komsomol" partisan brigade, which operated in Western Byelorussia in March 1944, Polish units burned down twenty-eight hamlets in the vicinity of the village of Bolshie Berezovcy, in the Vasil'shiki rayon in the Lida area, killing thirty local inhabitants.[279] In the Navahrudak area, the Armija Krajowa created "special clandestine courts," which pronounced death sentences on those Byelorussian collaborators who prior to September 1939 had been Polish citizens. These sentences were then carried out by the special flying troops of the Polish Home Army. Among those executed by these troops was the Minsk chief of police Yuljan Sakovič, who was killed on 11 June 1943 on his way to Ščučin in Western Byelorussia.[280]

As presented in this chapter, almost three years of Nazi occupation in Byelorussia had disastrous social implications. It would not be an exaggeration to state that the occupation reopened a Pandora's box of deep-seated conflicts and animosities. Gerald Reitlinger paints an accurate picture when he describes German rule in Byelorussia as the "law of the jungle." Like every other totalitarian regime, the Nazis suspected that the enemy was lurking behind every tree. In the occupied Eastern territories, the term "enemy" was a very loose concept: Jews, Poles, former members of the Communist Party, intelligentsia, straggling Soviet soldiers—ultimately, almost everybody—was looked upon with mistrust. From the very outset, the Germans came to Byelorussia resolute in their reliance on stereotypes and dogmas rather than on observation of the given local reality and, at the same time, prepared to quell any real or imaginary resistance with brutal force. When their approach led to the ever-growing partisan movement, the occupation authorities reacted in a characteristic manner, namely, using the method known as "the carrot and the stick." In their effort to ruthlessly eliminate all those who were merely suspected of supporting the partisans, including women and children, the Nazis also created a whole host of local military or paramilitary units and projects, such as the *Wehrdörfer*. The sole purpose of such projects was to serve as cannon-fodder in the anti-partisan warfare, to spare "precious" Aryan blood, and to assist the German authorities in controlling and exploiting the occupied country effectively. Of course, the occupation authorities refrained from making any clear promises to those serving in these units. At the same time, they were purposefully slow in supplying these units with the necessary equipment, hoping to get maximum cooperation for a minimum price.

It is not easy to compile a complete list of the motives prompting all those who joined the local units in fighting against the partisans, and those who participated in the persecution of those dubbed "undesirable" by the Germans. Their hatred towards the Soviet rule did not necessarily play a major role. In the case of Soviet POWs, the main motive was probably a prosaic desire to escape the appalling conditions of the POW camps. Many others, as in the situation described regarding the persecution of Jews, were simply ready to fight any enemy indicated by the rulers. As Jan Tomas Gross pointed out recently, "People subject to Stalin's or Hitler's rule were repeatedly set against each other and encouraged to act on the basest instincts of mutual dislike."[281] There were people, such as the guards of the Koldychevo camp, who became intoxicated with their power over the life and death of others and who were given the opportunity to give vent to their sadistic inclinations. The Germans were eager to inflame all the traditional conflicts, both social and national ones. In the case of Byelorussian–Polish relations, this led to a full-fledged war, characterized by mutual incrimination and physical assaults.

Notes

* This part of the chapter appeared in a somewhat altered and abridged version in *Holocaust and Genocide Studies* 20, no 3 (Winter 2006): 381–409.

1. The story, based on the unpublished memoirs of Dr. Ehrenfried Schütte, is quoted by Bernhard Chiari. See Chiari, *Alltag hinter der Front*, 2.
2. D. Goldhagen, *Hitler's Willing Executioners* (New York, 1996), 6.
3. See J. T. Gross, *Neighbors* (Princeton, 2001).
4. Gerd Robel, "Sowjetunion," in *Dimension des Völkermords*, ed. Wolfgang Benz (Munich, 1991), 526.
5. Vakar, *Belorussia*, 187.
6. Loftus, *Belarus Secret*, 29.
7. See Dean, *Collaboration in the Holocaust*.
8. Unfortunately, it is very difficult to establish the exact number of Byelorussian Jews that perished in the Holocaust. An additional difficulty lies in the fact that until recently many researchers treated Eastern and

Western Byelorussia separately. According to Israeli historian Leonid Smilovitsky, between 245,000 and one million Jews fell victim to the Nazi genocide in Byelorussia (see L. Smilovitsky, "Die Partizipation der Juden am Leben der Belorussischen Sozialistsichen Sowjetrepublik (BSSR) im ersten Nachkriegsjahrzehnt, 1944–1954," in *Existiert das Ghetto noch?*". *Weißrussland: Jüdisches Überleben gegen nationalsozialistische Herrschaft*, ed. Anne Klein et al. (Berlin, 2003), 277. According to *Enzyklopädie des Holocaust*, published in 1993, 1,075,000 Jews lived in both parts of Byelorussia on the eve of the German-Soviet war, while the first postwar census registered only 150,000. (Here, however, the Jews who left Byelorussia for various reasons, as well as those who returned from Soviet evacuation, must be taken into account. See "Belorussia," in *Encyclopedia of the Holocaust*, ed. Israel Gutman et al. (New York and London, 1990), 1:169–74.) Similar numbers to those in the *Enzyklopädie des Holocaust* can be found in Bernhard Chiari's study. According to Chiari, out of 820,000 Byelorussian Jews, survivors of the war numbered between 120,000 and 150,000 (see Chiari, *Alltag hinter der Front*, 231). Adolph Eichmann, in the report prepared for the Wansee conference, estimated the number of Byelorussian Jews (not including *Bezirk Bialystok*) in 1942, that is, after the first wave of extermination, to be 446,484. See "Minutes of the Wansee Conference," http://www.prorev.com/wannsee.htm.

9. The *Gaswagens* appeared in Byelorussia in the fall of 1941. On the development of the gas vans, see M. Beer, "Die Enwicklung der Gaswagen beim Mord an den Juden," *Vierteljahrshefte für Zeitgeschichte* 35 (1987): 403–17.

10. Hilberg, *The Destruction of the European Jews*, 1:53.

11. See Zvi Gitelman, "Soviet Jewry before the Holocaust," in *Bitter Legacy*, ed. Zvi Gitelman (Bloomington and Indianapolis, 1997), 1–13, esp. 7–11. Terry Martin gives an additional reason for the sharp condemnation of anti-Semitism on the part of Bolsheviks: "the large numbers of Jews in the Soviet government made anti-Semitism proxy for anti-Bolshevism" (Terry Martin, *The Affirmative Action Empire. Nations and Nationalism in the Soviet Union, 1923–1939* [Ithaca and London, 2001], 43). The People's Commissars' Council's Decree, dated 27 July 1918 and signed by Lenin himself, defined the anti-Semitic movement and pogroms as "a blow to the cause of the workers-and-peasants' revolution." See Solomon Schwartz, *Antisemitism v Sovetskom Soyuze* (New York, 1952), 70–71. A brief description of anti-Semitism in the Soviet Union before World War II and the official attitude toward it can be found in the author's article, published in *Holocaust and Genocide Studies* (see note * above).

12. "Fernschreiben Heydrichs an die Einsatzgruppenchefs vom 29.6.41," in Klein, *Einsatzgruppen in der besetzten Sowjetunion*, 319.

13. The problem of the personnel shortage was not limited to occupied Byelorussia. The same situation reigned, for example, in Galicia (Western Ukraine) and in the General Government, as stressed by German researcher Dieter Pohl. See Dieter Pohl, "The Murder of Jews in the General Government," in *National Socialist Extermination Policies*, ed. Ulrich. Herbert (New York and Oxford, 2000), 91.

14. See Gerlach, *Kalkulierte Morde*, 215.

15. Arad and Spector, *Einsatzgruppen Reports*, vi; Christian Gerlach, "Die Einsatzgruppe B 1941/1942," in Klein, *Einsatzgruppen in der besetzten Sowjetunion*, 52.

16. Gerlach, *Kalkulierte Morde*, 518.

17. Andrzej Zbikowski, "Local Anti-Jewish Pogroms in the Occupied Territo-
    ries of Eastern Poland, June-July 1941," in *The Holocaust in the Soviet
    Union,* ed. Lucjan Dobroszycki and Jeffrey S. Gurok (New York and Lon-
    don, 1993), 177; Cholawski, *The Jews of Bielorussia,* 81–82. The Hrodna
    pogrom is mentioned both in the testimonies of Jewish survivors and in the
    Nazi documents. See, for example, "Testimony of Yehudit Gliksmann"
    [Hebrew], YVA O 33/314; "Testimony of Leib Reizer," YVA O.33/296;
    "Operational Situation Report USSR No. 13, 5.7.41," in Arad and Spector,
    Einsatzgruppen Reports, 9. For more on the pogrom in Ivje, see M.
    Kaganovich, *"How It Has Been Destroyed"* [Hebrew], in *Memorial Book of
    the Ivie Country* [Hebrew], ed. M. Kaganovich (Tel Aviv, 1968), 499. It must
    be also remembered that according to the state on 22 June 1941 Jedwabne,
    too, was administratively part of Western Byelorussia.

18. As shown by German historian Dieter Pohl, who has treated the theme of
    anti-Jewish violence in Western Ukraine, there is little reason to associate
    these pogroms with the role the Jews played during the Soviet period. Pohl
    points out that first, pogroms were carried out in places where no NKVD
    mass shootings took place at all. Second, no perpetrators of those "NKVD
    crimes" were caught during the pogroms. Third, the victims of anti-Jewish
    violence during the first days of the war were not limited to those Jews who
    in the past had occupied State positions. Pohl, *Nationalsozialistische
    Judenverfolgung,* 55–56.

19. The reports draw a distinction between the population's attitude toward
    the invaders in Western Byelorussia, which was annexed to the Soviet
    Union only in 1939, and the attitude of the population in the old Soviet
    areas. See "Tätigkeits- und Lagebericht (TLB-L. R.) Nr. 1 der Einsatz-
    gruppen der Sicherheitspolizei und des SD in der UdSSR, 31.7.41," in
    Klein, *Einsatzgruppen in der besetzten Sowjetunion,* 125; "TLB Nr. 2
    (29.7.–14.8.41)," ibid., 136–37, 146; indirectly also: "Operational Situation
    Report No. 1, 2.7.41," in Arad and Spector, *Einsatzgruppen Reports,* 2.

20. "TLB Nr. 4, 1.9–15.9.41," in Klein, *Einsatzgruppen in der besetzten Sowje-
    tunion,* 183.

21. See "Operational Situation Report USSR No. 43, 5.8.41," Arad and Spector,
    Einsatzgruppen Reports, 68.

22. The extreme example, perhaps, of such views is the book by Wiktor
    Ostrowski, *Anti-Semitism in Byelorussia and its Origin* (London, 1960). In
    the last, very brief chapter, Ostrowski maintains that "Naturally, the local
    population took no part in these actions, on the contrary ... the Byeloruss-
    ian and Ukrainian local population met with the same fate as the Jews,
    though on a smaller scale" (65). Wiktor Ostrowski was the son of Radaslaŭ
    Astroŭski, the "President" of the Byelorussian Central Council created
    under the Nazi auspices at the closing stages of the Nazi occupation of
    Byelorussia.

23. Thus, according to Christian Gerlach (*Kalkulierte Morde,* 526–28, 623), eco-
    nomic considerations significantly influenced the whole extermination
    process, beginning with ghettoization, which Gerlach claims was intended
    to solve numerous problems, such as housing, food, and employment, and
    ending with the mass murders. This leads him to the conclusion that the
    initiative to apply anti-Jewish measures often came from the lower eche-
    lons, i.e., from the local authorities. As an example, Gerlach quotes
    Slonim's *Gebietskommissar* Gerhard Erren, who saw the big *Aktion* that

took place in Slonim in November 1941 as a way to get rid of "unnecessary eaters" (*unnützen Fressern*). Gerlach even comments on this statement, "The words about 'unnecessary eaters' was not merely a provocative remark; rather, this aspect was genuine ground for setting the murder at this time." Here, however, Gerlach confuses cause and pretext. It seems ahistorical to prefer one aspect, namely the economic factor, over another, the ideological factor. Moreover, as was shown earlier, many aspects of the Nazis' anti-Jewish policies did not serve economic interests but stood in blatant contradiction to them. For example, eliminating Jewish workers and replacing them with substantially less skilled non-Jewish workers was not economically justified. Another often cited example is that of the German trains, which were desperately needed at the front but were used instead until the very end for the transportation of Jews to extermination camps.

24. *Encyclopedia of the Holocaust*, 1: 171.
25. According to the data cited by Shalom Cholawski in Bobrujsk, 25%–30% of 30,000 city Jews managed to get evacuated. According to the same source, 80,000 people left the city of Gomel, many of them Jews. See Cholawski, *Be-Sufat Ha-Killayon*, 48. See also "TLB Nr.2, 29.7.–14.8.41," in Klein, *Einsatzgruppen in der besetzten Sowjetunion*, 136.
26. See "The testimony of David Vorobel" (in Yiddish), YVA O 33/174. Vorobel mentioned SS-men as being the perpetrators; however, Gerlach, quoting various sources, mentions the 1st company of 309th police battalion subordinated to the 221st Wehrmacht security division, which organized the burning of the synagogue. See Gerlach, *Kalkulierte Morde*, 542.
27. "Testimony of Ekaterina Matveeva (Rečica, Gomel oblast) before the Extraordinary State Commission for Investigation of Nazi Crimes (CHGK), 30.12.44," YVA M 41/265 (Gomel State Archive, 1345-1-4).
28. "Befehl Nr. 24 des Kommandants in Weißruthenien und Wehrmachtbefehlshabers Ostland von Bechtolsheim, 24.11.41," YVA M 41/104.
29. "Operational Situation Report USSR No.73," in Arad and Spector, *Einsatzgruppen Reports*, 124.
30. "Heydrichs nachträgliche schriftliche Einweisung der vier Höheren SS- und Polizeiführer im Osten vom 2.7.71," in Klein, *Einsatzgruppen in der besetzten Sowjetunion*, 323–28. Christoph Dieckmann, "The War and the Killing of Lithuanian Jews," in Ulrich Herbert (ed.), *National Socialist Extermination Policies* (New York and Oxford, 2000), 241. Gerlach, *Kalkulierte Morde*, 552–53. Thus, according to Dieckmann, "The approximately 10,000–12,000 (predominantly Jewish) victims of the first wave of killings in German-occupied Lithuania were in the first place Jewish men and communists. Jewish women and children were as a rule excluded from these shootings."
31. See Peter Longerich, *Politik der Vernichtung* (Munich and Zurich, 1998), 336f.; idem, *Der ungeschriebene Befehl* (Munich and Zurich, 2001), 98ff.
32. The date of the order is not clear. According to Gerlach, it was transferred to the SS Cavalry Brigade on 1 August, after the meeting between Himmler and Supreme Commander of SS and Police (HSSPF) for Central Russia Bach-Zelewski on 31 July. Yehoshua Büchler provides 30 July as the date of the Himmler–Bach-Zelewski meeting. See Gerlach, *Kalkulierte Morde*, 560; Yehoshua Büchler, "*Kommandostab Reichsführer-SS*: Himmler's Personal Murder Brigades in 1941," *Holocaust and Genocide Studies* 1:1 (1986), 15.
33. Büchler, "*Kommandostab Reichsführer-SS*," 15–16.

34. See Martin Cüppers, *Wegbereiter der Shoah* (Darmstadt, 2005), 142–214.

35. Ibid., 606; Cholawski, *Be Sufat ha-Killayon*, 178.

36. Gerlach, *Kalkulierte Morde*, 609.

37. Ibid.

38. Paul Kohl, "Trostenez – das Vernichtungslager bei Minsk," in *'Existiert das Ghetto noch?'* ed. Projektgruppe Belarus, 234–39.

39. Ibid., 225; Heinz Rosenberg, "Im Minsker Ghetto," ibid., 172. Jürgen Matthäus provides different figures: according to him, 30 out of 22,000 deported Jews survived the war. See Jürgen Matthäus, "'Reibungslos und planmäßig,'" *Jahrbuch für Antisemitismusforschung* 4 (1995), 260.

40. Document 3428-PS "Report by Kube, Commissioner General for White Ruthenia to Lohse, Reich Commissioner for the Eastern Territories [*Ostland*—L. R.], 31 July 1942," IMT, 279–82.

41. Daniel Romanovsky, "Das Minsker Ghetto," transl. A. Klein, in *'Existiert das Ghetto noch?'* ed. Anne Klein, 215.

42. Ibid., 217.

43. For Germans, it was unthinkable to ascribe to the Jews any active role in the resistance movement. See Matthäus, "'Reibungslos und planmäßig'," 266ff.

44. Leonid Smilovitsky, *Katastrofa Evreev v Belorussii 1941–1944* (Tel Aviv, 2000), 133–34; Yehuda Bauer, "Jewish Baranowicze in the Holocaust," Shoah Resource Center, The International School for Holocaust Studies, Yad Vashem, Israel, http://www.yadvashem.org.il/odot_pdf/Microsoft%20 Word%20-%207082.pdf.

45. See, for example: Cholawski, *Be-Sufat Ha-Killayon*, 107-109; Albert Lapidus, "Nas malo ostalos', nam mnogo dostalos," in *Vestnik Online* 2 (313), 22 January 2003, http://www.vestnik.com/issues/2003/0122/ koi/lapidus.htm. This publication was courteously sent to me by Dr. L. Smilovitsky.

46. Klein (ed.), *'Existiert das Ghetto noch?'*, 13–14.

47. Romanovsky, "Soviet Jews under Nazi Occupation in Northeastern Belarus and Eastern Russia," in Gitelman, *Bitter Legacy*, 242.

48. Quoted in Dean, *Collaboration in the Holocaust*, 52.

49. "TLB Nr.1, 31.7.41," Klein, *Einsatzgruppen in der besetzten Sowjetunion*, 116.

50. E. Baranovski, *"Vos ikh hob ibergelebt,"* in *Smorgon*, ed. E. Karpel et al. (Tel Aviv, 1965), 426.

51. Smilovitsky, *Katastrofa Evreev v Belorussii*, 83.

52. Lapidus, "Nas Malo ostalos'," see note 45.

53. Romanovsky, "Soviet Jews," 240.

54. See Ilya Altman, *Zhertvy Nenavisti* (Moscow, 2002), 217.

55. Romanovsky, "Soviet Jews," 240.

56. Loftus, *Belarus Secret*, 23n; "The Testimony of Isrol Lukhter," YVA, O 3/4692.

57. On the connection between the euphoria reigning in top Nazi echelons in the summer 1941 and the escalation of the extermination policies, see Christopher Browning, *The Origins of the Final Solution. The Evolution of Nazi Jewish Policy, September 1939-March 1942* (Jerusalem, 2004), 309–30.

58. This much quoted "prophecy" was made during Hitler's speech before the Reichstag on 30 January 1939, which is printed in abridged form in Wolfgang Michalka (ed.), *Deutsche Geschichte 1933–1945* (Frankfurt/Main,

1993), 163. It is interesting to note that this "prophecy" is quoted in letters of the soldiers who participated in the massacres. Thus, Walter Mattner, who participated in mass executions of Jews in Mogiljov, in letters to his wife describing the brutal killing of Mogiljov Jews—including little babies—stated explicitly, "The words of Hitler—who said once on the eve of the war, 'When Jewry believes that it can once again enflame war in Europe, then Jewry will not win, but it will be the end of Jewry in Europe'—will come true" (quoted in Gerlach, *Kalkulierte Morde*, 588–89). Could this prophecy have served as a kind of "indulgence" for the murder of innocent people?

59. "CBS: Trial by Insinuations," *Belarus*, May 1982; see also "File of Jan Awdziej," both in the Archives of Simon Weisenthal Center (SWCA), Jerusalem.

60. "Operational Situation Report USSR No. 31, 23.7.41," in Arad and Spector, *The Einsatzgruppen Reports*, 43; "TLB Nr. 1, 31.7.41," Klein (ed.), *Die Einsatzgruppen in der besetzten Soujetunion 1941/1942*, 127.

61. Minsk: "Testimony of Hanna Rubinchik, 22.2.44," "Order regarding creation of the Jewish ghetto in Minsk," both in YVA M 41/112, 3; Borisov: Loftus, *Belarus Secret*, 25–26; Stoŭbcy: "The File of Jan Awdziej," SWCA.

62. Dan Zhits, *Ghetto Minsk vetoledotav le'or hate'ud hehadash* [The History of the Minsk Ghetto (In the Light of the New Documentation)], (Ramat Gan, 2000), 18. I am grateful to Prof. Dan Michman for providing me with this study.

63. "File of Jan Awdziej," SWCA.

64. "Testimony of Hanna Rubinchik," see note 62.

65. "Order No. 51, 25.9.41," YVA M 41/274 (Original: State Archive, Mogiljov 260-1-15), 4–5.

66. "Testimony of Hanna Rubinchik," see note 61.

67. "Stanislav Stankevič: general information," "List of the Nazi collaborators, who after the war found refuge in United States," both in SWCA; "Letter of the chief of the Novo-Borisov police Mironchik to the administration of Borisov police, 6.09.41," YVA M 41/2396 (Original: State Archives of the Minsk Oblast, GAMO, 635-1-31), l. 22; Loftus, *Belarus Secret*, 25–28. See also: "The materials of interrogation of David Egof by the KGB," YVA M 41/119 (Original: KGB archives). According to Egof's personal testimony submitted before the Soviet interrogators after the war, he participated personally in killings.

68. See Martin Dean, "Jewish Property Seized in the Occupied Soviet Union in 1941 and 1942: The Records of the *Reichshauptkasse Baustelle*," *Holocaust and Genocide Studies* 14, no. 1 (Spring 2000): 99 n. 54.

69. See the entry on Stankevič in Solov'ev, *Belarusskaja Tsentral'naja Rada*, 172. Before 1939, Stankevič, living in Polish territory, was active in the Byelorussian national movement. See "The materials of interrogation of David Egof," see above, note 67.

70. Quoted in Matthäus, "'Reibungslos und planmäßig,'" 261.

71. Ibid.

72. See, for example, "Report of the chief of the local police of the city Novo-Borisov Bakhanovich to the administrative department of the rayon administration regarding the arrests by the order police (OD) of Novo-Borisov, 27.8.41," YVA M 41/2396, 6–7.

73. "Order of the Commander of the OD of the city Borisov Kovalevskij to the commander of the Novo-Borisov OD, 26.08.41," ibid., 8–9.

74. "Smert' Uchitel'nicy-Geroini," in Yitzhak Arad (ed.), *Neizvestnaja Chornaja Kniga*, (Jerusalem and Moscow, 1993), 272f.

75. This was the case, for example, in Borisov. See "Testimony of David Egof, former chief of Borisov district police (OD) before the Soviet investigators, undated," as in note 67.

76. Rufeisen was later converted to Christianity and died recently as Brother Daniel at the Carmelite monastery in Haifa, Israel.

77. Christopher Browning, *Ordinary Men* (New York, 1992), 2.

78. Matthäus, "'Reibungslos und planmäßig,'" 263–64.

79. According to the testimony of Boris Grushevskij, an eyewitness of the massacre of the Jews in the locality of Mir, the local policemen "behaved" during the massacre "as if they were celebrating a wedding." Quoted in Martin Dean, "Polen in der einheimischen Hilfspolizei," in Chiari (ed.), *Die polnische Heimatarmee*, 358.

80. See Chiari, *Alltag hinter der Front*, 184.

81. Nechama Tec, *In the Lion's Den* (New York and Oxford, 1990), 102.

82. "Order of the Commander of the OD in the city Borisov Kovalevskij to the commander of Novo-Borisov OD Bakhanovich, 26.8.41," YVA M 41/2396, 8–9.

83. Dean, *Collaboration in the Holocaust*, 76.

84. Quoted ibid., 76–77.

85. Cholawski, *Be-Sufat Ha-Killayon*, 110.

86. Smilovitsky, *Katastrofa Evreev v Belorussii*, 83.

87. See "Geheimer Bericht des Heinrich Carl, Gebietskommissar in Slutzk, an Wilhelm Kube, Generalkommissar für Weißruthenien, vom 30. Oktober 1941 über eine Vernichtungsaktion der Sicherheitspolizei und litauischer Kollaborateure gegen die jüdische Bevölkerung der Stadt Sluzk," in Kaden et al., *Dokumente des Verbrechens*, vol. 3, 57–61.

88. "Abschrift eines Funktelegramms des RSHA, Amt IV (Müller), an die Einsatzgruppen vom 30. August 1941," in W. Benz et al. (eds.), *Einsatz im "Reichskommissariat Ostland"* (Berlin, 1998), 69.

89. Wila Orbach, "The Destruction of the Jews in the Nazi-Occupied Territories of the USSR," *Soviet Jewish Affairs* 6, no. 2 (1976): 34–51; Marat Botvinnik, *Pamjatniki Genotsida Evreev Belarusi* (Minsk, 2000), 25–27, 60–82, 117–34, 166–86, 213–28, 254–69, 294–306; Smilovitsky, *Katastrofa Evreev v Belorussii*, 366–76; Emanuil Yoffe, *Belorusskije Evrei* (Minsk, 2003), 373–96.

90. See, for example, Daniel Romanovsky, "Kholokost v Vostochnoj Belorussii i Severo-Zapadnoj Rossii Glazami Neevreev," in *Vestnik Evrejskogo Universiteta* 2, no. 9 (1995): 68.

91. "Testimony of H. Vajner, the survivor of the Krinek ghetto" (in Yiddish), YVA 0.33/287.

92. "Testimony of Lev Lanskij, the former inmate of Trostenec concentration camp, undated," YVA M 41/100.

93. Dean, *Collaboration in the Holocaust*, 52.

94. Quoted in Gerlach, *Kalkulierte Morde*, 1059.

95. While there is no lack of vivid pictures of looting orgies following the *Aktionen* (see, for example, Smilovitsky, *Katastrofa Evreev v Belorussii*, 97–98), the whole scope of the phenomenon of misappropriation of Jewish property by the local population and local collaborationist bodies has not been sufficiently analyzed. For instance, Yitzhak Arad's article "Plunder of Jewish Property in the Nazi-Occupied Areas of the Soviet Union" (*Yad Vashem*

Studies 29 (2001): 109–48) concentrates mainly on the role of the German occupying bodies in the misappropriation of Jewish property, treating rather fragmentarily the role of local administrative bodies in this process. The same applies to Christian Gerlach's study *Kalkulierte Morde* (675–83). Gerlach treats the question of Jewish property in Byelorussia in the general context of German economic policy there. Gerlach tends to see the confiscation of Jewish property, particularly apartments, and their subsequent release to the local non-Jewish inhabitants as one of the ways in which economic problems were solved. In reality, as we will demonstrate, the needs of the homeless were by no means the top priority of the bodies responsible for registration and allocation of homes and apartments.

96. "TLB Nr. 11, 1.3.-31.3.42," in Klein, *Einsatzgruppen in der besetzten Sowjetunion*, 308.

97. Smilovitsky, *Katastrofa Evreev v Belorussii*, 95.

98. "Abschrift von Aktenvermerk des Stadtinspektors Loebel und Reichsangestellten Plenske, 16.11.42," YVA M 41/291 (Original: State Archive of Byelorussia, 370-1-486(21)).

99. "Schreiben Gemeindevorstehers von Samochwalowitschi Wasilev an die Minsker Rayonverwaltung, 1941," "Vasil'ev's report to the *Gebietskommissar* Kaiser, undated" (Russian), YVA M 41/290 (Original: State Archives of Byelorussia, 393-3-16), 9, 11.

100. Romanovsky, "Soviet Jews under Nazi occupation," 249.

101. "Testimony of Konstantin Mozolevsky 12–13.1.46," YVA M 41/2838 (KGB Archives), 1–5.

102. "Abschrift von Aktenvermerk des Stadtinspektors Loebel und Reichsangestellten Plenske, 16.11.42," YVA M 41/291 (State Archives of Byelorussia, 370-1-486(21)).

103. Chiari, *Alltag hinter der Front*, 183–84.

104. See "Testimony of Hanna Rubinchik," see note 61.

105. "Schnellbrief der Chefgruppe Wirtschaftspolitische Kooperation bei Reichsministerium f.d. bes. Ostgebiete betreffend Textilversorgung in den besetzten Ostgebieten tätigen deutschen, ausländischen und einheimischen Arbeitskräften, 13.4.42," YVA M 41/289 (Original: State Archives of Byelorussia, 370-1-634), 24–26.

106. "Instruction of city commandant's office in Bobrujsk to the city's and rayon's *Bürgermeistern* regarding Jewish property, 19.12.41," YVA M 41/273 (Original: State Archives, Mogilev 858-1-19), 1.

107. As can be noted, the total income of the Mogiljov's "city management" decreased between 1 May and 1 June 1942, while the income from the sales of the Jewish property increased in the same period. See "Report of the Mogiljov city financial department for May 1942 and for June 1942," YVA M 41/272 (Original: State Archives, Mogiljov, 260-1-45, 59), 1–2.

108. See, for example, "Directive of mayor of Mogiljov Felicyn to the commission for the sale of Jewish houses and the houses of the fled communists, 1941," YVA M 41/268 (Original: State Archives, Mogilev, 259-1-1), 1.

109. "Letter of the head of Novo-Borisov OD Bakhanovich to the *Rayonbürgermeister* in Borisov, undated," YVA M 41/2396 (GAMO, 635-1-31), 12–13.

110. "Report of the Bakhanovich to Stankevich, 28.08.41," ibid., 11.

111. "Stankevich's letter to the head of Borisov OD Kovalevskij and to the head of Novo-Borisov OD Bakhanovich, 7.7.42," M 41/2395 (Original: GAMO, 635-1-4), 2.

112. See "Abschrift des Schreibens Vertriebsabteilungs Minsk der Ostland Öl Vertriebsgesellschaft m.b.H., 11.12.42," YVA M 41/289 (GARB, State Archives of Republic of Belarus, 370-1-634), 3–4.

113. Ibid., 3.

114. "The testimony of Vladimir Kovachenok, 26.2.44," YVA M 41/2836 (Original: KGB archives).

115. Astroŭski, *Druhi Usebelaruski Kangres*, 23.

116. Chiari, *Alltag hinter der Front*, 259.

117. Ibid., 119–20.

118. Ibid., 262–63.

119. Chiari, *Alltag hinter der Front*, 5–6.

120. See, for example, Paul Kohl, *Der Krieg der deutschen Wehrmacht und der Polizei 1941–1944* (Gütersloh, 1990), 124.

121. The Ukrainians were members of the Ukrainian auxiliary police.

122. "Tagesmeldung der Kdtr. des Sich.-Gebietes Weißruthenien (Oberfeldkommandantur 392), 24.3.43," BA R 6/350, Mikrofiche 2.

123. "Schreiben an den SS- und Polizei-Gebietsführer von Borisov über die Vernichtung des Dorfes Chatyn," printed in Kohl, *Der Krieg der deutschen Wehrmacht*, 263.

124. Ibid., 124.

125. See the Reitlinger quotation above, Preface, note 3.

126. See "TLB Nr.1 (31.7.41)," in Klein, *Einsatzgruppen in der besetzten Sowjetunion*, 117–118; "TLB Nr. 2 (29.7.–14.8.41)," in ibid., 137; "TLB Nr. 3 (15.8.–31.8.41)," in ibid., 158; "Operational Situation Report USSR No. 21, 31.7.41," in Arad and Spector, *Einsatzgruppen Reports*, 24. To justify somehow the massacre of innocent people, in the first place of Jews, the units of all the *Einsatzgruppen* characterized the latter as "saboteurs," "looters," "shooters from behind," etc. For example, the activities of the 2nd SS Cavalry Brigade in the Polesje region during August 1941, whose main victims were Jewish men, women, and children including little babies, were officially characterized as "anti-partisan actions." See Gerlach, *Kalkulierte Morde*, 555f.

127. See Stalin, *The Great Patriotic War of the Soviet Union*, 15.

128. See Litvin, "Kak eto bylo," in *Akupacyja Belarusi (1941–1944)*, 24–25.

129. Among the punished were the first, second, and third secretaries of Lepel' (Vitebsk oblast) rayon' party committee (the latter was even excluded from the party and arrested by NKVD), the secretary of Bobrujsk city party committee, and the secretary of Minsk oblast' party committee. Litvin, "Kak eto bylo," 29–30.

130. See "Questioning of the Commander of the diversion group 2 Nikolaj Grek, 31.10.42," YVA, M 41/62 (Party Archives of the Institute of the Party History by Central Committee of CPB (in the following-PA), 3500-4-20), 3.

131. "From the report about the activity of the Chkalov detachment of the Sverdlov brigade, undated," YVA M41/91 (PA 3500-4-314c).

132. "TLB Nr.6, 1.10–31.10.41," "TLB Nr.7, 1.11–30.11.41," "TLB Nr. 9, 1.1.–31.1.42," "TLB Nr. 10, 1.2–28.2.42," in Klein, *Einsatzgruppen in der besetzten Sowjetunion*, 228, 251, 277, 289; Vakar, *Belorussia*, 195; Matthew Cooper, *The Nazi War against Soviet Partisans 1941–1944* (New York, 1979), 16.

133. According to Turonak, in Byelorussia there were the Soviet partisans as well as the Polish clandestine movement. See Turonak, *Belarus' pad nyameckaj Akupacyjaj*, 5–6.

134. Vakar, *Belorussia*.
135. See A. Dziarnoviä (ed.), *Antysaveckija Rukhi ? Belarusi 1944–1956* (Minsk, 1999), 120.
136. See Litvin, "Rol' Voennykh Sovetov, Shtabov i Politorganov Frontov i Armij v Koordinacii sovmestnykh Dejstvij s partizanskimi Otrjadami Belarusi," in *Akupacyja Belarusi*, 39–41.
137. "From the report of Vojtenkov to the Central Committee of KPB regarding the situation in the 1st Byelorussian partisan brigade, July 1942," YVA M 41/61 (PA 3500-4-11).
138. "Aktenvermerk vom 16. Juli 1941 über eine Besprechung Hitlers mit Rosenberg, Lammers, Keitel und Göring," Document 221-L, IMT, vol. 38, 88.
139. Quoted in French MacLean, *The Cruel Hunters* (Atglen, PA, 1998), 69. In the postwar period Heusinger was Inspector General of the Bundeswehr and NATO's representative in Washington. In 1961, the Soviets demanded Heusinger's extradition, accusing him of military crimes committed during World War II.
140. On the Prussian/German *franc-tireurs* complex, see Ben Shepherd, *War in the Wild East* (Cambridge, MA, and London, 2004), 41–44.
141. B. Tuchman, *August 1914* (London, 1994), 310.
142. Quoted in Shepherd, *War in the Wild East*, 42.
143. Ibid., 43.
144. In his diary entry for 20 August 1914, for example, Lieutenant Hermann Stegmaier of 124th Landwehr Infantry Regiment mentioned the burning of two French localities, Nomeny and Port sur Seille, and the execution of their inhabitants, "since they have shot on our troops from the houses" (Nachlaß Stegmaier, Archival Collection of Library for Modern History (Bibliothek für Zeitgeschichte, Stuttgart, Germany), N18, vol. 1). This is only one of many such statements I encountered during my post-doctoral research in Germany, both in the archives of the Library for Modern History as well as in the Main State Archives (Hauptstaatsarchiv) of Stuttgart.
145. Shepherd, *War in the Wild East*, 43.
146. Actually, as was shown above, already during the quelling of the Herero uprising this mixture of a *franc-tireurs* complex and racism produced horrendous results.
147. The most infamous of these orders are the so-called "Barbarossa order" and "Order regarding the Commissars" (*Kommissarbefehl*). See "Erlaß Hitlers [actually it was signed by Keitel—L. R., see below] über die Ausübung der Kriegsgerichtsbarkeit im Gebiet 'Barbarossa' und über besondere Maßnahmen der Truppe vom 13. Mai 1941," "OKW-Richtlinienzur Ermordung politischer Kommissare und Funktionäre der Roten Armee vom 6. Juni 1941," both in Kaden, *Dokumente des Verbrechens*, 1:134–39.
148. Quoted in Ch. Streit, *Keine Kameraden* (Bonn, 1997), 35.
149. "Erlaß Hilers über die Ausübung der Kriegsgerichtsbarkeit," in Kaden, *Dokumente des Verbrechens*, 1:134–37.
150. Quoted in Streit, *Keine Kameraden*, 39. See also "Law Reports of Trials of War Criminals selected and prepared by The United Nations War Crimes Commission, Volume XII", http://www.loc.gov/rr/frd/Military_Law/pdf/Law-Reports_Vol-12.pdf.
151. See, for example, the report by the head of the propaganda department in GKW, Schröter, quoted in the previous chapter (note 2).

152. "Obersturmführer Strauch über 'Die Aufgaben des Sicherheitsdienstes'-Protokoll über die Tagung," BA R 93/20, 141.

153. See note 149.

154. See, for example, "Schreiben Oberleutnant Hartenecks (AOK 2) 'Ausnutzung des russischen und ukrainischen menschen der besetzten Gebieten für die Kriegsführung,' 11.5.43," BA-MA RH 20-2/636.

155. "Schreiben der Abteilung Kriegsverwaltung bei Generalquartiermeister (OKH) 'Vorschläge für die Zersetzung der sowjetischen Widerstandskraft,' 8.1.42," BA R 90/257.

156. "Befehl des Kdt. r. A. [Geb.] 559 Generalleutnant von Unruh, 10.10.41," BA-MA RH 23/126.

157. Ibid.

158. "Divisionsbefehl Nr. 29 für 8. Infanterie-Division, 27.10.41," ibid.

159. See "Einsatzbefehl Nr. 12 des Chefs der Sicherheitspolizei und des SD vom 18.9.41," in Klein, *Einsatzgruppen in der besetzten Sowjetunion*, 352.

160. Schlootz, *Deutsche Propaganda in Weißrussland*, 37.

161. "Von Unruhs Schreiben an AOK 4 betreffend Propaganda, 2.11.41," BA-MA RH 23/126.

162. "Korpsbefehl Nr. 40, 16.08.41," BA-MA R 22/224.

163. Ibid.

164. "Abschließender Bericht der 137. Inf. Division über die Befriedung des Raumes Juchnow-Wjasma-Dorogobusch-Jelnja-Kirow in der Zeit vom 12. bis 25.10.41, 25.10.41," BA-MA RH 23/126.

165. "Tagesmeldung über die Säuberungsmaßnahmen, 20.7.41," BA-MA RH 22/226, 11. See also "Tagesmeldung des Ia beim Befehlshaber des rückw. Heeres-Gebietes Mitte, 8.11.41," ibid., 122.

166. D. Romanovsky, "Soviet Jews under Nazi Occupation," 240.

167. G. Fisher, *Soviet Opposition to Stalin* (Cambridge, MA, 1952), 6.

168. Cooper, *War against Soviet Partisans*, 16.

169. See, for example, "From the report about the activity of the Chkalov detachment, Sverdlov partisan brigade, undated," YVA M 41/91 (PA 3500-1-314c).

170. "Beurteilung der Lage in Heeresgebiet Mitte, 31.5.42," BA-MA RH 22/231, 193.

171. In the same report, Schenckendorff demanded the return of the following troops, which were necessary for the effective struggle against partisans: 354th infantry regiment from the 2nd army (AOK 2, Army Group "South"); the 2nd battalion of the same regiment from the 4th army (AOK 4); the 350th infantry regiment from the 2nd armored army (Pz. AOK 2); the 406th infantry regiment and the 2nd security regiment from the 4th army (AOK 4); and the 2nd battalion of 213th artillery regiment from the 3rd armored army (Pz. AOK 3). See ibid., 270.

172. Thus, according to Schenckendorff, the main problem with the growing partisan movement was that through it "the economic exploitation of the big areas is hampered or is made impossible." Ibid., 266.

173. "Schreiben Generals der Infanterie von Schenckendorff, Befehlshaber des rückw. Heeresgebiet Mitte 'Vorschläge zur Vernichtung der Partisanen im rückw. Heeresgebiet und in den rückw. Armeegebieten', 1.3.42," BA-MA RH 22/230.

174. "Schreiben Oberstleutnant Harteneck (AOK 2) 'Ausnutzung der russischen und ukrainischen Menschen der besetzten Gebiete für die Kriegsführung', 11.5.43," BA-MA RH 20-2/636.

175. It is difficult to establish the exact date of creation of the Lokot district. According to Matthew Cooper (*Nazi War against Soviet Partisans*, 112) as well as to Jürgen Thorwald (*Die Illusion*, 77–78), it was established at the end of 1941. A report by one of the officers from the Supreme Command of the Army Group Center speaks of July 1942 as the date of Schmidt's order regarding the creation of the district. See "Bericht des Oberkreisverwaltungsrates Dr. Günzel (Oberkommando der Heeresgruppe Mitte) über den Selbsverwaltungsbezirk Lokot', 25.5.43," BA R 6/309, Mikrofiche 1. According to German researcher Rolf Michaelis (*Russen in der Waffen-SS* [Berlin, 2002], 13), Schmidt's order, issued on 19 July 1942, merely expanded the Lokot district by adding several rayons to it as well as transferring to Bronislav Kaminski the title of supreme mayor (*Oberbüregermeister*) of autonomous district Lokot.

176. See "Aktennotiz für dem Führer bezüglich Russischer Selbstverwaltungsbezirk Lokotj, 8.1.43," BA R 6/18, Mikrofiche 5; Cooper, *Nazi War against Soviet Partisans*, 112; Ready, *Forgotten Axis*, 164.

177. Michaelis supposes that Kaminski stood behind the death of Voskobojnikov. See Michaelis, *Russen in der Waffen-SS*, 9. Bronislav Kaminski was born in 1899, the son of a Polish father and a German mother, near Vitebsk. He studied in Leningrad and worked subsequently as an engineer in the color industry. In the 1920s he belonged to the anti-Stalin opposition inside the Communist Party grouped around Nikolaj Bukharin and was among those who signed Bukharin's Declaration (1929), protesting against Stalin's agrarian policy. Kaminski was arrested in 1935, accused of maintaining contacts with Polish and German intelligence, and was sent to the labor camp in the Urals area. In 1941 he was released upon his mother's petition and came to Lokot, where he worked as an engineer at the local spirits factory. During this time, Kaminski met Voskobojnikov, who dreamed of creating a National Socialist State in Russia. See Kaminski's biography by Michaelis, *Russen in der Waffen-SS*, 119–20. Gerald Reitlinger's and Jürgen Thorwald's statements that Kaminski had already headed rayon administrations in the Soviet period seem to be erroneous. Reitlinger, *House Built on Sand*, 310; Thorwald, *Die Illusion*, 77.

178. "Bericht des Oberkreisverwaltungsrates Dr. Günzel (Oberkommando der Heeresgruppe Mitte) über den Selbsverwaltungsbezirk Lokot', 25.5.43," BA R 6/309, Mikrofiche 1.

179. "Aktennotiz für dem Führer," see note 176.

180. Cooper, *Nazi War against Soviet Partisans*, 112.

181. "Aktennotiz für dem Führer ..."

182. For example, on 5 August 1944 RONA men entered the Warsaw hospital for female cancer patients and raped both the staff and the patients. The 4th East Prussian Grenadier Regiment, which had taken part in suppressing the Warsaw Uprising, complained about the conduct both of Kaminski's and of Dirlewanger's men. See Ready, *Forgotten Axis*, 352. Especially repugnant, however, for the racial ideologues was the rape of BDM-girls reported by the 9th Army. See Michaelis, *Russen in der Waffen SS*, 51–53. Michaelis maintains, however, that many atrocities were ascribed wrongly to RONA men. Ibid., 51.

183. To prevent the mutiny of RONA men, the Germans at first presented Kaminski's death as the result of a partisan ambush. Later, they did acknowledge that Kaminski was executed, but for stealing jewelry. See Ready, *Forgotten Axis*, 354–55; Reitlinger, *House Built on Sand*, 311;

MacLean, *Cruel Hunters*, 187–88; Michaelis, *Russen in der Waffen SS*, 53–54.

184. MacLean, *Cruel Hunters*, 187; Michaelis, *Russen in der Waffen SS*, 55.
185. "Ausführungsbestimmungen zur Aufstellung der beiden Kampfbataillone Dnjepr u. Beresina, 29.4.42," BA-MA RH 22/231, 146.
186. "Schreiben des Kommandierenden General der Sicherungstruppen und Befehlshabers im Heeresgebiet Mitte an Oberkommando der Heeresgruppe Mitte betreffend Erfahrungen mit landeseigenen Verbänden, 5.8.42," BA-MA RH 22/233, 68.
187. "Schreiben des Kommandierenden General der Sicherungstruppen und Befehlshabers im Heeresgebiet Mitte an Oberkommando der Heeresgruppe Mitte betreffend landeseigene Verbände, 28.9.42," ibid., 224.
188. See above, note 186.
189. See ibid.
190. Ibid.
191. According to Alexej Litvin, the following Latvian police units operated in Byelorussia at various times: the 15th Latvian division (apparently 15th Waffen-Grenadier Division SS, known also as the 1st Latvian Waffen-SS Division); 2nd and 3rd police regiments; the border guards' regiment; the 15th, 17th, 18th, 24th, 25th, 26th, 208th, 231st, 266th "E," 268th, 271st, 273rd, 276th, 277th, 278th, 279th, 280th, 281st, 282nd, 313th, 316th, 317th, 347th, 432nd, 546th, 860th auxiliary police (*Schutzmannschaft*) battalions as well as motorcycle-infantry platoons. See Litvin, "Latyshskije policejskije (Schutzmannschaft) Batal'ony v Belarusi (1941–1944)," in *Akupacyja Belarusi (1941–1944)*, 240. Quite a number of Lithuanian units were deployed in Byelorussia at different times, including the infamous 2nd police battalion commanded by Impuljavičus, whose conduct during the massacre of Sluzk Jews provoked the rage of the local *Gebietskommissar* Carl.
192. See Ready, *Forgotten Axis*, 193.
193. Litvin, "Kazach'i formirovanija na territorii Belarusi (1941–1944)," in *Akupacyja Belarusi*, 204.
194. Ibid., 211.
195. Ibid. "Schreiben des Kommandierenden Generals der Sicherungstruppen und Befehlshabers im Heeresgebiet Mitte General der Infanterie Schenckendorff betreffend Bildung des Kosaken-Rgts. 102, 25.04.42," BA-MA RH 22/231.
196. Litvin, "Kazach'i formirovanija," 212.
197. For more on the prisoners-of-war "diet," see, among others, Streit, *Keine Kameraden*, 137–62.
198. "Besondere Anordnung Nr. 64 für die Versorgung von Hilfsmannschaften, Hilfswachmannschaften, Panjekolonnen, Hilfspolizei, Kosakenhundertschaften, Reiterhundertschaften und Pioniergruppen, 1.11.41," BA-MA RH 22/225.
199. Streit, *Keine Kameraden*, 131.
200. It must be noted, inter alia, that the cases of cannibalism, which were certainly solely the result of appalling conditions reigning in the POW camps, were interpreted by the Nazis as an expression of the "subhuman" nature of *Ostvölker*. Even today, more than sixty years after the fall of Nazism, there are historians in Germany who see it in more or less the same light. See Franz W. Seidler (ed.), *Verbrechen an der Wehrmacht* (Selent, 1998), 344 f.
201. See above, note 178.

202. Since the quoted document is undated, it is difficult to establish its exact author. From March 1941 *Wirtschaftsstab Ost* was headed by three different people: Generalleutnant Wilhelm Schubert (from 25 March 1941 to 30 June 1942), General Thomas (from 1 July to 3 August 1942), and then General Otto Stapf. See Gerlach, *Kalkulierte Morde*, 145. "Schreiben des Chefs des Wirtschaftsstabes Ost an dem Reichsminister für die besetzten Ostgebiete betreffend Belohnung von russischen Partisanen-Jäger (Sonderrecht), o. D.," BA R 6/430, Mikrofiche 1.

203. "10-Tagesmeldung (Stand 31.3.42) des Kommandierenden Generals der Sicherungstruppen und Befehlshaber in Heeresgebiet Mitte, 3.4.42," "Schreiben des Kommandierenden Generals der Sicherungstruppen und Befehlshaber in Heeresgebiet Mitte an Kosaken-Schwadron 102, 21.4.42," "Erfahrungsbericht beim Einsazt der Kosaken Sonderführers (K) Kuhr, Kosaken-Regiment 102 an dem Kommandierenden General der Sicherungstruppen und Befehlshaber in Heeresgebiet Mitte," all in BA-MA RH 22/231. See Gerlach, *Kalkulierte Morde*, 899–900.

204. Quoted in Litvin, "Kazach'i formirovanija," 215.

205. "Erfahrungsbericht beim Einsazt der Kosaken," see note 203.

206. "Bericht über den Einsatz der 3. Kom Res. Pol. Batl. 51 am 14. Juli 1942," BA-MA RH 22/233.

207. Ibid.

208. "Korpsbefehl des Kommandierenden Generals der Sicherungstruppen und Befehlshaber in Heeresgebiet Mitte, 27.9.42," ibid., 218–20. See "Bericht des Kommandierenden Generals der Sicherungstruppen und Befehlshaber in Heeresgebiet Mitte an Oberkommando der Heeresgruppe Mitte, 19.9.42," "Bericht des Leitendes Feldpolizeidirektor be der Sicherungs Division 203 betreffend Meuterei der 2. Kom des Batl. Beresina und Ermordung von 3 Angehörigen der GFP Gruppe 707, 20.9.42," "Bericht des Kommandierenden Generals der Sicherungstruppen und Befehlshaber in Heeresgebiet Mitte an Oberkommando der Heeresgruppe Mitte betreffend Meuterei bei 2./Kampf-Btl. 'Beresina', 25.9.42," all in BA-MA RH 22/233, 205–206, 213–16.

209. See, for example, "Conversation with the commander of the partisan detachment, Alexander Shramko, 27.12.42," YVA M 41/2446 (NARB 4-33a-263), 2–19, es 17.

210. "Aufrufe des Partisanenabteilung Nr. 112 an die litauischen Soldaten und an Kolchosbauern, Kolchosbäuerinnen, Arbeiter und Angestellte, o. D.," BA R 90/126. See also "Appeal of Ljakhviči RK KP(b)B 'To policemen and officials of German institutions' undated," BA R 90/158.

211. "The reactions of Cossack formations in Byelorussia to the partisan propaganda," YVA M 41/144 (NARB 3500-4-267).

212. Litvin's assertion that these people "knew" about Stalingrad (see Litvin, "Kazach'i formirovanija," 216) seems somewhat arguable, if one takes into account that they found themselves in camps in Germany, far away from the events and were moreover exposed to Nazi propaganda.

213. Litvin, "Kazach'i formirovanija," 217.

214. Ibid.

215. "Schreiben des Befehlshabers des rückw. Heeresgebiet Mitte betreffend Verstärkung der Kosakenschwadron 102 und der bei den Divisionen bezw. Brigaden aufgestellten Hundertschaften, 8.2.42," BA-MA RH 22/230.

216. "Aktenvermerk vom 16. Juli 1941 über eine Besprechung Hitlers mit Rosenberg, Lammers, Keitel und Göring," Document 221-L, IMT, 38:88. Ready, *Forgotten Axis*, 193.

217. See note 197. Also Litvin, "Kazach'i formirovanija," 213. Litvin is only speaking about the 102nd regiment here.

218. "Abschlußbericht des Gebietskommissar in Nowogrodek Gille, 18.7.44," BA R 93/13, 138–48. For more on the Cossacks in the Navahrudak area, see Litvin, "Kazach'i formirovanija," 223–30.

219. "Acknowledgment of Kube and SSPF Weißruthenien Zenner, 1.7.42," YVA M 41/112, 18.

220. See Turonak, *Belarus' pad nyameckaj Akupacyjaj*, 119–20.

221. Ibid., 120.

222. See ibid., as well as "Schreiben des Befehlshabers der Sicherheitspolizei u.d. SD Ostland an Lohse betreffend Tagesmeldung der Einsatzkommandos., 29.7.42," BA R 6/354, Mikrofiche 2.

223. "Die Referate des Zentralverwaltung des WSW: Schreiben Ermatschenkos an Rosenberg, 17.1.44," BA R 6/106, Mikrofiche 2.

224. Quoted in Turonak, *Belarus' pad nyameckaj Akupacyjaj*, 121.

225. Ibid.

226. "Abschrift von politischer Lagebericht Slonim verfaßt von Ehrenleitner, 21.3.43," BA R 6/27, Mikrofiche 4.

227. Quoted in Litvin, "Belorusskaja Krajovaja Oborona," 172.

228. "Ereignismeldung des Befehlshabers der Sicherheitspolizei u.d. SD Ostland, 5.10.42," BA R 6/348, Mikrofiche 2.

229. "Mit Generalkommissar Kube unterwegs. Zwei Tage im Hauptkommissariat Baranowitsche," *Deutscher Zeitung im Ostland*, 14 July 1942, BA R 90/95.

230. "Schreiben des Gebietskommissar Slonim und Reg. Rat Dr. Ludwig Ehernleitner an Generalkommissar für Weißruthenien Kube betreffend politische Lagebericht Slonim, 21.3.43," BA R 90/126.

231. See above, note 210.

232. "Bericht des Wehrmachtsbefehlshabers Ostland betreffend Bandenlage, 27.01.43," BA R 90/31, Mikrofiche 4.

233. See "Gefechtsbericht der Gruppe Jollasse (Stab/Pz. Gren. Brig. 18) über Unternehmen 'Dreieck' und 'Viereck' vom 17.9.–2.10.42," BA-MA RH 23/25.

234. See "Abschrift der Aufzeichnung des Generalkommissars von Weißruthenien v. Gottberg über die im weißruthensichen Raum zu treffenden politischen Maßnahmen, 1.12.43," BA R 6/281, Mikrofiche 2. Although the most important role in initiating the *Wehrdörfer* project was played by economic bodies such as the agricultural department in *Wirtschabsstab Ost*, as is shown by Gerlach (*Kalkulierte Morde*, 1010), it is still difficult to see this whole project, as does Gerlach, solely from the economic point of view. We must also take into account the political developments in occupied Byelorussia, especially remembering the fact that Gottberg announced his intention to create *Wehrdörfer* simultaneously with the announcement of the intention to create the BCR.

235. "Abschrift der Niederschrift des Militärverwaltungsrat Rother über der Besichtigung des Wehrdorf-Gruppenraumes Chidra (and der Straße von Marina-Gorka nach Bobruisk) am 8. und 9. 3.44, 13.3.44," BA R 6/94. See also Gerlach, *Kalkulierte Morde*, 1042.

236. "Schreiben des Führungsstabes Politik bei Ostministerium and den persönlichen Referenten des Chefs des Führungsstabes SS Hauptsturmführer Brandenburg betreffend Einrichtung von Wehrdörfer, 23.2.44," BA R 6/93.
237. "Schreiben des HSSPF Rußland-Mitte u. Weißruthenien and der Befehlshaber der Sicherheitspolizei und des SD Weißruthenien, Kommandeur der Ordnungspolizei im Generalbezirk Weißruthenien und Gebietskommissare Minsk-Land, Wilejka, Glebokie, Lida, Nowogrodek, Baranowitsche, Slonim, Hansewitsche, Sluzk und Borisow betreffend Ausbau es Stutzpunktesnetzes in Generalbezirk Weißruthenien-Errichtungs von Schutzmannschaftsdörfern, 19.10.43," BA R 6/308, Mikrofiche 2. "Abschrift der Niederschrift," see note 233.
238. "Schreiben des HSSPF Rußland-Mitte u. Weißruthenien betreffend Ausbau des Stützpunktnetzes in Generalbezirk Weißruthenien. Errichtung von Schutzmannschaftsdörfern, 19.10.43," BA R 6/93.
239. Ibid.
240. "Abschrift der Niederschrift," see note 236.
241. "Kundgebung in dem zu Wehrdorf ausgewählten Dorf, 29.1.44," BA R 6/93. This reveals the attitude of the German occupation authorities toward the local dwellers. Even at the end of the occupation period, the indigenous population was viewed and treated as a prehistoric people whose loyalty could be bought with some cheap items.
242. "Abschrift des Erlasses des Oberbefehlshabers der Heeresgebiet Mitte betreffend Einrichtung von Wehrdörfern, 29.1.44," ibid.
243. See note 236.
244. Quoted in Gerlach, *Kalkulierte Morde,* 1043.
245. "Vermerk über die Besprechung mit dem Stellvertretenden Generalkommissar von Weißruthenien, SS-Gruppenführer v. Gottberg am 1.3.44, 10.3.44," BA R 6/263, Mikrofiche 2.
246. Ibid.
247. Ibid.
248. See note 236.
249. "Niderschrift über die Besprechung am 24.1.44 beim Oberkommando der Heeresgruppe Mitte bezüglich Einrichtung von Wehrdörfern," BA R 6/93.
250. "Monatsbericht des Oberkommandos der Heeresgruppe Mite für Mai 1944," BA R 6/309, Mikrofiche 3.
251. Ibid.
252. "Tätigkeits- und Erfahrungsbericht des Gebietskommissars Baranowitsche Werner, 11.8.44," BA R 93/13.
253. "Bericht des Gebietskommissars Baranowitsche über die Auflockerungs- und Räumungsmassnahmen, 11.7.44," ibid.
254. The stories of survivors from the burned villages were collected in the 1970s by three Byelorussian writers, Ales' Adamovich, Janka Bryl', and Vladimir Kolesnik and published as a book in Russian and Byelorussian under the title *Ya iz ognennoj Derevni* ... [I am from the fiery village]. See Adamovich et al., *Ya iz ognennoj Derevni* ... (Minsk, 1977).
255. According to Soviet data, about 150,000 were exterminated in Malyj Trostenec. See "Akt ob ekspertize zakhoronenij okolo d. M. Trostenec, 13.8.44," YVA M 41/251 (original: National Archive, Minsk, 4-29-159a). The peculiarity of the Koldychevo camp lay in the fact that its personnel consisted almost exclusively of local people. After the war, four of them were brought to justice and sentenced to death. See Galina Paromchyk, *Kaldychoŭskaja Trahedyja* (Minsk, 1962)

256. These were people, Jews or relatives of the partisans, led on dog-collars and supplied with harrows, who were ordered to search and deactivate the mines with their own bodies. See "Befehl Nr. 1 für Unternehmen 'Dreieck,' 11.9.42," BA-MA RH 23/25.

257. In the fifty-five large and small anti-partisan operations that took place between March 1942 and June 1944, at least 142,223 people were killed (Gerlach, *Kalkulierte Morde*, 899–904). In providing these data, Gerlach apparently counts only those undertakings carried out in the Byelorussian territory proper and does not consider the operations carried out in the adjacent territories, for example, undertakings *Dreieck* (Triangle) and *Viereck* (Quadrangle) that took place between 17 September and 2 October 1942 in the present-day Bryansk oblast. According to the report of the so-called "Jollasse Group", this double operation was responsible for 1,064 victims. See "Gefechtsbericht der Gruppe Jollasse," see note 233.

258. See Gerlach, *Kalkulierte Morde*, 902.

259. "Übersicht über Zusammenstöße mit Banditen, Sabotageakte, Feind- und eigene Verluste sowie Beute u.a., November 1942," BA-MA, RH 22/235, 149.

260. See "Gefechtsbericht der Gruppe Jollasse," note 233.

261. One of Dirlewanger's favorite "amusements" was to inject strychnine into the captured Jewish girls and then watch their agony. After the girls were dead, Dirlewanger and his men cut the corpses into pieces and boiled them into soap. Quoted in MacLean, *Cruel Hunters*, 60–61.

262. See Chapter IV, note 41.

263. MacLean, *Cruel Hunters*, 282.

264. The important source on this camp is the work by Byelorussian researcher Galina Paromchyk published in 1962 and based on the materials of the legal proceedings against four former guards at Koldychevo: Nikolaj Kal'ko, Leonid Senkevich, Mikhail Kukhta, and Andrej Karalevich. See note 255.

265. Ibid., 14. According to Gerlach the camp had already been established in December 1941. See Gerlach, *Kalkulierte Morde*, 771.

266. Paromchyk, *Kaldychoŭskaja Trahedyja*, 15; Gerlach, *Kalkulierte Morde*, 771.

267. See Paromchyk, *Kaldychoŭskaja Tragedyja*, 27; Chiari, *Alltag hinter der Front*, 192.

268. "The protocol of the interrogation of Vera Parinskaja by the deputy chief of the 2nd department of Krupki rayon OD Karas', 17.6.43," YVA M 41/2394 (State Archive of the Minsk Oblast, GAMO 634-1-4), 2–4.

269. A photocopy of the document appears in Romanovskij, *Saudzel'niki ? zlachynstvakh*, 82.

270. Ibid.

271. Quoted in Turonak, *Belarus' pad nyameckaj Akupacyjaj*, 115. In many of its issues, the *Belaruskaja Hazeta* also described the damage done by Polish rule to Byelorussia in the interwar period and rejoiced about the replacement of Poles by Byelorussians in various bodies, such as the auxiliary police. See, for example, "Z pravincyi," BH, 11.2.42, 4, YVA C-762.

272. Turonak, *Belarus' pad nyameckaj Akupacyjaj*, 155.

273. Ibid.

274. "Bericht der Gebietskommissar Wilejka. Haase während der Tagung der Gebietskommissare etc. Vom 8.April bis 10. April 1943," BA R 93/20, 5.

275. Kazimierz Krajewski, "Der Bezirk Nowogródek der Heimatarmee. Nationalitätenkonflikte und politische Verhältnisse 1939 bis 1945," in Chiari, *Die polnische Heimatarmee*, 575.
276. Ibid.
277. "Erfahrung- und Abschlußbericht von Referent Sozialversicherung bei Generalkommissariat Weißruthenien über die Entwicklung der Sozialversicherung der einheimischen Arbeitskräfte im Generalbezirk Weißruthenien, 20.8.44," BA, R 93/12.
278. Turonak, *Belarus' pad nyameckaj Akupacyjaj*, 156.
279. "The history of the partisan brigade 'Leninskij Komsomol' (Western Byelorussia) for the period between May 1942 and July 12th, 1944," YVA, M 41/141 (NARB 3500-4-261).
280. See Krajewski, "Der Bezirk Nowogródek der Heimatarmee," in Chiari, *Die polnische Heimatarmee*, 575.
281. Gross, *Neighbors*, 4.

CHAPTER 8

MILITARY-POLICE COLLABORATION IN BYELORUSSIA

The Beginnings

For quite a long time military collaboration on the part of various Soviet nationalities during World War II was perceived by many historians as the only form of collaboration worth studying in depth. However, as the cold war threatened to turn into a "hot" one, especially during the 1950s and 1960s, the interest in this topic ceased to be a purely academic one; instead, it now pertained to the political sphere. It was almost axiomatically accepted that Hitler's failure in the war against the Soviet Union was due to his inability to attract and make proper use of the large scale anti-Stalinist military forces that encompassed various Soviet nationalities.

The military collaboration of Byelorussians, as well as that of other Soviet nationalities, once again constitutes an almost a perfect case study of the conflict between Nazi ideological dogmas and reality. It is noteworthy that the same people who were considered *Untermenschen* in 1941 by the Nazi hierarchy, were allowed, a mere three years later, to become members of what was originally thought of as "the shock troops" and the elite of the Aryan race, namely, the Waffen-SS.

Military collaboration as such was by no means a result of prewar planning. Rather, the opposite was true. For Hitler, who allegedly moved in his youth from Vienna to Munich to avoid serving in the Austro-Hungarian Army side by side with the representatives of the Habsburg Empire's minorities, the very thought of Slavs and other *Ostvölker* bearing arms was unbearable. In one of his well-known speeches made before his entourage on 16 July 1941, he proclaimed quite unambiguously: "No one but the Germans should ever be allowed to bear arms ... Only a German should bear arms: not a Slav, a Czech, a Cossack or a Ukrainian!"[1] He reiterated the same thoughts almost a year later, in April 1942, in one of his so-called "table talks":

> But the most stupid thing that could be done in the occupied territories would be to give weapons to the conquered peoples. History teaches us that ruling nations were always destined to perish after allowing their conquered peoples to bear arms. We might even say that giving weapons to the conquered people is *conditio sine quo non* [*sic*] for the downfall of a ruling nation. Therefore it is necessary that peace and order in the whole of occupied Russia be secured only by our own troops.[2]

Hitler and many of his generals believed that the Soviet campaign would end in a couple of weeks or months and that it would be superfluous to enlist the assistance of any external factions. On the eve of the invasion into the Soviet Union, the German military command turned down a proposal from the head of the émigrés' "Russian Common-to-All-Arms Union" (Russkij Obshchevoinskij Soyuz, ROVS), Major-General von Lampe, to mobilize the members of the union for the impending attack.[3] However, during the preparation stage for the invasion, some German bodies, in the first place the Abwehr, were eager to use the services of émigrés of various nationalities, including the Byelorussians, for espionage and sabotage purposes. However, this was done on an ad hoc basis and without any clear political obligations from the German side.

Only the confrontation with the reality of the front led to a change of approach, demonstrated first of all by the fighting units themselves. The initial battles of Operation Barbarossa had resulted in an enormous influx of Soviet POWs. According to Christian Streit, the Army Group "Center" alone reported 323,000 prisoners on 9 July 1941, merely a couple of weeks after the beginning of the invasion into the Soviet Union, while in December of the same year, 3.35 million Soviet POWs were reported by all three Army Groups.[4] These large numbers inevitably led to the following question: what were the Germans to do with all these prisoners? In most cases the problem was resolved quite simply. In accordance with the prewar orders, the most infamous of which was the "order regarding commissars" (*Kommissarbefehl*), all those defined as communist functionaries, Jews or "Asians" were to be executed on the spot. The rest were sent to POW camps, where they were exposed to the most terrible conditions, dying in the thousands, from hunger (cases of cannibalism were recorded in many places), the cold of winter, diseases, and mistreatment and abuse by camp personnel.[5]

There were those in the German military command, however, who thought differently. One must keep in mind that notwithstanding the great number of Soviet POWs captured in the first weeks of the war, the fighting against the Soviet Union was by no means a pleasure trip from the German point of view. Although there were cases of mass desertions, panic and demoralization on the part of Soviet soldiers in many places, in others the Soviet troops fought quite stubbornly, causing heavy losses on the Wehrmacht's side.[6] For example, the Wehrmacht met with tough resistance near the cities of Gomel and Mogiljov in Eastern Byelorussia, where the Soviet military command had more time to organize a decent defense. Here, the regular troops were strengthened by the "people's militia" (*narodnoje opolchenije*). The city of Mogiljov was put under strict military command and parts of the Soviet 13th Army held off German assaults until the end of July 1941, causing the attackers heavy losses.[7] Even the commander of the German Army Group "Center", Field Marshal Fedor von Bock, was compelled to acknowledge in his diary the "stubbornness" of the Russians.[8] As Omer Bartov showed, the German losses increased drastically in the winter of 1941/1942, especially during and after the Moscow battle.[9] Beyond the casualties of battle, additional losses were inflicted by "General Winter" as well as by diseases.[10]

The German *Ersaztheer* (Replacement Army), which bore the main responsibility for making up for the losses, could not cope with the ever-increasing demand for reinforcements. As a result, many Wehrmacht officers began to look for alternative sources for them, and their gaze fell upon the masses of Soviet POWs and civilians, who for various reasons were prepared to assist the Germans. Of course, hatred for the Stalinist regime was by no means the only motivating factor, although the terror inflicted by this rule had created no small number of opponents, who were just waiting for their hour. For many of the POWs, however, joining the Wehrmacht auxiliary units simply meant an escape from the hellish conditions of the POW camps.

It is very difficult to pinpoint the exact moment when the large-scale recruitment of Soviet auxiliaries began. The reason is very simple: initially recruitment was conducted surreptitiously, without the knowledge of either the Army's Supreme Command (OKH) or the Wehrmacht's Supreme Command (OKW). The new recruits were the "Army's black funds" (*schwarze Bestände des Heeres*), according to the expression used by Reinhard Gehlen, who during the war headed the Department of "Foreign Armies East" (*Fremde Heere Ost*, FHO), the military intelligence department of the OKH, and after the war was the founder and first head of the West German Federal Intelligence Service (*Bundesnachrichtendienst* or BND).[11] According to Wladyslaw Anders, the famous Polish commander, and Antonio Munoz, the massive recruitment of "eastern volunteers" by individual German troops began as early as autumn 1941.[12] These recruits were Soviet POWs and deserters as well as civilians. They received the name *Hilfswillige* (*Hiwis* for short), meaning "auxiliary volunteers," and were employed chiefly as munitions drivers, sentries, and cooks; however, there were some cases, for example in the Wehrmacht's 134th infantry division in July 1941, in which the *Hiwis*, most of whom were former Soviet Army soldiers, were supplied with weapons and enlisted as fighting troops.[13] According to different data sources, at the end of 1941, the *Hilfswillige* in various German units numbered between half a million and one million people.[14]

Local Auxiliary Security Forces: Strength, Structure and the German Attitude

In most cases, when German troops entered Soviet cities and villages, they found almost anarchical conditions. The Soviet functionaries, including militiamen, either fled or went into hiding and incidences such as shop lootings were quite frequent. Beyond the need to control the anarchy, the Germans also required assistance in spotting all those they defined as the "enemy," i.e., communists, Jews, and straggling Soviet soldiers. In the first days and weeks of the Nazi occupation, local police units were created, commonly referred to as "auxiliary police." Ultimately these auxiliary police became the very symbol of collaboration with the Germans; in fact, even today the German word *Polizei* in Russian designates *collaborator*. A short time after the German invasion, in many cities in Byelorussia, the *Einsatzgruppen* or the local military authorities (*Feldkommandanturen* or *Ortskommandanturen*) began recruiting volunteers into the local police.[15] This was accomplished mainly by posting recruitment notices on the walls.[16] Later, appeals to volunteer for the police were published from time to time in the vernacular periodical press.[17] The Germans also entrusted the local *Bürgermeistern* or *Dorfälteste* with the selection of men for the local auxiliary police force.[18] In Minsk, as well as in other cities, the members of the newly created police units, all named *Ordnungsdienst* ("order service" or "OD"), initially wore civilian clothes with an armband that read "Order service of city Minsk," and they were armed with Soviet weapons, which they succeeded in "organizing" on their own.[19]

As mentioned, it is not easy to establish the exact numerical strength of this *Ordnungsdienst*. According to Oberst (Colonel) Klepsch, who was a commander of the German order police (*Kommandeur der Ordnungspolizei*, KdO) in Minsk from autumn 1942 until at least April 1943, initially, in summer 1941, the local police force in this city comprised 910 men, while later this number was significantly reduced.[20] The Minsk auxiliary police unit existed until the autumn of 1941, when a unit of German *Schutzpolizei* (*schupo*, literally "guarding police") arrived in Minsk. This body was responsible for keeping order in the cities.[21] From the very beginning, the Germans intended to keep the local forces as small as possible. Officially, the maximum strength of the OD formation was supposed to be 300 men for every rayon or city, with the exception of cities such as Smolensk, Mogiljov, and Gomel, where at times the police forces reached 500 men.[22] These numbers, however, were not constant. In general, the lack of German forces led to the expansion of local police formations, although the Germans, obsessively seeing the germs of subversion in every corner, still strove to keep these forces within certain, well-defined limits. According to one of the service instructions regarding the OD issued by the authorities of the Rear Area of Army Group Center, it was recommended to keep one OD man for every hundred inhabitants in the countryside and one OD member for every three hundred people in the cities.[23]

In the countryside, the creation of local police units was often more spontaneous. In certain places, such as the village of

Zaostroviči in the Kleck area, where up to mid-1942 the inhabitants had seen almost no Germans at all, it did not start until the spring of 1942. Here the initiative for the formation of a local police force came from the *starosta*. The new force was supposed to be a kind of "self-defense" against the assaults of partisan groups who roamed the surrounding woods and raided the villages for food. It was only in the summer of 1942 that a fifty-year old German gendarme arrived to take control of the newly created *Schutzmannschaft* (consisting of some thirty men). Initially, the local policemen did not have uniforms and were armed with only three rifles. Almost up to the very end of the occupation, the policemen in Zaostroviči received no training.[24] Basically, as American researcher Martin Dean remarks, "The *Schutzmannschaft* was designed to take over much of the leg work from the predominantly middle-aged Gendarmes who supervised them."[25]

In the western part of Byelorussia, the Poles, who constituted a significant part of the population, initially provided the main source for the local auxiliary police units. Although the Germans spared no effort in forcing the Poles out of various offices and in replacing them with Byelorussians, even as late as 1943 in places such as Slonim, the Poles still constituted some thirty per cent of the local police (*Schutzmannschaft*), although it was officially designated "Byelorussian."[26]

With the establishment of the local self-administration, the selection, equipment, and feeding of the auxiliary policemen was entrusted to the *Rayonbürgermeistern* and *Bürgermeistern,* who had the right to propose the candidates. Preference was given to younger—the minimum age was seventeen—and single men, while, at least during the early stages of the occupation, special criteria were required for acceptance into the auxiliary police: "physical and spiritual fitness as well as political reliability."[27] The Jews and communists, at least theoretically, were excluded a priori. Even the so-called *Ortsfremde*, i.e., "strangers," were accepted into the *Ordnungsdienst* with some reservations. Upon entering the police, they received the status of "OD-candidates" (*OD-Anwärter*) and only after a certain period, in which their "reliability" was assessed, were they made full-fledged OD members. Those who volunteered for the auxiliary police underwent both a medical examination and a security check by the *Sicherheitsdienst* (German Security Service, SD).[28] Although former members of the Communist Party and the Komsomol were not officially eligible to serve in the police force, there are quite a number of examples where former communists and *komsomolcy* not only served as rank and file members but even occupied high positions. A former communist, Shvaj, served as chief of the Kojdanaŭ rayon (present-day Dzjarzhinsk, Minsk oblast) police, while his deputy, Khamenko, had been a Komsomol member before the war. One of the senior policemen in the same police division, Yarchuk, was a former candidate for Communist Party membership.[29] The Gomel police was headed by a former communist and Red Army colonel, Kardakov.[30] According to one of the testimonies submitted to the Israeli researcher Daniel Romanovsky, the police in the locality of Klimoviči in the Mogiljov area was led by a man named Ustinovič, who before the war allegedly was "deputy minister of trade of BSSR."[31] It is very difficult to confirm or disprove this testimony.

Little wonder then that the majority of the local policemen were peasants, since the majority of the population in Byelorussia during the Nazi occupation still lived in the countryside, and the Germans viewed the members of the intelligentsia with a high degree of suspicion. According to data quoted by Martin Dean, in *Schutzmannschaften* in the Baranaviči district, seventy-four of one hundred members were peasants.[32]

Regarding the age of the policemen, there were certain differences between western and eastern parts of Byelorussia. In the western part of Byelorussia, which had been conquered by the Germans earlier and so the Red Army had less time to recruit men of military age there, the majority of the auxiliary policemen were younger men. In the Mir police in 1944, of the 341 policemen 89 percent were between 20 and 34 years old, while almost half of them (46.4 percent) were 20 to 24 years old.[33] In Eastern Byelorussia, where the recruitment into the Red Army had been much more thorough, the age of many of the auxiliary policemen was higher. Thus, in the Klichev rayon (Bobrujsk, now Mogiljov oblast), almost half of the auxiliary policemen (46 percent) were between 25 and 50 years old.[34]

It is indeed very difficult to establish the motives that prompted people to join the local auxiliary police. Occasionally, these motives were diametrically opposed to each other, and they were often absolutely pragmatic. For many it was merely to obtain a job where employment was hard to find. Others—especially the members of the clandestine Byelorussian Independent Party, mentioned above—believed that by joining a police force that at least was officially designated as "Byelorussian," they were contributing to the building of a Byelorussian State. For many Poles, especially members of the Armija Krajowa, police service provided both a cover for their clandestine activities and the opportunity to get some kind of military training or even to supply the AK with arms and munitions.[35] For former Communists and Komsomol members, entering the auxiliary police provided an opportunity to conceal their past activities and to prove their loyalty to the new authorities. For those who suffered from the Soviet regime in one way or another, police service was seen as a chance to settle past scores. Later, with the beginning of mass deportation of workers to Germany, joining the local auxiliary police was also seen as a chance to evade deportation. Thus, Martin Dean quotes one policeman who joined the police in 1942 or 1943: "At the end of 1942 or the beginning of 1943 the Germans began to send former prisoners of war and young people to work in Germany. I wanted to stay at home and to make this possible I decided to go work for the Germans in the police and so to avoid transportation to Germany. At this time I voluntarily joined the police."[36]

Economic reasons figured prominently in this list of motives. The policemen received a salary, although its size left much to be desired. Moreover, the families of policemen killed in action were supposed to receive a certain amount of compensation. Apart from official salaries, service in the police also made possible the acquisition of additional provisions.

Service in the police force could also provide a feeling of protection in the generally insecure situation; however, one may question if this protection was indeed effective. Thus, Bernhard Chiari quotes the case of thirty-year old Byelorussian R., whose reason for joining the police was that on a number of occasions he had been beaten severely by the partisans and sought to put an end to his defenselessness through his police service.[37] The fact, however, that this man became in time not only "a brutal partisan hunter" but also an active participant in the murder of Jews may suggest that other motives, such as anti-Semitism, led him to volunteer in the local auxiliary police.[38]

Although this work uses the terms "police" and "policemen," the Israeli researcher Yehoshua Büchler has shown that in reality and according to Himmler's personal wish, the designation "policemen" was reserved for German policemen only.[39] It is obvious then that even in acknowledging their need to recruit local police forces, the Nazi authorities never freed themselves from racial dogmas.

Structurally, the local police units, called *Schutzmannschaften* in the civil administration areas and still known as *Ordnungsdienst* in the military administration areas, were organized in a similar way to that of German police. There were police units stationed in the cities and controlled by the German urban police (*Schutzpolizei*) commandos, while in the rural areas they were controlled by the Gendarmerie commandos and organized into "closed" mobile units consisting of companies and battalions.[40] The latter, inter alia, played a vital role in the extermination of the Jews. Moreover, the *Schutzmannschaften* had fire-fighting and technical-assistance units.[41] In the civil administration area in Byelorussia, the *Schutzmannschaften* were subordinate both administratively and operationally to the commander of the German order police (KdO) in Minsk.[42] In the military administration area, that is the area of Army Group Center, the situation was more complicated.

In the Army Group "Center", around the middle of 1942, the OD was divided into four departments in accordance with the tasks it was supposed to fulfill: a criminal police department (*OD I*, "prevention and persecution of criminal offenses"), a state police department (*OD II*, "investigation and persecution of anti-German hostile aspirations"), an order-police department (*OD III*, control of highway movement, checking of passes, fire-fighting), and a fighting department (*Kampfabteilung*) (*OD IV*, "defense from the bands, terrorists, paratroopers, skydivers ...").[43] Up to 1943, the operational activity of the first two departments was regulated by *Sicherheitspolizei* (*sipo*) and the SD. Then *OD I* and *OD II* were excluded from the joint OD system and subordinated to the local High SS and Police Leader (in the Rear Area of Army Group "Center" this position was occupied first by Erich von dem Bach Zelewski and then by Kurt von Gottberg). At that point, these two departments were also renamed the "security watch" (*Sicherheitswacht* or *Siwa*). Although the formal justification for such a change was that the functions of criminal police and state police departments overlapped those of the German *sipo*,[44] it was highly likely that either Bach-Zelewski or Gottberg, or both of them, were simply seeking to strengthen their own positions. Moreover, the splitting of the local police force was an expression of the Nazi authorities' obsessive fear of any kind of unification in the "eastern space." After the creation of the *Siwa,* when the third and fourth departments of the OD tried to form a kind of criminal police and state police groups of their own, they were not allowed to do so, the official reason being that such a step would result in "double work and erroneous decisions."[45]

The operational activities of both remaining departments, *OD III* and *OD IV*, were regulated by the German *Ortskom-*

mandante. During the anti-partisan operations, however, when units of the OD "fighting department" were allocated as auxiliary forces to German security troops, the overall command over these units was transferred to German troop commanders.[46] According to the letter of the 7th department of Ia (operational officer) by Schenckendorff, issued on 8 July 1942, security divisions were to participate actively in the military organization of *OD IV*, that is on issues relating to its overall organization, the provision of arms (only using captured weapons), and operational activities.[47] The letter also imposes on the security divisions the duty of dealing with the uniforms and insignia for the members of the "fighting" *OD* units.[48] In the case of units belonging to *OD III* (the order police), local military commanders (*Ortskommandante*) could allocate them to various economic bodies "for securing agriculture, forestry and industry" as well as to the local rayon administration for carrying out "special tasks" such as the organization of firewood or participation in *Sammelaktionen*.[49] Actually, the German authorities had an extremely vague concept of the duties of the order police.

Hierarchically, the *Ordnungsdienst* was divided in the following way: twenty OD men were united in a section (*Gruppe*) headed by a section commander, whose rank matched that of a non-commissioned officer (NCO). Five sections constituted a platoon (*Zug*), headed by the "police division leader" (*OD-Revierführer*), whose rank was equal to that of lieutenant. Three or four police stations (*Reviere*) were supposed to be united under a sector leader (*OD-Abschnittsführer*) with the rank of captain, who was to be subordinated to a district leader (*OD-Bezirksführer*), whose rank was equivalent to that of major. There was also a plan to introduce the level of OD inspector (*OD-Inspizient*), who would have the rank of colonel and who would oversee the *OD-Bezirksführer*; however, it is not known whether such a level was actually implemented.[50]

The quantitative increase in *Schutzmannschaften* personnel (*schumas*) reflected the worsening security situation, and yet, in the *GK Weißruthenien* this development was apparently somewhat slower than in the whole of the *Reichskommissariat Ostland*. According to data quoted by Yehoshua Büchler, in the whole of the *Reichskommissariat (RK) Ostland* there were 31,652 *schumas* in 1941, while a year later this number rose to 54,984.[51] In the *GK Weißruthenien* on 1 December 1941 there were 3,682 men in rural *Schutzmannschaften*, while at the beginning of April 1943 their number came to 6,850.[52] In the whole area of Army Group "Center" there were about 22,000 OD men in October 1942, and some 45,000 in 1943.[53] As for the remaining Byelorussian territories that were attached to *RK Ukraine* and to the Bialystok district, at the beginning of 1943 there were 11,870 *schumas* in *GK Wolhynien-Podolien*, which also encompassed the southwestern areas of Byelorussia and included cities such as Brest and Pinsk, and some 3000 *schumas* in the Bialystok district, which included the westernmost Byelorussian territories, with the cities of Hrodna and Valkavysk.[54]

Initially, at least in *GK Weißruthenien*, for every rayon reinforced by *Schutzmannschaften* the Germans organized one Gendarmerie post in the rayon's central city and four to five additional Gendarmerie posts throughout the rayon.[55] At the beginning of 1943, the whole of the *GK Weißruthenien* was partitioned into ten Gendarmerie areas (*Gendarmerie-Gebieten*), which in turn were distributed among three main groups (*Hauptmannschaften*): Minsk, Vilejka, and Baranaviči. These encompassed a total of fifty-five Gendarmerie posts reinforced by local *schumas* and seventy-two *Schutzmannschaft* posts under German command. Each Gendarmerie post also had a so-called "hunting commando" (*Jagdkommando*), consisting of thirty to forty local *schumas* and two to three German leaders intended to engage solely in the anti-partisan struggle.[56] As time passed, these *Jagdkommandos* also participated in the so-called *Erfassung* operations, the confiscation of agricultural products from the peasants.[57]

Minsk, the center of civil administration in Byelorussia, was in some respects a case apart. Here as many as five *schuma* posts existed in April 1943, with a total of 382 local policemen.[58] To this we should also add the German garrison of the city that, according to partisan intelligence, had reached the total strength of 2,500–3,000 men in the second half of 1942.[59]

It is not easy to establish how all of these forces were expected to adequately execute security duties, especially in the face of an ever-growing partisan movement. Bernhard Chiari, using the example of Baranaviči, seeks to destroy the image of a "lost island in a sea of terror."[60] According to Chiari, in the Baranaviči area in 1944 there were as many as 2,200 Byelorussian and Polish *schumas*. They served in 36 police posts in the area, each of which consisted of between 12 members, as in the village of Sevruki, and 212 members, as in the city of Lipsk, situated in the big forest area. The average distance between the posts was no more than ten kilometers. Furthermore, the local police forces were assisted by some additional troops, prominently Wehrmacht units.[61]

From a purely mathematical point of view, the data provided by Chiari are indeed irreproachable. When evaluating the adequacy of the local police, however, we must take into account additional factors, including their being equipped with weapons. Matthew Cooper clearly states in his book *The Nazi War against Soviet Partisans* that in 1943 "the partisans were, in general, better equipped than their enemies."[62] From the second half of 1942, the Soviet regime began to invest heavily in the partisan movement in the German rear areas. Weaponry such as anti-aircraft and anti-tank guns, artillery of various calibers, grenade launchers, and even tanks became in time an integral part of the partisan arsenal.[63] In contrast, the units, especially local ones, employed in anti-partisan warfare were very poorly equipped. Even the Germans could not deny this fact. Klepsch was compelled to acknowledge in his report that only in 1943 did the local *schumas* begin to receive weapons such as grenade launchers, heavy machine guns, and flamethrowers. All this booty either remained from the Soviet regular forces or had been captured during skirmishes with partisans.[64] Even in April 1943, ten per cent of the local auxiliary policemen stationed in *GK Weißruthenien* possessed no firearms at all.[65] The decision to shift responsibility for equipping local anti-partisan forces to the officials of the local self-administration disclosed once again the schizophrenic nature of the Germans, since it was not clear where these officials would obtain the weapons. Did not Kube himself, in his appeal to the population upon his entering the office of *Generalkommissar*, call upon the people to turn over all their firearms and ammunition, threatening them with death for non-compliance?[66] The slowness of the German authorities in supplying the *schumas* and OD men with weapons stemmed to a large degree from the paranoid fear that the local policemen one day would turn these arms against the Germans themselves. Even people such as Schenckendorff, who issued a number of memoranda and letters regarding the increased involvement of the local auxiliary forces in their anti-partisan struggle, were not free from such anxiety. In February 1942, Schenckendorff explicitly prohibited supplying the OD men with machine guns, and in October of the same year, in his regulations for guarding the railways, he once again prohibited the supply of automatic weapons and special devices to Ukrainian and other OD units participating in these activities.[67]

Supplying the local police units with food and uniforms as well as salaries did not help to make them an effective fighting force. The face that the peasants in Byelorussia, as well as having to send food deliveries to Germans using yields from the meager pieces of land they cultivated, were also compelled to allocate a certain amount of land to the officials of the local self-administration and policemen[68] did not make the latter very popular in the eyes of the local population, nor did it improve the atmosphere in the villages. In November 1941, the Germans in the military administration area established the food supply norms for various local units during anti-partisan activities. In the civil administration area, the supply of all necessary goods to the *schumas* was "entrusted," at least officially, to the local administration of either a municipality or rayon. But even the commander of the order police in the *GK Weißruthenien*, Klepsch, was forced to admit that "in reality they [the *schumas*—L. R.], especially in the countryside (*auf dem offenen Land*) had to be self sufficient and resort to supplying themselves" (*Selbstversorgung*).[69] The local policemen interpreted the notion of "self-supply" in a very broad way: there were repeated reports of looting and other serious crimes committed by the local auxiliary police.[70] The *Gebietskommissar* of Sluck, Carl, complained that "the local *Schutzmannschaften* are the greatest robbers; they are stealing all they are able to get hold of; they do what they want."[71]

The process of supplying the local policemen with uniforms also proceeded slowly. For Himmler, who as chief of the German police had the final word in all matters relating to both the German security forces and the auxiliary forces in the occupied areas, it was unthinkable that the *Untermenschen* should look like German policemen. Initially, the auxiliary policemen differed from the rest of the population only by wearing white armbands bearing the inscription *Ordnungsdienst* or *Schutzmann*.[72] Some policemen performed their duties in Soviet Army uniforms, while in Berdichev, in the Ukraine, the Gendarmerie demanded in February 1942 that the Soviet POWs who had been released to return home should surrender their greatcoats for use by the *schumas*.[73] Only in May 1942, did the *Schutzmannschaften* in *GK Weißruthenien* begin to appear in black uniforms with grey cuffs, which were actually SS uniforms modified for *schumas* stationed in cities and villages, and in green German police uniforms, also modified for the policemen serving in "closed" mobile formations.[74] In July 1943, Himmler issued a special instruction intended to regulate the service conditions, including the uniforms, of the *schumas* serving in "closed" units in *RK Ukraine*, in *GK Weißruthenien,* and in the "old Soviet areas." According to Himmler, the *schumas* of all ranks were to receive uniforms either from German stocks or from individuals captured during the fight against the partisans. Himmler insisted explicitly that "the service clothes *(Dienstkleidungsstücke)* given out from German stocks *(Bestände)* be of the older fashion or repaired clothes of the new fashion suitable for service."[75]

One of the most extreme examples of the poor equipment of the local police was provided by the OD in Smolensk, in the military administration area; Smolensk was a strategically important location, being—together with Mogiljov—the seat of command of Rear Area of Army Group "Center". The letter sent by the Smolensk rayon OD to the 588th unit of German *Feldgendarmerie* on 27 July 1943 depicted a truly lamentable picture. At the time of the letter, mid-1943, not all of the local policemen had yet received uniforms or shoes. Some of them performed their duties in Soviet or German uniforms, but the majority wore civilian clothes. The letter's authors complained that the OD men's appearance caused the local residents to mock them and that at the parade of OD men on 6 July 1943, the participants made a very bad impression on the spectators owing to the variety and poor condition of their clothes. Many policemen were even unable to take part in the parade because they lacked uniforms and shoes.[76]

One of the most revealing topics relating to the auxiliary police is that of their wages. In his study dealing with the treatment of Soviet POWs by the German authorities, Christian Streit showed that racial criteria played a paramount role in the attitude of Nazi rulers to POWs of various nationalities who fell into their hands during World War II. The whole racial scale was drawn up with Englishmen and Americans at the top, and Polish and Soviets (after 1943 also Italians) at the bottom.[77] A similar ranking was developed in relation to *schumas* of various nationalities employed in "occupied eastern territories." At the top were the representatives of Baltic peoples, while Slavs, Ukrainians and Byelorussians found themselves at the bottom. This expressed itself first in the wages and compensations the *schumas* received. According to the commander of the Order Police in *Weißruthenien,* Klepsch, at the beginning of 1943, some fourteen "closed" *Schutzmannschaft* battalions operated in the civil administration area, thirteen of them consisting of Lithuanians,

Latvians, and Ukrainians and one (49th) Byelorussian, but this number varied in different periods.[78] He stated that the wages of the *schumas* serving in Baltic battalions in April 1943 was almost five times higher than those received by Ukrainians and Byelorussians. Unmarried Byelorussian and Ukrainian rank-and-file policemen received a daily wage of 0.80 RM, married men received 1.80 RM. An unmarried battalion commander received 3.30 RM and a married one received 5.80 RM. At the same time, the daily wages of Lithuanian and Latvian auxiliary policemen fluctuated between 3.80 RM for rank-and-file *schumas* and 15.50 RM for battalion commander.[79] It seems, however, that until July 1943 there was no fixed wage for local policemen.

It was only on 22 July 1943 that Himmler issued the instructions quoted above to establish a clear "hierarchy" of wages for *schumas* serving in "closed" formations in the *Ostgebieten*, except for those in the Baltic area. According to this directive, the monthly wages of *Schutzmannschaften* members was to be between 375 rubles or 30 RM for *Schutzmann*, i.e., of the lowest rank, and 1,350 rubles or 108 RM for a battalion commander (*Batl.-Führer*).[80] All of these numbers only make sense when compared to the prices of various products and wares then current. In 1942, prices both in the civil and military administration areas were exorbitant. In the markets a Russian pound (16.38 kg) of flour cost 1,000–1,500 rubles; a pound of potatoes, 500–700 rubles; one liter of milk, 30–40 rubles; 10 eggs, 120–150 rubles; used shoes, 1,500–2,000 rubles; and woolen trousers, 300–1,000 rubles.[81] Although Klepsch spoke of the principle of "supplying themselves" as deriving from harsh necessity, it can be deduced from Himmler's instruction that this was desirable and even to be encouraged. Moreover, those policemen who could not use the "official supply" (*amtlichen Verpflegung*) during their "operational activities" were supposed to receive the "entire sum" of 0.60 RM as compensation for having to "supply themselves." In addition, "if during an individual operational assignment (*Einzeleinsatz*) ... the members of *Schutzmannschaft* had to rely on makeshift food supplies (*Selbstverpflegung*), they were to be awarded an additional sum of 0.30 RM (*Verpflegungsgeld*). An individual operational assignment could include up to four men."[82]

Even if Himmler may have intended the term "self-supply" to include the purchase of products, given the "additions" mentioned above and taking into account the market prices at the time, it is abundantly clear that this principle came to mean outright looting and stealing. The same directive reveals the German authorities' strong desire to cut costs relating to the local auxiliaries and indeed to turn a profit at their expense.

Himmler also introduced terms such as "partial supply" (*Teilverpflegung*), a mixture of "self-supply" and "official food supplies" (that is breakfast, lunch, and dinner provided at the point of service). The instruction foresaw in somewhat vague terms that "supply money would be reduced, by providing products instead of part of the sum (*Bei Inanspruchnahme von Teilverpflegung in Natur*) in the following way: participation in breakfast in the equivalent of 1/6; participation in lunch equivalent to 3/6 of the supply money; participation in dinner equivalent to 2/6."[83] Even prosaic items such as soap were to be given out to local *schumas* "according to need, but in amounts that would not exceed the norms for the police [*sic*], [albeit] 'free of charge'."[84]

On 17 July 1942 Himmler issued one of the most cynical documents regarding the treatment of local *schumas* and other auxiliary units serving in the Baltic as well as in the "old Soviet" regions. It provided a kind of "damage insurance" for the local auxiliaries and their families.[85] First of all, in this letter Himmler revealed once again his desire to rid himself—insofar as he could manage—of any material obligations towards the local policemen and other auxiliary units existing at this time. He opted to transfer the care for all of these units to other bodies. Thus, the units covered by these provisions, which were subordinated to the SS and the police apparatus, were the "closed" *Schutzmannschaften,* formed by the German police, the *schuma* units formed by the Wehrmacht, and the "auxiliary guards" (*Hilfsschutzmänner*), i.e., the units that the German police or Wehrmacht assembled on a temporary basis from the local population. All the other units, such as the Cossack and Tartar hundreds and *Hiwis,* which were used by the Wehrmacht front troops, were supposed to be governed by the Wehrmacht.[86] At the same time Himmler stated explicitly once again that "the administration (countryside, city, community) remains the bearer of supplies [for auxiliary units—L. R.]."[87]

The rules issued by Himmler also applied to compensation for "physical damage as a result of service" (*Körperschaden infolge des Dienstes*), that is, wounds, or for damage that was not the result of the service per se but was aggravated by it. These regulations seemed quite generous; however, any illusion of munificence disappeared when the exact amount of compensation was listed, and especially in the section defining damages. First of all, as in the hierarchy of the wages of individual *schumas,* there was a sharp distinction between the auxiliary policemen from the Baltic area and those from the "old Soviet area." Thus, a single rank-and-file *Schutzmann* from the "old Soviet area" with a first-degree wound, namely, the loss of a finger, eye, or "proved consequences of concussion," was supposed to receive 8 RM as compensation (10 RM for married men), or 32 RM (40 RM for married men) for a fourth-degree wound, meaning the complete loss of ability to perform one's duty.[88] For a first-degree wound, an unmarried battalion commander of non-Baltic origin was supposed to receive 16 RM and a married man 25 RM; for a fourth-degree wound, 64 RM for a single man and 100 RM for a married man. According to Himmler's regulations, a rank-and-file policeman of Estonian, Latvian, or Lithuanian origin could count on compensation ranging between 16 RM and 84 RM depending on marital status and the severity of the wounds, while battalion commanders were promised the sum of between 53 RM and 240 RM, based on the same criteria.[89] The families of policemen killed in action were also treated unfairly. The widow of a deceased ordinary policeman in the old Soviet areas was promised by Himmler a maximum monthly pension of 24 RM and his half-orphaned child 5 RM; a full orphan was to receive 8 RM; the widow of a battalion commander, 60 RM, a half-orphaned child 12 RM, and a full orphan 20 RM.[90] The maximum monthly allotment to the widow of a slain Baltic rank-and-file policeman was supposed to be 50 RM; to his half-orphaned child 10 RM; and to a fully orphaned child 17 RM. In the case of families of battalion commanders killed in action, the amounts were 144 RM, 29 RM, and 48 RM, respectively.[91] The definition of the degree of "physical damage" suffered by local policemen was quite vague as well as very cynical. The main criterion was the ability of the policemen to perform their duty. Roughly speaking, if the *Schutzmann* was able to move and shoot, his wounds were defined as light, entitling him to less compensation. The most radical definitions in this respect concerned "internal damage," which included tuberculosis or heart disease. According to Himmler, such "damage" did not prevent the policeman from performing his duties; it was therefore classified as first degree, the slightest degree of harm that received the lowest possible compensation.

Even on issues such as awards and leave for local forces in the "occupied eastern territories," the German authorities remained steadfast in their racial dogmas. It was unthinkable that *Untermenschen* should receive German awards, even if they were assisting the Germans in performing security duties. Only in November 1942, at Hitler's personal order, were local auxiliary policemen in Byelorussia and other occupied territories allowed to receive a special order, the "Order for Bravery and Merit" (*Tapferkeits- und Verdienstauzeichnung*, in the following TVAZ), with several classes: 1st and 2nd class in bronze, silver and gold.[92] The initiative for awarding "eastern auxiliaries" came from Rosenberg who, up to the very end of the occupation, sought to toy with "political warfare." Hitler and Bormann, even in 1944, were strongly opposed to awarding "eastern people" any orders or medals.[93] Yet reality overcame their opposition. The rates of desertion among local policemen and other forces engaged in anti-partisan warfare increased in 1942, 1943, and 1944, so some effort was needed to curtail this trend. In 1944, Rosenberg succeeded in obtaining a half-hearted concession from Hitler, according to which an *Ostvölker* could, in principle, receive the Iron Cross.[94] However, the precondition was that one must first have been awarded the "Order for Bravery and Merit." Thus, the award of the Iron Cross (2nd class) proceeded only after an award of TVAZ 2nd class in gold, and that of the Iron Cross (1st class) followed an award of TVAZ 1st class in gold.[95] One of the most popular forms of "awards" for those who excelled in anti-partisan warfare was the promise of economic advantages. In a letter composed in February 1943 regarding awards for "local auxiliary forces," the Supreme Command of the German Army (OKH) spoke of the "immediate enlargement of homestead land up to the maximum limit or the assignment of an individual homestead or municipal property etc. as private property." Also mentioned was a "gift of usable (*Nutztiere*) or draught animals, as well as agricultural tools etc. constituting a special award."[96] Of course these "awards," which in any case were never conferred, were hardly a result of German benevolence but rather a sign of the authorities' anxiety about economic interests and the effects of Nazi propaganda. Thus, the same letter states explicitly that "allowing leave (*Beurlaubung*) for individual candidates who have proven themselves outstanding (*hervorragend*) and who were generously awarded ... creates bearers of effective, positive German propaganda in the countryside, and is especially appropriate to overcome the mistrust of the rural population toward the German leadership."[97]

When we speak about the relationship between German and local policemen who served side by side, it is difficult to present a unified picture. According to Bernhard Chiari, the language barrier significantly influenced these relations. In numerous instances Germans beat or insulted local policemen. Chiari also relates that some German Gendarmes, being alcoholics, made themselves a laughing-stock in the eyes of both their local subordinates and the surrounding population when they begged for schnapps in the villages.[98] To a considerable degree relations were determined by the personality of the German heading the police post. When, as was the case of Mir, he was not a Nazi fanatic, relations were more or less "normal"—if such a term can be used in this situation. The head of the local Gendarmerie developed a special bond toward his "Polish" translator, not knowing of course that he was a Jew, Oswald Rufeisen.[99]

Relationships were somewhat different between the German front units and the *Hiwis* who were employed by them almost from the beginning of the Soviet campaign as well as between the German "framework personnel" and the various local "combat units." The *Hilfswillige* or *Hiwis* performed mainly logistic duties, but owing to increasing losses, some units, such as the 134th Infantry Division, also used them—albeit unofficially—as fighting troops. In 1942, several so-called "combat battalions" made up of POWs were created, with a number of Germans accompanying them as "framework personnel." The mutiny that occurred in the "Beresina" "combat battalion" in September 1942, during which a number of Germans were killed (see below), demonstrates that not all the relationships between Germans and locals in these units were trouble-free. The need to perform common combat duties, however, also helped to some degree in establishing normal and occasionally even friendly relations, especially when the Germans refrained from adhering strictly to their racial dogmas.

An interesting example in this respect is provided by an undated letter, apparently from 1943, written by the *Ostministerium* to the Supreme Command of the Wehrmacht (OKW). It discloses the true attitude of the Nazi leadership towards those who decided for various reasons to join the German side. The letter states that the higher echelons of the Nazi hierarchy were alarmed by the initiative of "a certain so-called Wehrmacht advice bureau (*Wehrmachtbetreuungsstelle*)," according to which Wehrmacht soldiers on leave in Germany could bring with them some "Eastern" "volunteers."[100] The indignation of people such as Rosenberg, the letter's author, was provoked by the possibility that representatives of *Ostvölker* might enter into

German families. The obsession of all Nazi leaders regarding sexual relations between "Eastern peoples" and German women was a decisive motive in Rosenberg's objections to the initiative. Generally, the objections and fears voiced in this regard were very similar to those raised during the discussions about the employment of Soviet POWs and civilians in the Reich's industry and agriculture. According to German historian Ulrich Herbert, fear of possible contact between the "Russians" and the German workers, especially German women, occupied a central place in what Herbert defines as "popular-political (*Volkstumspolitische*) objections" to the assignment of Soviet POWs and civilians in the Reich.[101] A relationship with a German woman was classified as the heaviest crime a "Russian" man could commit; punishment for the man was "special treatment" (that is execution) or being sent to a concentration camp, and for the woman being sent to a concentration camp until criminal proceedings took place.[102]

To prevent contact with the locals, Rosenberg proposed to place the "volunteers" who arrived for their leave in the Reich in "a common camp or possibly in Wehrmacht's hostels" (*Wehrmachtsheimen*).[103] The ambiguous attitude towards "Eastern" collaborators was demonstrated not only by the political leadership but also the military commanders as well. Even as late as 1943, when many thousands of Soviet civilians and POWs were part of various military bodies, such as the *Hiwis* and the *Osttruppen* or auxiliary police, it was still not clear how to refer to all these people. Field Marshal Ewald von Kleist, who in 1943 commanded Army Group "A" operating in the southern part of the former Soviet Union, was considered a relatively moderate commander. According to certain data, many thousands of various Soviet minorities, mainly Caucasians, served under his command.[104] Nevertheless, he too expressed the opinion that "the term *friends* [in reference to *Ostvölker* serving with Germans— L. R.] was going too far, and one should content himself with the term *allies* (*Bundesgenossen*). Allies need not always be friends. Perhaps it is possible to apply the word *comrades-in-arms* (*Mitkämpfer*) instead of the word *allies*."[105]

As this shows, the German attitude towards the "Eastern" collaborators differed very little from their general attitude towards the *Ostvölker*. As Rosenberg's letter shows, the same discordant and suspicious attitude was demonstrated towards the Soviet POWs. Roughly speaking, all *Hiwis* and members of *Osttruppen* were primarily regarded by the Germans as cannon fodder. Both the orders coming from above and those issued in the field clearly showed that "Eastern volunteers"—some of them indeed volunteers, others "volunteered" under the pressure of circumstances—were regarded as inferior; regardless of their function, they could not be regarded as equal to German soldiers or policemen.

The results of such an attitude were twofold and also quite predictable. As the fighters in the anti-partisan operations had poor equipment and lacked appropriate weapons, compared to their adversaries, they experienced significant losses. In addition, German racial dogmatism led to ever-increasing rates of desertion. From the second half of 1942, the losses among the local auxiliary policemen were quite high. In his report, Klepsch stated that between September 1942 and March 1943 alone, 268 *schumas* were killed in the territory of *GK Weißruthenien* and 236 were wounded.[106] This constitutes a significant loss of about seven per cent, since the total strength of rural *Schutzmannschaften* in April 1943 was 6,850 men. In the whole of the military administration area in just the month of September 1942, the total casualties of OD came to 188 (148 killed, 36 wounded, and 4 missing, possibly taken prisoners), and among the "local units" (*landeseigene Verbände*), i.e., the "combat battalions", to 43 (30 killed and 13 wounded).[107]

Desertion to the partisans, both by individuals in various auxiliary units and by entire units, also increased over time. The most famous case in this respect was that of the *Druzhina*, commanded by the former chief of staff of the Soviet 229th Infantry Division, Lieutenant-Colonel Gil (Rodionov).[108] This unit was created either in the winter of 1941/1942 or in the spring of 1942 in the Suvalki POW camp. Originally it was named the "Russian National Union."[109] *Druzhina*, which in ancient Rus' referred to the prince's personal armed force, was part of the so-called "Zeppelin" project, as worked out by the Reich Security Main Office (RSHA).[110] According to this project, the Soviet POWs (selected from the POW camps) were supposed to be dropped behind Soviet lines for intelligence and sabotage tasks, including "decomposing" the partisan units from within. According to Walter Schellenberg, all of those selected were volunteers, and this was only to be expected, as many of them were only too anxious to escape the conditions of the POW camps.[111] During their training, many of those involved in this project were formed into units, which were supposed to perform security duties in the German rear and to take part in anti-partisan warfare.[112]

Druzhina was one of these units. Although it was of battalion size, it was called a brigade and led by a number of former high-ranking Soviet officers, such as Rodionov; Major General Bogdanov, former commander of the Soviet 47th Riflemen Division; and a Major Yukhnov. It was originally stationed in the Pskov area, in northwestern Russia, but was later transferred to Byelorussia, where it actively engaged in anti-partisan warfare.[113]

The Germans were apparently satisfied with the unit's performance, since at the end of 1942 they allowed the creation of *Druzhina II* in Stalag— POWs camps located in the General-Government and in the Reich—319 A. *Druzhina II* was commanded by former Soviet Major Blazhevich.[114] In March 1943, both *Druzhina I* and *Druzhina II* were transferred to the Hlybokaje area in Byelorussia, where they were merged into the SS Brigade *Druzhina*.[115] In February 1943, a group of fifty *Druzhina* members made a trip to Germany. There, according to Steenberg, they saw the inmates of the Sachsenhausen concentration camp near Berlin as well as *Ostarbeitern*. According to both Steenberg and Littlejohn, it was this confrontation with the realities of the Third Reich that prompted a number of *Druzhina* leaders to have second thoughts about collaborating with Germans.[116] While stationed in Byelorussia, the *Druzhina* Brigade participated in several "anti-partisan" operations, including "Operation Cottbus" (20 May–23 June 1943) in eastern Byelorussia, an area between Lepel-Begoml-Ušači, to the north of Borisov, which claimed more than 10,000 victims.[117] Between battles and skirmishes, some people, such as the former commander of *Druzhina II*, Blazhevich, made contact with Soviet intelligence, sizing up the situation for changing sides. Apparently, German promises to create a Russian Liberation Army under Vlasov prompted *Druzhina* leaders to temporarily abandon their plans to defect. The data available are insufficient to reconstruct the whole process that ultimately led to the desertion of *Druzhina* to the partisans.

Sven Steenberg, who described the *Druzhina* from the German point of view, considers this desertion as the result of Rodionov's personal ambitions, characterizing him as a "coward and opportunist."[118] Steenberg feels that the arrival of Zhilenkov, one of the people close to General Vlasov, who was supposed to take over the training detachment that would be formed, strengthened the suspicions of Rodionov and other *Druzhina* commanders that they were going to be replaced due to the many complaints about their improper conduct, involving alcohol, women, and cards. When *Druzhina* was surrounded by partisans on 13 August 1943, in the course of one of the anti-partisan undertakings, Gil and his followers shot the Germans serving with the Brigade as well as the members of the unit who remained loyal to the Germans, which included all regimental commanders but one, and all battalion commanders, and went over to partisans.[119] Although the Command of the Partisan Movement regarded the former German collaborators who had joined their side with a great deal of distrust, somehow Rodionov's men managed to quickly allay these suspicions. Ultimately they were named the 1st Anti-Fascist Partisan Brigade and Gil was personally decorated with the Order of the Red Star, one of the highest Soviet awards.[120] The unit participated in numerous skirmishes with German forces, in one of which, during the winter of 1943–1944, Gil was killed.[121]

Although the case of *Druzhina* is the most famous of its kind, it was not the only instance of disobedience and defection within the *Osttruppen*. A similar event occurred, albeit on a lesser scale, in the "combat battalion" *Beresina* in September 1942. This happened during one of the "anti-partisan operations" carried out on 18 September 1942 to the southeast of Bobrujsk. Soldiers from the battalion's 2nd company, under the leadership of the company's commander Feldwebel (First Sergeant) Sorvin, a former officer in the Soviet Army, killed three German secret field police (GFP) members as well as two OD men, seriously wounded three OD men, and disarmed many others. Ultimately, some sixty-seven former *Beresina* members went over to the partisans, taking with them their personal weapons, three light machine guns and two grenade-launchers.[122]

For Germans this mutiny was a bolt out of the blue. About a month before it, on 5 August 1942, the operational department under the commander in the area of Army Group "Center" specifically praised the performance of the *Dnepr* and *Beresina* battalions during the fight against the partisans, stressing these soldiers' invulnerability to Soviet propaganda.[123] Yet, what happened on 18 September 1942 could not have been a sudden development. The Germans' attitude was undoubtedly a decisive factor among the causes that led to the mutiny and desertion. In July 1942, the inspection carried out in the *Beresina* battalion praised measures such as the organization of a balalaika-orchestra and a strong chorus. It also noted many "minor" shortcomings, includ-

ing a lack of basic needs, such as straw mattresses (which served
as the beds for battalion soldiers), bedclothes, and combs.[124]

For a long time, Western literature considered the Germans'
inability to create a Russian national anti-Stalinist army to be a
major reason for the dissatisfaction experienced by the soldiers
serving in the *Osttruppen*. According to Steenberg, in December
1942, Fieldmarshal von Klüge, the commander of Army Group
Center, came to two decisions: to split the majority of "combat
battalions" into companies and distribute these among the German troops; and to equip the "Eastern volunteers" with German
uniforms.[125] Steenberg depicts the enraged reaction of Colonel
Bojarskij to these ideas.

It is not unlikely that there were people among those joining
the various "Eastern troops" who hated Soviet rule and Stalin's
regime and who wanted to fight against the latter in a kind of
Russian national army. Such people, however, soon felt let down,
and there was almost nothing that Klüge could do about this disappointment. The guidelines for equipping the "volunteers" of
the "fighting battalions" with German uniforms were issued by
OKH and were supported by Schenckendorff, who is portrayed
as practically the "patron saint" of the "eastern collaborators"
in the Rear Area of Army Group Center. These instructions were
issued even before the *Beresina* mutiny took place.[126] In September 1942, a couple of weeks before the revolt, von Treskow's
office issued a directive regarding the "local auxiliary forces in
the east," which among other things foresaw the introduction of
a special oath for members of these forces, which read as follows:
"I swear in God's name by this solemn oath that I shall obey
unconditionally in the fight against Bolshevist enemies of my
homeland the Supreme Commander of German Wehrmacht
Adolph Hitler and as a brave soldier shall be ready at any time
to pay with my life for this oath."[127] Thus, any notion of independence and any illusion of national or nationalist ideas were
out of the question. Those who volunteered for the "combat battalions" were regarded with a great deal of mistrust, and the
word "control" (*Überwachung*) is frequently encountered in the
orders and directives related to these units.[128]

The mutiny executed by part of the *Beresina* battalion provided the Germans with an opportunity to tighten their control
over the *Osttruppen*. The fact that companies of these troops
were commanded by former Soviet officers drew suspicious
glances from the German military authorities. The revolt provided a pretext for correcting this situation—although there

were exceptions introduced by the German regulations. The commissar of field police, Pfeiffer, who investigated the *Beresina* events, presented the case as if "the men of the 2nd company [of *Beresina*—L. R.] expressed their wish for a German leadership, since they do not trust the former officers of the Red Army" and added that "German officers' strict control (*Überwachung*) over the employed *Beresina* companies is urgently demanded, since similar incidents could be repeated in other companies."[129]

The mutiny also led to a reorganization of the "combat battalions" and their subordination to German troops. The fact that the orders and letter regarding this reorganization were issued only a couple of days after the mutiny in *Beresina* makes it reasonable to assume that the German authorities had long been planning to limit what they already considered the excessive independence of the eastern auxiliary troops, and the mutiny simply provided an apt occasion. The documents issued by the operational department of the office of the commander of the Rear Area of Army Group "Center" on 27, 28, and 30 September 1942 led to the subordination "in every respect" of almost all of the "eastern troops" operating in the Rear Area of Army Group "Center" to the German security divisions. The only exceptions were the Cossack 102nd Regiment and the Voluntary Replacement Regiment "Center," *Freiwilligen Ersatzregiment Mitte*, which remained directly subordinate to Schenckendorff.[130] The same documents also called for the employment of these "eastern troops" only within the framework of German troops, only in companies, and only in the cases of *Dnjepr, Beresina,* and *Wolga.*[131] The companies of *Beresina* were to be used solely for sentry duty, either on the "less endangered parts of the railways" (owing to the fear of further desertions in the course of contact with the partisans) or at less strategically important points.[132]

The "corps order" dated 30 September 1942 also envisaged the renaming of the existing "fighting battalions," further stressing their subordination to Wehrmacht units. Thus, the 102nd Cossacks Regiment was renamed the 600th Cossack Regiment (*Kosakenabteilung 600*); the "combat battalion" *Beresina* became the 601st "Eastern Battalion" (*Ostbattaillon 601*); *Dnjepr* was renamed the 602nd "Eastern Battalion"; *Düna,* the 603rd *Ostbattaillon; Pripet,* the 604th *Ostbattaillon;* and *Wolga* was to be called the 605th "Eastern Battalion." The Voluntary Replacement Regiment "Center" became the "Eastern Replacement Regiment 'Center.'"[133]

Arguably, the most important point in all of these orders was the tightening of German control both over rank-and-file members of the battalions and over the local commanders. The first of the orders quoted above already envisaged the strengthening of the German "liaison commandos" (*Verbindungskommandos*) in all of the "combat battalions." The order demanded the appointment of an additional German officer to every *Kampfbataillon* and an additional officer or "older" NCO to every company. One of the most important duties of these officers was to constantly supervise the local commanders as well as submit evaluations of local battalion and company commanders.[134] That people positioned in "liaison commandos" were striving to increase their power within the battalions can be inferred indirectly from a phrase in the letter of 28 September 1942 cited above. In this document, issued from von Treskow's operational office by the commander of the Rear Area of Army Group Center, the author expresses the hope that the strengthening of the "liaison commando" of the *Pripet* battalion, by means of the 221st Security Division, would "guarantee that the battalion will come firmly under the control of the German liaison commando (*das Btl. fest in die Hand des deutschen Verbindungskommandos kommt*) before it starts its operational activities."[135]

Although the "Eastern troops" were regarded with a great deal of mistrust by the German military authorities, reality still dictated its own dynamic. At the end of 1942, in the area of Army Group "Center," more units composed of members of various Soviet nationalities were added, beyond the existing "combat battalions" mentioned above. According to data quoted by Alexej Litvin, in April 1943, as many as forty-three "eastern units" of various sizes were employed in the Rear Area of Army Group "Center."[136] These included twenty-six "eastern battalions," three Cossack battalions, two "eastern sentry battalions," eight battalions of "people's militia," two "Turkestan" battalions (389th and 785th), one Armenian battalion (2nd), one Azerbaijani battalion (807th), nineteen "eastern" companies, four "eastern" cavalry squadrons, and two "eastern" artillery batteries (582nd and 614th).[137] At this stage, all of these units were employed solely for anti-partisan warfare.

Dogmatism vs. Reality: Byelorussian "Self-Defense" and the "Home Guard"

During Kube's time in the part of Byelorussia belonging to the civil administration area, the auxiliary units often became playthings in the political games waged there. The creation of the 49th Byelorussian *schuma* battalion provides one of the best examples of this. Created in August 1942, when a number of Baltic and Ukrainian police battalions were already operating in Byelorussian territory, this unit was the first Byelorussian formation of battalion size.[138] The initiative to establish this battalion came from Walter Schimana who, at the end of July 1942, replaced Carl Zenner as SSPF *Weißruthenien*. The creation of the battalion was by no means a gesture of confidence toward Byelorussians, but just the opposite. What Schimana had in mind was the undermining of the BSA project.

Schimana, as well as his superior, HSSPF Ostland Friedrich Jeckeln, was alarmed by what he considered to be the undue independence of the "Self-Defense Corps."[139] The BNS was responsible for mobilizing people into the BSA and supplying it with weapons and clothes. Moreover, the head of the "Byelorussian Self-Aid Organization," Yermačenka, received the official title of Supreme Commandant of the BSA. In 1942, under the patronage of the BNS, special courses for future BSA officers were set up. The Byelorussian language was supposed to be the official language of the *Samaakhova*. All of these tendencies greatly troubled the SS authorities, both in *GK Weißruthenien* and in Ostland at large, although, at least according to Turonak, Kube supported the "Self-Defense" project and even pressed Lohse, the *Reichskommissar für Ostland*, with requests to speed up the supply of armor of the BSA units which had been recruited.[140]

Almost immediately upon entering office, Schimana began to torpedo the whole "Self-Defense" project. Yermačenka, the supreme commandant of the BSA, was summarily dismissed from his post of *Oberkommandant* without any explanation, only a short time after opening the three-week courses for retraining Byelorussian officers of the former Polish army in Minsk on 3 August 1942.[141] When Yury Sakovič, Yermačenka's deputy, turned to the *Generalkommissariat* with a request to create a seal for the Supreme Commandant of BSA, he received a letter from the head of the political department in *GK Weißruthenien* Jurda on 28 August 1942, informing him that "there is no office of Supreme Commandant of Byelorussian *Samaakhova*. With regard to the recruitment of volunteers into the BSA, the chief leadership of BNS is charged with the duty of ensuring that the supreme command is guided by the directives of police institutions. A separate supreme command is hereby rejected."[142]

The German authorities also dissolved the staff of *Samaakhova* and prohibited the use of any military ranks. The commanders were supposed to name only their functions, such as "company commander."[143] Yermačenka, who still remained head of the BNS, was allowed to have a personal advisor for BSA affairs, who was named "the chief military advisor of BSA" (Kušal was appointed), as well as district BSA advisors. The latter were subordinate not only to the local BNS leaders but also to the German district police authorities. According to Kušal's memoirs, quoted by Litvin, the sole function of these advisors was to recruit people for the BSA.[144]

Without completely dissolving the BSA, Schimana began to create new "closed" *schuma* battalions, the first one of which was the 49th battalion, mentioned above. He sought to undermine the status of the *Samaakhova* by calling upon the members of the existing *Samaakhova* units to accept the status of *Schutzmannschaften* under German command. Inevitably, such a step aroused protests from the BNS leadership, who saw in the BSA the seeds of a future Byelorussian national army.[145] Kube, eager to do everything to strengthen his own position, lent an attentive ear to these protests. Therefore, the creation of the 49th *schuma* battalion did not proceed smoothly. Although in his April 1943 report, written more than half a year after the events, Klepsch spoke of an initial "pleasing influx" (*erfreulicher Zustrom*) of volunteers, both Turonak and Litvin—quoting the testimonies of former BNS leaders—showed that young Byelorussians did not hurry to join the newly created battalion.[146] Even Klepsch could not conceal the fact that the initial "success," if success there was, very quickly became an inevitable failure. The initial number of 560 recruited to the 49th battalion quickly dwindled to a mere 180 men, due to the release of those who were physically unfit and through desertions. One may assume that the second factor was more significant than the first as Turonak speaks about "mass desertions" from the battalion.[147] At the end, the number of recruits was enough to man only two of the battalion's companies.[148]

Although the *Samaakhova* was allowed to carry on until 1943, the situation of the majority of its units was sorely lamentable.[149] Whole battalions had to arm themselves; the members of the "Self-Defense" battalion situated in the locality of Rudensk in the Minsk area simply bought all their weapons from German soldiers or acquired them in other ways.[150] Turonak also quotes the testimony of the former BSA commander in the Slonim area, Sergej Khmara, who described the barter system carried out in this area. Thus *Samaakhova* members bought machine guns from German and Italian soldiers who were on leave from the front in exchange for 9 kg of salted beef and 1.5 liters of homemade vodka (*samogon*).[151] The same source relates that "the ordinary automatic weapons were bought even ... from Soviet partisans—a couple of bottles of vodka was paid for them."[152] Although many *Samaakhova* members remained unarmed, dressed in civilian clothes, and wore bast shoes instead of boots, the BNS leadership continued to cherish the illusion of an autonomous Byelorussia with its own army even as late as the beginning of 1943. At a conference held in early March 1943, bringing together district BNS chiefs, military advisors, and members of the Central Council of the "Self-Aid Organization," a special memorandum was worked out that spoke explicitly about Byelorussian autonomy, the creation of a Byelorussian government and a Byelorussian army. The new government was supposed to proclaim the separation of Byelorussia from the Soviet Union and declare war upon the latter. One of the central points of the memorandum was the demand for the creation of Byelorussian national armed forces, a supply of weapons and ammunition, and permission to recruit for this army not only in the Byelorussian territory but also among Byelorussians living abroad. In return, the authors of the note promised to assist the Germans in securing the rear as well as the front and to supply the German forces with all necessary materials and products.[153] The German response to this memorandum, a month after the document was issued, was the release of Yermačenka from his post as well as the renaming of the "Byelorussian People's Self-Aid Organization" as the "Byelorussian Self-Aid Organization," carefully omitting the descriptive word "People's" (see Chapter IV).

At the same time the growing partisan activities required the Germans to reinforce their anti-partisan units. Whereas *Samaakhova* remained largely a stepchild, so to speak, of the German occupation authorities, between the summer and autumn of 1943, the Germans escalated forced mobilization into the local auxiliary police. While at the beginning of the occupation recruitment into the local police proceded almost exclusively on a voluntary basis, the second half of 1942 witnessed a change in this respect. The worsening of the security situation from the German point of view demanded an expansion of the police forces. Yet, after almost one year of occupation, it was clear that the existing methods were inadequate. The local populace began to turn its back on the new regime and was in no hurry to assist the occupiers. Partisan attacks against collaborators did not encourage people to join any of the collaborationist bodies. On 18 August 1942 Hitler issued "War Directive No. 46," which sought to intensify anti-partisan warfare and allowed for the extension of the local auxiliary forces.[154] Although Hitler spoke explicitly about the recruitment of volunteers, it was clear that proceding on a voluntary basis alone would not bring about the desired results, so coercion was widely applied. Martin Dean quotes the postwar testimonies of former local policemen who described the forceful methods of mobilization used: some of the people "were locked up and held until they expressed their agreement to join."[155] In another case, a potential recruit "and his family were threatened by the police chief with a pistol."[156] Given these methods, it is not surprising that the local police increased significantly in the second half of 1942. Dean's data shows that 134 (sixty-four per cent) of the 341 policemen who served in the Mir rayon police from July 1941 until the period shortly after 1 January 1944 joined between July 1942 and June 1943.[157]

This enforced recruitment did not meet with much enthusiasm among the local population, a fact noted with satisfaction by the Byelorussian Staff of the Partisan Movement. A report describing the conference of members of the Confidence Council (*Rada Daveru* or *Kamitet Daveru*), a body created following Kube's personal decision on 27 June 1943 (see Chapter IV), quoted the Slonim *Rayonbürgermeister* who explained that "forced recruitment of civilians into the police for the struggle against partisans [is necessary] since the police is not popular among the populace."[158]

The situation both on the German-Soviet front and in the German rear demanded that certain amendments be made to occupation policies. These included forceful mobilization into the local police forces mentioned above, which apart from being unpopular—a factor that certainly did not particularly trouble the German authorities—did little to solve the growing demand for security troops. Therefore, the acting *Generalkommissar für Weißruthenien*, von Gottberg, after proclaiming the creation of the Byelorussian Central Council on 23 February 1944, also ordered mobilization into the "Byelorussian Home Guard" (*Belaruskaja Krajova Abarona* or BKA).

From the very beginning the German civil authorities' perception of the BKA differed from that of the Byelorussian Central Council (BCR). The latter saw in it the seeds of the future Byelorussian army and a means to enhance its own prestige among the population. The initial public response to Gottberg's order appeared to be quite cautious. The people still remembered the unhappy fate of the *Samaakhova*. To demonstrate the seriousness of the matter this time, a mass meeting was organized in Minsk on 25 February 1944 at which the "deserter," the Red Army Captain Igor Kapor, appeared and proceeded to "reveal Stalin's secret plan" for the extermination of the Byelorussian people: of course, no one bothered to ask how a simple low-ranking officer could know the details of this plan if it was secret.[159] A short time after this gathering, on 6 March 1944, Astroŭski issued an order regarding total mobilization into the BKA, which encompassed all men born between 1908 and 1924. Not all of occupied Byelorussia and not even all of the *GK Weißruthenien* was affected by the BKA draft. According to Astroŭski's order, mobilization was to be carried out in only eight of eleven *Gebietskommissariate*, namely the Minsk area, the city of Minsk, Sluck, Baranaviči, Slonim, Vilejka, Hlybokaje, and Navahrudak. Areas such as Lida, where the population was predominantly Polish and which was a center of Armija Krajowa activities, were excluded from it. To carry out the mobilization in the districts, special officials were appointed, called district BKA heads.[160] In Minsk itself this task was assigned to the deputy presidents of the BCR, Nikolaj Škjaljonak and Yury Sabaleŭski. General supervision of the mobilization effort was assigned to former Polish army officer Major Franz (Francišak) Kušal, who was appointed head of the newly created Main Office of the BKA.[161] On 31 March 1944, this office established a special numbering system for future BKA battalions.[162] Astroŭski's order included a death threat against anyone who tried to avoid recruitment.[163] On 15 April 1944, when the mobilization efforts officially came to an end, anyone who was drafted but failed to appear was to be treated as an "enemy of the fatherland and a deserter."[164]

From the very beginning it was clear that Germans saw the
BKA as anything but a future Byelorussian army. By no means
did Gottberg want a mass army. According to his order of 23
February, only five hundred men were to be mobilized from each
district.[165] Moreover, on 1 March 1944, he presented to OMi a
project designed to create in Byelorussia a so-called "Combat
Group von Gottberg" (*Kampfgruppe von Gottberg*) that would
engage in anti-partisan warfare. It was to be composed of some
20,000 men, and would include all of the auxiliary forces stationed in Byelorussia, including the future units of the BKA.[166]
According to the data presented by Gottberg, it appears he
thought of the Byelorussian forces as a comprising 10,000
men.[167] As was the case with the "Self-Defense," here too Germans were slow to supply the BKA with weapons, ammunition,
and uniforms. The process of equipping the BKA troops with
various items such as bedding and crockery would proceed
through the "Byelorussian Self-Aid Organization" on the basis
of donations from the people.[168] Even as late as June 1944, in his
report to the Second All-Byelorussian Congress, Astroŭski could
not conceal the fact that only some of the BKA soldiers had
received uniforms and been provided with boots.[169] The majority
of weapons came from the local stockpiles and actually consisted
of weapons captured from partisans. In many units there was
one rifle for six or seven men.[170] On 1 April 1944, the commander of the 10th BKA battalion garrisoned in Zaslaŭl, Yanoŭski,
reported the lack of basic supplies such as soap, medicine, and
even beds ("people are sleeping on the floor").[171] On 30 April
1944, Astroŭski and Kušal turned directly to Gottberg, pointing
out the difficult situation in the BKA as a result of the lack of
weapons, clothing, and boots and asked him to issue an order
immediately to remedy this situation.[172]

The BKA mobilization did not proceed smoothly. The Germans in the Bialystok district as well as in Lithuania refused to
dispatch former Polish Army officers and NCOs of Byelorussian
origin to the BKA.[173] In its report about a conference of local officials held in Vilejka on 23 March 1944, partisan intelligence
quoted the president of the BCR, Astroŭski, who complained
that Germans who "ruled at the mobilization commissions ...
caused chaos, liberated [the recruits—L. R.] in return for bribes
etc., and thereby ruined to a certain degree the total mobilization."[174] Here, too, the desire to continue exploiting the local
resources until the very end of the occupation came into conflict
with military needs. Various economic bodies active in occupied

Byelorussia saw the call-up for the Home Guard as a loss of potential labor and did not shrink from actively recruiting people away from BKA service.[175] On 6 May 1944, Kušal issued a letter rejecting a request by the German construction firm "Ziendel und Fohl" to dismiss two of the soldiers from the BKA and to transfer them to the firm.[176] That such a practice was not unusual can be deduced from the order issued by the same Kušal on 12 April 1944 prohibiting the transfer of BKA soldiers to bodies such as Todt Organization (OT), which used the soldiers of the BKA engineering battalion for its works.[177] There were, however, cases in which those responsible for mobilization into the BKA were prepared to take into account German economic interests. On 4 March 1944, Kušal issued an order according to which all those defined during mobilization as politically unreliable were to be dispatched by the local *Rayonbürgermeister* into the district centers, where they were to be placed at the disposal of the local "working office" (*Arbeitsamt*).[178]

One of the main aims of the BKA was to prevent men from joining the partisans as well as to encourage desertions from among the partisans.[179] In reality, however, the partisans who decided to desert and join the BKA were not accepted as equals. The head of the Main Office of the BKA, Kušal, issued an order on 14 March 1944, stating that any partisans who had decided to leave the forest and wanted to join the "Home Guard" were to serve in special units consisting solely of such "deserters." They were also to be under constant control by the SD.[180]

Despite all the difficulties, the Byelorussian population initially reacted to mobilization into the BKA with surprising enthusiasm. The claim of Soviet historiography that "fascist mobilization into the BKA was a failure"[181] does not correspond to reality. Even a conservative historian such as Alexej Solov'ev could not deny the fact that "as a whole, the BCR's mobilization measures for the formation of BKA battalions produced quite good results."[182] In his telegram to Rosenberg on 20 March 1944, Gottberg himself reported that 40,000 had been mobilized, of which 19,000 were actually enlisted in BKA battalions.[183] It is difficult to confirm or deny these data, but Astroŭski repeatedly reported that between eighty-five to one hundred per cent had been mobilized.[184] In his speech before the officials of local self-administration in Vilejka, on 23 March 1944, he also noted that "Germans expected 20% to appear, we [that is the BCR leadership, "Astroŭski's gang" as they were defined in the partisan report—L. R.] expected 50%, but in fact about 85% appeared before the commission."[185]

Even the Germans, who certainly did not want to see a sizable national army, were not able to deny the success of the mobilization campaign. Thus, Werner, the *Gebietskommissar* of Baranaviči, reported as many as 20,000 recruits in his area up to August 1944; at the end of March 1944, the *Gebietskommissar* of Sluck reported 7,000 registered.[186] Only the *Gebietskommissar* of Navahrudak, Gille, defined the mobilization in his area as a failure, but this can be explained by there having been a significantly large Polish element in the population of this area.[187]

As time passed, the initial enthusiasm gave way to disappointment and fairly high rates of desertion; the chief local propagandist in the Baranaviči area, Bedritzki, reported to the area's police commander, Moche, that there were mass desertions of BKA soldiers in the area, while in the battalions stationed in Kleck, Nesviž, Stoŭbcy, and Mir alone the rates of desertion reached thirty-five to forty per cent.[188] This can be attributed mainly to the lack of clothes, boots, and weapons. Nevertheless, the initial zeal for recruitment into the BKA demands an explanation.

The whole range of motives for such enthusiasm is not easy to trace, especially given the progressive barbarization of the German regime. Yet, it is hardly deniable that in 1944 many people in occupied Byelorussia feared Stalin more than they feared Hitler. The legal press reported on the mistrust of the Soviet authorities towards all who remained in the occupied territories.[189] Various newspapers, such as *Belaruskaja Hazeta*, informed their readers about the enormous numbers of victims of the Stalinist terror of the 1930s. The lack of any reliable information resulted in a wave of rumors that spoke of real or imagined atrocities committed by Soviet soldiers in liberated areas.[190] Finally, there were Kapor's stories, mentioned above.

One may also assume that at least some of those who reported for service in the BKA sincerely believed in the slogans about the Byelorussian national army. The recruitment carried out by Byelorussians themselves, combined with the opening of the officers' school in Minsk in June 1944, gave the impression, at least initially, that this time something serious was happening. It should be noted that the Soviet picture of BKA soldiers as a gang of "professional criminals [*sic*] and killers as well as traitors" does not correspond to the actual situation then current. The fact that as many as thirty-nine BKA infantry battalions and six pioneer battalions were created also makes the views of Soviet historians appear unfounded.[191]

Strange Allies: Armija Krajowa and Germans

The growing partisan movement brought about not only an alliance of sorts between the German occupation regime and Byelorussian nationalism, but also another very strange union, namely, between the German authorities and parts of the Polish Armija Krajowa (the Home Army). Polish historians, quite understandably, prefer to remain silent about the contact at the end of the German occupation in Byelorussia between some AK units and Germans. Only Yerzy Turonak dedicates a few pages to the topic in his study on the German occupation of Byelorussia.[192] German historian Bernhard Chiari, in his study *Alltag hinter der Front,* treats the theme of Polish–German relations in Western Byelorussia in his portrayal of the Polish minority in *GK Weißruthenien.*[193] Chiari returned to the theme several years later in an article published in a collection dedicated to various aspects of the Home Army activities.[194] Recently, Byelorussian historian Alexej Litvin, in his article "Pol'sko-nemeckije Kontakty na Territorii Belarusi i Vilenshchiny v Otrazhenii nemeckikh Dokumentov" (Polish–German contacts in the Byelorussian territory and in the Vilna [Vilnius] area reflected by Germans documents), published a selection of documents from the famous Osoby Arkhiv which sheds light on the subject.[195]

The cooperation between various units of the Armija Krajowa and the German security authorities was a direct outcome of the situation created in Western Byelorussia in the last stages of the occupation, namely, the intensification of conflicts between Polish and Soviet partisans. The Soviets wanted to secure their hold on the territories they had annexed in 1939 as a result of the Molotov-Ribbentrop pact. Toward that end, partisan detachments that had been operating in the eastern part of Byelorussia were transferred to Western Byelorussia, and new partisan units were established.[196] At the same time, the Polish government-in-exile in London wanted to return to the status quo as it was before 1939. In 1943, the Poles began to accelerate the formation of new AK units and to tighten their control over the territories that Poland had lost in September 1939—not only Western Byelorussian and West Ukrainian territories, but also the Vilnius area. The agreement that had existed between

Moscow and the Polish government-in-exile since 1941 did not prevent constant, fierce skirmishes between members of the Armija Krajowa and Soviet partisans. In light of the "peaceful" relations between the Soviet government and the Polish government-in-exile in London, the latter ordered the AK to avoid armed conflicts with Soviets, but mutual attacks continued and even intensified during the summer of 1943.[197] In December 1943, an AK force consisting of 135 soldiers and nine officers was surrounded by Soviet partisans, who disarmed them, and then shot four Polish officers and nineteen soldiers.[198]

In 1943, the Germans decided to exploit the anti-Soviet sentiments of various AK units and their commanders for their own needs. According to Turonak, "At the end of 1943, occupation authorities decided to activate Polish forces for the struggle against the Soviet partisan movement and attract the cooperation of the AK detachments. Therefore, they abandoned their earlier anti-Polish course, which they had adopted in mid-1942."[199] The protocol of a conference held on 8 February 1944 in Vilna for Abwehr officers and the commander of security police in Lithuania Schmitz reveals the main goal of the cooperation between the Germans and the AK. The German authorities intended to supply the Armija Krajowa units with weapons and in return to obtain the AK's cooperation in securing various areas in Western Byelorussia and Lithuania. An additional aim was to ensure the continued economic exploitation of these areas.[200] A supply of weapons indeed proved to be an irresistible incentive to the numerous, relatively poorly armed AK units and their commanders. During the negotiations that took place with the Germans in Stoŭbcy on 4 February 1944, the commander of the Polish "Legion" in the Stoŭbcy area, First Lieutenant Adolf Pilch (nickname "Gura"), reported that around 18,000 cartridges had been received from the SD, and urgently demanded carbines, automatic weapons, 50mm mortars, light AT guns, especially rocket projectors, and more cartridges and hand grenades.[201]

This contact continued on both sides but not without reservations. The Supreme Command of the Home Army in Warsaw and the Polish government-in-exile in London severely condemned any kind of cooperation with the German authorities. On 17 January 1944 the Supreme Commander of the AK roundly condemned the acceptance of German weapons by Pilch's unit: "the weapons from the Germans should be taken by force and not accepted as a gift. We are expecting a report of who is guilty and what punishment he received."[202]

The Germans were also somewhat uneasy about an alliance with the people whom they regarded as their "hereditary foe" and against whom they carried out direct repressions during the occupation.[203] After the mysterious death of General Sikorski in the summer of 1943, the Poles turned to the commander of the security police in *Ostland,* Panzinger, with a proposal for negotiations; this was promptly turned down by Himmler, who stated explicitly that "no pact can be concluded with Slavs."[204] Eventually, after it had been established that the Wehrmacht would not carry on negotiations with irregular troops, such as the AK—although Abwehr officers, such as the head of Abwehr III, the counterintelligence unit in Vilna, Major Christiansen, figured quite prominently during the negotiations—the SD men were supposed to play a leading role in the contact with AK units.[205] Actually the question of who should carry out the negotiations on the German side was not clarified until the end. The first contacts with the commander of the Vilna (Vilnius) AK district, which also encompassed the northern areas of Byelorussia, Colonel Alexander Krzyżanowski (nicknamed "Wilk"), were made by the representative of the Vilejka SD office Seidler. At a later stage, negotiations with this Polish commander were supposed to be conducted by the head of the same SD office, an officer named Grave, but ultimately these negotiations were carried out by the head of the Vilna Abwehr, Christiansen.[206] During these negotiations, Germans remained bound to their dogmas and prejudices. They were not sure even about the definition of their negotiating partner. In their internal correspondence, they continued to use "White Polish bands" to describe Home Army units.[207]

Apart from the demands for weapons, the Poles participating in the negotiations also issued political demands, the first of which was the restoration of prewar Poland. One of the most steadfast positions in this respect was adopted by Wilk, who was also one of those most actively engaged in the Polish—German relations. The main political demand of Krzyżanowski, as well as of other AK commanders, was the acknowledgement of the Vilna area as an integral part of Poland.[208]

The result of all of these contacts and negotiations was an uneasy truce between various AK units and the Germans. Despite the prohibition of any contact with Germans issued by the Polish leadership in London and Warsaw, the local Home

Army's commanders continued to receive German weapons. Lieutenant Jusef Świda (nicknamed "Lech"), the commander of the AK Neman group, received five deliveries of weapons between January and March 1944. Both he and Pilch subsequently stated that they had acted with the consent of the commander of the Navahrudak AK district, Colonel Janush Praudzič-Šlyaski.[209] In order to sidestep the prohibitions from London regarding cooperation with the Germans, some ingenious methods were devised. During his negotiations with the Abwehr and the SS men, which took place on 10 and 12 February 1944, Krzyžanowski proposed that the Germans create poorly guarded arsenals, which would be then "attacked" by AK men.[210] It is not known whether the Germans accepted these proposals, but on 26 April 1944 the commander of the Wehrmacht in *GK Weißruthenien* reported thirty-two unprovoked attacks by AK units against the Wehrmacht and Todt organization buildings that had taken place between 5 March and 21 April that year in the Vilna area.[211] Turonak supposes that at least some of these attacks might have been secretly inspired by the Abwehr.[212]

The results of the cooperation between the AK and the German occupation authorities are not easy to evaluate. Gottberg, who supported the idea of using AK units for German security needs, informed the *Ostministerium* on 1 March 1944 that "four weeks ago three big Polish bands came over to our side and at the beginning fought well too."[213] According to AK reports, the Germans, who considered the Soviet partisan movement to be the greatest threat to themselves, were prepared to allow the Polish units a large degree of freedom of action in order to purge various areas of the Soviet partisans. In the *Gebietskommissariat* Lida, the head of the local German civil administration transferred the power in his *Gebietskommissariat* to the Home Army, with the aim of "cleansing" the area from "Bolsheviks."[214] A particularly favorable situation, from the Armija Krajowa's point of view, developed in the Ščuč in district of the same *Gebietskommissariat*. The AK report from the Navahrudak area quoted by Turonak even characterized the district as "a little island of Rzecz Pospolita, in which local German authorities express maximum tolerance and understanding in their relations toward an organized and armed Polish public ... In the whole of Poland there were no such favorable conditions for the creation of an underground army as in the Ščuč in district."[215] In this district, as in others, the AK was allowed to organize regular mobilization for the Home Army, sometimes even with German assistance.[216] In the spring of 1944, Gottberg even allowed mass mobilization in some areas, and in June 1944, the AK membership in the Navahrudak area alone reached 7,700 people.[217] In their public declarations, the Germans appeared to be supporters of Byelorussian nationalism; nevertheless, they were now prepared to close their eyes not only to the attacks against Byelorussian villages in which inhabitants were accused of pro-Soviet sympathies, but also the mobilization of Byelorussians into the AK.[218] (One may assume that in many cases, the mobilization was of an enforced nature. In any case, forty per cent of the 7,700 AK members in the Navahrudak area were Orthodox Byelorussians.)[219]

The German authorities' main interest vis-à-vis the AK was to obtain the Polish units' cooperation in weeding out Soviet partisans; they were, however, cautious not to over-emphasize this cooperation and thus refrained from making any promises. During the negotiations with Wilk, the Germans were opposed to his demand to create a Polish force consisting of eighteen infantry battalions (of eight hundred men each) and twelve cavalry squadrons, on the pretext that

> with such an enormous quantity ... it is impossible to keep the agreement secret and everyone will ask: "How did the Germans come to tolerate such a force at their side?" Further, such a large military force may indeed present a danger. It also would demand to be included in German fighting units. This would require additional liaison officers, staffs and a large apparatus would be necessary. All of this will certainly make the situation more difficult.[220]

Instead, Major Christiansen and other German participants in the negotiations presented Krzyżanowski with what they termed an "immediate aim" and a "long-term aim." The former foresaw the formation of a "Polish fighting group of 2,000–3,000 people [to be employed] only when battles with large Bolshevist units are at hand," while "the long-term aim" envisaged "Polish voluntary corps under German command."[221] Even as the Soviet Army was approaching, the Germans were still seized by an almost paranoid fear of any large military force consisting of "eastern people," which they would be unable to control and which one day might turn its weapons against them.

During the same negotiations the Germans avoided promising anything regarding the status of the Vilna area. Even in matters such as the deportation of Polish labor to Germany, the German negotiators were not ready to make any far-reaching concessions. So when Wilk refused to assist the Germans in the deportation of Poles to the Reich and protested against the methods of workforce recruitment, the Germans proposed that Poles mobilize Polish workers for Germany, and made it clear that "the required quota of workers should be fulfilled under any circumstances."[222]

On the Polish side, too, there was a great deal of uneasiness about cooperating with the Germans, who only a short time before had been considered the mortal enemy. Even the AK units were compelled to acknowledge that this cooperation "throws into confusion the political views of the Polish public and both in propagandistic and political senses can do great harm."[223] At the same time, at least officially, both the Polish government-in-exile in London and the Supreme Command of the Home Army in Warsaw vehemently opposed any cooperation with Germans. At the beginning of 1944, Lieutenant Jusef Świda, one of the first AK commanders to relying German assistance, was withdrawn from the Navahrudak area on direct orders from Warsaw.[224] Yet, it remains somewhat difficult to establish the true position of the Polish leadership regarding the contacts between Armija Krajowa commanders and the Germans. In various documents the Germans hinted that there had been secret attempts by the London government-in-exile to enter into negotiations. Patzinger, the commander of the security police in Ostland, mentioned in his letter to the commander of the security police in Lithuania, Fuchs, that "we once, just at the time of Sikorski's death, already received the Poles' invitation to negotiations."[225] During his negotiations with the Germans, Krzyżanowski also stressed that he "was authorized to carry out these negotiations by his higher institution in Warsaw," apparently referring to the Supreme Command of the AK.[226] Generally speaking, on the basis of the documents available, it is indeed very difficult to clarify this issue. According to Turonak, "Until the end of the occupation the German administration did not cease to flirt with AK members in Byelorussia and Lithuania, despite the noticeable increase of anti-German sabotage actions by the AK."[227] The speedy advance of the Soviet Army finally led to plans to increase cooperation with the Home Army. The Germans used the AK forces in the defense of Vilnius against the Soviet Army; they toyed with the idea of establishing a Polish representation in Lithuania as well as with granting some concessions to the Poles in fields such as education and culture.[228] However, the retreat from Byelorussia put an end to the short German flirtation with Polish nationalism.

"Untermenschen" in SS Uniforms*

During the summer of 1944, as a result of a large-scale Soviet military operation named after the hero of the anti-Napoleonic war of the nineteenth century, General Pjotr Bagration, the German forces left Byelorussia. The *GK Weißruthenien* ceased to exist. Not all those who collaborated with Germans during the occupation were able to leave with them westwards, and of those who could, not all desired to do so. The German retreat from Byelorussia was anything but orderly. In some places the officials of the German civil administration deceived themselves with the illusion that the German forces would hold on somehow, while in others a general panic ensued in the face of the advancing Soviet forces. In his final report, the *Gebietskommissar* of Slonim, Erren, described the atmosphere of panic reigning in Slonim during the last days of the Nazi occupation. He criticized those German officials who instead of organizing the retreat to Germany of war-important goods tried hard to take with them only those goods they had acquired during their stay in office.[229] In Minsk in the summer of 1944, the local *Stadtskommissar*, Johan Ewald Becker, was assured by the military authorities that not only would the German forces maintain their hold of the central front sector, but that the Wehrmacht was at the point of launching a new offensive against Moscow, one that would ultimately bring the Germans to the Urals.[230] Such an "assurance" makes clear the degree to which the German military authorities, both at the front and in the rear, had lost any sense of reality. Apparently, Becker considered the population of Minsk less susceptible to such assurances, and he chose to take various other measures to raise the morale in the city. He organized "voluntary" participation of the population in trench-digging around Minsk—an action which in itself did not support the German assurances about holding on—and in clearing the ruins, and held contests in garden-building and laying out a new cemetery [*sic*].[231]

Although during their retreat from the occupied Soviet territories in the summer of 1944, the Germans planned to leave "scorched earth" and deport masses of able-bodied civilians to work in Germany, the members of the local self-administration and auxiliary police, that is, the active collaborators, who at least theoretically might have been worried about their fate in the face of a return of Soviet rule, were not in a great hurry to leave with the Germans.[232] At the same time, the Germans assigned the highest priority to the "evacuation" of war-important materials and potential workers, and simply abandoned those who had collaborated with them during the occupation period, leaving them to contend with their own fate. For example, after the speedy evacuation from Minsk of the German liaison staff to the BKA, on 27 June 1944, the battalions of the "Byelorussian Home Guard" were guided solely by the decisions of their commanders. According to information provided by Turonak, Gottberg initially intended to issue an order for the general retreat of all BKA units westwards; ultimately, however, the de-mobilization of *Krajova Abarona* units was announced in several places. In the Baranaviči area, for example, the commanders of battalions gave their soldiers a choice: retreat with the Germans or stay at home. At least in one instance, that of the battalion's 700 soldiers, fewer than twenty, mainly NCOs, chose to retreat to the West.[233] A similar situation was reported elsewhere. The *Gebietskommissar* in Baranaviči, Rudolf Werner, reported that only fifty per cent of the peasants from the *Wehrdörfer* chose to leave with the Germans.[234] The *Gebietskommissar* in Navahrudak, Alfred Gille, reported that the total number of people in the city who chose to flee with the Germans amounted to some 5,000 to 6,000.[235] The author of the final report of the local office of "Central Trade Society for the East" (*Zentralhandelsgesellschaft Ost*) in Asipoviči complained that the office could not pay salaries to its local workers for June 1944, since "already on 26 June 1944, the majority of Russian personnel no longer showed up at work."[236]

Many of those who stayed in the territories liberated by the Soviet army were able, at least for the time being, to adjust to the new-old rule despite their past. Some of the former BKA soldiers who did not leave with the Germans joined the Soviet army and continued to fight, this time against the Germans. This should not be considered surprising. The circumstances of the occupation period, perhaps even more than those of the Soviet terror of the 1930s, eroded the distinction between friend and foe. Survival became a significant—if not the chief—motive for joining one side or another. Under the law of the jungle that reigned in the western areas of the Soviet Union in the 1930s and 1940s, especially in those annexed in and after 1939, notions such as "ideals" or "commitment" became mere figures of speech. Turonak, commenting on the former BKA soldiers who joined the Soviet Army, remarks aptly that "such 'commitment' was predetermined not by the population itself but by the ruling authority—it had changed too frequently in the last few years."[237]

For those who left Byelorussia with the Germans, the chapter of collaboration had not yet ended. In the summer of 1944, the remaining BKA and auxiliary police who had exited Byelorussia were concentrated in the territories of Eastern Prussia and in the territories of still-occupied Poland. According to Kušal, the total number of people evacuated in the framework of these units might have reached 10,000.[238] Although the leadership of the BCR, which was evacuated from Byelorussia, wanted to see all of those people organized in some kind of purely national force, such as a Byelorussian Legion that would take part in the war against the Soviets, Himmler, who had the last word in such matters, had his own plans. Already at the end of July 1944, all auxiliary policemen who had left Byelorussia were ordered to gather to the northeast of Warsaw. These units were then united into a Schutzmannschaft-Brigade. The leading role in this was played by SS Sturmbannführer and Police Major Hans Siegling, a former commander of 57th Schutzmannschaft-Battalion and then SS and Police Leader (SSPF) of "White Ruthenia and Pripjat." The newly created Schutzmannschaft-Brigade, named after its commander, Schutzmannschaft-Brigade "Siegling," consisted of four riflemen regiments, one artillery and one cavalry unit.[239]

Shortly after its formation, the Siegling Brigade drew the attention of Heinrich Himmler. After the failed anti-Hitler coup of 20 July 1944, he became the commander of the Replacement Army (*Ersatzheer*) and, as such, was responsible for reinforcing the front with fresh military units. On 31 July 1944, Himmler ordered the transformation of the Schutzmannschaft-Brigade Siegling into the 30th Waffen-Grenadier Division der SS (Russian No. 2).[240] This division was not the first Waffen-SS unit consisting of citizens of the former Soviet Union. On 28 April 1943, the Germans had begun to recruit volunteers into the Ukrainian SS Division "Galicia" (officially named the 14th SS voluntary division "Galicia").[241] In 1943, recruitment began into Latvian and Estonian SS units.[242] The creation of such units stood in blatant contradiction to Himmler's original conceptions of the Waffen-SS and SS at large. For the SS leader, the Waffen-SS were originally shock troops of the Aryan race. Even in 1940, when recruitment into the Waffen-SS was opened to West Europeans, the racial principle remained intact. American historian George Stein, who studied the whole Waffen-SS system in depth, described the recruitment into the first "Germanic" armed SS division, named "Wiking": "Just as King Frederick William of Prussia sent his recruiting officers throughout Europe to hunt for exceptionally tall soldiers for his Potsdam Guards, so Himmler sought recruits from all the Germanic countries for a racial show regiment."[243] In 1941 "Himmler refused to have French and Walloons in the Waffen-SS on the grounds that they were not 'Germanic' peoples."[244]

However, the heavy losses of the Waffen-SS during World War II inevitably led to the softening of a purely racial approach toward the formation of new units. The first blow to the original approach came from Hitler's February 1943 order regarding the creation of a Waffen-SS unit consisting of Moslems from Bosnia-Herzegovina, named later *Handschar.*[245] As previously noted, the same year also marked the recruitment of former Soviet citizens into the Waffen-SS. In mid-1944, when the 30th Division was established, there were already three Baltic divisions: the 15th Waffen-Grenadier Division der SS (Latvian No. 1); the 19th Waffen-Grenadier Division der SS (Latvian No. 2); and the 20th Waffen-Grenadier Division der SS (Estonian No. 1). There was also one Ukrainian division: the 14th Waffen-Grenadier Division der SS (Galician No. 1),[246] and the 29th Waffen-Grenadier Division der SS "RONA" (Russian No. 1).[247] With the creation of a Ukrainian division, there arose "certain inconveniences," since the division consisted of people who only a few years earlier had been defined as "subhuman" (*Untermenschen*) by Nazi propaganda. At the beginning of 1944, Himmler himself was compelled to call on German commanders of the division to demonstrate "comradeship" between Germans and Ukrainians.[248]

The process that led to the formation of 30th Waffen-Grenadier Division coincided with German plans to use General Vlasov, who had been captured as early as July 1942. At first, the idea to use a "Russian" anti-Soviet military force under Vlasov's command fascinated only a small group of officers in the Supreme Command of the Army (OKH), such as Wilfred Strik-Strikfeldt. However, the worsening military situation in which Nazi Germany found itself in 1944 enhanced interest in Vlasov and his plans for creating a Russian "liberation" army within the National Socialist hierarchy. On 16 September 1944, the former Soviet general and former Stalin favorite was received by the head of the SS, Himmler, and this meeting gave momentum to Vlasov's projects. On 14 November 1944, in Prague, Vlasov proclaimed the Manifesto of the "Committee for Liberation of the Peoples of Russia" (*Komitet Osvobozhdenija Narodov Rossii*, KONR). The Manifesto envisaged the building of a new "democratic" Russia after the overthrow of Stalin's regime, and demanded the "ending of the war and conclusion of an honorable peace."[249] It may be that one reason for the Germans' encouragement of Vlasov's movement was their desire to repeat the events of 1918 that had led to the Brest–Litovsk treaty. The KONR was supposed to include representatives of all the nationalities of the former Soviet Union.

The Vlasov projects had adversaries. Foremost among them was Rosenberg, who was still obsessed with "Great Russian imperialism" and saw General Vlasov and his committee as an expression of this "imperialism." In his letter to Lammers, the head of Hitler's chancellery, on 12 December 1944, Rosenberg warned, "Indeed, there is arising a Russian State on German soil ... [Those nationalities which] until now had been separately treated ultimately would be induced ... to see in the Russian General their representative too, and during critical days, such a central Russian organization could produce a number of sabotage acts, perhaps even more than that against the Reich."[250]

The representatives of the various Soviet nationalities who found themselves in the Reich after the retreat from liberated Soviet territories did not hurry to join Vlasov. Many among them, including the "president" of the BCR, Astroŭski, indeed feared that Vlasov had in mind the restoration of the Russian Empire, and all attempts to garner Astroŭski's support for the KONR failed. During a meeting between the BCR "president" and Vlasov, the former allegedly said, "Mr. General Vlasov, our ways are different. You are for a free Russia; I am for a free Byelorussia."[251]

Neither did the nationalists support Vlasov's ideas about the creation of a joint Armed Forces of the Committee for the Liberation of Peoples of Russia (*Vooruzhonnyje Sily Komiteta Osvobozhdenija Narodov Rossii*, VS KONR). BCR leaders insisted on the creation of a separate Byelorussian Legion for an anti-Soviet struggle. It seems that the idea of creating separate military forces for individual nationalities was also supported by the head of the SS main office, Gottlob Berger, who in 1944 was also the head of political department in the "Eastern Ministry."

In May 1944, he entrusted the *Sturmbannführer* of Waffen-SS, Fritz Rudolf Arlt, with the organization of an "eastern volunteers guiding office" (*Freiwilligen-Leitstelle Ost*) at the SS main office. This office, in turn, was supposed to be divided into individual "guiding offices" for various nationalities. The ultimate goal of the new body was the creation of military formations consisting of the "eastern volunteers."[252]

Two factors combined to speed up the decision regarding the formation of the 30th Waffen-Grenadier Division of the SS. The first was the landing of Allied forces in Normandy on 6 June 1944; the second was the pressure exerted by Astroŭski's letter on behalf of the Byelorussian Legion to the general of cavalry, Köstring, who in January 1944 had been appointed general of voluntary formations in the Wehrmacht.[253] But if Astroŭski and other Byelorussian nationalists hoped that this unit would take part in the fight against the Soviet Army, they were very soon disappointed.

The fact that Byelorussians were admitted—albeit *nolens volens*—to the Waffen-SS by no means indicated their equality with the Germans. The first taste of the German attitude to their new "comrades-in-arms" was received by the 30th Division's soldiers during its establishment in Poland. The family members of those enlisted into the division were dispersed and sent to work in Germany.[254] Although on 3 August 1944, the first officer of the division's general staff Hauptsturmführer SS and Hauptmann (Captain) Deutschbein issued a directive about the use of the Nazi salute and of Waffen-SS ranks for non-German members of the division, this did not alleviate the tension between the Germans and non-Germans in the unit.[255] The latter were constantly called "bandits" and "bolshevists," and cases of physical violence were not unknown.[256] Those who in the past had participated in "anti-partisan warfare" in Byelorussia were often used as coachmen and grooms.[257] Little wonder then that as early as the formation phase of the division, in August 1944, desertions became more and more frequent.[258]

Although the 30th Division was officially named Russian, its national composition was quite varied. Serving in the 3rd company of the division's 4th regiment alone were 447 Byelorussians, 53 Russians, 15 Ukrainians, 63 Poles, and even 3 Tartars. Germans, too, were part of the division, not only as officers but also as rank-and file-soldiers.[259] As can be seen from the 4th regiment's "regimental order," the company commanders in the division were mainly German officers who received the "foreign" (*fremdvölkische*) officers as assistants.[260] Although the Poles constituted a high percentage in the division, the suspicious attitude toward them did not waver during the entire period of the division's existence. Such an attitude derived not only from some Polish officers having made contact, during the division's stay in Poland, with Polish Armija Krajowa units, as German researcher Rolf Michaelis maintains, but also from the traditional mistrust, or even hostility, on the part of German authorities toward the Poles, which had already expressed itself in various forms during the German occupation of Byelorussia.[261] In November 1944, when the division had already left Poland and found itself in France, the division's commander Obersturmbannführer *SS* Siegling issued an order demanding that a list of the names of all of the soldiers and NCOs of Polish as well as Byelorussian origin "who registered as Poles" be submitted to him.[262]

The division's supply of weapons, food, and clothing left much to be desired, a situation that persisted during the entire period of the unit's existence. At no point did the division have heavy armor at its disposal. The majority of weapons supplied to the division's soldiers were captured arms. In September 1944, the 2nd company of the 77th division's regiment had at its disposal between 117 and 319 French rifles and only 35 German ones; 119 English and 4 Russian automatic weapons and only 3 of German origin.[263] At the beginning of August 1944, the commander of the 3rd company of the 61st Ukrainian *schuma* "F" battalion, which was a part of the division, reported a lack of 200 sets of underwear, 100 overcoats, and 200 pairs of socks.[264] The division's soldiers were former *schumas,* and upon entering it they continued to perform their duties in *Schutzmannschaften* uniform. The division members merely had black collars with a double cross on the right side, to show they belonged to the 30th Waffen-Grenadier Division.

The poor equipment of the 30th Division and the constant abuse by the German personnel led to uninterrupted waves of desertion by the non-German members of the division, mostly to the Armija Krajowa units. In July and August 1944, the division's commanders at various levels reported numerous cases of desertion of former *schumas* with or without weapons.[265] This defection to the Polish Home Army led to the German military command's decision at the beginning of August 1944 to transfer the division to East Prussia.[266] The division's stay there did not last long, however, as in the course of a few weeks the 30th Divi-

sion was transferred to France to fight the Résistance movement there as well as to cover the retreat of the German 19th
Army from the south of France. This retreat began a couple of
days after the landing of the 7th US Army on southern French
shores, on 15 August 1944 and was accompanied by the attacks
of French partisans on German soldiers, military objects, and
supply lines. The newly appointed German Supreme Commander "West," Walter Model, demanded additional troops to secure
the rear of the 19th Army. Since 30th Waffen-Grenadier Division
der SS consisted of experienced "partisan-hunters," Himmler
ordered the immediate transfer of this division to France.[267] It
was supposed to be deployed in the Pont de Roide and Vesoul
areas.[268] Both for the members of the division, as well as for the
Byelorussian nationalists in Berlin, who hoped to participate in
the fight against the advancing Soviet forces, the transfer of the
division to the West came as an unexpected blow. It also contradicted the oath taken by the division's members in Poland,
which spoke of the "fight against the Bolshevist enemies."[269]
Understandably, the division's morale, which had already suffered during its stay in Poland, sank even lower. On 27 August
1944, merely a couple of days after the arrival in France of the
first parts of the division, the 2nd battalions of both the 1st and
2nd regiments mutinied and killed the German framework personnel, subsequently deserting to the Maquis.[270] The following
day, Model directed a complaint to the SS head office: "[Mem-
bers of] the 30th SS-Panzer-Grenadier Division [*sic*] are deserting in battalions (*battaillonsweise*) to the bands, killing German
officers; completely unreliable. Division should be disarmed.
Immediate shipping off into the Reich for work assignment is
necessary."[271]

This did happen in the middle of September 1944, when the
main bulk of the division was transferred to Alsace, then still
under the control of the Third Reich. Here the division underwent a reformation. All "useless and unreliable elements"
(according to the division's commander, Siegling) were removed
from the division and transferred to the transport commanding
office (*Transportkommandantur*) of Karlsruhe, from where they
were later transferred to the building of the so-called Western
Wall. The remaining 6,200 men were placed in the reorganized
division, which now included division staff; two infantry regiments with three battalions each; a reconnaissance unit with
three cavalry squadrons; an armored infantry (Panzer-
Grenadier) unit with one armored infantry and one armored

scout company; an artillery unit with two batteries of 12.2 cm field howitzers and a throwers' battery; a pioneer company; a mixed intelligence company; one field reserve battalion with one riflemen company and one heavy company; and a logistics service unit.[272] On 19 October 1944 the division was reorganized once again on orders from the SS main leading office. The third infantry regiment was created, while the existing two regiments were reduced to two battalions each. The regiments were also newly numbered, receiving the numbers from 75 to 77 with the designation "Russian 4 to 6" in brackets.[273]

Most of the division's stay in Alsace was dedicated to raising the morale of the troops as well as to turning the division into a more or less combat-worthy unit. On 15 September 1944, the chief of staff of the 3rd battalion of the 1st regiment, Muravjov, issued order No. 1 in Russian, which was intended to improve the morale of the troops and put a stop to the desertions. The order spoke of "our victory" (less than a year before the collapse of the Third Reich) and informed the grenadiers that those who had deserted to the partisans in France had ultimately been transferred to the Soviets.[274] However, as may be deduced from Muravjov's subsequent orders, the morale and discipline in the division remained very low. The widespread drunkenness among the division's soldiers was an especially serious problem, leading to violence against the division's own commanders. An undated order, No. 14, also issued by Muravjov, mentions a case in which two drunken members of the 2nd company of the 1st regiment's 3rd battalion, Cherchin and Polomarenkov, stole weapons and tried to shoot their company commander before they could be disarmed. To prevent such occurrences in the future, Muravjov prohibited in that order the drinking of alcohol in the unit and threatened to send potential offenders to the concentration camps.[275]

To raise and maintain morale and discipline in the division, the "carrot and stick" method was employed. Those grenadiers who excelled in "anti-partisan warfare" during the division's short stay in France received the "Bravery Award for the Representatives of Eastern People" (*Tapferkeitsauszeichnung für Angehörige der Ostvölker*).[276] As for "the agitators," they— officers and NCOs—could expect to be demoted or be sent out on work service or even to concentration camps.[277] Lectures on the current situation delivered by both German and non-German division members were also intended to help raise morale. Given that many grenadiers still had not come to terms with their

transfer to the West, and that they bore no particular grudge
against the Western Allies, these lectures contrived to "reveal
the intimate connection between liberal and Bolshevist concepts
(*Weltanschauung*)," while describing "the appalling" conditions
in the territories liberated by the Allied forces.[278] Notwithstanding the difficult military situation of Germany at this time,
the grenadiers were incessantly barraged with slogans about
Germany's final victory, which would be achieved using the
"wonder weapons" (*Wunderwaffen*).[279]

Despite the "morale-raising" efforts and propaganda, the
morale of the 30th Waffen-Grenadier division remained
extremely low, a situation that even the division's commanding
officers could not conceal. The orders of Muravjov, housed today
in the military archive in Freiburg im Breisgau, Germany, depict
the truly lamentable conditions reigning in the division. The soldiers had no change of underwear and wore filthy, buttonless
clothing. Poor food supplies led to widespread buying, begging,
and stealing of food from the villages surrounding the encamp-
ments; attempts to curtail these occurrences by issuing numerous orders remained futile.[280]

The division also remained inadequately equipped in terms of
weaponry. Although officially it had artillery and armored
infantry units, in reality there were practically no heavy
weapons at its disposal. Formally, this situation was explained as
part of the general problem of shortage of supplies, but one may
assume that the German policy of "maximum collaboration for
a minimum price" as well as their traditional mistrust of "Eastern people" played a significant role.

The 30th Waffen-Grenadier Division der SS remained in
Alsace until the end of October 1944. Their stay was used by the
division's commanders to strengthen the division's combat ability. The lectures mentioned previously were part of the regimen
that included shooting, marching, and reconnaissance exercises.
On 2 October 1944, the 1st and parts of the 4th company of the
1st regiment's 3rd battalion were put on alert, following an
order to eliminate the Allied landing forces that intended to capture the Rhine, Rhone, and Calmar bridges on the
German–Dutch and German–French borders.[281]

On 24 October 1944, the commanders of the German Army
Group "G" operating in southern France recalled the 30th division, as the Germans were in need of any fresh and—to a certain
extent—armed troops. The commanders of the Army Group
asked the Supreme Commander "West" to subordinate the divi-

sion to the Army Group. In mid-November 1944, tension mounted significantly for the German troops in southern France, after the French troops of General Lattre de Tassigny succeeded in advancing in a short time through the Burgundian Gates almost as far as the Swiss border. When the commander of 30th Waffen-Grenadier Division, Siegling, offered his unit to the 19th German Army as support, the commanders of the latter decided to refuse "front-line use (*Fronteinsatz*) of the division that once was removed from combat because of mutiny. Only the division's artillery unit should be allocated to the Belfort area... The mission of the 30th Waffen-Grenadier Division should be ... to maintain the [German lines] in the rear."[282] In other words, the division was to be used solely for defensive duties in the German rear. On 19 November, when French troops reached the Rhine, Himmler allowed the use of the 30th division as a "security force at the Altkirch bolt."[283] Ultimately, the division was subordinated to German LXIIIrd corps. The 76th regiment (Russian No. 5) "occupied the line Dammerkirch-Altkirch-Hirtzbach" whereas the 75th regiment (Russian No. 4) was positioned "along the Rhine-Rhone canal between Montreux Chateau and Wolfersdorf."[284]

Although Model himself firmly insisted that the division should by no means participate in the offensive activities, the 76th Waffen-Grenadier regiment did take part in the German counterattack against Friesen-Überstraß.[285] Moreover, the 30th division was ordered by the Supreme Command of Army Group "G" to provide two "hunting teams" (*Jagdkommandos*) daily, armed with bazookas and pressure mines intended to interrupt the Allied supply lines in the Courtelevant-Ferette-Muesprach-Altkirch area.[286] The 30th Waffen-Grenadier Division also took part in the attack of 22 November 1944, headed by the combat group (*Kampfgruppe*) of Artillery General Loch, which proceeded from the area west of Altkirch towards the southwest. In the course of this attack, forty-one tanks of the French 1st armored division were destroyed, six of them by the soldiers of the 30th Division. The war diary of Supreme Command "West" even includes praise for the "bravery and steadfastness" of the soldiers of the 30th Waffen-Grenadier Division of the SS. But on 23 November 1944, the French counterattacked and pushed parts of the division back.[287]

The fact that the division members were forced to confront the French tanks and heavy artillery armed with only carbines, machine guns, bazookas, and no more than five 12.2 cm field howitzers significantly diminished the grenadiers' morale. Little wonder that already on 26 November the war diary of the German 19th Army reported that panic reigned among the soldiers of the 30th Division: "As soon as the tanks appear, the Russians abandon their positions without firing a single shot, and part of them [even] begin to fight against us."[288] After days of heavy fighting, even Siegling came to the conclusion that his division "is not capable of action anymore."[289] The division was transferred back to Germany, where it was disbanded on 31 December 1944. Some of the grenadiers were distributed among other troops, while the remaining Byelorussian grenadiers and German framework personnel were formed into a new unit, named Waffen-Grenadier Brigade der SS (Byelorussian No. 1), consisting of one infantry regiment, one reconaissance squadron, one armored and one field reserve company.[290] The brigade never saw action and remained, in the words of Turonak, merely a "paper unit."[291] The renaming of the brigade took place on 9 March 1945, but very soon after, by the beginning of April, it had already been disbanded.[292] Parts of the division still remained at the Grafenwöhr training camp in Wurttemberg, when it succumbed to units of the Third US Army. The former Waffen-Grenadiers were transferred to the POW camp near Regensburg in Bavaria. Since many of them were born in Western Byelorussia, which up to September 1939 had belonged to Poland, they posed as Poles to avoid extradition to the Soviet Union. After staying in Displaced Person's camps, many of them managed to escape to Western countries, where they were able to profit from the Cold War.[293]

After the war many of the soldiers of the 30th Waffen-Grenadier Division der SS found refuge in Western countries and were compelled to conceal the fact that they had once fought against the armies of those countries that now provided them with asylum. The skewed views of these postwar émigrés eventually found their way into historical research; so if the historical reports mentioned the division at all, they often downplayed its role in the fighting on the Western Front. Studies conducted in the 1990s and the first decade of the twenty-first century reflected a similar viewpoint. Turonak, quoted frequently throughout this work, while speaking about the 30th Division in France, mentions only the high rate of desertion among its soldiers, but says nothing about the fighting.[294] Martin Dean, whose study appeared in 2000, mentions the participation of the unit in fights against the Western Allies, but stresses the fact that the majority of soldiers fought without much enthusiasm and used the first opportunity to surrender.[295] In light of the information provided above, such views should be corrected. The 30th Waffen-Grenadier Division der SS (Russian No. 2), despite its poor appearance and short existence, was a fighting unit and did take part in the actions on the Western Front. Apparently, beyond the caution exercised by postwar émigrés, researchers were additionally confused by the frequent renamings and reorganizations of this unit.

The issue of military collaboration serves as a good example of the German vacillation between racial dogmatism and the demands of reality. While requiring some form of collaboration from the local population in the face of the growing resistance movement, the occupying authorities were not prepared to invest heavily in this collaboration, either politically or materially. As was the case with other forms of collaboration treated in this book, the various auxiliary military or paramilitary bodies very often became toys in the hands of the occupiers as they struggled to take over the "Eastern territories." Even though the Byelorussians, together with other representatives of *Ostvölker,* were allowed in the ranks of Waffen-SS towards the end of the war, this hardly changed the attitude of the German authorities towards these peoples. On the contrary, from beginning to end, their approach was based above all upon the *Herrenvolk* vs. *Untermenschen* principle. In this respect, the new Waffen-SS recruits were by no means seen as "comrades-in-arms," but rather as part of the human defenses of the crumbling Third Reich.

Notes

This section was published in somewhat altered form in the *Journal of Slavic Military Studies*. See L. Rein, *"Untermenschen* in SS Uniforms: 30th Waffen-Grenadier Division of Waffen SS," *Journal of Slavic Military Studies* 20 (April 2007): 329–45.

1. "Aktenvermerk vom 16. Juli 1941 über eine Besprechung Hitlers mit Rosenberg, Lammers, Keitel und Göring," Document 221-L, IMT, 38:88.
2. Picker, *Zastol'nye Razgovory Gitlera,* 199–200.
3. ROVS was created as early as September 1924 by Russian émigrés, veterans of General Wrangel's Army and members of other organizations, who found themselves in the West after the Bolshevist revolution and Russian civil war. *Soyuz* had its own military units, which were dispersed into several sections. The first included France with colonies, Italy, Czechoslovakia,

Poland, Denmark, Finland, and Egypt; the second Germany, Hungary, Austria, Danzig, Lithuania, Latvia, and Estonia; the third, Bulgaria and
Turkey; the fourth, Yugoslavia, Romania, and Greece; and the fifth, Belgium and Luxembourg. There were also one Far Eastern and two North
American sections. In all, ROVS included more than 100,000 men. See
Litvin, "Belorusskaja Krajovaja Oborona," in Litvin, *Akupacyja Belarusi*,
163–64.

4. Streit, *Keine Kameraden*, 83.
5. Ibid.; Reitlinger, *House Built on Sand*, 98–127.
6. See, for example, E. Manstein, *Uterjannye Pobedy*, transl. by V. Goncharov
   et al. (Moscow and St. Petersburg, 1999), 183f.
7. Gerlach, *Kalkulierte Morde*, 130.
8. Quoted ibid., 130n. According to Wilfried Strik-Strikfeldt, who initially
   served as translator on Bock's staff and later found his way into the FHO
   department of OKH (see below), as early as October 1941, the losses of the
   Army Group Center amounted to 18%–20%. See Strik-Strikfeldt, *Gegen
   Stalin und Hitler*, 42.
9. Thus, according to Omer Bartov, "During the first six months of the campaign ["Barbarossa"–L. R.], the *Ostheer* [the army fighting at the eastern
   front—L. R.] sustained close to 750,000 casualties, rising to over a million,
   or a third of the entire army in the East, by late March 1942." See Omer
   Bartov, *Hitler's Army* (New York and Oxford, 1991), 38–39.
10. Ibid., 23–24.
11. Thorwald, *Die Illusion*, 60. About Gehlen himself, see E. H. Cookridge,
    Gehlen. Spy of the Century, London 1972.
12. Wladyslaw Anders and Antonio Munoz, "Russian Volunteers in the Ger-
    man Wehrmacht in WWII," http://www.feldgrau.com/rvol.html.
13. See David Littlejohn, *Patriotic Traitors*, 297.
14. Ibid.; Fisher, *Soviet Opposition to Stalin*, 45; Joachim Hoffmann, *Die Ostle-
    gionen 1941–1943* (Freiburg, 1981), 11. In his memoirs Gehlen speaks
    about 700,000 to one million volunteers in the summer of 1942. See Rein-
    hard Gehlen, *Sluzhba*, transl. by V. Chernyavskij and Yu. Chuprov (Moscow,
    1997), 82. At the same time, Bartov, in his *Hitler's Army*, estimates the
    maximum number of *Hiwis* as 320,000. See Bartov, *Hitler's Army*, 44–45.
15. According to Schenckendorff's letter from October 1941, the OD was
    defined as the "organ of the SD." This letter foresaw the formation of the
    OD initially by the SD (that is *Einsatzgruppen*) or, if that was not possible,
    by the *Feld-* or *Ortskommandantur*, eventually also by the local *Bürger-
    meister*. See "Schreiben des Befehlshabers des rückw. Heeresgebietes Mitte
    betreffend Hilfsmannschaften, 30.10.41," BA-MA RH 23/126.
16. See Dean, *Collaboration in the Holocaust*, 65.
17. See, for example, *Belaruskaja Hazeta*, 15 February 1942, 4; 17 June 1942,
    4, both in YVA C-762.
18. "Trial of the War Crimes committed at Byelorussian territory, 1946-Inter-
    rogation of Hauptmann (Captain) Moll, former *Ortskommandant* in Pariči,
    24.01.46," YVA M 41/278II (National Archive, Minsk, NARB, 4-29-113).
19. "Vom Ordnungsdienst zum Schutzmannschaft," *Minsker Zeitung* (MZ), 26
    June 1942, BA R 90/107.
20. Specifically, it was lowered to 380 men. This occurred upon the arrival of
    the *schupo*-commando in the city, which was supposed to assume control
    over the local OD unit. See "Oberst Klepsch über die Schutzmannschaften:

Protokoll über die Tagung der GKW Funktionären, 8.4–10.4.43" (hereafter, Klepsch's report), BA R 93/20, 147ff.

21. Here too, there is a contradiction between the MZ article and Klepsch's report. The article refers to 8 September 1941 as the date of the *schupo*'s arrival, while according to Klepsch it was 1 October. See notes 19, 20.

22. "Abschlußbericht über die Tätigkeit der Militärverwaltung im Operationsgebiet des Ostens," 64, BA-MA RH 22/215.

23. "Dienstvorschrift für die Ordnungsdienst, o. D.," BA-MA RH 22/225.

24. See Chiari, *Alltag hinter der Front*, 163.

25. Dean, *Collaboration in the Holocaust*, 60.

26. "Schreiben des Leiters der Baranowitsche Propagandisten Bedritzkis an Propaganda-Referenten Lauch, 29.9.43," BA R 90/158.

27. "Abschlußbericht über die Tätigkeit der Militärverwaltung," 56.

28. Ibid.

29. "The partisan intelligence report regarding the situation in Dzerzhinsk rayon, 15.12.42," YVA M 41/128 (CGAOR RB, 3500-4-245).

30. "Vospominanija Vracha Cecilii Mikhajlovny Shapiro," in Arad, *Neizvestnaja Chornaja Kniga*, 255.

31. Romanovsky, "Kholokost v Vostochnoj Belorussii," 62.

32. See Dean, *Collaboration in the Holocaust*, 75.

33. Ibid., 74.

34. YVA JM/2000 (original-GARF 7021-82-3).

35. See Dean, "Polen in der einheimischen Hilfspolizei," in Chiari, *Die polnische Heimatarmee*, 359–60.

36. Quoted in Dean, *Collaboration in the Holocaust*, 67.

37. Chiari, *Alltag hinter der Front*, 171–72.

38. Ibid., 172.

39. See Büchler, "Local Police Force Participation," 81.

40. Ibid., 86.

41. Ibid.

42. See Ibid., 87. Apart from Klepsch, the following held this post from September 1941 on: Major of Police (*Major der Polizei*) Sokolowski, Major-General of Police (*General Major der Polizei*) Eberhard Herf (from October 1941), Colonel of Police (*Oberst der Polizei*) Erik von Heimburg (from March 1942), and Wilhelm Kurth (apparently Klepsch's successor). See Gerlach, *Kalkulierte Morde*, 190.

43. "Tätigkeitsbericht der Abt. Ia bei den Kommandierenden General der Sicherungstruppen und Befehlshaber im Heeresgebiet Mitte für Monat Mai 1942, 10.6.42," BA-MA RH 22/231. "Abschlußbericht über die Tätigkeit der Militärverwaltung," 64–65.

44. Ibid., 65

45. Ibid.

46. Ibid., 66. See also "Schreiben Abt. Ia/VII bei dem Kommandierenden General der Sicherheitstruppen und Befehlshaber in Heeresgebiet Mitte betreffend Einsatzes des OD und sein weiterer Ausbau," BA-MA RH 22/233, 20.

47. This post was occupied by Hennig von Treskow, one of the active participants of the 20 July plot.

48. BA-MA RH 22/233, 20.

49. "Abschlußbericht über die Tätigkeit der Militärverwaltung," 66.

50. "Gliederung des Ordnungsdienstes. Anlage zu Befh. H. Geb. Mitte Ia v. 8.7.42," BA-MA RH 22/233, 21.

51. Büchler, "Local Police Force Participation in the Extermination of Jews," 89.

52. Gerlach erroneously interpreted the term *Land-Schutzmannschaften* from Klepsch's report quoted above as meaning all *Schutzmannschaften* stationed in *GKW*. See Gerlach, *Kalkulierte Morde*, 204. These numbers are taken from Klepsch's report, 148, 151.

53. "Bericht des Beauftragter d. Reichsm. f. d. bes. Ostgebiete b. Kommand. General d. Sich.-Tr. u. Befh. i. H. G. Mitte Major O. W. Müller an das Reichsministerium für die besetzten Ostgebiete, Hauptabteilung I, 8.10.42," BA R 6/76, Mikrofiche 1. Gerlach, *Kalkulierte Morde*, 204.

54. Ibid.

55. See Klepsch's report, 148.

56. Ibid., 151.

57. "Schreiben der Kommandeur der Ordnungspolizei beim SS- u. Polizeiführer Weißruthenien an den Kommandeur der Gendarmerie Weißruthenien, 28.5.43," BA R 93/7, l. 6, See also "Hauptmann Moll's interrogation," see above note 18.

58. Klepsch's report, 150.

59. "Data about the enemy in Minsk and the Minsk oblast on 21.10.42, December 1942" (Russian), YVA M 41/2446, 20.

60. Chiari, *Alltag hinter der Front*, 164.

61. Ibid.

62. Cooper, *Nazi War against Soviet Partisans*, 64.

63. In October 1942, German forces reported the capture of weaponry such as numerous AT and AA guns, eight 15.2- and 12.2 cm howitzers, one light tank, and a number of SMGs in the course of operations *Dreieck* and *Viereck*, mentioned in the previous chapter. See "Gefechtsbericht der Gruppe Jollasse," ch. 7 n. 245.

64. Klepsch's report, 154.

65. Ibid., 153.

66. See Chapter III, n.94.

67. "Korpsbefehl Nr. 92 des Befehlshabers des rückw. Heeresgebietes Mitte, 18.2.42," BA-MA RH 22/230. "Einsatz von Ukrainern und OD-Leute: Merkblatt Schenckendorffs für Streckensicherung und Bahnschutz, 19.10.42," BA-MA RH 22/233.

68. Thus, in the Borisov area in 1942, the villages were forced to allocate between 0.5 and 1 hectare of rye fields, 0.10 to 0.5 hectare of spring crop fields, and 1 to 2.5 hectares of hay fields for the support of policemen, officials of the local administration, and local agronomists. See "Klimkovič's testimony," Chapter III, n.118.

69. Klepsch's report, 147.

70. See, for example, "Bericht des Gebietskommissars Baranowitsche über die Auflockerungsmassnahmen in Baranowitsche, 11.7.44," BA R 93/13.

71. "Bericht des Gebietskommissars Sluzk Carl während der Tagung von GKW Funktionäre, April 1943," BA R 93/20, 123.

72. See above and Dean, *Collaboration in the Holocaust*, 68.

73. Büchler, "Local Police Force Participation in the Extermination of Jews," 89. Dean, *Collaboration in the Holocaust*, 68.

74. Klepsch's report, 154; Büchler, "Local Police Force Participation in the Extermination of Jews," 89.

75. "Schreiben des Reichsführers SS und Chef der Deutscher Polizei betreffend Abfindung für die Angehörigen der geschlossenen Einheiten der Schutzmannschaft in der Ukraine und in Weißruthenien bezw. in den besetzten altsowjetischen Gebieten, 22.7.43," BA R 2/12147, Mikrofiche 5.
76. "Schreiben Rayon-OD Smolensk an die Feldgend. Truppe 588, 21.7.43," BA-MA RH 23/155.
77. Streit, *Keine Kameraden*, 69–70.
78. It is very difficult to distinguish all the *schuma* units that operated in Byelorussian territory during the occupation period. From various sources we may establish the following units: Muslim SS Regiment; Lithuanians: 3rd, 12th, 15th (*GKW*), 255th (*GKW*, military administration area); Latvians: 15th division, 2nd and 3rd regiments, 15th, 17th, 18th, 24th, 25th, 26th, 208th, 231st, 266th "E," 268th, 271st, 273rd, 276th, 277th, 279th, 280th, 281st, 282nd, 313th, 316th, 317th, 347th, 432nd, 546th, 860th battalions and 1st motorcycle-riflemen company; Estonians: 45th battalion; Ukrainians: 53rd, 56th artillery, 57th, 61st (temporary 102nd), 62nd, 63rd battalions (operating both in civil and in military administration areas); Byelorussians: 46th, 47th, 48th, 49th, 60th, 64th, 65th, 66th, 67th, 69th battalions (all operating solely in *GKW* territory); Caucasians: 70th, 71st battalions; 72nd and 73rd cavalry battalions; Cossacks: 74th battalions. See Klepsch's report, 152; Litvin, "Latyshskije batal'ony," in idem, *Akupacyja Belarusi*, 240; Aantonio J. Munoz, *The Kaminski Brigade* (Bayside, 2000), 35.
79. Klepsch's report, 155.
80. See above, note 75.
81. Ten rubles were worth one RM. "Information about the situation in the temporary occupied territory of Byelorussia, compiled at the Central Committee of Byelorussian Communist Party in Moscow, 22.11.42," YVA M 41/189 (NARB 4-33a-221), 15.
82. As note 75.
83. Ibid.
84. Ibid.
85. "Himmlers Schreiben an die HSSPF Rußland-Nord, Rußland-Mitte, Rußland-Süd betreffend Versorgung der Angehörigen der aus Landeseinwohnern gebildeten Schutzmannschaften in den Generalbezirken Estland, Lettland, Litauen und den besetzten ehem. sowjetischen Gebieten sowie ihrer Hinterblibenen (mit Anlagen), 17.7.42," BA R 90/303.
86. The letter was issued for the HSSPFs in all three Army Groups. The Tartar auxiliary units operated mainly in the Crimean peninsula.
87. That is "local self-administration." See note 85.
88. The definition of the degree of wounds was provided by Appendix E to Himmler's letter, entitled "The Guidelines for Definition of Gravity of Physical Damage." See "Anlage E-Richtlinien für die Bestimmung der Schwere der Körperschäden." The signature is similar to that indicated above, note 85. Actually fourth-degree wounds were not clearly defined, but it was certainly meant to imply heavier damage than blindness or damage to the spinal column, which were defined as third-degree wounds.
89. See above, note 85.
90. The definition of half-orphan is usually a child without a father, while full orphans are those who have lost both parents.
91. See above, note 85.

92. The order itself, unfortunately, has not been found. It was mentioned by Klepsch in the report cited above. See Klepsch's report, 156. See "Schreiben des Ostministeriums betreffend Tapferkeits- und Verdienstauszeichnungen für Angehörige der Ostvölker, 19.04.43," BA R 6/47. German "framework personnel" serving with various "eastern" auxiliary units were also eligible for the "Order for Bravery and Merit." A number of members of the infamous Dirlewanger unit received various degrees of this award. See MacLean, *Cruel Hunters*, 94, 108–9 etc.

93. "Schreiben des Staatsministers und Chefs der Präsidialkanzlei des Führers und Reichskanzlers Dr Meissners an Rosenberg, 3.04.44," BA R 6/47.

94. The document is undated.

95. "Vorschlag Rosenbergs betreffend Aufzeicnung, o. D.," BA R 6/47. In this document Rosenberg merely mentions Hitler's compliance, rather than an explicit order.

96. "Schreiben Oberkommmandos des Heeres betreffend landeseigene Hilfskräfte, 9.2.43," BA R 6/165.

97. Ibid.

98. Chiari, *Alltag hinter der Front*, 167.

99. Tec, *In the Lion's Den*.

100. "Schreiben des RMfdbOs an den OKW betreffend dem Urlaub in das Reich von Angehörigen der fremdvölkischen Freiwilligeneinheiten, o. D.," BA R 6/165, Mikrofiche 2.

101. Herbert, *Fremdarbeiter*, 139.

102. These proceedings were clearly established only at the beginning of 1943 by Gestapo chief Müller. Quoted in Streit, *Keine Kameraden*, 258.

103. See note 100.

104. See, for example, the entry "Kleist" in the recently issued Russian-language encyclopedia "Who was who in the Third Reich." See Konstantin Zalesskij, *Kto byl Kto v Tretjem Rejkhe* (Moscow, 2002), 355–58.

105. "Aufzeichnung Bräutigams bezüglich der Befehl des Oberkommandos des Heeresgruppe 'A' vom 17.2.43, o. D.," BA R6/165, Mikrofiche 1.

106. See Klepsch's report, 157.

107. "Anlage zu Bericht Nr. 21 von 8.10.42 über die militärische, politische und wirtschaftliche Lage in Heeresgebiet Mitte: Verluste während der Partisanenbekämpfung (September 1942)," BA R 6/51, Mikrofiche 4.

108. According to David Littlejohn (*Patriotic Traitors*, 300), Gil was his real name and Rodionov a nom de guerre, while according to Lee Ready (*Forgotten Axis*, 220), it was the opposite.

109. See Steenberg, *Vlasov*, 106.

110. Operation Zeppelin is described in depth in the memoirs of Walter Schellenberg, head of the RSHA's 6th department (foreign intelligence, *Ausland-SD*). See Schellenberg, *The Schellenberg Memoirs*, 308–20.

111. See ibid., 308.

112. Ibid., 293.

113. Steenberg, *Vlasov*, 105–6; Littlejohn, *Patriotic Traitors*, 300.

114. Steenberg, *Vlasov*, 106.

115. Ibid., 106–7.

116. Ibid., 107; Littlejohn, *Patriotic Traitors*, 300.

117. See "Bericht des Gebietskommissars in Wilejka von 12.06.43 betr. landwirtschaftliche Erfassung im Unternehmen 'Cottbus'," BA R 93/7a. According to the data quoted by Gerlach, "Cottbus" claimed 9,796 dead plus

2,000–3,000 killed during the "mine clearing." In addition, 500 "prisoners" were taken and 6,053 people deported to work in Germany. See Gerlach, *Kalkulierte Morde*, 902.

118. Steenberg, *Vlasov*, 107.

119. Ibid., 108–9. Some five hundred men who refused to go over to the partisans succeeded in reaching the German lines. See Littlejohn, *Patriotic Traitors*, 300.

120. Steenberg, *Vlasov*, 109; Littlejohn, *Patriotic Traitors*, 300.

121. Gil was killed by one of the officers who had previously served with him in *Druzhina*. See Steenberg, *Vlasov*, 109–10.

122. "Bericht des Leitenden Feldpolizeidirektors b. d. Sich. Div. 203 betreffend Meuterei der 2. Kom des Batl. Beresina und Ermordung von 3 Angehörigen der GFP Gruppe 707, 29.9.42," BA RH 22/233, 213.

123. "Schreiben des Ia bei dem Kommandierenden General der Sicherungstruppen und Befehlshaber im Heeresgebiet Mitte an Oberkdo. der Heeresgruppe Mitte betreffend die Erfahrungen mit landeseigenen Verbänden, 5.08.42," BA-MA RH 22/233, 68–72, especially 71.

124. "Notizen über Besichtigung des Btls. 'Beresina', 17.7.42," BA-MA RH 22/233, 47.

125. Klüge replaced von Bock at the end of 1941 after the failure of the Moscow offensive. Steenberg, *Vlasov*, 61.

126. They are mentioned in the Ia report by the commander of Rear Area of Army Group Center. See note 123, "Schreiben des Ia bei dem Kommandierenden General der Sicherungstruppen," 69.

127. "Schreiben Abt. Ia bei dem Kommandierenden General der Sicherungstruppen und Befehlshaber im Heeresgebiet Mitte 'Landeseigene Hilfskräfte im Osten,' 2.9.42," BA-MA RH 22/233, 153–55.

128. See all the directives and orders quoted above.

129. It was this company that led the mutiny. "Bericht des Feldpolizeikommissars Pfeiffers (Leitender Feldpolizeidirektoramt b. d. Sich. Div. 203) betreffend Meuterei der 2. Kom des Batl. Beresina, 20.9.42," BA-MA RH 22/233, 213.

130. "Korpsbefehl der Ia bei dem Kommandierenden General der Sicherungstruppen und Befehlshaber im Heeresgebiet Mitte, 27.9.42," ibid., 218. According to this order, the "fighting battalion" *Düna* was subordinated to 201st Security Division; *Dnjepr*, to 203rd Security Division; *Beresina* and *Wolga*, to 286th Security Division; and *Pripjat* (after 15 October 1942), to 221st Security Division.

131. See "Schreiben des Ia bei dem Kommandierenden General der Sicherungstruppen und Befehlshaber im Heeresgebiet Mitte an Obkdo. der Heeresgebiet Mitte betreffend Landeseigene Verbände, 28.9.42," ibid., 224–26.

132. Ibid., 224.

133. "Korpsbefehl der Ia bei dem Kommandierenden General der Sicherungstruppen und Befehlshaber im Heeresgebiet Mitte, 30.9.42," ibid., 227.

134. See note 129, "Bericht des Feldpolizeikommissars Pfeiffers," 219.

135. See note 130, "Korpsbefehl der Ia bei dem Kommandierenden General," 225.

136. Litvin, "Belorusskaja Krajovaja Oborona," 179.

137. Ibid.

138. See Klepsch's report, 149.
139. Up to November 1941, Jeckeln was HSSPF Southern Russia (*Rußland-Süd*) or Ukraine, in which capacity he played a prominent role in the massacre of Kiev Jews in Babij Yar. After his appointment to HSSPF Ostland, he also played a leading part in the genocide of the Jews in the Baltic region. See article "Jeckeln" in the dictionary *Kto byl Kto v Tretjem Rejkhe*. See Zalesskij, *Kto byl Kto*, 289–90.
140. Turonak, *Belarus' pad nyameckaj Akupacyjaj*, 122.
141. These courses encompassed some 80 participants. See "Schreiben des Befehlshabers der Sicherheitspolizei und SD Ostland an dem Reichskommissar für Ostland betreggend Erignismeldungen, 11.8.42," BA R 6/354, Mikrofiche 2.
142. Quoted by Litvin, "Belorusskaja Krajovaja Oborona," 176.
143. Ibid.; Turonak, *Belarus' pad nyameckaj Akupacyjaj*, 122.
144. See Litvin, "Belorusskaja Krajovaja Oborona," 176.
145. Ibid.; Turonak, *Belarus' pad nyameckaj Akupacyjaj*, 122.
146. Klepsch's report, 149. Turonak, *Belarus' pad nyameckaj Akupacyjaj*, 122–23; Litvin, "Belorusskaja Krajovaja Oborona," 177.
147. Turonak, *Belarus' pad nyameckaj Akupacyjaj*, 123. Klepsch's report, 149.
148. Ibid.
149. According to Kušal's memoirs, 20 BSA battalions were recruited in total. Quoted by Litvin, "Belorusskaja Krajovaja Oborona," 176–77; Turonak, *Belarus' pad nyameckaj Akupacyjaj*, 123.
150. According to Kušal's testimony. Quoted in Turonak, *Belarus' pad nyameckaj Akupacyjaj*, 123.
151. Quoted ibid., 123.
152. Ibid.
153. The memorandum is quoted in Litvin, "Belorusskaja Krajovaja Oborona," 179.
154. The English translation of the directive can be found in Cooper, *Nazi War against Soviet Partisans*, 176–78.
155. Dean, *Collaboration in the Holocaust*, 67.
156. Ibid.
157. Ibid.
158. Quoted in Litvin, "Belorusskaja Krajovaja Oborona," 181.
159. According to Kapor, Stalin intended to mobilize all Byelorussian men aged between fifteen and fifty-five into the Soviet Army and to assign them to penal battalions. The rest of the population, chiefly women, were to be resettled in the Ukraine, where they would work on the restoration of the Doneck basin. Children were to be taken away from their mothers, and those up to the age of fourteen were to be sent into the special NKVD children's homes. See "Stalin rottet auch die Weißruthenen aus," *Deutsche Zeitung in Wartegau*, 8 March 1944, BA R 90/89.
160. District BKA heads were as follows: in the Minsk district, Captain Mikhail Pugachjov; in the Navahrudak district, First Lieutenant Barys Rahulja; in the Sluck district, Captain Sciapan Šnek; in the Baranaviči district, Lieutenant Ryhor Zybajla; in the Slonim district, First Lieutenant Iosif Dakinevič; and in the Vilejka district, Lieutenant Jakov Babič. Litvin, "Belorusskaja Krajovaja Oborona," 184.
161. Ibid.
162. Ibid.

163. "Prikaz presidenta Belorusskoj Central'noj Rady R. K. Ostrovskogo o vseobschchej mobilizacii v Belorusskuju Krajovuju Oboronu," printed in Solov'ev, *Belarusskaja Tsentral'naja Rada*, 118–19.

164. Quoted in Litvin, "Belorusskaja Krajovaja Oborona," 184.

165. See ibid., 158.

166. Quoted in Turonak, *Belarus' pad nyameckaj Akupacyjaj*, 180.

167. Ibid.

168. "Prikaz namestnika BCR po Baranovichskomu okrugu o material'nom snabzhenii BKO s uchastiem Belorusskoj Samopomoshchi (BSP), 26.5.44," in Solov'ev, *Belarusskaja Tsentral'naja Rada*, 120–21.

169. Astroŭski, *Druhi Ŭsebelaruski Kangres*, 18.

170. Turonak, *Belarus' pad nyameckaj Akupacyjaj*, 181.

171. Quoted in Litvin, "Belorusskaja Krajovaja Oborona," 185.

172. "Otchyot-pis'mo prezidenta BCR R. K. Ostrovskogo general'nomu kommissaru Belorussii von Gottbergu o rezul'tatax mobilizacii v BKO, 30.4.44," in Solov'ev, *Belarusskaja Tsentral'naja Rada*, 121.

173. "Fernschreiben der Nachrichtensbetriebsstelle der Ordnungspolizei an Ostministerium betreffend weißruthenische Offiziere und Unterführer, 16.4. 44," BA R 6/165, Mikrofiche 2.

174. "Information about the conference carried out by the president BCR Astroŭski in the city Vilejka on 23rd March, 1944" (Russian), YVA, M 41/110 (BMVOV, 20-10a-4), 1-2.

175. See "Schreiben der RMfdbO an dem Leiter der Führungsgruppe P 3 Prof. von Mende betreffend Gründung des Weißruthenisches Zentralrates, 18.5.44," BA R 6/284, Mikrofiche 2.

176. An abridged form of the letter appears in Litvin, "Belorusskaja Krajovaja Oborona," 185–87.

177. The letter is printed ibid., 185, See also Turonak, *Belarus' pad nyameckaj Akupacyjaj*, 181.

178. Quoted in Litvin, "Belorusskaja Krajovaja Oborona," 189.

179. In March 1943, the newspaper leaflet of the propaganda department at *GK Weißruthenien* reported the desertion of two partisan units of about 2,000 people to the BKA in the Sluck area. It is difficult to verify these data. See "Weißruthenien steht auf zum Kampf," *Flügzeitung des Propagandaamtes bei Generalkommissar für Weißruthenien 'Nachrichten für Weißruthenien,'* 30 March 1944," BA R 90/156.

180. "Kušal's letter to the district officers of BKA regarding the treatment of the deserters from partisan detachments, 14.3.44" (translation from Byelorussian), YVA M 41/107, 1.

181. Romanovskij, *Saudzel'niki ? zlachynstvakh*, 160.

182. Solov'ev, *Belarusskaja Tsentral'naja Rada*, 35.

183. "Abschrift des Fernschreibens Generalkommissars für Weißruthenien von Gottberg bezüglich Mobilisierung des weißruthensiches Volkes gegen der Bolschewismus, 20.3.44," BA R 6/27, Mikrofiche 5.

184. "Otchyot-pis'mo prezidenta BCR R. K. Ostrovskogo," see note 172; "Spravazdacha Presidenta BCR praf. R. Astroŭskaha," Astroŭski, *Druhi Ŭsebelaruski Kangres*, 18.

185. See note 174.

186. "Tätigkeits-und Erfahrungsbericht des Gebietskommissars Baranowitsche Werner, 11.8.44," BA R 93/13. "Lagebericht des Gebietskommissars von

Sluzk für die Monate Januar, Februar u. März 1944, 25.3.44," BA R 6/308, Mikrofiche 2.

187. "Tätigkeits- Räumungs- und Erfahrungsbericht des Gebetskommissars für Nowogrodek Gille, 3.08.44," BA R 93/13, 145–48.

188. See "Bedritzkis Schreiben an den Polizeikommandanten d. Gb. Baranow-itsche Major Moche, o. D.," BA R 90/159.

189. See "Praŭda ab partisanskim rukhu," *Belarus na Varce*, No. 7–9 (1944): 12, quoted in Zhumar, *Okkupacionnaja Periodicheskaja Pechat'*, 115.

190. See, for example, Larissa Kotyeva, *Three Worlds of Larissa* (Brunswick, 1993), 127.

191. Romanovskij, *Saudzel'niki ŭ zlachynstvakh*, 160. The complete list of these battalions, with information about their deployment and the names of some of the commanders, can be found in Litvin, "Belorusskaja Krajovaja Oborona," 186–87. See also the document quoted in note 173. See Tur-onak, *Belarus' pad nyameckaj Akupacyjaj*, 181.

192. See ibid., 170–74.

193. Chiari, *Alltag hinter der Front*, 294f.

194. Chiari, "Kriegslist oder Bündnis mit dem Feind? Deutsch-polnische Kon-takte 1943/1944," in Chiari, *Die polnische Heimatarmee*, 497–527.

195. This article was published in the collection *Akupacyja Belarusi*, quoted above. See Litvin, "Pol'sko-nemeckije Kontakty na Territorii Belarusi i Vilenshchiny v Otrazhenii nemeckikh Dokumentov," in idem, *Akupacyja Belarusi*, 130–56.

196. Ibid., 130.

197. The order is mentioned by Chiari, see ibid., 289.

198. The case is quoted by Chiari, *Alltag hinter der Front*, 288–89.

199. Turonak, *Belarus' pad nyameckaj Akupacyjaj*, 170.

200. This and following documents appear in Litvin, "Pol'sko-nemeckije Kon-takty," 133f. Inter alia, the continuation of labor deportation into the Reich and of the "manual and carrier services by the local population" were fore-seen. See ibid., 137.

201. Ibid., 134–36.

202. Quoted ibid., 131.

203. In October 1941 the Wehrmacht commander in *Weißruthenien* Generalma-jor von Bechtolsheim defined the Poles as being "together with Jews and Bolsheviks our worst enemies." See "Lagebericht des Kommandanten in Weißruthenien in der Zeit vom 1.10.41 bis 15.10.41, 19.10.41," YVA M 41/303 (GARB, 651-1-1 [12, 14]). Nechama Tec mentions the arrest and gassing of twenty-five Poles from the Mir region defined by Germans as "intelligentsia," although she does not mention the date of this occurrence. See Tec, *In the Lion's Den*, 98–99.

204. See "The telegram from the commander of the security police in 'Ostland' Patzinger to the commander of security police and SD in Lithuania Fuchs, 16.2.44," printed in Litvin, "Pol'sko-nemeckije Kontakty," 141.

205. See "The report of Schmitz and Christiansen regarding the conference in Wilno, 8.02.44," appearing in Litvin, "Pol'sko-nemeckije Kontakty," 136–38.

206. According to the letter of *BdS* Lithuania Fuchs, Wilk himself refused to enter into negotiations with Grave, since the latter "is known as the enemy of the Poles." "Letter of *BdS* Lithuania Fuchs to RSHA, commander of *BdS Ostland*, *BdS Weißruthenien*, *BdS* General-Government regarding

White Polish bands, 15.2.44," Litvin, "Pol'sko-nemeckije Kontakty," 139–40.
207. Incidentally, the same definition was used also by the Soviets. See almost all the documents quoted in Litvin, "Pol'sko-nemeckije Kontakty," 136ff.
208. See "Attachment of the memorandum of the *BdS* Lithuania to the *BdS Ostland* regarding the White Polish bands," published ibid., 142–49. Vilna, today Vilnius, was captured by the Poles in the 1920s and was made part of Polish territory despite strong protests by Lithuania. The question of Vilna ultimately became the central issue of Lithuanian–Polish relations in the interwar period.
209. See Turonak, *Belarus' pad nyameckaj Akupacyjaj*, 170.
210. These prohibitions were not limited mere threats. Świda was ultimately expelled from the Navahrudak area. See ibid., 170. During the negotiations the German side was represented by Major Christiansen (Abwehr), Captain Eiberg, *Untersturmführer SS* Biebl and translator von Jakobi; the Polish by Krzyżanowski and the commander of 3rd AK brigade Staniewicz (nickname "Zabora"). Litvin, "Pol'sko-nemeckije Kontakty," 146.
211. "Report of the Wehrmacht commander in Byelorussia (*Weißruthenien*) to the intelligence department of the Supreme Command of 'Army Group Center,' regarding the Polish bandit movement, 26.4.44," printed ibid., 152–54.
212. Turonak, *Belarus' pad nyameckaj Akupacyjaj*, 172.
213. Quoted ibid., 171.
214. Ibid., 172.
215. Ibid., 173.
216. According to the same report, the Germans liberated nine people from the Ščučin prison on the condition that they join the AK. Ibid.
217. Ibid.
218. Ibid., 174.
219. Ibid.
220. Litvin, "Pol'sko-nemeckije Kontakty," 144.
221. Ibid.
222. Ibid., 143.
223. Quoted in Turonak, *Belarus' pad nyameckaj Akupacyjaj*, 173.
224. Ibid., 170.
225. See note 204. According to Chiari, Fuchs, then a member of the Gestapo office at Radom, met the commander of the Home Army, General Tadeusz "Bór" Komorowski, between 21 and 22 July 1941, near the Polish city of Józefów near Warsaw. See Chiari, "Kriegslist oder Bündnis mit dem Feind?" in Chiari, *Die polnische Heimatarmee*, 500.
226. See note 206.
227. Turonak, *Belarus' pad nyameckaj Akupacyjaj*, 174.
228. Ibid.
229. See "Ergänzung zum Räumungsbericht des Gebietskommissars Slonim vom 11.7. 44, 2.08.44," BA R 93/13.
230. "Abschlußbericht des Stadtskommissars Minsk über die Räumung der Stadt Minsk, 27.07.44," BA R 93/14.
231. Ibid.
232. See, for example, the Russian translation of "Order No. 609 of commandant's office No. 1901 (Pinsk area) regarding the capture of the civilian population," YVA M 41/100. The order envisaged a mass "evacuation" of able-bodied men and women from Pinsk and the area for work in German

industry and agriculture. Especially harsh measures were envisaged regarding localities situated in the so-called "partisan zones." From there, all able-bodied people were supposed to be evacuated, while families who had few or no members capable of working were not supposed to be evacuated to Germany but put into camps instead. It is highly probable that the latter option meant death.

233. Turonak, *Belarus' pad nyameckaj Akupacyjaj*, 189.
234. "Bericht des Gebietskommissars Baranowitsche Werner über Auflockerungs- und Räumungsmaßnahmen in Baranowitsche, 11.7.44," BA R 93/13.
235. "Abschlußbericht des Gebietskommissars in Nowogrodek Gille, 18.7.44," ibid.
236. "Räumungsbericht der Nebenstelle Osipowitschi, 31.07.44," BA R 33 I/1116.
237. Turonak, *Belarus' pad nyameckaj Akupacyjaj*, 189–90.
238. Quoted in Turonak, *Belarus' pad nyameckaj Akupacyjaj*, 193. Loftus speaks about 20,000 people, all of whom were incorporated into the 30th Waffen-Grenadier Division. See Loftus, *Belarus Secret*, 39.
239. R. Michaelis, *Russen in der Waffen-SS* (Berlin, 2002), 69f.
240. The designation "Division *der SS*" was used for the Waffen-SS units consisting of non-Germans and non-Germanic soldiers. As a rule, the Waffen-SS divisions consisting of the so-called "Reich's Germans" (i.e., Germans coming from Germany proper) were designated as SS Divisions while those consisting of either ethnic Germans or "Germanic" people bore the name SS Volunteers' Divisions (*SS Freiwilligedivisionen*). See Stein, *The Waffen SS* , 181n38.
241. Ibid., 185.
242. Ibid., 174–79.
243. Ibid., 143.
244. Ibid., 179.
245. On the history of this division, see G. Lepre, *Himmler's Bosnian Division. The Waffen-SS Handschar Division 1943–1945* (Atglen, PA, 1997).
246. About this unit, see the new, apologetic studies: M. O. Logusz, *Galician Division* (Atglen, 1997); T. Hunczak, *On the Horns of a Dilemma* (Lanham, 2000).
247. This unit was transformed from the former Waffen-Sturmbrigade (Waffen-Assault Brigade) "RONA" of Bronislav Kaminski (for more on this unit, see Chapter VII).
248. Stein, *Geschichte der Waffen SS*, 167.
249. See Steenberg, *Vlasov*, 158–60.
250. "Rosenbergs Schreiben an Lammers von 12.12.44," BA R 6/492, Mikrofiche 5.
251. Thorwald, *Die Illusion*, 287.
252. Ibid., 234–35.
253. Turonak, *Belarus' pad nyameckaj Akupacyjaj*, 193.
254. "Schreiben des Regimentsführers des Regiment 4 an 30. Waffen-Grenadier Division der SS betr. Vorfälle im letzten Quartierraum und auf dem Marsch 12.08.44," BA-MA RS 3-30/2.
255. Since units of Waffen-SS were field units, their officers had both SS and regular army ranks. "Großbestimmungen und Dienstgradangleichung, ausgegeben bei Hauptsturmführer u. Hptm. Deutschbein, der Erste Generalstabsoffizier der 30. Waffen-Grenadier Division der SS, 3.08.44," BA-MA RS 3-30/2.

256. "Regimentsbefehl Nr. 4 des SS Hauptssturmführers Hauptmann und Regiments Führers an 4. Regiment, 10.8.44," ibid.
257. "Schreiben an die 7., 8. und 9 Kompanien, 14.8.1944," BA-MA RS 3-30/2.
258. "Schreiben des SS-Untersturmführers u. Leutnant Kompanieführer Wüst betreffend flüchtige Waffengrenadiere, 5.08.44"; "Schreiben des Rev.-Hauptmanns und Gerichtsoffiziers bei Abt. III Brigade Siegling an die Regte 1–4., Artillerie-Reiter und Ausbildungsabteilung betreffend Fahndung nach entwichenen Schutzmänner, 30.7.44," BA-MA RS 3-30/2.
259. "SS-Grenadier Adolf Geyers Personalblatt," ibid.
260. "Regiments-Befehl Nr. 5 für Regiment 4 der 30. Waffen-Grenadier-Division der SS, 11.8.44," ibid.
261. Michaelis, *Russen in der Waffen-SS*, 75.
262. "Schreiben des Divisionskommandeur SS-Obersturmbannführer Siegling betreffend fremdvölkische polnischer Volkszugehörigkeit, 17.11.44," BA-MA RS 3-30/3.
263. "Waffenausstattung des Russ. Btl. 654, II/Waffen-Grenadier Rgm. SS 77 (russ. Nr.6), 30. Waff. Gren. Div. d. SS (russ. Nr. 2), 27.9.44," BA-MA RS 3-30/4.
264. "Schreiben des Regimentsführers des Regiment 4 an 30. Waffen-Grenadier Division betr. Vorfälle im letzten Quartierraum und auf dem Marsch, 12.08.44," "Meldung des Kompaniechefs der 3. Kom Ukr. Schutzm. F. Batl. 61," BA-MA RS 3-30/2.
265. "Schreiben des SS-Untersturmführer u. Leutnant Komapnieführer Wüst betreffend flüchtige Waffengrenadiere, 5.08.44"; "Schreiben des Rev.-Hauptmanns und Gerichtsoffiziers bei Abt. III Brigade Siegling an die Regte 1–4., Artillerie-Reiter und Ausbildungsabteilung betreffend Fahndung nach etwichenen Schutzmänner, 30.7.44"; "Schreiben des Kompaniesführers der 12. Komapnie III/Regt. 4 betreffend flüchtige Waffengrenadiere, 29.08.44," all in BA-MA RS 3-30/2.
266. Michaelis, *Russen in der Waffen-SS*, 76.
267. Ibid., 78.
268. See the map ibid., 80; see also "Durchsuchungsbefehl Batl.-Führers III/Regt. 4 an 11., 12. Kompanien und San.-Stelle, 29.8.44," BA-MA RS 3-30/2.
269. The entire text of the oath is quoted by Michaelis, *Russen in der Waffen-SS*, 73.
270. Ibid., 81.
271. Quoted ibid.
272. Ibid., 83.
273. Ibid., 86. Actually, the last reorganization should be dated to the end of September 1944, as shown by the report on the division's weapons equipment. See "Waffenausstattung des Russ. Btl. 654, II/Waffen-Grenadier Rgm. SS 77 (russ. Nr.6), 30. Waff. Gren. Div. d. SS (russ. Nr. 2), 27.9.44," BA-MA RS 3-30/4.
274. "Order no. 1 of Muravjov" (in Russian), BA-MA RS 3-30/8.
275. See "Order no. 14 to the riflemen battalion 'Muravjov' (in Russian), undated," BA-MA RS 3-30/6.
276. "Divisionsbefehl Nr. 9, 4.10.44," BA-MA RS 3-30/7.
277. "Schreiben des Stab. Btl. Kdr. Murawjev betreffend Überführung zum Arbeitseinsatz, 16.10.44," BA-MA RS 3-30/5.

278. "WE-Hinweis Nr. 16. 'Warum bekämpft uns Amerika?' 9.10.44," BA-MA RS 3-30/1. "WE-Hinweis Nr. 7–30. Waffen-Grenadier Division der SS (russ. Nr. 2) 'Warum wir siegen werden', 23.9.44," BA-MA RS 3-30/1.

279. Ibid.

280. See "Orders no.16 (undated), no. 17 (2.11.44), no. 19 (8.11.44), no. 23 (undated) to the riflemen battalion 'Muravjov'," (all in Russian), ibid.

281. "Fighting order no. 1 of commander of the staff battalion 'Muravjov,' 2.10.44" (in Russian), BA-MA RS 3-30/6. The area these units were supposed to hold stretched from the road crossings Duerenzen, Balzen-Heim, Kuen-Heim, to the north up to the Calmar canal, and to the east up to the canals crossing through the Rhine and the Rhone.

282. Quoted in Michaelis, *Russen in der Waffen-SS*, 90.

283. Quoted ibid, 91.

284. Ibid., 92.

285. Ibid.

286. Ibid, 92f.

287. Ibid, 94.

288. Ibid., 95.

289. Ibid.

290. They came mainly to 25th Waffen-Grenadier Division der SS "Hunyadi" (Hungarian No. 1) and 26th Waffen-Grenadier Division der SS "Hungaria" (Hungarian No. 2). The German framework personnel went to the newly formed 38th SS Grenadier Division "Niebelungen". Ibid., 98, A. J. Munoz, *Forgotten Legions* (Boulder, 1991), 278f. Michaelis, *Russen in der Waffen-SS*, 98.

291. Turonak, *Belarus' pad njameckaj Akupacyjaj*, 194.

292. Whereas for Antonio Munoz, the reason for this renaming is unclear, Rolf Michaelis assumes that it was supposed to deceive Allied intelligence. See Munoz, *Forgotten Legions*, 279; Michaelis, *Russen in der Waffen-SS*, 98, 99.

293. See Loftus, *Belarus Secret*.

294. Turonak, *Belarus' pad nyameckaj Akupacyjaj*, 194.

295. Dean, *Collaboration in the Holocaust*, 152–53.

Summary

Collaboration in Byelorussia, as well as in other German-occupied Soviet territories, was hardly a marginal phenomenon. The local self-administration apparatus together with the local auxiliary police—the two most noticeable forms of collaboration and the most important ones for the implementation of occupation policies—encompassed several thousands of people, while the rural *Schutzmannschaften* in *the GK Weißruthenien* alone included nearly 7,000 people. Local collaboration in Byelorussia was therefore an important element in the Nazi occupation policy of the country.

The occupation authorities did not have a set program regarding Byelorussian collaboration; their approach to the matter varied in accordance with the general situation and their immediate needs and interests. In the first weeks of the occupation, when the entire Byelorussian territory was under German military administration, their encouragement of local collaboration, chiefly in the form of "local self-administration" and auxiliary police, was primarily a matter of expedience. The German military, the first to arrive in Byelorussia, was almost totally ignorant of the local state of affairs and in the majority of cases found itself facing some very chaotic conditions resulting from the collapse of the Soviet administrative system. At the same time, the tendency of many Wehrmacht commanders was to stay

as far as possible from local political quarrels and concentrate
solely on fighting. Furthermore, the number of German personnel who arrived in Byelorussia was far too small to effectively
administer a country with a population of more than ten million
people. To all this one must add that *Einsatzgruppe B*, which
was entrusted with the task of killing between half a million
and one million Byelorussian Jews throughout most of the
Byelorussian territory, numbered merely 655 members. Little
wonder, then, that at least some kind of local administrative
apparatus was deemed essential for running the country.

Later, once the civil administration was established in part of
Byelorussia, issues of expedience took second place to the need
to be present since power struggles emerged among the various
occupation bodies. In the territory of *GK Weißruthenien*, at least
up to September 1943, a paramount role in the development of
various collaborationist bodies was played by *Generalkommissar*
Wilhelm Kube. His efforts to secure the establishment of the
Byelorussian Self-Aid Organization and the Self-Defense Corps,
as well as the institution of "men of confidence," were guided
not so much by a real or feigned "Byelorussophilia," but rather
by his obsessive desire to protect his authority from encroach-
ment by outside forces, mainly the SS apparatus. Moreover, the
growth of the partisan movement, especially from the second
half of 1942, compelled the Germans in Byelorussia to seek
approaches and solutions other than the use of sheer brutal
force. Not surprisingly, the term "political warfare" came to
mean prioritizing and encouraging more extensive native participation in the country's administration (although within very
rigid limits). Actually, beginning in 1942, many in the occupation apparatus, both in civilian and even more so in military
administration areas, fixated upon this notion, even though this
policy had nothing to do with the will of leaders such as Hitler,
Rosenberg, or Himmler. This situation, at least at first glance,
reveals a picture that supports those who claim that the Nazi
policies were no more than a collection of local improvisations,
an approach represented by "functionalist" historians (see
below).

In the final stages of the occupation, and with the Soviet
forces drawing near, and an ever-growing partisan movement
inside Byelorussia, the German attitude toward local collaboration once again became a matter of pure expedience. Even
Kube's successor, Curt von Gottberg, who initially looked upon
Byelorussian collaborationism with a great deal of disdain, was

eventually forced to encourage this same move, although he did it largely despite himself and with strong reservations.

The attitude of the Germans towards Byelorussian collaboration and collaborators derived from various factors. Figuring prominently among them were racial prejudices and stereotypes. The Germans came into the Soviet territories quite certain that the "Eastern peoples" were incapable of managing on their own. Moreover, according to the *Lebensraum* ideology which was the cornerstone of the Nazi *Ostpolitik*, the local inhabitants' participation in administering the areas destined for eventual German and Germanic colonization and exploitation was undesirable, to say the least, and a favorable view of such collaboration was considered extremely problematic. Towards the end of the occupation, all of these prejudices were shattered by harsh reality, yet many Nazi functionaries were still unable to shake them off completely.

In reviewing the German attitude towards collaboration in the whole of the Byelorussian territory—both the civil and the military administration areas— three different approaches emerge. The first, as presented above, was represented by the civil authorities, which, formally at least, were subordinate to Rosenberg's "Eastern Ministry." In the territory of *GK Weißruthenien*, the encouragement up to a certain degree of Byelorussian nationalism in general and of Byelorussian collaborationist bodies in particular, was the result not only of Kube's personal ambitions but also of the notion of a *cordon sanitaire*, which was to divide the German Reich from what would be left of Russia (or Muscovy as Rosenberg preferred to call it) after Germany's expected victory. When speaking of the entities that would form this barrier, it is unlikely that Rosenberg was referring to independent states. He undoubtedly shared the typical Nazi views regarding the *Ostvölker*'s lack of administrative skills, as explained earlier. It becomes clear, then, that Rosenberg could only have envisioned the creation of vassal bodies under rigid German patronage. To depict this approach as more or less "liberal" would be incorrect.

A more intransigent approach, based on racist, anti-Slavic dogmatism, was adopted by the SS and Himmler personally. In his capacity as head of both the SS and the police, Himmler exercised supreme authority over the local police units in the occupied territories, including Byelorussia. Guided by his perception of all Slavs as *Untermenschen* (Sub-Humans), the SS functionaries in the field were among those most "consistent" in

applying the *Herrenvolk* vs. *Untermensch* principles to various
local collaborationist bodies.

The third approach was adopted by the military authorities,
especially in the Rear Area of Army Group Center, which encompassed most of Byelorussia as it was prior to September 1939. It
was based primarily on considerations of expediency. Once again,
it must be stressed that it is inaccurate to refer to the "liberalism" of the Wehrmacht, even in comparison to the civil administration or the SS. From the beginning, both officers and
rank-and-file Wehrmacht personnel believed in the dogmas and
prejudices that had existed for generations in German society
regarding the *Ostvölker,* especially the Slavs; they also shared
the plans for colonization and exploitation as depicted by the
Nazi leadership. It is sufficient to recall the memorandum by
Hans von Seeckt, quoted in Chapter III, as well as those by
Schenckendorff, which are also quoted in this work. As demonstrated, the overtones in these written memoranda are reminiscent of those of Hitler's own writings and speeches. It was the
failure of the *Blitzkrieg* strategy, as well as the increase in German losses coupled with a growing resistance in the rear, that led
the more pragmatic among the Wehrmacht commanders to suggest certain amendments to the policies for the "Eastern space."
According to the memoranda written by these commanders, such
changes were to include an enhanced role for the local collaborationist bodies in the administration of occupied Soviet territories.
Such amendments, however, were to be introduced with great
caution, so as not to endanger German economic and geopolitical
interests. In light of this position, it is not surprising that occurrences such as the creation of the Lokot district, towards the end
of 1941, and the introduction of a new level of local self-administration, namely the *Bezirksverwaltung,* in the first half of 1942,
took place within the framework of the military administration.

A consideration of the factors that determined the Germans'
attitude towards Byelorussian collaboration would be incomplete without mentioning dogmatism and racial delusion. This
factor played an especially important role in the civilian administration. As known, the Germans arrived with a body of preset dogmas
and stereotypes regarding the country and its inhabitants. Although
after almost two years of occupation, there were some German functionaries who felt obliged to acknowledge [that Byelorussians] were
"quick on the uptake," the more common view considered Byelorussians to be passive, incapable of building an independent state,
and racially inferior (although Kube liked to talk publicly about

Byelorussians as "blond Arians"). These perceptions still had a decisive affect on Nazis' attitude towards Byelorussian collaboration. They also led German authorities to immediately thwart any hopes of an independent state or strivings for autonomy on the part of Byelorussians.

The anti-Slavist fear of "the Eastern flood," which existed in German society long before Hitler's rise to power,[1] was an ideology common to all occupation bodies at all levels. It was precisely this anti-Slavist approach, coupled with all the anti-Byelorussian stereotypes, that prevented the occupation authorities from considering the local collaborators as true partners; these prejudices also led the Germans to commit acts of brutality in both the civil and military administration areas. Basically, the main differences between the approaches to collaboration lay in the authorities' perception of the need for collaboration. Compared to the die-hard Nazi fanatics, who at least initially believed that they would be able to dispense with collaboration altogether or at most keep it at grassroots level, the more pragmatic leaders, such as Kube and several Wehrmacht commanders, thought it more expedient to pay some attention to national aspirations of the local peoples and to take into consideration a factor such as local collaboration.

Yet, the prevailing dogmatism alone cannot explain the Germans' relationship towards Byelorussian collaboration during the entire period of occupation. Opportunism also played a significant role in the Nazis' dealings with the collaborators. The fact that former communists and Poles, both of whom were officially defined as "hostile elements," were part of various collaborationist bodies such as the local self-administration and the local police, shows that in many cases reality and necessity took precedence over dogmatism. Likewise, the somewhat strange "alliance" between units of the Polish Armija Krajowa and the Germans at the very end of the occupation in 1944 reveals that the occupying authorities were not altogether oblivious to the prevailing situation.

The conflict between reality and dogmatism became increasingly evident in the second half of the occupation and expressed itself in the attitude of Kube's successor, Curt von Gottberg, towards Byelorussian collaboration. Owing to the growth of the partisan movement, Gottberg, an adherent of rigid occupation policies who typically disregarded the interests of the local inhabitants, was forced to encourage the creation of local bodies, such as the Byelorussian Home Guard (BKA) and the Byelorussian Central Council (BCR), whose members tried—albeit with dubious success—to display some degree of independence. Gottberg spared no effort, however, in belittling these bodies and turning them into mere executioners of German demands, demonstrating once again the Nazis' fierce and never-ending conflict between dogmatism and demands of reality. Perhaps the most blatant example of German opportunism was the employment of people with a communist past, especially in the auxiliary police and local self-administration. This step patently disregarded the "Commissar's Order" issued in the wake of Operation Barbarossa, which called for the immediate elimination of all communist functionaries and explicitly banned all former communists and komsomol members from joining any of the collaborationist bodies.

The lack of a unified position that resulted in multiple approaches to collaboration, as well as the rivalries among the various ruling bodies, were symptomatic not only of Nazi occupation policies in Byelorussia, but also of the Third Reich's policies as a whole. Historians adhering to what is known as the functionalist point of view[2] consider these chaotic conditions to be the decisive factor in the progressive radicalization and brutalization of the National-Socialist policies.[3] This administrative chaos certainly left its imprint upon the Nazi policies in Byelorussia in general, and upon the German attitude towards collaboration, in particular.

There was a clear distinction between the public attitude that the Germans displayed towards collaboration and the collaborationists, and the views that were intended "for internal use." Whereas in public declarations, various officials of the Nazi occupation administration proclaimed their sympathy towards Byelorussians in general and collaborators in particular, in different conferences of functionaries as well as in private conversations and in correspondence, the authorities' openly utilitarian and manipulative attitude towards collaboration received full expression. Within their own circles, the Nazis did not conceal the fact that the collaborationist bodies functioned as a mouthpiece for their policies, mere tools for their control and economic exploitation of the country. Outwardly, however, they spared no efforts in containing local collaborationism within well-defined limits. Any sign of independence from any of the various collaborationist bodies was to be suppressed, even if it meant using the most radical means, as exemplified in the case of Yermačenka, the one-time head of the Byelorussian Self-Aid Organization.

The degree of local collaboration in Byelorussia as well as in other occupied countries depended directly on the population's expectations from the occupation in general and from collaboration specifically. The political and material price the Germans were prepared to pay for collaboration was rather limited. Although the occupation authorities were quite interested in at least some form of collaboration to aid them in governing and exploiting Byelorussia, the Germans wanted to pay as little as possible for it, both in terms of political concessions and material compensation. The very idea of any form of political autonomy for Byelorussians, as well as for other *Ostvölker*, was absolute anathema for the Germans. Such an idea simply did not correspond with the *Lebensraum* plans, which envisaged ruthless exploitation and colonization of the "eastern territories." In addition, the Germans were prepared to invest only a very limited amount of resources in local collaboration. The most that local collaborators could hope for was to attain a better supply of food than the rest of the population. Auxiliary policemen participating in dangerous anti-partisan raids were fed promises of future material benefits, which would be delivered "after the war"; in the meantime they had to contend with less than modest salaries and "damage compensations." These, too, were allocated according to racial criteria. The Germans were in no hurry to protect those who chose their side. Whereas the Soviet authorities invested heavily in the partisan movement, those who were supposed to combat this movement were often inadequately supplied for such a task, owing to the Germans' obsessive fear that one day the collaborators would turn the weapons they had received against their occupiers.

In his study dealing with occupation policies in Byelorussia, German historian Christian Gerlach suggested that the chief factor guiding these policies was an economic interest, namely, the desire to exploit the country's resources to the maximum. Gerlach points to "the connections between German economic interests or German economic policy and the German extermination policy as well as other crimes,"[4] and rejects both the thesis about the "pre-eminence of Weltanschauung" in National-Socialist politics as well as the thesis expressed by Polish historian Wacław Długoborski, who claimed that German occupation policies were "senseless, from the economic point of view."[5] One must agree with Christian Gerlach that "it seems to be senseless to perceive and to discuss the ideological and economic motives as mutually exclusive contradictions."[6] Nevertheless, the picture presented in various chapters of this book implies that "Weltanschauung" indeed did take precedence over a well-calculated, economically strategic decision. Undoubtedly, at least in theory, one of the central purposes—if not the main intent—of the entire network of collaborationist bodies was to secure effective control and exploitation of Byelorussia's material and human resources for the German war effort. The question that arises, then, is what did the occupation authorities in fact do to make this apparatus effective and—indeed—was it effective?

An analysis of the way in which the apparatus of collaborationist bodies was manned shows that in practice its efficaciousness as an exploitation device was rather dubious from the start. The first telltale sign was the fact that abstract concepts such as "great activity" and "spiritual mobility" mattered more than professional skills in filling the posts in this administration. Secondly, the policies defined by the authorities of *GK Weißruthenien* as part of the "Byelorussification" of the collaborationist apparatus forced the Jews and the Poles out of various spheres of life. Yet, these were the two groups of people who possessed the professional skills necessary for the economic administration of the country. Even some German functionaries were forced to admit that many anti-Polish and anti-Jewish measures were "counterproductive." Thirdly, the German authorities in Byelorussia, as in other occupied countries such as Lithuania and the Ukraine, made it their priority to curtail any signs of independence or self-initiative by various local bodies, limiting their effectiveness still further.

Notwithstanding, it would appear utterly wrong to present the collaborators as blind pawns of the German occupiers. The German shortage of personnel, together with a lack of an elementary knowledge of the conditions reigning in Byelorussia, led to local bodies becoming important players in virtually every aspect of the occupation. Although the Germans spared no effort in tightening their control over them, their domination of these bodies weakened towards the end of the occupation, when large parts of Byelorussia became inaccessible to them due to the drastic growth of the partisan movement. Even inside the German administration, voices were heard calling for wider power for the local bodies.

One of the central questions in the research of the 1990s dealing with Nazi occupation policies was that of the relationship between decisions and initiatives taken at the local level and those that came from Berlin. The discussion of this issue represents the core of the argument between the "functionalists" and the "intentionalists." The treatment of the theme of collaboration in Byelorussia shows that the creation and promotion of the collaborationist movement as a whole proceeded on a local level and was dictated in the first place by local conditions, even if the actual approach to various collaborationist bodies was strongly permeated by dogmas originating in Berlin. The attitude of people such as Hitler, Göring, and even Rosenberg regarding the very possibility of collaboration on the part of the local populations was skeptical, to say the least. At the same time, the people who manned the occupation apparatus in the field understood very quickly that without a modicum of local collaboration they would be unable to manage the occupied countries or to achieve their war aims. Perhaps the most salient example is the recruitment of the *Hilfswillige* or *Hiwis* by various German troops in the east; at earlier stages of the invasion into the Soviet Union, this had proceeded without the knowledge of Berlin and was even contrary to the will of the Nazi bosses. Only very slowly did the Nazi central authorities come to acknowledge the existence of the wide-scale collaboration movement in the *Ostraum* and its usefulness for the German war effort. For example, Hitler's "War Directive No. 46," which allowed for the extension of the local auxiliary units in the "occupied eastern territories," appeared no earlier than August 1942.

Although from the German point of view, collaboration in Byelorussia was a mere tool in the execution of the occupation policy, in reality those engaged in it were not necessarily ready to play the role of pawns in the hands of the Germans. Collaboration in Byelorussia encompassed people with various motives, who did not always share the Nazis' aim. Apart from the relatively small group of Byelorussian National-Socialists, led by people such as Akinčyc and Kazloŭski, who dreamt of a National-Socialist Byelorussia as part of a Germany-dominated "New Europe," there were others who pursued their own goals by collaborating with the occupying power. On the surface, many collaborationist bodies appeared to be just what the Germans authorities desired: outwardly sharing the slogan of "Byelorussia for Byelorussians" and Rosenberg and Kube's chimeras about a *cordon sanitaire* around Russia, voicing anti-Polish, anti-Russian, anti-Semitic, and anti-communist views and repeatedly praising "victorious Germany and her leader Adolph Hitler." Inwardly, however, many collaborationists were hoping to pursue their own goals, which did not necessarily coincide with Nazi aims.

Among those collaborating with the Germans during the occupation period in Byelorussia, one could find side by side Byelorussians who wanted to resurrect the ill-fated Byelorussian Popular Republic (BNR) and Poles who strove for the status quo ante September 1939. For a time, some people were even able to combine outward collaboration with secret resistance, as did for example Poles, members of Armija Krajowa, or Byelorussians, members of the clandestine Byelorussian Independent Party. As shown in the chapter dealing with the collaboration of the Orthodox Church in Byelorussia, collaboration was not necessarily unlimited and unconditional. In the case of the Church, the readiness to collaborate with the occupation authorities ended—or at least faded—once matters of the Church canon were involved.

Overall, as in other occupied countries, both in the West and in the East, readiness to collaborate with the occupation authorities in Byelorussia was not static and constant, but was influenced both by internal and external factors. So, at the initial stage of occupation, when Germany seemed invincible, it was considered advantageous to side with the Germans rather than resist them. The change of the situation at the front, the inability of German authorities to dam the growing partisan movement, and especially the progressive brutalization of their policies led those who initially had been ready to collaborate or at least to cooperate with the Germans to have second thoughts. Moreover, the fact that collaborationists, especially those serving in the local self-administration, found themselves between a rock and a hard place, i.e., between partisan violence and German pressure, also influenced their readiness to collaborate. The Germans themselves were compelled to acknowledge that as the occupation continued it became increasingly difficult to find people to man the local self-administration, especially at its lowest levels.

It is indeed very difficult to substantiate claims made by former Soviet and some post-Soviet historians stating that from the outset the majority of Byelorussians categorically rejected the very notion of collaborating with the Germans and despised those who did accept this option. Yet, as has been shown throughout this work, the Germans did all they could to make the collaborators quite unpopular. The German authorities did not hesitate in involving local collaborators in all the measures that were associated with the brutal nature of their regime; they also discriminated quite openly between those who collaborated with them and those who did not.

The local collaborators were not necessarily blind tools of the occupation authorities; even so, the importance of the role played by various collaborationist bodies in propagating and implementing occupation policies cannot be denied. The bodies engaged in political collaboration, such as the local self-administration, the Byelorussian Self-Aid Organization (BNS), the Union of Byelorussian Youth, and the Byelorussian Central Council, all of which saw themselves as contributors to the building of a "New Byelorussia," fulfilling an important function in controlling the moods of the local population and in quelling the anti-German attitudes—the anti-partisan struggle was actually the main *raison d'être* of the BCR. They also mobilized local resources, both material and human, for the German war effort. The Orthodox Church was also used for the needs of the Germans, although not all of its exploitative ploys came to fruition. While the Orthodox Church was not opposed to providing the propagandistic cover for various measures by the occupiers, many Orthodox priests were quite reluctant to go along on the question of the Autocephaly of the Byelorussian Church, since such a step contradicted the Church canon. The only body that gave full support to virtually all the measures of the occupation authorities, however unpopular and harsh, was the so-called "legal" press, especially the largest publication, *Belaruskaja Hazeta*, which was controlled by the adherents of Byelorussian National-Socialism. The *BH* became both the loyal mouthpiece of the Germans and the forum for the most radical and chauvinistic elements in Byelorussian society of that period.

As noted above, the elimination of anti-Nazi resistance was the central cause for encouraging collaboration. Ultimately, this struggle developed into the outright purging of all elements that the Germans defined as "undesirable." The long-established traditions of ethnic, social, and political hatred provided fertile soil for collaboration in the persecution of various categories of the population, in the first place the Jews and the communists, as well as the Poles and the *Ortsfremde*.

Local collaborators played an important role in the implementation of the "Final Solution of the Jewish Question" in Byelorussia. This role was prominent at virtually every stage of the extermination process, beginning with the ghettoization and finishing with the misappropriation of the property of the Jews murdered during the massacres. After the war, many of those collaborators who found refuge in the West tried hard to persuade those eager to listen that their participation in anti-Jewish repressions proceeded literally at gunpoint; as shown in the current work, however, in the majority of cases the collaborators demonstrated their eagerness to participate in the persecution of Jews. In some cases the local officials and policemen went beyond what was demanded by the Germans. Even if collabora-tors had the option not to participate in mass murders and to step aside, it was very seldom exercised. On the contrary, in most cases local policemen participated enthusiastically in the massacres, displaying a measure of cruelty that the Germans themselves often found repulsive. From the Nazi point of view, the participation of local people in the persecution of the Jews was important both practically, due to the shortage of German personnel, and propagandistically. Local participation in the hounding of the Jews made it possible for Nazi propaganda to present the anti-Jewish actions as something spontaneous, an expression of the popular will, a sign of an indulgent attitude towards murderous Nazi politics. The cruelty displayed by local policemen during the *Aktionen* was used by Nazi racial ideolo-gists as additional evidence of the "barbaric nature" of the "Eastern people." The active collaboration in the atrocities of the Holocaust can be explained neither by anti-Semitism alone nor by the general difficult conditions created by the occupa-tion; only the integration of both factors creates a more or less comprehensive picture. While it is undeniable that traditional anti-Semitism had a very strong footing in all of the territories that only a quarter of a century before the Nazi invasion had been part of the Russian Empire, the general atomization of society should also be taken into account. The process had begun prior to the German invasion into the Soviet Union, but it intensified significantly during the Nazi occupation. As a result, the desire to survive physically even at the cost of some-one else's life became—arguably—the strongest motive for con-duct during the entire occupation period. To illustrate this point, the image of Byelorussian society as a raft drifting in the stormy waters—a figure used by Bernhard Chiari, who is quoted often in this work—should suffice.

It must also be remembered that the active involvement of local people in the persecution of Jews was not unique to Byelorussia. In all the occupied countries, both in the West and in the East, local collaborators were an important element in the implementation of the "Final Solution." In countries such as France or Holland, however, collaborationists exercised certain reservations in this respect, for example by trying to draw a distinction, at least initially, between "their" Jews and "foreign" Jews. By contrast, such reservations were virtually non-existent in the East.

In conclusion, the analysis of the phenomenon of Byelorussian collaboration ultimately revealed the general nature of the occupation regime in that country, one that was never able to bridge the gap between the *Lebensraum* and racist dogmatism and the demands of the reality of the occupation. The analysis of collaboration also exposed motives for conduct and the reactions of a society that found itself in an extreme, abnormal situation. This book is not intended as either an indictment or an apology. Rather, it attempts to cope with this phenomenon. While its treatment is still quite marginalized in historiography, without directly addressing the phenomenon of collaboration, it would be impossible to create a coherent picture of Byelorussia under Nazi occupation. This work does not bring discussion of the subject to a close; rather, it is intended as a stimulus for further and more detailed research.

Notes

1. See, for example, the recent study by German historian Wolfram Wette, *Die Wehrmacht* (Frankfurt/Main, 2005), esp. 14–25.
2. The argument between historians adhering to the "functionalist" point of view and those representing the "intentionalist" position is discussed by Tim Mason. See T. Mason, "Intention and Explanation: A Current Controversy about the Interpretation of National-Socialism," in *Der 'Führerstaat': Mythos und Realität*, ed. G. Hirschfeld and L. Kettenacker (Stuttgart, 1981), 23–42. It should be noted that today most historians tend to speak more and more about the combination of the institutional chaos and the body of preset ideological dogmas as the factor in Nazi policy making at various levels.
3. Thus, German historian Hans Mommsen introduced the term "cumulative radicalization," speaking in the first place about the development of the Third Reich's anti-Jewish policies. Quoted ibid., p. 24.
4. Gerlach, *Kalkulierte Morde*, 19.
5. Quoted ibid., 1145.
6. Ibid.

APPENDIX:
SS AND MILITARY RANKS

SS	Wehrmacht	US Army
Sturmann	Gefreiter	Private 1st Class
Rottenführer	Obergefreiter	Corporal
Unterscharführer	Unteroffizier	NCO
Scharführer	Unterfeldwebel	Sergeant
Oberscharführer	Feldwebel	1st Sergeant
Untersturmführer	Leutnant	Lieutenant
Obersturmführer	Oberleutnant	1st Lieutenant
Hauptsturmführer	Hauptmann	Captain
Sturmbannführer	Major	Major
Obersturmbannfürer	Obersleutnant	Lt.-Colonel
Standartenführer	Oberst	Colonel
Oberführer	Oberst	
Brigadeführer	Generalmajor	Major General
Gruppenführer	Generalleutnant	Lt.-General
Obergruppenführer	General	General
Oberstgruppenführer	Generaloberst	

GLOSSARY

General terms

Abwehr. The Abwehr was a German intelligence organization from 1921 to 1944. The term Abwehr (German: defense) was used as a concession to Allied demands that Germany's post-World War I intelligence activities be for "defensive" purposes only. After 4 February 1938 it was called the Foreign Affairs/Defense Office of the Armed Forces High Command (German: Amt Ausland/Abwehr im Oberkommando der Wehrmacht).

Despite its name implying counterespionage, the Abwehr was an intelligence-gathering agency and dealt exclusively with human intelligence, especially raw intelligence reports from field agents and other sources. The Chief of the Abwehr reported directly to the German High Command. Intelligence summaries and intelligence dissemination were the prerogative of the Operations Branch (as distinct from the Intelligence Branch), of the *Oberkommando der Wehrmacht* (OKW), and through it to the intelligence-evaluation sections of the army, navy, and air force (*Heer, Kriegsmarine,* and *Luftwaffe,* respectively, in German).

Autocephaly. The independent administration of the local Church in a particular area.

Blut und Boden ("Blubo") (literally "Blood-and-Soil"). Nazi agrarian romanticism.

Einsatzgruppe (literally "Task Force"). Mobile SS and Police squad for the extermination of "German-hostile elements," primarily Jews and Communists, in Protectorate Bohemia and Moravia, in occupied Poland, and in the Soviet territories.

Exarchate. In the Orthodox Church, a district consisting of several dioceses with some degree of independence. The head of the Exarchate is an exarch.

Gauleiter. In Nazi Germany, the head of the *Gau*, the main administrative unit of the Third Reich and simultaneously the regional leader of the National-Socialist party.

Gymnasium. A secondary school in European countries as well as in Russia before the Bolshevist Revolution, providing a general education and preparing pupils for university. The gymnasia were abolished in Soviet Russia after the Bolshevist revolution. From 1989 in the former USSR and then in Russia, the name "gymnasium" designates general education schools which specialize in humanities.

Lebensraum. (literally "living space"). According to Hitler, the area that should secure the Germans "a healthy viable natural relation between the nation's population and growth on the one hand and the quantity and quality of its soil on the other hand."

Metropolitan. in the Roman Catholic, Eastern Orthodox, and Anglican Churches, the head of the ecclesiastical province (subordinate to the *Patriarch*).

Oberkommando des Heeres (OKH). Germany's Army High Command from 1936 to 1945. In theory the *Oberkommando der Wehrmacht* (OKW) commanded the OKH. However, the de facto situation after 1941 was that the OKW directly commanded operations on the Western Front while the OKH commanded the Russian Front.

Oblast. The largest administrative unit inside the Union Republics (or Autonomous Republics) constituting the Soviet Union.

Ordnungsdienst (literally "order service"). (a) auxiliary police unit, mainly in the military administration area; (b) *jüdische Ordnungsdienst*, ghetto police.

Patriarch. The highest rank in the Orthodox Church; in some cases also the head of the *Autocephalous* Church.

Rayon. In the former USSR, an administrative unit below the level of oblast and part of a city with a population above 100,000.

Schutzmannschaft. Auxiliary police unit, mainly in the civil administration area.

Sel'sovet. In the former USSR, the lowest administrative level encompassing several villages.

Völkisch. Racial-nationalist.

Wehrdörfer. Defensive villages.

Wehrmacht (literally "defense force"). The name of the unified armed forces of Germany from 1935 to 1945, it consisted of the Heer (army), the Kriegsmarine (navy) and the Luftwaffe (air force).

BIBLIOGRAPHY

Primary Sources

Unpublished Sources

Archival Collection of the Library for Modern History-Stuttgart, Germany:
N 18 – Private archives of Hermann Stegmaier (*Nachlaß Stegmaier*).
Archives of Simon Wisenthal Center (SWCA)-Jerusalem, Israel:
"CBS: Trial by Insinuations." *Belarus*, May 1982.
"File of Jan Awdziej."
"File of Stanislav Stankevich."
"File of Vitaut Tumash."
Astroŭski, R. ed. *Druhi Ŭsebelaruski Kangres (Second All-Byelorussian Congress)*, 1954.
Bundesarchiv (BA)-Berlin-Lichterfelde:
Microfilm 44 832 "Interrogations by the Office of US Chief of Council for the War Crimes."
R 6 – Reich's Ministry for the Occupied Eastern Territories (*Reichsministerium für die besetzte Ostgebiete*).
R 90 – Reich's Ministry Department for Ostland (*Reichskommissariat für Ostland*).
R 91 Borissow – Area Ministry Department Borisov (*Gebietskommissariat Borissow*).
R 91 Minsk – Area Ministry Department Minsk (*Gebietskommissariat Minsk*).
R 93 – General Ministry Department for "Weißruthenien" (*Generalkommissariat für Weißruthenien*).
Bundesarchiv (BA)-Berlin-Dallwitz-Hoppegarten:
R 33 I, II-Central Trade Society for the East (*Zentralhandelsgesellschaft Ost*).
Bundesarchiv-Militärarchiv(BA-MA)-Freiburg im Breisgau:

RH 19 II-Army Group "Center" (*Heeresgruppe Mitte*).
RH 22-Commander of the Rear Area of Army Group "Center" (*Befehlshaber des rückwärtigen Heeresgebiet Mitte*).
RS 3-30-30th Waffen SS Infantry Division (2nd Russian, 1st Byelorussian) (*30. Waffen-Grenadier-Division der SS*).
Hauptstaatsarchiv Stuttgart (HStAS):
E 40 – Foreign Ministry of Kingdom of Wurttemberg.
Yad Vashem Archives-Jerusalem, Israel:
C 762-*Belaruskaja Hazeta* (issues 1942–1944, photocopy).
M 33-The Soviet National Committee for Research into Nazi Crimes (*ChGK-Chrezvychajnaja Gosudarstvennaja Kommissija po Rassledovaniju Fashistskikh Prestuplenij na Okkupirovannykh Territorijakh Sovetskogo Sojuza*, original-GARF, Moscow).
M 41-Byelorussian Archives (copies; originals are in various archives in Byelorussia).
O 33-Collection of Testimonies of Holocaust Survivors.

Published Sources

Arad, Yitzhak, and Shmuel Spector, eds. *The Einsatzgruppen Reports: Selections from the dispatches of the Nazi Death Squads' campaign against the Jews July 1941–January 1943*. New York, 1989.
Benz, Wolfgang et al., eds. *Einsatz im "Reichskommissariat Ostland:" Dokumente zum Volkermord im Baltikum und in Weissrussland, 1941–1944*. Berlin, 1998.
Der Prozess gegen die Hauptkriegsverbrecher vor dem Internationalen Militärgerichtshof (IMT), vol 38. Nuremberg, 1949.
Gorshenin, K. P. et al., eds. *Niurnbergskij Protsess: Sbornik Materialov*, 2 vols. 3rd ed. Moscow, 1955.
Halder, Franz. "Kriegstagebuch, 30.3.41." *NS-Archiv. Dokumente zum Nationalsozialismus:* http://www.ns-archiv.de/krieg/sowjetunion/halder1941-30-03.shtml.
Heiber, Helmut. "Aus den Akten des Gauleiters Kube," *Vierteljahrshefte für Zeitgeschichte* 1 (1956): 67–92.
Hitler's Table Talk 1941–1944. Translated by N. Cameron and R. H. Stevens. 2nd ed. London, 1973.
Jacobsen, Hans-Adolph, ed. *Kriegstagebuch des Oberkommandos der Wehrmacht (Wehrmachtführungsstab)*. Franfurt/Main, 1965.
Kaden, Helma, et al., eds. *Dokumente des Verbrechens: Aus Akten des Dritten Reiches 1933–1945*, 3 vols. Berlin, 1993.
Kaslas, Bronis J., ed. *The USSR-German Aggression against Lithuania*. New York, 1973.
Klein, Peter, ed. *Die Einsatzgruppen in der besetzten Sowjetunion 1941/1942: Die Tatigkeits- und Lageberichte des Chefs der Sicherheitspolizei und des SD*. Berlin, 1997.
Madajczyk, Czeslaw, ed. *Vom Generalplan Ost zum Generalsiedlungsplan*. Munich, 1994.
Michalka, Wolfgang, ed. *Deutsche Geschichte 1933–1945. Dokumente zur Innen- und Aussenpolitik*. Frankfurt/Main, 1993.
"Minutes of the Wansee Conference." http://www.prorev.com/wannsee.htm.
Moritz, Erhard, ed. *Fall Barbarossa*. Berlin, 1970.

Picker, Henry. *Zastol'nye Razgovory Gitlera.* Translated by I. Rozanov.
Smolensk, 1993. ·
Stalin, Josef. *The Great Patriotic War of the Soviet Union.* New York, 1945.
Reprint of 1969 edition.
"The Nuremberg War Crimes Trials."
http://avalon.law.yale.edu/subject_menus/imt.asp.
*Trial of the Major War Criminals before the International Military Tribunal
(IMT),* Nuremberg 1947–1948.
Zalesskij, A., and A. Azarov, eds. *Dokumenty Oblichajut.* Minsk, 1964.

Secondary Sources

Memoirs, Diaries, Autobiographies, Testimonies

Arad, Yitzhak, ed. *Neizvestnaja Chornaja Kniga: Svidetel'stva Ochevidcev o
Katastrofe Sovetskikh Evreev (1941–1944).* Jerusalem and Moscow,
1993.
Gehlen, Reinhard. *Sluzhba.* Translated by V. Chernyavskij and Yu. Chuprov.
Moscow, 1997.
Hitler, Adolph. *Mein Kampf.* Translated by R. Manheim, 2 vols. Boston and
Cambridge, 1943.
Kleist, Peter. *Zwischen Hitler und Stalin: Aufzeichnungen.* Bonn, 1950.
Kotyeva, Larissa. *Three Worlds of Larissa. A Story of Survival.* Brunswick,
1993.
Lapidus, Albert. "Nas malo ostalos', nam mnogo dostalos'," *Vestnik Online* 2
(313), 22 January 2003.
http://www.vestnik.com/issues/2003/0122/koi/lapidus.htm.
Manstein, Erich. *Uterjannye Pobedy.* Translated by V. Goncharov et al. Moscow
and St. Petersburg, 1999.
Seraphim, Hans-Günther, ed. *Das Politische Tagebuch Alfred Rosenbergs.* Göt-
tingen, Berlin, Frankfurt, 1956.
Schellenberg, Walter. *The Schellenberg Memoirs*, ed. and transl. Louis Hagen.
London, 1956.
_____. *Memuary.* Minsk, 1998.
Slavinas, Alexander. *Gibel Pompeji: Zapiski Ochevidtsa.* Tel Aviv, 1997.
Speer, Albert. *Inside the Third Reich.* Translated by R. and C. Winston. New
York, 1970.
Strik-Strikfeldt, Wilfried. *Gegen Stalin und Hitler: General Wlassow und die
Russische Freiheitsbewegung.* Mainz, 1970.
Warlimont, Walter. *Im Hauptquartier der deutschen Wehrmacht.*
Franfurt/Main, 1962.

The Literature Published before 1945

Borkenau, Franz. *The New German Empire.* Paulton and London, 1939.
Chamberlain, Houston Stewart. *The Foundations of the Nineteenth Century.* 2
vols. Translated by J. Lees. London and New York, 1911.
Engelhardt, Eugen Freiherr von. *Weißruthenien: Volk und Land.* Berlin, 1943.
Lastoŭski, Vaclaŭ. *Karotkaja Historyja Belarusi.* Vilna, 1910. Reprint, Minsk,
1993.

Rauschning, Hermann. *Hitler Speaks: A series of Political Conversations with Adolph Hitler on his real Aims.* London, 1939.
Rosenberg, Alfred. *Der Mythus des 20. Jahrhunderts: Eine Wertung der seelisch-geistigen Gestaltenkämpfe unserer Zeit.* Munich, 1935.
Seraphim, Peter-Heinz. *Das Judentum im osteuropäischen Raum.* Essen, 1938.

The Literature Published after 1945

Adamovich, Ales et al. *Ya iz ognennoj Derevni.* Minsk, 1977.
Alexeev, Vasilij, and Theofanis Stavrou. *The Great Revival: The Russian Church under German Occupation.* Minneapolis, 1976.
Alexiev, Alex. *Soviet Nationalities in German Wartime Strategy, 1941–1945.* Santa Monica, Calif., 1982.
Altman, Ilya. *Zhertvy Nenavisti.* Moscow, 2002.
Anders, Wladyslaw, and Antonio Munoz. "Russian Volunteers in the German Wehrmacht in WWII." http://www.feldgrau.com/rvol.html.
Andreyev, Catherine. *Vlasov and the Russian Liberation Movement: Soviet Reality and Emigré Theories.* Cambridge, UK, 1987.
Arad, Yitzhak. "'The Final Solution in Lithuania' in the Light of German Documentation," *Yad Vashem Studies* 11 (1976): 240.
_____. *Ghetto in Flames: The Struggle and Destruction of the Jews in Vilna in the Holocaust.* Jerusalem, 1980.
_____. "Plunder of Jewish Property in the Nazi-Occupied Areas of the Soviet Union," *Yad Vashem Studies* 29 (2001): 109–48.
Armstrong, John Alexander. *Ukrainian Nationalism.* 2nd ed. New York, 1963.
_____. "Collaborationism in World War II: The Integral Nationalist Variant in Eastern Europe," *Journal of Modern History* 40, no. 3 (1968): 396–410.
Azéma, J. P. *La Collaboration (1940–1944).* Paris, 1975.
Bartov, Omer. *Hitler's Army. Soldiers, Nazis and War in the Third Reich.* New York and Oxford, 1991.
Bauer, Yehuda. "Jewish Baranowicze in the Holocaust." Shoah Resource Center. The International School for Holocaust Studies, Yad Vashem, Israel, http://www.yadvashem.org.il/odot_pdf/Microsoft%20Word%20-%207082.pdf.
Beer, Mathias. "Die Enwicklung der Gaswagen beim Mord an den Juden," *Vierteljahrshefte für Zeitgeschichte* 35 (1987): 403–17.
Bethge, Eberhard. *Dietrich Bonhoffer: Man of Vision, Man of Courage.* Translated by E. Mosbacher et al. New York and London, 1970.
Bojzow, Valentin. "Aspekte der militärischen Kollaboration in der UdSSR von 1941–1944." In *Europa unter Hakenkreuz. Vol 1: Okkupation und Kollaboration,* ed. Werner Röhr. Heidelberg, 1994.
Boltin, Yevgenij et al., eds. *Nemecko-Fashistskij okkupacionnyj Rezhim (1941–1944).* Moscow, 1965.
Botvinnik, Marat. *Pamjatniki Genotsida Evreev Belarusi.* Minsk, 2000.
Browning, Christopher. *Ordinary Men: Reserve Police Battalion 101 and the Final Solution in Poland.* New York, 1992.
_____. *Die Entfesselung der "Endlösung."* Translated by K.-D. Schmidt. Munich, 2003.
_____. *The Origins of the Final Solution. The Evolution of Nazi Jewish Policy, September 1939-March 1942.* Jerusalem, 2004.

Büchler, Yehoshua R. "Local Police Force Participation in the Extermination of Jews in occupied Soviet Territory 1941–1942," *Shvut* 4, no. 20 (1996): 79–99.

Carroll, Wallace. "It takes a Russian to beat a Russian," *Life Magazine* (19 December 1949), 80–88.

Chiari, Bernhard. *Alltag hinter der Front: Besatzung, Kollaboration und Widerstand in Weißrussland 1941–1944.* Düsseldorf, 1998.

———. "Geschichte als Gewalttat. Weißrussland als Kind zweier Weltkriege." In *Erster Weltkrieg. Zweiter Weltkrieg: Ein Vergleich. Krieg, Kriegserlebnis, Kriegserfahrung in Deutschland,* ed. Bruno Thoß and Hans-Erich Volkmann, 615–31. Paderborn, 2002.

———. "Kriegslist oder Bündnis mit dem Feind? Deutsch-polnische Kontakte 1943/1944." In *Die ponische Heimatarmee. Geschichte und Mythos der Armia Krajowa seit dem Zweiten Weltkrieg,* ed. Bernhard Chiari, 497–527. Munich, 2003.

Cholawski, Shalom. *Be-Sufat Ha-Kilayyon: Yahadut Belorussia ha-mizrakhit be-Milkhemet ha-Olam ha-Shniyya* [In the Eye of the Hurricane: The East Byelorussian Jewry during World War II]. Tel Aviv, 1988.

———. *The Jews of Bielorussia during World War II.* Amsterdam, 1998.

Conway, Martin. *Collaboration in Belgium: Leon Degrelle and the Rexist Movement, 1940–1944.* New Haven and London, 1993.

Cookridge, E. H. *Gehlen: Spy of the Century.* 2nd ed. London, 1972.

Cooper, Matthew. *The Nazi War against Soviet Partisans 1941–1944.* New York, 1979.

Cüppers, Martin. *Wegbereiter der Shoah. Die Waffen SS, der Kommandostab Reichsführer SS und die Judenvernichtung 1939-1945.* Darmstadt, 2005.

Dallin, Alexander. *German Rule in Russia, 1941–1945: A Study of Occupation Policies.* 2nd ed. Boulder, Colo., 1981.

Dean, Martin. *Collaboration in the Holocaust: Crimes of the Local Police in Belorussia and Ukraine, 1941–44.* New York, 2000.

———. "Jewish Property Seized in the Occupied Soviet Union in 1941 and 1942: The Records of the *Reichshauptkasse Baustelle,*" *Holocaust and Genocide Studies* 14, no. 1 (Spring 2000), 83-101.

———. "Polen in der einheimischen Hilfspolizei: Ein Aspekt der Besatzungsrealität in den deutsch besetzten ostpolnischen Gebieten." In *Die polnische Heimatarmee: Geschichte und Mythos der Armia Krajowa seit dem Zweiten Weltkrieg,* ed. Bernahrd Chiari, 355–68. Munich, 2003.

Dieckmann, Christoph. "The War and the Killing of Lithuanian Jews." In *National Socialist Extermination Policies: Contemporary German Perspectives and Controversies,* ed. Ulrich Herbert, 240–75. New York and Oxford, 2000.

Diner, Dan. "Beyond the Conceivable: The Judenrat as Borderline Experience." In *Beyond the Conceivable: Studies on Germany, Nazism and the Holocaust,* ed. Dan Diner, 117–29. Berkeley, 2000.

———. *Das Jahrhundert verstehen: Eine universalhistorische Deutung.* 2nd ed. Frankfurt/Main, 2001.

Eichholz, Dietrich. "Wirtschaftskollaboration und 'Ostgesellschaften' in NS-besetzten Ländern." In *Europa unter Hakenkreuz,* Ergänzungsband 1, ed. W. Röhr, 433–60. Berlin and Heidelberg, 1994.

Even-Shoshan, Shlomo, ed. *Minsk: Ir ve-Em* [Minsk. City and Mother], The Minsk Community in Israel, 2 vols. Tel-Aviv, 1988.

Fireside, Harvey. *Icon and Swastika: The Russian Orthodox Church under Nazi and Soviet Control.* Cambridge, Mass., 1971.

Fisher, George. *Soviet Opposition to Stalin: A Case Study in World War II.* Cambridge, Mass., 1952.

Gerlach, Christian. *Krieg, Ernährung, Völkermord: Forschungen zur deutschen Vernichtungspolitik im Zweiten Weltkrieg.* Hamburg, 1998.

_____. *Kalkulierte Morde: Die deutsche Wirtschafts- und Vernichtungspolitik in Weißrußland 1941 bis 1944.* Hamburg, 1999.

Gitelman, Zvi. "Soviet Jewry before the Holocaust." In *Bitter Legacy: Confronting the Holocaust in the USSR*, ed. Zvi Gitelman, 1–13. Bloomington and Indianapolis, 1997.

Goldhagen, Daniel Jonah. *Hitler's Willing Executioners: Ordinary Germans and the Holocaust.* New York, 1996.

Gordon, Bertram M. *Collaborationism in France during the Second World War.* Ithaca and London, 1980.

Gross, Jan Tomasz. *The Revolution from Abroad: The Soviet Conquest of Poland's Western Ukraine and Western Belorussia.* Princeton, 1988.

_____. *Neighbors: The Destruction of the Jewish Community in Jedwabne, Poland.* Princeton and Oxford, 2001.

Gur'janov, Alexander. "Überblick über die Deportationen der Bevölkerung in der UdSSR in den Jahren 1930–1950." In *Vertreibung europäisch erinnern? Historische Erfahrungen. Vergangenheitspolitik – Zukunftskonzeptionen*, ed. Dieter Binge et al. Wiesbaden, 2003.

Heer, Hannes, and Klaus Naumann, eds. *War of Extermination: the German Military in World War II, 1941–1944.* New York, 2000.

Herbert, Ulrich. *Fremdarbeiter: Politik und Praxis des "Auslander-Einsatzes" in der Kriegswirtschaft des Dritten Reiches.* 2nd ed. Berlin and Bonn, 1986.

_____. "The German Military Command in Paris and the Deportation of the French Jews." In *National Socialist Extermination Policies*, ed. Ulrich Herbert, 128–62. New York and Oxford, 2000.

Herzstein, Robert. *Vojna kotoruju vyigral Gitler.* Translated by A. Utkin et al. Smolensk, 1996.

Hilberg, Raul. *The Destruction of the European Jews.* New York, 1961.

Hillgruber, Andreas, *Hitlers Strategie: Politik und Kriegsführung.* Frankfurt/Main, 1965.

Hirschfeld, Gerhard. *Nazi Rule and Dutch Collaboration: The Netherlands under German Occupation, 1940–1945.* Translated by L. Willmot. Oxford, 1988.

_____. "Collaboration in Nazi-Occupied France." In *Collaboration in France*, ed. Gerhard Hirschfeld and P. Marsh, 1–14. Oxford, 1989.

Hoffmann, J. *Ostlegionen 1941–1943.* 2nd ed. Freiburg im Breisgau, 1981.

Hoffmann, Stanley, "Collaborationism in France during World War II," *Journal of Modern History* 40, no. 3 (September 1968): 375–95.

Hunczak, Taras. *On the Horns of a Dilemma.* Lanham, 2000.

Kaganovich, M., ed. *Sefer Zikaron Likehilath Ivje* [The Memorial Book of the Ivje Community]. Tel Aviv, 1968.

Kalush, Viktor. *In the Service of the People for a Free Byelorussia: Biographical Notes on Professor Radoslav Ostrowsky.* London, 1964.

Karpel, Eliezer et al., eds. *Smorgon: Makhoz Vilna* [Smorgon: Vilna District]. Tel Aviv, 1965.

Katkovič, A. and V. Katkovič-Klentak, *Uspaminy.* Bialystok, 1999.

Klein, Anne et al., eds. *Existiert das Ghetto noch?"*: *Weißrussland: Jüdisches Überleben gegen nationalsozialistische Herrschaft.* Berlin, 2003.

Kljuchevskij, Vasilij. *Russkaja Istoriia. Polnyj Kurs Lektsij v Trjokh Knigakh,* 3 vols. Moscow, 1995.

Kohl, Paul. *Der Krieg der deutschen Wehrmacht und der Polizei 1941–1944: Sowjetische Überlebende berichten.* Gütersloh, 1990.

Krajewski, Kazimierz. "Der Bezirk Nowogródek der Heimatarmee: National-itätenkonflikte und politische Verhältnisse 1939 bis 1945." In *Die polnische Heimatarmee. Geschichte und Mythos der Armia Krajowa seit dem Zweiten Weltkrieg,* ed. Bernhard Chiari, 563–84. Munich, 2003.

Kravchenko, Ivan. "Nemecko-Fashistskij okkupacionnyj Rezhim v Bjelorussii." In *Nemetsko-Fashistskij Okkupatsionnyj Rezhim (1941–1944),* ed. Yevgeny Boltin et al. Moscow, 1965.

Lang, Armin. "Zakhvat Norvegii s nemeckoj i norvezhskoj tochek zreniia." In *Vtoraja Mirovaja Vojna,* ed. W. Michalka, trans. N. Zakharchenko et al. Moscow, 1997.

Lemberg, Hans. "Kollaboration in Europa mit dem Dritten Reich um das Jahr 1941." In *Das Jahr 1941 in der europäischen Politik,* ed. K. Bosl. Munich and Vienna, 1972.

Lemkin, Raphael. *Axis Rule in Occupied Europe: Laws of Occupation, Analysis of Government, Proposals for Redress.* New York, 1973.

Lepre, George. *Himmler's Bosnian Division: The Waffen-SS Handschar Division 1943–1945.* Atglen, Pa., 1997.

Levy, C. *Le Nouveaux Temps et l'idéologie de la collaboration.* Paris, 1974.

Littlejohn, David. *The Patriotic Traitors: A History of Collaboration in German-occupied Europe, 1940–1945.* London, 1972.

Litvin, Alexej. *Akupacyja Belarusi (1941–1944): Pytanni Supracivu i Kalabaracyi.* Minsk, 2000.

———. "K Voprosu o Kolichestve lyudskikh Poter' Belarusi v Gody Velikoj Otechestvennoj Vojny (1941–1945 gg.)." In *Belarus v XX Veke. Sbornik nauchnykh Rabot,* ed. Yakov Basin, Yakov. 1st issue, 127–38. Minsk, 2002.

Liulevicius, Vejas, Gabriel. *War Land on the Eastern Front: Culture, National Identity and German Occupation in World War I.* Cambridge, 2000.

Loftus, John. *The Belarus Secret.* New York, 1982.

Logusz, Michael O. *Galicia Division: The Waffen-SS 14th Grenadier Division 1943–1945.* Atglen, Pa., 1997.

Longerich, Peter. *Politik der Vernichtung.* Munich and Zurich, 1998.

———. *Der ungeschriebene Befehl.* Munich and Zurich, 2001.

Lubachko, Ivan S. *Belorussia under Soviet Rule 1917–1957.* Lexington, 1972.

MacLean, French L. *The Cruel Hunters: SS-Sonderkommando Dirlewanger, Hitler's most notorious Anti-partisan Unit,* Atglen, Pa., 1998.

Madajczyk, Czeslaw. *Die Okkupationspolitik Nazideutschlands in Polen 1939–1945.* Berlin, 1987.

———. "Zwischen neutraler Zusammenarbeit der Bevölkerung okkupierter Gebiete und Kollaboration mit den Deutschen." In *Europa unterm Hakenkreuz,* vol. 1, *Okkupation und Kollaboration (1938–1945),* ed. Werner Röhr. Berlin and Heidelberg, 1994.

Mader, Julius. *Abver: Shchit i Mech Tret'ego Rejkha.* Translated by Nikolaj Lavrov. Rostov/Don, 1999.

Martin, Terry. *The Affirmative Action Empire: Nations and Nationalism in the Soviet Union, 1923-1939.* Ithaca and London, 2001.

Mason, Tim. "Intention and Explanation: A Current Controversy about the Interpretation of National-Socialism." In _Der "Führerstaat:" Mythos und Realität. Studien zur Struktur und Politik des Dritten Reiches_, ed. Gerhard Hirschfeld and Lothar Kettenacker, 23–42. Stuttgart, 1981.

Matthäus, Jürgen, "'Reibungslos und Planmäßig:' Die zweite Welle der Judenvernichtung im Generalkommissariat Weißruthenien (1942–1944)," _Jahrbuch für Antisemitismusforschung_ 4 (1995): 254–74.

McMillan, James F. _Twentieth-Century France: Politics and Society, 1898–1991_. London, 1992.

Michaelis, Rolf. _Russen in der Waffen-SS_. Berlin, 2002.

Michalka, Wolfgang, ed. _Vtoraja Mirovaja Vojna. Diskussii. Osnovnyje Tendencii. Rezul'taty Issledovanij_. Translated by N. Zakharchenko et al. Moscow, 1997.

Michman, Dan. _Holocaust Historiography: a Jewish Perspective: Conceptualizations, terminology, approaches, and fundamental issues_. London and Portland, Oreg., 2003.

Misiunas, Romuald J., and Rein Taagepera. _The Baltic States, Years of Dependence, 1940–1990_. 2nd ed. Berkeley and Los Angeles, 1993.

Moorehead, Alan. _The Russian Revolution_. 4th ed. New York, 1959.

Munoz, Antonio J. _Forgotten Legions_. Boulder, Colo., 1991.

_____. _The Kaminski Brigade: A History, 1941–1945_. Bayside, N.Y., 2000.

Musial, Bogdan. _"Konterrevolutionäre Elemente sind zu erschießen:" Die Brutalisierung des deutsch-sowjetischen Krieges in Sommer 1941_. Berlin and Munich, 2000.

Neshamit, Sara, "Bein Shittuf Pe'ula le-Meri" [Between the Collaboration and Resistance]. _Dappim le-Heker ha-Shoa ve ha-Mered_, 2nd series, 1st supplement (1970), 152–77.

Orbach, Wila. "The Destruction of the Jews in the Nazi-Occupied Territories of the USSR," _Soviet Jewish Affairs_ 6, no. 2 (1976): 14–51.

Ory, P. _Les Collaborateurs, 1940–1945_. Paris, 1976.

_____. _La France allemande: Paroles du collaborationisme français (1933–1945)_. Paris, 1977.

Ostmann, Eckehard. _Russlands Fremdvölker: seine Stärke und Schwäche_. Munich, 1915.

Ostrowski, Wiktor. _Anti-Semitism in Byelorussia and its Origin_. London, 1960.

Paromchyk, Galina. _Kaldychoŭskaja Tragedyja_. Minsk, 1962.

Paxton, Robert O. _Vichy France. Old Guard and New Order, 1940–1944_. New York, 1972.

Pinchuk, Ben-Cion. _Yehudei Brit ha-Mo'atzot mul Pnei ha-Sho'a. Mekhkar be-Beayot Haglaya u-Pinui_ [Soviet Jews in the Face of the Holocaust: Research into the Problems of Exile and Evacuation]. Tel Aviv, 1979.

_____. _Shtetl Jews under Soviet Rule; Eastern Poland on the Eve of the Holocaust_, 2nd ed. Cambridge, Mass., 1991.

Piper, Ernst. _Alfred Rosenberg: Hitlers Chefideologe_. Munich, 2005.

Pohl, Dieter. "Der Mörderische Sommer von 1941 aus politischer Sicht." http://www.fritz-bauer-institut.de/rezensionen/nl20/pohl.htm.

_____. _Nationalsozialistische Judenverfolgung in Ostgalizien 1941–1944: Organisation und Durchführung eines staatlichen Massenverbrechens_. Munich, 1996.

_____. "The Murder of Jews in the General Government." In _National Socialist Extermination Policies_, ed. Ulrich Herbert, 83–103. New York and Oxford, 2000.

Poljan, Pavel. *Ne po svoej Vole: Istoria i Geografija prinuditel'nykh Migracij v SSSR.* Moscow, 2001.

_____. *Zhertvy Dvukh Diktatur.* Moscow, 2002.

Pospelov, Pjotr et al., eds. *Istoria Velikoj Otechestvennoj Vojny Sovetskogo Sojuza 1941–1945.* Moscow, 1961.

Pospielovsky, Dimitry. *The Russian Church under the Soviet Regime, 1917–1982,* 2 vols. New York, 1984.

Poznanski, Renee. *Jews in France during World War II.* Translated by N. Bracher. Hanover and London, 2001.

Ready, J. Lee. *The Forgotten Axis: Germany's Partners and Foreign Volunteers in World War II.* Jefferson, N.C., and London, 1987.

Redlich, Shimon. "Metropolitan Andrii Sheptyts'kyi and the Complexities of Ukrainian-Jewish Relations." In *Bitter Legacy,* ed. Zvi Gitelman, 61–76. Bloomington and Indianapolis, 1997.

Rein, Leonid. "Otnosheniie belorusskogo naseleniia k evreyam vo vremya Katastrofy. 1941–1944 gody." *Evrei Belarusi. Istoriia i Kul'tura* 6 (2001), 181–205.

_____. "The Orthodox Church in Byelorussia under Nazi Occupation (1941–1944)," *East European Quarterly* 39, no. 1 (Spring 2005): 13–46.

Reitlinger, Gerald. *The House Built on Sand. The Conflicts of German Policy in Russia, 1939–1945.* London, 1960.

_____. *The Final Solution: The Attempt to Exterminate the Jews of Europe, 1939–1945.* 2nd ed. London, 1961.

Rings, Werner. *Life with the Enemy: Collaboration and Resistance in Hitler's Europe, 1939–1945.* New York, 1982.

Robel, Gert. "Sowjetunion." In *Dimension des Völkermords: Die Zahl der jüdischen Opfer des Nationalsozialismus,* ed. Wolfgang Benz, 499–560. Munich, 1991.

Röhr, Werner, "Einleitung." In *Europa unterm Hakenkreuz: Okkupation und Kollaboration,* ed. Werner Röhr, 17–30. Berlin and Heidelberg, 1994.

_____. "Okkupation und Kollaboration." In *Europa unter Hakenkreuz,* vol. *Okkupation und Kollaboration (1938–1945).* Berlin and Heidelberg, 1994, 59–84.

_____. "Forschungsprobleme zur deutschen Okkupationspolitik im Spiegel der Reihe Europa unter Hakenkreuz." In *Europa unter Hakenkreuz: Analysen-Quellen-Register,* ed. Werner Röhr, 25–341. Heidelberg, 1996.

Romanovskij, Vasilij. *Saudzel'niki ŭ zlachynstvakh.* Minsk, 1964.

Romanovsky, Daniel. "Kholokost v Vostochnoj Belorussii i Severo-Zapadnoj Rossii Glazami Neevreev," *Vestnik Evrejskogo Universiteta* 2, no. 9 (1995): 56–92.

_____. "Soviet Jews under Nazi Occupation in Northeastern Belarus and Eastern Russia." In *Bitter Legacy,* ed. Zvi Gitelman, 230–52. Bloomington and Indianapolis, 1997.

Rosenblat, Yevgenij. "Evrei v sisteme mezhnacional'nykh otnoshenij v zapadnykh oblastyakh Belarusi, 1939-1941," *Belaruski Histarychny Sbornik,* 13 (2000).

Sabaliŭnas, Leonas. *Lithuania in Crisis: Nationalism to Communism, 1939–1940.* Bloomington and London, 1972.

Sandkühler, Thomas. "Anti-Jewish Policy and the Murder of the Jews in the District of Galicia, 1941/1942." In *National Socialist Extermination Policies,* ed. Ulrich Herbert, 104–27. New York and Oxford, 2000.

Schlootz, Johannes, ed. *Deutsche Propaganda in Weißrussland, 1941–1944: Eine Konfrontation von Propaganda und Wirklichkeit: Ausstellung in Berlin und Minsk.* Berlin, 1996.

Schünnemann, K. "Die Neue Agrarordnung für den Osten." In *Der Alemanne* (Freiburg im Breisgau), 28 February 1942.

Schwarz, Solomon. *Antisemitism v Sovetskom Soyuze.* New York, 1952.

———. *Evrei v Sovetskom Soyuze s Nachala Vtoroj Mirovoj Vojny, 1939–1965.* New York, 1966.

Seidler, Franz W., ed. *Verbrechen an der Wehrmacht: Kriegsgreuel der Roten Armee 1941/1942.* 3rd ed. Selent, 1998.

Servachinskij, I. *Kollaboracionizm na okkupirovannoj Territorii Belarusi.* Minsk, 1999.

Shepherd, Ben. *War in the Wild East.* Cambridge, Mass., and London, 2004.

Shokhat, Azriel. *"Helkam shel ha-Lita'im be-Hashmadat Yehudei Lita"* [Particpation of Lithuanians in the Extermination of Lithuanian Jews], *Dappim le-Heker Tekufat ha-Sho'a,* 1st issue (1979), 77–95.

Skorokhod, Fanja. *"Rimonim beli napatzim"* (Grenades without detonators). In *Minsk. Ir ve-Em* (Minsk. City and Mother), ed. Sh. Even-Shoshan, vol. 2. Tel Aviv, 1988.

Slezkine, Yuri. "The USSR as a Communal Apartment, or How a Socialist State Promoted Ethnic Particularism," *Slavic Review* 53, no. 2 (Summer 1994).

Smilovitsky, Leonid. "Righteous Gentiles, the Partisans, and Jewish Survival in Belorussia, 1941–1944." Translated by M. Gelb. *Holocaust and Genocide Studies* 11, no. 3 (winter 1997): 301–29.

———. *Katastrofa Evreev v Belorussii 1941–1944.* Tel Aviv, 2000.

Solov'ev, Alexej. *Belarusskaja Tsentral'naja Rada: Sozdanie, Dejatel'nost', Krakh.* Minsk, 1995.

Steenberg, Sven. *Vlasov.* Translated by A. Farbstein. New York, 1970.

Stein, George H. *The Waffen SS: Hitler's Elite Guard at War.* London, 1966.

Sternhell, Zeev. *Ni droit ni gauche: L'idéologie fasciste en France.* Paris, 1983.

———. *Yesodot ha-Fashizm: Meymad Tarbuti le-Mahapeikha Politit* [The Basics of Fascism: The Cultural Aspect of Political Revolution]. 3rd ed., Tel Aviv, 1996.

Strazhas, Abba. *Deutsche Ostpolitik im Ersten Weltkrieg: Der Fall Ober Ost 1915–1917.* Wiesbaden, 1993.

Streit, Christian. *Keine Kameraden: Die Wehrmacht und die Sowjetischen Kriegsgefangenen, 1941–1945.* 2nd ed. Bonn, 1997.

Sweets, J. F. *Choices in Vichy France.* Oxford and New York, 1986.

Tec, Nechama. *In the Lion's Den: The Life of Oswald Rufeisen.* New York and Oxford, 1990.

Thorwald, Jürgen. *Die Illusion. Rotarmisten in Hitlers Heeren.* Zurich, 1974.

Tomaszewski, Jerzy. "Belorussians in the Eyes of the Poles, 1918–1939," *Acta Poloniae Historica* 51 (1985): 101–22.

Trunk, Isaiah. *Judenrat: The Jewish Councils in Eastern Europe under Nazi Occupation.* 2nd ed. Lincoln, 1996.

Tsanava, Lavrenty. *Vsenarodnaja Partisanskaja Vojna v Belorussii protiv Fashistskikh Zakhvatchikov,* part 2. Minsk, 1951.

Tuchman, Barbara Wertheim. *August 1914.* 2nd ed. London, 1994.

Turonak, Yury. *Belarus' pad nyameckaj Akupacyjaj.* Minsk, 1993.

Vakar, Nicholas P. *Belorussia: The Making of a Nation, a Case Study.* Cambridge, Mass., 1956.

Weisberg, Richard H. *Vichy Law and the Holocaust in France*. Amsterdam, 1996.

Wette, Wolfram. *Die Wehrmacht*. 2nd ed. Frankfurt/Main, 2005.

Wilhelm, Hans-Heinrich, "Die Rolle der Kollaboration für die deutsche Besatzungspolitik in Litauen und 'Weißruthenien'." In *Europa unter Hakenkreuz*, Band: *Okkupation und Kollaboration*, ed. Werner Röhr. Heidelberg, 1994.

Yoffe, Emanuil. *Belorusskije Evrei: Tragedija i Geroizm*. Minsk, 2003.

Yurevič, Lyavon. *Vyrvanaja Bachyny. Da Historyi Sayuzu Belaruskaje Moladzi*. Minsk, 2001.

Zalesskij, A. *V Tylu Vraga: Bor'ba Krest'janstva Belorussii protiv sotsial'no-ekonomicheskikh Meroprtijatij nemetsko-fahistskikh Okkupantov*. Minsk, 1969.

Zaprudnik, Janka (Jan). *Belarus': Na gistraychnykh skryzhavannyakh*. Minsk, 1996.

Zbikowski, Andrzej. "Local Anti-Jewish Pogroms in the Occupied Territories of Eastern Poland, June–July 1941." In *The Holocaust in the Soviet Union. Studies and Sources on the Destruction of the Jews in the Nazi-occupied Territories of the USSR, 1941–1945*, ed. Lucjan Dobroszycki and Jeffrey S. Gurok, 173–79. New York and London, 1993.

Zhits, Dan. *Ghetto Minsk ve-toledotav le-or ha-te'ud he-hadash* [The History of the Minsk Ghetto (In the Light of the New Documentation)]. Ramat Gan, 2000.

Zhumar, Sergej. *Okkupacionnaja Periodicheskaja Pechat' na Territorii Belarusi v Gody Velikoj Otechestvennoj Vojny*. Minsk, 1996.

Reference Literature

Belaruski Nacyjanalizm. Davednik. http://slounik.org/nac/

Dear, I. C. B., and M. R. D. Foot, M.R.D, eds. *The Oxford Companion to World War II*. Oxford, 2001.

Dziarnovič, Aleh, ed. *Antysaveckija Rukhi ǔ Belarusi 1944–1956: Davednik*. Minsk, 1999.

Egazarov, Albert, ed. *Encyklopedija Tret'ego Rejkha*. Moscow, 1996.

Gutman, Israel et al., eds. *Enzyklopädie des Holocaust: Die Verfolgung und Ermordung der europäischen Juden*, 3 vols. Berlin, 1993.

Klee, Ernst. *Das Personenlexikon zum Dritten Reich: Wer war was vor und nach 1945*, 2nd ed. Frankfurt/Main, 2005.

Sachenka, Barys, ed. *Belarus: Encyklapedychny Davednik*. Minsk, 1995.

Zalesskij, Konstantin. *Kto byl Kto v Tret'em Rejkhe: Biograficheskij encyklopedicheskij Slovar'*. Moscow, 2002.

INDEX OF PLACES

Names such as Byelorussia (or *Weißruthenien*), Germany and USSR (or Soviet Union) are omitted from this index. Also omitted are the archives' locations as well as places at which the books quoted in this work were published. Not included are also such general names as Europe, Baltic region, Scandinavia etc. Italics means the place is mentioned in the endnotes.

INDEX OF PERSONS

The persons whose first names I was unable to find are omitted from this index. Also omitted are the authors of the books I am quoting in this work. Italics means the name is mentioned in the endnotes.